Lecture Notes in Computer Science 13560

More information about this series at https://link.springer.com/bookseries/558

Nils Jansen · Mariëlle Stoelinga ·
Petra van den Bos (Eds.)

A Journey from Process Algebra via Timed Automata to Model Learning

Essays Dedicated to Frits Vaandrager
on the Occasion of His 60th Birthday

Springer

Editors
Nils Jansen (ID)
Radboud University Nijmegen
Nijmegen, The Netherlands

Mariëlle Stoelinga (ID)
University of Twente
Enschede, The Netherlands

Petra van den Bos
University of Twente
Enschede, The Netherlands

ISSN 0302-9743   ISSN 1611-3349   (electronic)
Lecture Notes in Computer Science
ISBN 978-3-031-15628-1   ISBN 978-3-031-15629-8   (eBook)
https://doi.org/10.1007/978-3-031-15629-8

This Springer imprint is published by the registered company Springer Nature Switzerland AG
The registered company address is: Gewerbestrasse 11, 6330 Cham, Switzerland

Frits Vaandrager

Preface

We are happy to present this Festschrift, written for the occasion of the 60th birthday of Frits Vaandrager.

We all know Frits as a highly passionate researcher: He can immerse himself in a new idea and then forget everything around him. During his career, Frits focused on several scientific passions:

- In the early days, as a PhD student of Jan Bergstra at the Centre for Mathematics and Computer Science in Amsterdam, Frits worked in the area of process algebras. Together with his office mate Rob van Glabbeek and colleague Jan Friso Groote they hammered down several fundamental papers on concurrency theory and operational semantics.
- After his PhD, he flew to MIT, working as a postdoc with Nancy Lynch on his second passion: I/O automata.
- After a short stay in France, he returned to the Netherlands, first working in Amsterdam. Finally, he became a professor in Nijmegen, working on model checking of timed automata, contributing to the famous model checker Uppaal.
- Then, a bit more than a decade ago, Frits switched to the area of model learning, being one of the area's founding fathers.

We are sure that his scientific journey does not end here—Frits is always open to research collaboration in his own research fields and sometimes takes a step somewhere else: most astoundingly, he has a publication on polymers. Further, his passion does not only lead to theoretical results. Frits also has stunning success with industrial applications, applying model learning to the TCP protocol and Dutch biometric passports, model checking the very complex machines at ASML's wafer steppers, the data paths of industrial printers at Canon, and many more.

The Festschrift contains contributions of (former) colleagues, PhD students, and researchers Frits collaborated with. The papers exemplify the rainbow of Frits' research interests and show the great appreciation Frits receives in the scientific community.

As part of our work on the volume, we organized a review process that involved a program committee consisting of all contributing authors.

We thank Frits for inspiring all of us and congratulate him on his 60th birthday!

July 2022

Nils Jansen
Mariëlle Stoelinga
Petra van den Bos

Organization

Program Committee

Luca Aceto	Reykjavik University, Iceland
Elli Anastasiadi	National Technical University of Athens, Greece
Christel Baier	TU Dresden, Germany
Henk Barendregt	Radboud University, The Netherlands
Twan Basten	TU Eindhoven, The Netherlands
Jan Bergstra	University of Amsterdam, The Netherlands
Benedikt Bollig	LMF, ENS Paris-Saclay, CNRS, France
Valentina Castiglioni	Reykjavik University, Iceland
Vincenzo Ciancia	Consiglio Nazionale delle Ricerche, Italy
Rance Cleaveland	University of Maryland, USA
Carlos Diego Nascimento Damasceno	Radboud University, The Netherlands
Rocco De Nicola	IMT School for Advanced Studies Lucca, Italy
Erik De Vink	TU Eindhoven, The Netherlands
Luca Di Stefano	University of Gothenburg, Sweden
Clemens Dubslaff	TU Dresden, Germany
Ansgar Fehnker	Macquarie University, Australia
Tiago Ferreira	University College London, UK
Wan Fokkink	Vrije Universiteit Amsterdam, The Netherlands
Markus Frohme	TU Dortmund University, Germany
Martin Fränzle	Carl von Ossietzky Universität Oldenburg, Germany
Florian Funke	TU Dresden, Germany
Hubert Garavel	Inria, France
Herman Geuvers	Radboud University, The Netherlands
Jan Friso Groote	TU Eindhoven, The Netherlands
Jozef Hooman	TNO-ESI and Radboud University, The Netherlands
Falk Howar	TU Dortmund, Germany
Marieke Huisman	University of Twente, The Netherlands
Omar Inverso	University of Southampton, UK
David N. Jansen	Chinese Academy of Sciences, China
Nils Jansen	Radboud University, The Netherlands
Simon Jantsch	TU Dresden, Germany
Sebastian Junges	Radboud University, The Netherlands
Ivan Kurtev	Capgemini Engineering and TU Eindhoven, The Netherlands
Frédéric Lang	CONVECS, Inria Grenoble - Rhône-Alpes, France
Diego Latella	ISTI-CNR, Italy
Martin Leucker	University of Luebeck, Germany

Xinxin Liu	Chinese Academy of Sciences, China
Nancy Lynch	Massachusetts Institute of Technology, USA
Mieke Massink	CNR-ISTI, Italy
Joshua Moerman	RWTH Aachen University, Germany
Jakob Piribauer	TU Dresden, Germany
Jurriaan Rot	Radboud University, The Netherlands
Alexandra Silva	University College London, UK
Marielle Stoelinga	University of Twente, The Netherlands
Daniel Strüber	Chalmers University of Technology, Sweden, and Radboud University, The Netherlands
Jan Tretmans	TNO-ESI and Radboud University, The Netherlands
Serenella Valiani	IMT School for Advanced Studies Lucca, Italy
Petra van den Bos	University of Twente, The Netherlands
Rob van Glabbeek	University of New South Wales, Australia
Tim Willemse	TU Eindhoven, The Netherlands
Hans Zantema	TU Eindhoven, The Netherlands
Robin Ziemek	TU Dresden, Germany

Contents

Non-finite Axiomatisability Results via Reductions: CSP Parallel Composition and CCS Restriction

Luca Aceto[1,2]([✉]) [iD], Elli Anastasiadi[1] [iD], Valentina Castiglioni[1] [iD], and Anna Ingólfsdóttir[1] [iD]

[1] ICE-TCS, Department of Computer Science, Reykjavik University, Reykjavik, Iceland
luca@ru.is
[2] Gran Sasso Science Institute, L'Aquila, Italy

Abstract. This paper studies the existence of finite, ground-complete axiomatisations of CSP-like parallel composition operators, and the restriction operator from CCS, modulo bisimilarity. More specifically, we build on Moller's result to the effect that bisimilarity does not have a finite, ground-complete equational axiomatisation over a minimal fragment of CCS, and we use a reduction technique by Aceto et al. to lift it to various extensions of BCCSP with CSP-like parallel operators, and to the recursion and relabelling free fragment of CCS.

1 Introduction

Some of Frits Vaandrager's early seminal contributions were firmly rooted in the theory and applications of process algebras and their semantics. Having been brought up in the tradition of Bergstra and Klop's Algebra of Communicating Processes (ACP) [14, 16, 17], Frits Vaandrager studied semantic models of algebraic process description languages [25, 26], equational axiomatisations of process equivalences [15] and their application in verification (see, for instance, [24, 39]). Moreover, together with Aceto and Bloom, in [3] he initiated the study of methods for generating finite, ground-complete, equational axiomatisations of bisimilarity [32, 36] from operational specifications given in the GSOS format [18]. The techniques proposed in [3] can be used to synthesise auxiliary operators, such as Bergstra and Klop's left- and communication-merge operators, that make finite axiomatisations possible and paved the way to several further studies in the literature—see, for instance, the developments presented in [10, 21, 27, 31].

The use of auxiliary operators to obtain finite, equational, ground-complete axiomatisations of bisimilarity, even for very inexpressive process algebras, was justified by Moller in [33–35], where he showed that bisimilarity has no finite axiomatisation

This work has been partially supported by the project *"Open Problems in the Equational Logic of Processes"* (OPEL) of the Icelandic Research Fund (grant No. 196050-051). E. Anastasiadi has been supported by the project *"Runtime and Equational Verification Of Concurrent Programs"* (REVOCOP) of the Reykjavik University Research Fund (grant No. 222021-051). V. Castiglioni has been supported by the project *"Programs in the wild: Uncertainties, adaptabiLiTy and veRificatiON"* (ULTRON) of the Icelandic Research Fund (grant No. 228376-051).

N. Jansen et al. (Eds.): Vaandrager Festschrift 2022, LNCS 13560, pp. 1–26, 2022.
https://doi.org/10.1007/978-3-031-15629-8_1

over minimal fragments of Milner's Calculus of Communicating Systems (CCS) [32] and Bergstra and Klop's ACP. (Henceforth, we will consider the recursion, relabelling and restriction free fragment of CCS, which, for simplicity, we still denote as CCS.) Moller's above-mentioned, path-breaking, negative results have been followed by a wealth of research on non-finitely-based fragments of process algebras—see, for instance, [1,2,4–8,12,20].

Our Contribution. In this paper, we celebrate Frits Vaandrager's early contributions to the study of algebraic process description languages by answering the two questions that Rob van Glabbeek[1] asked the first author after his invited talk at LICS 2021[2]:

> Would Moller's non-finite axiomatisability result for CCS remain true if we replaced CCS parallel composition with the parallel operators from Hoare's Communicating Sequential Processes (CSP) [29]? And what if we added the restriction operator to CCS instead?

Our first contributions concern the existence of finite, ground-complete axiomatisations of bisimilarity over process algebras that extend the language BCCSP [22,28,32] with parallel operators from CSP. (BCCSP is a common fragment of Milner's CCS and Hoare's CSP suitable for describing finite process behaviour.)

For each set of actions A, the CSP parallel operator $|_A$ behaves like interleaving parallel composition for all actions that are not contained in A, but requires transitions of its operands that are labelled with some action $a \in A$ to synchronise. The result of such a synchronisation is an a-labelled transition of the composite parallel process, which can itself synchronise further with a-labelled steps from its environment. Therefore, unlike CCS parallel composition that is based on hand-shaking communication, the parallel operators from CSP support multi-way synchronisation and span the whole spectrum from pure interleaving parallel composition (the operator $|_\emptyset$) to synchronous composition (the operator $|_{\text{Act}}$, where Act is the whole collection of actions that processes may perform).

We start our investigations by considering the languages $\text{BCCSP}_A^{\text{p}}$, which extend BCCSP with the parallel operator $|_A$ for some subset A of the whole set of actions Act, and $\text{BCCSP}_\tau^{\text{p}}$, which contains the parallel operator $|_A$ for each $A \subseteq \text{Act}$, and the τ-prefixing operator for a distinguished action $\tau \notin \text{Act}$. We show that Moller's non-finite axiomatisability result for bisimilarity still holds over $\text{BCCSP}_A^{\text{p}}$, when A is a strict subset of Act, and $\text{BCCSP}_\tau^{\text{p}}$. On the other hand, bisimilarity affords a finite, ground-complete axiomatisation over $\text{BCCSP}_{\text{Act}}^{\text{p}}$.

The proofs of the above-mentioned negative results for $\text{BCCSP}_A^{\text{p}}$, when A is a strict subset of Act, and $\text{BCCSP}_\tau^{\text{p}}$ employ a reduction-based technique proposed in [11] for showing new, non-finite axiomatisability results over process algebras from already-established ones. In our setting, such reductions are translations from terms in the languages $\text{BCCSP}_A^{\text{p}}$ ($A \subset \text{Act}$) and $\text{BCCSP}_\tau^{\text{p}}$ to those in the fragment of CCS studied by Moller that

---

[1] Rob van Glabbeek was one of Frits Vaandrager's early collaborators and fellow doctoral student at CWI.

[2] See https://www.youtube.com/watch?v=2PxM3f0QWDM for a recording of that talk.

- preserve sound equations and equational provability over the source language, and
- reflect an infinite family of equations responsible for the non-finite axiomatisability of the target language.

No reduction from $BCCSP^P_{Act}$ to CCS satisfying the former property modulo bisimilarity reflects Moller's family of equations witnessing his negative result over CCS. Therefore, the reduction technique cannot be applied to $BCCSP^P_{Act}$. Indeed, we present a finite, ground-complete axiomatisation of bisimilarity over $BCCSP^P_{Act}$.

We also show that, if we consider the language $BCCSP^P$, namely BCCSP with a parallel operator $|_A$ for each $A \subseteq Act$, then no reduction that is structural, i.e. that does not introduce new variables and it is defined compositionally over terms, can reflect Moller's family of equations. However, we conjecture that bisimilarity does not admit a finite, ground-complete axiomatisation over $BCCSP^P$.

For our final contribution, we consider the language CCS^r, namely CCS enriched with *restriction operators* of the form $\cdot \backslash R$. Informally, $R \subseteq Act$ is a set of actions that are restricted, meaning that the execution of a-labelled transitions (and of their "complementary actions") is prevented in $t \backslash R$ for all $a \in R$. By exploiting the reduction technique described above, we show that Moller's negative result can be lifted to CCS^r, giving thus that bisimilarity admits no finite, ground-complete axiomatisation over CCS with restriction.

Our contributions can then be summarised as follows:

1. We consider $BCCSP^P_A$, i.e., BCCSP enriched with *one* CSP-style parallel composition operator $|_A$, with $A \subset Act$, and we show that, over that language, bisimilarity admits no finite, ground-complete axiomatisation (Theorem 4).
2. We consider $BCCSP^P$, i.e., BCCSP enriched with *all* CSP-style parallel composition operators $|_A$, and we show that there is no structural reduction from $BCCSP^P$ to CCS that can reflect the family of equations used by Moller to prove the negative result for bisimilarity over CCS (Theorem 5).
3. We consider $BCCSP^P_\tau$, i.e., $BCCSP^P$ enriched with the τ-prefixing, and we show that this algebra admits no finite, ground-complete axiomatisation modulo bisimilarity (Theorem 6).
4. We consider $BCCSP^P_{Act}$, i.e., BCCSP enriched with the CSP-style parallel composition operator $|_{Act}$, and we present a finite, ground-complete axiomatisation for it, modulo bisimilarity (Theorem 7).
5. We consider CCS^r, i.e., CCS with the restriction operator, and we show that bisimilarity has no finite, ground-complete axiomatisation over it (Theorem 8).

Organisation of Contents. In Sect. 2 we review basic notions on process semantics, behavioural equivalences, and equational logic. We also briefly recap Moller's negative result for bisimilarity over CCS. In Sect. 3 we give a bird's-eye view of the reduction technique from [11]. In Sect. 4, we present the lifting of Moller's negative result to $BCCSP^P_A$ (for $A \subset Act$) and $BCCSP^P_\tau$, we study the case of $BCCSP^P$, and then we discuss the collapse of the negative result in the case of $BCCSP^P_{Act}$. In Sect. 5, we use the reduction technique to prove the non-finite axiomatisability result for CCS^r. We conclude by discussing some directions for future work in Sect. 6.

2 Preliminaries

In this section we present some background notions on process algebras and equational logic. To make our contribution self-contained, we also briefly recap Moller's work on the nonexistence of finite axiomatisations modulo bisimilarity over the recursion, rela-belling, and restriction free fragment of CCS (henceforth simply referred to as CCS).

Labelled Transition Systems and Bisimilarity. As semantic model for the algebraic process description languages that we will study, we consider classic *Labelled Transition Systems* [30].

Definition 1 (Labelled Transition System). *A* labelled transition system *(LTS) is a triple* $(\mathcal{P}, \mathrm{Act}, \rightarrow)$, *where* $\mathcal{P}$ *is a set of* processes *(or states),* Act *is a set of* actions *(or labels), and* $\rightarrow \subseteq \mathcal{P} \times \mathrm{Act} \times \mathcal{P}$ *is a (labelled)* transition relation.

In what follows, we assume that the set of actions Act is finite and non-empty. We let $p, q, \ldots$ range over $\mathcal{P}$, and $a, b, \ldots$ over Act. Moreover, as usual, we use $p \xrightarrow{a} p'$ in lieu of $(p, a, p') \in \rightarrow$. For each $p \in \mathcal{P}$ and $a \in \mathrm{Act}$, we write $p \xrightarrow{a}$ if $p \xrightarrow{a} p'$ holds for some p', and $p \xrightarrow{a}\!\!\!/$ otherwise. For a sequence of actions $\rho = a_1 \cdots a_n$ $(n \geq 0)$, and processes p, p', we write $p \xrightarrow{\rho} p'$ if and only if there exists a sequence of transitions $p = p_0 \xrightarrow{a_1} p_1 \xrightarrow{a_2} \cdots \xrightarrow{a_n} p_n = p'$. If $p \xrightarrow{\rho} p'$ holds for some process p', then ρ is a *trace* of p. All the LTSs we will consider in this paper are finite and loop-free. The *depth* of a process p in such an LTS, denoted by $\mathrm{depth}(p)$, is then defined as the length of a longest trace of p.

Behavioural equivalences have been introduced as a tool to establish whether the behaviours of two processes are *indistinguishable for their observers*. In the literature we can find several notions of behavioural equivalence based on the observations that an external observer can make on a process. In this paper we consider the classic notion of *bisimilarity* [32, Chapter 4, Definition 1].

Definition 2 (Bisimilarity). *Let* $(\mathcal{P}, \mathrm{Act}, \rightarrow)$ *be a LTS. A binary symmetric relation* $\mathcal{R} \subseteq \mathcal{P} \times \mathcal{P}$ *is a* bisimulation *if, and only if, whenever* $(p, q) \in \mathcal{R}$ *and* $p \xrightarrow{a} p'$ *then there exists a process* q' *such that* $q \xrightarrow{a} q'$ *and* $(p', q') \in \mathcal{R}$. *We say that* p *and* q *are* bisimilar *if there is a bisimulation relation* $\mathcal{R}$ *such that* $(p, q) \in \mathcal{R}$.

The union of all the bisimulation relations is called bisimilarity, *and denoted by* $\sim$.

It is well known that $\sim$ is an equivalence relation over $\mathcal{P}$, and it is the largest bisim-ulation relation [32, Chapter 4, Proposition 2].

Remark 1. Bisimilarity preserves the depth of processes, i.e., whenever $p \sim q$, then $\mathrm{depth}(p) = \mathrm{depth}(q)$.

The Language BCCSP. In this paper we will consider several algebraic process description languages, each characterised by the presence of a particular operator, or sets of operators. As all those languages are extensions of BCCSP [28], consisting of the basic operators from CCS [32] and CSP [29], in this section we use that language

Table 1. The SOS rules for BCCSP operators ($a \in$ Act).

$$(\text{act}) \frac{}{a.t \xrightarrow{a} t} \qquad (\text{lSum}) \frac{t \xrightarrow{a} t'}{t+u \xrightarrow{a} t'} \qquad (\text{rSum}) \frac{u \xrightarrow{a} u'}{t+u \xrightarrow{a} u'}$$

to introduce some general notions and notations on term algebras that will be useful throughout the remainder of the paper.

BCCSP terms are defined by the following grammar:

$$t ::= \quad \mathbf{0} \quad | \quad x \quad | \quad a.t \quad | \quad t+t, \tag{BCCSP}$$

where x is drawn from a countably infinite set of variables Var, a is an action from Act, $a.(\cdot)$ is the prefixing operator, defined for each $a \in$ Act, and $\cdot + \cdot$ is the nondeterministic choice operator. We shall use the meta-variables $t, u, \ldots$ to range over process terms, and write var(t) for the collection of variables occurring in the term t. The *size* of a term t, denoted by size(t), is the number of operator symbols in t. A term is *closed* if it does not contain any variables. Closed terms, or *processes*, will be denoted by $p, q, \ldots$. In particular, we denote the set of all BCCSP terms by $\mathbb{T}(\text{BCCSP})$, and the set of closed BCCSP terms (or BCCSP processes) by $\mathcal{P}(\text{BCCSP})$. This notation can be directly extended to all the languages that we will consider. Moreover, we omit trailing $\mathbf{0}$'s from terms and we use a *summation* $\sum_{i=1}^{k} t_i$ to denote the term $t = t_1 + \cdots + t_k$, where the empty sum represents $\mathbf{0}$. Henceforth, for each action $a \in$ Act and natural number $m \geq 0$, we let a^0 denote $\mathbf{0}$ and a^{m+1} denote $a.(a^m)$.

We use the *Structural Operational Semantics* (SOS) framework [37] to equip processes with an operational semantics. The SOS rules (also called inference rules, or deduction rules) for the BCCSP operators given above are reported in Table 1. A (*closed*) *substitution* σ is a mapping from process variables to (closed) terms. Substitutions are extended from variables to terms, transitions, and rules in the usual way. Note that $\sigma(t)$ is closed, if so is σ. The inference rules in Table 1 allow us to derive valid transitions between closed BCCSP terms. The operational semantics for BCCSP is then modelled by the LTS whose processes are the closed terms in $\mathcal{P}(\text{BCCSP})$, and whose labelled transitions are those that are provable from the SOS rules. The same approach will be applied to all the extensions of BCCSP that we will consider. The SOS rules of each language will be presented in the respective sections.

We call an equivalence relation a *congruence* over a language if it is compositional with respect to the operators of the language, i.e., the replacement of a component with an equivalent one does not affect the overall behaviour. Formally, the congruence property for bisimilarity over BCCSP, and its extensions, consists in verifying whether, given any n-ary operator f,

$$f(p_1, \ldots, p_n) \sim f(q_1, \ldots, q_n) \text{ whenever } p_i \sim q_i \text{ for all } i = 1, \ldots, n.$$

Since all the operators considered in this paper are defined by inference rules in the de Simone format [38], by [23, Theorem 4] we have that bisimilarity is a *congruence* over BCCSP and over all the languages that we will study.

Table 2. Rules of equational logic (f is any n-ary operator in L).

$$\frac{}{t \approx t} \qquad \frac{t_1 \approx t_2, \; t_2 \approx t_3}{t_1 \approx t_3} \qquad \frac{t \approx t'}{t' \approx t}$$

$$\frac{}{\sigma(t) \approx \sigma(t')} \; t \approx t' \in E \qquad \frac{t_1 \approx t'_1, \; \ldots, \; t_n \approx t'_n}{f(t_1, \ldots, t_n) \approx f(t'_1, \ldots, t'_n)}$$

Table 3. Finite equational basis for BCCSP modulo bisimilarity.

(A1) $x \approx x + x$

(A2) $x + y \approx y + x$

(A3) $(x + y) + z \approx x + (y + z)$

(A4) $x + \mathbf{0} \approx x$

Equational Logic. An *equational axiomatisation* (or *axiom system*) over a language L is a collection E of equations $t \approx u$, which are referred to as *axioms*, over the terms in L. We write $E \vdash t \approx u$ if the equation $t \approx u$ is derivable from the axioms in E using the rules of equational logic, presented in Table 2, that express, respectively, reflexivity, symmetry, transitivity, substitution, and closure under L contexts. Without loss of generality, we assume that substitution can be used *only* when $(t \approx u) \in E$. In this case, $\sigma(t) \approx \sigma(u)$ is called a *substitution instance* of an axiom in E.

We are interested in equations that are valid modulo some congruence relation $\mathcal{R}$ over the closed terms in the language L. An equation $t \approx u$ is *sound* modulo $\mathcal{R}$, written $t \, \mathcal{R} \, u$, when $\sigma(t) \, \mathcal{R} \, \sigma(u)$ for all closed substitutions σ. An axiomatisation E is *sound* modulo $\mathcal{R}$ over L if for all terms t, u in $\mathbb{T}(L)$, we have that whenever $E \vdash t \approx u$, then $t \, \mathcal{R} \, u$. E is *(ground-)complete* modulo $\mathcal{R}$ if $t \, \mathcal{R} \, u$ implies $E \vdash t \approx u$, for all (closed) L terms t and u. A congruence $\mathcal{R}$ is said to be *finitely based* if there exists a finite axiomatisation E that is sound and complete modulo $\mathcal{R}$.

A classic question is whether an algebra modulo the chosen notion of behavioural congruence (in this work, bisimilarity) affords a finite equational axiomatisation. For example, as shown by Hennessy and Milner in [28], the equations in Table 3 are a finite axiomatisation of bisimilarity over BCCSP. We denote by $\mathcal{E}_0$ the axiom system consisting of the equations in Table 3. Later on, we will extend this set of axioms to present our positive result for $\text{BCCSP}^{\text{P}}_{\text{Act}}$.

Moller's Result over CCS. In his thesis [33], Moller gave a celebrated non-finite axiomatisability result in the field of process algebra, namely:

Theorem 1. *Bisimilarity admits no finite, ground-complete axiomatisation over CCS.*

Specifically, Moller considered the language CCS_a with interleaving parallel composition, defined over $\text{Act} = \{a\}$ by the following syntax:

$$t ::= \quad \mathbf{0} \quad | \quad x \quad | \quad a.t \quad | \quad t + t \quad | \quad t \parallel t \qquad (\text{CCS}_a)$$

Table 4. The SOS rules for CCS_a interleaving parallel composition.

$$(\text{lPar}) \ \frac{t \xrightarrow{a} t'}{t \parallel u \xrightarrow{a} t' \parallel u} \qquad (\text{rPar}) \ \frac{u \xrightarrow{a} u'}{t \parallel u \xrightarrow{a} t \parallel u'}$$

where $x \in \text{Var}$, and $\parallel$ denotes the interleaving parallel composition operator. The SOS rules for CCS_a operators are given by the rules in Table 1, plus the rules for the interleaving parallel operator presented in Table 4.

In detail, for his result, Moller applied the following proof strategy, later referred to as the proof-theoretic approach to negative results [9]. He considered the infinite family of equations Φ with

$$\Phi = \{\varphi_n \mid n \geq 0\}$$

$$\varphi_n : \ a \parallel \left(\sum_{i=1}^{n} a^i\right) \approx a.\left(\sum_{i=1}^{n} a^i\right) + \left(\sum_{i=2}^{n+1} a^i\right) \qquad (n \geq 0)$$

and he proved that whenever n is larger than the size of any term occurring in the equations in a finite, sound axiom system E, then equation φ_n cannot be derived from E. Hence, Theorem 1 specialised to the following result, which will play a fundamental role in the technical development of our contributions:

Theorem 2 (Moller's negative result [33, **Theorem 5.2.12]).** *No finite axiom system that is sound modulo bisimilarity over CCS_a can prove the whole family of equations Φ. Thus no finite, ground-complete axiom system can exist for CCS_a modulo bisimilarity.*

3 The Proof Strategy: Reduction Mappings

The non-finite axiomatisability results that we will present in this paper are all obtained by means of a proof technique, proposed in [11], that allows for transferring this kind of negative results across process languages. Even though we only apply that technique out-of-the-box towards establishing new results, we decided to give, in this section, an overview of the terminology and results presented in [11], to improve the readability of our paper. As our studies are focused on the axiomatisability of bisimilarity, we consider only this behavioural congruence in the presentation below.

We consider two processes description languages defined over the same set of variables: L_{neg} and L_{new}. L_{neg} is known to be non-finitely axiomatisable modulo bisimilarity, whereas L_{new} is the language for which we want to prove this negative result. The aim of the proof technique proposed in [11] is to establish whether it is possible to *lift* the known result for L_{neg} to L_{new}. This approach is based on a variation of the classic idea of *reduction mappings* that, in this setting, are *translations* from $\mathbb{T}(L_{\text{new}})$ to $\mathbb{T}(L_{\text{neg}})$ that preserve soundness and provability.

Given a translation mapping $\widehat{\cdot} : \mathbb{T}(L_{\text{new}}) \to \mathbb{T}(L_{\text{neg}})$ and a collection E of equations over L_{new} terms, we let $\widehat{E} = \{\widehat{t} \approx \widehat{u} \mid t \approx u \in E\}$. The notion of *reduction* is then formalised as follows:

Definition 3 (Reduction). *A mapping* $\widehat{\cdot} \colon \mathbb{T}(L_{\text{new}}) \to \mathbb{T}(L_{\text{neg}})$ *is a reduction from* $\mathbb{T}(L_{\text{new}})$ *to* $\mathbb{T}(L_{\text{neg}})$, *when for all* $t, u \in \mathbb{T}(L_{\text{new}})$:

1. $t \sim u \implies \widehat{t} \sim \widehat{u}$, *i.e.,* $\widehat{\cdot}$ *preserves sound equations, and*
2. $E \vdash t \approx u \implies \widehat{E} \vdash \widehat{t} \approx \widehat{u}$, *for each axiom system E over* L_{new}, *i.e.,* $\widehat{\cdot}$ *preserves provability.*

   Interestingly, in [11, Theorem 2] it is proved that if a mapping is *structural*, then it automatically satisfies Definition 3.2. Hence, the notion of structural mapping will be crucial in the development of our results, as it allows for a significant simplification of the technical proofs.

Definition 4 (Structural mapping). *A mapping* $\widehat{\cdot} \colon \mathbb{T}(L_{\text{new}}) \to \mathbb{T}(L_{\text{neg}})$ *is structural if:*

- *It is the identity function over variables, i.e.,* $\widehat{x} = x$ *for each variable* x.
- *It does not introduce new variables, i.e., the set of variables occurring in the term* $\widehat{f(x_1, \ldots, x_n)}$ *is included in* $\{x_1, \ldots, x_n\}$, *for each operator* f *in* L_{new} *and sequence of distinct variables* $x_1, \ldots, x_n$.
- *It is defined compositionally, i.e.* $\widehat{f(t_1, \ldots, t_n)} = \widehat{f(x_1, \ldots, x_n)}[\widehat{t_1}/x_1, \ldots, \widehat{t_n}/x_n]$ *for each operator* f *in* L_{new}, *sequence of distinct variables* $x_1, \ldots, x_n$ *and sequence of terms* $t_1, \ldots, t_n$. *(Here* $[\widehat{t_1}/x_1, \ldots, \widehat{t_n}/x_n]$ *stands for the substitution mapping each variable* x_i *to* $\widehat{t_i}$ *($1 \le i \le n$), and acting like the identity function on all the other variables.)*

   Given a substitution $\sigma \colon \text{Var} \to \mathbb{T}(L_{\text{new}})$, we let $\widehat{\sigma} \colon \text{Var} \to \mathbb{T}(L_{\text{neg}})$ denote the substitution that maps each variable x to $\widehat{\sigma(x)}$.

Proposition 1. *Assume that* $\widehat{\cdot} \colon \mathbb{T}(L_{\text{new}}) \to \mathbb{T}(L_{\text{neg}})$ *is a structural mapping. Then*

- $\widehat{\sigma(t)} = \widehat{\sigma}(\widehat{t})$, *for each term* $t \in \mathbb{T}(L_{\text{new}})$, *and for each substitution* $\sigma \colon \text{Var} \to \mathbb{T}(L_{\text{new}})$.
- *The mapping satisfies Definition 3.2.*

   Assume now that we have an infinite collection E of equations that are sound modulo bisimilarity, but that are not derivable from any finite, sound axiom system over L_{neg}. The idea in [11] is then that if a structural mapping $\widehat{\cdot}$ is a reduction from $\mathbb{T}(L_{\text{new}})$ to $\mathbb{T}(L_{\text{neg}})$ that contains all the equations in E in its range, then the "malicious" collection of equations that map to those in E cannot be derivable from any finite, sound axiom system over L_{new}. In fact, if those derivations were possible, then the equational properties of $\widehat{\cdot}$ would allow us to write derivations (obtained via the translations of the equational proofs) of the equations in E from a finite, sound axiom system over L_{neg}. As this contradicts the established negative result over L_{neg}, the non-finite axiomatisability result over L_{new} follows.

   The intuitions above are formalised in the following definition and theorem.

Definition 5 (E-reflection). *Let E be a collection of equations over* L_{neg}. *A reduction* $\widehat{\cdot}$ *is E-reflecting, when for each* $t \approx u \in E$, *there are terms* $t', u' \in \mathbb{T}(L_{\text{new}})$ *such that the equation* $t' \approx u'$ *is sound modulo* $\sim$, $\widehat{t'} = t$ *and* $\widehat{u'} = u$. *A reduction is ground E-reflecting, if the conditions above are satisfied over closed equations.*

Theorem 3 (The lifting theorem). *Assume that there is a collection of (closed) equations E over L_{neg} that is sound modulo $\sim$ and that is not derivable from any finite sound axiom system over L_{neg}. If there exists a (ground) E-reflecting reduction from L_{new} to L_{neg}, then there is no sound and (ground-)complete finite axiom system for $\sim$ over L_{new}.*

We remark that the notion of (ground) E-reflecting reduction requires that only the equations in E are reflected. This means that to establish the negative result over L_{neg} it is enough to identify a particular family of equations that is reflected, disregarding the effects of the reduction on other sound equations. For our purposes, it will be enough to consider the family of equations Φ used by Moller to prove Theorem 2. Hence, our target language will always be CCS_a, for some action a, and we will use the lifting technique presented in this section to prove negative results for the languages $BCCSP_A^p$ (Sect. 4.2), $BCCSP_\tau^p$ (Sect. 4.3), and CCS^τ (Sect. 5).

4 Axiomatisability Results for CSP Parallel Composition

In this section we investigate the existence of finite, ground-complete axiomatisations of bisimilarity over the process description languages $BCCSP_A^p$ (for all $A \subset Act$), $BCCSP_{Act}^p$, $BCCSP^p$ and $BCCSP_\tau^p$. In detail, we apply the reduction technique presented in Sect. 3 to lift Moller's negative result to $BCCSP_A^p$, for each $A \subseteq Act$, and to $BCCSP_\tau^p$ (Theorem 4 and Theorem 6, respectively). In between, we show that the reduction technique cannot be applied to $BCCSP^p$ (Theorem 5). Conversely, we establish a positive result for $BCCSP_{Act}^p$, providing a finite, ground-complete axiomatisation for bisimilarity over this language (Theorem 7).

4.1 The Languages $BCCSP_A^p$, $BCCSP_{Act}^p$, $BCCSP^p$ and $BCCSP_\tau^p$

The languages that we consider in this section are obtained by extending BCCSP with instances of the CSP-like parallel composition operator $|_A$, where $A \subseteq Act$ is the set of actions that must be performed synchronously by the parallel components. For this reason, we shall henceforth refer to A in $|_A$ as to the *synchronisation* set. The operator then behaves like interleaving parallel composition on the complement of A.

In detail, the languages are defined by the following grammar

$$t ::= \quad \mathbf{0} \quad | \quad x \quad | \quad a.t \quad | \quad t+t \quad | \quad t\,|_A\,t,$$

with $x \in Var$ and $a \in Act$, and they differ in the choice of the synchronisation set(s) $A \subseteq Act$ as follows:

$BCCSP_A^p$ The parallel operator $|_A$ is defined only over the fixed set $A \subset Act$ (notice that the inclusion is strict).

$BCCSP_{Act}^p$ The only synchronisation set is the entire set of actions Act.

$BCCSP^p$ There are no restrictions on the choice of synchronisation sets, i.e. the signature of the language contains the operator $|_A$ for all $A \subseteq Act$.

Table 5. SOS rules for the parallel operator $|_A$, $A \subseteq \text{Act}$.

$$(\text{lParA}) \ \frac{t \xrightarrow{a} t'}{t \mid_A u \xrightarrow{a} t' \mid_A u} \ a \notin A \qquad (\text{rParA}) \ \frac{u \xrightarrow{a} u'}{t \mid_A u \xrightarrow{a} t \mid_A u'} \ a \notin A$$

$$(\text{syncA}) \ \frac{t \xrightarrow{a} t', \quad u \xrightarrow{a} u'}{t \mid_A u \xrightarrow{a} t' \mid_A u'} \ a \in A$$

BCCSP$_\tau^{\text{P}}$ This is like BCCSP^{P} with the additional property that the prefixing operator is of the form $\mu.t$, with $\mu \in \text{Act} \cup \{\tau\}$ for a special action label $\tau \notin \text{Act}$ (see Sect. 4.3 for further details).

The SOS rules for the CSP-like parallel composition operator $|_A$ are given in Table 5. The operational semantics of each of the above-mentioned languages is then given by the rules in Table 1 and those in Table 5, in which A is instantiated according to the considered language.

Let $L \in \{\text{BCCSP}_A^{\text{P}}, \text{BCCSP}_{\text{Act}}^{\text{P}}, \text{BCCSP}^{\text{P}}, \text{BCCSP}_\tau^{\text{P}}\}$. Since in the technical results to follow we will need to distinguish between transitions over L processes and transitions over CCS_a processes, to avoid possible confusion we will denote the transition relation over $\mathcal{P}(L)$ induced by the rules in Tables 1 and 5 by $\rightarrow_{\text{p}}$. Similarly, we can properly instantiate the definition of bisimilarity over L processes:

Definition 6 (Bisimilarity over BCCSP$_A^{\text{P}}$, BCCSP$_{\text{Act}}^{\text{P}}$, BCCSP^{P} and BCCSP$_\tau^{\text{P}}$). *Let L be any of $\text{BCCSP}_A^{\text{P}}, \text{BCCSP}_{\text{Act}}^{\text{P}}, \text{BCCSP}^{\text{P}}, \text{BCCSP}_\tau^{\text{P}}$. Bisimulation relations over L processes are defined by applying Definition 2 to the LTS $(\mathcal{P}(L), \text{Act}, \rightarrow_{\text{p}})$ induced by the SOS rules in Tables 1 and 5. We use the symbol $\sim_{\text{p}}$ to denote bisimilarity over L processes.*

It is worth noticing that, as briefly outlined above, when the parallel components t, u in $t \mid_A u$ contain only actions that are not in A, then the semantics of $|_A$ coincides with the semantics of CCS interleaving parallel composition. On the other hand, when t and u contain only actions in A, then $|_A$ behaves like "synchronous" parallel composition. The following example highlights these observations.

Example 1. Let $A \subseteq \text{Act}$ and $b \in A$. It is not difficult to see that

$$b \mid_A \sum_{i=1}^{n} b^i \sim_{\text{p}} b \qquad\qquad (n \geq 1)$$

and therefore

$$b \mid_A \sum_{i=1}^{n} b^i \sim_{\text{p}} b \mid_A \sum_{j=1}^{m} b^j \qquad\qquad (n, m \geq 1).$$

In particular, we have that the axiom

$$b.x \mid_A (b.y + z) \approx (b.x \mid_A b.y) + (b.x \mid_A z) \qquad \text{if } b \in A$$

is sound modulo $\sim_{\text{p}}$ over the languages considered in this section.

Conversely, if we pick an action $a \notin A$, then we have

$$a \mid_A \sum_{i=1}^{n} a^i \sim_{\mathrm{p}} a . \sum_{i=1}^{n} a^i + \sum_{j=1}^{n} a^{j+1} \qquad (n \geq 0)$$

and thus

$$a \mid_A \sum_{i=1}^{n} a^i \nsim_{\mathrm{p}} a \mid_A \sum_{j=1}^{m} a^j \qquad (n \neq m).$$

◄

Notice that, for $a \notin A$, if we let

$$\varphi_A^n : a \mid_A \sum_{i=1}^{n} a^i \approx a . \sum_{i=1}^{n} a^i + \sum_{j=1}^{n} a^{j+1} \qquad (n \geq 0), \tag{1}$$

then the family of equations $\Phi_A = \{\varphi_A^n \mid n \in \mathbb{N}\}$ can be thought of as the counterpart in $\mathrm{BCCSP}_A^{\mathrm{p}}$ of the family Φ used by Moller to prove Theorem 2. As we will see, this correspondence will be instrumental in applying the reduction technique to those languages.

4.2 The Negative Result for $\mathrm{BCCSP}_A^{\mathrm{p}}$

We start our investigations with $\mathrm{BCCSP}_A^{\mathrm{p}}$, for a given set $A \subset \mathrm{Act}$. In particular, by applying the proof methodology discussed in Sect. 3, we prove that:

Theorem 4. *$\mathrm{BCCSP}_A^{\mathrm{p}}$ does not have a finite, ground-complete axiomatisation modulo bisimilarity.*

Our first step consists in defining a mapping allowing us to rewrite $\mathrm{BCCSP}_A^{\mathrm{p}}$ terms into CCS_a terms. As the target language is built over a specific action, it is natural to have a definition of our mapping that is parametric in that action. Hence, choose an action $a \in \mathrm{Act} \setminus A$. Notice that the requirement that the inclusion $A \subset \mathrm{Act}$ be strict guarantees that such an action a exists.

Definition 7 (The mapping p_a^A). *The mapping $\mathrm{p}_a^A : \mathbb{T}(BCCSP_A^{\mathrm{p}}) \to \mathbb{T}(CCS_a)$ is defined inductively over the structure of terms as follows:*

$$\mathrm{p}_a^A(0) = 0 \qquad \mathrm{p}_a^A(x) = x \qquad \mathrm{p}_a^A(t + u) = \mathrm{p}_a^A(t) + \mathrm{p}_a^A(u)$$

$$\mathrm{p}_a^A(b.t) = \begin{cases} a.\mathrm{p}_a^A(t) & \text{if } b = a, \\ 0 & \text{otherwise.} \end{cases} \qquad \mathrm{p}_a^A(t \mid_A u) = \mathrm{p}_a^A(t) \parallel \mathrm{p}_a^A(u).$$

By Definition 7, for each $t \in \mathbb{T}(\mathrm{BCCSP}_A^{\mathrm{p}})$, the only action occurring in $\mathrm{p}_a^A(t)$ is a.

In order to lift the negative result in Theorem 2 to $\mathrm{BCCSP}_A^{\mathrm{p}}$, we need to prove that the proposed mapping p_a^A is a ground Φ-reflecting reduction. Let us first focus on showing that p_a^A is a reduction, i.e., we need to show that it satisfies the two constraints in Definition 3.

Remark 2. For simplicity, we shall sometimes extend the mapping notation from terms to equations. For instance, if $e : t \approx u$ is an equation over $BCCSP_A^p$ terms, we shall write $p_a^A(e)$ to denote the equation over CCS_a terms $p_a^A(t) \approx p_a^A(u)$.

The following lemma is immediate from Definition 7.

Lemma 1. *The mapping p_a^A is structural.*

Hence, in light of Proposition 1, the mapping p_a^A satisfies Definition 3.2. Our order of business will now be to show that p_a^A preserves sound equations.

Lemma 2. *For all $p \in \mathcal{P}(BCCSP_A^p)$ and $q \in \mathcal{P}(CCS_a)$, if $p_a^A(p) \xrightarrow{a} q$, then there exists a $BCCSP_A^p$ process p' such that $p \xrightarrow{a}_p p'$ and $p_a^A(p') = q$.*

Proof. We proceed by structural induction over p.

- Case $p = 0$. This is vacuous, since $p_a^A(p)$ has no outgoing transition.
- Case $p = b.p_0$. By Definition 7 and the assumption that $p_a^A(p) \xrightarrow{a} q$, we have that $b = a \notin A$ and $p_a^A(p_0) = q$. As $p \xrightarrow{a}_p p_0$, the claim follows.
- Case $p = p_1 \mid_A p_2$. By Definition 7, we have that $p_a^A(p) = p_a^A(p_1) \parallel p_a^A(p_2)$. Moreover, by the proviso of the lemma, $p_a^A(p_1) \parallel p_a^A(p_2) \xrightarrow{a} q$, for some CCS_a process q. This follows by an application of either rule (lPar) or rule (rPar) from Table 4. We can assume, without loss of generality, that rule (lPar) was applied. (The case of an application of rule (rPar) follows from a similar reasoning.) Hence $p_a^A(p_1) \xrightarrow{a} q'$ for some CCS_a process q' such that $q' \parallel p_a^A(p_2) = q$. By the induction hypothesis, we obtain that $p_1 \xrightarrow{a}_p p_1'$ for some $p_1' \in \mathcal{P}(BCCSP_A^p)$ such that $p_a^A(p_1') = q'$. Hence, as $p_1 \xrightarrow{a}_p p_1'$ and $a \notin A$, we can apply rule (lParA) from Table 5 and obtain that $p = p_1 \mid_A p_2 \xrightarrow{a}_p p_1' \mid_A p_2$. Since $p_a^A(p_1' \mid_A p_2) = p_a^A(p_1') \parallel p_a^A(p_2) = q' \parallel p_a^A(p_2) = q$, the claim follows.
- Case $p = p_1 + p_2$. This case is similar to the case of parallel composition discussed above. The only difference is that rules (lSum) and (rSum) from Table 1 are applied in place of rules (lParA) and (rParA), respectively. □

Lemma 3. *For all $p, p' \in \mathcal{P}(BCCSP_A^p)$, if $p \xrightarrow{a}_p p'$ then $p_a^A(p) \xrightarrow{a} p_a^A(p')$.*

Proof. We proceed by induction on the size of the proof for the transition $p \xrightarrow{a}_p p'$. We distinguish three cases, according to the last inference rule from Tables 1 and 5 that is applied in the proof. (Notice that the analysis of symmetric rules is omitted.) We remark that since $a \notin A$, rule (syncA) cannot be applied as the last rule in the proof for $p \xrightarrow{a}_p p'$.

- Rule (act). In this case, we have that $p = a.p'$ and $p \xrightarrow{a}_p p'$. By Definition 7, we have that $p_a^A(a.p') = a.p_a^A(p')$, and, thus, we can apply rule (act) and obtain that $p_a^A(p) = p_a^A(a.p') = a.p_a^A(p') \xrightarrow{a} p_a^A(p')$. Hence the claim follows in this case.
- Rule (lSum). In this case, we have that $p = p_0 + p_1$, $p_0 \xrightarrow{a}_p p'$, and $p_a^A(p) = p_a^A(p_0) + p_a^A(p_1)$. By the inductive hypothesis we get that $p_a^A(p_0) \xrightarrow{a} p_a^A(p')$. By applying now rule (lSum), we conclude that $p_a^A(p) = p_a^A(p_0) + p_a^A(p_1) \xrightarrow{a} p_a^A(p')$.

– Rule (lParA). In this case, as $a \notin A$, we have that $p = p_0 \mid_A p_1$, $p_0 \xrightarrow{a}_{\mathrm{P}} p_0'$ for some $p_0' \in \mathcal{P}(\mathrm{BCCSP}_A^{\mathrm{P}})$, and $p' = p_0' \mid_A p_1$. By induction, we obtain that $\mathrm{p}_a^A(p_0) \xrightarrow{a} \mathrm{p}_a^A(p_0')$. Hence, by applying rule (lPar) from Table 4 to $\mathrm{p}_a^A(p)$, we get that $\mathrm{p}_a^A(p) = \mathrm{p}_a^A(p_0) \parallel \mathrm{p}_a^A(p_1) \xrightarrow{a} \mathrm{p}_a^A(p_0') \parallel \mathrm{p}_a^A(p_1) = \mathrm{p}_a^A(p_0' \mid_A p_1) = \mathrm{p}_a^A(p')$. □

We can now proceed to prove that p_a^A satisfies Definition 3.1 as well. Moreover, we show that it is also ground Φ-reflecting.

Proposition 2. *The mapping p_a^A satisfies the following properties:*

1. *For all $t, u \in \mathbb{T}(BCCSP_A^{\mathrm{P}})$, if $t \sim_{\mathrm{p}} u$ then $\mathrm{p}_a^A(t) \sim \mathrm{p}_a^A(u)$.*
2. *The mapping p_a^A is ground Φ-reflecting.*

Proof. We prove the two items separately.

1. First, observe that for every (closed) term t in CCS_a there is a (closed) term $t_a^{\mathrm{P},A}$ in $\mathrm{BCCSP}_A^{\mathrm{P}}$ such that $\mathrm{p}_a^A(t_a^{\mathrm{P},A}) = t$. The term $t_a^{\mathrm{P},A}$ is defined as follows:

$$0_a^{\mathrm{P},A} = 0 \qquad x_a^{\mathrm{P},A} = x \qquad (a.t)_a^{\mathrm{P},A} = a.t_a^{\mathrm{P},A}$$
$$(t + u)_a^{\mathrm{P},A} = t_a^{\mathrm{P},A} + u_a^{\mathrm{P},A} \qquad (t \parallel u)_a^{\mathrm{P},A} = t_a^{\mathrm{P},A} \mid_A u_a^{\mathrm{P},A}.$$

Given a CCS_a substitution σ, we define $\sigma_a^{\mathrm{P},A}$ to be the $\mathrm{BCCSP}_A^{\mathrm{P}}$ substitution given by $\sigma_a^{\mathrm{P},A}(x) = (\sigma(x))_a^{\mathrm{P},A}$. By Proposition 1 and since the mapping p_a^A is structural (Lemma 1), we have that

$$\mathrm{p}_a^A(\sigma_a^{\mathrm{P},A}(t)) = \mathrm{p}_a^A(\sigma_a^{\mathrm{P},A})(\mathrm{p}_a^A(t)) = \sigma(\mathrm{p}_a^A(t)),$$

for all $t \in \mathbb{T}(\mathrm{BCCSP}_A^{\mathrm{P}})$.

To prove the claim, it is then enough to show that the following relation

$$\mathcal{R} = \{(\sigma(\mathrm{p}_a^A(t)), \sigma(\mathrm{p}_a^A(u))) \mid t \sim_{\mathrm{p}} u \text{ and } \sigma \colon \mathrm{Var} \to \mathcal{P}(\mathrm{CCS}_a)\}$$

is a bisimulation relation over CCS_a processes.

Notice, first of all, that since $\sim_{\mathrm{p}}$ is symmetric, then so is $\mathcal{R}$. Assume now that $\sigma(\mathrm{p}_a^A(t)) \mathcal{R} \sigma(\mathrm{p}_a^A(u))$, where $t, u \in \mathbb{T}(\mathrm{BCCSP}_A^{\mathrm{P}})$ and σ is a closed CCS_a substitution. By the definition of $\mathcal{R}$, we have that $t \sim_{\mathrm{p}} u$. Assume now that $\sigma(\mathrm{p}_a^A(t)) \xrightarrow{a} q$ for some $q \in \mathcal{P}(\mathrm{CCS}_a)$. By the observation above, this means that $\mathrm{p}_a^A(\sigma_a^{\mathrm{P},A}(t)) \xrightarrow{a} q$. By Lemma 2, we get that $\sigma_a^{\mathrm{P},A}(t) \xrightarrow{a}_{\mathrm{p}} p'$ for some $p' \in \mathcal{P}(\mathrm{BCCSP}_A^{\mathrm{P}})$ such that $\mathrm{p}_a^A(p') = q$. As $t \sim_{\mathrm{p}} u$ implies that $\sigma_a^{\mathrm{P},A}(t) \sim_{\mathrm{p}} \sigma_a^{\mathrm{P},A}(u)$, we have that $\sigma_a^{\mathrm{P},A}(u) \xrightarrow{a}_{\mathrm{p}} p''$, for some $p'' \in \mathcal{P}(\mathrm{BCCSP}_A^{\mathrm{P}})$ such that $p' \sim_{\mathrm{p}} p''$. Additionally, by Lemma 3 we have that $\sigma(\mathrm{p}_a^A(u)) = \mathrm{p}_a^A(\sigma_a^{\mathrm{P},A}(u)) \xrightarrow{a} \mathrm{p}_a^A(p'')$. We can then conclude by noticing that, since $p' \sim_{\mathrm{p}} p''$, by definition of $\mathcal{R}$ it holds that $q = \mathrm{p}_a^A(p') \mathcal{R} \mathrm{p}_a^A(p'')$, i.e., $\mathcal{R}$ is a bisimulation relation over CCS_a processes.
2. In order to show that p_a^A is ground Φ-reflecting, it is enough to argue that the family Φ_A consisting of the closed equations φ_A^n defined in Eq. 1 is mapped exactly onto Φ. Since $a \notin A$ we have that p_a^A simply replaces all the occurrences of $\mid_A$ in each equation φ_A^n with $\parallel$. Hence, we have that $\mathrm{p}_a^A(\varphi_A^n) = \varphi_n$, for each $n \geq 0$. □

From Lemma 1 and Proposition 2, we can infer that p_a^A is a well-defined reduction as in Definition 3, and it is also ground Φ-reflecting. Theorem 4 then follows by Theorem 2 and Theorem 3.

4.3   The Case of BCCSP^P and the Negative Result for BCCSP$^P_\tau$

Given the negative result over BCCSP^P_A, it is natural to wonder what happens when we extend that language to BCCSP^P, namely BCCSP enriched with an operator $|_A$, for each $A \subseteq$ Act.

One might expect that bisimilarity does not have a finite, ground-complete axiomatisation over BCCSP^P and indeed we conjecture that such a results holds. However, the reduction method cannot be applied to prove such a claim. Specifically, consider the language BCCSP^P over Act $= \{a\}$. We can prove the following result:

Theorem 5. *There is no structural reduction from BCCSP^P to CCS$_a$ that is ground Φ-reflecting.*

Proof. To simplify notation, let us use $|_a$ in place of $|_{\{a\}}$.

Assume that $\widehat{\cdot}$ is a structural reduction from BCCSP^P to CCS$_a$. Our aim is to prove that $\widehat{\cdot}$ is not ground Φ-reflecting.

To this end, we start by recalling that, since $\widehat{\cdot}$ is structural (Definition 4), then:

$$\widehat{at} = \widehat{ax}[\widehat{t}/x], \text{ for each } t \in \mathbb{T}(\text{BCCSP}^P) \tag{2}$$

$$\widehat{t_1 \odot t_2} = \widehat{x_1 \odot x_2}[\widehat{t_1}/x_1, \widehat{t_2}/x_2], \text{ for each } t_1, t_2 \in \mathbb{T}(\text{BCCSP}^P) \tag{3}$$

$$\text{and binary operator } \odot \in \{+, |_\emptyset, |_a\}.$$

Moreover, as $\widehat{\cdot}$ preserves sound equations (Definition 3), we have that:

$$\widehat{ax \,|_a\, \mathbf{0}} \sim \widehat{\mathbf{0}} \sim \widehat{\mathbf{0} \,|_a\, ax}; \tag{4}$$

$$\widehat{a^n \,|_a\, a^n} \sim \widehat{a^n}, \text{ for all } n \geq 0; \tag{5}$$

$$\widehat{\mathbf{0} + \mathbf{0}} \sim \widehat{\mathbf{0}}; \tag{6}$$

$$\widehat{\mathbf{0} \,|_\emptyset\, \mathbf{0}} \sim \widehat{\mathbf{0}}. \tag{7}$$

Assume now that

$$\widehat{x_1 |_a x_2} = t \tag{8}$$

for some $t \in \mathbb{T}(\text{CCS}_a)$ with $\text{var}(t) \subseteq \{x_1, x_2\}$ (as $\widehat{\cdot}$ is structural).

We can distinguish two cases, according to whether t is a closed term or not. In both cases, we shall show that $\widehat{\cdot}$ is not ground Φ-reflecting.

– CASE 1: t IS A CLOSED CCS$_a$ TERM. In this case, for each $n \geq 0$, we have that

$$t \sim \widehat{a^n} \sim \mathbf{0}. \tag{9}$$

Indeed,

$$\widehat{a^n} \sim \widehat{a^n \,|_a\, a^n} \qquad\qquad \text{(by 5)}$$
$$\sim t[\widehat{a^n}/x_1, \widehat{a^n}/x_2] \qquad\qquad \text{(by 3 and 8)}$$
$$\sim t[\widehat{\mathbf{0}}/x_1, \widehat{\mathbf{0}}/x_2] \qquad\qquad \text{(since } t \text{ is closed)}$$
$$\sim \widehat{\mathbf{0}} \qquad\qquad \text{(by 3 and 5 with } n = 0\text{)}.$$

We now claim that

Claim 1: *For each* $p \in \mathcal{P}(BCCSP^P)$, *it holds that* $\widehat{p} \sim \widehat{0}$.

Before proving Claim 1 above, we observe that by using it we can immediately show that the mapping $\widehat{}$ is not ground Φ-reflecting. Indeed, since

$$a \parallel a \not\sim a \parallel (a + a^2),$$

by Claim 1 there cannot be two processes $p, q \in \mathcal{P}(BCCSP^P)$ such that $\widehat{p} = a \parallel a$ and $\widehat{q} = a \parallel (a + a^2)$. Let us now prove Claim 1.

Proof of Claim 1: We proceed by induction on the structure of process p.

- The case $p = 0$ is trivial.
- Case $p = aq$. We have

$$\widehat{p} = \widehat{ax}[\widehat{q}/x] \qquad \qquad \text{(by 2)}$$
$$\sim \widehat{ax}[\widehat{0}/x] \qquad \text{(by induction and } \sim \text{ is a congruence)}$$
$$\sim \widehat{a0} \qquad \qquad \text{(by 2)}$$
$$\sim \widehat{0} \qquad \qquad \text{(by 9).}$$

- Case $p = p_1 \odot p_2$ for some binary operator $\odot \in \{+, |_\emptyset, |_a\}$. In this case,

$$\widehat{p} = \widehat{x_1 \odot x_2}[\widehat{p_1}/x_1, \widehat{p_2}/x_2] \qquad \qquad \text{(by 3)}$$
$$\sim \widehat{x_1 \odot x_2}[\widehat{0}/x_1, \widehat{0}/x_2] \qquad \text{(by induction and } \sim \text{ is a congruence)}$$
$$\sim \widehat{0 \odot 0} \qquad \qquad \text{(by 3)}$$
$$\sim \widehat{0} \qquad \qquad \text{(by 5−7 according to the form of } \odot \text{).}$$

This concludes the Proof of Claim 1.

The proof of Case 1 is now complete.

- CASE 2: t IS AN OPEN CCS_a TERM. Assume, without loss of generality, that t contains at least an occurrence of x_1. (The cases of $x_2 \in var(t)$ and $x_1, x_2 \in var(t)$ can be treated in a similar fashion and are therefore omitted.) Firstly, we observe that for each $p \in \mathcal{P}(BCCSP^P)$

$$\widehat{0} \sim \widehat{ap |_a 0} \qquad \qquad \text{(by 4)}$$
$$= t[\widehat{ap}/x_1, \widehat{0}/x_2] \qquad \text{(by 3 and 8).}$$

Moreover, we recall that for every $u \in CCS_a$ and $y \in Var$, it holds that whenever $y \in var(u)$ then $\text{depth}(\sigma(y)) \leq \text{depth}(\sigma(u))$ for every closed substitution σ. Hence, since $t \in \mathbb{T}(CCS_a)$ and $x_1 \in var(t)$, we have that

$$\text{depth}(\widehat{ap}) \leq \text{depth}(\widehat{ap |_a 0}) = \text{depth}(\widehat{0}). \qquad \qquad (10)$$

We claim that

Claim 2: *For each $n \geq 0$ and processes $p_1, \ldots, p_n \in \mathcal{P}(BCCSP^P)$, it holds that* $\text{depth}(\widehat{\sum_{i=1}^n ap_i}) \leq \text{depth}(\widehat{\mathbf{0}})$.

Proof of Claim 2: We proceed by induction on $n \geq 0$.

- The case $n = 0$ is trivial.
- For the inductive step, we have that:

$$\text{depth}(\widehat{\sum_{i=1}^{n+1} ap_i})$$

$$= \text{depth}(\widehat{\sum_{i=1}^n ap_i + ap_{n+1}})$$

$$= \text{depth}(\widehat{x_1 + x_2}[\widehat{\sum_{i=1}^n ap_i}/x_1, \widehat{ap_{n+1}}/x_2]) \qquad \text{(by 3)}$$

$$\leq \text{depth}(\widehat{x_1 + x_2}[\widehat{\mathbf{0}}/x_1, \widehat{\mathbf{0}}/x_2]) \qquad\qquad \text{(by induction and 10)}$$

$$= \text{depth}(\widehat{\mathbf{0} + \mathbf{0}}) \qquad\qquad\qquad\qquad \text{(by 3)}$$

$$= \text{depth}(\widehat{\mathbf{0}}) \qquad\qquad\qquad\qquad\quad \text{(by 6 and Remark 1)}.$$

This concludes the Proof of Claim 2.

Claim 3: *For each $p \in \mathcal{P}(BCCSP^P)$ it holds that* $\text{depth}(\widehat{p}) \leq \widehat{(\mathbf{0})}$.

Proof of Claim 3: First of all, we notice that each $BCCSP^P$ process can be rewritten into *head normal form* up to bisimilarity. This means that, given any $p \in \mathcal{P}(BCCSP^P)$, we have that $p \sim \sum_{i=1}^n ap_i$ for some $n \geq 0$ and $p_1, \ldots, p_n \in \mathcal{P}(BCCSP^P)$.

Since $\widehat{\cdot}$ preserves sound equations, we have

$$\widehat{p} \sim \widehat{\sum_{i=1}^n ap_i}.$$

Hence, by Claim 2 above, it follows that

$$\text{depth}(\widehat{p}) = \text{depth}(\widehat{\sum_{i=1}^n ap_i}) \leq \text{depth}(\widehat{\mathbf{0}}). \qquad (11)$$

This concludes the Proof of Claim 3.

We can now proceed to show that $\widehat{\cdot}$ is not ground Φ-reflecting. Let $k = \text{depth}(\widehat{\mathbf{0}})$. We have that equation $\varphi_k \in \Phi$ is of the form:

$$a \parallel \left(\sum_{i=1}^k a^i\right) \approx a.\left(\sum_{i=1}^k a^i\right) + \sum_{i=2}^{k+1} a^i.$$

In particular, the depth of $a \parallel (\sum_{i=1}^k a^i)$ is $k + 1$. Therefore, by 11, there is no $p \in \mathcal{P}(BCCSP^P)$ such that $\widehat{p} = a \parallel (\sum_{i=1}^k a^i)$.

The proof of Case 2 is now concluded.

This completes the proof of the Theorem 5.   □

Although we proved Theorem 5 in the simplified setting of Act = $\{a\}$, it is not difficult to see that the proof can be extended to the general case $\{a\} \subset$ Act in a straightforward manner.

Since the reduction method cannot be applied, one might show the non-existence of a finite, ground-complete axiomatisation of bisimilarity over BCCSP^p by adapting the strategy employed by Moller in his proof of Theorem 2. However, since that proof would require several pages of technical results, we leave it as an avenue for future research, and we deal with the presence of all the operators $|_A$ in a simplified setting.

The basic idea behind the reduction defined for BCCSP^p_A is that we can always identify an action $a \in$ Act $\setminus A$ such that the parallel operator $|_A$ always allows for interleaving of a-moves of its arguments. Clearly, if we add an operator $|_A$ for each $A \subseteq$ Act to the language, it is no longer possible to identify such an action. There is, however, a special action that is not used to build syntactically CSP terms, but it is however necessary to express their semantics: the silent action $\tau \notin$ Act. CSP terms are defined over Act, which means that the language does not offer a τ-prefixing operator; however, in order to properly define the operational semantics of the internal choice operator, the set of action labels in the LTS is Act $\cup \{\tau\}$. In particular, as explained in [19], the operational semantics of the parallel operators always allow for the interleaving of τ-moves of their arguments.

Hence, we now consider BCCSP$^p_\tau$, i.e., the extension of BCCSP^p that includes the τ-prefixing operator, and we prove the following result:

Theorem 6. *BCCSP$^p_\tau$ modulo bisimilarity does not afford a finite, ground-complete axiomatisation.*

To this end, we apply the same proof technique that we used in Sect. 4.2 for BCCSP^p_A. The reduction mapping for BCCSP$^p_\tau$ is almost identical to the mapping p^A_a defined for BCCSP^p_A, the only difference being that now we consider the language CCS$_\tau$ as target language, i.e., CCS$_a$ with $a = \tau$.

Remark 3. Theorem 2 remains true over CCS$_\tau$. In fact, as we are considering strong bisimilarity, there is no difference between τ and any other observable action $a \in$ Act. Specifically, if we let Φ_τ be the family of equations in Φ in which each occurrence of a is replaced by τ, then we can repeat Moller's arguments in a step-by-step fashion to obtain that no finite axiom system, that is sound modulo bisimilarity, can prove the whole family of equations Φ_τ.

Definition 8 (The mapping p_τ). *The mapping $p_\tau \colon \mathbb{T}(BCCSP^p_\tau) \to \mathbb{T}(CCS_\tau)$ is defined inductively over the structure of BCCSP$^p_\tau$ terms as follows:*

$$p_\tau(0) = 0 \qquad p_\tau(x) = x \qquad p_\tau(t + u) = p_\tau(t) + p_\tau(u)$$

$$p_\tau(\mu.t) = \begin{cases} \tau.p_\tau(t) & \text{if } \mu = \tau, \\ 0 & \text{otherwise;} \end{cases} \qquad p_\tau(t \mid_A u) = p_\tau(t) \parallel p_\tau(u).$$

Intuitively, we use the mapping p_τ to eliminate any action $b \neq \tau$ from terms, so that a process $p_\tau(p \mid_A q)$ can perform a transition $p_\tau(p \mid_A q) \xrightarrow{\tau} p'$, for some CCS_a process p', if and only if $b = \tau$. (Recall that, by construction $\tau \notin A$ for each $A \subseteq \text{Act.}$)

First, we note that this mapping is a structural mapping.

Lemma 4. *The mapping p_τ is structural.*

We now state the corresponding results over $BCCSP_\tau^P$ to Lemma 2 and Lemma 3.

Lemma 5. *For all $p \in \mathcal{P}(BCCSP_\tau^P)$ and $q \in \mathcal{P}(CCS_\tau)$, if $p_\tau(p) \xrightarrow{\tau} q$, then there exists a $BCCSP_\tau^P$ process p', such that $p \xrightarrow{\tau}_p p'$ and $p_\tau(p') = q$.*

Proof. The proof is by structural induction over p. We omit it since it is similar to that of Lemma 2. $\qquad\square$

Lemma 6. *For all $p, p' \in \mathcal{P}(BCCSP_\tau^P)$, if $p \xrightarrow{\tau}_p p'$ then $p_\tau(p) \xrightarrow{\tau} p_\tau(p')$.*

Proof. The proof proceeds by induction over the size of the proof for $p \xrightarrow{\tau}_p p'$. It is analogous to the proof of Lemma 3, and it is therefore omitted. $\qquad\square$

The following result, which extends Proposition 2 to $BCCSP_\tau^P$, allows us to prove that p_τ is a well-defined reduction mapping that is also ground Φ_τ-reflecting.

Proposition 3. *The following properties hold for the mapping p_τ:*

1. *For all $t, u \in \mathbb{T}(BCCSP_\tau^P)$, if $t \sim_p u$, then $p_\tau(t) \sim p_\tau(u)$.*
2. *The mapping p_τ is ground Φ_τ-reflecting.*

Proof. 1. We start by observing that for every (closed) term t in CCS_τ there is a (closed) term t_τ^P in $BCCSP_\tau^P$ such that $p_\tau(t_\tau^P) = t$. The term t_τ^P is defined as follows:

$$0_\tau^P = 0 \qquad\qquad x_\tau^P = x \qquad\qquad (\tau.t)_\tau^P = \tau.t_\tau^P$$
$$(t + u)_\tau^P = t_\tau^P + u_\tau^P \qquad\qquad (t \parallel u)_\tau^P = t_\tau^P \mid_\emptyset u_\tau^P.$$

Then, given a CCS_τ substitution σ, we define the $BCCSP_\tau^P$ substitution σ_τ^P by $\sigma_\tau^P(x) = (\sigma(x))_\tau^P$. By Lemma 4 and Proposition 1, we have that $p_\tau(\sigma_\tau^P(t)) = p_\tau(\sigma_\tau^P)(p_\tau(t)) = \sigma(p_\tau(t))$ for all $t \in \mathbb{T}(BCCSP_\tau^P)$.
The proof of this statement then proceeds as that of the corresponding statement in Proposition 2, and it is therefore omitted.

2. Consider the family of equations $\Phi_{\tau,\emptyset} = \{\varphi_{\tau,\emptyset}^n \mid n \in \mathbb{N}\}$, where the closed equations $\varphi_{\tau,\emptyset}^n$ are defined as in Eq. 1, using the set $\emptyset$ as synchronisation set, and replacing each occurrence of a with τ. It is straightforward to prove that $p_\tau(\varphi_{\tau,\emptyset}^n) = \varphi_{\tau,n}$ for each $n \in \mathbb{N}$. Hence, p_τ is ground Φ_τ-reflecting. $\qquad\square$

Theorem 6 is then obtained as a direct consequence of Lemma 4, Proposition 3, Theorem 3, and Theorem 2.

Table 6. Additional axioms for BCCSP$^{\text{p}}_{\text{Act}}$.

(P1) $x \mid_{\text{Act}} y \approx y \mid_{\text{Act}} x$

(P2) $(x + y) \mid_{\text{Act}} z \approx (x \mid_{\text{Act}} z) + (y \mid_{\text{Act}} z)$

(P3) $(x \mid_{\text{Act}} 0) \approx 0$

(P4) $(a.x \mid_{\text{Act}} a.y) \approx a.(x \mid_{\text{Act}} y)$, for each $a \in$ Act

(P5) $(a.x \mid_{\text{Act}} b.y) \approx 0$, for $b \neq a$, and $a, b \in$ Act.

4.4   The Case of BCCSP$^{\text{p}}_{\text{Act}}$

We now argue that the requirement that the inclusion $A \subset$ Act be strict, used in Sect. 4.2, is indeed necessary for Theorem 4 to hold. We also notice that a similar requirement is not explicitly expressed for the validity of Theorem 6, proved in Sect. 4.3, because having $\mid_A$ defined for all $A \subseteq$ Act automatically guaranteed the existence of at least one synchronisation set A such that $a \notin A$ for some action $a \in$ Act, namely the synchronisation set $A = \emptyset$. Moreover, as discussed in Example 1, given a synchronisation set A, the requirement $a \notin A$ is crucial to guarantee the soundness modulo bisimilarity of equation φ^n_A, for any $n \in \mathbb{N}$ (see Eq. 1).

In this section, we handle the border case of the language BCCSP$^{\text{p}}_{\text{Act}}$, which includes only the parallel operator $\mid_{\text{Act}}$, and we show that for this special case a positive result holds: we provide a *finite, ground-complete axiomatisation* of bisimilarity over this language. Let us consider the axiom system $\mathcal{E}_{\text{p}} = \mathcal{E}_0 \cup \{\text{P1}, \text{P2}, \text{P3}, \text{P4}, \text{P5}\}$, where $\mathcal{E}_0$ consists of the axioms in Table 3, and axioms P1–P5 are reported in Table 6. Notice that the axiom schemata P4 and P5 generate only finitely many axioms. More precisely, P4 generates $|$Act$|$ axioms, and P5 generates $|$Act$| \times (|$Act$| - 1)$ axioms. We will now prove the following result:

Theorem 7. $\mathcal{E}_{\text{p}}$ *is a finite, ground-complete axiomatisation of* BCCSP$^{\text{p}}_{\text{Act}}$ *modulo bisimilarity.*

The idea behind the proof of Theorem 7 is that the axioms in Table 6 allow us to eliminate all occurrences of the parallel operator $\mid_{\text{Act}}$ from BCCSP$^{\text{p}}_{\text{Act}}$ processes. Hence, every BCCSP$^{\text{p}}_{\text{Act}}$ process can be proven equal to a BCCSP process using $\mathcal{E}_{\text{p}}$. The ground-completeness of $\mathcal{E}_{\text{p}}$ then follows from that of $\mathcal{E}_0$ proven in [28]. To that end, we first show:

Lemma 7. *For all closed BCCSP terms p and q, there exists a closed BCCSP term r such that $\mathcal{E}_{\text{p}} \vdash p \mid_{\text{Act}} q \approx r$.*

Proof. The proof is by induction on size$(p \mid_{\text{Act}} q)$. First of all we notice that, given any closed BCCSP term p, we can assume, without loss of generality, that $p = \sum_{i \in I} a_i p_i$ for some finite index set I, actions $a_i \in$ Act, and closed BCCSP terms p_i, for $i \in I$. In fact, in case p is not already in this shape, then by applying axioms A2 and A4 in Table 3 we can remove superfluous occurrences of 0 summands. In particular, we remark that this transformation does not increase the number of operator symbols occurring in p.

Thus we proceed under the assumption that

$$p = \sum_{i \in I} a_i.p_i \quad \text{and} \quad q = \sum_{j \in J} b_j.q_j.$$

We proceed by a case analysis on the cardinality of the sets of indexes I and J.

- If either $I = \emptyset$ or $J = \emptyset$, then $p = \mathbf{0}$ or $q = \mathbf{0}$. In light of P1, without loss of generality, we can assume that $q = \mathbf{0}$ and we have that $p \mid_{\text{Act}} q = p \mid_{\text{Act}} \mathbf{0}$. Thus by applying axiom P3, we get $\mathcal{E}_p \vdash p \mid_{\text{Act}} q \approx \mathbf{0}$ and we are done.
- If both I and J are singletons, then we have that $p = a.p'$ and $q = b.q'$, for some $a, b \in \text{Act}$ and BCCSP processes p' and q'.
  If $a = b$, then we use axiom P4 to get $\mathcal{E}_p \vdash a.p' \mid_{\text{Act}} a.q' \approx a.(p' \mid_{\text{Act}} q')$. Since the size of $p' \mid_{\text{Act}} q'$ is smaller than that of $p \mid_{\text{Act}} q$, by the induction hypothesis, there exists a BCCSP process r' such that $\mathcal{E}_p \vdash p' \mid_{\text{Act}} q' \approx r'$. Thus we have $\mathcal{E}_p \vdash a.p' \mid_{\text{Act}} a.q' \approx a.r'$, which is a BCCSP process.
  In the case that $a \neq b$, then we can use axiom P5, to infer $\mathcal{E}_p \vdash a.p' \mid_{\text{Act}} b.q' \approx \mathbf{0}$ and we are done.
- We can now assume, without loss of generality, that $|I| > 1$ and $|J| \geq 1$. This means that we can express p as the summation of two summands of smaller size that are different from $\mathbf{0}$, i.e. $p = p_1 + p_2$, for some BCCSP processes p_1 and p_2. Then, we use axiom P2 to get $\mathcal{E}_p \vdash (p_1 + p_2) \mid_{\text{Act}} q \approx (p_1 \mid_{\text{Act}} q) + (p_2 \mid_{\text{Act}} q)$. Since both $p_1 \mid_{\text{Act}} q$ and $p_2 \mid_{\text{Act}} q$ have size less than that of $p \mid_{\text{Act}} q$, by the induction hypothesis, we have that there exist BCCSP processes r' and r'' such that $\mathcal{E}_p \vdash p_1 \mid_{\text{Act}} q \approx r'$ and $\mathcal{E}_p \vdash p_2 \mid_{\text{Act}} q \approx r''$. We thus have that $\mathcal{E}_p \vdash p \mid_{\text{Act}} q \approx r' + r''$, which is a BCCSP process, and we are done. □

The above lemma is the key step in the elimination of $\mid_{\text{Act}}$ from closed terms. Namely:

Proposition 4. *For every closed $BCCSP_{\text{Act}}^p$ process p there exists a closed BCCSP process q such that $\mathcal{E}_p \vdash p \approx q$.*

Proof. The proof is straightforward by structural induction on p and using Lemma 7 in the case that p is of the form $p_1 \mid_{\text{Act}} p_2$, for some $BCCSP_{\text{Act}}^p$ processes p_1, p_2.   □

The ground-completeness of $\mathcal{E}_p$ over $BCCSP_{\text{Act}}^p$ follows from Proposition 4 and the ground-completeness of $\mathcal{E}_0$ over BCCSP [28].

5   The Case of Restriction

In this section we apply the reduction technique described in Sect. 3 to show that bisimilarity does not have a finite, ground-complete equational axiomatisation over the recursion and relabelling free fragment of CCS. In detail, we assume a finite set of action names Act, and we let $\overline{\text{Act}}$ denote the set of action co-names, i.e., $\overline{\text{Act}} = \{\overline{a} \mid a \in \text{Act}\}$. As usual, we postulate that $\overline{\overline{a}} = a$ and $a \neq \overline{a}$ for all $a \in \text{Act}$.

Table 7. The SOS rules for CCS^τ operators ($\mu \in Act_\tau$, $\alpha \in Act \cup \overline{Act}$).

$$(r1)\ \frac{t \xrightarrow{\mu} t'}{t \mid u \xrightarrow{\mu} t' \mid u} \qquad (r2)\ \frac{u \xrightarrow{\mu} u'}{t \mid u \xrightarrow{\mu} t \mid u'} \qquad (r3)\ \frac{t \xrightarrow{\alpha} t' \quad u \xrightarrow{\overline{\alpha}} u'}{t \mid u \xrightarrow{\tau} t' \mid u'}$$

$$(r4)\ \frac{t \xrightarrow{\alpha} t'}{t \backslash L \xrightarrow{\alpha} t' \backslash R}\ \alpha, \overline{\alpha} \notin R \qquad (r5)\ \frac{t \xrightarrow{\tau} t'}{t \backslash L \xrightarrow{\tau} t' \backslash R}$$

Then, we let $Act_\tau = Act \cup \overline{Act} \cup \{\tau\}$, where $\tau \notin Act \cup \overline{Act}$. Henceforth, we let $\mu, \nu, \ldots$ range over actions in Act_τ, $\alpha, \beta, \ldots$ range over actions in $Act \cup \overline{Act}$, and $a, b, \ldots$ range over actions in Act.

We denote by CCS^τ the recursion and relabelling free fragment of CCS with the full merge operator (denoted by $\mid$) generated by the following grammar:

$$t ::= \ \mathbf{0} \ \mid \ x \ \mid \ \mu.t \ \mid \ t + t \ \mid \ t \mid t \ \mid \ t \backslash R \qquad (CCS^\tau)$$

where $x \in Var$, $\mu \in Act_\tau$ and $R \subseteq Act \cup \overline{Act}$.

Following [32], the action symbol τ will result from the synchronised occurrence of the complementary actions α and $\overline{\alpha}$, as described by the inference rules in Table 7.

We recall that the *restriction operator* $t \backslash R$ prevents t (and its derivatives) from performing any α-transition, for all $\alpha \in R$.

The operational semantics of CCS^τ is obtained by adding the inference rules for the full merge and the restriction operator given in Table 7 to the rules for BCCSP operators given in Table 1. In the technical results that follow, we will need to distinguish between transitions over CCS^τ processes, and transitions over CCS_a processes. Hence, to avoid possible confusion and favour thus readability, we adopt the same strategy we used in Sect. 4, and use special symbols to distinguish them: we denote the transition relation induced by the rules in Tables 1 and 7 by $\rightarrow_r$, and bisimilarity over $\mathcal{P}(CCS^\tau)$ by $\sim_r$.

Definition 9 (Bisimulation over CCS^τ). *Bisimulation relations over CCS^τ processes are defined by applying Definition 2 to the LTS $(\mathcal{P}(CCS^\tau), Act_\tau, \rightarrow_r)$ induced by the SOS rules in Table 7. We use the symbol $\sim_r$ to denote bisimilarity over CCS^τ processes.*

5.1 The Negative Result

Our main goal in this section is to prove the following theorem:

Theorem 8. *Bisimilarity has no finite, ground-complete axiomatisation over CCS^τ.*

To this end, as already done in Sects. 4.2 and 4.3, we exploit the reduction technique from [11] and Moller's non-finite axiomatisability result from CCS_a (Theorem 2). In detail:

- We select a particular action $a \in Act$.
- We consider the language CCS_a and the instantiation of the equations φ_n in the family Φ over processes defined using only that action.

– We provide a translation mapping from CCS^τ to CCS_a, denoted by r_a, whose definition will be parametric in the chosen action a, that will allow us to eliminate all CCS^τ terms in which the execution of a is restricted, while ensuring the possibility to perform any a-transition that is unrestricted.

It will be then enough to show that the mapping r_a is structural, it preserves the soundness of equations from CCS^τ to CCS_a, and it is ground Φ-reflecting, to obtain the validity of the lifting of the negative result in Theorem 2 to CCS^τ, proving thus Theorem 8.

5.2 The Reduction

Choose an action a from the action set Act. Then we define a mapping $r_a \colon \mathbb{T}(CCS^\tau) \to \mathbb{T}(CCS_a)$ allowing us to rewrite any CCS^τ term into a CCS_a term.

Definition 10 (The mapping r_a). *The mapping* $r_a \colon \mathbb{T}(CCS^\tau) \to \mathbb{T}(CCS_a)$ *is defined inductively as follows:*

$$r_a(0) = 0 \qquad\qquad r_a(t + u) = r_a(t) + r_a(u)$$

$$r_a(x) = x \qquad\qquad r_a(t \mid u) = r_a(t) \parallel r_a(u)$$

$$r_a(\mu.t) = \begin{cases} a.r_a(t) & \text{if } \mu = a \\ 0 & \text{otherwise} \end{cases} \qquad r_a(t \backslash R) = \begin{cases} r_a(t) & \text{if } a, \bar{a} \notin R \\ 0 & \text{otherwise.} \end{cases}$$

Notice that a is the only action that may possibly occur in $r_a(t)$, for each $t \in \mathbb{T}(CCS^\tau)$.

We now proceed to show that the mapping r_a is a well-defined reduction, according to Definition 3. As a first step, we notice that r_a is structural by definition.

Lemma 8. *The mapping r_a is structural.*

We now proceed to prove two technical lemmas, that will be useful to prove that r_a is a reduction.

Lemma 9. *For all $p \in \mathcal{P}(CCS^\tau)$, and $q \in \mathcal{P}(CCS_a)$, if $r_a(p) \xrightarrow{a} q$, then there exists some $p' \in \mathcal{P}(CCS^\tau)$ such that $p \xrightarrow{a}_r p'$ and $r_a(p') = q$.*

Proof. The proof proceeds by structural induction over the $\mathcal{P}(CCS^\tau)$ process p. As for prefixing, nondeterministic choice, and parallel composition the proof is analogous to that of the corresponding steps in Lemma 2, we limit ourselves to present only the inductive step related to the restriction operator.

Let $p = p_1 \backslash R$. We can distinguish two cases, according to whether $a \in R$ or $\bar{a} \in R$, or not (see Definition 10):

– Assume that $a \in R$ or $\bar{a} \in R$. Then $r_a(p) = 0$, and this case becomes vacuous as $r_a(p) \xrightarrow{a}\!\!\!\!\!/\,$.
– Assume now that $a, \bar{a} \notin R$. Then $r_a(p) = r_a(p_1)$ and $r_a(p_1) \xrightarrow{a} q$. By induction over p_1, there is some $p_1' \in \mathcal{P}(CCS^\tau)$ such that $p_1 \xrightarrow{a}_r p_1'$ and $r_a(p_1') = q$. Since $a, \bar{a} \notin R$, by an application of rule (r4) from Table 7 we obtain that $p \xrightarrow{a}_r p_1' \backslash R$. Finally, by Definition 10, since $a, \bar{a} \notin R$ it follows that $r_a(p_1' \backslash R) = r_a(p_1') = q$ as required. $\qquad\square$

Lemma 10. *For all $p, p' \in \mathcal{P}(CCS^{\tau})$, if $p \overset{a}{\longrightarrow}_{\mathbf{r}} p'$, then $\mathbf{r}_a(p) \overset{a}{\longrightarrow} \mathbf{r}_a(p')$.*

Proof. The proof proceeds by induction over the size of the proof for the transition $p \overset{a}{\longrightarrow}_{\mathbf{r}} p'$. Also in this case, given the similarities with the proofs of the corresponding cases in Lemma 3, we limit ourselves to analyse only the case in which the last inference rule from Table 7 that is applied in the proof for $p \overset{a}{\longrightarrow}_{\mathbf{r}} p'$ is rule (r4), i.e., the rule for restriction. (In particular, we remark that since $a \neq \tau$, rules (r3) and (r5) cannot be applied as the last rules in the proof for $p \overset{a}{\longrightarrow}_{\mathbf{r}} p'$.)

Let (r4) be the last rule applied in the proof. In this case, $p = p_1 \backslash R$, $p_1 \overset{a}{\longrightarrow}_{\mathbf{r}} p_1'$, and $p' = p_1' \backslash R$. In particular, the application of rule (r4) guarantees that $a, \bar{a} \notin R$, so that $\mathbf{r}_a(p) = \mathbf{r}_a(p_1)$, by Definition 10. By induction we obtain that $\mathbf{r}_a(p_1) \overset{a}{\longrightarrow} \mathbf{r}_a(p_1')$. Clearly, this directly gives $\mathbf{r}_a(p) \overset{a}{\longrightarrow} \mathbf{r}_a(p_1')$. Since, moreover, $a, \bar{a} \notin R$, by Definition 10 we also get that $\mathbf{r}_a(p') = \mathbf{r}_a(p_1' \backslash R) = \mathbf{r}_a(p_1')$. We can then conclude that $\mathbf{r}_a(p) \overset{a}{\longrightarrow} \mathbf{r}_a(p')$. □

We now have all the ingredients necessary to prove that the mapping $\mathbf{r}_a$ is a well-defined ground Φ-reflecting reduction.

Proposition 5. *The mapping $\mathbf{r}_a$ satisfies the following properties:*

1. *For each $t, u \in \mathbb{T}(CCS^{\tau})$, $t \sim_{\mathbf{r}} u$ implies $\mathbf{r}_a(t) \sim \mathbf{r}_a(u)$.*
2. *The mapping $\mathbf{r}_a$ is ground Φ-reflecting.*

Proof. We prove the two statements separately.

1. First of all, for each $t \in \mathbb{T}(CCS_a)$ we define $t_a^{\tau} \in \mathbb{T}(CCS^{\tau})$ as follows:

$$\mathbf{0}_a^{\tau} = \mathbf{0} \qquad x_a^{\tau} = a \qquad (a.t)_a^{\tau} = a.t_a^{\tau}$$
$$(t + u)_a^{\tau} = t_a^{\tau} + u_a^{\tau} \qquad (t \parallel u)_a^{\tau} = t_a^{\tau} \mid u_a^{\tau}.$$

   It is then immediate to check that for each $t \in \mathbb{T}(CCS_a)$ we have that $\mathbf{r}_a(t_a^{\tau}) = t$. Then, given any CCS_a substitution σ, we define σ_a^{τ} as the CCS^{τ} substitution such that $\sigma_a^{\tau}(x) = (\sigma(x))_a^{\tau}$. The claim then follows by applying the same reasoning used in the proof of Proposition 2.

2. Consider the family of equations $\Phi_{\mathbf{r}}$ defined as follows:

$$\varphi_{\mathbf{r}}^n : a \mid \sum_{i=1}^{n} a^i \approx a. \sum_{i=1}^{n} a^i + \sum_{j=1}^{n} a^{j+1} \qquad (n \geq 0)$$

$$\Phi_{\mathbf{r}} = \{\varphi_{\mathbf{r}}^n \mid n \geq 0\}.$$

   It is straightforward to prove that $\mathbf{r}_a(\varphi_{\mathbf{r}}^n) = \varphi_n$ for each $n \in \mathbb{N}$, and thus that $\mathbf{r}_a$ is ground Φ-reflecting. □

Theorem 8 is then a immediate consequence of Lemma 8, Proposition 5, Theorem 3, and Theorem 2.

6   Concluding Remarks

In this paper, we have exploited the reduction technique from [11], for the lifting of negative results across process algebras, to prove the non-finite axiomatisability of various extensions of BCCSP modulo bisimilarity. In detail, we have proved that bisimilarity does not admit a finite, ground-complete axiomatisation 1. over $BCCSP_A^p$, i.e., BCCSP enriched with a CSP-like parallel operator $|_A$, with $A \subset Act$, 2. over $BCCSP_\tau^p$, i.e., BCCSP enriched with τ-prefixing, $\tau \notin Act$, and CSP-like parallel operators with any possible synchronisation set, and 3. over CCS^r, i.e., the recursion and relabelling free fragment of CCS. Interestingly, among all these negative results, we found a positive one: if we consider only the CSP-like parallel operator $|_{Act}$, forcing all the actions in the parallel components to be synchronised, then a finite, ground-complete axiomatisation of bisimilarity over $BCCSP_{Act}^p$ exists. Moreover, we have proved that the reduction technique from [11] cannot be applied in the case of $BCCSP^p$, i.e., BCCSP enriched with all parallel operators $|_A$ for $A \subseteq Act$.

As a natural step for future work, we will provide a direct proof of the fact that bisimilarity does not admit a finite, ground-complete axiomatisation over $BCCSP^p$.

Moreover, we plan to investigate how far the lifting technique of [11] can be pushed. In particular, we are interested in studying whether (some variations of) it can be used to lift known results for strong behavioural equivalences to their weak counterparts or to potentially extend results over weak behavioural congruences (such as Theorem 10 presented in [1]) to new settings.

Another possible direction for future work, would be to focus on full recursion free CCS. Aceto, Ingólfsdóttir, Luttik and van Tilburg gave an equational axiomatisation of bisimilarity over recursion-free CCS with interleaving parallel composition and the left-merge operator in [13]. That result crucially depends on the fact that restriction and relabelling distribute over interleaving parallel composition. On the other hand, neither restriction nor relabelling distribute over parallel composition in the presence of synchronisation. Obtaining a complete axiomatisation of full recursion free CCS modulo bisimilarity, with restriction, relabelling and parallel composition that allows for synchronisation is a natural, and very challenging, avenue for future research.

Acknowledgements. The first author thanks Frits Vaandrager for the joint work they did about thirty years ago and Rob van Glabbeek for asking the questions that led to the research presented in this article.

We thank the reviewers for their valuable comments on our paper. In particular, we are very grateful to the reviewer who spotted a technical error in the original manuscript.

References

1. Aceto, L., Anastasiadi, E., Castiglioni, V., Ingólfsdóttir, A., Luttik, B.: In search of lost time: axiomatising parallel composition in process algebras. In: Proceedings of LICS 2021, pp. 1–14. IEEE (2021). https://doi.org/10.1109/LICS52264.2021.9470526
2. Aceto, L., Anastasiadi, E., Castiglioni, V., Ingólfsdóttir, A., Luttik, B., Pedersen, M.R.: On the axiomatisability of priority III: priority strikes again. Theor. Comput. Sci. **837**, 223–246 (2020). https://doi.org/10.1016/j.tcs.2020.07.044

3. Aceto, L., Bloom, B., Vaandrager, F.W.: Turning SOS rules into equations. Inf. Comput. **111**(1), 1–52 (1994). https://doi.org/10.1006/inco.1994.1040

4. Aceto, L., Castiglioni, V., Fokkink, W., Ingólfsdóttir, A., Luttik, B.: Are two binary operators necessary to finitely axiomatise parallel composition? In: Proceedings of CSL 2021. LIPIcs, vol. 183, pp. 8:1–8:17 (2021). https://doi.org/10.4230/LIPIcs.CSL.2021.8

5. Aceto, L., Castiglioni, V., Ingólfsdóttir, A., Luttik, B., Pedersen, M.R.: On the axiomatisability of parallel composition: a journey in the spectrum. In: Proceedings of CONCUR 2020. LIPIcs, vol. 171, pp. 18:1–18:22 (2020). https://doi.org/10.4230/LIPIcs.CONCUR.2020.18

6. Aceto, L., Fokkink, W., van Glabbeek, R.J., Ingólfsdóttir, A.: Nested semantics over finite trees are equationally hard. Inf. Comput. **191**(2), 203–232 (2004). https://doi.org/10.1016/j.ic.2004.02.001

7. Aceto, L., Fokkink, W., Ingólfsdóttir, A.: A menagerie of non finitely based process semantics over BPA* - from ready simulation to completed traces. Math. Struct. Comput. Sci. **8**(3), 193–230 (1998). http://journals.cambridge.org/action/displayAbstract?aid=44743

8. Aceto, L., Fokkink, W., Ingólfsdóttir, A., Luttik, B.: CCS with Hennessy's merge has no finite-equational axiomatization. Theor. Comput. Sci. **330**(3), 377–405 (2005). https://doi.org/10.1016/j.tcs.2004.10.003

9. Aceto, L., Fokkink, W., Ingolfsdottir, A., Luttik, B.: Finite equational bases in process algebra: results and open questions. In: Middeldorp, A., van Oostrom, V., van Raamsdonk, F., de Vrijer, R. (eds.) Processes, Terms and Cycles: Steps on the Road to Infinity. LNCS, vol. 3838, pp. 338–367. Springer, Heidelberg (2005). https://doi.org/10.1007/11601548_18

10. Aceto, L., Fokkink, W., Ingólfsdóttir, A., Luttik, B.: A finite equational base for CCS with left merge and communication merge. ACM Trans. Comput. Log. **10**(1), 6:1–6:26 (2009). https://doi.org/10.1145/1459010.1459016

11. Aceto, L., Fokkink, W., Ingólfsdóttir, A., Mousavi, M.R.: Lifting non-finite axiomatizability results to extensions of process algebras. Acta Inf. **47**(3), 147–177 (2010). https://doi.org/10.1007/s00236-010-0114-7

12. Aceto, L., Fokkink, W., Ingólfsdóttir, A., Nain, S.: Bisimilarity is not finitely based over BPA with interrupt. Theor. Comput. Sci. **366**(1–2), 60–81 (2006). https://doi.org/10.1016/j.tcs.2006.07.003

13. Aceto, L., Ingólfsdóttir, A., Luttik, B., van Tilburg, P.: Finite equational bases for fragments of CCS with restriction and relabelling. In: Ausiello, G., Karhumäki, J., Mauri, G., Ong, L. (eds.) TCS 2008. IIFIP, vol. 273, pp. 317–332. Springer, Boston, MA (2008). https://doi.org/10.1007/978-0-387-09680-3_22

14. Baeten, J.C.M., Basten, T., Reniers, M.: Process Algebra: Equational Theories of Communicating Processes. Cambridge Tracts in Theoretical Computer Science, Cambridge University Press (2009). https://doi.org/10.1017/CBO9781139195003

15. Baeten, J.C.M., Vaandrager, F.W.: An algebra for process creation. Acta Informatica **29**(4), 303–334 (1992). https://doi.org/10.1007/BF01178776

16. Bergstra, J.A., Klop, J.W.: Process algebra for synchronous communication. Inf. Control **60**(1–3), 109–137 (1984). https://doi.org/10.1016/S0019-9958(84)80025-X

17. Bergstra, J.A., Klop, J.W.: Algebra of communicating processes with abstraction. Theor. Comput. Sci. **37**, 77–121 (1985). https://doi.org/10.1016/0304-3975(85)90088-X

18. Bloom, B., Istrail, S., Meyer, A.R.: Bisimulation can't be traced. J. ACM **42**(1), 232–268 (1995). https://doi.org/10.1145/200836.200876

19. Brookes, S.D., Roscoe, A.W., Walker, D.J.: An operational semantics for CSP. Report, University of Oxford (1986)

20. Chen, T., Fokkink, W., van Glabbeek, R.J.: On the axiomatizability of impossible futures. Log. Methods Comput. Sci. **11**(3) (2015). https://doi.org/10.2168/LMCS-11(3:17)2015

21. Fokkink, W.J., Luttik, S.P.: An ω-complete equational specification of interleaving. In: Montanari, U., Rolim, J.D.P., Welzl, E. (eds.) ICALP 2000. LNCS, vol. 1853, pp. 729–743. Springer, Heidelberg (2000). https://doi.org/10.1007/3-540-45022-X_61

22. Glabbeek, R.J.: The linear time - branching time spectrum. In: Baeten, J.C.M., Klop, J.W. (eds.) CONCUR 1990. LNCS, vol. 458, pp. 278–297. Springer, Heidelberg (1990). https://doi.org/10.1007/BFb0039066

23. van Glabbeek, R.J.: Full abstraction in structural operational semantics (extended abstract). In: Proceedings of AMAST 1993, pp. 75–82. Workshops in Computing (1993)

24. van Glabbeek, R., Vaandrager, F.: Modular specifications in process algebra. In: Wirsing, M., Bergstra, J.A. (eds.) Algebraic Methods 1987. LNCS, vol. 394, pp. 465–506. Springer, Heidelberg (1989). https://doi.org/10.1007/BFb0015049

25. van Glabbeek, R., Vaandrager, F.: Petri net models for algebraic theories of concurrency. In: de Bakker, J.W., Nijman, A.J., Treleaven, P.C. (eds.) PARLE 1987. LNCS, vol. 259, pp. 224–242. Springer, Heidelberg (1987). https://doi.org/10.1007/3-540-17945-3_13

26. Groote, J.F., Vaandrager, F.W.: Structured operational semantics and bisimulation as a congruence. Inf. Comput. **100**(2), 202–260 (1992). https://doi.org/10.1016/0890-5401(92)90013-6

27. Groote, J.F., de Vink, E.P.: An axiomatization of strong distribution bisimulation for a language with a parallel operator and probabilistic choice. In: ter Beek, M.H., Fantechi, A., Semini, L. (eds.) From Software Engineering to Formal Methods and Tools, and Back. LNCS, vol. 11865, pp. 449–463. Springer, Cham (2019). https://doi.org/10.1007/978-3-030-30985-5_26

28. Hennessy, M., Milner, R.: Algebraic laws for nondeterminism and concurrency. J. ACM **32**(1), 137–161 (1985). https://doi.org/10.1145/2455.2460

29. Hoare, C.A.R.: Communicating Sequential Processes. Prentice-Hall (1985)

30. Keller, R.M.: Formal verification of parallel programs. Commun. ACM **19**(7), 371–384 (1976). https://doi.org/10.1145/360248.360251

31. Middelburg, C.A.: Probabilistic process algebra and strategic interleaving. Sci. Ann. Comput. Sci. **30**(2), 205–243 (2020). https://doi.org/10.7561/SACS.2020.2.205

32. Milner, R.: Communication and Concurrency. PHI Series in Computer Science. Prentice Hall (1989)

33. Moller, F.: Axioms for Concurrency. Ph.D. thesis, Department of Computer Science, University of Edinburgh, July 1989. https://era.ed.ac.uk/bitstream/handle/1842/11182/Moller1989.pdf, report CST-59-89. Also published as ECS-LFCS-89-84

34. Moller, F.: The importance of the left merge operator in process algebras. In: Paterson, M.S. (ed.) ICALP 1990. LNCS, vol. 443, pp. 752–764. Springer, Heidelberg (1990). https://doi.org/10.1007/BFb0032072

35. Moller, F.: The nonexistence of finite axiomatisations for CCS congruences. In: Proceedings of LICS 1990, pp. 142–153 (1990). https://doi.org/10.1109/LICS.1990.113741

36. Park, D.: Concurrency and automata on infinite sequences. In: Deussen, P. (ed.) GI-TCS 1981. LNCS, vol. 104, pp. 167–183. Springer, Heidelberg (1981). https://doi.org/10.1007/BFb0017309

37. Plotkin, G.D.: A structural approach to operational semantics. Report DAIMI FN-19, Computer Science Department, Aarhus University (1981)

38. de Simone, R.: Higher-level synchronising devices in Meije-SCCS. Theor. Comput. Sci. **37**, 245–267 (1985). https://doi.org/10.1016/0304-3975(85)90093-3

39. Vaandrager, F.W.: Algebraic techniques for concurrency and their application. Ph.D. thesis, University of Amsterdam, February 1990

Operational Causality – Necessarily Sufficient and Sufficiently Necessary

Christel Baier[✉], Clemens Dubslaff[✉], Florian Funke[✉], Simon Jantsch[✉], Jakob Piribauer[✉], and Robin Ziemek[✉]

Technische Universität Dresden, Dresden, Germany
{christel.baier,clemens.dubslaff,florian.funke,simon.jantsch,
jakob.piribauer,robin.ziemek}@tu-dresden.de

Abstract. Necessity and sufficiency are well-established notions in logic and causality analysis, but have barely received attention in the formal methods community. In this paper, we present temporal logic characterizations of necessary and sufficient causes in terms of state sets in operational system models. We introduce degrees of necessity and sufficiency as quality measures for sufficient and necessary causes, respectively, along with a versatile weight-based approach to find "good causes". The resulting optimization problems of finding optimal causes are shown to be solvable in polynomial time.

1 Introduction

The classical model-checking task is to verify whether a given formal system satisfies a property usually expressed in some temporal logic [19,66]. Much effort has been devoted to enriching classical yes/no answers of model checkers with useful diagnostic information. If the system does not meet the prescribed condition, many model checkers produce *counterexample traces* [21] that can further be investigated in order to localize precisely where the error lies or how far the trace is from satisfying the formula [8,35–37,69,73]. However, realistic system models can usually produce errors for a variety of reasons so that more diverse analysis techniques are required. In the case of a positive model-checking result, *coverage estimation* aims at determining which parts of the system are essential to ensure satisfaction [16–18,45], and *vacuity detection* analyzes whether it is due to some unintended, trivial behavior [12,54,65].

In this paper we tackle the explication of the behavior of transition systems through novel notions of cause–effect relationships. Both cause and effect are represented as subsets of the state space of the transition system, and formulas in linear temporal logic (LTL, [64]) are used to express the principles of necessity

The authors are supported by the DFG through the Collaborative Research Center TRR 248 (CPEC, project ID 389792660, https://perspicuous-computing.science), the Cluster of Excellence EXC 2050/1 (CeTI, project ID 390696704, as part of Germany's Excellence Strategy) and the Research Training Groups QuantLA (GRK 1763) and RoSI (GRK 1907).

and sufficiency in causal reasoning. A *necessary cause* is a state set that necessarily needs to be passed before reaching the effect set. A *sufficient cause* is a state set where every extension of a path reaching that set eventually sees an effect state. Therefore, necessary and sufficient causes provide orthogonal views on causality in operational systems. To estimate the explanatory power of such causes and determine "good causes", we exploit counterbalances on these orthogonal views: We determine necessary causes with maximal *degree of sufficiency* and sufficient causes with maximal *degree of necessity*. In order to admit use-case specific quality criteria for necessary causes, a rather general weight-based approach is finally presented. Weight-minimal necessary causes in this framework can be computed in polynomial time via a reduction to a min-cut problem in weighted graphs.

Despite being loosely inspired by philosophical theories of causation, the theory put forth in this paper concentrates on formal operational system models and does not transcend the borders of computer science. There have been philosophical attempts to understand causality in terms of necessity and sufficiency [31,59,60,71]. Perhaps most elaborate in this direction is the INUS condition ("insufficient but necessary part of a condition which is itself unnecessary but sufficient") [59] that is closely related to the NESS test (necessary element of sufficient subset) from jurisprudence [42,72]. Our contributions are in some sense also orthogonal to Halpern and Pearl's *actual causality*, the perhaps most influential instance of causality in the computer science community [39–41]. Halpern and Pearl express causal dependencies in structural equation models [29,30,38,63] and employ the counterfactuality principle that has a rich history in philosophical theories of causal reasoning [46,47,58]. Counterfactuality proclaims to consider alternative worlds in which the cause has not occurred and then check whether the effect still happened. To what extend necessity, sufficiency, counterfactuality, and conditionality etc. relate to each other and emerge to meaningful notions of causality is a matter of ongoing debate.

Related Work. Notions of causality inspired by Halpern and Pearl's actual causes have been employed in the verification landscape to analyze counterexample traces for temporal logic specifications in transition systems [11], LTL model checking [10,13,52,57], concurrent interacting programs [23], and timed systems [53]. To deal with the limited expressive power of propositional structural equation models, Hopkins and Pearl [44] introduced a notion of actual causality defined in the framework of the *situation calculus* [68]. This line of work has recently been picked up again [9,48]. Causal reasoning in component-based systems [32–34] and causality-based notions on responsibility [14] have also been considered in the model-checking community [15,26,61].

Rather than defining cause–effect relationships *within* a system, there are also approaches to use causal reasoning as a basis for verification algorithms *on* transition systems [55,56] and two-player reachability games [2]. From a conceptual viewpoint, the latter article defines necessary and sufficient subgoals in the same spirit as our formalization of necessary and sufficient causes (which, nevertheless, serve a different purpose there).

Recently, notions of causality have been considered in the realm of stochastic operational systems. Based on the probability-raising principle [67], Kleinberg and Mishra [49–51] presented an approach towards causal inference in time series modeled as Markov chains. This has recently sparked novel probabilistic causality notions [4,5], including notions of precision and recall that are closely connected to our notion of degrees of sufficiency and necessity [5]. Probabilistic causation has also been expressed in terms of hyperproperties [1,25].

Finally, the survey article [3] exhibits how the notion of causality entered and influenced the verification landscape over the course of the past two decades.

2 Preliminaries

In the sequel, we briefly present our notation regarding transition systems, Markov chains, and linear temporal logic (LTL). For more details, see standard textbooks on systems modeling and verification [6].

A *transition system* $\mathcal{T}$ is a tuple (S, R, I) comprising a finite set of states S, a transition relation $R \subseteq S \times S$, and a set of initial states $I \subseteq S$. A state that does not have any outgoing transition is called terminal. A path π in $\mathcal{T}$ is a sequence of states $s_0 s_1 \ldots$ such that $s_0 \in I$ and $(s_i, s_{i+1}) \in R$ for all appropriate i and where π is either infinite or ends in a terminal state. A state $s \in S$ is called reachable if there is a path that contains s. We assume that all states in a transition system are reachable.

A *Markov chain* $\mathcal{M}$ is a tuple $(S, \mathbf{P}, \iota)$ comprising a finite set of states S, a transition probability function $\mathbf{P} \colon S \times S \to [0,1]$ where we require $\sum_{s' \in S} \mathbf{P}(s, s') \in \{0, 1\}$ for all $s \in S$, and an initial state distribution $\iota \colon S \to [0,1]$ satisfying $\sum_{s \in S} \iota(s) = 1$. We say that a state s is terminal if $\sum_{s' \in S} \mathbf{P}(s, s') = 0$. A path π in $\mathcal{M}$ is a state sequence $s_0 s_1 \ldots$ such that $\iota(s_0) > 0$ and $\mathbf{P}(s_i, s_{i+1}) > 0$ for all appropriate i, and π is either infinite or ends in a terminal state. The σ-algebra of the probability space over sets of paths of $\mathcal{M}$ is generated by cylinder sets $\mathrm{Cyl}(\hat{\pi})$ comprising all path extensions of path prefixes $\hat{\pi}$. The probability measure $\mathrm{Pr}_{\mathcal{M}}$ on paths of $\mathcal{M}$ is induced by $\mathrm{Pr}_{\mathcal{M}}\big(\mathrm{Cyl}(s_0 \ldots s_n)\big) = \iota(s_0) \cdot \mathbf{P}(s_0, s_1) \cdot \ldots \cdot \mathbf{P}(s_{n-1}, s_n)$ [6, Chapter 10]. We write Pr_s for the probability measure that arises for $\mathcal{M}$ with $\iota(s) = 1$.

A formula in *linear temporal logic* (LTL) over a set AP of atomic propositions is formed according to the following grammar

$$\varphi ::= true \mid a \mid \varphi \wedge \varphi \mid \neg \varphi \mid \bigcirc \varphi \mid \varphi \, \mathsf{U} \, \varphi$$

where $a \in$ AP. In this paper, we consider LTL over sets of states as atomic propositions with the intended meaning that the atomic proposition A holds in a state s iff $s \in A$. We use the standard syntactic derivations $\varphi \vee \psi \equiv \neg(\neg\varphi \wedge \neg\psi)$, $\varphi \to \psi \equiv \neg\varphi \vee \psi$, $\Diamond\varphi \equiv true \, \mathsf{U} \, \varphi$ ("eventually"), $\Box\varphi \equiv \neg\Diamond\neg\varphi$ ("always"), $\varphi \, \mathsf{W} \, \psi \equiv \Box\varphi \vee \varphi \, \mathsf{U} \, \psi$ ("weak until") and $\varphi \, \mathsf{R} \, \psi \equiv \neg(\neg\varphi \, \mathsf{U} \, \neg\psi)$ ("release").

The semantics of LTL over sequences of atomic proposition sets is defined the standard way (see, e.g., [6]). For example, a path $\pi = s_0 s_1 \ldots$ satisfies $\varphi \mathsf{R} \psi$, denoted by $\pi \models \varphi \mathsf{R} \psi$, iff there is a position $k \in \mathbb{N}$ such that $s_i s_{i+1} \ldots$ satisfies ψ for $i \leq k$ and $s_k s_{k+1} \ldots$ satisfies φ. A transition system $\mathcal{T}$ is said to satisfy an LTL formula φ, denoted by $\mathcal{T} \models \varphi$, if all paths π of $\mathcal{T}$ satisfy φ. We write $\mathcal{T}, s \models \varphi$ in case $\mathcal{T}$ satisfies φ under the assumption that $I = \{s\}$ is the only initial state of $\mathcal{T}$. The set of states satisfying a formula φ in $\mathcal{T}$ is denoted by $\mathrm{Sat}_{\mathcal{T}}(\varphi) = \{s \in S \mid \mathcal{T}, s \models \varphi\}$, or simply $\mathrm{Sat}(\varphi)$ if $\mathcal{T}$ is clear from the context.

3   Necessary and Sufficient Causes

In this section, we define two notions of causes in transition systems, namely necessary and sufficient causes. Both notions lead to a binary relation on events, stating that an event is a cause for an effect event. Here, we focus on reachability events as causes and effects, such that they can be represented by sets of states. Our focus is motivated by the fact that numerous properties can be expressed by reachability properties on transition systems obtained by well-known automata-theoretic transformations [22,24,43,70].

3.1   Necessary Causes

Informally spoken, an event C is considered to be a *necessary cause* of an event E whenever the presence of E necessarily implies the prior occurrence of C. The presence of C, on the other hand, does not necessarily imply that E will occur. This idea can be expressed formally using LTL formulas over state sets:

Definition 1 (Necessary cause). *Let* $\mathcal{T} = (S, R, I)$ *be a transition system and let* $C, E \subseteq S$ *be sets of states. We say that* C *is a* necessary cause *for* E, *denoted by* $C \prec_{\mathsf{nec}} E$, *if* E *is non-empty and*

$$\mathcal{T} \models C \mathsf{R} \neg E \qquad (\equiv \Box \neg E \vee (\neg E \mathsf{U} (\neg E \wedge C))).$$

The formula $C \mathsf{R} \neg E$ is fulfilled whenever E is not reached *before* reaching C. In particular, there needs to be at least one transition between reaching C and E. Note that if the set E consists only of terminal states, i.e., states without any outgoing transitions, and C and E are disjoint, then C is a necessary cause of E iff $\mathcal{T} \models \Diamond E \rightarrow \Diamond C$. The set I of initial states is a trivial necessary cause for any effect $E \subseteq S$ if its intersection with the effect states E is empty. For any effect E not containing an initial state, it is thus clear that necessary causes always exist. Saying that the set of initial states is a necessary cause, however, does of course not carry much explanatory information.

Example 1. Consider the transition system $\mathcal{T}$ depicted in Fig. 1. We are interested in necessary causes for the effect $E = \{e\}$. Any set containing the initial state s_0 is trivially a necessary cause. More interesting are necessary causes that do not contain s_0. There are two such causes containing two states: $C_1 = \{a_1, b\}$

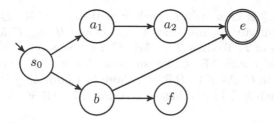

Fig. 1. The transition system $\mathcal{T}$ for Example 1.

and $C_2 = \{a_2, b\}$. C_1 occurs at least as early as C_2 on all paths. Nevertheless, $C_1 \prec_{\mathsf{nec}} C_2$ does not hold since we required causes to occur strictly before their effects: when entering state b the events to reach C_1 and C_2 occur simultaneously.

In order to compare simultaneously occurring causes for the same effect, we introduce a second type of 'necessary cause'-relation between sets of states that we call *necessary quasi-cause* in the following definition. For a quasi-cause, we do not require that to occur *strictly* before its effect.

Definition 2 (Necessary quasi-cause). *Let $\mathcal{T} = (S, R, I)$ be a transition system and let $C, E \subseteq S$ be sets of states. We say that C is a* necessary quasi-cause *for E, denoted by $C \preceq_{\mathsf{nec}}^{q} E$, if E is non-empty and*

$$\mathcal{T} \models \neg E \,\mathsf{W}\, C \qquad (\equiv \Box \neg E \vee (\neg E \,\mathsf{U}\, C)).$$

For a quasi-cause, we only require non-strict temporal priority. Hence, on any path reaching an effect E, it is sufficient if the quasi-cause C is reached simultaneously with E. Returning to Example 1, we therefore have $C_1 \preceq_{\mathsf{nec}}^{q} C_2$ even though $C_1 \prec_{\mathsf{nec}} C_2$ does not hold. As indicated by the name quasi-cause, we do not claim that this notion itself constitutes a meaningful cause–effect relationship. For example, any effect set provides a quasi-cause for itself. The notion is useful, however, when comparing different causes for the same effect.

We now establish first fundamental properties of the relations $\prec_{\mathsf{nec}}$ and $\preceq_{\mathsf{nec}}^{q}$:

Lemma 1. *Let $\mathcal{T} = (S, R, I)$ be a transition system. Then:*

(1) The relation $\prec_{\mathsf{nec}}$ is a strict partial order (irreflexive, asymmetric, and transitive) on the powerset of the state space S of $\mathcal{T}$.
(2) The relation $\preceq_{\mathsf{nec}}^{q}$ is a preorder (reflexive and transitive) on the powerset of the state space S of $\mathcal{T}$.
(3) For all $C, E \subseteq S$, we have that $C \prec_{\mathsf{nec}} E$ implies $C \preceq_{\mathsf{nec}}^{q} E$.
(4) For all $C_1, C_2, E \subseteq S$, if $C_1 \preceq_{\mathsf{nec}}^{q} C_2$ and $C_2 \prec_{\mathsf{nec}} E$, then $C_1 \prec_{\mathsf{nec}} E$.
(5) For all $C, E_1, E_2 \subseteq S$, if $C \prec_{\mathsf{nec}} E_1$ and $E_1 \preceq_{\mathsf{nec}}^{q} E_2$, then $C \prec_{\mathsf{nec}} E_2$.

Proof. Ad (1): $\prec_{\mathsf{nec}}$ is irreflexive since $C \,\mathsf{R}\, \neg C$ does not hold on paths that reach C (recall that $\neg C$ still has to hold when C releases the requirement of $\neg C$ to hold) and every state of $\mathcal{T}$ is assumed to be reachable in $\mathcal{T}$. Similarly asymmetry of $\prec_{\text{nec}}$ is clear as any path π with $\pi \models C\,R\,\neg E$ cannot satisfy $E\,R\,\neg C$. For transitivity, assume that $A \prec_{\text{nec}} B$ and $B \prec_{\text{nec}} C$ for three sets A, B, and C of states of $\mathcal{T}$. To show $\mathcal{T} \models A\,R\,\neg C$, let $\pi = s_0 s_1 s_2 \ldots$ be a path in $\mathcal{T}$. If $\pi \models \Box \neg C$, we have $\pi \models A\,R\,\neg C$. So, suppose that $\pi \models \Diamond C$. Let s_i be the first state in π that is in C. As $\mathcal{T} \models B\,R\,\neg C$, there is a position $j < i$ with $s_j \in B$. Analogously, there is $k < j$ such that $s_k \in A$. So, $\pi \models A\,R\,\neg C$. We conclude that $\prec_{\text{nec}}$ is transitive.

Ad (2): As for any set of states A the formula $\neg A\,W\,A$ is a tautology, reflexivity of $\preceq_{\text{nec}}^q$ is clear. Transitivity is shown analogously to the proof of transitivity above, where the strict inequalities on the positions i, j, and k are replaced by non-strict ones.

Ad (3): This is a direct consequence of $C\,R\,\neg E \equiv \Box \neg E \lor \left(\neg E\,U\,(\neg E \land C) \right)$ entailing $\neg E\,W\,C \equiv \Box \neg E \lor (\neg E\,U\,C)$.

Ad (4) and (5): The proofs are again analogous to the proof of transitivity above, where this time one of the strict inequalities between positions is replaced by a non-strict one. □

These definitions and basic properties of the two relations will help us to find "good causes" later on. There is no gold standard what precisely constitutes a good necessary cause. One common approach also within other notions of causality is to only consider minimal representatives as causes [26,39], i.e., events where removing some part leads to loosing the property of being a cause. In our setting, necessary causes may contain redundant states that do not affect the causal relationships to potential effect sets and could be removed towards more concise causes. To provide an intuition, consider again the transition system $\mathcal{T}$ depicted in Fig. 1. The necessary cause $C_3 = \{a_1, a_2, b\}$ contains the redundant state a_2. This state can only be reached if the set C_3 is visited already before in state a_1. As only the first visit to the set is relevant in the relations $\prec_{\text{nec}}$ and $\preceq_{\text{nec}}^q$, the fact that a_2 belongs to C_3 does not play a role at all for causal relationships. To remove such redundant states, we define the following pruning of sets of states.

Definition 3 (Pruning of state sets). *Let* $\mathcal{T} = (S, R, I)$ *be a transition system and let* $A \subseteq S$ *be a set of states. We define the* pruning $\lfloor A \rfloor$ *of* A *by*

$$\lfloor A \rfloor = \{\, a \in A \mid \text{ there is a path } \pi \text{ in } \mathcal{T} \text{ with } \pi \models \neg A\,U\,a \,\}.$$

Recall that paths always start in an initial state of the transition system. The pruning $\lfloor A \rfloor$ includes precisely those states in A that are reachable without previously seeing A. It satisfies the following properties related to the necessary (quasi-)cause relations defined above.

Lemma 2. *Let* $\mathcal{T} = (S, R, I)$ *be a transition system.*

(1) For all $A \subseteq S$, *we have* $A \preceq_{\text{nec}}^q \lfloor A \rfloor$ *and* $\lfloor A \rfloor \preceq_{\text{nec}}^q A$.
(2) For $A, B \subseteq S$, *we have that* $A \preceq_{\text{nec}}^q B$ *and* $B \preceq_{\text{nec}}^q A$ *implies* $\lfloor A \rfloor = \lfloor B \rfloor$.
(3) For all $C, E \subseteq S$ *with* $C \prec_{\text{nec}} E$, *we have* $C \prec_{\text{nec}} \lfloor E \rfloor$.

Proof. Ad (1): First, we will show $\mathcal{T} \models (\neg A) \mathsf{W} \lfloor A \rfloor$ which is equivalent to $\mathcal{T} \models \Diamond A \to (\neg A) \mathsf{U} \lfloor A \rfloor$. Let $\pi = s_0 s_1 \ldots$ be a path in $\mathcal{T}$ that satisfies $\Diamond A$ and let $i \in \mathbb{N}$ be the first position such that $s_i \in A$. Then, by definition of $\lfloor A \rfloor$, we have $s_i \in \lfloor A \rfloor$. This shows $\pi \models (\neg A) \mathsf{U} \lfloor A \rfloor$. In the other direction, $\mathcal{T} \models (\neg \lfloor A \rfloor) \mathsf{W} A$ holds because $\lfloor A \rfloor \subseteq A$.

Ad (2): Assume $A \preceq_{\mathsf{nec}}^q B$ and $B \preceq_{\mathsf{nec}}^q A$ and suppose towards a contradiction that $\lfloor A \rfloor \neq \lfloor B \rfloor$. Assume w.l.o.g. that there is an $a \in \lfloor A \rfloor \setminus \lfloor B \rfloor$. By the definition of $\lfloor A \rfloor$, there is a path $\pi = s_0 s_1 \ldots s_n \ldots$ with $s_0 \in I$ and $s_n = a$ such that $s_i \notin A$ for all $i < n$. As $A \preceq_{\mathsf{nec}}^q B$, it follows that also $s_i \notin B$ for all $i < n$. Since $a \notin \lfloor B \rfloor$, also $a \notin B$ since otherwise the path π would witness that a also belongs to $\lfloor B \rfloor$. Thus, $\pi \not\models (\neg A) \mathsf{W} B$ and hence $B \not\preceq_{\mathsf{nec}}^q A$, which yields a contradiction.

Ad (3): The claim follows from $E \preceq_{\mathsf{nec}}^q \lfloor E \rfloor$ by (1) and Lemma 1(5). □

The preorder $\preceq_{\mathsf{nec}}^q$ induces an equivalence relation defined by

$$A \sim B \qquad \text{iff} \qquad A \preceq_{\mathsf{nec}}^q B \text{ and } B \preceq_{\mathsf{nec}}^q A.$$

Statements (1) and (2) of Lemma 2 tell us that in each of these equivalence classes, there is exactly one pruned set. Choosing the respective pruned set as representative for each equivalence class, we obtain that $\preceq_{\mathsf{nec}}^q$ is a partial order (reflexive, transitive, and anti-symmetric) on the set of pruned subsets of S. In the light of Lemma 1 and Lemma 2(3), we can conclude that for sets $C_1, C_2, E_1, E_2 \subseteq S$ with $C_1 \sim C_2$ and $E_1 \sim E_2$, we have

$$C_1 \prec_{\mathsf{nec}} E_1 \qquad \text{iff} \qquad C_2 \prec_{\mathsf{nec}} E_2.$$

In words, $\prec_{\mathsf{nec}}$ is well-defined on the equivalence classes induced by $\preceq_{\mathsf{nec}}^q$ and it is therefore reasonable to restrict ourselves to the canonical representatives for necessary causes in terms of pruned sets.

3.2   Sufficient Causes

Intuitively, a sufficient cause C for an event E means that the presence of C necessarily implies the subsequent occurrence of E. This intuition can be formalized using LTL formulas over state sets:

Definition 4 (Sufficient cause). *Let $\mathcal{T} = (S, R, I)$ be a transition system. A non-empty set $C \subseteq S$ is a sufficient cause for $E \subseteq S$ if*

$$\mathcal{T} \models \Box(C \to \bigcirc \Diamond E).$$

The formula basically states that whenever we see a state $c \in C$ we will also see E at some point in the future. Note that if E comprises terminal states only and C and E are disjoint, the above characterization of sufficient causes is equivalent to $\Diamond C \to \Diamond E$.

Example 2. Consider the transition system depicted in Fig. 2, modeling a coffee machine that has a defect and sometimes only produces hot water instead of

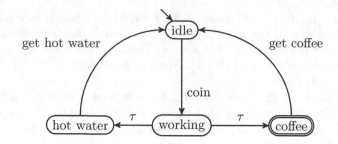

Fig. 2. A defect coffee machine that sometimes produces hot water

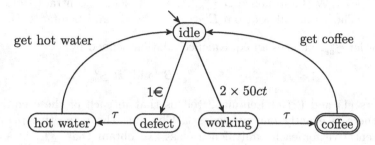

Fig. 3. A refined transition system for the defect coffee machine

delicious coffee. We consider the effect $E = \{\text{coffee}\}$. Within this model, there are no sufficient causes for E since it is unclear how the non-deterministic choice in the working state is resolved. However, both $C_1 = \{\text{working}\}$ and $C_2 = \{\text{idle}\}$ are necessary causes for E.

Suppose now that we have additional knowledge about the defect and can refine the transition system model towards the one in Fig. 3. Here, we assume that a person with strong desire of getting more insights about the defect, let us call him Frits, figured out a trick: when using two coins instead of one, the defect does not occur and the machine always delivers coffee. For the effect $E = \{\text{coffee}\}$, we then still have $C_1 = \{\text{working}\}$ and $C_2 = \{\text{idle}\}$ as necessary causes. In this model, C_1 is additionally a sufficient cause since all paths that visit C_1 will visit E afterwards eventually.

In analogy to necessary causes, we can observe sufficient causes are transitive:

Lemma 3 (Transitivity of sufficient causes.). *Let $\mathcal{T} = (S, R, I)$ be a transition system and $C, W, E \subseteq S$. If C is a sufficient cause for W and W is a sufficient cause for E, then C is a sufficient cause for E.*

Proof. Assume that C is a sufficient cause for W, which in turn is a sufficient cause for E. Let $\pi = s_0 s_1 \ldots$ be a path in $\mathcal{T}$. Then, since $\mathcal{T} \models \Box(C \rightarrow \bigcirc \Diamond W)$ we have for each $i \in \mathbb{N}$ with $s_i \in C$ that there is $j > i$ with $s_j \in W$. Likewise, by $\mathcal{T} \models \Box(W \rightarrow \bigcirc \Diamond E)$ for each $j \in \mathbb{N}$ with $s_j \in W$ there is $k > j$ with $s_k \in E$. We conclude that $\pi \models \Box(C \to \bigcirc\Diamond E)$ for all paths π in $\mathcal{T}$. Hence, C is a sufficient cause for E. $\qquad\square$

Since all states in a transition system $\mathcal{T}$ are assumed to be reachable, a set C is a sufficient cause for E in $\mathcal{T}$ iff the sufficiency condition holds for all states included in C. That is, for all $a \in C$ the formula $\Box(a \to \bigcirc\Diamond E)$ holds in $\mathcal{T}$. Equivalently, a set $C \subseteq S$ is a sufficient cause for E iff $\varnothing \neq C \subseteq \mathrm{Sat}_{\mathcal{T}}(\bigcirc\Diamond E)$. Therefore, existence of a sufficient cause can be checked in polynomial time with standard model-checking algorithms [6,20].

The satisfaction set of $\bigcirc\Diamond E$ is consequently the inclusion-maximal sufficient cause for the effect E in $\mathcal{T}$. This set, however, might be very large and does not necessarily point to "good causes" for the effect. To this end, we define the *canonical sufficient* cause as $C_c^E = \lfloor \mathrm{Sat}_{\mathcal{T}}(\bigcirc\Diamond E) \rfloor$, i.e., the set of all states in $\mathrm{Sat}_{\mathcal{T}}(\bigcirc\Diamond E)$ that are either initial or are reachable from some initial state by visiting only non-sufficient states. The name "canonical" sufficient cause is justified by the following observation:

Proposition 1. *Let $\mathcal{T}$ and E be as above. The canonical sufficient cause C_c^E is the unique pruned and $\preceq_{\mathrm{nec}}^q$-least sufficient cause for E.*

Proof. By Lemma 1(1), we know that $C_c^E \preceq_{\mathrm{nec}}^q \mathrm{Sat}_{\mathcal{T}}(\bigcirc\Diamond E)$, and therefore also $C_c^E \preceq_{\mathrm{nec}}^q C$ for all $C \subseteq \mathrm{Sat}_{\mathcal{T}}(\bigcirc\Diamond E)$ by the definition of $\preceq_{\mathrm{nec}}^q$. But the sufficient causes of E are exactly the non-empty subsets of $\mathrm{Sat}_{\mathcal{T}}(\bigcirc\Diamond E)$. Thus, the canonical sufficient cause C_c^E is a $\preceq_{\mathrm{nec}}^q$-least sufficient cause. By Lemma 2, we know that there is only one pruned cause in the equivalence class (induced by $\preceq_{\mathrm{nec}}^q$) of $\preceq_{\mathrm{nec}}^q$-least sufficient causes, rendering C_c^E unique. $\qquad\square$

While Proposition 1 already shows that C_c^E is a distinguished sufficient cause, we will see later on that it is also optimal with respect to other criteria, namely the degree of necessity introduced in the next section.

4   Finding Good Causes

We have seen that causes may differ in their information they provide and their ability to concisely explain reasons for the effect. For example, the set of initial states is a necessary cause for any effect E that does not contain an initial state. In this section, we introduce different ways to quantify the quality of a cause and show how to find optimal causes with respect to the introduced quality measures.

4.1   Degrees of Sufficiency and Necessity

The notions of sufficiency and necessity defined in the previous section are qualitative: either a set satisfies the corresponding criterion, or it does not. However, one can think of situations where a set C is *almost* sufficient or necessary, e.g., that a very large part of the executions which see the effect set E are preceded by C in the case of necessity. To quantify how close a set is a necessary cause for an effect (resp. a sufficient cause), we define degrees of necessity (resp. degree of sufficiency). Here, we rely on the probability measure on paths that we obtain by equipping the outgoing transitions from each state with a uniform probability distribution. In particular, we are interested in the trade-off between sufficiency and necessity and aim toward sufficient causes with a high degree of necessity, and vice versa.

For the remainder of this section, let us fix a transition system $\mathcal{T} = (S, R, I)$ and a non-empty effect set $E \subseteq S$. Then we can construct the Markov chain $\mathcal{M}_{\mathcal{T},E} = (S, \mathbf{P}, \iota)$ as follows. For each transition $(s, s') \in R$ with $s \notin E$, we have $\mathbf{P}(s, s') = 1/|\operatorname{Post}(s)|$, where $\operatorname{Post}(s)$ denotes the set of direct successors of s. For all $s, s' \in S$ where $(s, s') \notin R$ or $s \in E$, we set $\mathbf{P}(s, s') = 0$, i.e., all effect states are terminal in $\mathcal{M}_{\mathcal{T},E}$. Further, we set $\iota(s) = 1/|I|$ for all $s \in I$. In the following, we denote by Pr the probability measure $\operatorname{Pr}_{\mathcal{M}_{\mathcal{T},E}}$ on measurable sets of paths of $\mathcal{M}_{\mathcal{T},E}$.

The degree of sufficiency of a non-empty candidate cause $C \subseteq S \backslash E$ intuitively provides a measure how many of the paths that see C will also see E. It is defined as a conditional probability in the following way:

$$\text{suff-deg}(C, E) \; = \; \operatorname{Pr}(\Diamond E \mid \Diamond C) \; = \; \frac{\operatorname{Pr}(\Diamond E \wedge \Diamond C)}{\operatorname{Pr}(\Diamond C)}$$

With a similar reasoning, the degree of necessity of C is defined as:

$$\text{nec-deg}(C, E) \; = \; \operatorname{Pr}(\Diamond C \mid \Diamond E) \; = \; \frac{\operatorname{Pr}(\Diamond E \wedge \Diamond C)}{\operatorname{Pr}(\Diamond E)}$$

Note that these degrees can be computed in polynomial time by standard techniques for computing conditional probabilities on Markov chains [7].

If C is a sufficient cause as defined above, then its degree of sufficiency clearly is 1. The analogous statement holds for necessary causes, but the reverse directions do not hold in general. Since multiple sufficient causes may exist, it makes sense to look for those with maximal degree of necessity. In case C is a sufficient cause, the above expression for nec-deg(C, E) simplifies to

$$\text{nec-deg}(C, E) \; = \; \frac{\operatorname{Pr}(\Diamond C)}{\operatorname{Pr}(\Diamond E)} \tag{$*$}$$

as the formula $\Diamond C \to \Diamond E$ holds in $\mathcal{M}_{\mathcal{T},E}$ with E comprising terminal states only by construction. Analogously, if C is a necessary cause we have

$$\text{suff-deg}(C, E) \; = \; \frac{\operatorname{Pr}(\Diamond E)}{\operatorname{Pr}(\Diamond C)} \tag{$**$}$$

The above definitions raise the question of how to find a sufficient cause with maximal degree of necessity, or, a necessary cause with maximal degree of sufficiency. Observe that causes that are sufficient *and* necessary may not exist in general. The following lemma connects the degrees of necessity and sufficiency to the necessary quasi-cause relation $\preceq^q_{\text{nec}}$.

Lemma 4. *Let $C_1, C_2 \subseteq S$ be two necessary causes for E, i.e., $C_1 \prec_{\mathsf{nec}} E$ and $C_2 \prec_{\mathsf{nec}} E$. Then, $C_1 \preceq^q_{\mathsf{nec}} C_2$ implies that suff-deg$(C_1, E) \leq$ suff-deg(C_2, E).*

Let $D_1, D_2 \subseteq S$ be two sufficient causes for E. Then, $D_1 \preceq^q_{\mathsf{nec}} D_2$ implies that nec-deg$(D_1, E) \geq$ nec-deg(D_2, E).

Proof. For any sets $A_1, A_2 \subseteq S$ with $A_1 \preceq^q_{\mathsf{nec}} A_2$, we have that $\mathcal{T} \models \Diamond A_2 \rightarrow \Diamond A_1$. So, $\Pr(\Diamond A_1) \geq \Pr(\Diamond A_2)$. Applied to the necessary causes C_1 and C_2, we conclude the claim due to equation $(**)$. For the sufficient causes D_1 and D_2, the claim follows analogously using equation $(*)$. □

Sufficient Causes with Maximal Degree of Necessity. The story of how to find a sufficient cause with maximal degree of necessity is quickly told: By Lemma 4, we know that $\preceq^q_{\mathsf{nec}}$-least sufficient causes have maximal degree of necessity. In Proposition 1, we have seen that the canonical sufficient cause $C^E_c = \lfloor \mathrm{Sat}_{\mathcal{T}}(\bigcirc \Diamond E) \rfloor$, is a $\preceq^q_{\mathsf{nec}}$-least sufficient cause. We conclude:

Proposition 2. *Let $\mathcal{T} = (S, R, I)$ a transition system and $E \subseteq S$. The canonical sufficient cause C^E_c has maximal degree of necessity among all sufficient causes for E.*

Necessary Causes with Maximal Degree of Sufficiency. While sufficient causes are always non-empty subsets of an LTL satisfaction set, this is not the case for necessary causes. Indeed, the set of all states S is always a necessary cause for any effect that is disjoint from the initial states but not all state sets have to be a necessary cause. Following the definition of a canonical sufficient cause suggests considering the pruned maximal necessary cause as a candidate. However, in the case above, $I = \lfloor S \rfloor$, which does not attain the maximal degree of sufficiency among all necessary causes (on the contrary, it achieves the minimal degree of sufficiency). A necessary cause with maximal degree of sufficiency is the *direct-predecessor cause*: It is denoted by $C^E_{\mathsf{dp}} = \{s \in S \mid$ there is $e \in E$ such that $(s, e) \in R\}$ and comprises all those states that have at least one transition to E.

Proposition 3. *Let $\mathcal{T} = (S, R, I)$ a transition system and $E \subseteq S \backslash I$. The direct-predecessor cause C^E_{dp} is a necessary cause that achieves the maximal degree of sufficiency among all necessary causes for E.*

Proof. Clearly, C^E_{dp} is a necessary cause by definition, since for all paths π in $\mathcal{T}$ that visit E we clearly have $\pi \models \neg E \mathsf{U} (\neg E \wedge C^E_{\mathsf{dp}})$ (recall that $E \cap I = \varnothing$). We show that $\Pr(\Diamond C^E_{\mathsf{dp}}) \leq \Pr(\Diamond C)$ for every necessary cause $C \subseteq S$ by proving

$$\{\pi \mid \pi \models \Diamond C^E_{\mathsf{dp}}\} \quad \subseteq \quad \{\pi \mid \pi \models \Diamond C\}.$$

Let $\pi = s_0 s_1 \ldots$ be a path in $\mathcal{T}$ with $\pi \models \Diamond C^E_{\mathsf{dp}}$ and let $i \in \mathbb{N}$ be the smallest position such that $s_i \in C^E_{\mathsf{dp}}$. Then clearly $s_j \notin E$ for all $j \leq i$ and there is a path $\pi' = s_0 s_1 \ldots s_i s'_{i+1} \ldots$ where $s'_{i+1} \in E$ and thus, $\pi' \models \neg E \mathsf{U} (\neg E \wedge C)$ as C is a necessary cause. But then there is $k \leq i$ with $s_k \in C$ and thus $\pi \models \Diamond C$. □

The motivation for pruned necessary causes is also applicable to direct-predecessor causes, asking for the "earliest" necessary cause C that has the same degree of sufficiency as C_{dp}^E. To this end, we consider the set of states $C_{\Diamond \text{dp}}^E = \{s \in S \mid \Pr_s(\Diamond C_{\text{dp}}^E) = 1\}$, which is a necessary cause due to $C_{\text{dp}}^E \subseteq C_{\Diamond \text{dp}}^E$. By Lemma 1, its pruned set is also a necessary cause, i.e. $\lfloor C_{\Diamond \text{dp}}^E \rfloor \prec_{\text{nec}} E$. In $\mathcal{M}_{\mathcal{T},E}$ we have $\Pr(\Diamond \lfloor C_{\Diamond \text{dp}}^E \rfloor) \leq \Pr(\Diamond C_{\Diamond \text{dp}}^E) = \Pr(\Diamond C_{\text{dp}}^E)$. On the other hand, $\lfloor C_{\Diamond \text{dp}}^E \rfloor \preceq_{\text{nec}}^q C_{\Diamond \text{dp}}^E$ (again by Lemma 1) implies $\Pr(\Diamond C_{\text{dp}}^E) \leq \Pr(\Diamond \lfloor C_{\Diamond \text{dp}}^E \rfloor)$. Therefore, we have $\Pr(\Diamond C_{\text{dp}}^E) = \Pr(\Diamond \lfloor C_{\Diamond \text{dp}}^E \rfloor)$ and hence the degrees of sufficiency of C_{dp}^E and $\lfloor C_{\Diamond \text{dp}}^E \rfloor$ are the same.

Moreover, $\lfloor C_{\Diamond \text{dp}}^E \rfloor$ is a necessary quasi-cause for all necessary causes of E that achieve the same degree of sufficiency:

Proposition 4. *Let $\mathcal{T} = (S, R, I)$ a transition system and $E \subseteq S \setminus I$. For all necessary causes C of E that satisfy* suff-deg$(C, E) = $ suff-deg(C_{dp}^E, E) *we have* $\lfloor C_{\Diamond \text{dp}}^E \rfloor \preceq_{\text{nec}}^q C$.

Proof. It suffices to show $C \subseteq C_{\Diamond \text{dp}}^E$. Since C is a necessary cause for E, we can apply the same argumentation as in the proof of Proposition 3, showing that

$$\{\pi \mid \pi \models \Diamond(C \wedge \Diamond C_{\text{dp}}^E)\} \quad = \quad \{\pi \mid \pi \models \Diamond C_{\text{dp}}^E\} \quad \subseteq \quad \{\pi \mid \pi \models \Diamond C\}.$$

Due to suff-deg$(C, E) = $ suff-deg(C_{dp}^E, E), we have $\Pr(\Diamond C) = \Pr(\Diamond C_{\text{dp}}^E)$ and thus, $\{\pi \mid \pi \models \Diamond(C \wedge \Diamond C_{\text{dp}}^E)\} = \{\pi \mid \pi \models \Diamond C\}$. Now fix some arbitrary $s \in C$. Then, every path that visits s has to visit C_{dp}^E eventually afterwards. Thus, $\Pr_s(\Diamond C_{\text{dp}}^E) = 1$, which is equivalent to $s \in C_{\Diamond \text{dp}}^E$, leading to $C \subseteq C_{\Diamond \text{dp}}^E$. $\qquad \square$

This leads to a $\preceq_{\text{nec}}^q$-least necessary cause $\lfloor C_{\Diamond \text{dp}}^E \rfloor$ with maximal degree of sufficiency that can be computed in polynomial time by standard methods.

4.2   Weight-Minimal Necessary Causes

The previous section showed how to determine necessary causes with maximal degree of sufficiency and $\preceq_{\text{nec}}^q$-least ones among them. We now describe a different technique to find optimal necessary causes with respect to a generic optimization criterion, employing a natural connection to minimal cuts from flow networks.

Let $\mathcal{T} = (S, R, I)$ be a transition system and $A, B \subseteq S$ be two sets of states. We call $X \subseteq S \setminus B$ an *AB-separator* if every finite path through $\mathcal{T}$ that starts in A and ends in B sees a vertex in X. The following observation follows directly from the definition of necessary causes.

Proposition 5. *The necessary causes for E which do not intersect E in $\mathcal{T}$ are exactly the IE-separators of $\mathcal{T}$.*

Let us augment $\mathcal{T}$ by a weight function $w \colon S \to \mathbb{Q}_{\geq 0}$. The weight of a set $X \subseteq S$ is defined to be $w(X) = \sum_{v \in X} w(v)$. In the presence of such a weight function, it makes sense to ask for weight-minimal AB-separators in $\mathcal{T}$, for some given

$A, B \subseteq S$. Via a polynomial reduction to the problem of computing minimal cuts, we get the following result.[1]

Proposition 6. *Weight-minimal AB-separators can be computed in polynomial time.*

Proof. We reduce the problem of computing minimal AB-separators to the problem of computing a weight-minimal s-t-cut. An s-t-cut of $T = (S, R, I)$ is a partition S_1, S_2 of S such that $s \in S_1$, $t \in S_2$. Let $w: R \to \mathbb{Q}$ be a weight function on the edges of T. The *bridging edges* of an s-t-cut S_1, S_2 are defined to be $\mathrm{br}(S_1, S_2) = R \cap (S_1 \times S_2)$, and its weight is $\sum_{(u,v) \in \mathrm{br}(S_1, S_2)} w(u, v)$. Weight-minimal cuts can be computed in polynomial time [62].

We show how to reduce the problem of computing weight-minimal AB-separators to the problem of computing weight-minimal cuts. Let $T = (S, R, I)$, w, $A, B \subseteq S$ be an instance of the weight-minimal AB-separator problem. We may assume that $A \cap B = \varnothing$ and that B is a singleton set $\{b\}$. If $A \cap B \neq \varnothing$, then there are no AB-separators by definition. If B is not singleton, we can first collapse all states in B into a single state b, and let $B = \{b\}$. This transformation preserves AB-separators and their weights.

Now we transform the transition system T as follows. Define $T' = (S \cup S' \cup \{a\}, R', I)$, where $S' = \{s' \mid s \in S\}$, and with edges

$$v \to v' \qquad \text{for all } v \in S \tag{1}$$
$$v' \to u \qquad \text{for all } (v, u) \in R \tag{2}$$
$$a \to v \qquad \text{for all } v \in A \tag{3}$$

Consider the weight function $w': R' \to \mathbb{Q}_{\geq 0}$ defined by $w'(v, v') = w(v)$ for all $v \in S \setminus B$ and $w'(x, y) = w(S) + 1$ for all other edges (x, y) of T'. Note that these transformations are all possible in polynomial time.

Each AB-separator X in T induces an a-b-cut in T' as follows. Take S_1 to be the union of X and the states of T' reachable from a without seeing X. As X is an AB-separator in T, the partition $(S_1, (S \cup S') \setminus S_1)$ forms an a-b-cut in T'. Furthermore, as the outgoing edges of S_1 are exactly $\{(u, u') \mid u \in X\}$, the weight of this cut is $w(X)$.

Conversely, every a-b-cut (S_1, S_2) in T' satisfying $\mathrm{br}(S_1, S_2) \subseteq \{(u, u') \mid u \in S \setminus B\}$ induces the AB-separator $X = \{u \in S \mid (u, u') \in \mathrm{br}(S_1, S_2)\}$ with the same weight. Finally, any a-b-cut (S_1, S_2) in T' which does not satisfy $\mathrm{br}(S_1, S_2) \subseteq \{(u, u') \mid u \in S \setminus B\}$ cannot be weight-minimal, as it has larger weight than any cut with this property. The a-b-cut induced by the set $A \cup \{a\}$ has this property, and hence such an a-b-cut exists (this uses our assumption $A \cap B = \varnothing$). Hence, a weight-minimal a-b-cut in T' induces a weight-minimal AB-separator in T. $\qquad\square$

---

[1] The problem of finding *balanced vertex separators*, as studied by Feige et al. [27, 28], is NP-complete and differs from the one we study in that it requires that the vertex separator partitions the graph into approximately equally sized components.

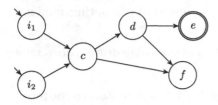

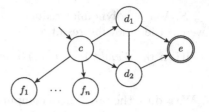

Fig. 4. Transition system $\mathcal{T}_1$ from Example 3

Fig. 5. Transition system $\mathcal{T}_2$ from Example 4

This gives us a tool to compute weight-optimal necessary causes in polynomial time. In the following, we consider two natural choices for weight functions which lead to different notions of optimality for necessary causes.

State-Minimal Necessary Causes. Let $\mathcal{T} = (S, R, I)$ be a transition system as above and $E \subseteq S$ a set of states. Consider the weight function $w \colon S \to \mathbb{Q}_{\geq 0}$ where $w(s) = 1$ for all $s \in S$. Then, a weight-minimal necessary cause with respect to w is a necessary cause C such that $|C|$ is minimal among all necessary causes. By the above observations, such a cause can be computed in polynomial time.

If $|I| = 1$, then I itself is always a state-minimal necessary cause, which renders the optimization problem trivial. However, I has the worst possible degree of sufficiency among all necessary causes due to $\Pr(\lozenge I) = 1$ in the corresponding Markov chain $\mathcal{M}_{\mathcal{T}, E}$. The following paragraph considers a weight function that aims to achieve a trade-off between the size of a necessary cause and its degree of sufficiency.

A Trade-Off Between Size and Degree of Sufficiency. Consider the weight function w defined by $w(v) = \Pr(\lozenge v)$, again with respect the probability measure in the Markov chain $\mathcal{M}_{\mathcal{T}, E}$. A weight-minimal necessary cause with respect to this weight function is a necessary cause X minimizing

$$w(X) = \sum_{v \in X} \Pr(\lozenge v). \qquad (\dagger)$$

Recall that the degree of sufficiency of X is given by suff-deg$(X, E) = \frac{\Pr(\lozenge E)}{\Pr(\lozenge X)}$ if X is a necessary cause. We have $w(X) \geq \Pr(\lozenge X)$, and therefore minimizing the weight encourages necessary causes with high degree of sufficiency. At the same time, the number of states corresponds to the number of summands in $w(X)$, and hence few states are also encouraged.

Example 3. Consider the transition system $\mathcal{T}_1$ from Fig. 4, where $I = \{i_1, i_2\}$ are the initial states and consider $E = \{e\}$ as the effect. Then both $C = \{c\}$ and $D = \{d\}$ are necessary causes of minimal size $|C| = |D| = 1$, as removing these states would separate I and E. This means that under the state-counting weight function, both C and D are weight-minimal necessary causes. However,

D has a higher degree of sufficiency and would thus be optimal for both size and degree of sufficiency. Specifically, we have $\Pr(\Diamond C) = 1$ and $\Pr(\Diamond D) = 1/2$. Hence, suff-deg$(C, E) = \Pr(\Diamond E) = 1/4$, and suff-deg$(D, E) = 1/2$. Under the weight function defined in (†), only D is optimal, since $w(C) = \Pr(\Diamond C) = 1$ and $w(D) = \Pr(\Diamond D) = 1/2$.

Example 4. Consider the transition system $\mathcal{T}_2$ from Fig. 5, with initial states $I = \{c\}$ and the effect $E = \{e\}$. Then I and $D = \{d_1, d_2\}$ are the only inclusion-minimal necessary causes. According to the weight function defined in (†) we have $w(I) = 1$ and $w(D) = \frac{5}{2(n+2)}$. For $n = 0$ we have $w(D) = 5/4 > 1 = w(I)$ and thus, I would be trade-off optimal. On the other hand, for $n > 0$ we have $w(D) < 1 = w(I)$, which turns D into the trade-off optimal necessary cause. Intuitively, increasing n makes I less sufficient, as it increases the set of paths that start in c but never reach E.

5   Conclusion

We have formalized well-known notions of necessity and sufficiency in the context of transition systems using temporal logic formulas over state sets that stand for causes and effects. Based on these formalizations, we addressed several trade-offs between necessity and sufficiency and presented three optimality criteria that differ in their properties with respect to conciseness and explainability: the degree of necessity, the degree of sufficiency, and through state weights. Causes that maximize the former two were explicitly characterized, and a polynomial-time algorithm for the computation of weight-optimal causes was described relying on known algorithms to determine minimal cuts in flow networks. Which notion of causality is appropriate to identify the reason for an effect, e.g., such that the imaginary person Frits from Example 2 can fix the broken coffee machine, highly depends on the considered system and it might be required to consider all our notions of causality to draw a conclusion.

In practice, also state sets with high degree of necessity *and* sufficiency might be interesting to consider also when they are neither sufficient nor necessary causes. In this direction it is promising to investigate trade-off values between the two degrees such as the f-score from statistics, as done for probability-raising causes in MDPs [5]. In future work we also plan to examine relaxations of the cause conditions studied here, following the more articulate INUS condition [59] or the NESS test [42,72].

References

1. Ábrahám, E., Bonakdarpour, B.: HyperPCTL: a temporal logic for probabilistic hyperproperties. In: McIver, A., Horvath, A. (eds.) QEST 2018. LNCS, vol. 11024, pp. 20–35. Springer, Cham (2018). https://doi.org/10.1007/978-3-319-99154-2_2
2. Baier, C., Coenen, N., Finkbeiner, B., Funke, F., Jantsch, S., Siber, J.: Causality-based game solving. In: Silva, A., Leino, K.R.M. (eds.) CAV 2021. LNCS, vol. 12759, pp. 894–917. Springer, Cham (2021). https://doi.org/10.1007/978-3-030-81685-8_42

3. Baier, C., et al.: From verification to causality-based explications. In: Bansal, N., Merelli, E., Worrell, J. (eds.) 48th International Colloquium on Automata, Languages, and Programming (ICALP 2021). Leibniz International Proceedings in Informatics (LIPIcs), Dagstuhl, Germany, vol. 198, pp. 1:1–1:20. Schloss Dagstuhl - Leibniz-Zentrum für Informatik (2021)

4. Baier, C., Funke, F., Jantsch, S., Piribauer, J., Ziemek, R.: Probabilistic causes in Markov chains. In: Hou, Z., Ganesh, V. (eds.) ATVA 2021. LNCS, vol. 12971, pp. 205–221. Springer, Cham (2021). https://doi.org/10.1007/978-3-030-88885-5_14

5. Baier, C., Funke, F., Piribauer, J., Ziemek, R.: On probability-raising causality in Markov decision processes. In: Bouyer, P., Schröder, L. (eds.) FoSSaCS 2022. LNCS, vol. 13242, pp. 40–60. Springer, Cham (2022). https://doi.org/10.1007/978-3-030-99253-8_3

6. Baier, C., Katoen, J.-P.: Principles of Model Checking. MIT Press, Cambridge (2008)

7. Baier, C., Klein, J., Klüppelholz, S., Märcker, S.: Computing conditional probabilities in Markovian models efficiently. In: Ábrahám, E., Havelund, K. (eds.) TACAS 2014. LNCS, vol. 8413, pp. 515–530. Springer, Heidelberg (2014). https://doi.org/10.1007/978-3-642-54862-8_43

8. Ball, T., Naik, M., Rajamani, S.K.: From symptom to cause: localizing errors in counterexample traces. SIGPLAN Not. 38(1), 97–105 (2003)

9. Batusov, V., Soutchanski, M.: Situation calculus semantics for actual causality. In: Proceedings of the AAAI Conference on Artificial Intelligence, vol. 32, no. 1, April 2018

10. Beer, A., Heidinger, S., Kühne, U., Leitner-Fischer, F., Leue, S.: Symbolic causality checking using bounded model checking. In: Fischer, B., Geldenhuys, J. (eds.) SPIN 2015. LNCS, vol. 9232, pp. 203–221. Springer, Cham (2015). https://doi.org/10.1007/978-3-319-23404-5_14

11. Beer, I., Ben-David, S., Chockler, H., Orni, A., Trefler, R.J.: Explaining counterexamples using causality. Formal Methods Syst. Des. 40(1), 20–40 (2012)

12. Beer, I., Ben-David, S., Eisner, C., Rodeh, Y.: Efficient detection of vacuity in ACTL formulas. In: Grumberg, O. (ed.) CAV 1997. LNCS, vol. 1254, pp. 279–290. Springer, Heidelberg (1997). https://doi.org/10.1007/3-540-63166-6_28

13. Caltais, G., Guetlein, S.L., Leue, S.: Causality for general LTL-definable properties. In: Proceedings of the 3rd Workshop on Formal Reasoning About Causation, Responsibility, and Explanations in Science and Technology (CREST), pp. 1–15 (2018)

14. Chockler, H., Halpern, J.Y.: Responsibility and blame: a structural-model approach. J. Artif. Int. Res. 22(1), 93–115 (2004)

15. Chockler, H., Halpern, J.Y., Kupferman, O.: What causes a system to satisfy a specification? ACM Trans. Comput. Logic 9(3), 1–26 (2008)

16. Chockler, H., Kupferman, O., Kurshan, R.P., Vardi, M.Y.: A practical approach to coverage in model checking. In: Berry, G., Comon, H., Finkel, A. (eds.) CAV 2001. LNCS, vol. 2102, pp. 66–78. Springer, Heidelberg (2001). https://doi.org/10.1007/3-540-44585-4_7

17. Chockler, H., Kupferman, O., Vardi, M.: Coverage metrics for formal verification. Int. J. Softw. Tools Technol. Transf. (STTT) 8(4–5), 373–386 (2006)

18. Chockler, H., Kupferman, O., Vardi, M.Y.: Coverage metrics for temporal logic model checking. In: Margaria, T., Yi, W. (eds.) TACAS 2001. LNCS, vol. 2031, pp. 528–542. Springer, Heidelberg (2001). https://doi.org/10.1007/3-540-45319-9_36

19. Clarke, E.M., Emerson, E.A.: Design and synthesis of synchronization skeletons using branching time temporal logic. In: Grumberg, O., Veith, H. (eds.) 25 Years of Model Checking. LNCS, vol. 5000, pp. 196–215. Springer, Heidelberg (2008). https://doi.org/10.1007/978-3-540-69850-0_12
20. Clarke, E.M., Emerson, E.A., Sistla, A.P.: Automatic verification of finite-state concurrent systems using temporal logic specifications. ACM Trans. Program. Lang. Syst. **8**, 244–263 (1986)
21. Clarke, E.M., Grumberg, O., McMillan, K.L., Zhao, X.: Efficient generation of counterexamples and witnesses in symbolic model checking. In: Proceedings of the 32nd Annual ACM/IEEE Design Automation Conference (DAC), New York, NY, USA, pp. 427–432. ACM (1995)
22. Courcoubetis, C., Yannakakis, M.: The complexity of probabilistic verification. J. ACM **42**(4), 857–907 (1995)
23. Datta, A., Garg, D., Kaynar, D., Sharma, D., Sinha, A.: Program actions as actual causes: a building block for accountability. In: Proceedings of the 28th IEEE Computer Security Foundations Symposium (CSF), pp. 261–275 (2015)
24. Alfaro, L.: Temporal logics for the specification of performance and reliability. In: Reischuk, R., Morvan, M. (eds.) STACS 1997. LNCS, vol. 1200, pp. 165–176. Springer, Heidelberg (1997). https://doi.org/10.1007/BFb0023457
25. Dimitrova, R., Finkbeiner, B., Torfah, H.: Probabilistic hyperproperties of Markov decision processes. In: Hung, D.V., Sokolsky, O. (eds.) ATVA 2020. LNCS, vol. 12302, pp. 484–500. Springer, Cham (2020). https://doi.org/10.1007/978-3-030-59152-6_27
26. Dubslaff, C., Weis, K., Baier, C., Apel, S.: Causality in configurable software systems. In: Proceedings of the 44th International Conference on Software Engineering (ICSE) (2022)
27. Feige, U., Hajiaghayi, M., Lee, J.R.: Improved approximation algorithms for minimum weight vertex separators. SIAM J. Comput. **38**(2), 629–657 (2008)
28. Feige, U., Mahdian, M.: Finding small balanced separators. In: Kleinberg, J.M. (ed.) Proceedings of the 38th Annual ACM Symposium on Theory of Computing, Seattle, WA, USA, 21–23 May 2006, pp. 375–384. ACM (2006)
29. Galles, D., Pearl, J.: Axioms of causal relevance. Artif. Intell. **97**(1–2), 9–43 (1997)
30. Galles, D., Pearl, J.: An axiomatic characterization of causal counterfactuals. Found. Sci. **3**, 151–182 (1998)
31. Gomes, G.: Are necessary and sufficient conditions converse relations? Australas. J. Philos. **87**(3), 375–387 (2009)
32. Gössler, G., Le Métayer, D.: A general trace-based framework of logical causality. In: Fiadeiro, J.L., Liu, Z., Xue, J. (eds.) FACS 2013. LNCS, vol. 8348, pp. 157–173. Springer, Cham (2014). https://doi.org/10.1007/978-3-319-07602-7_11
33. Gössler, G., Le Métayer, D.: A general framework for blaming in component-based systems. Sci. Comput. Program. **113**, 223–235 (2015)
34. Gössler, G., Stefani, J.-B.: Causality analysis and fault ascription in component-based systems. Theoret. Comput. Sci. **837**, 158–180 (2020)
35. Groce, A.: Error explanation with distance metrics. In: Jensen, K., Podelski, A. (eds.) TACAS 2004. LNCS, vol. 2988, pp. 108–122. Springer, Heidelberg (2004). https://doi.org/10.1007/978-3-540-24730-2_8
36. Groce, A., Chaki, S., Kroening, D., Strichman, O.: Error explanation with distance metrics. Int. J. Softw. Tools Technol. Transfer **8**(3), 229–247 (2006)
37. Groce, A., Visser, W.: What went wrong: explaining counterexamples. In: Ball, T., Rajamani, S.K. (eds.) SPIN 2003. LNCS, vol. 2648, pp. 121–136. Springer, Heidelberg (2003). https://doi.org/10.1007/3-540-44829-2_8

38. Halpern, J.Y.: Axiomatizing causal reasoning. J. Artif. Intell. Res. **12**(1), 317–337 (2000)
39. Halpern, J.Y.: A modification of the Halpern-Pearl definition of causality. In: Proceedings of the 24th International Joint Conference on AI (IJCAI), pp. 3022–3033. AAAI Press (2015)
40. Halpern, J.Y., Pearl, J.: Causes and explanations: a structural-model approach. Part I: causes. Br. J. Philos. Sci. **56**(4), 843–887 (2005)
41. Halpern, J.Y., Pearl, J.: Causes and explanations: a structural-model approach. Part II: explanations. Br. J. Philos. Sci. **56**(4), 889–911 (2005)
42. Hart, H.L.A., Honoré, A.M.: Causation in the Law. Oxford University Press, Oxford (1959)
43. Hart, S., Sharir, M., Pnueli, A.: Termination of probabilistic concurrent program. ACM Trans. Program. Lang. Syst. **5**(3), 356–380 (1983)
44. Hopkins, M., Pearl, J.: Causality and counterfactuals in the situation calculus. J. Log. Comput. **17**(5), 939–953 (2007)
45. Hoskote, Y., Kam, T., Ho, P.-H., Zhao, X.: Coverage estimation for symbolic model checking. In: Proceedings of the 36th Annual ACM/IEEE Design Automation Conference (DAC), pp. 300–305 (1999)
46. Hume, D.: A Treatise of Human Nature. John Noon (1739)
47. Hume, D.: An Enquiry Concerning Human Understanding. London (1748)
48. Khan, S.M., Soutchanski, M.: Necessary and sufficient conditions for actual root causes. In: 24th European Conference on Artificial Intelligence (ECAI 2020), Including 10th Conference on Prestigious Applications of Artificial Intelligence (PAIS 2020), pp. 800–808 (2020)
49. Kleinberg, S.: A logic for causal inference in time series with discrete and continuous variables. In: Proceedings of the 22nd International Joint Conference on AI (IJCAI), pp. 943–950 (2011)
50. Kleinberg, S., Mishra, B.: The temporal logic of causal structures. In: Proceedings of the 25th Conference on Uncertainty in AI (UAI), pp. 303–312 (2009)
51. Kleinberg, S., Mishra, B.: The temporal logic of token causes. In: Proceedings of the 12th International Conference on Principles of Knowledge Representation and Reasoning (KR) (2010)
52. Kölbl, M., Leue, S.: An efficient algorithm for computing causal trace sets in causality checking. In: Chen, Y.-F., Cheng, C.-H., Esparza, J. (eds.) ATVA 2019. LNCS, vol. 11781, pp. 171–186. Springer, Cham (2019). https://doi.org/10.1007/978-3-030-31784-3_10
53. Kölbl, M., Leue, S., Schmid, R.: Dynamic causes for the violation of timed reachability properties. In: Bertrand, N., Jansen, N. (eds.) FORMATS 2020. LNCS, vol. 12288, pp. 127–143. Springer, Cham (2020). https://doi.org/10.1007/978-3-030-57628-8_8
54. Kupferman, O., Vardi, M.Y.: Vacuity detection in temporal model checking. In: Pierre, L., Kropf, T. (eds.) CHARME 1999. LNCS, vol. 1703, pp. 82–98. Springer, Heidelberg (1999). https://doi.org/10.1007/3-540-48153-2_8
55. Kupriyanov, A., Finkbeiner, B.: Causality-based verification of multi-threaded programs. In: D'Argenio, P.R., Melgratti, H. (eds.) CONCUR 2013. LNCS, vol. 8052, pp. 257–272. Springer, Heidelberg (2013). https://doi.org/10.1007/978-3-642-40184-8_19
56. Kupriyanov, A., Finkbeiner, B.: Causal termination of multi-threaded programs. In: Biere, A., Bloem, R. (eds.) CAV 2014. LNCS, vol. 8559, pp. 814–830. Springer, Cham (2014). https://doi.org/10.1007/978-3-319-08867-9_54

57. Leitner-Fischer, F., Leue, S.: Causality checking for complex system models. In: Giacobazzi, R., Berdine, J., Mastroeni, I. (eds.) VMCAI 2013. LNCS, vol. 7737, pp. 248–267. Springer, Heidelberg (2013). https://doi.org/10.1007/978-3-642-35873-9_16
58. Lewis, D.: Causation. J. Philos. **70**(17), 556–567 (1973)
59. Mackie, J.L.: Causes and conditions. Am. Philos. Q. **2**(4), 245–264 (1965)
60. Mackie, J.L.: The Cement of the Universe: A Study of Causation. Clarendon Press, Oxford (1974)
61. Mascle, C., Baier, C., Funke, F., Jantsch, S., Kiefer, S.: Responsibility and verification: importance value in temporal logics. In: 2021 36th Annual ACM/IEEE Symposium on Logic in Computer Science (LICS), pp. 1–14 (2021)
62. Papadimitriou, C.H., Steiglitz, K.: Combinatorial Optimization: Algorithms and Complexity. Prentice-Hall, Hoboken (1982)
63. Pearl, J.: Causal diagrams for empirical research. Biometrika **82**(4), 669–688 (1995)
64. Pnueli, A.: The temporal logic of programs. In: Proceedings of the 18th Annual Symposium on Foundations of Computer Science (FOCS), pp. 46–57 (1977)
65. Purandare, M., Somenzi, F.: Vacuum cleaning CTL formulae. In: Brinksma, E., Larsen, K.G. (eds.) CAV 2002. LNCS, vol. 2404, pp. 485–499. Springer, Heidelberg (2002). https://doi.org/10.1007/3-540-45657-0_39
66. Queille, J.P., Sifakis, J.: Specification and verification of concurrent systems in CESAR. In: Dezani-Ciancaglini, M., Montanari, U. (eds.) Programming 1982. LNCS, vol. 137, pp. 337–351. Springer, Heidelberg (1982). https://doi.org/10.1007/3-540-11494-7_22
67. Reichenbach, H.: The Direction of Time. University of California Press, Berkeley and Los Angeles (1956)
68. Reiter, R.: Knowledge in Action: Logical Foundations for Specifying and Implementing Dynamical Systems. MIT Press, Cambridge (2001)
69. Renieres, M., Reiss, S.P.: Fault localization with nearest neighbor queries. In: Proceedings of the 18th IEEE International Conference on Automated Software Engineering (ASE), pp. 30–39 (2003)
70. Vardi, M.Y.: Automatic verification of probabilistic concurrent finite state programs. In: Proceedings of the 26th Annual Symposium on Foundations of Computer Science, SFCS 1985, pp. 327–338. IEEE Computer Society (1985)
71. Wertheimer, R.: Conditions. J. Philos. **65**(12), 355–364 (1968)
72. Wright, R.W.: Causation in tort law. Calif. Law Rev. **73**(6), 1735–1828 (1985)
73. Zeller, A.: Isolating cause-effect chains from computer programs. In: Proceedings of the 10th ACM SIGSOFT Symposium on Foundations of Software Engineering (FSE), New York, NY, USA, pp. 1–10. ACM (2002)

Axiomatizing Consciousness
with Applications

Henk Barendregt[1(✉)] and Antonino Raffone[2]

[1] Faculty of Science, Radboud University, Nijmegen, The Netherlands
`henk.barendregt@ru.nl`
[2] Department of Psychology, Sapienza University of Rome, Rome, Italy
`antonino.raffone@uniroma1.it`

Abstract. Consciousness will be introduced axiomatically, inspired by classical Buddhist insight meditation and psychology, computer science, and cognitive neuroscience, as belonging to *agents* that observe and act, in the form of a stream of *configurations* that is *compound, discrete*, and *probabilistic-computable*.

Within the axiomatic context the notions of *self, concentration, mindfulness*, and various forms of suffering can be defined. As an application of this setup, it will be shown how a combined development of concentration and mindfulness can attenuate and eventually eradicate some major forms of suffering.

The main message of this paper is that advanced mindfulness consists of knowledge of the state an agent finds itself in and can be used to defuse mental/behavioral scenarios. From the computer science point of view it is trivial that being in the position to access and modify state is powerful and enables a greater flexibility. This paper is an attempt to bridge the gap between computer science and cognitive psychology. The other explanatory gap of the hard problem (How do physics and consciousness relate?) is not discussed in this paper, but is quite possibly an extension of it.

1 Towards Consciousness

Studying phenomena in the 'external world' by making conceptual models has led to physics. Its success gives the impression that also the human mind could be studied similarly, answering questions like "How does consciousness (experience) arise?" There is, however, a persistent 'explanatory gap' between models of the universe and 'first-person' awareness. This gap is called the 'hard problem' [12]. Whatever model of consciousness is proposed, the question "And where is awareness in all of this?" cannot be bypassed [8]. Not only is the consciousness problem hard to solve, it even seems impossible to properly state it[1].

In contrast to the third person description of consciousness, the phenomenological approach employs a first person perspective, in which the experience of consciousness comes prior to anything else. In this view, matter and the whole

---

[1] Personal communication by Bill Phillips.

N. Jansen et al. (Eds.): Vaandrager Festschrift 2022, LNCS 13560, pp. 46–62, 2022.
https://doi.org/10.1007/978-3-031-15629-8_3

universe derive from consciousness as a construction of the world with predictive value. But then another problem pops up: "Why does the external world gives the impression to be stable?" [22]. In this paper the hard consciousness problem will not be discussed as such. See [30,35] for recent discussions. We position ourselves among the phenomenologists: there is the experience of phenomena that can be studied phenomenologically. In this way consciousness will be described as an objective personal phenomenon, not from the brain side, but from the other side of the explanatory gap: direct experience. The description will be called objective, since it is claimed that the description is universally valid, and personal, since it takes place in the mind of a given person.

The difficulty of defining what consciousness is will be dealt with by the methodology of the axiomatic method [2]. In a given setting there are *primitive (undefined) objects* (also called *concepts*, as the objects are mental) and *axioms* about these that are taken to be valid. In this way, following [19], the axioms form an *implicit definition*[2] of the primitive objects. In the next sections a setting and axiomatization of consciousness will be proposed using the notions object (input), state, and action (output) of consciousness[3]. The details are inspired by Buddhist psychology, the Abhidhamma [1], and Abhidharma[4], translated into the language of science: cognitive neuroscience, mathematical logic and computability. Intended is an axiomatization of those aspects of consciousness that are shared by adult humans in possession of their ordinary faculties. The axiomatization will not touch the hard problem, but aims at describing certain aspects of consciousness to arrive at some applications in the domain of computability, learning and deconditioning, and the cause and eradication of existential suffering.

---

[2] In planar geometry one has as setting that there are points and lines, and that there is a relation *"point P lies on line l"*, in notation $P|l$. In this setting an example of an axiom is

For distinct points P, Q there is exactly one line l such that both $P|l$ and $Q|l$.

What actually is a point and a line doesn't matter, as long as the axioms are valid for these. Since the axioms do not always fully determine the objects, one better speaks about an 'implicit specification' of the primitive concepts.

[3] This paper is a continuation of [4]. Another axiomatic approach to consciousness is Integrated Information Theory (IIT) [31]. That theory also contains the triples object-state-action (using different terminology). The model IIT diverges from ours, wanting to propose a solution to the hard problem of consciousness. Although [8] argues convincingly that this is impossible, IIT is an interesting further analysis of the mechanisms needed for consciousness. Our axiomatization focuses on several applications, mentioned in the abstract and detailed below. Further comparison between IIT and our model is beyond the scope of this paper.

[4] See [34] for a thorough description of discreteness of phenomenological time in Buddhism.

2 Consciousness as Discrete, Probabilistic-Computable Actor

Change

Science doesn't know what is consciousness. But we know. Consciousness consists of phenomena, called *configurations* and are members of a space $\mathcal{C}$, that change in time. We write c_t for the configuration at time $t \in \mathbf{T}$, to be thought of as 'what is perceived at moment t'. Time is not to be seen as a given from the outside, but as a construct from the phenomena themselves. Time has passed from t to t' if there is a change from c_t to $c_{t'}$ and there is memory part of c_t within $c_{t'}$. This is called the *primordial intuition of time*, [9].

The changing configurations create the *stream of consciousness*, which is a function $\mathbf{c} \colon \mathbf{T} \to \mathcal{C}$ that assigns to a moment t in time the configuration c_t:

$$\boxed{\mathbf{c}(t) = c_t, \text{ with } t \in \mathbf{T}.} \tag{2.1}$$

Actors in a World

The stream of consciousness $\mathbf{c}$ may seem like a dynamical system that changes in time, in which a future state is determined by the state at present. Examples of such systems are the following. 1. A single planet orbiting a star. 2. Conway's Game of Life. But (the stream of) consciousness is not a dynamical system. The consciousness is embedded in an environment, the world. These two mutually influence each other. Thus consciousness may be better compared to one planet among other ones in the gravitational field of a star and the (other) planets. For example the orbit of Uranus could not be explained by the laws of mechanics w.r.t the sun alone: it had an aberration that led to the hypothetical existence of a further planet. In this way the planet Neptune was discovered. The mathematics involved is becoming complex: the three body problem (c.q. predicting the movements of Uranus and Neptune with respect to the sun) has chaotic solutions.

An *agent* A living in a *world* W consists of the following. Both A and W consists of changing configurations; those of A are denoted by $c, c', c'', c_0, c_1, \ldots$ and similarly those of W by variations of the letter w. Agent A in configuration c enacts with the world W in configuration w. This enacting is denoted by $c|w$, thereby changing both configurations[5]. The resulting combined stream of the agent A thrown in the world W will be denoted as $(\mathbf{c}, \mathbf{w})$ so that for $t \in \mathbf{T}$ one has

$$\boxed{(\mathbf{c}, \mathbf{w})(t) = (c_t, w_t).} \tag{2.2}$$

---

[5] Dynamical systems are a special case, having a world that doesn't change (e.g. Conway's game of Life). On the other hand an agent and its world can be considered as a pair, forming a single dynamical system. The choice is pragmatic.

Discreteness of Time

We postulate that the stream of consciousness is temporally discrete. This view can be related to Buddhist texts, in which it is asserted that the continuum of awareness is characterized by successive moments, or pulses of cognition, [1] and [34]. Also it stems from psychophysical investigations and neural models of consciousness: [15] suggested that conscious cognition is temporally discrete and parsed into sensory sampling intervals or 'perceptual frames', estimated to be about 70–100 ms in average duration. More recently, this time range has been interpreted as an attentional object-based sampling rate for visual motion, [28] and [33].

This means that $\mathbf{T}$ is not modeled by the set $\mathbb{R}$ of real numbers, but by

$$\mathbb{Z} = \{\ldots, -2, -1, 0, 1, 2, \ldots\}$$

the set of integers. So

$$\boxed{\mathbf{T} = \mathbb{Z}.} \tag{2.3}$$

Now an agent A in world W develops by a repeated interaction $c|w = (c', w')$, as follows:

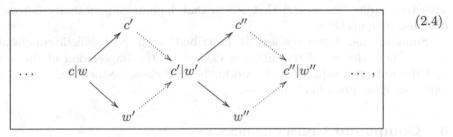

(2.4)

creating *streams* $\mathbf{c}: c \to c' \to c'' \to \ldots$ and $\mathbf{w}: w \to w' \to w'' \to \ldots$ of configurations and states of the world. The $\mathbf{w}$ could be called the *trace* or *footprint* of the agent in the world. The transitions from the interacting c and w to c' and w' take place in *discrete time*, that imaginatively could be called *stroboscopic*. This creates phenomenological time. We have chosen $\mathbf{T} = \mathbb{Z}$ and not $\mathbf{T} = \mathbb{N} = \{0, 1, 2, \ldots\}$ to make time without beginning. The reader may like to make another choice.

In [36] it is explained that discreteness of the stream of consciousness neatly answers the question of von Neumann how it is possible that the human mind, being based on a biological substrate with its inherent imprecision, is capable to arrive at the precision that is available in e.g. mathematics. This is similar to a digital CD that represents sound with less noise than an analogue record.

Stream of Consciousness is Probabilistic-Computable

The stream of consciousness proceeds in mutual dependency with the stream of the world. The progression is determined by repeatedly applying the operation $c|w$. In this way one obtains a new pair of configurations (c', w') that are being subject to their interaction $c'|w'$, et cetera. We assign the task of obtaining the next c' or w' to the agent A and its world W; so we have

$$\boxed{\begin{aligned} A(c, w) &= c'; \\ W(c, w) &= w'. \end{aligned}} \tag{2.5}$$

That is $c|w = (A(c, w), W(c, w))$. The functions A, W with

$$\boxed{A \colon \mathcal{A} \times \mathcal{W} \to \mathcal{A}, \ W \colon \mathcal{A} \times \mathcal{W} \to \mathcal{W}} \tag{2.6}$$

are postulated to be probabilistic-computable[6]. The non-determinism causing probabilistic-computability comes from the following. 1. There are neural nets in the brain of an animal/human agent that act adequately but not with 100% precision; 2. What happens in the world depends on other agents and on quantum fluctuations.

As motivation for the axiom of probabilistic-computability of the stream of consciousness one can refer to: functioning of neurons, see [25]. The Buddhist view, and corresponding meditation experience, that everything has a cause (dependent origination) also motivates this axiom. The axiom also is consistent with the Turing Thesis [32] that states that human computability is exactly machine computability.

Summarizing. Consciousness is described as a probabilistic-computable agent, where the non-determinism is caused by the imprecision of the agent and the unknown aspects of the world. Nevertheless, because the actions are digitized, great precision is possible.

3   Compound Consciousness

Input, state, action

Acting in a world is made efficient by sensors, channels for input (i), and actuators, for action (a). Behaviorism took as position that humans could be described by the set of pairs (i, a) (in short ia), also called 'stimulus and reaction'. In this line of thinking one could write

---

[6]   A multivariate function $f \colon D^k \to D$ is called *probabilistic-computable* if for some computable function $g \colon D^{k+1} \to D$ one has

$$f(d) = g(s(d), d),$$

where $s \colon D^k \to D$ is some stochastic function. A prime example of a probabilistic-computable agent is a particular goose in the well-known child's Game of Goose, whose actions depend on non-deterministic factors, like the throwing of a pair of dice and the stack of cards that determine special actions. Viable animal agents in our biological world, depending on a probabilistic-computable function f, are usually good in performing actions, maximizing the chance that $f(d)$ is in some set of suitable outcomes, [17].

$$\boxed{\mathbf{c}(t) = c_t = i_t a_t, \text{ with } t \in \mathbb{Z}} \tag{3.1}$$

This, however, is a limited view, as a person doesn't always behave in the same way if being subject to the same input. Therefore next to i and a one needs an (internal) 'state' s to describe the agent. This 'mind-state' s can be considered as 'the tendency to act in a certain way'. This results in postulating that for the configurations c of an agent A one has $c = isa$, so that the stream of consciousness $\mathbf{c}$ can be considered to consist of three streams[7].

$$\mathbf{c} = \ldots \rightarrow \underbrace{i_{-1}s_{-1}a_{-1}}_{c_{-1}} \rightarrow \underbrace{i_0 s_0 a_0}_{c_0} \rightarrow \underbrace{i_1 s_1 a_1}_{c_1} \rightarrow \ldots = \begin{cases} \ldots, i_{-1}, i_0, i_1, \ldots \\ \ldots, s_{-1}, s_0, s_1 \ldots \\ \ldots, a_{-1}, a_0, a_1, \ldots \end{cases} \tag{3.2}$$

Feeling tone: reward system

For humans (and other species) it is useful to make a further division. 1. Writing $s = s^f s^c$, where s^f is the feeling tone and s^c is the rest of the state of consciousness. The s^f is an element of $\{--, -, 0, +, ++\}$ and indicates whether the present configuration is felt as very unpleasant, unpleasant, neutral, pleasant, very pleasant. It is the reward-punishment for humans and other species; nature makes certain things pleasant, like eating and making children, in order to make Homo Sapiens thrive.

Cognition: memory, language, mental programs

Another subdivision, notably for humans, is to add a group i^m for 'cognition'[8], consisting of concepts and images and split i as follows: $i = i^b i^m$. The objects of i^b consist of input from the physical senses, hence the superscript 'b' refering to 'body'. The objects of i^m consist of mental images, concepts, and intentions to act. Except for pathological cases, humans can distinguish these respectively from actual input i^b and from actual execution of an intended act a.

The elements of the streams in $c = i^b i^m s^f s^c a$ are acting in an associative way. The sound of a bell (i^b) preceding a meal for a dog that triggers saliva, after a couple of times is enough to trigger the saliva without a meal. In general associations between elements of the *isa* may trigger occurrences of other objects possibly in another stream. The group i^m has a rich potential of elements that can be triggered by an event coming in through i^b, and causing in its turn the right reaction in a.

For this to work well there is *cued recall*. After a particular object o_1 in say i^b is presented several times and followed by another object o_2, the presentation

---

[7] This is how the transitions in a Turing Machine can be seen. The Read/Write device (R/W-head) is positioned on a cell and reads i. Then depending on this and on the state s an action is performed: either moving the R/W-head, or writing a symbol on the cell where the R/W-head is positioned, or changing the inner state.

[8] Traditionally this is called the group of 'perception'.

of just o_1 may trigger the memory of o_2. In a small brain cued recall has limited reliability (the recalled o_2 may not be correct) and capacity (only a limited numbers of pairs (o_1, o_2) may be stored. This limitation can be increased considerably, [10], at the cost of brain tissue and energy consumption. In this way language and mental programs can be developed.

Another integrative model of human cognition and emotion was proposed by [7], in terms of an interacting cognitive subsystems (ICS) model of the organization and function of the resources underlying human cognition, see also [6]. This model provides a conceptual framework for understanding normal and dysfunctional cognitive/affective relationships and their modification. ICS includes nine interacting cognitive subsystems, which individually handle a specific type of information. Information arrives in a subsystem, is copied into an image record and is transformed for use in another subsystem. The subsystems differ in their inputs and outputs, as they each specialise in storing and processing a qualitatively different form of mental representation. ICS stresses that mental activity occurs in multiple domains in parallel. This model emphasizes the importance, of schematic, synthetic level of processing that integrates both propositional meaning and direct sensory contributions as part of the total cognitive configuration producing emotion. ICS also includes a body state subsystem.

The five groups

Taken together one obtains the five groups, aka aggregates/skandhas:

$$c = \underbrace{i^b i^m}_{i} \underbrace{s^f s^c}_{s} a, \tag{3.3}$$

so that the stream of consciousness has five substreams. The new substreams

$$s^f = \ldots \to s^f_{-1} \to s^f_0 \to s^f_1 \to \ldots$$
$$i^m = \ldots \to i^m_{-1} \to i^m_0 \to i^m_1 \to \ldots \tag{3.4}$$

are the stream of feeling tones and that of mental activities, like thinking or imagining. These two streams often are being hypertrophied (in the sense of getting much attention) in human existence, notably reinforcing each other.

Finer details of consciousness

A triple $c_t = i_t s_t a_t$ (or more accurately a quintuple $c_t = i^b_t i^m_t s^f_t s^c_t a_t$) is called a *ceta* (aka *citta* or *mind-moment*). A state can be approximately seen as a large array of values (parameters). Think of a possible state of the weather, e.g. a local snowstorm. Relevant for that state are the temperature, humidity, wind, and more at the different relevant local positions. In Buddhist psychology, the Abhidhamma, the mind-state s is seen as such an array of many so called mental factors, called *cetasikas*. As feeling tone s^f is such an important factor, that is always present, it is singled out in the five groups. Other mental factors, that however are not always present, are *aversion, desire* on the unwholesome side, and *mindfulness*, to be introduced below, and *compassion* on the wholesome side.

4 Self

The following second part of this paper will apply the given model of consciousness to understanding mechanisms of human sufferng that are possible to relinquish.

That an agent in the world proceeds with a probabilistic-computable stream of consciousness may be expressed by saying that it is 'impersonal'. It just follows the laws of nature, depending on the configuration of A and the state of the world. Another way of expressing this is by saying that A is self-less. It proceeds without independent existence, just like like a glider crawls diagonally over the field of Conway's Game of Life, [13] and [23], or like a wave towards the shore, that seems to proceed from a pebble thrown into the middle of a pool. In the latter case water only moves up and down, not sideways, as becomes clear when placing a ping-pong ball in the water.

Nevertheless within the life-stream of the agent it can happen that a self is being formed. It is a dynamical process consisting of a collection of behavioral strategies that protect and take care of the individual. For humans a self-pattern integrates as a dynamic whole or 'Gestalt' a very heterogeneous set of processes: bodily, experiential, affective, behavioral, cognitive, narratival, social, worldly and normative processes, [18]. This self needs some balance: fine tuning of the different sub-strategies.

Healthy Attachments

When homo sapiens considered as agent grows up, it learns as a baby first the following: relating a and i, so that some control over the environment can be obtained. Shortly after in the development of a child, as each i is coupled with s^f, the actions will be directed towards avoiding input with unpleasant s^f.

With the capacities so far: acting towards pleasant input in an intelligent way, learned from the social environment, agent A develops strategies that are good for A, for itself. If this happens in the right way, one has developed a healthy self through healthy attachments.

Selfing

If one doesn't have enough empathy, the capacity to imagine the state of others in a given situation, the notion of self may become too central and becomes counter-productive. If one mentions too often 'I, me, mine', and acts accordingly, then one will be avoided by people in one's environment.

Wrong View

The self that has been described as a dynamical process is used so often, that it gets reified as a thing. In the same way as the wave is seen as an object that moves towards the shore, the self is perceived as an entity with independent existence. This is called 'Wrong View'. In the first place this causes fear of death. But many more problems will result, as Wrong View creates the idea that one needs to defend self. Also it leads to the unwholesome habit of selfing.

5 Mindfulness: Mechanism and Application to ER

Mechanism of Mindfulness

In the given model of consciousness one can define mindfulness. In this way one primitive term can be eliminated.

Mindfulness at c_{t+1} is a mental factor that has (part of) the previous ceta c_t as object. If $c_t = isa$, then the next ceta being mindful means that it is $c_{t+1} = ('isa')s'a'$. One speaks of the 'right' mindfulness if s' contains friendliness.

Mindfulness can help emotional regulation (ER). Suppose $c_t = i(\text{\includegraphics{}} + s)a$ is a ceta in which the mind-state contains the cetasika (mental factor) of angriness. The presence of this unwholesome factor makes it probable that the action a is unwholesome, increasing the chance of suffering at some or more future consciousness moments. Being mindful of the angriness at the next ceta can be seen as $c_{t+1} = (i + \text{'\includegraphics{}'})s'a'$. The transition

$$i(\text{\includegraphics{}} + s)a \longmapsto (i + \text{'\includegraphics{}'})s'a' \tag{5.1}$$

is said to be the transformation of *being angry*, possibly with unwholesome act a, to *seeing angriness*, with an equanimous mental state s' and wholesome act a'.

Application of mindfulness: purification. *Mindfulness training* consists of exercising the transition (5.1) so that mindfulness becomes easy to apply. To increase the effect of mindfulness in the direction of ER one may train it so that it becomes strong and sharp. Strong means that it is being applied during a longer time period; sharp means that it is being applied with a high frequency.

Mindfulness as Liberating Factor

A strong and sharp form of mindfulness is useful for removing counterproductive mind-states. When mindfulness has been sufficiently developed, so that it possesses a high resolution and can be maintained for an extended period, eventually it will show that consciousness is

$$\boxed{\text{compound, fluctuating, impersonal,}} \qquad (5.2)$$

and therefore a cause of suffering. In the Buddhist tradition, [11], one mentions the *three fundamental characteristics of existence* (and thereby of consciousness):

$$\boxed{\text{non permanence, suffering, non self.}} \qquad (5.3)$$

Experiencing this causes further 'insights': feelings of (irrational) fear, delusions of seeing (non existing) danger and (utter) disgust/nausea, often experienced in quick succession. These form an impressive cross-section of psychiatric conditions. From the Buddhist point of view these are caused by attachment to self. Provided there is 'wisdom' (understanding that the experience is real), this leads to a balanced and flexible form of being, described in Sect. 7.

6 Suffering

One can distinguish three essentially different forms of suffering and distress.

1. Distress: 2. Distress: stable, rigidly   3. Chaos & Lack:
avoiding pain   avoiding change   existential fear 'no escape'

The three diagrams represent stylistically the dynamic character of three forms of suffering.

6.1 Suffering as Pain

The most basic form of suffering comes in the form of feeling-tone s^f having a negative value. Things are unpleasant or even very much so. The agent tries to avoid this by changing position or the situation and becomes restless, repeatedly running away from unpleasant feeling. The shape of this attractor is constantly changing, but keeps some of its patterns.

6.2   Suffering as Change

Holding tightly onto some object of craving, resisting change. The shape of this attractor from a distance looks stable, even rigid. The strategies constituting the self have as goal to minimize pain and maximize pleasure. If one has some success in this, then one likes to keep the life style one lives. For that reason change is felt as a threat and is felt as cause of suffering. Next to this there is also a mechanism of trying to hold onto one's lifestyle, even if it is not conductive to decreasing suffering in the form of pain. This will be explained in the next subsection. Both the drive to accomplish what one wants and to cover up what one fears lead to rigidity.

6.3   Suffering from Lack

The fact that consciousness is progressing as a stream that is compound, fluctuating as a stroboscope, and impersonal, is a serious blow to self, when there is the Wrong View of it being permanent and substantial (having independent existence). One falls apart, not succeeding to hold a stable image of the world (derealization) or ourselves (depersonalization). Various kinds of defense mechanisms create a 'cover-up' that hides this fundamental fact. Rigidly holding on to unwholesome habits happens if one fears that the cover-up is taken away. This explains the second reason why change may be experienced as suffering, mentioned in the previous subsection: one is forced to hold on to unwholesome habits.

If, on the other hand, one doesn't succeed in maintaining the cover-up, then outright existential fear appears. This fear is not related to objects, like a wild animal, that appear in the world. It is related to the failure of basic mechanism of consciousness. It therefore is difficult to understand by friends that would like to provide help, but are unfamiliar to the experience of the three fundamental characteristics.

(Un)wholesome Actions

An action is (un)wholesome if it (increases) decreases the chance of later occurring states with negative s^f (that are painful). A mindstate is (un)wholesome if it leads to (un)wholesome acts. While hedonist acts are intended to lead to immediate pleasure, wholesome acts are intended to lead to sustainably avoiding suffering.

7   Release: ↓Suffering and ↑Freedom

To increase resilience against stress and make it sustainable one needs to release existential suffering. For this the insight meditation tradition [11] has created *the triple training*:

$$\boxed{\text{behavior} \longmapsto \text{concentration} \longmapsto \text{wisdom.}} \tag{7.1}$$

The development of behavior, also called *discipline* or *ethics*, is towards having respect for oneself, others, and the world. This prevents necessary actions in the future and simplifies life. For example if one doesn't steal one will not risk to come into contact with the police and be charged for theft. This helps enabling to develop a lifestyle apt to build concentration, i.e. being able to restrict attention to fewer objects. Details how to do this are beyond the scope of this paper, but can be found in many meditation manuals, e.g. [26]. Then, finally, it becomes possible to obtain insight into the functioning of our body-mind system so that unwholesome mental loops (vicious circles) can be defused and avoided.

An important aspect of the training of behavior and concentration is that also mental activity i^m, which is both an action and an input, decreases.

It is not the case that one first fully develops ethical behavior, then concentration, and only then insight arises. With some discipline in behavior, some concentration may be developed, and then some wisdom arises. With that wisdom one is motivated to increase discipline, so that concentration and wisdom can be developed further. This then leads to an upward spiral.

Discipline means that one follows a mental program, a plan. Concentration means that one is able to keep one's attention to a desired object, the meditation object, for example the physical sensations of the movements related to breathing. This is practiced by taking a meditation object with as aim to keep it as long as possible in focus. Each time when attention has drifted somewhere else, often without even noticing this, as soon as one is aware of this, one gently brings attention back to the chosen object. When this is done continuously, eventually concentration grows and the period to remain focused on the meditation object increases considerably.

With enough discipline and concentration one is able to restrict the i and a such that they are approximately constant and become i_0 and a_0. Then a usual stream of consciousness like

$$\boxed{\ldots \to isa \to i'a's' \to i''a''s'' \to \ldots} \tag{7.2}$$

becomes

$$\boxed{\ldots \to i_0 s a_0 \to i_0 s' a_0 \to i_0 s'' a_0 \to \ldots} \tag{7.3}$$

with the input and action fixed to i_0, a_0, respectively. This means that the only change is happening in the stream of mind-states

$$\boxed{\ldots \to s \to s' \to s'' \to \ldots} \tag{7.4}$$

Being for some longer time in this scenario is restful. But certain tendencies remain present. After stopping meditation, going back to sensory and mental input one returns to the usual scenario (7.2). Nevertheless having felt the quietness of (7.3) is already refreshing, wholesome, and increasing one's resilience.

But it is possible to develop something better: sustainable resilience. Not counting mental or sensory input, it can be assumed that there are only a limited number of mind-states. Therefore the stream of mind-states will enter a loop:

$$\boxed{s \to s' \to s'' \to \ldots s^{(k)} \to s} \tag{7.5}$$

If one is fully aware of this loop, or at least of a subloop jumping now and then a few positions, then habituation occurs and consciousness occurs without an object arises where even i_0 disappears. This is called *nibbana/nirvana*. It causes a powerful reset, enabling the stream of consciousness to escape from the quasi-attractor in which it was caught for a long time. Wrong View becomes Right View, that was already intuitively clear during the insight of Lack, but it was not yet accepted.

The transitions $(7.2) \longmapsto (7.3) \longmapsto (7.5)$ can be intuitively depicted as follows:

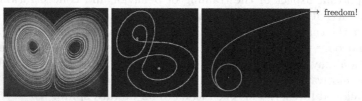

   a. ego (cover-up) b. concentration c. release

a. Holding on to a repeated scenario, giving some stability at the cost of rigidity. b. Using concentration that keeps input and actions constant, simplifying the scenario depicted in a. During sleep the scenario also may become simpler, but then usually one is not mindful so that one cannot go to the next stage of liberation. c. When scenario b is followed fully mindfully, only possible after the simplification, then one realzes that one is in a loop, makes a reset, and exits the pseudo-attractor.

8 Freedom Paradox

There is a remarkable pseudo paradox. Being fully aware of the loop (7.5) one intuitively understands what is called 'Dependent origination'. Basically this states that the stream of consciousness (7.5), but then also (7.2), is subject to a probabilistic-computable process. This is liberating, as one is no longer obliged to pretend one has an essential say in the propagation of our stream of consciousness. No longer pretending frees us from rigidity fixated on the self-image we held on to for a long time. Therefore there is the freedom paradox:

> We become free by realizing that we are fully determined. (8.1)

To understand this, we may compare homo sapiens to a goat that is attached by a rope around its neck to a pole in the grass. Consequently the animal can graze only in a circle around the pole. The goat learns from someone, or invents it autodidactically, that to become free one should gnaw on the rope. When the goat has succeeded to break the rope, it is free to walk away from the farm where it is being held, walk into the fields, forests, and mountains to find other goats for playing and mating. Thereby the goat follows its way of being conditioned. It even can go back to the farm. In this simile the rope for homo sapiens consists of the image one has of oneself, including our desires and fears. One is attached to this self-image, in order not to feel the fundamental Lack [24] of self, of substantial independent being. Freedom consists of having 'algorithms' that are pretty good in calculating in an intelligent and compassionate way what is our best surviving strategy. This way our actions are based on a flow and no longer on ideas that create our narrative being. Another way of stating the freedom paradox is the following[9].

$$\boxed{\text{There is freedom, but it is not ours.}} \qquad (8.2)$$

A similar statement, in a literary style, is in [27].

I am a psychological and historical structure. Along with existence, I received a way of existing, or a style. All of my actions and thoughts are related to this structure, and even a philosopher's thought is merely a way of making explicit his hold upon the world, which is all he is. And yet, I am free, not in spite of or beneath these motivations, but rather by their means. For that meaningful life, that particular signification of nature and history that I am, does not restrict my access to the world; it is rather my means of communication with it.

Merleau-Ponty: *Phenomenology of perception*

9 Layers of Consciousness

Using our physical senses and possibly also the mental sense through which the i^m arrive), is overwhelming. Therefore the human mind has a mechanism of attention that makes a selection. This can be modeled by allowing each i to be a large set of values, together with a (chosen) subset $F \subseteq i$ of values to which attention is being paid. In the same way action a can be seen as a large set of possible actions to which one needs to apply attention as subset $G \subseteq a$, to select the intended actions.

Forms of Consciousness

One can ride over a well-known bridge in town without realizing that one does this. Arrived in the other part of town suddenly one realizes 'We are here, so I

---

[9] Formulation by Karin Videc, personal communication.

must have crossed the bridge.' Consciousness is sometimes described as proto-consciousness plus knowing. As the example shows, this knowing part is not always there. In the theory presented so far this can be modeled as having a (series of) mind-moment(s) including the mental factor of mindfulness that enables input not via the physical senses, but more directly from the information of the previous mind-moment.

One may even differentiate further. Pre-consciousness of an object i_0 may be described as a $((\{i\}; F), s, a)$ in which i_0 is among the i, but is not attended to, i.e. not in F. Proto consciousness of an object i_0 is such that F focuses on at least i_0. And as stated, full consciousness arises when i_0 is also observed in the next mind-moment by mindfulness.

$$\boxed{\begin{array}{l} \text{(full) consciousness} = \text{proto-consciousness} + \text{knowing} \\ \text{proto-consciousness} = \text{pre-consciousness} + \text{attention} \end{array}} \quad (9.1)$$

See [20] and [14] where these distinctions have been made, using slightly different terminology.

Layers of Agents

Conscious agents A, B can be combined by diverting the actions of A towards the input of B and vice versa the actions of B towards the input of A. This has been done in an attractive way by [21] and [16]. By also considering the physical base as agent interaction, as is done in quantum physics, these authors and also [29] coin the interesting possibility that the explanatory gap of the body-mind problem may be bridged.

10   Conclusion

Consciousness is

$$\boxed{\text{compound, fluctuating, impersonal.}} \quad (10.1)$$

Experiencing this has strong psychological implications. This may explain on the one hand part of the psychiatric phenomena: fear (panic attacks and phobias[10]), delusion (paranoia), disenchantment (depression). On the other hand that it is possible to develop the mind in impressive ways. Through combined phenomeno-logical and neurophysiological investigations this may eventually give full insight into the objective nature of consciousness, its ailments and possibilities.

---

[10] It also has been described in [5, Ch. XIII] that phobias appear after one has had experience of non-permanence and non-self. In that Chapter phobias are described as repersonalization after a depersonalization. In [3] this idea is generalized to the so-called 'cover-up' model.

References

1. Anuruddha, A.: A comprehensive manual of Abhidhamma (Abhidhammattha Sangaha). In: Bodhi, B., Rewata-Dhamma, U. (eds.) Buddhist Publication Society, Kandy (±1200/1993), translation by Mahathera Nārada
2. Aristotle: Organon: Posterior Analytics. Web Edition, University of Adelaide. https://ebooks.adelaide.edu.au/a/aristotle/a8poa/ (±350BC/1928), translation by GRG Mure of the Greek original
3. Barendregt, H.P.: Mysticism and beyond. Eastern Buddhist XXIX, 262–287 (1996). http://ftp.science.ru.nl/CSI/CompMath.Found/bp2.pdf. Attachments are ways to cover-up emptiness
4. Barendregt, H.P., Raffone, A.: Conscious cognition as a discrete, deterministic, and universal Turing machine process. In: Cooper, S., van Leeuwen, J. (eds.) Alan Turing, His Work and Impact, pp. 92–97. Elsevier, Amsterdam (2013)
5. Barendregt, J.T.: De Zielenmarkt, over psychotherapie in alle ernst. Boom (1982). English translation. www.cs.ru.nl/henk/JTBarendregtFobias.pdf
6. Barnard, P.J.: Interacting cognitive subsystems: modeling working memory phenomena within a multiprocessor architecture. In: Shah, A.M.P. (ed.) Models of Working Memory: Mechanisms of Active Maintenance and Executive Control, pp. 298–339. Cambridge University Press (1999)
7. Barnard, P.J., Teasdale, J.D.: Interacting cognitive subsystems: a systemic approach to cognitive-affective interaction and change. Cogn. Emot. **5**(1), 1–39 (1991)
8. Bitbol, M.: Is consciousness primary? NeuroQuantology, pp. 53–71 (2008)
9. Brouwer, L.E.J.: Historical background, principles and methods of intuitionism. S. Afr. J. Sci. **49** (1952)
10. de Bruijn, N.G.: A mathematical model for biological memory and consciousness. In: Kamareddine, F. (ed.) Thirty Five Years of Automating Mathematics, vol. 28, pp. 9–23. Kluwer Academic Publishers, Dordrecht (2003). https://doi.org/10.1007/978-94-017-0253-9_1
11. Buddhaghosa, B.: The Path of Purification: Visuddhimagga. Buddhist Publication Society, Pariyatti Publishing (±400 AD/1999), pali original appeared around 400 AD. Translator: Bhikkhu Ñānamoli. www.urbandharma.org/pdf1/PathofPurification2011.pdf
12. Chalmers, D.J.: Facing up to the problem of consciousness. J. Conscious. Stud. **2**, 200–219 (1995)
13. Conway, J., et al.: The game of life. Sci. Am. **223**(4), 4 (1970)
14. Dehaene, S., Changeux, J.P., Naccache, L., Sackur, J., Sergent, C.: Conscious, preconscious, and subliminal processing: a testable taxonomy. Trends Cogn. Sci. **10**(5), 204–211 (2006)
15. Efron, R.: Effect of stimulus duration on perceptual onset and offset latencies. Percept. Psychophysics **8**(4), 231–234 (1970). https://doi.org/10.3758/BF03210211
16. Fields, C., Hoffman, D.D., Singh, M., Prakash, C.: Conscious agent networks: formal analysis and application to cognition. Cogn. Syst. Res. **47**(6), 186–213 (2018)
17. Friston, K.: The free-energy principle: a unified brain theory? Nat. Rev. Neurosci. **11**, 127–138 (2010). https://doi.org/10.1038/nrn2787
18. Gallagher, S.: A pattern theory of self. Front. Hum. Neurosci. **7**, 443 (2013)
19. Hilbert, D.: Mathematical problems. Bull. (New Series) Am. Math. Soc. **37**(4), 407–436 (2000), reprint of Bull. Amer. Math. Soc. **8**, 437–479 (1902)
20. Hobson, A.: REM sleep and dreaming: towards a theory of protoconsciousness. Nat. Rev. Neurosci. **10**(11), 803–862 (2009)

21. Hoffman, D.D., Prakash, C.: Objects of consciousness. Front. Psychol. **5**, 577 (2014). https://doi.org/10.3389/fpsyg.2014.00577
22. Hut, P., Shepard, R.N.: Turning the hard problem upside-down and sideways. J. Conscious. Stud. **3**(4), 313–329 (1996)
23. Izhikevich, E.M., Conway, J.H., Seth, A.: Game of life. Scholarpedia **10**(6), 1816 (2015)
24. Loy, D.: Lack and Transcendence: The Problem of Death and Life in Psychotherapy, Existentialism, and Buddhism. Humanities Press, London (1996)
25. Maaß, W., Markram, H.: On the computational power of circuits of spiking neurons. J. Comput. Syst. Sci. **69**(4), 593–616 (2004)
26. Mahasi, S.: Manual of Insight. Wisdom Books, Kerala (2016)
27. Merleau-Ponty, M.: Phenomenology of Perception. Routledge, England (1945/2013)
28. Pascual-Marqui, R.D., Michel, C.M., Lehmann, D.: Segmentation of brain electrical activity into microstates: model estimation and validation. IEEE Trans. Bio-Med. Eng. **42**, 658–665 (1995)
29. Rovelli, C.: Helgoland. Taylor & Francis, Oxfordshire (2021)
30. Slors, M., de Bruijn, L., Strijbos, D.: Philosophy of Mind, Brain and Behaviour. Boom (2015)
31. Tononi, G.: Integrated information theory of consciousness: an updated account. Arch. Ital. Biol. **150**, 290–326 (2012)
32. Turing, A.M.: On computable numbers, with an application to the entscheidungsproblem. Proc. Lond. Math. Soc. **2**(42), 230–265 (1937)
33. VanRullen, R., Reddy, L., Koch, C.: The continuous wagon wheel illusion is associated with changes in electroencephalogram power at $\sim$ 13 Hz. J. Neurosci. **26**(2), 502–507 (2006)
34. Von Rospatt, A.: The Buddhist Doctrine of Momentariness a Survey of the Origins and Early Phase of this Doctrine up to Vasubandhu. F. Steiner, Stuttgart (1995)
35. Weisberg, J.: Consciousness. Polity (2014). The Hard Problem of Consciousness, Internet Encyclopedia of Philosophy. www.iep.utm.edu/hard-con/#SH3a
36. Zylberberg, A., Dehaene, S., Roelfsema, P.R., Sigman, M.: The human Turing machine: a neural framework for mental programs. Trends Cogn. Sci. **15**(7), 293–300 (2011)

Symmetric Transrationals: The Data Type and the Algorithmic Degree of its Equational Theory

Jan A. Bergstra[1(✉)] and John V. Tucker[2]

[1] Informatics Institute, University of Amsterdam, Science Park 904, 1098 XH Amsterdam, The Netherlands
j.a.bergstra@uva.nl
[2] Department of Computer Science, Swansea University, Bay Campus, Fabian Way, Swansea SA1 8EN, UK
j.v.tucker@swansea.ac.uk

Abstract. We introduce and investigate an arithmetical data type designed for computation with rational numbers. Called the *symmetric transrationals*, this data type comes about as a more algebraically symmetric modification of the arithmetical data type of transrational numbers [9], which was inspired by the transreals of Anderson et.al. [1]. We also define a bounded version of the symmetric transrationals thereby modelling some further key semantic properties of floating point arithmetic. We prove that the bounded symmetric transrationals constitute a data type. Next, we consider the equational theory and prove that deciding the validity of equations over the symmetric transrationals is 1-1 algorithmically equivalent with deciding unsolvability of Diophantine equations over the rational numbers, which is a longstanding open problem. The algorithmic degree of the bounded case remains open.

Keywords: rational numbers · data types · computer arithmetic · common meadows · transrationals · diophantine problem · floating-point

1 Introduction

Whilst the design of many computing systems depends upon the real numbers, the deployment depends upon computer arithmetics, which are data types contained within the rational numbers. Starting with [8], we have been developing a theory of arithmetical data types based on rational numbers. Classical mathematics has viewed the rationals as a field, i.e., a commutative ring in which each non-zero element has a unique multiplicative inverse, equipped with the constants $0, 1$ and operations $x + y$, $-x$, and $x \cdot y$. However, with these operators the rationals do not qualify as a data type, for the field is not a minimal algebra, i.e., not every element of the algebra can be constructed by applying

---

To Frits Vaandrager on the occasion of his 60th Birthday.

N. Jansen et al. (Eds.): Vaandrager Festschrift 2022, LNCS 13560, pp. 63–80, 2022.
https://doi.org/10.1007/978-3-031-15629-8_4

the operations to its constants. For minimality, we need to add inverse x^{-1} or division $x \div y$, which are not total operators on 0; such an algebra with inverse or division is called a meadow [8]. For computation, we must turn one of these into a total function; there are several semantic options, each of which has its own motivation and significant implications for the algebra of the rationals.

The Data Type. Using the theory of abstract data types, we present new algebraic models of the rational numbers motivated by common floating point conventions. The data type implements these three features:

   (i) having total operations only;
  (ii) accommodating overflows and underflows; and
 (iii) computations are sensitive when values come close to 0.

The new data type is one of a number of adaptations of the rationals that address totality (i), but is novel in the semantic matters of (ii) and (iii).

We begin the development of the model by enlarging the rational numbers with an 'absorptive element' $\perp$ that is used to totalise partial operations; by absorbtive we mean that if $\perp$ is an argument of an operator then the result is also $\perp$. In particular, $0^{-1} = \perp$. This design decision has been studied in some detail through a general algebraic theory of *common meadows*, as introduced in [5,6].

Secondly, we further enlarge the common meadow with flags for signed infinities $\infty, -\infty$ and signed infinitesimals $\iota, -\iota$ to model sensitivities close to 0. This done, we also introduce upper and lower bounds $p, -p$ to model overflow and underflow. These two new data types of rational numbers we call the *symmetric transrationals* and the *bounded symmetric transrationals*, respectively.

Our new models, and the terminology 'transrational', owes much to the *transreal* model of computer arithmetic proposed in [1,13]. The transreals use the infinities so that $1/0$ and $-1/0$ behave as infinite elements ∞ and $-\infty$, respectively. Whilst they assume that $\infty^{-1} = (-\infty)^{-1} = 0$, they also feature an asymmetry as follows:

$$(\infty^{-1})^{-1} = \infty \text{ while } (-\infty^{-1})^{-1} = \infty \neq -\infty.$$

We analysed the (non-symmetric) transrationals as an abstract data type in [9].

In addition to our use of common meadows to tackle totality, $1/0 = \perp$, our new model of symmetric transrational numbers restores symmetry by adopting

$$(\infty^{-1})^{-1} = \infty \text{ and } (-\infty^{-1})^{-1} = -\infty$$

and the infinitesimals

$$\infty^{-1} = \iota \text{ and } \iota^{-1} = \infty.$$

The five new elements $\perp, \infty, -\infty, \iota, -\iota$ we call *peripheral numbers*; they have a profound effect on all the operations as familiar equations fail and need to be replaced – e.g., most obviously, $0 \cdot x \neq 0$ because $0 \cdot \perp = \perp$.

Our notations are as follows. The rationals Q are built in various ways from the integers Z, which are built from the naturals N. We assume that $N \subseteq Z$

and that Z is embedded in Q; as this dependency matters, we write Q_Z for a set of rationals. As data types these sets have algebraic structures and we use the symbols $\mathbb{N}$, $\mathbb{Z}$ and $\mathbb{Q}$ when some operations are placed on the sets of numbers, N, Z and Q. Thus, the first stage of the model building was to create the common meadow, which we denote $\mathbb{Q}_{Z,\perp}$. In the second stage, the data type of symmetric transrationals was obtained from $\mathbb{Q}_{Z,\perp}$, which we denote $\mathbb{Q}_{Z,\pm\infty,\pm\iota,\perp}$. The bounded symmetric transrationals we denote $\mathbb{Q}^p_{Z,\pm\infty,\pm\iota,\perp}$. In Theorem 3 we prove that bounded transrationals actually constitute a data type, i.e., a minimal algebra; this result is quite tricky compared with the ease of minimality for $\mathbb{Q}_{Z,\perp}$ and $\mathbb{Q}_{Z,\pm\infty,\pm\iota,\perp}$.

Equational theories. Abstract data type theory uses equations to axiomatise the operations of data types. The equational theory of a data type is the set of all equations valid in the data type. An important algorithmic problem, connected to the power of the axioms and completeness of equational reasoning, is to decide whether or not any given equation is valid. Earlier, in [11], we showed:

Proposition 1. *The equational theory of the common meadow $\mathbb{Q}_{Z,\perp}$ has the same 1-1 algorithmic degree as the complement of solvability of Diophantine equations over $\mathbb{Q}_Z$.*

Now enlargements are an expansion (i.e., adding new operations on the domain) of an extension (i.e., adding new data to the domain), but they cannot be relied upon to preserve desirable properties. Yet, with quite some effort, we extend Proposition 1 to the symmetric transrationals. Combining Proposition 7 and Theorem 4 below, we have:

Theorem 1. *The equational theory of the symmetric transrationals $\mathbb{Q}_{Z,\pm\infty,\pm\iota,\perp}$ has the same 1-1 algorithmic degree as the complement of solvability of Diophantine equations over $\mathbb{Q}_Z$.*

The Diophantine Problem for the rationals Q_Z is a difficult long-standing open problem, in contrast with the algorithmic unsolvability of the Diophantine Problem for the naturals, established by Matiyasevich in 1972. Both Proposition 1 and Theorem 1 are somehow theoretically significant for developing arithmetical data types based on rational numbers.

We leave open the question whether or not the validity of equations in bounded symmetric transrationals is 1-1 reducible to the complement of Diophantine solvability over $\mathbb{Q}_Z$.

Contents. In Sect. 2, we recall some working methods for abstract data types. In Sect. 3, we add the peripheral numbers to an ordered field and define the symmetric transfield and bounded symmetric transfield. Applying these constructions to the rationals yields our symmetric transrationals and bounded symmetric transrationals and we prove that bounded symmetric transrationals are minimal in Sect. 4. In Sect. 5, we tackle the algorithmic degree of the equational theory. In Sect. 6, we reflect on the model's connection to floating point and a role in reasoning about analogue-digital systems.

This paper is dedicated to Frits Vaandrager whose work covers a wide range of system design formalisms, including process algebras, hybrid systems, and timed automata. Although this paper is independent of these themes, we study data types which we hope to be relevant when contemplating abstract versions of floating point arithmetic and reasoning about systems involving analogue data.

2 Basic Theory of Abstract Data Types

For abstract data types we mention [15] for motivation, and [14] for technical information. The theory of abstract data types starts from four basic concepts as follows. An implementation of a data type is modelled by a many-sorted algebra A of signature Σ; our algebras will be single-sorted and have a non-empty carrier. A signature Σ is an interface to some (model of an) implementation of the data type, and the constants and operations declared in Σ provide the only means of access for the programmer to the data. This means that the data in an algebra A should be constructible from its constants and operations, technically: A Σ-algebra A is Σ-minimal if it is generated by the constants and operations of its signature Σ. Axiomatisations of the operations in a signature define a whole range of implementations. Implementations are equivalent if, and only if, their algebraic models are isomorphic.

Definition 1. *A* data type *is a minimal algebra. An* abstract data type *is an isomorphism class of a data type.*

The properties of interest to abstract data types are isomorphism invariants – typical examples are properties that are definable by first order formulae and forms of computability. This means that if a property is true of *any* data type A, and is an isomorphism invariant, then the property will be true of its abstract data type.

We will use an informal notation for data types and signatures. For instance, $(V \mid c_1, \ldots, c_k, f_1, \ldots, f_l)$ denotes a data type with domain V and constants c_1, ..., c_k from V, and functions $f_1, .., f_k$, where it is assumed that arities for the functions on V are known from the context. Similarly, for signatures, we use names instead of sets, constants and functions. Given a data type A, and a valuation σ for variables in a term t over its signature, $(A, \sigma \models t)$ denotes the result of evaluating t in A using the values of the variables in σ.

2.1 Expansions, Extensions, and Enlargements

Algebras can be *expanded* by adding new constants and operations to their signature. Algebras can be *extended* by adding new elements to their domain. Combining expansions and extensions comprises what we call *enlargements* of an algebra. Thus, we will be enlarging the rationals with inverse and peripheral numbers. These notions carry over from data types to abstract data types.

Adding and taking away data and operations from an algebra, such as peripheral numbers and inverse, is not straightforward.

Proposition 2. *There exists a single sorted computable algebra B and a restriction A of B to a smaller signature such that the domain of A is not a computable subset of the domain of B.*

Proof. Let N be a set of natural numbers and let $V \subseteq N$ be a computably enumerable non-computable splinter generated from 0 by means of a computable function $f{:}N \to N$ [26]. So $V = \{f^k(0) \mid k \in N\}$. Let B be the algebra $(N \mid 0, 1, +, f)$ with signature $\Sigma = (nat \mid 0, 1, +, F)$. Now, let A be the restriction of B to the signature Σ' containing only 0 and F, obtained by forgetting 1 and $+$ and taking the minimal subalgebra w.r.t. Σ. Thus, $A = (V \mid 0, f)$ whose domain V is not a computable subset of the domain of B. $\qquad\square$

Proposition 3. *There is an enlargement B of the algebra $A = (N \mid 0, S, P)$ such that* every *finite equational specification of A fails to hold in B.*

Proof. A is well known as the naturals with constant 0 and successor function (named S) and predecessor function (here named P, while also known as monus, written $\div$), for which an equational specification is: $\Sigma = (nat \mid 0, S, P), \{P(0) = 0, P(S(x)) = x\})$. Let $T(c, S, P)$ be the term algebra over Σ with 0 replaced by c; we can assume that $A \cap T(c, S, P) = \emptyset$. Now, by taking the union of both domains as well as the union of both structures we obtain a joint enlargement of both structures, say $B = A \oplus T(c, S, P)$. In this algebra no non-trivial equation can hold because no such equations are valid in $T(c, S, P)$. It follows that no equational specification of the data type A can be given with equations that are valid in B. $\qquad\square$

The finiteness condition is essential because there is always an infinite ground term specification which will be satisfied in each enlargement. Proposition 3 is an extreme example where enlargement leads to a reduction of the collection of valid equations. Similarly, the addition of peripheral numbers to rationals reduces the set of valid equations. Whether removing all non-trivial equations, as in Proposition 3, can be achieved by means of an enlargement with finitely many new elements we do not know:

Problem 1. For which data types A is there an enlargement which consists of an expansion of an extension by finitely many elements, B of A with the property that only trivial equations over the signature of A are valid in B.

3   The Symmetric Transfields

3.1   Algebra of Peripheral Numbers and their Equational Specification

Consider the data type $P^5_{\pm\infty,\pm\iota,\bot}(0)$ with 6 elements, one ordinary number 0 and five peripheral numbers $\bot, \infty, -\infty, \iota, -\iota$. Let Σ_P be a signature for the algebra with four constants $0, \infty, \iota$ and $\bot$, and four operations $+, \cdot, -, ^{-1}$.

As a finite structure, the operators can be defined by the finite set E_P of equations in Table 1. In fact, omitting the proof, we have:

Theorem 2. *The equational specification* (Σ_P, E_P) *is an initial algebra specification for the algebra of peripheral numbers* $P^5_{\pm\infty,\pm\iota,\perp}(0)$.

Table 1. (Σ_P, E_P): An initial algebra equational specification of the peripheral numbers.

$x + y = y + x$	(1)	$0 \cdot \infty = \perp$	(15)
$x \cdot y = y \cdot x$	(2)	$0 \cdot \iota = 0$	(16)
$-(-x) = x$	(3)	$\infty + \infty = \infty$	(17)
$(-x) + (-y) = -(x + y)$	(4)	$\infty + (-\infty) = \perp$	(18)
$(-x) \cdot y = -(x \cdot y)$	(5)	$\infty + \iota = \infty$	(19)
$(-x)^{-1} = -(x^{-1})$	(6)	$\infty + (-\iota) = \infty$	(20)
$-\perp = \perp$	(7)	$\infty \cdot \infty = \infty$	(21)
$x + \perp = \perp$	(8)	$\infty \cdot \iota = \perp$	(22)
$x \cdot \perp = \perp$	(9)	$\infty^{-1} = \iota$	(23)
$\perp^{-1} = \perp$	(10)	$\iota + \iota = \iota$	(24)
$-0 = 0$	(11)	$\iota + (-\iota) = \perp$	(25)
$x + 0 = x$	(12)	$\iota \cdot \iota = \iota$	(26)
$0^{-1} = \perp$	(13)	$\iota^{-1} = \infty$	(27)
$0 \cdot 0 = 0$	(14)		

3.2   Making a Symmetric Transfield

Proposition 4. *Let* $F_<$ *be an ordered field such that* $F \cap P^5_{\pm\infty,\pm\iota,\perp}(0) = \{0\}$. *Then* F *and* $P^5_{\pm\infty,\pm\iota,\perp}(0)$ *have a common enlargement* $F_{\pm\infty,\pm\iota,\perp}$ *with domain* $F \cup \{\infty, -\infty, \iota, -\iota, \perp\}$.

Proof. Both data types can be combined while some values of functions must still be defined. To begin with: a^{-1} for nonzero $a \in F$ is defined as the unique $b \in F$ with $a \cdot b = 1$; for other arguments to inverse the value in $P^5_{\pm\infty,\pm\iota,\perp}(0)$ applies. For both addition and multiplication 5 new arguments have to be taken into account: $\infty, -\infty, \iota, -\iota$ and $\perp$. Both functions are extended in such a manner that $\perp$ is absorptive (e.g., $a + \perp = \perp$ etc.). For nonzero positive $a \in F$: $a + \infty = \infty$, $a + (-\infty) = -\infty$, $a + \iota = a$, $a + (-\iota) = a$, $a \cdot \infty = \infty$, $a \cdot (-\infty) = -\infty$, $a \cdot \iota = \iota$, $a \cdot (-\iota) = -\iota$. For nonzero negative $a \in F$: $a + \infty = \infty$, $a + (-\infty) = -\infty$, $a + \iota = a$, $a + (-\iota) = a$, $a \cdot \infty = -\infty$, $a \cdot (-\infty) = \infty$, $a \cdot \iota = -\iota$, $a \cdot (-\iota) = \iota$. All other values for the addition and multiplication of peripherals are determined such as to make both operations commutative. $\square$

Definition 2. *The algebra* $F_{\pm\infty,\pm\iota,\perp}$ *is called the* symmetric transfield *of the ordered field* $F_<$. *Let* Σ_{str} *be the signature of symmetric transfields.*

$F_{\pm\infty,\pm\iota,\perp}$ is a so-called joint amalgamation of $F_<$ and $P^5_{\pm\infty,\pm\iota,\perp}(0)$.

3.3   Making a Bounded Symmetric Transfield

Again, let $F_<$ be an ordered field. The idea of creating a bounded symmetric transfield for $F_<$ is roughly this. We choose some positive $p \in F$, with $p > 1$ and build a new algebraic structure $F^p_{\pm\infty,\pm\iota,\perp}$ using surgery on $F_{\pm\infty,\pm\iota,\perp}$. The carrier set is the subset of $F_{\pm\infty,\pm\iota,\perp}$ consisting of

$$F^p = (-p, -1/p) \cup (1/p, p) \cup \{0, \perp, \iota, -\iota, \infty, -\infty\}.$$

and its operations are either restrictions or adaptations of the operations of $F_{\pm\infty,\pm\iota,\perp}$. Thus, the signature of bounded symmetric transfields is also Σ_{str}.

The constants of the bounded transfield are the constants of $F_{\pm\infty,\pm\iota,\perp}$. Note the carrier F^p contains all these constants; in particular, because $p > 1$, $1 \in (1/p, p)$. But the bound p is *not* a constant as it is not in F^p.

The unary operations minus and inverse are simply the restrictions of the corresponding functions in $F_{\pm\infty,\pm\iota,\perp}$ to $F^p \subseteq F_{\pm\infty,\pm\iota,\perp}$.

However, the addition and multiplication operations are not restrictions because of the over and underflows and calculations: addition is interpreted by $\_ +_p \_$ and multiplication is interpreted by $\_ \cdot_p \_$ in $F^p_{\pm\infty,\pm\iota,\perp}$. These functions are defined as follows. Given $x, y \in F^p$,

- if $x + y \in F^p$ then $x +_p y = x + y$,
- if $x \cdot y \in F^p$ then $x \cdot_p y = x \cdot y$
- if $x + y \in [-\infty, -p]$ then $x +_p y = -\infty$,
- if $x + y \in [-1/p, 0)$ then $x +_p y = -\iota$,
- if $x + y \in (0, 1/p]$ then $x +_p y = \iota$,
- if $x + y \in [p, \infty]$ then $x +_p y = \infty$,
- if $x \cdot y \in [-\infty, -p]$ then $x \cdot_p, y = -\infty$,
- if $x \cdot y \in [-1/p, 0)$ then $x \cdot_p y = -\iota$,
- if $x \cdot y \in (0, 1/p]$ then $x \cdot_p y = \iota$,
- if $x \cdot y \in [p, \infty]$ then $x \cdot_p y = \infty$.

Definition 3. *The algebra* $F^p_{\pm\infty,\pm\iota,\perp}$ *is called the* bounded symmetric transfield *of the ordered field* $F_<$. *Let* Σ_{str} *be the signature of bounded symmetric transfields.*

$F^p_{\pm\infty,\pm\iota,\perp}$ is an infinite algebra because in an ordered field with $p > 0$ the interval $(1/p, p)$ is infinite.

4   Rationals and Transrationals

4.1   Transrationals and Bounded Transrationals

We will now specialise the general constructions above to the case of rational numbers. First, we construct a non-minimal algebra $\mathbb{Q}_Z$ of rationals with domain $SFP_Z = \{(n, m) : n, m \in Z, m > 0, and \ gcd(n, m) = 1\}$. SFP_Z stands for *simplified fracpairs*. For information on fracpairs we refer to [7].

The additive identity is uniquely defined by $(0, 1)$ and the multiplicative unit is $(1, 1)$. We define the operations in stages starting with addition: $(n, m) + (p, q) = (a, b)$ where $a = \frac{np+mq}{gcd(np+mq,mq)}$ and $b = \frac{mq}{gcd(np+mq,mq)}$. Secondly, we define multiplication: $(n, m).(p, q) = (a, b)$ where $a = \frac{np}{gcd(np,mq)}$ and $b = \frac{mq}{gcd(np,mq)}$ Thirdly, we define additive inverse: $-(n, m) = (-n, m)$,

Now: $\mathbb{Q}_Z = (SFP_Z \mid (0, 1), (1, 1), +, -, \cdot)$. $\mathbb{Q}_Z$ is *not* a data type because it is not minimal. In order to turn $\mathbb{Q}_Z$ into a data type, an additional operator *must* be included in the signature and interpreted in SFP_Z. The common meadow $\mathbb{Q}_{Z,\perp}$ provides an enlargement of $\mathbb{Q}_Z$ which qualifies as a data type.

The field $\mathbb{Q}_Z$ has a natural ordering and the construction of a transfield for $\mathbb{Q}_Z$ can be applied, leading to $\mathbb{Q}_{Z,\pm\infty,\pm\iota,\perp}$, a data type of transrationals and to $\mathbb{Q}^p_{Z,\pm\infty,\pm\iota,\perp}$, a data type of p bounded transrationals.

4.2   Minimality of the Bounded Transrationals

The two abstract data types of common meadows of rationals $\mathbb{Q}_{Z,\perp}$ and symmetric transrationals $\mathbb{Q}_{Z,\pm\infty,\pm\iota,\perp}$ are easily shown to be minimal and hence data types. To see this, one notices that the rational numbers are generated from 1, as in [8], while the new constants allow to express the 5 peripheral elements.

Similarly, $\mathbb{Q}^p_{Z,\pm\infty,\pm\iota,\perp}$ is a Σ_{str}-minimal algebra and a data type, although this is not immediately obvious.

Proposition 5. *For* $1 < p \leq 2$: $\mathbb{Q}^p_{Z,\pm\infty,\pm\iota,\perp}$ *is* Σ_{str}-*non-minimal.*

Proof. $\mathbb{Q}^p_{Z,\pm\infty,\pm\iota,\perp}$ is infinite but its minimal subalgebra has 8 elements only, the 6 elements of $P^5_{\pm\infty,\pm\iota,\perp}(0)$ plus $\{1, -1\}$. It is immediate that this set of 8 elements is closed under $\_ +_p \_$ and $\_ \cdot_p \_$, as well as under the unary operators. □

Theorem 3. *Let* $p \in \mathbb{N}$, *with* $p > 2$, *then* $\mathbb{Q}^p_{Z,\pm\infty,\pm\iota,\perp}$ *is* Σ_{str}-*minimal.*

Proof. We write $\mathbb{Q}^p = \mathbb{Q}^p_{Z,\pm\infty,\pm\iota,\perp}$ and we will further assume that N is the set of decimal naturals, i.e., $N_d = \{0, 1, 2, ..., 9, 10, 11, ...\}$. Moreover, we will assume that rationals are the non-$\perp$ elements of $\mathbb{Q}_{Z,\perp}$, and that for naturals n and $m > 0$, n/m denotes the value of $(\mathbb{Q}_{Z,\perp} \models \underline{n} \cdot (\underline{m})^{-1}) \in \mathbb{Q}_{Z,\perp}$. All functions and constants of Σ_{stf} as well as $\_ +_p \_$ and $\_ \cdot_p \_$ are interpreted as functions on and constants in $\mathbb{Q}_{Z,\perp}$.

First, notice that $1 +_p 1 = \underline{2}$ because $2 < p$. It follows that $(\mathbb{Q}^p \models (1 + 1)^{-1}) = 1/\underline{2}$, and, as $1 + 1/\underline{2} = \underline{3/2} < p$ also $(\mathbb{Q}^p \models 1 + (1 + 1)^{-1}) = \underline{3/2}$. Let $t_1 \equiv 1 + (1 + 1)^{-1}$, and for natural $n \geq 1$, $t_{n+1} \equiv (1 + 1) + (-(t_n^{-1}))$. We will first show by induction (assertion $\star$ for use below) that:

for natural $n \geq 1$: $Q_{Z,\perp} \models t_n = 1 + (n+1)^{-1}$ $(\star)$

For the base case $n = 1$ this is immediate.

For the induction step: $Q_{Z,\perp} \models t_{n+1} = (1+1) + (-t_n^{-1}) =_{IH} (1+1) + (-(1 + (n+1)^{-1})^{-1}) = (1+1) + (-((n+\underline{2}) \cdot (n+1)^{-1})^{-1}) = (1+1) + (-((n+\underline{2})^{-1} \cdot (n+1))) = (1+1) + (-((n+1) \cdot (n+\underline{2})^{-1})) = ((1+1) \cdot (n+\underline{2}) + (-(n+1))) \cdot (n+\underline{2})^{-1} = (n+\underline{3}) \cdot (n+\underline{2})^{-1}$. Thus, $(Q_{Z,\perp} \models t_{n+1}) = (n+\underline{3})/(n+\underline{2})$.

With induction on n, we will show that for $n \geq 1$:

$$(\mathbb{Q}^p \models t_n) = (Q_{Z,\perp} \models t_n) = (n+\underline{2})/(n+1).$$

The base case $n = 1$ has been established already. For the induction step: $(\mathbb{Q}^p \models t_{n+1}) = (\mathbb{Q}^p \models (1+1) + (-(t_n^{-1}))) = (1 +_p 1) +_p (-((Q_{Z,\perp} \models t_n)^{-1})) = (1 +_p 1) +_p (-((n+\underline{2})/(n+1))^{-1}))) = (1 +_p 1) +_p (-((n+1)/(n+\underline{2})))$.

Now, $0 < (n+1)/(n+\underline{2}) < 1$ so that $(1 +_p 1) +_p (-((n+1)/(n+\underline{2}))) < 2$ and so that $(1 +_p 1) +_p (-((n+1)/(n+\underline{2}))) \in (1/p, p)$ whence $(\mathbb{Q}^p \models t_{n+1}) = (Q_{Z,\perp} \models t_{n+1}) =_\star (n+\underline{3})/(n+\underline{2})$.

The proof is now completed with the following Lemma. $\qquad\Box$

Lemma 1. *For each rational number $q \in (1, p)$ (with $p > 2$) there is a term t_q such that $(\mathbb{Q}^P \models t_q) = q$.*

Proof. It suffices to find t_q for $q \in (1, p)$; as for the case $q \in (1/p, 1)$ we may choose $t_q = (t_{1/q})^{-1}$. Assume that $q = 1 + m/n$ with positive naturals m and n, and $n \geq 2$. With induction on k we prove that for $k \geq 1$ with $1 + k/n < p$ there is a term r_k^n such that $(\mathbb{Q}^p \models r_k^n) = 1 + k/n$.

For $k = 1$ the result has been obtained above: $r_1^n \equiv t_{n-1}$ will work.

For the induction step, we assume $(\mathbb{Q}^p \models r_k^n) = 1 + \underline{k}/\underline{n}$. Now $(\mathbb{Q}^p \models (r_k^n + (-\underline{2}^{-1})) + (r_k^n + (-\underline{2}^{-1}))) = ((1 + \underline{k}/\underline{n}) +_p (-1/2) +_p ((1 + 1/\underline{n}) +_(-1/\underline{2})) = (1/\underline{2} + \underline{k}/\underline{n}) + (1/\underline{2} + 1/\underline{n}) = 1 + \underline{k+1}/\underline{n}$. $\qquad\Box$

According to the standard theory [23], it is easy to check the following:

Proposition 6. *Symmetric transrationals and bounded symmetric transrationals are computable algebras.*

5 One-One Degree of Equations in Symmetric Transrationals

5.1 The Diophantine Problem for the Rationals

First, note that a classical polynomial $p(x_1, \ldots, x_n)$ with rational or integer coefficients can be understood as an expression over the signature of a commnutative ring with 1, and as a division-free expression over the signature Σ_m of a meadow.

A *Diophantine equation* is an equation of the form

$$p(x_1, \ldots, x_n) = 0$$

with p an integer polynomial.

The question whether or not $p(x_1, \ldots, x_n) = 0$ has a solution in the rationals Q is clearly computably enumerable: all Diophantine equations that have a rational solution can be effectively enumerated. However, the algorithmic decidability of solvability of Diophantine equations over Q is a long standing open problem, originating in Hilbert's 10th Problem of 1900. Hilbert's 10th Problem asked for an algorithm to decide if there are solutions to Diophantine equations in the natural numbers. After many years, in 1972, this was shown to be algorithmically undecidable by Matiyasevich – see [18]. Expectations are that the problem for rationals is undecidable, too. For an easy introduction to the Diophantine problem for rationals see [21].

5.2 Equational Theories

We will first show that solvability of Diophantine equations in Q is computably one-one reducible to determining validity of equations over the symmetric transrationals. This means that *if* the corresponding equational theory is decidable then the Diophantine problem for Q is solved!

Proposition 7. *Unsolvability of Diophantine equations over* $\mathbb{Q}_Z$ *is 1-1 reducible to the validity of equations over* $\mathbb{Q}_{Z, \pm\infty, \pm\iota, \perp}$.

Proof. Let there be given a Diophantine equation $p = 0$ with p a polynomial, i.e., a term over the signature of commutative rings. Then it is easy to see that: $\mathbb{Q}_Z \models p \neq 0$ (i.e., $p = 0$ has no solution in $\mathbb{Q}_Z$) if, and only if,

$$\mathbb{Q}_{Z, \pm\infty, \pm\iota, \perp} \models \frac{p}{p} = 1 + (p + (-p))$$

$\square$

To simplify work in $\mathbb{Q}_{Z, \pm\infty, \pm\iota, \perp}$, we will make use of a dedicated quantifier $\forall^+ x$, defined by:
$$\forall^+ x.\phi \equiv_{\text{def}} \forall x \in Q_Z(x > 0 \rightarrow \phi).$$

We will write $\mathbb{Q}_{Z, \pm\infty, \pm\iota, \perp} \models^+ \phi$ in order to express that all variables in ϕ are universally quantified with $\forall^+$ rather than with $\forall$.[1]

Proposition 8. *There is a uniform transformation* η *which assigns to each equation* $t = r$ *over* $\mathbb{Q}_{Z, \pm\infty, \pm\iota, \perp}$ *a conjunction of equations* $\eta_{t=r}$ *such that:*

$$\mathbb{Q}_{Z, \pm\infty, \pm\iota, \perp} \models t = r \text{ if, and only if, } \mathbb{Q}_{Z, \pm\infty, \pm\iota, \perp} \models^+ \eta_{t=r}.$$

---

[1] We notice that an alternative presentation of the proof may use, in addition, the quantifier $\forall^- x.\phi \equiv_{\text{def}} \forall x \in Q_Z(x < 0 \rightarrow \phi)$. The advantage of using the second quantifier for the proof is very limited, while the bookkeeping of variables will become more involved, and for that reason it will not be used.

Proof. We need to work with conjunctions of equations where the first m variables are quantified by way of $\models^+$ and the remaining variables are quantified with a quantifier over all elements of the structure. We assume that variables come from a set V_{var}. Let $x_1, \ldots, x_n$ be the variables free in ϕ and assume that variable x_m has to be dealt with.

The universal quantification over x_m can be replaced by a quantification over positive rationals as follows:

$\mathbb{Q}_{Z,\pm\infty,\pm\iota,\perp} \models \forall x_m.\phi(x_m) \iff$

$\mathbb{Q}_{Z,\pm\infty,\pm\iota,\perp} \models \phi(0) \wedge \phi(\iota) \wedge \phi(-\iota) \wedge \phi(\infty) \wedge \phi(-\infty) \wedge \phi(\perp) \wedge \forall^+ x_m.\phi(x_m) \wedge$
$\forall^+ x_m.\phi(-x_m) \iff$

$\mathbb{Q}_{Z,\pm\infty,\pm\iota,\perp} \models^+ \phi(0) \wedge \phi(\iota) \wedge \phi(-\iota) \wedge \phi(\infty) \wedge \phi(-\infty) \wedge \phi(\perp) \wedge \phi(x_m) \wedge \phi(-x_m)$.

This transformation is applied successively for all variables. We notice that a combinatorial explosion in size may occur where the blow up is exponential in the number of variables of an equation. $\qquad \square$

Proposition 9. *The validity of conjunctions of conditional equations over $\mathbb{Q}_Z$ w.r.t. $\models^+$ is 1-1 reducible to the unsolvability of Diophantine equations over $\mathbb{Q}_Z$.*

Proof. We write $\theta \equiv \bigwedge_{i=1}^k \theta_i \equiv \bigwedge_{i=1}^k (\Phi_i \to t_i = r_i)$ with $\Phi_i = \bigwedge_{h=1}^{k_i} u_{i,h} = v_{i,h}$. In view of $p = q \iff p - q = 0$ it may be assumed that the righthand side of each equation occurring in θ is 0.

Next, we notice that $(\bigwedge_{h=1}^k u_h = 0) \to t = 0$ is equivalent in $\mathbb{Q}_Z$ (w.r.t. $\models$ as well as w.r.t. $\models^+$) to $(\sum_{h=1}^k u_h^2) = 0 \to t = 0$. Hence it may be assumed that the various Φ_i consist of a single equation only. So θ has now been rewritten, keeping the semantics w.r.t. $\models^+$ unchanged, in the form

$$\theta \equiv \bigwedge_{i=1}^k (u_i = 0 \to v_i = 0).$$

Now, consider the conditional equation $p = 0 \to q = 0$ with free variables $x_1, \ldots, x_n$. For $i \in [1, n]$, let $y_1^i, \ldots, y_4^i, z_1^i, \ldots, z_4^i, u_1^i, \ldots, u_4^i, v_1^i, \ldots, v_4^i$ be variables not occurring in p and q, and, more generally, not in θ. Then we notice that

$$\mathbb{Q}_Z \models^+ p = 0 \to q = 0$$

if, and only if, the Diophantine equation $H_{p,q} = 0$ has no solution, with $H_{p,q} \equiv$

$$\sum_{i=1}^n (x_i \cdot (1 + \sum_{j=1}^4 (y_j^i)^2) - (1 + \sum_{j=1}^4 (z_j^i)^2)) + p^2 + (q^2 \cdot (1 + \sum_{j=1}^4 (u_j)^2) - (1 + \sum_{j=1}^4 (v_j)^2))^2$$

To see this, one may notice that a counter example to $p = 0 \to q = 0$ involves positive rational values for the x_i together with $p = 0$ and $q \neq 0$ (i.e., $q^2 > 0$). Now, a rational number z is positive if, and only if, there are positive naturals z_d and z_n such that $z \cdot z_d - z_n = 0$. This idea is applied 4 times in the expression

$H_{p,q}$ using the fact that 1 plus the sum of four squares expresses all positive naturals.

Finally, $\mathbb{Q}_Z \models^+ \theta$ if, and only if, for all $i \in [1, k]$, $Q \models^+ u_i = 0 \to v_i = 0$ if, and only if, all Diophantine equations $H_{u_i,v_i} = 0$ are unsolvable if, and only if, the Diophantine equation $\prod_{i=1}^n H_{u_i,v_i} = 0$ is unsolvable over $\mathbb{Q}_Z$.   □

Theorem 4. *Validity of equations over $\mathbb{Q}_{Z,\pm\infty,\pm\iota,\perp}$ is 1-1 reducible to unsolvability of Diophantine equations over $\mathbb{Q}_Z$.*

Proof. We consider open formulae of the following form

$$\theta \equiv \bigwedge_{i=1}^k \theta_i \equiv \bigwedge_{i=1}^k (\Phi_i \to t_i = r_i)$$

where the Φ_i are conjunctions of equations over the signature of fields (commutative rings) and assume that satisfaction requires universal quantification over positive rational values, i.e., we will focus on $\mathbb{Q}_{Z,\pm\infty,\pm\iota,\perp} \models^+ \theta$. These open formulae are called formulae of the form *CCeqURc* (conjunctions of conditional equations with conditions over the signature of unital rings).

Given an equation $t = r$ for which we intend to assess $\mathbb{Q}_{Z,\pm\infty,\pm\iota,\perp} \models t = r$ via a reduction to another problem, upon expanding all of its quantifiers as suggested in the manner of Proposition 8, a formula $\phi_{t=r}$ of the form CCeqURc is obtained:

$$\mathbb{Q}_{Z,\pm\infty,\pm\iota,\perp} \models t = r \iff \mathbb{Q}_{Z,\pm\infty,\pm\iota,\perp} \models^+ \phi_{t=r}$$

with $\phi_{t=r} \equiv \bigwedge_{i=1}^k (\Phi_i \to t_i = r_i)$, and where the Φ_i are all identical to *true* and the equations $t_i = r_i$ result from $t = r$ by substituting values from the peripheral algebra for various variables in $t = r$. The latter transformation may create an exponential blow-up in size in terms of the number of variables in the equation. We write $|s|$ for the size of a term s as determined by the total number of constants, variables and function symbols in s.

We let $V_{1,2}$ be the following set of expressions:

$$V_{1,2} = \{0, 1, -1, \perp, \iota, -\iota, \infty, -\infty\} \cup \{x, -x \mid x \in V_{var}\}.$$

$V_{1,2}$ contains the terms with norm 1 and norm 2 with the exception of -0 and $-\perp$ both of which can be simplfied.

We introduce the following norm $|\phi|$ for a CCeqURc-formula ϕ:

$$\left| \bigwedge_{i=1}^k (\Phi_i \to t_i = r_i) \right| = (l_{|t|+|r|}, \ldots, l_2)$$

with l_n, for $n \in [1, |t| + |r|]$ equal to the number of indices $i \in [1, k]$ with the property that $|t_i| + |r_i| = n$. We will identify norm $l_{k+1}, \ldots l_2$ with $0, l_{k+1}, \ldots l_2$. We notice that under this assumption norms can be added pointwise and that for CCeqURc-formulae θ_1 and θ_2, $\theta_1 \wedge \theta_2$ is a CCeqURc formula such that: $|\theta_1 \wedge \theta_2| = |\theta_1| + |\theta_2|$.

CCeqURc-formulae with lowest norms have $l_2 > 0$, and $l_n = 0$ for $n > 2$. If any of the s_i or t_i for $i \in [1, k]$ contains a subterm of the form $-(-s))$, say $t_i \equiv C[-(-s)]$ replacing that subterm by s thereby changing $\theta_i \equiv \Phi_i \to t_i = r_i$ to $\Phi_i \to C[s] = r_i$, the result is logically equivalent over $\mathbb{Q}_{Z, \pm\infty, \pm\iota, \perp}$ and leads to a lower norm: $|\Phi_i \to t_i = r_i| > |\Phi_i \to C[s] = r_i|$ which extents to a lower norm for the modified CCeqURc-formula having θ_i as a conjunct.

We will next outline a transformation step ρ which transforms each CCeqURc-formula $\theta \equiv \bigwedge_{i=1}^{k} \theta_i$ with $\theta_i \equiv \Phi_i \to t_i = r_i$ for which for some $j \in [1, k]$ either t_j or r_j has norm above 2 to a formula $\rho(\theta)$, such that $\rho(\theta)$ is equivalent to θ over $\mathbb{Q}_{Z, \pm\infty, \pm\iota, \perp}$ w.r.t. $\models^+$, and such that $|\rho(\theta)| < |\theta|$. More specifically $\rho(\theta) \equiv \bigwedge_{i=1}^{k} \theta_j'$ where $\theta_j' = \theta_j$ for $j \neq i$, where j is chosen, and θ_j' is obtained, as follows.

The value $j \in \mathbb{N}$ used in the above description of ρ is chosen as a minimal value such that at least one of t_j or r_j contains a subterm outside $V_{1,2}$. Write $t_j \equiv C[t]$ with t a smallest subterm outside $V_{1,2}$, if t_j contains such a subterm; otherwise, write $r_j \equiv C[t]$. Both cases are dealt with similarly, and we will focus on the case that t can be written as $t_j \equiv C[t]$ with t a term outside $V_{1,2}$ of which, by consequence of the choice of the context $C[-]$, all subterms are elements of $V_{1,2}$.

As all of the subterms of t are in $V_{1,2}$ we may distinguish for t the following cases, with $r, r' \in V_{1,2}$: (i) $t \equiv -r$, (ii) $t \equiv r^{-1}$, (iii) $t = r + r'$, and (iv) $t \equiv r \cdot r'$.

In each case we will find a CCeqURc-formula θ_j' such that $\mathbb{Q}_{Z, \pm\infty, \pm\iota, \perp} \models^+$ $\theta_i' \iff \theta_j$ and such that $|\theta_j'| < |\theta_j|$. In consequence: $\mathbb{Q}_{Z, \pm\infty, \pm\iota, \perp} \models^+ \rho(\theta) \iff \theta$ and $|\rho(\theta)| < |\theta|$.

Case (i): Because $t \notin V_{1,2}$, and $r \in V_{1,2}$, the following cases can be ruled out (making use also of the fact that subterms of the form $-(-s)$ have been removed): $r \equiv 1, r \equiv -1, r \equiv \iota, r \equiv -\iota, r \equiv \infty, r \equiv -\infty, r \equiv x, r \equiv -\infty$ so that the cases $r \equiv 0, r \equiv \perp$ remain. In the case that $r \equiv 0$ $\theta_j' \equiv \Phi_j \to C[0] = r_j$ is equivalent to $\theta_j \equiv \Phi_i \to C[-0] = r_i$, in view of $-0 = 0$, while $|\theta_j'| = |\Phi_j \to C[0] = r_j| < |\Phi_i \to C[-0] = r_i| = |\theta_j|$ so that $|\theta| < |\theta'|$. In case $r \equiv \perp$, $\theta_j' \equiv \Phi_i \to C[\perp] = r_j$ can be chosen in view of $-\perp = \perp$.

Case (ii) $t \equiv r^{-1}$. We first consider cases $r \equiv 0, 1, -1, \iota, -\iota, \infty, -\infty, \perp$. Replacing t by t' as follows produces a formula with the same semantics but with a lower $|-|$ size: $t' \equiv \perp, 1, -1, \infty, -\infty, \iota, -\iota, \perp$ respectively. The cases $x, -x$ require the introduction of an additional condition. Let y be a variable with is not free in θ, $\theta_j' \equiv \Phi_i \to C[x^{-1}] = r_j$ can be chosen as: $\Phi_i \wedge x \cdot y = 1 \to C[y] = r_j$. In case $r \equiv -x$ one may choose $\theta_j' \equiv \Phi_i \wedge x \cdot y = 1 \to C[-y] = r_j$.

Case (iii) $t \equiv r + r'$. We have to deal with cases $r \equiv 0, 1, -1, \iota, -\iota, \infty, -\infty, \perp, x, -x$ and $r \equiv 0, 1, -1, \iota, -\iota, \infty, -\infty, \perp, y, -y$ (where x and y may be the same variable). The treatment of various cases is somewhat ad hoc. After each step, it must be checked if any subterm of the form $-(-s)$ has been introduced, and if so that subterm must be simplified before applying the next step in the manner that was outlined above.

If $r \equiv 0$ then t may be replaced by r', and if $r' \equiv 0$ then t may be replaced by r, so that all cases involving a 0 are done. In both cases a simplification w.r.t. $|-|$ results. If either r or r' is identical to $\bot$, t can be replaced by $\bot$. If $r \equiv \infty$ then: if $r' \equiv \infty$, t can be replaced by ∞, if $r' \equiv -\infty$, t can be replaced by $\bot$ and in all other cases t can be replaced by ∞. If $r \equiv -\infty$ then: if $r' \equiv -\infty$, t can be replaced by $-\infty$, if $r' \equiv \infty$, t can be replaced by $\bot$ and in all other cases t can be replaced by $-\infty$. Making use of the symmetry of $+$ all cases involving ∞ or $-\infty$ are dealt with in this manner. Next let $r \equiv \iota$, the cases that must be considered for r' are $r' \equiv 1, -1, \iota, -\iota, x, -x$. The following replacements t' for t work for these cases respectively: $1, -1, \iota, \bot, x, -x$. The cases that $r \equiv -\iota$ is dealt with similarly and so are the cases $r' \equiv \iota$ and $r' \equiv -\iota$. We are left with all cases with r and r' in $1, -1, x, -x$ (where r and r' may be different variables). Let $r \equiv 1$, then if $r' \equiv -1$ one may replace t by $t' \equiv 0$. The other the cases require more care: chose variable y outside the free variables of θ. Now if $r' \equiv 1$ let $\theta_j' \equiv \Phi_j \wedge y = 1 + 1 \to C[y] = r_j$, if $r' \equiv x$ let $\theta_j' \equiv \Phi_j \wedge y = 1 + x \to C[y] = r_j$, and if $r' \equiv -x$ let $\theta_j' \equiv \Phi_j \wedge y = 1 + (-x) \to C[y] = r_j$. The cases $r \equiv -1$, $r' \equiv 1, r' \equiv -1$ are dealt with similarly.

Next, let $r \equiv x$, now four cases can be distinguished: $r' \equiv x, -x, z, -z$ with z a variable different from x. In case $r' \equiv -x$, t can be replaced by $t' \equiv 0$. In case $r' \equiv x$ choose y a variable outside θ and take $\theta_j' \equiv \Phi_j \wedge y = x + x \to C[y] = r_j$. In case $r' \equiv z$, z a variable different from x and y. As it is impossible to predict the sign of $x + z$, conditions are used to distinguish the three cases for that sign by taking $\theta_j' \equiv$

$$(\Phi_i \wedge y = x + z \to C[y] = r_j) \wedge (\Phi_i \wedge 0 = x + z \to C[0] = r_j) \wedge$$
$$(\Phi_i \wedge -y = x + z \to C[-y] = r_j).$$

To see that $|\theta_j'| < |\theta_j|$, notice that the three conjuncts of θ_j' each have the highest non-zero value of the size $|-|$ at a lower position than θ_j so that the sum of these sizes is lexicographically lower than $|\theta_j|$. The case $r \equiv -x$ is dealt with similarly.

Having dealt with all four cases for t the definition of the transformation ρ is completed. Given that $|-|$ imposes a well-founded relation on terms and so that infinite descending chains do not exist, the above considerations allow us to conclude that after repeatedly performing the transformation ρ every CCeqURc-formula θ can be uniformly (i.e., in a computable manner) transformed into an equivalent formula θ^* where both sides of the various equations are terms in $V_{1,2}$.

Now θ^* can be simplified further: for each conclusion $t_j = r_j$ with t_j and r_j both closed the equation $t_j = r_j$ is either true in $\mathbb{Q}_{Z,\pm\infty,\pm\iota,\bot}$ in which case said equation can be replaced by $0 = 0$; or it is false in which case it can be replaced by $0 = 1$. In other cases if one side amounts to x or to $-x$ and the other side is in $\iota, -\iota, \infty, -\infty, \bot$ then the equation cannot hold for any value of x and therefore it can be replaced by $0 = 1$. By repeatedly using the latter simplification step a CCeqURc-formula is found which involves no peripheral constants, i.e., it is a conjunction of conditional equations over the signature of unital rings.

Next, we show that for CCeqURc-formulae θ not involving peripheral constants, satisfaction w.r.t. $\models^+$, i.e., $\mathbb{Q}_Z \models^+ \theta$, is 1-1 reducible to the complement of Diophantine solvability over a ring of rationals. This observation immediately follows from Proposition 9 and the fact that θ is a conjunction of conditional equations over $\mathbb{Q}_Z$ thereby completing the proof of Theorem 4.   □

6 Concluding Remarks

One aim of our series of papers on data types of rational numbers is a theory of abstract data types for numerical computation. There is no shortage of semantic problems yet to be tackled and many arose in the early days of computing [25].

6.1 Background on the Rationals and Their Enlargements

A first logical account of the "problem of division by zero" can be found in [24], where adopting $1/0 = 0$ is suggested as a plausible solution; see also [2]. A finite equational initial algebra specification of the rationals was accomplished in [8] by taking option $1/0 = 0$. Upon defining $0^{-1} = 0$, inverse becomes an involution and by enriching Q in this manner a so-called *involutive meadow* is obtained. We refer to [4] for the notion of an involutive meadow. Earlier, meadows, with a focus on first order axiomatisations, had been studied under the name of pseudofields in [19].

As an alternative for involutive meadows, common meadows with the external option $1/0 = \bot$ were first developed in [5,7]. The option $1/0 = \infty$ (unsigned) leads to the wheel of rational numbers (see [12,22]) for which a finite equational initial algebra specification is developed in [10]. One option with two signed infinities leads to the transrationals, for which a finite equational initial algebra specification is developed in [9]. A survey of options for division by zero is [3].

6.2 Practical Computer Arithmetics

Consider the key semantic features of computer arithmetics as they are handled in floating point arithmetic. Viewed as a data type, a floating point arithmetic is an algebra on a *finite* subset of the rational numbers. Its actual design strives for an approximation of rational number arithmetic that is "best possible" according to certain working criteria, and can be implemented in computer hardware. It involves semantic enhancements such as the following:

1. Every number must be represented in a bit pattern of fixed length.
2. Except for zero 0, each number is coded by a pair containing a decimal number $1 \leq d \leq 10$ of fixed length l and a power $e \in [-k, k]$ of 10. A finite set of rationals can be represented in this way.
3. Arithmetical operations on rational numbers may need rounding.

4. Partial arithmetical operations are avoided by using the special values ∞ (infinity) and $-\infty$ (minus infinity) to represent $\frac{1}{0}$ and $\frac{-1}{0}$, respectively, and an error value NaN to represent $\frac{0}{0}$,
5. Partial operations may lead to exceptions and interrupts that are modelled by special signalling error values (viz. *signalling* sNaN).
6. Due to the presence of error values there is no total ordering of the domain of floating point arithmetic.
7. In some models of floating point arithmetic $\frac{1}{\infty} = 0$ and $\frac{1}{-\infty} = -0$ with -0 different from 0.

The arithmetical data type of transrationals adapts the data type of rational numbers by including ∞ and $-\infty$ and a single quiet NaN, which is here called $\perp^2$. It sets $\frac{1}{\infty} = \frac{1}{-\infty} = 0$. Seen from the point of view of the rationals, the transrationals are a semantic model of some key features to be found in floating point arithmetic, though possessing an unfortunate asymmetry for infinities.

Symmetric transrationals deviate from the conventions of floating point arithmetic concerning division by zero. The idea is that positive infinity can arise only from a positive overflow, and that the positive infinitesimal arises from a positive underflow, as well as from division by positive zero - infinity. This phenomenon is present in the bounded symmetric transrationals. Notice the peripheral elements have separated the issue of 0^{-1} from overflows and underflows.

What of the finiteness of floating point? The construction of the transrational models arise from a general construction on an ordered field. This means that the constructions fail to apply to finite fields, which do not have orderings. Obtaining finite structures for symmetric transrationals requires working with a finite but ordered set of numbers, which is what happens in floating point arithmetic. The transition to a finite set of numbers is decomposable in two steps that can be made in either order: (i) imposing a bound on the size of numbers, and (ii) imposing a bound on the relative precision of numbers while taking the view that each number serves as an approximation of its close neighbours as rationals. We have investigated the result of taking size bounds into account only.

6.3   Hybrid Systems

Mathematical models of analogue-digital systems, including hybrid automata of various kinds, combine the methods of the calculus on real and complex number continua with algorithmic methods on discrete data types. In this area Frits Vaandrager has been active for many years (see, e.g., [16,17]). However, in applications, idealised or actual, the analogue data is the result of making measurements, which is the business of data types of rational numbers. Calibrations in terms of units and subunits are the raison d'être of the rational numbers, a fact known to ancient Greek mathematics. Thus, computations with hybrid systems, neither in theory nor practice, take place on data types with real numbers. The

---

[2] Anderson denotes this by Φ and calls it *nullity*, thereby emphasising that its role may be more significant than simply representing an error.

analogue data types are computer arithmetics, which by their nature are composed of rational numbers. Thus, theoretically, data types of rational numbers can faithfully represent the analogue data, drawn from the working environment of the system.

Our studies of various total data types of rational numbers has relevance to foundational thinking about hybrid computational systems. The study of hybrid systems that is most advanced – especially in matters of modelling, specification and verification – are based on automata of different forms [20]. It is a matter for further research to explore what data types of rationals might offer theories of hybrid automata. However, the fundamental role of the calculus in modelling physical systems prioritises floating point arithmetics, being the orthodox computer arithmetics for numerical methods in science and engineering. In the case of data types of rationals akin to floating point we propose the symmetric transrationals as a semantical model.

References

1. Anderson, J.A., Völker, N., Adams, A.A.: Perspecx Machine VIII, axioms of transreal arithmetic. In: Latecki, J., Mount, D.M., Wu, A.Y. (eds.) Proceeding SPIE 6499. Vision Geometry XV, p. 649902, (2007). https://www.spiedigitallibrary. org/conference-proceedings-of-spie/6499/1/Perspex-Machine-VIII-axioms-of-transreal-arithmetic/10.1117/12.698153.short?SSO=1
2. Anderson, J.A., Bergstra, J.A.: Review of Suppes 1957 proposals for division by zero. Transmathematica (2021). https://doi.org/10.36285/tm.53
3. Bergstra, J.A.: Division by zero, a survey of options. Transmathematica (2019). https://doi.org/10.36285/tm.v0i0.17
4. Bergstra, J.A., Middelburg, C.A.: Division by zero in non-involutive meadows. J. Appl. Logic **13**(1), 1–12 (2015). https://doi.org/10.1016/j.jal.2014.10.001
5. Bergstra, J.A., Ponse, A.: Division by zero in common meadows. In: De Nicola, R., Hennicker, R. (eds.) Software, Services, and Systems. LNCS, vol. 8950, pp. 46–61. Springer, Cham (2015). https://doi.org/10.1007/978-3-319-15545-6_6
6. Bergstra, J.A., Ponse, A.: Division by zero in common meadows. Improved version of [5] (2021). https://arxiv.org/abs/1406.6878v4
7. Bergstra, J.A., Ponse, A.: Fracpairs and fractions over a reduced commutative ring. Indigationes Math. **27**(2016), 727–748 (2016). https://doi.org/10.1016/j.indag.2016.01.007
8. Bergstra, J.A., Tucker, J.A.: The rational numbers as an abstract data type. J. ACM, **54**(2) (2007), Article 7. https://doi.org/10.1145/1219092.1219095
9. Bergstra, J.A., Tucker., J.V.: The transrational numbers as an abstract data type. Transmathematica (2020). https://doi.org/10.36285/tm.47
10. Bergstra, J.A., Tucker., J.V.: The wheel of rational numbers as an abstract data type. In: Roggenbach, M. (ed.) WADT 2020. LNCS, vol. 12669, pp. 13–30. Springer, Cham (2021). https://doi.org/10.1007/978-3-030-73785-6_2
11. Bergstra, J.A., Tucker., J.V.: Eager equality for rational number arithmetic. Submitted for publication (2021)
12. Carlström, J.: Wheels-On division by zero. Math. Struct. Comput. Sci. **14**(1), 143–184 (2004). https://doi.org/10.1017/S0960129503004110

13. dos Reis, T.S., Gomide, W., Anderson, J.A.: Construction of the transreal numbers and algebraic transfields. IAENG Int. J. Appl. Math. **46**(1), 11–23 (2016). http:// www.iaeng.org/IJAM/issues_v46/issue_1/IJAM_46_1_03.pdf

14. Ehrich, H.-D., Wolf, M., Loeckx, J.: Specification of Abstract Data Types, Vieweg Teubner (1997)

15. Goguen, J.A.: Memories of ADJ. Bulletin of the EATCS no. 36, October (1989). https://cseweb.ucsd.edu/goguen/pubs/other.html

16. Kaynar, D.K., Lynch, N., Segala, R., Vaandrager, F.: The Theory of Timed I/O Automata. 2nd edn. Morgan Claypool 2010 (2010). https://doi.org/10.2200/ S00310ED1V01Y201011DCT005

17. Lynch, N., Segala, R., Vaandrager, F.: Hybrid I/O automata. Inf. Comput. **185**(1), 105–157 (2003). https://doi.org/10.1016/S0890-5401(03)00067-1

18. Manin, Y.: A Course in Mathematical Logic. Springer (1977). 2nd edn 2010

19. Ono, H.: Equational theories and universal theories of fields. J. Math. Soc. Jpn. **35**(2), 289–306 (1983). https://doi.org/10.2969/jmsj/03520289

20. Platzer, A.: Logical Analysis of Hybrid Systems. Springer (2010). https://doi.org/ 10.1007/978-3-642-14509-4

21. Poonen, B.: Undecidability in number theory. Not. AMS, **55**(3), 344–350 (2008). https://www.ams.org/notices/200803/tx080300344p.pdf

22. Setzer, A.: Wheels (Draft) (1997). http://www.cs.swan.ac.uk/csetzer/articles/ wheel.pdf

23. Stoltenberg-Hansen, V., Tucker, J.V.: Effective algebras. In: Abramsky, S., Gabbay, D., Maibaum, T. (eds.) Handbook of Logic in Computer Science. Volume IV: Semantic Modelling, Oxford University Press, pp. 357–526 (1995)

24. Suppes, P.: Introduction to Logic. Van Nostrand Reinhold (1957)

25. Tucker, J.V.: Unfinished Business: abstract data types and computer arithmetic. BCS FACS FACTS, The Newsletter of the Formal Aspects of Computing Science (FACS) Specialist Group, issue 2022–1, February 2022, pp. 60–68 (2022). https:// www.bcs.org/media/8289/facs-jan22.pdf

26. Ullian, J.S.: Splinters of recursive functions. J. Symbolic Logic **25**(1), 33–38 (1960). https://doi.org/10.2307/2964335

A Survey of Model Learning Techniques for Recurrent Neural Networks

Benedikt Bollig[1] , Martin Leucker[2] , and Daniel Neider[3]($\boxtimes$)

[1] Université Paris-Saclay, CNRS, ENS Paris-Saclay, LMF, Gif-sur-Yvette, France
[2] Institute for Software Engineering and Programming Languages,
Universität zu Lübeck, Lübeck, Germany
[3] Safety and Explainability of Learning Systems Group,
Carl von Ossietzky Universität Oldenburg, Oldenburg, Germany
daniel.neider@uni-oldenburg.de

Abstract. Ensuring the correctness and reliability of deep neural networks is a challenge. Suitable formal analysis and verification techniques have yet to be developed. One promising approach towards this goal is model learning, which seeks to derive surrogate models of the underlying neural network in a model class that permits sophisticated analysis and verification techniques. This paper surveys several existing model learning approaches that infer finite-state automata and context-free grammars from Recurrent Neural Networks, an essential class of deep neural networks for sequential data. Most of these methods rely on Angluin's approach for learning finite automata but implement different ways of checking the equivalence of a learned model with the neural network. Our paper presents these distinct techniques in a unified language and discusses their strengths and weaknesses. Furthermore, we survey model learning techniques that follow a novel trend in explainable artificial intelligence and learn models in the form of formal grammars.

Keywords: Model learning · Recurrent Neural Networks · Automata learning

1   Introduction

Rather than programming manually, it seems charming to simply provide examples of the intended input-output behavior of a given function and derive the function's implementation using algorithmic means. That is the promise of machine learning, in which often some form of classification problem is addressed by adjusting the parameters of a (deep) neural network until it fits the sample set appropriately.

While machine learning has shown to provide excellent solutions in many cases, it is not surprising that this approach also has deficiencies. Starting

This work was partly supported by the Deutsche Forschungsgemeinschaft (DFG, German Research Foundation) grant number 434592664.

with the question to which extent the examples are characteristic, it is unclear whether the learning algorithm considers the characteristic aspects of the examples, whether the resulting system really realizes or closely approximates the intended function, or whether it meets privacy requirements, to name but a few challenges. As such, sophisticated analysis and verification techniques for the learned artifacts seem extremely important to make sure that the resulting system meets its intended goals.

In the area of *formal methods* (see Garavel, ter Beek, and van de Pol [10] for a recent survey), a vast number of analysis and verification methods have been developed to analyze systems, often given as programs. As such, it seems promising to apply these methods also for the analysis of deep neural networks. To this end, two general approaches seem possible. First, one could adapt the procedures developed in the area of formal methods to analyze the artifacts encountered in machine learning directly. Second, one may translate the artifacts found in machine learning (e.g., deep neural networks) into formal models that are well-studied in program verification. In other words, the actual object of study is translated into a so-called *surrogate model* that mimics relevant aspects of the underlying system and is easier to analyze or may be used for explaining some of its aspects.

This paper gives a short overview of several techniques following the latter of the two approaches above. More precisely, we consider *Recurrent Neural Networks (RNNs)*, an essential subclass of deep neural networks for classification and regression of sequential data, and survey a recent trend in the literature that employs *model learning* techniques [30]. The core insight is that RNNs can be seen as deep neural networks with a notion of state, which may be approximated by finite automata. This view permits using the wealth of existing verification and analysis techniques for automata (e.g., model checking) to reason about RNNs.[1]

In Sect. 2, we precisely define the object of study (i.e., recurrent neural networks) and introduce basic notation from automata theory. Then, Sect. 3 surveys three state-of-the-art model learning approaches for inferring finite-state abstractions of a given RNN. All three approaches build on Angluin's L* automata-learning algorithm but differ in how they check whether a learned automaton is equivalent to the RNN—or at least an approximation thereof that is good enough. While Mayr and Yovine [23, 24] use ideas underlying Valiant's Probably Approximately Correct (PAC) learning [31] to this end (Sect. 3.1), Khmelnitsky et al. [18] rely on an approach based on Hoeffding's inequality bound [15] (Sect. 3.2), which is also used in statistical model checking [19]. The third approach by Weiss, Goldberg, and Yahav [32] (Sect. 3.3), on the other hand, does not use probabilistic sampling but instead proposes an abstraction refinement technique to perform the equivalence check.

---

[1] We refer to the comprehensive overview article by Frits Vaandrager [30] for a gentle introduction to the field of automata-based model learning, which highlights the milestones until the state-of-the art and identifies the challenges faced today.

Recurrent neural networks have also often been employed for language recognition and other language processing tasks. Since (controlled) natural languages often have a context-free nature, context-free grammars seem to be a more suitable object of study than finite automata. Hence, we sketch an approach in Sect. 4 that infers a context-free grammar as a surrogate model instead of a finite automaton. This approach follows a current trend in explainable artificial intelligence, where formal grammars are used to explain how the underlying RNN processes language artifacts.

2   Recurrent Neural Networks as Language Acceptors

The term *Recurrent Neural Network (RNN)* is an umbrella term for a variety of artificial neural networks that process sequential data. In contrast to feed-forward networks, RNNs are designed to process sequential data of varying lengths, which is essential in domains such as natural language processing and time-series prediction.

Following the recent literature on model learning for RNNs [5,18,22–24,32], we make two assumptions throughout this paper:

1. We assume that the inputs to an RNN are sequences over a fixed, finite set of symbols (e.g., letters). Such inputs are typically vectors in a one-hot encoding, but we abstract from these kinds of implementation details and instead view data series as words over a finite alphabet.
2. We consider settings where an RNN is used as a binary (or a one-vs-all) classifier.

A popular example for such a setting is sentiment analysis [21], where the task is to classify whether a text, such as a product review, expresses a positive or negative opinion.

To make the setting above mathematically precise, let us first introduce the required notation. An *alphabet* Σ is a nonempty finite set, whose elements are called *letters*. A (finite) word w over Σ is a sequence $a_1 \ldots a_n$ of letters $a_i \in \Sigma$ for $i \in \{1, \ldots, n\}$. The length of a word $w = a_1 \ldots a_n$ is defined as $|w| = n$. The unique word of length 0 is called the *empty word* and denoted by λ. We let Σ^* refer to the set of all words over Σ and call a sub-set $L \subseteq \Sigma^*$ a *language* (over Σ). The complement of a language $L \subseteq \Sigma^*$ is $\overline{L} = \{w \in \Sigma^* \mid w \notin L\}$. For two languages $L_1, L_2 \subseteq \Sigma^*$, we let $L_1 \backslash L_2 = L_1 \cap \overline{L_2}$. The symmetric difference of L_1 and L_2 is defined as $L_1 \oplus L_2 = (L_1 \backslash L_2) \cup (L_2 \backslash L_1)$.

We are now ready to define RNNs, which we view in this paper as language acceptors (i.e., computational devices that "accept" or "reject" words). There are several popular architectures to implement RNNs in practice, such as (simple) Elman RNNs, long short-term memory (LSTM) [14], and GRUs [7]. However, we abstract away from the actual implementation details and view RNNs as abstract computational devices, as defined next.

Definition 1. *A recurrent neural network (RNN) is a tuple* $\mathcal{R} = (\ell, f, h_0, g)$ *where* $\ell \in \mathbb{N}$ *is the dimension of the state space* $\mathbb{R}^\ell$, $h_0 \in \mathbb{R}^\ell$ *is the initial state,*

$f: \mathbb{R}^{\ell} \times \Sigma \rightarrow \mathbb{R}^{\ell}$ *is the* transition function *describing the effect of applying an input letter in a given source state, and* $g: \mathbb{R}^{\ell} \rightarrow \{0,1\}$ *is a function that defines whether a state is accepting or rejecting (indicated by 1 and 0, respectively).*

The language of an RNN $\mathcal{R} = (\ell, f, h_0, g)$ is defined as

$$L(\mathcal{R}) = \{w \in \Sigma^* \mid g(f(h_0, w)) = 1\},$$

where we extend the transition function f to words in the usual way: $f(h, \lambda) = h$ and $f(h, ua) = f(f(h, u), a)$. In other words, a word w is contained in $L(\mathcal{R})$ if and only if, starting from h_0, the state that the RNN reaches by successively applying f to the letters of w is accepting.

Model learning for RNNs now seeks to extract a finite-state representation from a given RNN, typically in the form of a deterministic finite automaton. Formally, a *deterministic finite automaton (DFA)* is a tuple $\mathcal{A} = (Q, \Sigma, \delta, q_0, F)$ where Q is a finite, nonempty set of states, Σ is the input alphabet, $\delta: Q \times \Sigma \rightarrow Q$ is the transition function, $q_0 \in Q$ is the initial state, and $F \subseteq Q$ is the set of final states. We assume familiarity with basic automata theory and just mention that the language $L(\mathcal{A})$ of $\mathcal{A}$ is defined as the set of words from Σ^* that δ guides into a final state when starting in q_0. A language $L \subseteq \Sigma^*$ is called *regular* if there exists a DFA $\mathcal{A}$ with $L(\mathcal{A}) = L$.

The expressive power of RNNs depends on the exact architecture and generally goes beyond regular languages. Hence, we can—in general—not expect to be able to extract a DFA that accepts the same language as a given RNN. Instead, we can only hope that our DFA approximates its language. The following section surveys various recent approaches that can learn such approximate DFAs.

3   Model Learning for Recurrent Neural Networks

The key idea underlying the majority of model learning approaches for RNNs is to use Angluin's L* algorithm [3]. We do not detail the algorithm here but only define its interfaces and sketch its working principles.[2]

Given a (regular) language $L \subseteq \Sigma^*$, Anlguin's algorithm seeks to learn a DFA accepting L by interacting with an information source, often called the *teacher*. The algorithm can ask two different types of queries: membership and equivalence queries.

- On a *membership query (MQ)*, the learning algorithm proposes a word $w \in \Sigma^*$ and wants to know whether $w \in L$. The teacher answers either "yes" (if $w \in L$) or "no" (if $w \notin L$).

---

[2]   Various improvements have been proposed over the years, such as Rivest and Shapire's algorithm [28] and Kearns and Vazirani's algorithm [17]. However, all of these operate within Angluin's *minimally adequate teacher* framework [3] and can seamlessly be swapped if desired. Hence, for the sake of a more straightforward exposition, this paper focuses on Angluin's L* algorithm as a prototypical example. The reader may substitute L* with any other learning algorithm that operates in the minimal adequate teacher framework.

– On an *equivalence query*, the learning algorithm proposes a DFA $\mathcal{A}$ and wants to know whether $L(\mathcal{A}) = L$. The teacher answers either "yes" (if $L(\mathcal{A}) = L$) or returns a so-called *counterexample* $w \in L(\mathcal{A}) \oplus L$ (if $L(\mathcal{A}) \neq L$).

Figure 1 shows an outline of Angluin's L^* algorithm. The algorithm asks membership queries until it has collected sufficient information to construct a hypothesis DFA $\mathcal{A}$. It then proposes $\mathcal{A}$ on an equivalence query. If $\mathcal{A}$ passes the test and the teacher returns "yes", the learning process stops, and $\mathcal{A}$ is returned. Otherwise, Angluin's algorithm uses the counterexample and potentially further membership queries to refine the current hypothesis. The process of asking membership and equivalence queries then continues until the teacher replies with "yes". If the target language L is regular, Angluin's algorithm guarantees to learn the minimal DFA accepting L in polynomial time (in the size of the minimal DFA and the length of the longest counterexample).

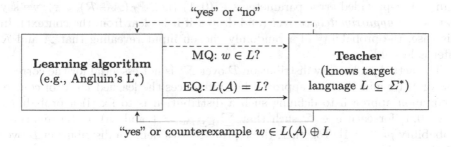

Fig. 1. Overview of Angluin's L^* algorithm

In the context of model learning for an RNN $\mathcal{R}$, the target language for Angluin's algorithm is $L(\mathcal{R})$. It is not hard to verify that membership queries can be answered straightforwardly by passing the input words through the network, which can be parallelized and efficiently performed on a GPU. Note that answering membership questions is also possible if the RNN is a black box and only offers input-output access.

Equivalence queries, on the other hand, are much more complex. In a black-box setting, one does not have access to the network's internals and, thus, can only interact with the network through a finite number of input-output queries. However, even if an RNN is given (as a white box), reasoning about it is often computationally intractable due to the enormous size of today's networks. Hence, most approaches in the literature approximate equivalence queries. In the remainder, we survey three such techniques.

3.1 Answering Equivalence Queries Probably Approximately Correct

Mayr and Yovine [23,24] proposed a simple yet effective way to approximate equivalence queries, which relies on Valiant's paradigm of *Probably Approxi-*

mately Correct (PAC) learning [31] and has first been applied to automata learning by Angluin [3]. Instead of reasoning about an RNN symbolically, the core idea is to replace an equivalence query with a series of membership queries with randomly sampled words. If the number of membership queries is large enough, we can guarantee with high confidence that the learned DFA makes only minor errors. Note that this approach is particularly suited for black-box settings, when only input-output queries to the RNN are possible.

To make the above idea mathematically precise, let us fix a probability distribution $\mathcal{D}$ over Σ^* such that $\sum_{w \in \Sigma^*} \mathbb{P}_{\mathcal{D}}(w) = 1$. This distribution allows us to determine the probability

$$\mathbb{P}_{\mathcal{D}}(\mathcal{A} \oplus \mathcal{R}) := \sum_{w \in L(\mathcal{A}) \oplus L(\mathcal{R})} \mathbb{P}_{\mathcal{D}}(w)$$

that the languages of a DFA $\mathcal{A}$ and an RNN $\mathcal{R}$ differ. If this quantity is smaller than a user-provided error parameter $\varepsilon \in (0,1)$ (i.e., $\mathbb{P}_{\mathcal{D}}(\mathcal{A} \oplus \mathcal{R}) < \varepsilon$), we say that $\mathcal{A}$ is ε-*approximately correct* (and drop ε if it is clear from the context). In this case, the probability of a randomly chosen input revealing that $\mathcal{A}$ and $\mathcal{R}$ differ is less than ε.

The actual probability distribution $\mathcal{D}$ over Σ^* is not essential for the correctness of Mayr and Yovine's approach but influences the learned DFA, of course. A common approach to defining such a distribution is to fix (i) a probability $p_a \in [0,1]$ for each $a \in \Sigma$ such that $\sum_{a \in \Sigma} p_a = 1$ and (ii) a "termination" probability $p_t \in (0,1]$. Together, these probabilities define a distribution $\mathcal{D}$ over Σ^* that is given by

$$\mathbb{P}_{\mathcal{D}}(a_1 \ldots a_n) := \left(\prod_{i=1}^{n} p_{a_i} \right) \cdot (1 - p_t)^n \cdot p_t.$$

Note that the expected length of a randomly drawn word is then $1/p_t - 1$ with a variance of $(1-p_t)/p_t^2$.

Fixing a *confidence parameter* $\gamma \in (0,1)$, Mayr and Yovine now replace an equivalence query with a set of random tests large enough to conclude that $\mathcal{A}$ is ε-approximately correct with confidence at least $1-\gamma$. Apart from the parameters ε and γ, the size of this test suite also depends on the number of approximate equivalence queries that have been made so far. To make the i-th equivalence query, where $i \geq 1$, one requires a test suite of size

$$r_i := \left\lceil \frac{1}{\varepsilon} (i \cdot \ln 2 - \ln \gamma) \right\rceil.$$

Once r_i words have been drawn according to $\mathcal{D}$, a membership query is posed with each of them. Then, the result is compared to the hypothesis DFA $\mathcal{A}$. If one of the membership queries shows a difference between the target language and $\mathcal{A}$, the corresponding word is returned as a counterexample. Otherwise, the teacher returns "yes" and the learning stops.

Clearly, the exact version of Angluin's algorithm either returns a DFA eventually or repeats forever (the latter happens if $L(\mathcal{R})$ is not regular). If the learning algorithm returns a DFA $\mathcal{A}$, say after $m \geq 1$ equivalence queries, then Angluin's results [3] imply that $\mathcal{A}$ is ε-approximately correct with probability at least $1 - \gamma$. To prove that this is true, we observe that the probability of $\mathcal{A}$ not being ε-approximately correct (i.e., $\mathbb{P}_D(\mathcal{A} \oplus \mathcal{R}) \geq \varepsilon$) if all test inputs have passed all of the m equivalence queries is at most

$$\sum_{i=1}^{m}(1 - \varepsilon)^{r_i} \leq \sum_{i=1}^{m} e^{-\varepsilon r_i} \leq \sum_{i=1}^{m} 2^{-i}\gamma \leq \gamma.$$

Thus, $\mathcal{A}$ is indeed ε-approximately correct with probability of at least $1 - \gamma$. It is also worth noting that this approach is guaranteed to terminate if $L(\mathcal{R})$ is regular.

To cope with RNNs whose language is not regular, Mayr and Yovine impose two bounds on the teacher: the maximum number $k \geq 1$ of equivalence queries and the maximum length $b \geq 0$ of random words. Once one of those two bounds is reached, the learning process stops, and the most recent hypothesis DFA is returned.

If the learning terminates prematurely, one can no longer hope that $\mathcal{A}$ has the desired (ε, γ)-guarantee. However, one can still derive statistical information. To make this precise, let us assume that the learning stopped after $i \geq 1$ equivalence queries and the test suite still contained $k > 0$ counterexamples (i.e., k membership queries revealed a difference between $\mathcal{A}$ and $\mathcal{R}$). Then, Mayr and Yovine show that one can still accept the hypothesis that $\mathcal{A}$ is ε-approximately correct with confidence $\gamma' > \binom{r_i}{k} e^{-\varepsilon(r_i - k)}$. Similarly, one can accept the hypothesis that $\mathcal{A}$ is ε'-approximately correct with probability at least $1 - \gamma$ for every $\varepsilon' > \frac{1}{r_i - k}\left(\ln\binom{r_i}{k} - \ln\gamma\right)$, provided $r_i - k \neq 0$. However, Mayr and Yovine have observed that both ε' and γ' can be larger than 1 in practice and, hence, carry no meaning in such cases.

3.2   Equivalence Queries Inspired by Statistical Model Checking

Khmelnitsky et al. [18] propose a method that is similar to the one by Mayr and Yovine but takes its inspiration from *statistical model checking (SMC)* [19]. Instead of increasing the number of random tests with each equivalence query, Khmelnitsky et al. fix it to

$$r := \left\lceil \frac{\log \frac{2}{\gamma}}{2\varepsilon^2} \right\rceil.$$

By applying Hoeffding's inequality bound [15], one then obtains that the probability of a DFA being ε-approximately correct if it passes such an equivalence query is at least $1 - \gamma$.

Figure 2 compares the number of membership queries per equivalence query of Mayr and Yovine's approach as well as Khmelnitsky et al.'s approach for $\varepsilon = \gamma = 0.1$, $\varepsilon = \gamma = 0.05$, and $\varepsilon = \gamma = 0.01$. In all three cases, Mayr and

Yovine's number of membership queries per equivalence query is initially lower but grows with the number of equivalence queries asked. Since Khmelnitsky et al.'s approach always asks the same constant number of membership queries, Mayr and Yovine's approach eventually asks more per equivalence query, and this difference grows over time. This observation indicates that Khmelnitsky et al.'s approach is preferable if the language of an RNN is expected to be complex and, hence, Angluin's algorithms has to ask a large number of equivalence queries.

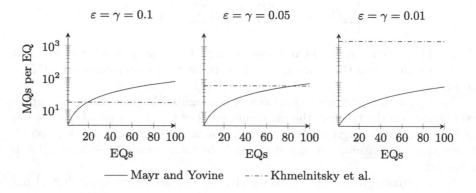

Fig. 2. Comparison of the number of membership queries (MQ) per equivalence query (EQ) of Mayr and Yovine's approach [23] and Khmelnitsky et al.'s approach [18]

While this approach and the one of Sect. 3.1 work in principle, both have drawbacks in practice. On the one hand, the size of the test suite may be huge, and finding a counterexample or proving equivalence might take a substantial time (cf. Fig. 2). On the other hand, the chosen random distribution also has to take the RNN into account because the statistical guarantee is meaningless if this is not the case. Due to these problems, it has been reported that random sampling does often not work well in practice [18,32].

To mitigate this severe practical limitation, Weiss, Goldberg, and Yahav [32] have proposed an abstraction refinement approach, which we describe in the next section. However, before we do so, let us briefly sketch how Khmelnitsky et al. address this issue.

Khmelnitsky et al.'s precise setting is not a mere extraction of a DFA from an RNN but the verification of the RNN. More precisely, given an RNN $\mathcal{R}$ and a formal specification in the form of a language $S \subseteq \Sigma^*$, the task is to prove that $L(\mathcal{R}) \subseteq S$. The language S can be given as a DFA or in any other form that compiles into one (e.g., temporal logics, such as Linear Temporal Logic (LTL) [27] or the IEEE Property Specification Language (PSL) [9]).

The core idea of Khmelnitsky et al. is to use Angluin's algorithm to learn a DFA $\mathcal{A}$ as a surrogate model of $\mathcal{R}$ and then perform model checking on $\mathcal{A}$. This process is sketched in Fig. 3 and modifies the teacher as follows.

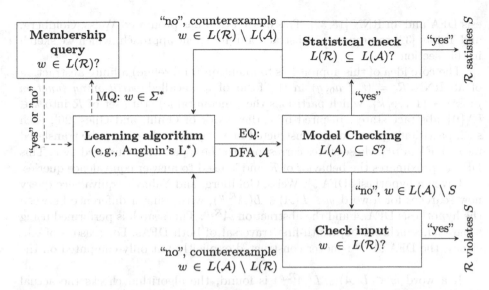

Fig. 3. Property directed verification of RNNs as proposed by Khmelnitsky et al. [18]

As in Angluin's classical setting, membership queries are answered by passing the input straightforwardly through the RNN and reporting the outcome. However, equivalence queries with a hypothesis DFA $\mathcal{A}$ are answered in a so-called *property-directed manner*. More specifically, Khmelnitsky et al.'s algorithm first checks $L(A) \subseteq S$ and then proceeds depending on the outcome of this test:

- If a word $w \in L(\mathcal{A}) \setminus S$ is found (i.e., $L(\mathcal{A}) \not\subseteq S$), the algorithm checks whether $w \in L(\mathcal{R})$ holds using a membership query. If this is the case, an input violating the property S was detected, and the algorithm returns that the RNN violates the property. If $w \notin L(\mathcal{R})$, then w is returned as a counterexample to Angluin's algorithm, witnessing that the surrogate model $\mathcal{A}$ and the RNN $\mathcal{R}$ differ (i.e., $w \in L(\mathcal{A}) \setminus L(\mathcal{R})$).
- If $L(\mathcal{A}) \subseteq S$, then the teacher performs an approximate equivalence query using membership queries as described above with the exception that it checks $L(\mathcal{R}) \subseteq L(\mathcal{A})$ instead of $L(\mathcal{R}) = L(\mathcal{A})$. If a counterexample $w \in L(\mathcal{R}) \setminus L(\mathcal{A})$ is found, it is returned as a counterexample to Angluin's algorithm. If all tests pass, on the other hand, the teacher returns "yes" and the learning stops. In the latter case, the RNN is ε-approximately correct with respect to the property S with confidence at least $1 - \gamma$.

As Khmelnitsky et al. show, this property-directed approach empirically performs better than a purely statistical test. In the following section, we survey another method that replaces the statistical test with symbolic reasoning.

3.3   An Abstraction Refinement Approach to Equivalence Queries

While random sampling is an established way to answer equivalence queries, experiments show that it often fails to detect differences between a given hypothesis DFA and an RNN [18,32]. This observation has prompted Weiss, Goldberg, and Yahav [32] to propose an abstraction refinement approach, which we sketch in this section.

The core idea of this approach is to maintain (and refine) a finite abstraction of an RNN $\mathcal{R} = (\ell, f, h_0, g)$ in the form of a so-called *partitioning function* $p\colon \mathbb{R}^\ell \to \{1, \ldots, k\}$, which partitions the (uncountable) state set of $\mathcal{R}$ into $k \in \mathbb{N}\setminus\{0\}$ abstract states. Inspired by earlier work of Omlin and Giles [26], each such partitioning function is constructed in a way such that it can be translated into a DFA $\mathcal{A}^{\mathcal{R},p}$, whose states correspond to the k partitions induced by p. This DFA approximates the behavior of $\mathcal{R}$ and is used to answer equivalence queries.

Given a hypothesis DFA $\mathcal{A}$, Weiss, Goldberg, and Yahav's equivalence query now searches for a word $w \in L(\mathcal{A}) \oplus L(\mathcal{A}^{\mathcal{R},p})$, witnessing a difference between the hypothesis DFA $\mathcal{A}$ and the abstraction $\mathcal{A}^{\mathcal{R},p}$. This search is performed using a parallel, synchronized, depth-first traversal of both DFAs. For reasons of efficiency, the DFA $\mathcal{A}^{\mathcal{R},p}$ is never constructed explicitly but only computed on the fly.

If a word $w \in L(\mathcal{A}) \oplus L(\mathcal{A}^{\mathcal{R},p})$ is found, the algorithm checks the actual behavior of $\mathcal{R}$ on w using a membership query (i.e., it checks whether $w \in L(\mathcal{R})$) and proceeds as follows:

- If $\mathcal{A}$ and $\mathcal{R}$ disagree on w (i.e., $w \in L(\mathcal{A}) \Leftrightarrow w \notin L(\mathcal{R})$), then $\mathcal{A}$ is incorrect and w is returned as a counterexample.
- If $\mathcal{A}$ and $\mathcal{R}$ agree on w (i.e., $w \in L(\mathcal{A}) \Leftrightarrow w \in L(\mathcal{R})$), then the partitioning function p is refined (as sketched shortly). This refinement is necessary to account for the fact that p is too coarse, causing $\mathcal{A}^{\mathcal{R},p}$ to classify w incorrectly. Once p has been refined, the parallel depth-first search begins anew.

Note that refining p causes the abstraction $\mathcal{A}^{\mathcal{R},p}$ gradually to converge to a state-based representation of the RNN $\mathcal{R}$.

Let us now turn to the description of the refinement step, which initializes p to $p(h) = 1$ for $h \in \mathbb{R}^\ell$ before the first equivalence query. To understand which partition of p has to be refined, we must carefully analyze the synchronized depth-first search. Recall that the refinement step is triggered once a word $w \in L(\mathcal{A}) \oplus L(\mathcal{A}^{\mathcal{R},p})$ with $w \in L(\mathcal{A}) \Leftrightarrow w \in L(\mathcal{R})$ is found (see above). As illustrated in Fig. 4, Weiss, Goldberg, and Yahav show that this situation arises when the search has identified two words $u_1, u_2 \in \Sigma^*$ such that

- u_1 and u_2 lead to the same state q in abstraction DFA $\mathcal{A}^{\mathcal{R},p}$; and
- u_1, u_2 lead to two distinct states $q_1 \neq q_2$ in the hypothesis DFA $\mathcal{A}$.

Since Angluin's algorithm always constructs hypothesis DFAs that are minimal for the language it has learned so far, q_1 and q_2 cannot be equivalent, and there must exist a separating word $v \in \Sigma^*$ such that $u_1 v \in L(\mathcal{A}) \Leftrightarrow u_2 v \notin L(\mathcal{A})$. However, $u_1 v \in L(\mathcal{A}^{\mathcal{R},p}) \Leftrightarrow u_2 v \in L(\mathcal{A}^{\mathcal{R},p})$ since u_1 and u_2 lead to the same state q in $\mathcal{A}^{\mathcal{R},p}$.

In the situation of Fig. 4, the synchronized search performs two membership queries with $u_1 v$ and $u_2 v$. However, we already know that $\mathcal{A}$ and $\mathcal{R}$ agree on

both u_1v and u_2v—otherwise, one of them would have been returned as a counterexample, avoiding the refinement step. Hence, the DFA $\mathcal{A}^{\mathcal{R},p}$ is incorrect, and
we obtain $w = u_iv$ for the unique $i \in \{1,2\}$ with $u_iv \in L(\mathcal{A}) \oplus L(\mathcal{A}^{\mathcal{R},p})$.

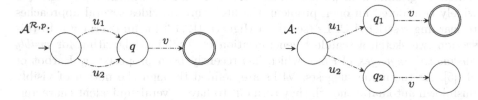

Fig. 4. Illustration of the situation arising when refining the partintioning function p

Let $h_1 = f(h_0, u_1) \in \mathbb{R}^\ell$ and $h_2 = f(h_0, u_2) \in \mathbb{R}^\ell$ now be the states of $\mathcal{R}$
reached after reading u_1 and u_2, respectively. Since u_1 and u_2 lead to the same
state in $\mathcal{A}^{\mathcal{R},p}$, we know that $p(u_1) = p(u_2)$. However, as shown in Fig. 4, this
is incorrect, and the partition $p(u_1) = p(u_2)$ needs to be split because it is too
coarse (causing the state q in $\mathcal{A}^{\mathcal{R},p}$ to be refined). To this end, Weiss, Goldberg,
and Yahav use a Support Vector Machine (SVM) classifier [6] with a radial basis
function kernel. The choice of SVM is motivated by their maximum-margin
property, meaning that they seek to find a decision boundary that maximizes
the margin between h_1 and h_2.

Since RNNs are more expressive than regular languages, the refinement step
can be necessary an infinite number of times, causing the hypothesis DFA $\mathcal{A}$ and
the abstraction DFA $\mathcal{A}^{\mathcal{R},p}$ to grow indefinitely. To counter this problem, Weiss,
Goldberg, and Yahav place a time or size limit on the interaction between the
learner and teacher, after which the teacher replies "yes" and the last hypothesis DFA $\mathcal{A}$ is returned. The authors observe empirically that these DFAs still
generalize well to their respective networks [32].

Finally, it is worth pointing out that Weiss, Goldberg, and Yahav have generalized the work presented in this section to a probabilistic setting under noise, in
which they propose a modification of Angluin's L* algorithm for learning probabilistic DFAs [34]. In addition, there exist several other approaches to extract
finite-state machines from recurrent neural networks [4,16,25]. While these works
present many vital insights into the topic, we skip an in-depth discussion here.
Instead, let us now turn to model learning techniques that follow a novel trend
in explainable artificial intelligence and learn models in the form of formal grammars.

4   Explainability Beyond Regular Languages

As Weiss et al. [33] point out, RNNs can simulate several types of counters or
stacks. The high expressive power of RNNs and their applicability in natural
language processing motivate extensions of the inference techniques described

above beyond the class of regular languages. Since explainability becomes more critical the more expressive the models are, it is worth representing the languages of RNNs with human-readable grammars.

Grammatical inference for context-free languages (CFLs), which are represented by grammars or pushdown automata, has a long tradition. Though it is widely considered an open problem, the literature provides several approaches to learning restricted CFLs (see de la Higuera [12,13] for an overview). In this section, we sketch a seamless generalization of Angluin's algorithm for *visibly pushdown languages (VPLs)*, which has recently been proposed by Barbot et al. [5]. As the name suggests, VPLs are defined through the notion of visibly pushdown automata, though they turn out to have several equivalent characterizations. Examples include Monadic Second-Order Logic or specific context-free grammars [2] (we come back to this point shortly). VPLs reside strictly between regular languages and deterministic CFLs. They enjoy a close link with regular tree languages, making them just as robust.

The key feature of VPLs is that the given input alphabet Σ is partitioned into *push*, *pop*, and *internal* letters, which determines—once and for all—the effect on the pushdown stack: (i) along with a push letter, depending only on the current state, one stack symbol is pushed onto the stack; (ii) consuming a pop letter allows one to read, and will remove, the topmost stack symbol; and (iii) internal letters are read without touching the stack. Moreover, modifying the stack without consuming a letter is prohibited (i.e., λ-transitions are not allowed). A typical VPL is $\{a^n b^n \mid n \in \mathbb{N}\}$ with a being a push and b a pop symbol. By contrast, the CFL $\{a^n b a^n \mid n \in \mathbb{N}\}$, no matter what partitioning, is not a VPL (we leave it to the reader to verify this).

It is not hard to see that, over such an alphabet Σ, there are close connections between words and trees. This is illustrated in Fig. 5, where a and b are push letters, $\underline{a}$ and $\underline{b}$ are pop letters, and c is an internal letter. First, a word $w \in \Sigma^*$ determines a unique nesting structure that associates with every push position at most one pop position and vice versa (see Fig. 5a).[3] Second, omitting some of the direct-successor edges of the word reveals a tree $tree(w)$ over a suitable *ranked alphabet*, such as the one shown in Fig. 5b.

The set $tree(L) = \{tree(w) \mid w \in L\}$ of trees associated with a VPL L turns out to be a regular tree language. Therefore, a unique minimal deterministic bottom-up tree automaton exists for this language, which is the model that Barbot et al.'s algorithm infers. More precisely, Barbot et al. build on the tree-automata learning algorithm by Drewes and Högberg [8], an extension of L* to finite ranked trees. Note that this detour via tree-automata is necessary because visibly pushdown automata do not have a minimal canonical representation [1]. The learned tree automaton for $tree(L)$ can then be translated into a grammar, or a pushdown automaton, for L.

As the target device is a tree automaton representing the tree representation $tree(L)$ of the unknown word language $L \subseteq \Sigma^*$, a membership query is asked in

---

[3] For the sake of convenience, Barbot et al. [5] restrict their focus to *well-formed words* as this entails a bijection between push and pop positions.

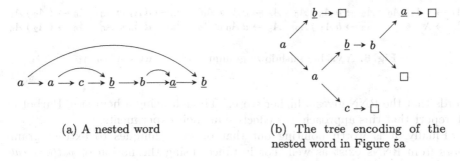

(a) A nested word

(b) The tree encoding of the nested word in Figure 5a

Fig. 5. A nested word (left) and its tree encoding (right)

terms of a tree t. However, the teacher still expects words and word languages as queries. Accordingly, we implement the following main changes to the general learning setup of Fig. 1 (on Page 5):

- The target language being of the form $tree(L)$, queries for trees that are not of the form $tree(w)$ with $w \in \Sigma^*$ can directly be answered negatively.
- For a membership query of the form $tree(w)$ with $w \in \Sigma^*$, it is actually this *unique* w that is sent to the teacher. The learner applies the outcome of the query to $tree(w)$ and refines its data structure accordingly.
- A hypothesis tree automaton is transformed into a model representing the encoded visibly pushdown language. In particular, an equivalence query can be asked in terms of a visibly pushdown automaton or visibly pushdown grammar. It practical cases, however, it may also be possible to directly compare the tree automata hypothesis to the given black-box system.

When restricting to well-formed words, a visibly pushdown grammar generates a matching pair of push and pop letters (i.e., in one rule). For example, consider the context-free grammar

$$S \rightarrow \alpha A \beta \quad A \rightarrow \alpha A \beta \mid AA \mid \lambda$$

with $\alpha = \langle abcd$ and $\beta = wxyz \rangle$, where A is a non-terminal symbol, $\langle, a, b, c, d$ are push letters, and $w, x, y, z, \rangle$ are pop letters. This grammar generates a VPL L that is equivalent to the visibly pushdown grammar given in Fig. 6. It is worth pointing out that the grammar in Fig. 6 was automatically inferred by Barbot et al.'s algorithm [5] from an RNN trained on sample words for L.

As in the case of finite automata, a significant challenge remains the equivalence query, which has to check whether a hypothesis approximates the RNN good enough. Barbot et al. [5] complement the statistical approach described in Sect. 3 with an A*-based search [11] to find counterexample words that the RNN accepts but that are currently not contained in the hypothesis language. The underlying idea is to explore the prefix tree Σ^* while giving preference to

$$A_1 \rightarrow \langle A_2 \rangle A_0 \quad A_2 \rightarrow a A_3 z A_0 \quad A_4 \rightarrow c A_5 x A_0 \quad A_5 \rightarrow d A_1 w A_0 \quad A_6 \rightarrow \langle A_2 \rangle A_1$$
$$A_0 \rightarrow \lambda \qquad\quad A_3 \rightarrow b A_4 y A_0 \quad A_5 \rightarrow d A_0 w A_0 \quad A_5 \rightarrow d A_6 w A_0 \quad A_6 \rightarrow \langle A_2 \rangle A_6$$

Fig. 6. A visibly pushdown grammar with start symbol A_1

words that the RNN gives a higher score.[4] Though being a heuristic, Barbot et al. report that this approach was effective in their experiments.

Finally, it is worth pointing out that other techniques to extract grammars from RNNs exist as well. For instance, using the notion of *pattern rule sets (PRSs)*, Yellin and Weiss [36] have devised an algorithm to extract grammars from RNNs for a subclass of context-free languages that is orthogonal to VPLs.

5   Conclusion

Model learning has become a valuable tool for establishing the correctness of systems, especially when a system is highly complex or only accessible as a black box. This paper has focussed on recurrent neural networks (RNNs), an important class of artificial neural networks for sequential data, and surveyed various model learning techniques for this class. Most of these techniques share the idea of using Angluin's L* algorithm to learn a finite-state model from an RNN, but they differ on their specific implementation of the equivalence queries. Furthermore, we have surveyed a learning technique that follows a novel trend in explainable artificial intelligence and learns models in the form of formal grammars.

While model learning promises an effective way to prove artificial intelligence correct, it is often not clear what the term "correctness" actually means in this context: the popularity of machine learning stems from the fact that no formal specification exists, which renders traditional verification seemingly inappropriate [20]. Thus, future work on verifying artificial intelligence cannot just focus on the algorithmic aspects of verifying intelligent systems but must also explore novel ways to specify their correctness formally [29,35].

References

1. Alur, R., Kumar, V., Madhusudan, P., Viswanathan, M.: Congruences for visibly pushdown languages. In: Caires, L., Italiano, G.F., Monteiro, L., Palamidessi, C., Yung, M. (eds.) ICALP 2005. LNCS, vol. 3580, pp. 1102–1114. Springer, Heidelberg (2005). https://doi.org/10.1007/11523468_89
2. Alur, R., Madhusudan, P.: Adding nesting structure to words. J. ACM **56**(3), 16:1–16:43 (2009). https://doi.org/10.1145/1516512.1516518

---

[4] Here, we assume that the acceptance function $g \colon \mathbb{R}^\ell \rightarrow \{0,1\}$ of the given RNN is obtained as the composition of a function *score* $\colon \mathbb{R}^\ell \rightarrow \mathbb{R}$ and a threshold function *thr* $\colon \mathbb{R} \rightarrow \{0,1\}$ such that, for a given threshold $\tau \in \mathbb{R}$, we have $thr(x) = 1$ iff $x \geq \tau$.

3. Angluin, D.: Learning regular sets from queries and counterexamples. Inf. Comput. **75**(2), 87–106 (1987). https://doi.org/10.1016/0890-5401(87)90052-6
4. Ayache, S., Eyraud, R., Goudian, N.: Explaining black boxes on sequential data using weighted automata. In: Unold, O., Dyrka, W., Wieczorek, W. (eds.) Proceedings of the 14th International Conference on Grammatical Inference, ICGI 2018, Wrocław, Poland, 5–7 September 2018. Proceedings of Machine Learning Research, vol. 93, pp. 81–103. PMLR (2018). http://proceedings.mlr.press/v93/ayache19a.html
5. Barbot, B., Bollig, B., Finkel, A., Haddad, S., Khmelnitsky, I., Leucker, M., Neider, D., Roy, R., Ye, L.: Extracting context-free grammars from recurrent neural networks using tree-automata learning and a* search. In: Chandlee, J., Eyraud, R., Heinz, J., Jardine, A., van Zaanen, M. (eds.) Proceedings of the Fifteenth International Conference on Grammatical Inference. Proceedings of Machine Learning Research, vol. 153, pp. 113–129. PMLR, 23–27 August 2021. https://proceedings.mlr.press/v153/barbot21a.html
6. Boser, B.E., Guyon, I., Vapnik, V.: A training algorithm for optimal margin classifiers. In: Haussler, D. (ed.) Proceedings of the Fifth Annual ACM Conference on Computational Learning Theory, COLT 1992, Pittsburgh, PA, USA, 27–29 July 1992, pp. 144–152. ACM (1992). https://doi.org/10.1145/130385.130401
7. Cho, K., et al.: Learning phrase representations using RNN encoder-decoder for statistical machine translation. In: Moschitti, A., Pang, B., Daelemans, W. (eds.) Proceedings of the 2014 Conference on Empirical Methods in Natural Language Processing, EMNLP 2014, 25–29 October 2014, Doha, Qatar, A Meeting of SIGDAT, a Special Interest Group of the ACL, pp. 1724–1734. ACL (2014). https://doi.org/10.3115/v1/d14-1179
8. Drewes, F., Högberg, J.: Query learning of regular tree languages: How to avoid dead states. Theory Comput. Syst. **40**(2), 163–185 (2007). https://doi.org/10.1007/s00224-005-1233-3
9. Eisner, C., Fisman, D.: A Practical Introduction to PSL. Series on Integrated Circuits and Systems. Springer, Heidelberg (2006). https://doi.org/10.1007/978-0-387-36123-9
10. Garavel, H., Beek, M.H., Pol, J.: The 2020 expert survey on formal methods. In: ter Beek, M.H., Ničković, D. (eds.) FMICS 2020. LNCS, vol. 12327, pp. 3–69. Springer, Cham (2020). https://doi.org/10.1007/978-3-030-58298-2_1
11. Hart, P.E., Nilsson, N.J., Raphael, B.: A formal basis for the heuristic determination of minimum cost paths. IEEE Trans. Syst. Sci. Cybern. **4**(2), 100–107 (1968). https://doi.org/10.1109/TSSC.1968.300136
12. de la Higuera, C.: A bibliographical study of grammatical inference. Pattern Recognit. **38**(9), 1332–1348 (2005). https://doi.org/10.1016/j.patcog.2005.01.003
13. de la Higuera, C.: Grammatical Inference. Cambridge University Press, Cambridge (2010). https://doi.org/10.1017/CBO9781139194655
14. Hochreiter, S., Schmidhuber, J.: Long short-term memory. Neural Comput. **9**(8), 1735–1780 (1997). https://doi.org/10.1162/neco.1997.9.8.1735
15. Hoeffding, W.: Probability inequalities for sums of bounded random variables. J. Am. Stat. Assoc. **58**(301), 13–30 (1963). https://doi.org/10.2307/2282952
16. Jacobsson, H.: Rule extraction from recurrent neural networks: A taxonomy and review. Neural Comput. **17**(6), 1223–1263 (2005). https://doi.org/10.1162/0899766053630350
17. Kearns, M.J., Vazirani, U.V.: An Introduction to Computational Learning Theory. MIT Press, Cambridge (1994). https://doi.org/10.7551/mitpress/3897.001.0001

18. Khmelnitsky, I., et al.: Property-directed verification and robustness certification of recurrent neural networks. In: Hou, Z., Ganesh, V. (eds.) ATVA 2021. LNCS, vol. 12971, pp. 364–380. Springer, Cham (2021). https://doi.org/10.1007/978-3-030-88885-5_24

19. Legay, A., Lukina, A., Traonouez, L.M., Yang, J., Smolka, S.A., Grosu, R.: Statistical model checking. In: Steffen, B., Woeginger, G. (eds.) Computing and Software Science. LNCS, vol. 10000, pp. 478–504. Springer, Cham (2019). https://doi.org/10.1007/978-3-319-91908-9_23

20. Leucker, M.: Formal verification of neural networks? In: Carvalho, G., Stolz, V. (eds.) SBMF 2020. LNCS, vol. 12475, pp. 3–7. Springer, Cham (2020). https://doi.org/10.1007/978-3-030-63882-5_1

21. Liu, B.: Sentiment analysis and subjectivity. In: Indurkhya, N., Damerau, F.J. (eds.) Handbook of Natural Language Processing, 2nd edn., pp. 627–666. Chapman and Hall/CRC (2010). http://www.crcnetbase.com/doi/abs/10.1201/9781420085938-c26

22. Mayr, F., Visca, R., Yovine, S.: On-the-fly black-box probably approximately correct checking of recurrent neural networks. In: Holzinger, A., Kieseberg, P., Tjoa, A.M., Weippl, E. (eds.) CD-MAKE 2020. LNCS, vol. 12279, pp. 343–363. Springer, Cham (2020). https://doi.org/10.1007/978-3-030-57321-8_19

23. Mayr, F., Yovine, S.: Regular inference on artificial neural networks. In: Holzinger, A., Kieseberg, P., Tjoa, A.M., Weippl, E. (eds.) CD-MAKE 2018. LNCS, vol. 11015, pp. 350–369. Springer, Cham (2018). https://doi.org/10.1007/978-3-319-99740-7_25

24. Mayr, F., Yovine, S., Visca, R.: Property checking with interpretable error characterization for recurrent neural networks. Mach. Learn. Knowl. Extr. 3(1), 205–227 (2021). https://doi.org/10.3390/make3010010

25. Okudono, T., Waga, M., Sekiyama, T., Hasuo, I.: Weighted automata extraction from recurrent neural networks via regression on state spaces. In: The Thirty-Fourth AAAI Conference on Artificial Intelligence, AAAI 2020, The Thirty-Second Innovative Applications of Artificial Intelligence Conference, IAAI 2020, The Tenth AAAI Symposium on Educational Advances in Artificial Intelligence, EAAI 2020, New York, NY, USA, 7–12 February 2020, pp. 5306–5314. AAAI Press (2020). https://ojs.aaai.org/index.php/AAAI/article/view/5977

26. Omlin, C.W., Giles, C.L.: Extraction of rules from discrete-time recurrent neural networks. Neural Netw. 9(1), 41–52 (1996). https://doi.org/10.1016/0893-6080(95)00086-0

27. Pnueli, A.: The temporal logic of programs. In: 18th Annual Symposium on Foundations of Computer Science, Providence, Rhode Island, USA, 31 October–1 November 1977, pp. 46–57. IEEE Computer Society (1977). https://doi.org/10.1109/SFCS.1977.32

28. Rivest, R.L., Schapire, R.E.: Inference of finite automata using homing sequences. Inf. Comput. 103(2), 299–347 (1993). https://doi.org/10.1006/inco.1993.1021

29. Seshia, S.A., et al.: Formal specification for deep neural networks. In: Lahiri, S.K., Wang, C. (eds.) ATVA 2018. LNCS, vol. 11138, pp. 20–34. Springer, Cham (2018). https://doi.org/10.1007/978-3-030-01090-4_2

30. Vaandrager, F.W.: Model learning. Commun. ACM 60(2), 86–95 (2017). https://doi.org/10.1145/2967606

31. Valiant, L.G.: A theory of the learnable. Commun. ACM 27(11), 1134–1142 (1984). https://doi.org/10.1145/1968.1972

32. Weiss, G., Goldberg, Y., Yahav, E.: Extracting automata from recurrent neural networks using queries and counterexamples. In: Dy, J.G., Krause, A. (eds.) Proceedings of the 35th International Conference on Machine Learning, ICML 2018, Stockholmsmässan, Stockholm, Sweden, 10–15 July 2018. Proceedings of Machine Learning Research, vol. 80, pp. 5244–5253. PMLR (2018). http://proceedings.mlr.press/v80/weiss18a.html

33. Weiss, G., Goldberg, Y., Yahav, E.: On the practical computational power of finite precision RNNs for language recognition. In: Gurevych, I., Miyao, Y. (eds.) Proceedings of the 56th Annual Meeting of the Association for Computational Linguistics, ACL 2018, Melbourne, Australia, 15–20 July 2018, Volume 2: Short Papers, pp. 740–745. Association for Computational Linguistics (2018). https://doi.org/10.18653/v1/P18-2117

34. Weiss, G., Goldberg, Y., Yahav, E.: Learning deterministic weighted automata with queries and counterexamples. In: Wallach, H.M., Larochelle, H., Beygelzimer, A., d'Alché-Buc, F., Fox, E.B., Garnett, R. (eds.) Advances in Neural Information Processing Systems 32: Annual Conference on Neural Information Processing Systems 2019, NeurIPS 2019, 8–14 December 2019, Vancouver, BC, Canada, pp. 8558–8569 (2019). https://proceedings.neurips.cc/paper/2019/hash/d3f93e7766e8e1b7ef66dfdd9a8be93b-Abstract.html

35. Xie, X., Kersting, K., Neider, D.: Neuro-symbolic verification of deep neural networks. In: Proceedings of the Thirty-First International Joint Conference on Artificial Intelligence, IJCAI 2022. ijcai.org (2022, to appear). https://doi.org/10.48550/arXiv.2203.00938

36. Yellin, D.M., Weiss, G.: Synthesizing context-free grammars from recurrent neural networks. In: Groote, J.F., Larsen, K.G. (eds.) TACAS 2021. LNCS, vol. 12651, pp. 351–369. Springer, Cham (2021). https://doi.org/10.1007/978-3-030-72016-2_19

Back-and-Forth in Space: On Logics and Bisimilarity in Closure Spaces

Vincenzo Ciancia[1], Diego Latella[1]([✉]), Mieke Massink[1], and Erik P. de Vink[2]

[1] CNR-ISTI, Pisa, Italy
{V.Ciancia,D.Latella,M.Massink}@cnr.it
[2] Eindhoven University of Technology, Eindhoven, The Netherlands
evink@win.tue.nl

Abstract. We adapt the standard notion of bisimilarity for topological models to closure models and refine it for quasi-discrete closure models. We also define an additional, weaker notion of bisimilarity that is based on paths in space and expresses a form of *conditional* reachability in a way that is reminiscent of *Stuttering Equivalence* on transition systems. For each bisimilarity we provide a characterisation with respect to a suitable spatial logic.

Keywords: Closure Spaces · Topological Spaces · Spatial Logics · Spatial Bisimilarities · Stuttering Equivalence

1 Introduction

The use of modal logics for the description of properties of topological spaces—where a point in space satisfies formula $\diamond\,\Phi$ whenever it belongs to the *topological closure* of the set $[\![\Phi]\!]$ of the points satisfying formula Φ—has a well established tradition, dating back to the fourties, and has given rise to the research area of *Spatial Logics* (see e.g. [5]). More recently, the class of underlying models of space have been extended to include, for instance, *closure spaces*, a generalisation of topological spaces (see e.g. [20]). The relevant logics have been extended accordingly. The approach has been enriched with algorithms for spatial (and spatio-temporal) logic *model checking* [13,14] and associated tools [4,11,12,23,24], and has been applied in various domains, such as bike-sharing [17], Turing patterns [30], medical image analysis [2–4,10]. An example of the latter is shown in Fig. 1, where the segmentation of a nevus (Fig. 1a) and a segmentation of a cross-section of brain grey matter (Fig. 1b) are presented. The original manual segmentation of both the nevus [29] and the grey matter [1] is shown in blue, while that resulting using spatial model checking is shown in cyan for the nevus

Research partially supported by the MIUR Project PRIN 2017FTXR7S "IT-MaTTerS". The authors are listed in alphabetical order; they contributed to this work equally.

and in red for grey matter. As the figures show, the manual segmentation of the nevus and that obtained using spatial model-checking have a very good correspondence; those of the grey matter coincide almost completely, so that very little blue is visible.

Notions of spatial bisimilarity have been proposed as well, and their potential for model minimisation plays an important role in the context of model-checking optimisation. Consequently, a key question, when reasoning about modal logics and their models, is the relationship between logical equivalences and notions of bisimilarity on their models.

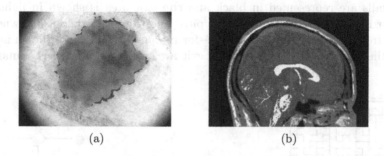

(a)   (b)

Fig. 1. Segmentation of (a) nevus and (b) grey matter in the brain.

In this paper we study three different notions of bisimilarity for closure models, i.e. models based on closure spaces. The first one is *closure model bisimilarity* (CM-bisimilarity for short). This bisimilarity is an adaptation for closure models of classical *topo-bisimilarity* for topological models [5]. The former uses the interior operator where topo-bisimilarity uses open sets. Actually, due to monotonicity of the interior operator, CM-bisimilarity is an instantiation to closure models of *monotonic bisimulation* on neighbourhood models [6,25,27].

We provide a logical characterisation of CM-bisimilarity, using Infinitary Modal Logic, a modal logic with infinite conjunction [8].

We show that, for *quasi-discrete* closure models, i.e. closure models where every point has a minimal neighbourhood, CM-bisimilarity gets a considerably simpler definition—based on the the closure operator instead of the interior operator—that is reminiscent of the definition of bisimilarity for transition systems. The advantage of the direct use of the closure operator, which is the foundational operator of closure spaces, is given by its intuitive interpretation in quasi-discrete closure models that makes several proofs simpler. We then present a refinement of CM-bisimilarity, specialised for *quasi-discrete* closure models. In *quasi-discrete* closure spaces, the closure of a set of points—and so also its interior—can be expressed using an underlying binary relation; this gives rise to both a *direct* closure and interior of a set, and a *converse* closure and interior, the latter being obtained using the inverse of the binary relation. This, in turn, induces a refined notion of bisimilarity, *CM-bisimilarity with converse*, CMC-bisimilarity, which is shown to be strictly stronger than CM-bisimilarity. We also present a closure-based definition for CMC-bisimilarity [15]. Interestingly, the latter resembles *Strong Back-and-Forth bisimilarity* proposed by De Nicola, Montanari and Vaandrager in [19].

We extend the Infinitary Modal Logic with the converse of its unary modal operator and show that the resulting logic characterises CMC-bisimilarity.

CM-bisimilarity, and CMC-bisimilarity, play an important role as they are the closure model counterpart of classical topo-bisimilarity. On the other hand, they turn out to be too strong, when considering intuitive relations on space, such as scaling or reachability, that may be useful when dealing with models representing images[1]. Consider, for instance, the image of a maze in Fig. 2a, where walls are represented in black and the exit area is shown in light grey (the floor is represented in white). A typical question one would ask is whether, starting from a given point (i.e. pixel)—for instance one of those shown in dark grey in the picture—one can reach the exit area, at the border of the image.

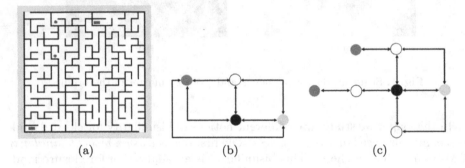

(a)   (b)   (c)

Fig. 2. A maze (a) and its path- and CoPa-minimal models ((b) and (c))

Essentially, we are interested in those paths in the picture, rooted at dark grey points, leading to light grey points *passing only* through white points. In [18] we introduced path-bisimilarity; it requires that, in order for two points to be equivalent, for every path rooted in one point there must be a path rooted in the other point and the end-points of the two paths must be bisimilar. Path-bisimilarity is too weak; nothing whatsoever is required about the internal structure of the relevant paths. For instance, Fig. 2b shows the minimal model for the image of the maze shown in Fig. 2a according to path-bisimilarity. We see that all dark grey points are equivalent and so are all white points. In other words, we are unable to distinguish those dark grey (white) points from which one can reach an exit from those from which one cannot. So, we look for *reachability* of bisimilar points by means of paths over the underlying space. Such reachability is not unconditional; we want the relevant paths to share some common structure. For that purpose, we resort to a notion of "compatibility" between relevant paths

---

[1] Images can be modeled as quasi-discrete closure spaces where the underlying relation is a pixel/voxel adjacency relation; see [2–4,10] for details.

that essentially requires each of them to be composed by a sequence of non-empty "zones", with the total number of zones in each of the paths being the same, while the length of each zone being arbitrary; each element of one path in a given zone is required to be related by the bisimulation to all the elements in the corresponding zone in the other path. This idea of compatibility gives rise to the third notion of bisimulation we present in this paper, namely *Compatible Path bisimulation*, CoPa-bisimulation. We show that, for quasi-discrete closure models, CoPa-bisimulation is strictly weaker than CMC-bisimilarity[2]. Figure 2c shows the minimal model for the image of the maze shown in Fig. 2 according to CoPa-bisimilarity. We see that, in this model, dark grey points from which one can reach light grey ones passing only by white points are distinguished from those from which one cannot. Similarly, white points through which an exit can be reached from a dark grey point are distinguished both from those that can't be reached from dark grey points and from those through which no light grey point can be reached.

We provide a logical characterisation of CoPa-bisimularity too. The notion of CoPa-bisimulation is reminiscent of that of the *Equivalence with respect to Stuttering* for transition systems [9,22], although in a different context and with different definitions as well as different underlying notions. The latter, in fact, is defined via a convergent sequence of relations and makes use of a different notion of path than the one of CS used in this paper. Finally, stuttering equivalence is focussed on CTL/CTL*, which implies a flow of time with single past (i.e. trees), which is not the case for structures representing space.

The paper is organised as follows: after having settled the context and offered some preliminary notions and definitions in Sect. 2, in Sect. 3 we present CM-bisimilarity. Section 4 deals with CMC-bisimularity. Section 5 addresses CoPa-bisimilarity. We conclude the paper with Sect. 6.

2   Preliminaries

In this paper, given a set X, $\mathcal{P}(X)$ denotes the powerset of X; for $Y \subseteq X$ we use $\overline{Y}$ to denote $X \setminus Y$, i.e. the complement of Y. For a function $f : X \to Y$ and $A \subseteq X$, we let $f(A)$ be defined as $\{f(a) \,|\, a \in A\}$. We briefly recall several definitions and results on closure spaces, most of which are taken from [20].

Definition 1 (Closure Space – CS). *A closure space, CS for short, is a pair $(X, \mathcal{C})$ where X is a non-empty set (of points) and $\mathcal{C} : \mathcal{P}(X) \to \mathcal{P}(X)$ is a function satisfying the following axioms: (i) $\mathcal{C}(\emptyset) = \emptyset$; (ii) $A \subseteq \mathcal{C}(A)$ for all $A \subseteq X$; and (iii) $\mathcal{C}(A_1 \cup A_2) = \mathcal{C}(A_1) \cup \mathcal{C}(A_2)$ for all $A_1, A_2 \subseteq X$.* •

The structures defined by Definition 1 are often known as *Čech Closure Spaces* [33] and provide a convenient common framework for the study of several different kinds of spatial models, both discrete and continuous [31]. In particular, topological spaces coincide with the sub-class of CSs that satisfy the *idempotence* axiom $\mathcal{C}(\mathcal{C}(A)) = \mathcal{C}(A)$.

---

[2] CoPa-bisimilarity is stronger than path-bisimilarity (see [18] for details).

The *interior* operator is the dual of closure: $\mathcal{I}(A) = \overline{\mathcal{C}(\overline{A})}$. It holds that $\mathcal{I}(X) = X$, $\mathcal{I}(A) \subseteq A$, and $\mathcal{I}(A_1 \cap A_2) = \mathcal{I}(A_1) \cap \mathcal{I}(A_2)$. A *neighbourhood* of a point $x \in X$ is any set $A \subseteq X$ such that $x \in \mathcal{I}(A)$. A minimal neighbourhood of a point x is a neighbourhood A of x such that $A \subseteq A'$ for every other neighbourhood A' of x. We recall that the closure operator, and consequently the interior operator, is monotonic: if $A_1 \subseteq A_2$ then $\mathcal{C}(A_1) \subseteq \mathcal{C}(A_2)$ and $\mathcal{I}(A_1) \subseteq \mathcal{I}(A_2)$. We have occasion to use the following property of closure spaces[3]:

Lemma 1. *Let $(X, \mathcal{C})$ be a CS. For $x \in X$, $A \subseteq X$, it holds that $x \in \mathcal{C}(A)$ iff $U \cap A \neq \emptyset$ for each neighbourhood U of x.* □

Definition 2 (Quasi-discrete CS – QdCS). *A quasi-discrete closure space is a CS $(X, \mathcal{C})$ such that any of the two following equivalent conditions holds: (i) each $x \in X$ has a minimal neighbourhood; or (ii) for each $A \subseteq X$ it holds that $\mathcal{C}(A) = \bigcup_{x \in A} \mathcal{C}(\{x\})$.* •

Given a relation $R \subseteq X \times X$, define the function $\mathcal{C}_R : \mathcal{P}(X) \to \mathcal{P}(X)$ as follows: for all $A \subseteq X$, $\mathcal{C}_R(A) = A \cup \{x \in X \mid a \in A \text{ exists s.t. } (a, x) \in R\}$. It is easy to see that, for any R, $\mathcal{C}_R$ satisfies all the axioms of Definition 1 and so $(X, \mathcal{C}_R)$ is a CS. The following theorem is a standard result in the theory of CSs [20]:

Theorem 1. *A CS $(X, \mathcal{C})$ is quasi-discrete if and only if there is a relation $R \subseteq X \times X$ such that $\mathcal{C} = \mathcal{C}_R$.* □

The above theorem implies that graphs coincide with QdCSs. We prefer to treat graphs as QdCSs since in this way we can formulate key definitions at the level of closure spaces and so we can have, in general, a uniform treatment for graphs and other kinds of models for space (e.g. topological spaces) [31]. Note furthermore that if X is finite, any closure space $(X, \mathcal{C})$ is quasi-discrete.

In the sequel, whenever a CS $(X, \mathcal{C})$ is quasi-discrete, we use $\vec{\mathcal{C}}$ to denote $\mathcal{C}_R$, and, consequently, $(X, \vec{\mathcal{C}})$ to denote the closure space, abstracting from the specification of R, when the latter is not necessary. Moreover, we let $\overleftarrow{\mathcal{C}}$ denote $\mathcal{C}_{R^{-1}}$. Finally, we use the simplified notation $\vec{\mathcal{C}}(x)$ for $\vec{\mathcal{C}}(\{x\})$ and similarly for $\overleftarrow{\mathcal{C}}(x)$. An example of the difference between $\vec{\mathcal{C}}$ and $\overleftarrow{\mathcal{C}}$ is shown in Fig. 3.

Regarding the interior operator $\mathcal{I}$, the notations $\vec{\mathcal{I}}$ and $\overleftarrow{\mathcal{I}}$ are defined in the obvious way: $\vec{\mathcal{I}}(A) = \overline{\vec{\mathcal{C}}(\overline{A})}$ and $\overleftarrow{\mathcal{I}}(A) = \overline{\overleftarrow{\mathcal{C}}(\overline{A})}$.

In the context of the present paper, *paths* over closure spaces play an important role. Therefore, we give a formal definition of paths based on continuous functions below.

Definition 3 (Continuous function). *Function $f : X_1 \to X_2$ is a continuous function from $(X_1, \mathcal{C}_1)$ to $(X_2, \mathcal{C}_2)$ if and only if for all sets $A \subseteq X_1$ we have $f(\mathcal{C}_1(A)) \subseteq \mathcal{C}_2(f(A))$.* •

---

[3] See also [33] Corollary 14.B.7.

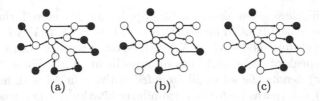

Fig. 3. In white: (a) a set of points A, (b) $\vec{\mathcal{C}}(A)$, and (c) $\breve{\mathcal{C}}(A)$.

Definition 4 (Index space). *An* index space *is a connected[4] CS* $(I,\mathcal{C})$ *equipped with a total order* $\leqslant \subseteq I \times I$ *with a bottom element* 0. *We often write* $\iota_1 < \iota_2$ *whenever* $\iota_1 \leqslant \iota_2$ *and* $\iota_1 \neq \iota_2$, (ι_1, ι_2) *for* $\{\iota \mid \iota_1 < \iota < \iota_2\}$, $[\iota_1, \iota_2)$ *for* $\{\iota \mid \iota_1 \leq \iota < \iota_2\}$, *and* $(\iota_1, \iota_2]$ *for* $\{\iota \mid \iota_1 < \iota \leq \iota_2\}$.   •

Definition 5 (Path). *A* path *in CS* $(X,\mathcal{C})$ *is a continuous function from an index space* $\mathcal{J} = (I, \mathcal{C}^{\mathcal{J}})$ *to* $(X,\mathcal{C})$. *A path* π *is* bounded *if there exists* $\ell \in I$ *such that* $\pi(\iota) = \pi(\ell)$ *for all* ι *such that* $\ell \leqslant \iota$; *we call the minimal such* ℓ *the* length *of* π, *written* $\mathtt{len}(\pi)$.   •

Particularly relevant in the present paper are *quasi-discrete* paths, i.e. paths having $(\mathbb{N}, \mathcal{C}_{\mathtt{succ}})$ as index space, where $\mathbb{N}$ is the set of natural numbers and $\mathtt{succ}$ is the *successor* relation $\mathtt{succ} = \{(m,n) \mid n = m + 1\}$.

The following lemmas state some useful properties of closure and interior operators as well as of paths.

Lemma 2. *For all QdCSs* $(X, \vec{\mathcal{C}})$, $A, A_1, A_2 \subseteq X, x_1, x_2 \in X$, *and* $\pi : \mathbb{N} \to X$ *the following holds:*

1. $x_1 \in \breve{\mathcal{C}}(\{x_2\})$ *if and only if* $x_2 \in \vec{\mathcal{C}}(\{x_1\})$;
2. $\breve{\mathcal{C}}(A) = \{x \mid x \in X \text{and exists } a \in A \text{ such that } a \in \vec{\mathcal{C}}(\{x\})\}$;
3. π *is a path over* X *if and only if for all* $j \neq 0$ *the following holds:*
   $\pi(j) \in \vec{\mathcal{C}}(\pi(j-1))$ *and* $\pi(j-1) \in \breve{\mathcal{C}}(\pi(j))$.   □

Lemma 3. *Let* $(X, \vec{\mathcal{C}})$ *be a QdCS. Then* $\vec{\mathcal{C}}(x) \subseteq A$ *iff* $x \in \breve{\mathcal{I}}(A)$ *and* $\breve{\mathcal{C}}(x) \subseteq A$ *iff* $x \in \vec{\mathcal{I}}(A)$, *for all* $x \in X$ *and* $A \subseteq X$.   □

In the sequel we will assume a set **AP** of *atomic proposition letters* is given and we introduce the notion of closure *model*.

Definition 6 (Closure model – CM). *A closure model, CM for short, is a tuple* $\mathcal{M} = (X, \mathcal{C}, \mathcal{V})$, *with* $(X, \mathcal{C})$ *a CS, and* $\mathcal{V} : \mathtt{AP} \to \mathcal{P}(X)$ *the (atomic proposition) valuation function, assigning to each* $p \in \mathtt{AP}$ *the set of points where* p *holds.*   •

---

[4] Given CS $(X,\mathcal{C})$, $A \subseteq X$ is *connected* if it is *not* the union of two non-empty separated sets. Two subsets $A_1, A_2 \subseteq X$ are called *separated* if $A_1 \cap \mathcal{C}(A_2) = \emptyset = \mathcal{C}(A_1) \cap A_2$. CS $(X,\mathcal{C})$ is *connected* if X is connected.

All the definitions given above for CSs apply to CMs as well; thus, a *quasi-discrete closure model* (QdCM for short) is a CM $\mathcal{M} = (X, \vec{\mathcal{C}}, \mathcal{V})$ where $(X, \vec{\mathcal{C}})$ is a QdCS. For a closure model $\mathcal{M} = (X, \mathcal{C}, \mathcal{V})$ we often write $x \in \mathcal{M}$ when $x \in X$. Similarly, we speak of paths in $\mathcal{M}$ meaning paths in $(X, \mathcal{C})$. For $x \in \mathcal{M}$, we let $\texttt{BPaths}^{\mathsf{F}}_{\mathcal{J}, \mathcal{M}}(x)$ denote the set of all *bounded* paths π in $\mathcal{M}$ with indices in $\mathcal{J}$, such that $\pi(0) = x$ (paths *rooted* in x); similarly $\texttt{BPaths}^{\mathsf{T}}_{\mathcal{J}, \mathcal{M}}(x)$ denotes the set of all *bounded* paths π in $\mathcal{M}$ with indices in $\mathcal{J}$, such that $\pi(\texttt{len}(\pi)) = x$ (paths *ending* in x). We refrain from writing the subscripts $\mathcal{J}, \mathcal{M}$ when not necessary.

In the sequel, for a logic $\mathcal{L}$, a formula $\Phi \in \mathcal{L}$, and a model $\mathcal{M} = (X, \mathcal{C}, \mathcal{V})$ we let $\llbracket \Phi \rrbracket^{\mathcal{M}}_{\mathcal{L}}$ denote the set $\{x \in X \mid \mathcal{M}, x \models_{\mathcal{L}} \Phi\}$ of all the points in $\mathcal{M}$ that satisfy Φ, where $\models_{\mathcal{L}}$ is the satisfaction relation for $\mathcal{L}$. For the sake of readability, we refrain from writing the subscript $_{\mathcal{L}}$ when this does not cause confusion.

3 Bisimilarity for Closure Models

In this section, we introduce the first notion of bisimilarity that we consider, namely CM-bisimilarity, for which we also provide a logical characterisation.

3.1 CM-bisimilarity

Definition 7. *Given a CM $\mathcal{M} = (X, \mathcal{C}, \mathcal{V})$, a symmetric relation $B \subseteq X \times X$ is a CM-bisimulation for $\mathcal{M}$ if, whenever $(x_1, x_2) \in B$, the following holds:*

1. *for all $p \in \mathsf{AP}$ we have $x_1 \in \mathcal{V}(p)$ if and only if $x_2 \in \mathcal{V}(p)$;*
2. *for all $S_1 \subseteq X$ such that $x_1 \in \mathcal{I}(S_1)$ exists $S_2 \subseteq X$ such that $x_2 \in \mathcal{I}(S_2)$ and for all $s_2 \in S_2$ exists $s_1 \in S_1$ such that $(s_1, s_2) \in B$.*

Two points $x_1, x_2 \in X$ are called CM-bisimilar in $\mathcal{M}$ if $(x_1, x_2) \in B$ for some CM-bisimulation B for $\mathcal{M}$. Notation, $x_1 \rightleftharpoons^{\mathcal{M}}_{\mathsf{CM}} x_2$. ●

The above notion is the natural adaptation for CMs of the notion of topo-bisimulation for topological models [5]. In such models the underlying set is equiped with a topology, i.e. a special case of a CS. For a topological model $\mathcal{M} = (X, \tau, \mathcal{V})$ with τ a topology on X the requirements for a relation $B \subseteq X \times X$ to be a topo-bisimulation are similar to those in Definition 7; see [5] for details.

3.2 Logical Characterisation of CM-bisimilarity

Next, we show that CM-bisimilarity is characterised by an infinitary version of Modal Logic, IML for short, where the classical modal operator $\diamond$ is interpreted as closure and is denoted by $\mathcal{N}$—for "near". We first recall the definition of IML [15], i.e. Modal Logic with infinite conjunction.

Definition 8. *The abstract language of IML is defined as follows:*

$$\Phi ::= p \mid \neg\Phi \mid \bigwedge_{i \in I} \Phi_i \mid \mathcal{N}\Phi$$

where p ranges over AP *and* I *ranges over a collection of index sets.*

The satisfaction relation for all CMs $\mathcal{M}$, points $x \in \mathcal{M}$, and IML formulas Φ is recursively defined on the structure of Φ as follows:

$$\mathcal{M}, x \models_{\mathrm{IML}} p \qquad\qquad \Leftrightarrow x \in \mathcal{V}(p);$$
$$\mathcal{M}, x \models_{\mathrm{IML}} \neg\Phi \qquad \Leftrightarrow \mathcal{M}, x \models_{\mathrm{IML}} \Phi \text{ does not hold;}$$
$$\mathcal{M}, x \models_{\mathrm{IML}} \bigwedge_{i \in I} \Phi_i \Leftrightarrow \mathcal{M}, x \models_{\mathrm{IML}} \Phi_i \text{ for all } i \in I;$$
$$\mathcal{M}, x \models_{\mathrm{IML}} \mathcal{N}\Phi \qquad \Leftrightarrow x \in \mathcal{C}(\llbracket\Phi\rrbracket^{\mathcal{M}}). \qquad\qquad\bullet$$

Below we define IML-equivalence, i.e. the equivalence induced by IML.

Definition 9. *Given CM $\mathcal{M} = (X, \mathcal{C}, \mathcal{V})$, the equivalence relation $\simeq_{\mathrm{IML}}^{\mathcal{M}} \subseteq X \times X$ is defined as: $x_1 \simeq_{\mathrm{IML}}^{\mathcal{M}} x_2$ if and only if for all IML formulas Φ the following holds: $\mathcal{M}, x_1 \models_{\mathrm{IML}} \Phi$ if and only if $\mathcal{M}, x_2 \models_{\mathrm{IML}} \Phi$.* $\qquad\bullet$

It holds that IML-equivalence $\simeq_{\mathrm{IML}}^{\mathcal{M}}$ includes CM-bisimilarity.

Lemma 4. *For all points x_1, x_2 in a CM $\mathcal{M}$, if $x_1 \rightleftharpoons_{\mathrm{CM}}^{\mathcal{M}} x_2$ then $x_1 \simeq_{\mathrm{IML}}^{\mathcal{M}} x_2$.* $\quad\square$

The converse of the lemma follows from Lemma 5 below.

Lemma 5. *For a CM $\mathcal{M}$, it holds that $\simeq_{\mathrm{IML}}^{\mathcal{M}}$ is a CM-bisimulation for $\mathcal{M}$.* $\quad\square$

From this lemma we immediately obtain that $x_1 \simeq_{\mathrm{IML}}^{\mathcal{M}} x_2$ implies $x_1 \rightleftharpoons_{\mathrm{CM}}^{\mathcal{M}} x_2$, for all points x_1, x_2 in a CM $\mathcal{M}$. Summarizing, we get the following result.

Theorem 2. *For every CM $\mathcal{M}$ it holds that IML-equivalence $\simeq_{\mathrm{IML}}^{\mathcal{M}}$ coincides with CM-bisimilarity $\rightleftharpoons_{\mathrm{CM}}^{\mathcal{M}}$.* $\qquad\qquad\qquad\qquad\qquad\qquad\qquad\qquad\qquad\qquad\square$

4   CMC-bisimilarity for QdCMs

Definition 7 defines CM-bisimilarity in terms of the interior operator $\mathcal{I}$. In the case of QdCMs, an alternative formulation, exploiting the symmetric nature of the operators in such spaces, can be given that uses the closure operator explicitly and directly, as we will see below.

Definition 10. *Given a QdCM $\mathcal{M} = (X, \vec{\mathcal{C}}, \mathcal{V})$, a symmetric relation $B \subseteq X \times X$ is a CM-bisimulation for $\mathcal{M}$ if, whenever $(x_1, x_2) \in B$, the following holds:*

1. *for all $p \in$ AP we have $x_1 \in \mathcal{V}(p)$ if and only if $x_2 \in \mathcal{V}(p)$;*
2. *for all x_1' such that $x_1 \in \vec{\mathcal{C}}(x_1')$ exists x_2' with $x_2 \in \vec{\mathcal{C}}(x_2')$ and $(x_1', x_2') \in B$.* $\bullet$

The above definition is justified by the next lemma.

Lemma 6. *Let $\mathcal{M} = (X, \vec{\mathcal{C}}, \mathcal{V})$ be a QdCM and $B \subseteq X \times X$ a relation. It holds that B is a CM-bisimulation according to Definition 7 if and only if B is a CM-bisimulation according to Definition 10.* $\qquad\qquad\qquad\qquad\qquad\square$

As noted above, when dealing with QdCMs, we can exploit the symmetric nature of the operators in such spaces. Recall in fact that, whenever $\mathcal{M}$ is quasi-discrete, there are actually two interior functions, namely $\vec{\mathcal{I}}(S)$ and $\overleftarrow{\mathcal{I}}(S)$. It is then natural to exploit both functions for the definition of a notion of CM-bisimilarity specifically designed for QdCMs, namely CMC-bisimilarity, presented below.

4.1   CMC-bisimilarity for QdCMs

Definition 11. *Given QdCM* $\mathcal{M} = (X, \vec{\mathcal{C}}, \mathcal{V})$, *a symmetric relation* $B \subseteq X \times X$ *is a CMC-bisimulation for* $\mathcal{M}$ *if, whenever* $(x_1, x_2) \in B$, *the following holds:*

1. *for all* $p \in \mathtt{AP}$ *we have* $x_1 \in \mathcal{V}(p)$ *if and only if* $x_2 \in \mathcal{V}(p)$;
2. *for all* $S_1 \subseteq X$ *such that* $x_1 \in \vec{\mathcal{I}}(S_1)$ *exists* $S_2 \subseteq X$ *such that* $x_2 \in \vec{\mathcal{I}}(S_2)$ *and for all* $s_2 \in S_2$, *exists* $s_1 \in S_1$ *with* $(s_1, s_2) \in B$;
3. *for all* $S_1 \subseteq X$ *such that* $x_1 \in \overleftarrow{\mathcal{I}}(S_1)$ *exists* $S_2 \subseteq X$ *such that* $x_2 \in \overleftarrow{\mathcal{I}}(S_2)$ *and for all* $s_2 \in S_2$, *exists* $s_1 \in S_1$ *with* $(s_1, s_2) \in B$.

Two points $x_1, x_2 \in X$ *are called CMC-bisimilar in* $\mathcal{M}$, *if* $(x_1, x_2) \in B$ *for some CMC-bisimulation* B *for* $\mathcal{M}$. *Notation,* $x_1 \rightleftharpoons^{\mathcal{M}}_{\mathsf{CMC}} x_2$.   ●

For a QdCM $\mathcal{M}$, as for CM-bisimilarity, we have that CMC-bisimilarity $\rightleftharpoons_{\mathsf{CMC}}$ on $\mathcal{M}$ is a CMC-bisimulation itself, viz. the largest CMC-bisimulation for $\mathcal{M}$, thus including each CMC-bisimulation for $\mathcal{M}$. Also for CMC-bisimilarity, a formulation directly in terms of closures is possible.

Definition 12. *Given a QdCM* $\mathcal{M} = (X, \vec{\mathcal{C}}, \mathcal{V})$, *a symmetric relation* $B \subseteq X \times X$ *is a CMC-bisimulation for* $\mathcal{M}$ *if, whenever* $(x_1, x_2) \in B$, *the following holds:*

1. *for all* $p \in \mathtt{AP}$ *we have* $x_1 \in \mathcal{V}(p)$ *in and only if* $x_2 \in \mathcal{V}(p)$;
2. *for all* $x_1' \in \vec{\mathcal{C}}(x_1)$ *exists* $x_2' \in \vec{\mathcal{C}}(x_2)$ *such that* $(x_1', x_2') \in B$;
3. *for all* $x_1' \in \overleftarrow{\mathcal{C}}(x_1)$ *exists* $x_2' \in \overleftarrow{\mathcal{C}}(x_2)$ *such that* $(x_1', x_2') \in B$.   ●

The next lemma shows the interchangability of Definitions 11 and 12.

Lemma 7. *Let* $\mathcal{M} = (X, \vec{\mathcal{C}}, \mathcal{V})$ *be a QdCM and* $B \subseteq X \times X$ *a relation. It holds that* B *is a CMC-bisimulation according to Definition 11 if and only if* B *is a CMC-bisimulation according to Definition 12.*   □

Remark 1. Note the correspondence of criterium (3) of Definition 12 and criterium (2) of Definition 10. Recall that in the context of QdCMs we have that $x_1 \in \mathcal{C}(x_1')$ if and only if $x_1 \in \vec{\mathcal{C}}(x_1')$ if and only if $x_1' \in \overleftarrow{\mathcal{C}}(x_1)$—see Lemma 2(1).

Definition 12 was proposed originally in [15], in a slightly different form, and resembles (strong) Back-and-Forth bisimulation of [19], in particular for the presence of condition (3). Should we have deleted that condition, thus making our definition more similar to classical strong bisimulation for transition systems, we would have to consider points v_{12} and v_{22} of Fig. 4a bisimilar where $X = \{v_{11}, v_{12}, v_{21}, v_{22}\}$, $\vec{\mathcal{C}}(v_{11}) = \{v_{11}, v_{12}\}$, $\vec{\mathcal{C}}(v_{12}) = \{v_{12}\}$, $\vec{\mathcal{C}}(v_{21}) = \{v_{21}, v_{22}\}$, $\vec{\mathcal{C}}(v_{22}) = \{v_{22}\}$, $\mathcal{V}(w) = \{v_{11}\}, \mathcal{V}(b) = \{v_{21}\}$, and $\mathcal{V}(g) = \{v_{12}, v_{22}\}$, for the atomic propositions g, b, and w.

We instead want to consider them as not being bisimilar because they are in the closure of points that are *not* bisimilar, namely v_{11} and v_{21}. For instance, v_{21} might represent a poisoned physical location (whereas v_{11} is not poisoned) and so v_{22} should not be considered equivalent to v_{12} because the former can be reached (by poison aerosol) from the poisoned location while the latter cannot. The following proposition follows directly from the relevant definitions, keeping in mind that for QdCSs the interior operator $\mathcal{I}$ coincides with the operator $\vec{\mathcal{I}}$.

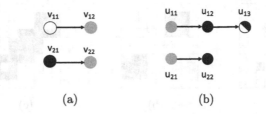

(a)   (b)

Fig. 4. v_{12} and v_{22} are not bisimilar (a); $u_{11} \rightleftharpoons_{\mathrm{CM}} u_{21}$ but $u_{11} \not\rightleftharpoons_{\mathrm{CMC}} u_{21}$ (b).

Proposition 1. *For x_1, x_2 in QdCM $\mathcal{M}$, if $x_1 \rightleftharpoons_{\mathrm{CMC}}^{\mathcal{M}} x_2$, then $x_1 \rightleftharpoons_{\mathrm{CM}}^{\mathcal{M}} x_2$.*   □

As can be expected, the converse of the proposition does *not* hold. A counter example to Proposition 1 is shown in Fig. 4b.

Here, $X = \{u_{11}, u_{12}, u_{13}, u_{21}, u_{22}\}$, $\mathcal{C}(u_{11}) = \{u_{11}, u_{12}\}$, $\mathcal{C}(u_{12}) = \{u_{12}, u_{13}\}$, $\mathcal{C}(u_{13}) = \{u_{13}\}$, $\mathcal{C}(u_{21}) = \{u_{21}, u_{22}\}$, $\mathcal{C}(u_{22}) = \{u_{22}\}$, and $\mathcal{V}(g) = \{u_{11}, u_{21}\}$, $\mathcal{V}(b) = \{u_{12}, u_{13}, u_{22}\}$, and $\mathcal{V}(w) = \{u_{13}\}$, for the atomic propositions g, b, and w.

It is easy to see, using Definition 10, that the symmetric closure of relation $B = \{(u_{11}, u_{21}), (u_{12}, u_{22})\}$ is a CM-bisimulation. Thus, we have $u_{11} \rightleftharpoons_{\mathrm{CM}} u_{21}$. Note, the checking of the various requirements does not involve the point u_{13} at all. However, there is no CMC-bisimulation containing the pair (u_{11}, u_{21}). In fact, any such relation would have to satisfy condition (2) of Definition 12. Since $u_{12} \in \vec{\mathcal{C}}(u_{11})$ we would have $(u_{12}, u_{21}) \in B$ or $(u_{12}, u_{22}) \in B$. Since $u_{13} \in \vec{\mathcal{C}}(u_{12})$, similarly, we would have that $(u_{13}, u_{21}) \in B$ or $(u_{13}, u_{22}) \in B$, because $\vec{\mathcal{C}}(u_{21}) = \{u_{21}, u_{22}\}$ and $\vec{\mathcal{C}}(u_{22}) = \{u_{22}\}$. However, $u_{13} \in \mathcal{V}(w)$ and neither $u_{21} \in \mathcal{V}(w)$, nor $u_{22} \in \mathcal{V}(w)$, violating requirement (1) of Definition 12, if $(u_{13}, u_{21}) \in B$ or $(u_{13}, u_{22}) \in B$.

4.2 Logical Characterisation of CMC-bisimilarity

In order to provide a logical characterisation of CMC-bisimilarity, we extend IML with a "converse" of its modal operator. The result is the *Infinitary Modal Logic with Converse* (IMLC), a logic with the two modalities $\vec{\mathcal{N}}$ and $\bar{\mathcal{N}}$ expressing *proximity*. For example, with reference to the QdCM shown in Fig. 5a—where points and atomic propositions are shown as grey-scale coloured squares and the underlying relation is orthodiagonal adjacency[5]—Figure 5b shows in black the points satisfying $\vec{\mathcal{N}}$black in the model shown in Fig. 5a.

Definition 13. *The abstract language of IML is defined as follows:*

$$\Phi ::= p \mid \neg\Phi \mid \bigwedge_{i \in I} \Phi_i \mid \vec{\mathcal{N}}\,\Phi \mid \bar{\mathcal{N}}\,\Phi.$$

where p ranges over AP and I ranges over a collection of index sets.

---

[5] In orthodiagonal adjacency, two squares are related if they share a face or a vertex.

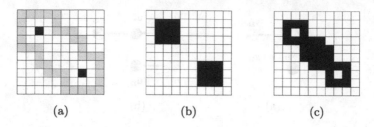

(a)	(b)	(c)

Fig. 5. A model (a). In black the points satisfying $\vec{\mathcal{N}}$black (b), and those satisfying $\vec{\zeta}$black[white] (c)

The satisfaction relation for all QdCMs $\mathcal{M}$, points $x \in \mathcal{M}$, and IMLC formulas Φ is defined recursively on the structure of Φ as follows:

$$
\begin{aligned}
\mathcal{M}, x \models_{\text{IMLC}} p &\Leftrightarrow x \in \mathcal{V}(p); \\
\mathcal{M}, x \models_{\text{IMLC}} \neg\Phi &\Leftrightarrow \mathcal{M}, x \models_{\text{IMLC}} \Phi \text{ does not hold}; \\
\mathcal{M}, x \models_{\text{IMLC}} \bigwedge_{i \in I} \Phi_i &\Leftrightarrow \mathcal{M}, x \models_{\text{IMLC}} \Phi_i \text{ for all } i \in I; \\
\mathcal{M}, x \models_{\text{IMLC}} \vec{\mathcal{N}}\Phi &\Leftrightarrow x \in \vec{\mathcal{C}}(\llbracket\Phi\rrbracket^{\mathcal{M}}); \\
\mathcal{M}, x \models_{\text{IMLC}} \tilde{\mathcal{N}}\Phi &\Leftrightarrow x \in \breve{\mathcal{C}}(\llbracket\Phi\rrbracket^{\mathcal{M}}).
\end{aligned}
$$

IMLC-equivalence is defined in the usual way:

Definition 14. *Given QdCM $\mathcal{M} = (X, \vec{\mathcal{C}}, \mathcal{V})$, the equivalence relation $\simeq_{\text{IMLC}}^{\mathcal{M}} \subseteq X \times X$ is defined as: $x_1 \simeq_{\text{IMLC}}^{\mathcal{M}} x_2$ if and only if for all IMLC formulas Φ the following holds: $\mathcal{M}, x_1 \models_{\text{IMLC}} \Phi$ if and only if $\mathcal{M}, x_2 \models_{\text{IMLC}} \Phi$.*

Next we derive two lemmas which are used to prove that CMC-bisimilarity and IMLC-equivalence coincide.

Lemma 8. *For x_1, x_2 in QdCM $\mathcal{M}$, if $x_1 \rightleftharpoons_{\text{CMC}}^{\mathcal{M}} x_2$ then $x_1 \simeq_{\text{IMLC}}^{\mathcal{M}} x_2$.* □

For what concerns the other direction, i.e. going from IMLC-equivalence to CMC-bisimilarity, we have the following result.

Lemma 9. *For a QdCM $\mathcal{M}$, $\simeq_{\text{IMLC}}^{\mathcal{M}}$ is a CMC-bisimulation for $\mathcal{M}$.* □

With the two lemmas above in place, we can establish the correspondence of CMC-bisimilarity and IMLC-equivalence.

Theorem 3. *For a QdCM $\mathcal{M}$ it holds that $\simeq_{\text{IMLC}}^{\mathcal{M}}$ coincides with $\rightleftharpoons_{\text{CMC}}^{\mathcal{M}}$.* □

Remark 2. In previous work of Ciancia et al., versions of the *Spatial Logic for Closure Spaces*, SLCS, have been defined that are based on the *surrounded* operator $\mathcal{S}$ and/or the *reachability* operator ρ (see e.g. [4,14,15,18]). A point x satisfies $\Phi_1 \mathcal{S} \Phi_2$ if it lays in an area whose points satisfy Φ_1, and that is delimited (i.e., surrounded) by points that satisfy Φ_2; x satisfies $\rho \Phi_1[\Phi_2]$ if there is a path rooted in

x that *can reach* a point satisfying Φ_1 and whose *internal* points—if any—satisfy Φ_2. In [4], it has been shown that $\mathcal{S}$ can be derived from the logical operator ρ; more specifically, $\Phi_1\,\mathcal{S}\,\Phi_2$ is equivalent to $\Phi_1 \wedge \neg\rho(\neg(\Phi_1 \vee \Phi_2))[\neg\Phi_2]$. Furthermore, for QdCM, ρ gives rise to two symmetric operators, namely $\vec{\rho}$—coinciding with ρ—and $\overleftarrow{\rho}$—meaning that x *can be reached* from a point satisfying Φ_1, via a path whose internal points satisfy Φ_2. It is easy to see that, for such spaces, $\vec{\mathcal{N}}\,\Phi$ $(\overleftarrow{\mathcal{N}}\,\Phi)$ is equivalent to $\vec{\rho}\,\Phi[\texttt{false}]$ $(\overleftarrow{\rho}\,\Phi[\texttt{false}])$ and that $\vec{\rho}\,\Phi_1[\Phi_2]$ $(\overleftarrow{\rho}\,\Phi_1[\Phi_2])$ is equivalent to a suitable combination of (possibly infinite) disjunctions and nested $\vec{\mathcal{N}}$ $(\overleftarrow{\mathcal{N}})$; the interested reader is referred to [16]. Thus, on QdCMs, IMLC and ISLCS—the infinitary version of SLCS [18]—share the same expressive power.

5   CoPa-Bisimilarity for QdCM

CM-bisimilarity, and its refinement CMC-bisimilarity, are a fundamental starting point for the study of spatial bisimulations due to their strong links to topo-bisimulation. On the other hand, they are rather fine-grained relations for reasoning about general properties of space. For instance, with reference to the model of Fig. 6a, where all black points satisfy only atomic proposition b while the grey ones satisfy only g, the point at the center of the model is *not* CMC-bisimilar to any other black point. This is because CMC-bisimilarity is based on the fact that points reachable "in one step" are taken into consideration, as it is clear also from Definition 12. This, in turn, gives bisimilarity a sort of "counting" power, that goes against the idea that, for instance, all black points in the model could be considered spatially equivalent. In fact, they are black and can reach black or grey points. Furthermore, they could be considered equivalent to the black point of a smaller model consisting of just one black and one grey point mutually connected—that would in fact be minimal.

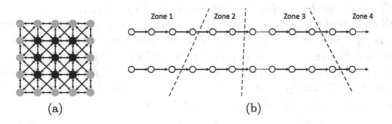

Fig. 6. A model (a); zones in paths (b).

In order to relax such "counting" capability of bisimilarity, one could think of considering *paths* instead of single "steps"; and in fact in [18] we introduced such a bisimilarity, called path-bisimilarity. The latter requires that, in order for two points to be equivalent, for every bounded path rooted in one point there must be a bounded path rooted in the other point and the end-points of the two paths must be bisimilar.

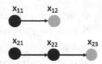

Fig. 7. $x_{11} \leftrightharpoons_{\text{CoPa}} x_{21}$ but $x_{11} \not\leftrightharpoons_{\text{CMC}} x_{21}$.

As we have briefly discussed in Sect. 1, however, path-bisimilarity is too weak. A deeper insight into the structure of paths is desirable as well as some, relatively high-level, requirements over them. For that purpose we resort to a notion of "compatibility" between relevant paths that essentially requires each of them be composed of a non-empty sequence of non-empty, adjacent "zones". More precisely, both paths under consideration in a transfer condition should share the same structure, as follows (see Fig. 6b):

- both paths are composed by a sequence of (non-empty) "zones";
- the number of zones should be the same in both paths, *but*
- the length of "corresponding" zones can be different, *as well as* the length of the two paths;
- *each* point in one zone of a path should be related by the bisimulation to *every* point in the corresponding zone of the other path.

This notion of compatibility gives rise to *Compatible Path bisimulation*, CoPa-bisimulation, defined below.

5.1   CoPa-bisimilarity

Definition 15. *Given CM* $\mathcal{M} = (X, \mathcal{C}, \mathcal{V})$ *and index space* $\mathcal{J} = (I, \mathcal{C}^{\mathcal{J}})$, *a symmetric relation* $B \subseteq X \times X$ *is a* CoPa-bisimulation *for* $\mathcal{M}$ *if, whenever* $(x_1, x_2) \in B$, *the following holds:*

1. *for all* $p \in \text{AP}$ *we have* $x_1 \in \mathcal{V}(p)$ *in and only if* $x_2 \in \mathcal{V}(p)$;
2. *for all* $\pi_1 \in \text{BPaths}^{\text{F}}{}_{\mathcal{J},\mathcal{M}}(x_1)$ *such that* $(\pi_1(i_1), x_2) \in B$ *for all* $i_1 \in [0, \text{len}(\pi_1))$ *there is* $\pi_2 \in \text{BPaths}^{\text{F}}{}_{\mathcal{J},\mathcal{M}}(x_2)$ *such that the following holds:* $(x_1, \pi_2(i_2)) \in B$ *for all* $i_2 \in [0, \text{len}(\pi_2))$, *and* $(\pi_1(\text{len}(\pi_1)), \pi_2(\text{len}(\pi_2))) \in B$;
3. *for all* $\pi_1 \in \text{BPaths}^{\text{T}}{}_{\mathcal{J},\mathcal{M}}(x_1)$ *such that* $(\pi_1(i_1), x_2) \in B$ *for all* $i_1 \in (0, \text{len}(\pi_1)]$ *there is* $\pi_2 \in \text{BPaths}^{\text{T}}{}_{\mathcal{J},\mathcal{M}}(x_2)$ *such that the following holds:* $(x_1, \pi_2(i_2)) \in B$ *for all* $i_2 \in (0, \text{len}(\pi_2)]$, *and* $(\pi_1(0), \pi_2(0)) \in B$.

Two points $x_1, x_2 \in X$ *are called* CoPa-bisimilar *in* $\mathcal{M}$ $(x_1, x_2) \in B$ *for some CoPa-bisimulation* B *for* $\mathcal{M}$. *Notation,* $x_1 \leftrightharpoons_{\text{CoPa}}^{\mathcal{M}} x_2$. •

CoPa-bisimilarity is strictly weaker than CMC-bisimilarity, as shown below:

Proposition 2. *For* x_1, x_2 *in QdCM* $\mathcal{M}$, *if* $x_1 \leftrightharpoons_{\text{CMC}}^{\mathcal{M}} x_2$, *then* $x_1 \leftrightharpoons_{\text{CoPa}}^{\mathcal{M}} x_2$. □

The converse of Proposition 2 does not hold; with reference to Fig. 7, with $\mathcal{V}(b) = \{x_{11}, x_{21}, x_{22}\}$ and $\mathcal{V}(g) = \{x_{12}, x_{23}\}$, it is easy to see that the symmetric closure of $B = \{(x_{11}, x_{21}), (x_{11}, x_{22}), (x_{12}, x_{23})\}$ is a CoPa-bisimulation, and so $x_{11} \leftrightharpoons_{\text{CoPa}} x_{21}$ but $x_{11} \not\leftrightharpoons_{\text{CMC}} x_{21}$ since $x_{12} \in \mathcal{V}(g)$ and $\vec{\mathcal{C}}(x_{21}) \cap \mathcal{V}(b) = \emptyset$.

5.2   Logical Characterisation of CoPa-bisimilarity

In order to provide a logical characterisation of CoPa-bisimilarity, we replace the proximity modalities $\vec{\mathcal{N}}$ and $\bar{\mathcal{N}}$ of IMLC by the *conditional reachability modalities* $\vec{\zeta}$ and $\bar{\zeta}$. Again with reference to the QdCM shown in Fig. 5a, Fig. 5c shows in black the points satisfying $\bar{\zeta}$black[white], i.e. those white points from which a black point can be reached via a white path. We thus introduce the *Infinitary Compatible Reachability Logic* (ICRL).

Definition 16. *The abstract language of* ICRL *is defined as follows:*

$$\Phi ::= p \mid \neg\,\Phi \mid \bigwedge_{i \in I} \Phi_i \mid \vec{\zeta}\,\Phi_1[\Phi_2] \mid \bar{\zeta}\,\Phi_1[\Phi_2].$$

where p ranges over AP *and I ranges over a collection of index sets.*

*   The satisfaction relation for all CMs* $\mathcal{M}$, *points* $x \in \mathcal{M}$, *and* ICRL *formulas* Φ *is defined recursively on the structure of* Φ *as follows:*

$\mathcal{M}, x \models_{\text{ICRL}} p \qquad \Leftrightarrow x \in \mathcal{V}(p);$

$\mathcal{M}, x \models_{\text{ICRL}} \neg\,\Phi \qquad \Leftrightarrow \mathcal{M}, x \models_{\text{ICRL}} \Phi \ does \ not \ hold;$

$\mathcal{M}, x \models_{\text{ICRL}} \bigwedge_{i \in I} \Phi_i \Leftrightarrow \mathcal{M}, x \models_{\text{IRL}} \Phi_i \ for \ all \ i \in I;$

$\mathcal{M}, x \models_{\text{ICRL}} \vec{\zeta}\,\Phi_1[\Phi_2] \Leftrightarrow path \ \pi \ and \ index \ \ell \ exist \ such \ that \ \pi(0) = x,$
$\qquad\qquad\qquad\qquad \pi(\ell) \models_{\text{ICRL}} \Phi_1, \ and \ \pi(j) \models_{\text{ICRL}} \Phi_2 \ for \ j \in [0, \ell)$

$\mathcal{M}, x \models_{\text{ICRL}} \bar{\zeta}\,\Phi_1[\Phi_2] \Leftrightarrow path \ \pi \ and \ index \ \ell \ exist \ such \ that \ \pi(\ell) = x,$
$\qquad\qquad\qquad\qquad \pi(0) \models_{\text{ICRL}} \Phi_1, \ and \ \pi(j) \models_{\text{ICRL}} \Phi_2 \ for \ j \in (0, \ell].$ •

Remark 3. With reference to Remark 2, we note that, clearly, $\vec{\zeta}$ can be derived from $\vec{\rho}$, namely: $\vec{\zeta}\,\Phi_1[\Phi_2] \equiv \Phi_1 \vee (\Phi_2 \wedge \vec{\rho}\,\Phi_1[\Phi_2])$ and similarly for $\bar{\zeta}\,\Phi_1[\Phi_2]$.

Also for ICRL we introduce the equivalence induced on $\mathcal{M}$:

Definition 17. *Given CM* $\mathcal{M} = (X, \mathcal{C}, \mathcal{V})$, *the equivalence relation* $\simeq^{\mathcal{M}}_{\text{ICRL}} \subseteq X \times X$ *is defined as:* $x_1 \simeq^{\mathcal{M}}_{\text{ICRL}} x_2$ *if and only if for all* ICRL *formulas* Φ, *the following holds:* $\mathcal{M}, x_1 \models_{\text{ICRL}} \Phi$ *if and only if* $\mathcal{M}, x_2 \models_{\text{ICRL}} \Phi$.   •

Lemma 10. *For* x_1, x_2 *in QdCM* $\mathcal{M}$, *if* $x_1 \rightleftharpoons^{\mathcal{M}}_{\text{CoPa}} x_2$ *then* $x_1 \simeq^{\mathcal{M}}_{\text{ICRL}} x_2$.   □

The converse of Lemma 10 is given below.

Lemma 11. *For QdCM* $\mathcal{M}$, $\simeq^{\mathcal{M}}_{\text{ICRL}}$ *is a CoPa-bisimulation for* $\mathcal{M}$.   □

The correspondence between ICRL-equivalence and CoPa-bisimilarity is thus established by the following theroem.

Theorem 4. *For every QdCM* $\mathcal{M}$ *it holds that* ICRL*-equivalence* $\simeq^{\mathcal{M}}_{\text{ICRL}}$ *coincides with CoPa-bisimilarity* $\rightleftharpoons^{\mathcal{M}}_{\text{CoPa}}$.   □

6   Conclusions

In this paper we have studied three main bisimilarities for closure spaces, namely CM-bisimilarity, its specialisation for QdCMs, CMC-bisimilarity, and CoPa-bisimilarity.

CM-bisimilarity is a generalisation for CMs of classical topo-bisimilarity for topological spaces. We can take into consideration the fact that, in QdCMs, there is a notion of "direction" given by the binary relation underlying the closure operator. This can be exploited in order to get an equivalence—namely CMC-bisimilarity—that, for QdCMs, refines CM-bisimilarity. Interestingly, the latter resembles *Strong Back-and-Forth bisimilarity* proposed by De Nicola, Montanari and Vaandrager in [19].

Both CM-bisimilarity and CMC-bisimilarity turn out to be too strong for expressing interesting properties of spaces. Therefore, we introduce CoPa-bisimilarity, that expresses a notion of path "compatibility" resembling the concept of *stuttering* equivalence for transition systems [9]. For each notion of bisimilarity we also provide an infinitary modal logic that characterises it. Obviously, for finite closure spaces, finitary versions of the logics are sufficient.

Note that, in the context of space, and in particular when dealing with notions of directionality (e.g. one way roads, public area gates), it is essential to be able to distinguish between the concept of "reaching" and that of "being reached". A formula like $\vec{\zeta}(\texttt{rescue} - \texttt{area} \land \neg(\overleftarrow{\zeta}\,\texttt{danger} - \texttt{area})[\texttt{true}])[\texttt{safe} - \texttt{corridor}]$ expresses the fact that, via a safe corridor, a rescue area can be reached that cannot be reached from a dangerous area. This kind of situations have no obvious conterpart in the temporal domain, where there can be more than one future, like in the case of branching time logics, but there is typically only *one*, fixed past, i.e. the one that occurred[6]. The "back-and-forth" nature of CMC-bisimilarity and CoPa-bisimilarity, conceptually inherited from Back-and-Forth bisimilarity of [19], allows for such distinction in a natural way.

In this paper we did not address the problem of space minimisation explicitly. In [15] we have presented a minimisation algorithm for $\rightleftharpoons_{\texttt{CMC}}$[7]. We plan to investigate the applicability of the results presented in [21] for stuttering equivalence to minimisation modulo CoPa-bisimilarity.

Most of the results we have shown in this paper concern QdCMs. The investigation of their extension to continuous or general closure spaces is an interesting line of research. In [7] Ciancia et al. started this by approaching continuous multidimentional space using polyhedra and their representation as so-called simplicial complexes for which a model checking procedure and related tool have been developed. A similar approach is presented in [28], although the underlying model is based on an adjacency relation and the usage of simplicial complexes therein is aimed more at representing objects and higher-order relations between them than at the identification of properties of points / regions of volume meshes in a particular kind of topological model.

---

[6] There are a few exception to this interpretation of past-tense operators, e.g. [26,32].

[7] The implementation is available at https://github.com/vincenzoml/MiniLogicA.

References

1. Aubert-Broche, B., Griffin, M., Pike, G., Evans, A., Collins, D.: Twenty new digital brain phantoms for creation of validation image data bases. IEEE Trans. Med. Imaging **25**(11), 1410–1416 (2006). https://doi.org/10.1109/TMI.2006.883453
2. Belmonte, G., Broccia, G., Ciancia, V., Latella, D., Massink, M.: Feasibility of spatial model checking for nevus segmentation. In: Bliudze, S., Gnesi, S., Plat, N., Semini, L. (eds.) 9th IEEE/ACM International Conference on Formal Methods in Software Engineering, FormaliSE@ICSE 2021, Madrid, Spain, 17–21 May 2021, pp. 1–12. IEEE (2021). https://doi.org/10.1109/FormaliSE52586.2021.00007
3. Belmonte, G., Ciancia, V., Latella, D., Massink, M.: Innovating medical image analysis via spatial logics. In: ter Beek, M.H., Fantechi, A., Semini, L. (eds.) From Software Engineering to Formal Methods and Tools, and Back. LNCS, vol. 11865, pp. 85–109. Springer, Cham (2019). https://doi.org/10.1007/978-3-030-30985-5_7
4. Belmonte, G., Ciancia, V., Latella, D., Massink, M.: VoxLogicA: a spatial model checker for declarative image analysis. In: Vojnar, T., Zhang, L. (eds.) TACAS 2019. LNCS, vol. 11427, pp. 281–298. Springer, Cham (2019). https://doi.org/10.1007/978-3-030-17462-0_16
5. Benthem, J.v., Bezhanishvili, G.: Modal logics of space. In: Aiello, M., Pratt-Hartmann, I., Benthem, J.v. (eds.) Handbook of Spatial Logics, pp. 217–298. Springer (2007). https://doi.org/10.1007/978-1-4020-5587-4_5
6. Benthem, J.V., Bezhanishvili, N., Enqvist, S., Yu, J.: Instantial neighbourhood logic. Rev. Symb. Log. **10**(1), 116–144 (2017). https://doi.org/10.1017/S1755020316000447
7. Bezhanishvili, N., Ciancia, V., Gabelaia, D., Grilletti, G., Latella, D., Massink, M.: Geometric model checking of continuous space. CoRR abs/2105.06194 (2021). arxiv.org/abs/2105.06194
8. Blackburn, P., van Benthem, J.F.A.K., Wolter, F. (eds.): Handbook of Modal Logic, Studies in Logic and Practical Reasoning, vol. 3. North-Holland (2007).https://www.sciencedirect.com/bookseries/studies-in-logic-and-practical-reasoning/vol/3/suppl/C
9. Browne, M.C., Clarke, E.M., Grumberg, O.: Characterizing finite Kripke structures in propositional temporal logic. Theor. Comput. Sci. **59**, 115–131 (1988). https://doi.org/10.1016/0304-3975(88)90098-9
10. Banci Buonamici, F., Belmonte, G., Ciancia, V., Latella, D., Massink, M.: Spatial logics and model checking for medical imaging. Int. J. Softw. Tools Technol. Transfer **22**(2), 195–217 (2019). https://doi.org/10.1007/s10009-019-00511-9
11. Ciancia, V., Gilmore, S., Grilletti, G., Latella, D., Loreti, M., Massink, M.: Spatio-temporal model checking of vehicular movement in public transport systems. Int. J. Softw. Tools Technol. Transfer **20**(3), 289–311 (2018). https://doi.org/10.1007/s10009-018-0483-8
12. Ciancia, V., Grilletti, G., Latella, D., Loreti, M., Massink, M.: An experimental spatio-temporal model checker. In: Bianculli, D., Calinescu, R., Rumpe, B. (eds.) SEFM 2015. LNCS, vol. 9509, pp. 297–311. Springer, Heidelberg (2015). https://doi.org/10.1007/978-3-662-49224-6_24
13. Ciancia, V., Latella, D., Loreti, M., Massink, M.: Specifying and verifying properties of space. In: Diaz, J., Lanese, I., Sangiorgi, D. (eds.) TCS 2014. LNCS, vol. 8705, pp. 222–235. Springer, Heidelberg (2014). https://doi.org/10.1007/978-3-662-44602-7_18

14. Ciancia, V., Latella, D., Loreti, M., Massink, M.: Model checking spatial logics for closure spaces. Log. Meth. Comput. Sci. **12**(4) (2016). https://doi.org/10.2168/LMCS-12(4:2)2016
15. Ciancia, V., Latella, D., Massink, M., de Vink, E.: Towards spatial bisimilarity for closure models: logical and coalgebraic characterisations (2020). arxiv.org/pdf/2005.05578pdf
16. Ciancia, V., Latella, D., Massink, M., de Vink, E.: On the expressing power of ISLCS and IMLC (2022). unpublished manuscript
17. Ciancia, V., Latella, D., Massink, M., Paškauskas, R., Vandin, A.: A tool-chain for statistical spatio-temporal model checking of bike sharing systems. In: Margaria, T., Steffen, B. (eds.) ISoLA 2016. LNCS, vol. 9952, pp. 657–673. Springer, Cham (2016). https://doi.org/10.1007/978-3-319-47166-2_46
18. Ciancia, V., Latella, D., Massink, M., de Vink, E.P.: On bisimilarities for closure spaces - preliminary version. CoRR abs/2105.06690 (2021). arxiv.org/abs/2105.06690
19. De Nicola, R., Montanari, U., Vaandrager, F.: Back and forth bisimulations. In: Baeten, J.C.M., Klop, J.W. (eds.) CONCUR 1990. LNCS, vol. 458, pp. 152–165. Springer, Heidelberg (1990). https://doi.org/10.1007/BFb0039058
20. Galton, A.: A generalized topological view of motion in discrete space. Theor. Comput. Sci. **305**(1–3), 111–134 (2003). https://doi.org/10.1016/S0304-3975(02)00701-6
21. Groote, J.F., Jansen, D.N., Keiren, J.J.A., Wijs, A.: An O(mlog n) algorithm for computing stuttering equivalence and branching bisimulation. ACM Trans. Comput. Log. **18**(2), 13:1–13:34 (2017). https://doi.org/10.1145/3060140
22. Groote, J.F., Vaandrager, F.: An efficient algorithm for branching bisimulation and stuttering equivalence. In: Paterson, M.S. (ed.) ICALP 1990. LNCS, vol. 443, pp. 626–638. Springer, Heidelberg (1990). https://doi.org/10.1007/BFb0032063
23. Grosu, R., Smolka, S.A., Corradini, F., Wasilewska, A., Entcheva, E., Bartocci, E.: Learning and detecting emergent behavior in networks of cardiac myocytes. Commun. ACM **52**(3), 97–105 (2009). https://doi.org/10.1145/1467247.1467271
24. Haghighi, I., Jones, A., Kong, Z., Bartocci, E., Grosu, R., Belta, C.: Spatel: a novel spatial-temporal logic and its applications to networked systems. In: Girard, A., Sankaranarayanan, S. (eds.) Proceedings of the 18th International Conference on Hybrid Systems: Computation and Control, HSCC 2015, Seattle, WA, USA, 14–16 April 2015, pp. 189–198. ACM (2015). https://doi.org/10.1145/2728606.2728633
25. Hansen, H.: Monotonic modal logics. Master's thesis, University of Amsterdam, ILLC (2003)
26. Kurtonina, N., de Rijke, M.: Bisimulations for temporal logic. J. Log. Lang. Inf. **6**(4), 403–425 (1997). https://doi.org/10.1023/A:1008223921944
27. Linker, S., Papacchini, F., Sevegnani, M.: Analysing spatial properties on neighbourhood spaces. In: Esparza, J., Král', D. (eds.) 45th International Symposium on Mathematical Foundations of Computer Science, MFCS 2020, August 24–28, 2020, Prague, Czech Republic. LIPIcs, vol. 170, pp. 66:1–66:14. Schloss Dagstuhl - Leibniz-Zentrum für Informatik (2020) https://doi.org/10.4230/LIPIcs.MFCS.2020.66
28. Loreti, M., Quadrini, M.: A spatial logic for a simplicial complex model. CoRR abs/2105.08708 (2021). arxiv.org/abs/2105.08708
29. Marchetti, M.A., et al.: Results of the 2016 international skin imaging collaboration international symposium on biomedical imaging challenge: Comparison of the accuracy of computer algorithms to dermatologists for the diagnosis of melanoma from

dermoscopic images. J. Am. Acad. Dermatol. **78**(2), 270-277.e1 (2018). https://doi.org/10.1016/j.jaad.2017.08.016

30. Nenzi, L., Bortolussi, L., Ciancia, V., Loreti, M., Massink, M.: Qualitative and quantitative monitoring of spatio-temporal properties with SSTL. Log. Methods Comput. Sci. **14**(4) (2018). https://doi.org/10.23638/LMCS-14(4:2)2018

31. Smyth, M.B., Webster, J.: Discrete spatial models. In: Aiello, M., Pratt-Hartmann, I., van Benthem, J. (eds.) Handbook of Spatial Logics, pp. 713–798. Springer (2007). https://doi.org/10.1007/978-1-4020-5587-4_12

32. Stirling, C.: Modal and temporal logics. In: Abramsky, S., Gabbay, D., Maibaum, T. (eds.) Handbook of logic in computer science, chap. V, p. 477?563. Oxford University Press (1993)

33. Čech, E.: Topological spaces. In: Pták, V. (ed.) Topological Spaces, chap. III, pp. 233–394. Publishing House of the Czechoslovak Academy of Sciences/Interscience Publishers, John Wiley & Sons, Prague/London-New York-Sydney (1966), Revised edition by Zdeněk Frolíc and Miroslav Katětov. Scientific editor, Vlastimil Pták. Editor of the English translation, Charles O. Junge. MR0211373

Better Automata Through Process Algebra

Rance Cleaveland(✉)

Department of Computer Science, University of Maryland,
College Park, MD 20742, USA
rance@cs.umd.edu

Abstract. This paper shows how the use of Structural Operational Semantics (SOS) in the style popularized by the process-algebra community can lead to a succinct and pedagogically satisfying construction for building finite automata from regular expressions. Techniques for converting regular expressions into finite automata have been known for decades, and form the basis for the proofs of one direction of Kleene's Theorem. The purpose of the construction documented in this paper is, on the one hand, to show students how small automata can be constructed, *without the need for empty transitions*, and on the other hand to show how the construction method admits closure proofs of regular languages with respect to many operators beyond the standard ones used in regular expressions. These results point to an additional benefit of the process-algebraic approach: besides providing fundamental insights into the nature of concurrent computation, it also can shed new light on long-standing, well-known constructions in automata theory.

Keywords: Process algebra · Finite automata · Regular expressions · Operational semantics

1 Introduction

It is an honor to write this paper in celebration of Frits Vaandrager on the occasion of the publication of his *Festschrift*. It is safe to say that Frits and I came of age, research-wise, at the same time and in a very similar intellectual milieu. In 1987, after finishing my PhD at Cornell University on using the Nuprl theorem prover [7] to reason about Milner's Calculus of Communicating Systems [16], I spent two years as a postdoctoral research scientist in Matthew Hennessy's group at the University of Sussex in the UK. Coming from North America, I was largely self-educated in process algebra but intoxicated by the subject and highly desirous of deepening my background in, and making research contributions to, the field. It was during this time that I became aware of two "superstar" Dutch PhD students that people in the UK process-algebra were talking excitedly

Research supported by US Office of Naval Research Grant N000141712622.

about. One was Rob van Glabbeek; the other was Frits! I read several of Frits' papers during this time and was struck by the depth, and also clarity, of their insights, especially given that Frits was still a PhD student. I was particularly enamored of two papers from that time: "Petri net models for algebraic theories of concurrency" [22], by Rob and Frits, and "Structured operational semantics and bisimulation as a congruence" [11], by Frits and Jan Friso Groote (himself a PhD student at the time). The former was pivotal in unifying different models of concurrency, and represented an entry point for me into non-process-algebraic theories of concurrency; the latter was a *tour de force* on congruence properties for a whole family of process operators based on the form of the operational rules used to define their behavior. I was transfixed by this result then, and remain so to this day; it also spawned a number of fruitful follow-on papers and was highly influential in my own work, performed with Steve Sims, on the Process Algebra Compiler [6].

Frits and I have never worked together, and starting in the late 1990s our interests, while still inspired by process algebra, diverged somewhat. I retain a deep affection, however, for process algebra; the field has remained an inspiration throughout my career. Frits, along with other members of the so-called "Dutch School" of concurrency, had a quite significant influence on my development as a researcher, and I remain a great admirer of their work to this day.

In this paper I wish to pay an homage of sorts to the process-algebra community in general and to Frits in particular by elaborating on a particular process-algebraic construction that I have used in teaching automata theory over the years. In particular, I will show how, using ideas from process algebra, one can derive a method for constructing finite automata from regular expressions. I believe this method has certain advantages from a pedagogical point of view to the traditional construction, usually attributed to Ken Thompson [21], found in textbooks such as [13,20]. The construction I present has been present in the folklore for years; indeed, I have lecture notes that are more than 25 years old describing it. However, to the best of my knowledge the construction has never been published, and hence remains inaccessible outside the process-algebraic community; thus, another purpose of this paper is to document the construction and its properties so that others may know about it. I also briefly situate the work in the setting of another, highly optimized technique [3] used in practice for converting regular expressions to finite automata. The message I hope to convey is that in addition to contributing foundational understanding to notions of concurrent computation, process algebra can also cast new light on well-understood automaton constructions as well, and that early luminaries in the field process algebra, including Frits Vaandrager, are doubly deserving of the accolades they receive from the research community.

2   Languages, Regular Expressions and Automata

This section reviews the definitions and notation used later in this paper for formal languages, regular expressions and finite automata.

2.1 Alphabets and Languages

At their most foundational level digital computers are devices for computing with symbols. Alphabets and languages formalize this intuition mathematically.

Definition 1 (Alphabet, word).

1. *An* alphabet *is a finite non-empty set Σ of symbols.*
2. *A* word *over alphabet Σ is a finite sequence $a_1 \ldots a_k$ of elements from Σ. We say that k is the* length *of w in this case. If $k = 0$ we say w is* empty; *we write ε for the (unique) empty word over Σ. Note that every $a \in \Sigma$ is also a (length-one) word over Σ. We use Σ^* for the set of all words over Σ.*
3. *If $w_1 = a_1 \ldots a_k$ and $w_2 = b_1 \ldots b_n$ are words over Σ then the* concatenation, *$w_1 \cdot w_2$, of w_1 and w_2 is the word $a_1 \ldots a_k b_1 \ldots b_n$. Note that $w \cdot \varepsilon = \varepsilon \cdot w = w$ for any word w. We often omit $\cdot$ and write $w_1 w_2$ for $w_1 \cdot w_2$.*
4. *A* language *L over alphabet Σ is a subset of Σ^*. The set of all languages over Σ is the set of all subsets of Σ^*, and is written 2^{Σ^*} following standard mathematical conventions.*

Since languages over Σ^* are sets, general set-theoretic operations, including $\cup$ (union), $\cap$ (intersection) and $-$ (set difference) may be applied to them. Other, language-specific operations may also be defined.

Definition 2 (Language concatenation, Kleene closure). *Let Σ be an alphabet.*

1. *Let $L_1, L_2 \subseteq \Sigma^*$ be languages over Σ. Then the* concentation, *$L_1 \cdot L_2$, of L_1 and L_2 is defined as follows.*

$$L_1 \cdot L_2 = \{w_1 \cdot w_2 \mid w_1 \in L_1 \text{ and } w_2 \in L_2\}$$

Note that $L \cdot \emptyset = \emptyset \cdot L = \emptyset$ and $L \cdot \{\varepsilon\} = \{\varepsilon\} \cdot L = L$ for any language L.
2. *Let $L \subseteq \Sigma^*$ be a language over Σ. Then the* Kleene closure, *L^*, of L is defined inductively as follows.*
   - *$\varepsilon \in L^*$*
   - *If $w_1 \in L$ and $w_2 \in L^*$ then $w_1 \cdot w_2 \in L^*$.*

2.2 Regular Expressions

Regular expressions provide a notation for defining certain languages.

Definition 3 (Regular expressions). *Let Σ be an alphabet. Then the set, $\mathcal{R}(\Sigma)$, of* regular expressions *over Σ is defined inductively as follows.*

   - *$\emptyset \in \mathcal{R}(\Sigma)$.*
   - *$\varepsilon \in \mathcal{R}(\Sigma)$.*
   - *If $a \in \Sigma$ then $a \in \mathcal{R}(\Sigma)$.*
   - *If $r_1 \in \mathcal{R}(\Sigma)$ and $r_2 \in \mathcal{R}(\Sigma)$ then $r_1 + r_2 \in \mathcal{R}(\Sigma)$ and $r_1 \cdot r_2 \in \mathcal{R}(\Sigma)$.*
   - *If $r \in \mathcal{R}(\Sigma)$ then $r^* \in \mathcal{R}(\Sigma)$.*

It should be noted that $\mathcal{R}(\Sigma)$ is a set of expressions; the occurrences of $\emptyset, \varepsilon, +, \cdot$ and $*$ are symbols that do not innately possess any meaning, but must instead be given a semantics. This is done by interpreting regular expressions mathematically as languages. The formal definition takes the form of a function, $\mathcal{L} \in \mathcal{R}(\Sigma) \rightarrow 2^{\Sigma^*}$ assigning a language $\mathcal{L}(r) \subseteq \Sigma^*$ to regular expression r.

Definition 4 (Language of a regular expression, regular language). *Let Σ be an alphabet, and $r \in \mathcal{R}(\Sigma)$ a regular expression over Σ. Then the* language, *$\mathcal{L}(r) \subseteq \Sigma^*$, associated with r is defined inductively as follows.*

$$\mathcal{L}(r) = \begin{cases} \emptyset & \text{if } r = \emptyset \\ \{\varepsilon\} & \text{if } r = \varepsilon \\ \{a\} & \text{if } r = a \text{ and } a \in \Sigma \\ \mathcal{L}(r_1) \cup \mathcal{L}(r_2) & \text{if } r = r_1 + r_2 \\ \mathcal{L}(r_1) \cdot \mathcal{L}(r_2) & \text{if } r = r_1 \cdot r_2 \\ (\mathcal{L}(r'))^* & \text{if } r = (r')^* \end{cases}$$

A language $L \subseteq \Sigma^*$ is regular *if and only if there is a regular expression $r \in \mathcal{R}(\Sigma)$ such that $\mathcal{L}(r) = L$.*

2.3   Finite Automata

Traditional accounts of finite automata typically introduce three variations of the notion: deterministic (DFA), nondeterministic (NFA), and nondeterministic with ε-transitions (NFA-ε). I will do the same, although I will do so in a somewhat different order than is typical.

Definition 5 (Nondeterministic Finite Automaton (NFA)). *A nondeterministic finite automata (NFA) is a tuple $(Q, \Sigma, \delta, q_I, F)$, where:*

- *Q is a finite non-empty set of states;*
- *Σ is an alphabet;*
- *$\delta \subseteq Q \times \Sigma \times Q$ is the transition relation;*
- *$q_I \in Q$ is the initial state; and*
- *$F \subseteq Q$ is the set of accepting, or final, states.*

This definition of NFA differs slightly from e.g. [13] in that δ is given as relation rather than function in $Q \times \Sigma \rightarrow 2^Q$. The next definition explains how NFAs process words for acceptance or rejection, thereby associating a language $\mathcal{L}(M)$ with any NFA M.

Definition 6 (Language of a NFA). *Let $M = (Q, \Sigma, \delta, q_I, F)$ be a NFA.*

1. *Let $q \in Q$ be a state of M and $w \in \Sigma^*$ be a word over Σ. Then M accepts w from q if and only if one of the following holds.*
    - *$w = \varepsilon$ and $q \in F$; or*
    - *$w = aw'$ some $a \in \Sigma$ and $w' \in \Sigma^*$, and there exists $(q, a, q') \in \delta$ such that M accepts w' from q'.*

2. *The* language, $\mathcal{L}(M)$, *accepted by M is defined as follows.*

$$\mathcal{L}(M) = \{w \in \Sigma^* \mid M \text{ accepts } w \text{ from } q_I\}$$

Deterministic Finite Automata (DFAs) constitute a subclass of NFAs whose transition relation is deterministic, in a precisely defined sense.

Definition 7 (Deterministic Finite Automaton (DFA)). *An NFA $M = (Q, \Sigma, \delta, q_I, F)$ is a* deterministic finite automaton *(DFA) if and only if δ satisfies the following: for every $q \in Q$ and $a \in \Sigma$, there exists exactly one q' such that $(q, a, q') \in \delta$.*

Since DFAs are NFAs the definition of $\mathcal{L}$ in Definition 6 is directly applicable to them as well. NFAs with ϵ-transitions are now defined as follows.

Definition 8 (NFA with ε-Transitions (NFA-ε)). *A nondeterministic automaton with ε-transitions (NFA-ε) is a tuple $(Q, \Sigma, \delta, q_I, F)$, where:*

– *Q, Σ, q_I and F are as in the definition of NFA (Definition 5); and*
– *$\delta \subseteq Q \times (\Sigma \cup \{\varepsilon\}) \times Q$ is the transition relation.*

An NFA-ε is like an NFA except that some transitions can be labeled with the empty string ε rather than a symbol from Σ. The intuition is that a transition of form (q, ε, q') can occur without consuming any symbol as an input. Formalizing this intuition, and defining $\mathcal{L}(M)$ for NFA-ε, may be done as follows.

Definition 9 (Language of a NFA-ε). *Let $M = (Q, \Sigma, \delta, q_I, F)$ be a NFA-ε.*

1. *Let $q \in Q$ and $w \in \Sigma^*$. Then M accepts w from q if and only if one of the following holds.*
    – *$w = \varepsilon$ and $q' \in F$; or*
    – *$w = aw'$ for some $a \in \Sigma$ and $w' \in \Sigma^*$ and there exists $q' \in Q$ such that $(q, a, q') \in \delta$ and M accepts w' from q'; or*
    – *there exists $q' \in Q$ such that $(q, \varepsilon, q') \in \delta$ and M accepts w from q'.*
2. *The language, $\mathcal{L}(M)$, accepted by M is defined as follows.*

$$\mathcal{L}(M) = \{w \in \Sigma^* \mid M \text{ accepts } w \text{ from } q_I\}$$

Defining the language of a NFA-ε requires redefining the notion of word acceptance from state q in order to accommodate the difference between ε-transitions and those labeled by alphabet symbols.

The three types of automata have differences in form, but equivalent expressive power. It should first be noted that, just as every DFA is a NFA, every NFA is also a NFA-ε, namely, a NFA-ε with no ε-transitions. Thus, every language accepted by some DFA is also accepted by some NFA, and every language accepted by some NFA is accepted by some NFA-ε. The next theorem establishes the converses of these implications.

Theorem 1 (Equivalence of DFAs, NFAs and NFA-εs).

1. Let M be a NFA. Then there is a DFA $D(M)$ such that $\mathcal{L}(D(M)) = \mathcal{L}(M)$.
2. Let M be a NFA-ε. Then there is a NFA $N(M)$ such that $\mathcal{L}(N(M)) = \mathcal{L}(M)$.

Proof. The proof of Case 1 involves the well-known subset construction, whereby each subset of states in M is associated with a single state in $D(M)$. The proof of Case 2 typically relies on defining the ε-closure of a set of states, namely, the set of states reachable from the given set via a sequence of zero or more ε-transitions. This notion is used to define the transition relation $N(M)$ as well as its set of accepting states. The details are standard and are omitted.   □

3   Kleene's Theorem

Given the definitions in the previous section it is now possible to state Kleene's Theorem succinctly.

Theorem 2 (Kleene's Theorem). *Let Σ be an alphabet. Then $L \subseteq \Sigma^*$ is regular if and only if there is a DFA M such that $\mathcal{L}(M) = L$.*

The proof of this theorem is usually split into two pieces. The first involves showing that for any regular expression r, there is a finite automaton M (DFA, NFA or NFA-ε) such that $\mathcal{L}(M) = \mathcal{L}(r)$. Theorem 1 then ensures that the resulting finite automaton, if it is not already a DFA, can be converted into one in a language-preserving manner. The second shows how to convert a DFA M into a regular expression r so that $\mathcal{L}(r) = \mathcal{L}(M)$; there are several algorithms for this in the literature, including one based on dynamic programming due to Kleene [15] and equation-solving methods based on Arden's Lemma [1].

From a practical standpoint, the conversion of regular expressions to finite automata is the more important of these two pieces, since regular expressions are textual and are used consequently as the basis for string search and processing. For this reason, I believe that teaching this construction is especially key in automata-theory classes, and this where my complaint with the approaches in traditional automata-theory texts originates.

To understand the source of my dissatisfaction, let us review the construction presented in [13], which explains how to convert regular expression r into NFA-ε M_r in such a way that $\mathcal{L}(r) = \mathcal{L}(M_r)$. The method is based on the construction due to Ken Thompson [21] and produces NFA-ε M_r with the following properties.

– The initial state q_I has no incoming transitions: that is, there exists no $(q, \alpha, q_I) \in \delta$ for any $\alpha \in \Sigma \cup \{\varepsilon\}$.
– There is a single accepting state q_F, and q_F has no outgoing transitions: that is, $F = \{q_F\}$, and there exists no $(q_F, \alpha, q') \in \delta$ for any $\alpha \in \Sigma \cup \{\varepsilon\}$.

The approach proceeds inductively on the structure of r. For example, if $r = (r')^*$, then assume that $M_{r'} = (Q, \Sigma, \delta, q_I, \{q_F\})$ meeting the above constraints has been constructed from r'. Then M_r is built as follows. First, let $q'_I \notin Q$ and $q'_F \notin Q$ be new states. Then $M_r = (Q \cup \{q'_I, q'_F\}, \Sigma, \delta', \{q'_F\})$, where

$$\delta' = \delta \cup \{(q'_I, \varepsilon, q_I), (q'_I, \varepsilon, q'_F), (q_F, \varepsilon, q_I), (q_F, \varepsilon, q'_F)\}.$$

It can be shown that M_r satisfies the requisite properties and that $\mathcal{L}(M_r) = \mathcal{L}(r) = (\mathcal{L}(r'))^*$.

Mathematically, the construction of M_r is wholly satisfactory: it has the required properties and can be defined straightforwardly. The proof of correctness is a bit complicated, owing to the definition of $\mathcal{L}(M)$ when M is an NFA-ε and thus has ε-transitions, but it does acquaint students with definitions via structural induction on regular expressions. That said, there are a couple of drawbacks to teaching the construction. On the one hand, it does require the introduction of the notion of NFA-ε, which is more complex that that of NFA. If ε-transitions were used for other purposes in the course, this might not be problematic. However, in my years teaching automata theory NFA-εs were only used as a basis for defining the construction of automata from regular languages. On the other hand, the accretion of the introduction of new states at each state in the construction makes it difficult to test students on their understanding of the construction in an exam setting. Specifically, even for relatively small regular expressions the literal application of the construction yields automata with too many states and transitions to be doable during the typical one-hour midterm exam for which US students would be tested on the material.

In practice the Berry-Sethi procedure is used to construct DFAs from regular expressions, so one might imagine using that algorithm in an automata-theory class. The procedure is subtle and elegant, but it relies on concepts, such as Brzozowski derivatives [4], that I would view as too specialized for an undergraduate course on automata theory. The resulting automata can also become large relative to the regular expression from which they are constructed, due to the implicit determinization of the constructed automata. Consequently, I would not be in favor of covering them in an undergraduate classroom setting. Instead, in the next section I give a technique, based on operational semantics in process algebra, for construction NFAs from regular expressions. The resulting NFAs are small enough for students to construct during exams, and the construction has other properties, including the capacity for introducing other operations that preserve regularity, that are pedagogically useful.

4 NFAs via Structural Operational Semantics

This section describes an approach based on *Structural Operational Semantics* (SOS) [18,19] for constructing NFAs from regular expressions. Specifically, I will define an operational semantics for regular expressions on the basis of the structure of regular expressions, and use the semantics to construct the requisite NFAs. The construction requires no ε-transitions and yields automata with at most one more state than the size of the regular expression from which they are derived.

Following the conventions in the other parts of this paper I give the SOS rules in natural language, as a collection of if-then statements, and not via inference rules. I use this approach in the classroom to avoid having to introduce notations for inference rules. The appendix contains the more traditional SOS presentation.

4.1   An Operational Semantics for Regular Expressions

In what follows fix alphabet Σ. The basis for the operational semantics of regular expressions consists of a relation, $\rightarrow \subseteq \mathcal{R}(\Sigma) \times \Sigma \times \mathcal{R}(\Sigma)$, and a predicate $\sqrt{} \subseteq \mathcal{R}(\Sigma)$. In what follows I will write $r \xrightarrow{a} r'$ and $r\sqrt{}$ in lieu of $(r, a, r') \in \rightarrow$ and $r \in \sqrt{}$. The intuitions are as follows.

1. $r\sqrt{}$ is intended to hold if and only if $\varepsilon \in \mathcal{L}(r)$. This is used in defining accepting states of the constructed automata.
2. $r \xrightarrow{a} r'$ is intended to reflect the following about $\mathcal{L}(r)$: one way to build a word in $\mathcal{L}(r)$ is to start with $a \in \Sigma$ and then finish it with a word from $\mathcal{L}(r')$.

Using these relations, I then show how to build a NFA from r whose states are regular expressions, whose transitions are given by $\rightarrow$, and whose final states are defined using $\sqrt{}$. We first define $\sqrt{}$.

Definition 10 (Definition of $\sqrt{}$). *Predicate $r\sqrt{}$ is defined inductively on the structure of $r \in \mathcal{R}(\Sigma)$ as follows.*

- *If $r = \varepsilon$ then $r\sqrt{}$.*
- *If $r = (r')^*$ for some $r' \in \mathcal{R}(\Sigma)$ then $r\sqrt{}$.*
- *If $r = r_1 + r_2$ for some $r_1, r_2 \in \mathcal{R}(\Sigma)$, and either $r_1\sqrt{}$ or $r_2\sqrt{}$, then $r\sqrt{}$.*
- *If $r = r_1 \cdot r_2$ for some $r_1, r_2 \in \mathcal{R}(\Sigma)$, and $r_1\sqrt{}$ and $r_2\sqrt{}$, then $r\sqrt{}$.*

From the definition, one can see it is not the case that $\emptyset\sqrt{}$ or $a\sqrt{}$, for any $a \in \Sigma$, while $\varepsilon\sqrt{}$ is true and $r^*\sqrt{}$ always holds, regardless of r. This accords with the definition of $\mathcal{L}(r)$; $\varepsilon \notin \mathcal{L}(\emptyset) = \emptyset$, and $\varepsilon \notin \mathcal{L}(a) = \{a\}$, while $\varepsilon \in \mathcal{L}(\varepsilon) = \{\varepsilon\}$ and $\varepsilon \in \mathcal{L}(r^*) = (\mathcal{L}(r))^*$ for any regular expression r. The other cases in the definition reflect the fact that $\varepsilon \in \mathcal{L}(r_1 + r_2)$ can only hold if $\varepsilon \in \mathcal{L}(r_1)$ or $\varepsilon \in \mathcal{L}(r_2)$, since $+$ is interpreted as set union, and that $\varepsilon \in \mathcal{L}(r_1 \cdot r_2)$ can only be true if $\varepsilon \in \mathcal{L}(r_1)$ and $\varepsilon \in \mathcal{L}(r_2)$, since regular-expression operator $\cdot$ is interpreted as language concatenation. Table 1 gives examples of when $\sqrt{}$ does and does not hold for different regular expressions.

We also use structural induction to define $\rightarrow$.

Definition 11 (Definition of $\rightarrow$). *Relation $r \xrightarrow{a} r'$, where $r, r' \in \mathcal{R}(\Sigma)$ and $a \in \Sigma$, is defined inductively on r.*

- *If $r = a$ and $a \in \Sigma$ then $r \xrightarrow{a} \varepsilon$.*
- *If $r = r_1 + r_2$ and $r_1 \xrightarrow{a} r_1'$ then $r \xrightarrow{a} r_1'$.*
- *If $r = r_1 + r_2$ and $r_2 \xrightarrow{a} r_2'$ then $r \xrightarrow{a} r_2'$.*
- *If $r = r_1 \cdot r_2$ and $r_1 \xrightarrow{a} r_1'$ then $r \xrightarrow{a} r_1' \cdot r_2$.*

Table 1. Examples of $r\sqrt{}$.

r	$r\sqrt{}$?	Reason
$\varepsilon \cdot a^*$	Yes	$\varepsilon\sqrt{}$ and $a^*\sqrt{}$
$a + b$	No	Neither $a\sqrt{}$ nor $b\sqrt{}$ hold
$01 + (1 + 01)^*$	Yes	$(1 + 01)^*\sqrt{}$
$01(1 + 01)^*$	No	$01\sqrt{}$ does not hold

- If $r = r_1 \cdot r_2$, $r_1\sqrt{}$ and $r_2 \xrightarrow{a} r_2'$ then $r \xrightarrow{a} r_2'$.
- If $r = (r')^*$ and $r' \xrightarrow{a} r''$ then $r \xrightarrow{a} r'' \cdot (r')^*$.

The definition of this relation is somewhat complex, but the idea that it is aiming to capture is relatively simple: $r \xrightarrow{a} r'$ should hod if one can build words in $\mathcal{L}(r)$ by taking the a labeling $\rightarrow$ and appending a word from $\mathcal{L}(r')$. So we have the rule $a \xrightarrow{a} \varepsilon$ for $a \in \Sigma$, while the rules for $+$ follow from the fact that $\mathcal{L}(r_1 + r_2) = \mathcal{L}(r_1) \cup \mathcal{L}(r_2)$. The cases for $r_1 \cdot r_2$ in essence state that $aw \in \mathcal{L}(r_1 \cdot r_2)$ can hold either if there is a way of splitting w into w_1 and w_2 such that aw_1 is in the language of r_1 and w_2 is in the language of r_2, or if ε is in the language of r_1 and aw is in the language of r_2. Finally, the rule for $(r')^*$ essentially permits "looping". As examples, we have the following.

$$a + b \xrightarrow{a} \varepsilon \qquad\qquad \text{by the rules for } a \text{ and } +.$$
$$(abb + a)^* \xrightarrow{a} \varepsilon bb(abb + a)^* \quad \text{by the rules for } a, \cdot, +, \text{ and } {}^*.$$

In this latter example, note that applying the definition literally requires the inclusion of the ε in $\varepsilon bb(abb + a)^*$. This is because the case for a says that $a \xrightarrow{a} \varepsilon$, meaning that $abb \xrightarrow{a} \varepsilon bb$, etc.

The following lemmas about $\sqrt{}$ and $\rightarrow$ formally establish the intuitive properties that they should have.

Lemma 1. *Let* $r \in \mathcal{R}(\Sigma)$ *be a regular expression. Then* $r\sqrt{}$ *if and only if* $\varepsilon \in \mathcal{L}(r)$.

Proof. The proof proceeds by structural induction on r. Most cases are left to the reader; we only consider the $r = r_1 \cdot r_2$ case here. The induction hypothesis states that $r_1\sqrt{}$ if and only if $\varepsilon \in \mathcal{L}(r_1)$ and $r_2\sqrt{}$ if and only if $\varepsilon \in \mathcal{L}(r_2)$. We now reason as follows.

$r\sqrt{}$ iff	$r_1\sqrt{}$ and $r_2\sqrt{}$	Def. of $\sqrt{}$
iff	$\varepsilon \in \mathcal{L}(r_1)$ and $\varepsilon \in \mathcal{L}(r_2)$	Induction hypothesis
iff	$\varepsilon \in (\mathcal{L}(r_1)) \cdot (\mathcal{L}(r_2))$	Def. of $\cdot$ for languages, $\varepsilon \cdot \varepsilon = \varepsilon$
iff	$\varepsilon \in \mathcal{L}(r_1 \cdot r_2)$	Def. of $\mathcal{L}(r_1 \cdot r_2)$
iff	$\varepsilon \in \mathcal{L}(r)$	$r = r_1 \cdot r_2$

$\square$

Before stating and proving the desired result about $\rightarrow$ we first establish the following technical lemma about non-empty words in the Kleene closure, L^*, of language L.

Lemma 2. *Let Σ be an alphabet, with $a \in \Sigma$, $w \in \Sigma^*$, and $L \subseteq \Sigma^*$. Then $a \cdot w \in L^*$ if and only if there exist $w_1, w_2 \in \Sigma^*$ such that $w = w_1 \cdot w_2$, $a \cdot w_1 \in L$ and $w_2 \in L^*$.*

Proof. Fix alphabet $\Sigma, a \in \Sigma, w \in \Sigma^*$ and $L \subseteq \Sigma^*$. We must prove both the "if" and "only if" directions. For the "if" direction, assume that there exist w_1 and w_2 such that $w = w_1 \cdot w_2$, $a \cdot w_1 \in L$ and $w_2 \in L^*$. We must show that $a \cdot w \in L^*$. From the definition of L^* it immediately follows that $a \cdot w_1 \cdot w_2 \in L^*$, and as $w = w_1 \cdot w_2$, we have that $a \cdot w \in L^*$.

For the "only if" direction, we prove the following equivalent statement: for all $w' \in L^*$, if $w' = a \cdot w$ then there exist w_1 and w_2 such that $w = w_1 \cdot w_2$, $a \cdot w_1 \in L$, and $w_2 \in L^*$. The proof proceeds by induction on the definition of L^*. In the base case $w' = \varepsilon$; as $a \cdot w \neq \varepsilon$ the implication to be proven is vacuously true. Now assume that $w' = w_1' \cdot w_2'$ for some $w_1' \in L$ and $w_2' \in L^*$; the induction hypothesis asserts that the result holds for w_2'. Now assume that $w' = a \cdot w$. There are two cases to consider. In the first, $w_1' = \varepsilon$; in this case $w' = w_2' = a \cdot w$, and the induction hypothesis delivers the desired result. In the second case, $w_1' \neq \varepsilon$; this means that $w_1' = a \cdot w_1''$ for some w_1''. Take $w_1 = w_1''$ and $w_2 = w_2'$. We immediately have that $a \cdot w_1 = w_1' \in L$ and $w_2 = w_2' \in L^*$. □

In the above lemma, $a \cdot w$ is a non-empty word; the lemma in effect says that when non-empty word $a \cdot w$ is in the Kleene closure, L^*, of language L then there must be a non-empty word $a \cdot w_1$ in L that is a prefix of $a \cdot w$. (In the lemma w_2 consists of the remainder of $a \cdot w$ that is not in $a \cdot w_1$.) We can now state and prove the following key property of $\rightarrow$.

Lemma 3. *Let $r \in \mathcal{R}(\Sigma)$, $a \in \Sigma$, and $w \in \Sigma^*$. Then $a \cdot w \in \mathcal{L}(r)$ if and only if there is an $r' \in \mathcal{R}(\Sigma)$ such that $r \xrightarrow{a} r'$ and $w \in \mathcal{L}(r')$.*

Proof. The proof proceeds by structural induction on r. We only consider the case $r = s^*$, where $s \in \mathcal{R}(\Sigma)$, in detail; the others are left to the reader. The induction hypothesis asserts that for all $a \in \Sigma$ and $w \in \Sigma^*$, $a \cdot w \in \mathcal{L}(s)$ if and only if there is an s' such that $s \xrightarrow{a} s'$ and $w \in \mathcal{L}(s')$. Now fix $a \in \Sigma$ and $w \in \Sigma^*$. We reason as follows.

$a \cdot w \in \mathcal{L}(r)$

iff $a \cdot w \in \mathcal{L}(s^*)$ $\qquad\qquad\qquad\qquad\qquad\qquad\qquad\qquad\qquad$ $r = s^*$

iff $a \cdot w \in (\mathcal{L}(s))^*$ $\qquad\qquad\qquad\qquad\qquad\qquad\qquad\qquad\quad$ Def. of $\mathcal{L}(s^*)$

iff $a \cdot w = a \cdot w_1 \cdot w_2$ some $a \cdot w_1 \in \mathcal{L}(s), w_2 \in (\mathcal{L}(s))^*$ $\quad$ Lemma 2 ($L = \mathcal{L}(s)$)

iff $s \xrightarrow{a} s'$ some s' with $w_1 \in \mathcal{L}(s'), w_2 \in (\mathcal{L}(s))^*$ $\qquad$ Induction hypothesis

iff $s^* \xrightarrow{a} s' \cdot s^*$ with $w_1 \in \mathcal{L}(s'), w_2 \in (\mathcal{L}(s))^*$ $\qquad$ Def. of $\rightarrow$

iff $s^* \xrightarrow{a} s' \cdot s^*$ with $w_1 \cdot w_2 \in \mathcal{L}(s') \cdot (\mathcal{L}(s))^*$ $\qquad$ Def. of $\cdot$ for languages

iff $s^* \xrightarrow{a} s' \cdot s^*$ with $w_1 \cdot w_2 \in \mathcal{L}(s' \cdot s^*)$ $\qquad\qquad$ Def. of $\mathcal{L}(s' \cdot s^*)$

Since $r = s^*$ and $w = w_1w_2$, if we take $r' = s' \cdot r$ we have demonstrated an r' such that $r \xrightarrow{a} r'$ and $w \in \mathcal{L}(r')$, thereby completing the proof of this case. $\square$

4.2 Building Automata Using $\sqrt{}$ and $\rightarrow$

That $\sqrt{}$ and $\rightarrow$ may be used to build NFAs derives from how they may be used to determine whether a word is in the language of a regular expression. Consider the following sequence of transitions starting from regular expression $(abb + a)^*$.

$$(abb + a)^* \xrightarrow{a} bb(abb + a)^* \xrightarrow{b} b(abb + a)^* \xrightarrow{b} (abb + a)^* \xrightarrow{a} (abb + a)^*$$

Using Lemma 3 four times, we can conclude that if $w \in \mathcal{L}((abb + a)^*)$, then $abba \cdot w \in \mathcal{L}((abb + a)^*)$ also. In addition, since $(abb + a)^*\sqrt{}$, it follows from Lemma 1 that $\varepsilon \in \mathcal{L}((abb + a)^*)$. As $abba \cdot \varepsilon = abba$, we know that $abba \in \mathcal{L}((abb + a)^*)$.

More generally, if there is a sequence of transitions $r_0 \xrightarrow{a_1} r_1 \cdots \xrightarrow{a_n} r_n$ and $r_n\sqrt{}$, then it follows that $a_1 \ldots a_n \in \mathcal{L}(r_0)$, and vice versa. This observation suggests the following strategy for building a NFA from a regular expression r.

1. Let the states be all possible regular expressions that can be reached by some sequence of transitions from r.
2. Take r to be the start state.
3. Let the transitions be given by $\rightarrow$.
4. Let the accepting states be those regular expressions r' reachable from r for which $r'\sqrt{}$ holds.

Of course, this construction is only valid if the set of all possible regular expressions mentioned in Step 1 is finite, since NFAs are required to have a finite number of states. In fact, a stronger result can be proved. Define the size, $|r|$, of regular expression r as follows.

Definition 12 (Size of a regular expression). *The size, $|r|$, of $r \in \mathcal{R}(\Sigma)$ is defined inductively as follows.*

$$|r| = \begin{cases} 1 & \text{if } r = \varepsilon, r = \emptyset, \text{ or } r = a \text{ for some } a \in \Sigma \\ |r'| + 1 & \text{if } r = (r')^* \\ |r_1| + |r_2| + 1 & \text{if } r = r_1 + r_2 \text{ or } r = r_1 \cdot r_2 \end{cases}$$

Intuitively, $|r|$ counts the number of regular-expression operators in r. The *reachability set* of regular expression r can now be defined in the usual manner.

Definition 13. *Let $r \in \mathcal{R}(\Sigma)$ be a regular expression. Then the set $RS(r) \subseteq \mathcal{R}(\Sigma)$ of regular expressions reachable from r is defined recursively as follows.*

- $r \in RS(r)$.
- *If $r_1 \in RS(r)$ and $r_1 \xrightarrow{a} r_2$ for some $a \in \Sigma$, then $r_2 \in RS(r)$.*

As an example, note that $|(abb + a)^*| = 8$ and that (In this example we have retained the leading instances of ε obtained by applying the operational semantics. This is why both $(abb+a)^*$ and $\varepsilon(abb+a)^*$ are in $RS((abb+a)^*)$, even though they are semantically equivalent. One could employ algebraic simplifiers during the construction of RS to eliminate these redundant expressions, although we do not explore this point further in this paper.)

$$RS((abb + a)^*) = \{(abb + a)^*, \varepsilon bb(abb + a)^*, \varepsilon b(abb + a)^*, \varepsilon(abb + a)^*\}.$$

The following theorem establishes a tight connection between $|r|$ and $|RS(r)|$, where $|RS(r)|$ is the number of elements in $RS(r)$.

Theorem 3. *Let $r \in \mathcal{R}(\Sigma)$ be a regular expression. Then $|RS(r)| \leq |r| + 1$.*

Proof. The proof proceeds by structural induction on r. There are six cases to consider.

$r = \emptyset$. In this case $RS(r) = \{\emptyset\}$, and $|RS(r)| = 1 = |r| < |r| + 1$.

$r = \varepsilon$. In this case $RS(r) = \{\varepsilon\}$, and $|RS(r)| = 1 = |r| < |r| + 1$.

$r = a$ **for some** $a \in \Sigma$. In this case $RS(r) = \{a, \varepsilon\}$, and $|RS(r)| = 2 = |r| + 1$.

$r = r_1 + r_2$. In this case, $RS(r) \subseteq RS(r_1) \cup RS(r_2)$, and induction hypothesis guarantees that $|RS(r_1)| \leq |r_1| + 1$ and $RS(r_2) \leq |r_2| + 1$. It follows that

$$|RS(r)| \leq |RS(r_1)| + |RS(r_2)| \leq |r_1| + |r_2| + 2 = |r| + 1.$$

$r = r_1 \cdot r_2$. In this case it can be shown that $RS(r) \subseteq \{r_1' \cdot r_2 \mid r_1' \in RS(r_1)\} \cup RS(r_2)$. Since $|\{r_1' \cdot r_2 \mid r_1' \in RS(r_1)\}| = |RS(r_1)|$, similar reasoning as in the $+$ case applies.

$r = (r')^*$. In this case we have that $RS(r) \subseteq \{r\} \cup \{r'' \cdot r \mid r'' \in RS(r')\}$. Thus

$$|RS(r)| \leq |RS(r')| + 1 \leq |r'| + 2 = |r| + 1.$$

$\square$

This result shows not only that the NFA construction sketched above yields a finite number of states for given r, but also that this set of states is no larger than $|r| + 1$. We can now formally define the construction of NFA M_r from regular expression r as follows.

Definition 14. *Let $r \in \mathcal{R}(\Sigma)$ be a regular expression. Then $M_r = (Q, \Sigma, q_I, \delta, A)$ is the NFA defined as follows.*

- $Q = RS(r)$.
- $q_I = r$.
- $\delta = \{(r_1, a, r_2) \mid r_1 \xrightarrow{a} r_2\}$.
- $F = \{r' \in Q \mid r'\sqrt{}\}$.

The next theorem establishes the desired correspondence between the languages of r and M_r.

Theorem 4. *Let $r \in \mathcal{R}(\Sigma)$ be a regular expression. The $\mathcal{L}(r) = \mathcal{L}(M_r)$.*

Proof. Relies on the fact that Lemmas 1 and 3 guarantee that $w = a_1 \ldots a_n \in \mathcal{L}(r)$ if and only if there is a regular expression r' such that $r \xrightarrow{a_1} \cdots \xrightarrow{a_n} r'$ and $r'\sqrt{}$.

4.3 Computing M_r

This section gives a routine for computing M_r in an "on-the-fly" manner. In particular, it intertwines the computation of the reachability set from regular expression r with the construction of the transition relation and the set of accepting states. It relies on the computation of the so-called *outgoing transitions* of r; these are defined as follows.

Definition 15. *Let $r \in \mathcal{R}(\Sigma)$ be a regular expression. Then the set of* outgoing transitions *from r is defined as the set $\{(a, r') \mid r \xrightarrow{a} r'\}$.*

The outgoing transitions from r consists of pairs (a, r') that, when combined with r, constitute a valid transition $r \xrightarrow{a} r'$. Figure 1 defines a recursive function, *out*, for computing the outgoing transitions of r. The routine uses the structure of r and the definition of $\rightarrow$ to guide its computation. For regular expressions of the form $\emptyset, \varepsilon$ and $a \in \Sigma$, the definition of $\rightarrow$ in Definition 11 immediately gives all the transitions. For regular expressions built using $+, \cdot$ and $*$, one must first recursively compute the outgoing transitions of the subexpressions of r and then combine the results appropriately, based on the cases given in the Definition 11.

$$
out(r) = \begin{cases}
\emptyset & \text{if } r = \emptyset \text{ or } r = \varepsilon \\
\{(a, \varepsilon)\} & \text{if } r = a \in \Sigma \\
out(r_1) \cup out(r_2) & \text{if } r = r_1 + r_2 \\
\{(a, r_1' \cdot r_2) \mid (a, r_1') \in out(r_1)\} & \\
\quad \cup \{(a, r_2') \mid (a, r_2') \in out(r_2) \wedge r_1\sqrt{}\} & \text{if } r = r_1 \cdot r_2 \\
\{(a, r'' \cdot (r')^*) \mid (a, r_1') \in out(r_1)\} & \text{if } r = (r')^*
\end{cases}
$$

Fig. 1. Calculating the outgoing transitions of regular expressions.

The next lemma states that $out(r)$ correctly computes the outgoing transitions of r.

Lemma 4. *Let $r \in \mathcal{R}(\Sigma)$ be a regular expression, and let $out(r)$ be as defined in Fig. 1. Then $out(r) = \{(a, r') \mid r \xrightarrow{a} r'\}$.*

Proof. By structural induction on r. The details are left to the reader.

Algorithm 1 contains pseudo-code for computing M_r. It maintains four sets.

- Q, a set of states computed so far for M_r.
- F, a set that contains the accepting states so far for M_r.
- δ, a set that contains the transition relation so far M_r.
- W, the *work set*, a subset of Q containing states that have not yet had their outgoing transitions computed or acceptance status determined.

Algorithm 1: Algorithm for computing NFA M_r from regular expression r

---

1 **Algorithm** $NFA(r)$
   Input   : Regular rexpression $r \in \mathcal{R}(\Sigma)$
   Output: NFA $M_r = (Q, \Sigma, q_I, \delta, F)$
2 $Q := \{r\}$ // State set
3 $q_I := r$ // Start state
4 $W := \{r\}$ // Work set
5 $\delta := \emptyset$ // Transition relation
6 $F := \emptyset$ // Accepting states
7 **while** $W \neq \emptyset$ **do**
8 | choose $r' \in W$
9 | $W := W - \{r'\}$
10 | **if** $r'\surd$ **then**
11 | | $F := F \cup \{r'\}$ // r' is an accepting state
12 | $T = out(r')$ // Outgoing transitions of r'
13 | $\delta := \delta \cup \{r', a, r'') \mid (a, r'') \in T\}$ // Update transition relation
14 | **foreach** $(a, r'') \in T$ **do**
15 | | **if** $r'' \notin Q$ **then**
16 | | | $Q := Q \cup \{r''\}$ // r'' is a new state
17 | | | $W := W \cup \{r''\}$
18 | |
19 | **end**
20 **end**
21 **return** $M_r = (Q, \Sigma, \delta, q_I, F)$

The procedure begins by adding its input r to both Q and W. It then repeatedly removes a state from W, determines if it should be added to F, computes its outgoing transitions and updates δ appropriately, and finally adds the target states in the outgoing transition set to both Q and W if they are not yet in Q (meaning they have not yet been encountered in the construction of M_r). The algorithm terminates when W is empty.

Figure 2 gives the NFA resulting from applying the procedure to $(abb + a)^*$. Figure 3, by way of contrast, shows the result of applying the routine in [13] to produce a NFA-ε from the same regular expression.

5 Discussion

The title of this paper is "Better Automata through Process Algebra," and I want to revisit it in order to explain in what respects I regard the method presented here as producing "better automata." Earlier I identified the following motivations that prompted me to incorporate this approach in my classroom instruction.

– I wanted to produce NFAs rather than NFA-εs. In large part this was due to my desire not cover the notion of NFA-ε. The only place this material is used

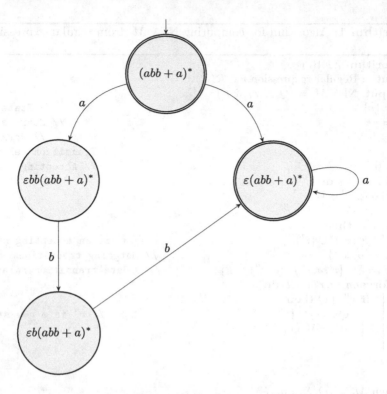

Fig. 2. NFA(r) for $r = (abb + a)^*$.

in typical automata-theory textbooks is as a vehicle for converting regular expressions into finite automata. By giving a construction that avoids the use of ε-transitions, I could avoid covering NFA-εs and devote the newly freed lecture time to other topics. Of course, this is only possible if the NFA-based construction does not require more time to describe than the introduction of NFA-ε and the NFA-ε construction.

– I wanted to be able to confirm that students understood how automata can be constructed from regular expressions, and thus the construction I gave them needed to be one that they could apply manually during an exam. The classical construction found in [13, 20] and other books fails this test, in my opinion; while the inductive definitions are mathematically pleasing, they yield automata with too many states for students to be expected to apply them in a time-constrained setting.

– Related to the preceding point, I wanted a technique that students could imagine being implemented and used in the numerous applications to which regular expressions are applied. In such a setting, fewer states is better than more states, all things considered.

This paper has attempted to argue these points by giving a construction in Definition 14 for constructing NFAs directly from regular expressions.

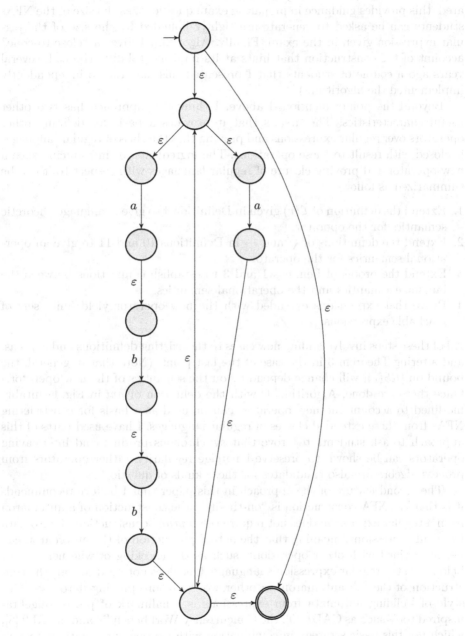

Fig. 3. NFA-ε for $(abb + a)^*$.

Theorem 3 establishes that the number of states in these NFAs is at most one larger than the size of the regular expression from which the NFAs are generated; this provides guidance in preparing exam questions, as the size of the NFAs students can be asked to generate are tightly bounded by the size of the regular expression given in the exam. Finally, Algorithm 1 gives a "close-to-code" account of the construction that hints at its implementability. (Indeed, several years ago a couple of students that I presented this material to independently implemented the algorithm.)

Beyond the points mentioned above, I think this approach has two other useful characteristics. The first is that it provides a basis for defining other operators over regular expressions and proving that the class of regular languages is closed with result to these operations. The ingredients for introducing such a new operator and proving closure of regular languages with respect to it can be summarized as follows.

1. Extend the definition of $\mathcal{L}(r)$ given in Definition 4 to give a language-theoretic semantics for the operator.
2. Extend the definitions of $\sqrt{}$ and $\rightarrow$ in Definitions 10 and 11 to give an operational semantics for the operator.
3. Extend the proofs of Lemmas 1 and 3 to establish connections between the language semantics and the operational semantics.
4. Prove that expressions extended with the new operator yield finite sets of reachable expressions.

All of these steps involve adding new cases to the existing definitions and lemmas, and altering Theorem 3 in the case of the last point. (Note that in general, the bound on $|RS(r)|$ will change depending on the semantics of the new operator.) Once these are done, Algorithm 1, with the definition of *out* in Fig. 1 suitably modified to account the new operator, can be used as a basis for constructing NFAs from these extended classes of regular languages. I have used parts of this approach to ask students to prove that synchronous product and interleaving operators can be shown to preserve language regularity. Other operators from process algebra are also candidates for these kinds of questions.

The second feature of the approach in this paper that I believe recommends it is that the NFA construction is "on-the-fly"; the construction of a automaton from a regular expression does not require the *a priori* construction of automata from subexpressions, meaning that the actual production of the automaton can be intertwined with other operations, such as the checking of whether a word belongs to the regular expression's language. One does not need to wait the construction of the full automaton, in other words, before putting it to use. This style of building automata from expressions is a hallmark of process-algebra-inspired tools such as CADP [9], the Concurrency Workbench [5] and mCRL2 [8], which use this basic strategy in combination with various optimizations to generate *labeled transition systems* (automata without designated accepting states) encoding the behavior of systems.

Criticisms that I have heard of this approach center around two issues. The first is that the construction of NFA M_r from regular expression r does not use structural induction on r, unlike the classical constructions in e.g. [13,20,21], and this removes an opportunity for the students to be exposed to structural induction. This is indeed the case; in fact, the on-the-fly construction is really a co-inductive construction rather than an inductive one, although I do not make this point to my students. However, the concepts that M_r is built on, namely $\sqrt{}$ and $\rightarrow$, are defined inductively, and the results proven about them require substantial use of induction, so students still receive substantial instruction in inductive constructions and proof techniques. The other complaint is that the notion of $r \xrightarrow{a} r'$ is "hard to understand." It is indeed the case that equipping regular expressions with an operational semantics is far removed from the language-theoretic semantics typically given to these expressions. That said, I would argue that the operational semantics considered here in fact exposes the essence of the relationship between regular expressions and finite automata: this semantics enables regular expressions to be executed, and in a way that can be captured via automata. In this respect the disconnect between my favored approach and the traditional one reflects the traditional dichotomy between denotational and operational semantics.

The Berry-Sethi algorithm [3] is widely used in practice and produces DFAs rather than NFAs. This feature enables their technique to accommodate complementation, an operation with respect to which regular languages are closed but which fits uneasily with NFAs, so one may wonder about using this routine in automata-theory classes. From a pedagogical perspective, however, the algorithm suffers somewhat as the number of states in a DFA can be exponentially larger than that size of the regular expression from which it is derived. A similar criticism can be made of other techniques that rely on Brzozowsky derivatives [4], which also produce DFAs. There are interesting connections between our operational semantics and these derivatives, but we exploit nondeterminacy to keep the sizes of the resulting finite automata small.

I close this section by remarking on work done in the process-algebra community on so-called *regular behaviors*. In this area researchers study various syntactic presentations of systems, often inspired by regular expressions, with respect to equivalences based on bisimulation rather than language equivalence. Milner [17] presented a theory of recursive expressions with an algebra of operators and gave a complete axiomatization of bisimulation equivalence for these expressions. He conjectured that his axiomatization was also complete for regular expressions and bisimulation; this has remained open until very recently [10]. Baeten, Corradini and Grabmayer [2] studied the question of which finite automata are bisimulation equivalent to regular expressions and showed that the set of so-called *well-behaved* finite behaviors exactly describe this class.

6   Conclusions and Directions for Future Work

In this paper I have presented an alternative approach for converting regular expressions into finite automata. The method relies on defining an operational semantics for regular expressions, and as such draws inspiration from the work on process algebra undertaken by leaders in that field, including Frits Vaandrager. In contrast with classical techniques, the construction here does not require transitions labeled by the empty word ε, and it yields automata whose state sets are proportional in size to the regular expressions they come from. The procedure can also be implemented in an on-the-fly manner, meaning that the production of the automaton can be intertwined with other analysis procedures.

Other algorithms studied in process algebra also have pedagogical promise, in my opinion. One method, the Kanellakis-Smolka algorithm for computing bisimulation equivalence [14], is a case in point. Partition-refinement algorithms for computing language equivalence of deterministic automata have been in existence for decades, but the details underpinning them are subtle and difficult to present in an undergraduate automata-theory class, where instructional time is at a premium. While not as efficient asymptotically as the best procedures, the simplicity of the K-S technique recommends it, in my opinion, both for equivalence checking and state-machine minimization. Simulation-checking algorithms [12] can also be used as a basis for checking language containment among finite automata; these are interesting because they do not require determinization of both automata being compared, in general.

A   SOS Rules for $\sqrt{}$ and $\rightarrow$

Inference rules are given in the form

$$\frac{premises}{conclusion}$$

with $-$ denoting an empty list of premises. Here are the rules for $\sqrt{}$.

$$\frac{-}{\varepsilon\sqrt{}} \qquad \frac{-}{r^*\sqrt{}} \qquad \frac{r_1\sqrt{}}{(r_1+r_2)\sqrt{}} \qquad \frac{r_2\sqrt{}}{(r_1+r_2)\sqrt{}} \qquad \frac{r_1\sqrt{} \quad r_2\sqrt{}}{(r_1\cdot r_2)\sqrt{}}$$

Next are the rules for $\rightarrow$.

$$\frac{-}{a \xrightarrow{a} \varepsilon} \qquad \frac{r_1 \xrightarrow{a} r_1'}{r_1+r_2 \xrightarrow{a} r_1'} \qquad \frac{r_2 \xrightarrow{a} r_2'}{r_1+r_2 \xrightarrow{a} r_2'}$$

$$\frac{r_1 \xrightarrow{a} r_1'}{r_1\cdot r_2 \xrightarrow{a} r_1'\cdot r_2} \qquad \frac{r_1\sqrt{} \quad r_2 \xrightarrow{a} r_2'}{r_1\cdot r_2 \xrightarrow{a} r_2'} \qquad \frac{r \xrightarrow{a} r'}{r^* \xrightarrow{a} r'\cdot (r^*)}$$

References

1. Arden, D.N.: Delayed-logic and finite-state machines. In: 2nd Annual Symposium on Switching Circuit Theory and Logical Design, pp. 133–151. IEEE (1961)
2. Baeten, J.C.M., Corradini, F., Grabmayer, C.A.: A characterization of regular expressions under bisimulation. J. ACM **54**(2), 6-es (2007)
3. Berry, G., Sethi, R.: From regular expressions to deterministic automata. Theor. Comput. Sci. **48**, 117–126 (1986)
4. Brzozowski, J.A.: Derivatives of regular expressions. J. ACM **11**(4), 481–494 (1964)
5. Cleaveland, R., Parrow, J., Steffen, B.: The concurrency workbench: a semantics-based tool for the verification of concurrent systems. ACM Trans. Program. Lang. Syst. (TOPLAS) **15**(1), 36–72 (1993)
6. Cleaveland, R., Sims, S.T.: Generic tools for verifying concurrent systems. Sci. Comput. Program. **42**(1), 39–47 (2002). Special Issue on Engineering Automation for Computer Based Systems
7. Constable, R.L., et al.: Implementing Mathematics with the Nuprl Proof Development System. Prentice-Hall, Englewood Cliffs (1986)
8. Cranen, S., et al.: An overview of the mCRL2 toolset and its recent advances. In: Piterman, N., Smolka, S.A. (eds.) TACAS 2013. LNCS, vol. 7795, pp. 199–213. Springer, Heidelberg (2013). https://doi.org/10.1007/978-3-642-36742-7_15
9. Garavel, H., Lang, F., Mateescu, R., Serwe, W.: CADP 2011: a toolbox for the construction and analysis of distributed processes. Int. J. Softw. Tools Technol. Transfer **15**(2), 89–107 (2013)
10. Grabmayer, C.: Milner's proof system for regular expressions modulo bisimilarity is complete. In: Symposium on Logic in Computer Science (2022, to appear)
11. Groote, J.F., Vaandrager, F.: Structured operational semantics and bisimulation as a congruence. In: Ausiello, G., Dezani-Ciancaglini, M., Della Rocca, S.R. (eds.) ICALP 1989. LNCS, vol. 372, pp. 423–438. Springer, Heidelberg (1989). https://doi.org/10.1007/BFb0035774
12. Rauch Henzinger, M., Henzinger, T.A., Kopke, P.W.: Computing simulations on finite and infinite graphs. In: Proceedings of IEEE 36th Annual Foundations of Computer Science, pp. 453–462. IEEE (1995)
13. Hopcroft, J.E., Motwani, R., Ullman, J.D.: Introduction to Automata Theory, Languages, and Computation, 3rd edn. Addison-Wesley Longman (2006)
14. Kanellakis, P.C., Smolka, S.A.: CCS expressions, finite state processes, and three problems of equivalence. Inf. Comput. **86**(1), 43–68 (1990)
15. Kleene, S.C.: Representation of events in nerve nets and finite automata. In: Automata Studies, pp. 3–41. Princeton University Press (1956)
16. Milner, R. (ed.): A Calculus of Communicating Systems. LNCS, vol. 92. Springer, Heidelberg (1980). https://doi.org/10.1007/3-540-10235-3
17. Milner, R.: A complete inference system for a class of regular behaviours. J. Comput. Syst. Sci. **28**(3), 439–466 (1984)
18. Plotkin, G.D.: A structural approach to operational semantics. Technical report, Aarhus University, Denmark (1981)
19. Plotkin, G.D.: The origins of structural operational semantics. J. Logic Algebraic Program. **60**, 3–15 (2004)

20. Sipser, M.: Introduction to the Theory of Computation, 3rd edn. Cengage Learning, Boston (2013)
21. Thompson, K.: Programming techniques: regular expression search algorithm. Commun. ACM **11**(6), 419–422 (1968)
22. van Glabbeek, R., Vaandrager, F.: Petri net models for algebraic theories of concurrency. In: de Bakker, J.W., Nijman, A.J., Treleaven, P.C. (eds.) PARLE 1987. LNCS, vol. 259, pp. 224–242. Springer, Heidelberg (1987). https://doi.org/10.1007/3-540-17945-3_13

Family-Based Fingerprint Analysis:
A Position Paper

Carlos Diego N. Damasceno[1]([✉]) [ID] and Daniel Strüber[1,2] [ID]

[1] Radboud University, Nijmegen, The Netherlands
d.damasceno@cs.ru.nl
[2] Chalmers University of Technology, Gothenburg, Sweden
danstru@chalmers.se

Abstract. Thousands of vulnerabilities are reported on a monthly basis
to security repositories, such as the National Vulnerability Database.
Among these vulnerabilities, software misconfiguration is one of the top
10 security risks for web applications. With this large influx of vulnerability reports, software fingerprinting has become a highly desired
capability to discover distinctive and efficient signatures and recognize
reportedly vulnerable software implementations. Due to the exponential worst-case complexity of fingerprint matching, designing more efficient methods for fingerprinting becomes highly desirable, especially for
variability-intensive systems where optional features add another exponential factor to its analysis. This position paper presents our vision of
a framework that lifts model learning and family-based analysis principles to software fingerprinting. In this framework, we propose unifying
databases of signatures into a featured finite state machine and using
presence conditions to specify whether and in which circumstances a
given input-output trace is observed. We believe feature-based signatures
can aid performance improvements by reducing the size of fingerprints
under analysis.

Keywords: Model Learning · Variability Management · Family-Based
Analysis · Software Fingerprinting

1 Introduction

Automatically recognizing vulnerable black-box components is a critical requirement in security analysis, especially considering the fact that modern systems
typically include components borrowed from free and open-source projects.
Besides, with the large influx of versions released over time and vulnerabilities
reported in security data sources, such as the National Vulnerability Database
(NVD) [25], engineers should dedicate a special attention to the efficiency and
the scalability of techniques for automated software analysis. Providing such a
capability can dramatically reduce engineer's workload and greatly increase the
efficiency as well as the accuracy of security analysis. One of such techniques is
software fingerprinting [33].

N. Jansen et al. (Eds.): Vaandrager Festschrift 2022, LNCS 13560, pp. 137–150, 2022.
https://doi.org/10.1007/978-3-031-15629-8_8

Software fingerprinting aims to produce a distinctive and efficient *signature* from syntactic, semantic, or structural characteristics of a system under test (SUT). It is an important technique with many security applications, ranging from malware detection, digital forensics, copyright infringement, to vulnerability analysis [3]. To produce a signature that is both expressive and identifiable, fingerprint discovery and matching can be pursued using different techniques and representation models [3], such as text-based models (e.g., code instruction or strings), structural models (e.g., call graphs or control/data-flow graphs), and behavioral-based models (e.g., execution traces and finite state machines). When source code is unavailable, model learning [4,38] and testing [8] techniques may be used as means to capture the behavioral signatures of an SUT in terms of states and transitions of a finite state machine.

Model learning has emerged as an effective bug-finding technique for black-box hardware and software components [38]. In active model learning [4], a learning algorithm interacts with an SUT to construct and validate a hypothesis $\mathcal{H}$ about the "language" of its external behavior. In general, this hypothesis is expressed as a Mealy finite state machine (FSM) that, once established, can be deployed as a *behavioral signature* to recognize an SUT. Model learning has been reported effective in building models of different network protocols, including TCP [16], TLS [20,31], Bluetooth [29], and MQTT [34]. In this work, we focus on fingerprinting techniques based upon model learning and model-baseed testing techniques.

Once a group of fingerprints is produced for a set of SUTs, two naive approaches may take place to identify whether an unidentified SUT matches with any of the signatures in a group of fingerprints [20]: (a) re-run model learning over the unidentified SUT and compare the resulting hypothesis to all known signatures; (b) perform conformance testing [8] for each model to see which one matches. While both methods can be effective, they are resource and time intensive and hence, inefficient for large groups of candidate fingerprints. As a matter of fact, active group fingerprinting has an exponential worst-case complexity for the number of fingerprints in a database of signatures [33]. Therefore, finding more efficient ways to perform fingerprint group matching becomes highly desirable.

Fingerprinting is especially challenging in variability-intensive systems, in which particular system variants can be generated by switching features on or off. Optional features lead a combinatorial explosion of the overall set of possible system variants and hence, significant challenges for software analyses [14]. A recent survey indicates that software security of variability-intensive systems is an under-studied topic [22]. To the best of our knowledge, fingerprinting in particular has not been addressed in this context. To date, Shu et al. [33] and Janssen [20] are the most prominent studies exploring model learning [7] and conformance testing [23] in fingerprint group matching. Nevertheless, further investigations are still needed to evaluate the efficiency and scalability of their approaches in large fingerprint databases [20], as expected in variability-intensive systems. In this paper, we envision optimizing fingerprinting techniques towards variability-intensive and evolving systems.

In our vision, we propose principles from variability-aware software analysis [37] as means to achieve an efficient framework for family-based fingerprint discovery and matching. The term *family-based* [37] refers to an analysis that is performed at the level of the whole product line, instead of individual products, thus allowing to efficiently derive statements about *all* products. In our proposed framework, we aim at combining groups of behavioral signatures into a family model, e.g., featured finite state machine [18], and use presence conditions to specify whether (and in which circumstances) a given input-output (IO) trace can be observed.

In combination with SAT/SMT solvers and state-based model comparison algorithms [12,40], this family-based representation can pave the way for efficient fingerprint discovery and matching techniques where the size of the fingerprints under analysis can be reduced in orders of magnitude. It would also contribute to addressing the general lack of family-based analyses in the field: Kenner et al.'s survey [22] mentions a single previous family-based security analysis [27].

This position paper is organized as follows: In Sect. 2, we introduce software fingerprinting, with an emphasis in active model learning [38]. In Sect. 3, we draw our vision of family-based fingerprint analysis upon the concept of family-based analysis [37] and testing [18]. We close this article, in Sect. 4, with our final remarks about this framework for family-based fingerprint analysis.

2   Software Fingerprinting

Software fingerprinting aims at discovering a distinctive and efficient signature of syntactic, semantic, or structural characteristics of a SUT and matching unidentified SUTs against one or more fingerprints in a database. It is a fundamental approach with various applications in software security, including malware detection, software infringement, vulnerability analysis, and digital forensics [3]. To construct signatures that are both expressive and identifiable, fingerprint discovery and matching can be addressed using different kinds of techniques. In this work, we focus on active model learning [4] as a means to achieve fingerprint discovery and matching [20,33].

2.1   Model Learning

Active model learning [4] has been proven effective in fingerprinting behavioral signatures from black-box software implementations [15,20,31,33]. For an overview on model learning, we refer the interested reader to Frits Vaandrager's cover article[1] of the Communications of the ACM Volume 60 [38]. Active model learning is often described in terms of the Minimally Adequate Teacher (MAT) framework [4] shown in Fig. 1.

---

[1] In fact, we would like to thank for this well-crafted introduction that sparked our interest to the topic and led to the initial ideas of the first author's doctoral thesis.

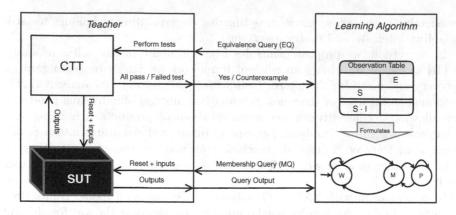

Fig. 1. The MAT framework (adapted from [38])

In the MAT framework, a learning algorithm is used to interact with a black-box system and construct a hypothesis $\mathcal{H}$ about the "language" of a system's external behavior. To construct $\mathcal{H}$, the learning algorithm poses membership queries (MQ) formed by prefixes and suffixes to respectively access and distinguish states in the SUT. Traditionally, these input sequences are maintained in an observation table that guides the formulation of a hypothesis $\mathcal{H}$ of the SUT behavior as a finite state machine (FSM) [8].

Once a hypothesis is formulated, equivalence queries (EQ) are used to check whether $\mathcal{H}$ fits in the SUT behavior, otherwise it replies a counterexample that exposes any differences. EQs are typically derived using conformance testing techniques [8]. To handle more complex behavior, learning algorithms can also enrich hypotheses with time intervals [1,35] and data guards [33]. Whenever a hypothesis is consistent with an SUT, it can be deployed as a fingerprint [3,20,38].

2.2   A Methodology and Taxonomy for Formal Fingerprint Analysis

Software fingerprinting has been the focus of previous research from multiple angles [3]. A formal methodology for fingerprinting problems is introduced by Shu et al. [33]. They introduce the Parameterized Extended Finite State Machine (PEFSM) model as an extension of the FSM formalism that incorporates state variables, guards, and parameterized IO symbols to represent behavioral signatures of network protocols. Using the PEFSM model, the authors discuss a taxonomy of network fingerprinting problems where these are distinguished by their type (active or passive experiments), and goal (matching or discovery). A summary of the taxonomy for fingerprinting problems is shown in Table 1.

In active fingerprinting, security analysts are able to pose queries to an unidentified SUT whenever they want. In contrast, in passive experiments, fingerprint analysis is limited to a finite set of IO traces as source of information. While active experiments are known to be more effective for providing freedom to query as much as wanted, passive experiments have the advantage that the

Table 1. Taxonomy of fingerprinting problems (adapted from [33])

Fingerprinting problem	Experiment type	
	Active	Passive
Single matching	Conformance testing	Passive testing
Group matching	Online matching separation	Concurrent passive testing
Discovery with spec.	Model enumeration and separation	Back-tracking based testing
Discovery without spec.	Model learning	No efficient solution

SUT stays completely unaware that it is under analysis. The process of building a fingerprint signature for an SUT is named *fingerprint discovery*.

In fingerprint discovery [33], the goal is to systematically build a distinctive and efficient fingerprint for a SUT. This can be performed by retrieving as much information as possible with the guidance of a pre-existing specification. Otherwise, if no specification is available, model learning [38] can be still applied to build behavioral signatures. Once a database of signatures is established, the task of *fingerprint matching* can take place.

Typically, the goal of fingerprint matching is to determine whether the behavior of an unidentified SUT matches a single fingerprint signature. However, in cases where there are multiple signatures, it may be interesting to consider matching the SUT against a set of fingerprints of different versions of an implementation [33].

Active group fingerprinting has been reported to require an exponential worst-case execution time defined by the number of fingerprints in a group [33]. Therefore, it is highly desirable to have group matching approaches that are more efficient than checking fingerprints one by one.

Example 1. (Running example of fingerprint analysis) In Fig. 2, we depict three alternative versions of an FSM describing the behavior of characters in a game platform, namely $v1, v2, v3$.

In the first version $v1$, we have a character that stays in constant movement, once it starts walking. In version $v2$, the character can toggle its moving mode. And, in version $v3$, the character skills are extended with another feature to temporary **pause** its movement. To distinguish versions $v1$ and $v2$, we have the input sequence **start · end**.

Limitations and Related Work. The algorithms for fingerprint matching introduced by Shu et al. [33] have been specifically designed for PEF-SMs. Hence, they cannot be directly applied to other notations, such as Mealy machines [38,39] and timed automata [1,35]; that have more consolidated and ongoing research. To fill this gap, Janssen [20] introduced two novel methods for group fingerprinting matching in his Master's dissertation, under the supervision of prof. Frits Vaandrager.

In this work, Janssen [20] explores state-of-the-art conformance testing techniques [7] in active fingerprint group matching. Despite the empirical evidences

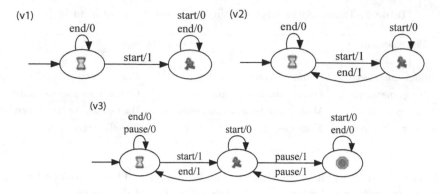

Fig. 2. Family of product FSMs

using an extensive list of TLS implementations, the author points out that further research is still needed to evaluate the efficiency and scalability of their fingerprint matching methods when models are added over time [20]. This limitation becomes particularly interesting if we consider the large number of release versions that can emerge over time and the influx of vulnerability reports available in security databases. For instance, at the moment this manuscript was produced, the GitHub repository of the OpenSSL project [26] has 338 release versions and more than 31 thousand commits and, the NVD has more than 300 vulnerabilities associated with the keyword "*openssl*". This reinforces the need for designing fingerprinting techniques able to efficiently handle large sets of signatures.

3   Family-Based Fingerprint Analysis

As previously discussed, the efficiency of fingerprinting heavily depends on the number of fingerprints under analysis. In fact, the size of a candidate group of fingerprints is an exponential factor in the worst-case complexity of fingerprint group matching [33]. In variability-intensive systems, this factor may become more noticeable because the number of valid products is up-to exponential in the number of features [37]. Thus, to minimize costs and effort, while maximizing the effectiveness, we propose looking at fingerprint discovery and matching from a feature-oriented perspective [21].

Feature modeling allows software engineers to design and manage families of similar, yet customized products by enabling or disabling features. A feature is any prominent or distinctive user-visible behavior or characteristic of a software system [21]. Features are typically managed in association with other assets, including feature models [21], source code [5], and test models [18].

In fingerprinting, the notion of features may be used to capture variability in IO interfaces, optional build parameters, or even release version identifiers.

However, when fingerprinting variability-intensive, evolving software systems, it becomes essential to represent behavioral signatures in a way that is succinct [9,17] and aid the design and implementation of *variability-aware* analysis strategies [37]. To pursue performance improvements, there is a research direction dedicated to raise variability-awareness in software analysis by lifting modeling languages and analysis strategies to the so called family-based level [37].

3.1 Family-Based Modeling and Analysis

In family-based analysis, domain artifacts, such as feature models [21], are exploited to efficiently reason about product variants and feature combinations. To make it feasible, software modeling and analysis principles are extended to become aware of variability knowledge and avoid redundant computations across multiple products; an issue that typically occurs when standard software analysis is applied in an exhaustive, product-based fashion [37].

Product-based analysis techniques are known to be effective but *infeasible* because of the potentially exponential number of valid implementations; or, in the best case, *inefficient*, due to redundant computations over assets shared among multiple products [37].

Family-based analysis operates on a unified representation of a family of product-specific representations, namely the *family model*. A Featured Finite State Machine (FFSM) [18] is one example of variability-aware modeling notation proposed to express families of FSMs as a unified artifact. In FFSMs, states and transitions are annotated with presence conditions described as propositional logic formulae defined over the set of features. These FSM fragments are called conditional transition [18] as they occur only when the feature constraints involved in a concerned state or transition are satisfied.

Using SAT solvers, family models are amenable to automated derivation of product-specific models [17], family-based model checking [9], and configurable test case generation [18], where redundant analysis over shared states/transitions are mitigated. Thus, the cost of family-based analysis becomes determined by the feature size and amount of feature sharing, instead of the number of valid products [37].

To guide the creation and maintenance of family models, recent studies have proposed the application of model comparison algorithms, such as LTS_diff [40] and FFSM_diff [12], to match and merge product-specific FSMs. These approaches can provide efficient means to find differences between models [40] and produce succinct FFSM representations from families of FSMs [11,12].

Motivated by these benefits, we introduce our vision of how family-based learning [11,12] and testing [9,18] principles could be lifted to behavior-based fingerprint analysis. These notions should aid an efficient framework for family-based fingerprint analysis where a group of behavioral signatures are handled, matched and merged as a family model, rather than a group of individual signatures.

Example 2. (Running example of behavioral variability models) In Fig. 3, we depict a family-based representation for the set of alternative product FSMs shown in the previous example.

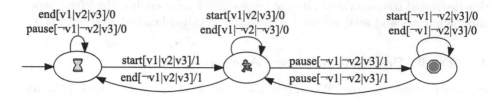

Fig. 3. Example of family model expressed as a FFSM

3.2 A Framework for Family-Based Fingerprint Analysis

In this paper, we propose the development of a framework for family-based fingerprint analysis. We suggest principles from model learning [11,12] and testing [9,18] as means to kick-off the automated creation and maintenance of family-based signatures from a set of SUT binaries. In Fig. 4, we depict this framework, which, inspired by [32,33], we divided in two stages: (a) *Fingerprint discovery*, where a family signature is generated by learning, matching, and merging SUT-specific signatures; and (b) *Fingerprint Matching*, where the family signature is employed as a *configuration query oracle* to answer *if* or *under which circumstances* a given IO trace has been observed.

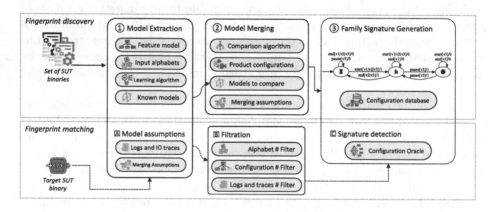

Fig. 4. A framework for family-based fingerprint analysis

Family Fingerprint Discovery. When fingerprinting a set of SUT binaries that are akin, it is reasonable to assume that they share behavioral commonalities due to similar requirements or even reused components. Hence, we believe adaptive model learning [19] is a variant that can aid in reducing the costs required for fingerprint discovery. In adaptive learning, pre-existing models are used to derive MQs to steer learning algorithms to states maintained after updates, and potentially speed up the model learning process for systems evolving over time [10] and in space [36]. Hence, we believe these benefits may also hold in fingerprint discovery.

Once a group of signatures is obtained, fingerprint matching may be performed in its standard way. However, as the cost for fingerprint group matching may increase exponentially to the number of alternative versions and the size of its candidate signatures, we suggest a model merging step to combine a set of behavioral signatures into a unified FFSM representation [18]. To support this step, we find that state-based model comparison algorithms (e.g., LTS_diff [40], FFSM_diff [12]) can provide efficient means to construct a *family signature*. Merging assumptions can be used to preset state pairs matching [40] and aid the creation of a more succinct representation [12] for groups of fingerprints. This concept of family signature provides the basis for a key entity in family-based fingerprinting experiments, namely the *configuration query oracle* (CQ).

Our idea for a CQ is an abstract entity able to report *if* or *under which circumstances* (e.g., feature combinations, versions) a given IO trace has been previously observed. We believe that CQs can also be repurposed to recommend configurable test cases for distinguishing SUT versions from their *observed outputs* or *satisfiable presence conditions*. Thus, family-based signatures are amenable to be deployed in both passive and active fingerprint experiments for discovery and matching.

Family Fingerprint Matching. Once a family signature is created, variability-aware, model-based testing concepts can enable an efficient fingerprint matching. Particularly, we see that family-based testing principles, such as configurable test suites [18], could be repurposed as queries to check whether a particular IO trace has been previously observed. If so, the presence conditions assigned to the conditional transitions traversed by an IO trace can be used to constraint the configuration space of a family of SUT binaries, e.g., "the following presence conditions must hold because the IO traces matches with this list of conditional state/transition". To automate the task of fingerprint matching, SAT/SMT solvers can be used to reply what (or even how many) configurations can potentially match to a given SUT behavior, as EQs do.

Example 3. (Example of fingerprint matching) In Fig. 5, we illustrate an example of configurable test cases derived from the FFSM in Fig. 3.

From this configurable test case, we can find that the trace start/1 · end/1 implies the constraint $(v1|v2|v3) \land (\neg v1|v2|v3)$ and, from it, we can discard a match between the SUT and version v1. Also, we can find that this same input is able to distinguish versions v1 and v2. In this case, if the trace start/1 · end/0

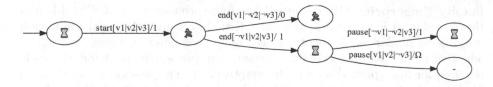

Fig. 5. Example of configurable test case for fingerprint matching

is observed, then the constraint $(v1|v2|v3) \wedge (v1|\neg v2|\neg v3)$ is derived and hence, a match to v1 is found.

3.3 Practical and Theoretical Implications

In this section, we outline a few implications of this framework on software analysis. These include (a) Combining passive and active fingerprinting experiments, (b) Family-based fingerprinting in model learning, and (c) Fingerprint Analysis in the Open-World.

Hybrid Fingerprinting Experiments. When fingerprinting, traces from passive experiments can be incorporated in fingerprint matching to constraint the configuration space of family-based fingerprints. Then, presence conditions derived from these IO traces can be used to steer fingerprint analysis to parts of the signature to reduce the uncertainty of what configuration is inside some unidentified SUT. Similar concepts have been used in adaptive learning to speed up update learning and should also aid performance improvements.

Family Signatures in Active Model Learning. Family-based fingerprints may also support active model learning, particularly by providing *EQ*s based on multiple merged hypotheses. Typically, equivalence queries are approximated via conformance testing techniques applied over a single hypothesis [4]. However, some learning techniques may construct hypothesis non-deterministically [39] and hence, potentially lead to "hypotheses mutants". Aichernig et al. [2] has shown that EQs can be efficiently generated using mutation analysis over hypothesis. We believe these results may also hold when combined with family models. In fact, a similar idea has been already investigated by Devroey et al. [13] within the context of family model-based testing where behavioral variability models have been deployed to optimize the generation, configuration and execution of mutants. Nevertheless, there are still no studies deploying family model-based testing in active learning.

Towards Fingerprinting Highly-Configurable Systems. As our long term vision, we aim at making our approach suitable for highly-configurable systems, where it is infeasible to enumerate all variants or the complete SUT behavior.

Hence, fingerprinting must rely on samples of traces. Currently, if the SUT does not have an *exact match* with any signature, Shu et al. [33] recommends applying model learning [4] to the SUT. However, in highly-configurable systems, exhaustive learning becomes impractical due to the potentially exponential number of valid configurations. Thus, it becomes interesting to inform whether an *unindetified trace* has an *inexact match* with patterns associated to a particular configuration or parameter. To address this, we believe that other variability-aware representations, e.g., composition-based models [6] or control-flow graphs [30], and analysis techniques, e.g., statistical classification or clustering [28], may be more suitable to capture fingerprints as small behavioral or structural patterns, rather than an exact annotative-based model [9,17] of the SUT behavior.

4 Final Remarks

This paper discusses a generic framework for lifting fingerprint analysis to the family-based level. We suggest that state-based model comparison algorithms [40] can aid the creation of concise FFSM representations [11,12] from a set of fingerprints and enable efficient fingerprint analysis. We envision there are a plenty of real-world artifacts and alternative analysis and modeling approaches that could be used to start exploring and expanding this problem. Many artifacts are available in the Automata Wiki [24]. We believe this repository constitutes a great opportunity to future investigations in this novel topic which we call **family-based fingerprinting analysis.**

References

1. Aichernig, B.K., Pferscher, A., Tappler, M.: From passive to active: learning timed automata efficiently. In: Lee, R., Jha, S., Mavridou, A., Giannakopoulou, D. (eds.) NFM 2020. LNCS, vol. 12229, pp. 1–19. Springer, Cham (2020). https://doi.org/10.1007/978-3-030-55754-6_1

2. Aichernig, B.K., Tappler, M.: Efficient active automata learning via mutation testing. J. Autom. Reason. **63**(4), 1103–1134 (2018). https://doi.org/10.1007/s10817-018-9486-0

3. Alrabaee, S., Debbabi, M., Wang, L.: A survey of binary code fingerprinting approaches: taxonomy, methodologies, and features. ACM Comput. Surv. **55**(1), 1–41 (2022). https://doi.org/10.1145/3486860

4. Angluin, D.: Learning regular sets from queries and counterexamples. Inf. Comput. **75**(2), 87–106 (1987). https://doi.org/10.1016/0890-5401(87)90052-6

5. Apel, S., Batory, D., Kästner, C., Saake, G.: Feature-Oriented Software Product Lines. Springer, Berlin, Heidelberg (2013). https://doi.org/10.1007/978-3-642-37521-7

6. Benduhn, F., Thüm, T., Lochau, M., Leich, T., Saake, G.: A survey on modeling techniques for formal behavioral verification of software product lines. In: Proceedings of the Ninth International Workshop on Variability Modelling of Software-intensive Systems, pp. 80:80–80:87. VaMoS 2015. ACM, New York (2015). https://doi.org/10.1145/2701319.2701332, event-place: Hildesheim, Germany

7. van den Bos, P., Vaandrager, F.: State identification for labeled transition systems with inputs and outputs. Sci. Comput. Program. **209**, 102678 (2021). https://doi.org/10.1016/j.scico.2021.102678

8. Broy, M., Jonsson, B., Katoen, J.-P., Leucker, M., Pretschner, A. (eds.) Model-Based Testing of Reactive Systems. LNCS, vol. 3472. Springer, Heidelberg (2005). https://doi.org/10.1007/b137241

9. Classen, A., Cordy, M., Schobbens, P.Y., Heymans, P., Legay, A., Raskin, J.F.: Featured transition systems: foundations for verifying variability-intensive systems and their application to LTL model checking. IEEE Trans. Softw. Eng. **39**(8), 1069–1089 (2013). https://doi.org/10.1109/TSE.2012.86

10. Damasceno, C.D.N., Mousavi, M.R., da Silva Simao, A.: Learning to reuse: adaptive model learning for evolving systems. In: Ahrendt, W., Tapia Tarifa, S.L. (eds.) IFM 2019. LNCS, vol. 11918, pp. 138–156. Springer, Cham (2019). https://doi.org/10.1007/978-3-030-34968-4_8

11. Damasceno, C.D.N., Mousavi, M.R., Simao, A.: Learning from difference: an automated approach for learning family models from software product lines [research]. In: Proceedings of the 23rd International Systems and Software Product Line Conference - Volume A. SPLC 2019. ACM, New York (2019). https://doi.org/10.1145/3336294.3336307

12. Damasceno, C.D.N., Mousavi, M.R., Simao, A.S.: Learning by sampling: learning behavioral family models from software product lines. Empir. Softw. Eng. **26**(1), 1–46 (2021). https://doi.org/10.1007/s10664-020-09912-w

13. Devroey, X., Perrouin, G., Papadakis, M., Legay, A., Schobbens, P.Y., Heymans, P.: Featured model-based mutation analysis. In: Proceedings of the 38th International Conference on Software Engineering, pp. 655–666. ICSE 2016, New York (2016). https://doi.org/10.1145/2884781.2884821

14. Elmaghbub, A., Hamdaoui, B.: LoRa device fingerprinting in the wild: disclosing RF Data-driven fingerprint sensitivity to deployment variability. IEEE Access **9**, 142893–142909 (2021). https://doi.org/10.1109/ACCESS.2021.3121606

15. Fiterau-Brostean, P., Jonsson, B., Merget, R., de Ruiter, J., Sagonas, K., Somorovsky, J.: Analysis of DTLS implementations using protocol state fuzzing. In: 29th USENIX Security Symposium (USENIX Security 20), pp. 2523–2540. USENIX Association, August 2020. https://www.usenix.org/conference/usenixsecurity20/presentation/fiterau-brostean

16. Fiterău-Broştean, P., Janssen, R., Vaandrager, F.: Combining model learning and model checking to analyze TCP implementations. In: Chaudhuri, S., Farzan, A. (eds.) CAV 2016. LNCS, vol. 9780, pp. 454–471. Springer, Cham (2016). https://doi.org/10.1007/978-3-319-41540-6_25

17. Fragal, V.H., Simao, A., Mousavi, M.R.: Validated test models for software product lines: featured finite state machines. In: Kouchnarenko, O., Khosravi, R. (eds.) Formal Aspects of Component Software: 13th International Conference, FACS 2016. Springer, Cham (2017). https://doi.org/10.1007/978-3-319-57666-4_13

18. Fragal, V.H., Simao, A., Mousavi, M.R., Turker, U.C.: Extending HSI test generation method for software product lines. Comput. J. (2018). https://doi.org/10.1093/comjnl/bxy046

19. Huistra, D., Meijer, J., van de Pol, J.: Adaptive learning for learn-based regression testing. In: Howar, F., Barnat, J. (eds.) FMICS 2018. LNCS, vol. 11119, pp. 162–177. Springer, Cham (2018). https://doi.org/10.1007/978-3-030-00244-2_11

20. Janssen, E.: Fingerprinting TLS implementations using model learning. Master's thesis, Radboud Universit, Nijmegen, March 2021

21. Kang, K., Cohen, S., Hess, J., Novak, W., Peterson, A.: Feature-Oriented Domain Analysis (FODA) Feasibility Study. Technical report CMU/SEI-90-TR-021, Software Engineering Institute, Carnegie Mellon University, Pittsburgh, PA (1990)
22. Kenner, A., May, R., Krüger, J., Saake, G., Leich, T.: Safety, security, and configurable software systems: a systematic mapping study. In: Proceedings of the 25th ACM International Systems and Software Product Line Conference - Volume A. New York, September 2021. https://doi.org/10.1145/3461001.3471147
23. Lee, D., Yannakakis, M.: Principles and methods of testing finite state machines-a survey. Proc. IEEE **84**(8), 1090–1123 (1996). https://doi.org/10.1109/5.533956
24. Neider, D., Smetsers, R., Vaandrager, F., Kuppens, H.: Benchmarks for automata learning and conformance testing. In: Margaria, T., Graf, S., Larsen, K.G. (eds.) Models, Mindsets, Meta: The What, the How, and the Why Not? LNCS, vol. 11200, pp. 390–416. Springer, Cham (2019). https://doi.org/10.1007/978-3-030-22348-9_23
25. NVD: The National Vulnerability Database (2022). https://nvd.nist.gov/
26. OpenSSL Foundation Inc: OpenSSL Releases on Github (2022). https://github.com/openssl/openssl/releases
27. Peldszus, S., Strüber, D., Jürjens, J.: Model-based security analysis of feature-oriented software product lines. In: Proceedings of the 17th ACM SIGPLAN International Conference on Generative Programming: Concepts and Experiences, pp. 93–106 (2018). https://doi.org/10.1145/3278122.3278126
28. Pereira, J.A., Acher, M., Martin, H., Jézéquel, J.M., Botterweck, G., Ventresque, A.: Learning software configuration spaces: a systematic literature review. J. Syst. Softw. **182**, 111044 (2021). https://doi.org/10.1016/j.jss.2021.111044
29. Pferscher, A., Aichernig, B.K.: Fingerprinting Bluetooth low energy devices via active automata learning. In: Huisman, M., Păsăreanu, C., Zhan, N. (eds.) FM 2021. LNCS, vol. 13047, pp. 524–542. Springer, Cham (2021). https://doi.org/10.1007/978-3-030-90870-6_28
30. Rhein, A.V., Liebig, J., Janker, A., Kästner, C., Apel, S.: Variability-aware static analysis at scale: an empirical study. ACM Trans. Softw. Eng. Methodol. **27**(4), 1–33 (2018). https://doi.org/10.1145/3280986
31. Ruiter, J.: A tale of the OpenSSL state machine: a large-scale black-box analysis. In: Brumley, B.B., Röning, J. (eds.) NordSec 2016. LNCS, vol. 10014, pp. 169–184. Springer, Cham (2016). https://doi.org/10.1007/978-3-319-47560-8_11
32. Shirani, P., Wang, L., Debbabi, M.: BinShape: scalable and robust binary library function identification using function shape. In: Polychronakis, M., Meier, M. (eds.) DIMVA 2017. LNCS, vol. 10327, pp. 301–324. Springer, Cham (2017). https://doi.org/10.1007/978-3-319-60876-1_14
33. Shu, G., Lee, D.: A formal methodology for network protocol fingerprinting. IEEE Trans. Parallel Distrib. Syst. **22**(11), 1813–1825 (2011). https://doi.org/10.1109/TPDS.2011.26
34. Tappler, M., Aichernig, B.K., Bloem, R.: Model-based testing IoT communication via active automata learning. In: 2017 IEEE International Conference on Software Testing, Verification and Validation (ICST), March 2017. https://doi.org/10.1109/ICST.2017.32
35. Tappler, M., Aichernig, B.K., Larsen, K.G., Lorber, F.: Time to learn – learning timed automata from tests. In: André, É., Stoelinga, M. (eds.) FORMATS 2019. LNCS, vol. 11750, pp. 216–235. Springer, Cham (2019). https://doi.org/10.1007/978-3-030-29662-9_13

36. Tavassoli, S., Damasceno, C.D.N., Khosravi, R., Mousavi, M.R.: Adaptive behavioral model learning for software product lines. In: Proceedings of the 26th International Systems and Software Product Line Conference, SPLC 2022 (2022)

37. Thüm, T., Apel, S., Kästner, C., Schaefer, I., Saake, G.: A classification and survey of analysis strategies for software product lines. ACM Comput. Surv. **47**(1), 1–45 (2014). https://doi.org/10.1145/2580950

38. Vaandrager, F.: Model learning. Commun. ACM **60**(2) (2017). https://doi.org/10.1145/2967606

39. Vaandrager, F., Garhewal, B., Rot, J., Wißmann, T.: A new approach for active automata learning based on apartness. In: Proceedings of the 28th International Conference on Tools and Algorithms for the Construction and Analysis of Systems (TACAS), January 2022. http://arxiv.org/abs/2107.05419

40. Walkinshaw, N., Bogdanov, K.: Automated comparison of state-based software models in terms of their language and structure. ACM Trans. Softw. Eng. Methodol. **22**(2), 1–37 (2013). https://doi.org/10.1145/2430545.2430549

What's in School? – Topic Maps for Secondary School Computer Science

Ansgar Fehnker[✉]

Macquarie University, Sydney, Australia
ansgar.fehnker@mq.edu.au

Abstract. Computer science education in secondary schools has transformed in the last decade, both in content and status. Whereas, initially the subject focused mostly on digital skills – if it was taught at all – different institutions and countries have adopted teaching and examination plans that introduce computer science as a science.

Even before the adoption of computer science as a regular subject in schools, individual researchers and academics created content to be used in schools. One such example is the model checking unit developed by Vaandrager et al. in the 2000s. While these activities are not aimed to give a complete view of computer science, they can serve as a proxy to determine which topics researchers consider important and suitable for secondary school.

This paper will focus on secondary school computer science in the UK, the Netherlands, and the state North Rhine-Westphalia in Germany. It will map the content of examination or teaching plans to a common classification by the scientific community – the ACM subject classification. The comparison reveals choices made by the different countries. We furthermore compare it to one of the first model checking units for secondary school, developed by Vaandrager et al., which is still being used today.

Keywords: Computer science education · Computing education programs · Model curricula

1 Introduction

While computer science established itself as a separate subject at universities from the 1980s onwards – either in its own right or in the context of other fields such as bioinformatics – computer science in schools was treated differently. The UK Royal Society observed in their 2012 report *Shut-down or restart?* that despite individual instances of imaginative and inspiring teaching, many pupils learned not much more than basic digital literacy skills such as the use of a word processor [12]. A committee of the Royal Dutch Academy of Sciences observed in 2012 that after an initial push in the 1990s for computer science in secondary school, it withered away, due to understaffing and lack of curriculum development [10]. The committee observed that most primary school pupils in 2012

N. Jansen et al. (Eds.): Vaandrager Festschrift 2022, LNCS 13560, pp. 151–163, 2022.
https://doi.org/10.1007/978-3-031-15629-8_9

could use computing technology at a level that just 10 years was taught in secondary school. They criticised henceforth secondary school *computer science* education, which did not aim at more than teaching the use of devices or building a web page. The German *Gesellschaft für Informatik* (GI) warned in 2015 in the *3rd Dagstuhl Declaration* not to confuse computer science education with the training of computer usage [14]. Interestingly, the call to treat computer science in school as more than the training of computer usage was already a core recommendation in the *1st Dagstuhl Declaration* from 1992 [5].

In the second decade of this century, new curricula were developed, combined with efforts to improve the status of computer science as a subject. Computer science became a mandatory subject in secondary school in the UK from age 10 to 16, and the UK Department of Education published the first guidelines for GCSE and A-level computer science in 2014 [18]. In 2013 the German GI was tasked with developing a joint computer science standard for the different German states [1]. North-Rhine Westfalia, the German state adjacent to the Netherlands, implemented a new curriculum in 2014 [11]. In 2016 the Stichting Leerplanontwikkeling (SLO) proposed a new curriculum [4], which became the new curriculum that came into effect in 2019 [3,16]. While there have been comparable efforts in other countries, this paper focuses on these three.

The official recognition of computer science as a regular subject in schools was preceded by individual researchers and academics who created content to be used in schools. One such example is the model checking material developed by Vaandrager et al. [19]. While these activities are often insular and not aimed to give a complete picture, they serve as a proxy to determine which topics are considered important and suitable for secondary school by researchers from the field. This is relevant since an aim of teaching computer science is should be "exposure to Computer Science as a rigorous academic discipline" [12].

This paper examines which topics from the field of computer science are covered by the new computer science curricula. It maps topics that are mentioned in the curricula, teaching or examination plan to the 2012 ACM Computing Classification System [2]. This classification provides an ontology of concepts and categories that reflect the state of the computing discipline. The choice to use the ACM Computing Classification – a tool made for and by the computing community – instead of a tool by the educational community, such as model curricula, is intentional. It separates the topic areas that appear in the curriculum, from educational considerations, such as complexity, specificity and cognitive domain. This paper looks at the senior years of secondary school, which prepare pupils for a study at a university.

This mapping exercise identifies topics that are relevant across different countries, as well as differences. It helps to answer the question of whether topics that are prominent in one curriculum, are equally important in the others. The paper will also derive a topic map for a specific learning activity. This is not done to check for compliance with the curriculum – in this case, the learning activity precedes either of the curricula considered in this paper – but to assess to what extent content developed by an active research group fits in with current curricula, and whether it can inform its further development.

2   Computer Science Learning and Teaching Standards

The *core teaching plan* for the senior years of secondary school in North Rhine-Westphalia (NRW) was published in 2014 by the state minister of education [11]. NRW borders the Netherlands, has a similar population size in a slightly smaller area, and includes the Ruhr area. The core teaching plan provides a framework for the *Gymnasiale Oberstufe*, which leads to the *Abitur*, which is comparable to the *A-level* exam in the UK, or the *vwo* exam in the Netherlands.

The NRW teaching plan states explicitly that it aims to concentrate on fundamental and timeless computer science ideas, concepts, and methods. The teaching plan distinguishes between competence areas and topic areas. Competence areas are *reasoning, modelling, implementation, presentation and interpretation*, as well as *communication and cooperation*. The top-level topic areas are *data and structure, algorithms, formal languages and automata, information systems*, and *computer science, humans and society*. This paper focuses on the topic areas.

The core teaching plan of NRW precedes the report of the *Gesellschaft für Informatik* (GI) from 2015. This report was produced at the request of the joint federal conference of education ministers. Setting education standards is a responsibility of the individual German states, but the joint federal conference can set agreed standards. The GI recommendation distinguishes between competencies and topics, like the NRW core teaching plan does, with some adjustments to the specific competency and topic areas. The 2014 NRW core teaching plan met the criteria of the GI recommendation, as it is still in effect today.

In 2014 the UK department of education (DoE) published a guideline on *GCE AS and A level subject content* for computer science [18]. The guideline became effective in 2015. An explicitly stated objective was that pupils develop an understanding of fundamental principles and concepts of computer science. The subject content was divided between *knowledge and understanding*, which includes the *understanding of programming, data structures, networks* and *algorithms*, and *skills*, which includes *problem-solving, designing, testing and debugging*, and *applying relevant mathematics*.

The guideline by DoE does not provide a detailed teaching plan. It leaves room for different accreditation providers to develop their own. Schools in England can be accredited by several accreditation providers. This paper will the consider the 2021 *Cambridge Assessment International Examination* (CAIE) syllabus for AS& A-Level computer science [6]. CAIE is targeting international schools inside and outside of the UK, that want to offer a degree that is equivalent to the UK AS or A-level.

The syllabus defines four sections: *computational thinking and problem-solving, fundamental problem-solving and programming skills, advanced theory* and *further problem-solving and programming skills*. Each of these sections is then further refined. Whereas the DoE guideline gives too little detail for comparison of the covered topics, the CAIE syllabus refines it for some topics down to specific examples that can be expected in class.

The Minister of Education in the Netherlands appointed a committee that presented 2016 an advisory report on a future computer science exam program [4]. The advice uses a concept-context approach that separates between concept, and the context in which the concept is applied. This is a similar approach to the one taken in both the NRW teaching plan and the CAIE syllabus. This advisory report formed the basis for a new curriculum which came into effect in 2019 [16].

The curriculum is divided into a core curriculum and elective themes. The core curriculum covers 6 domains: *skills, foundations, information, programming, architecture* and *interaction*. The elective themes define 12 different domains, of which a vwo pupil has to choose four. All students that take the computer science subject have to cover the core curriculum.

The curriculum tries to strike a balance between giving guidance as well as the freedom to schools when implementing the curriculum [3]. This places it between the general guidelines of the UK DoE, and the more specific NRW and CAIE curriculum. For the topic mapping, we include in addition example specifications that are provided by Stichting Leerplanontwikkeling (SLO) [17]. They provide additional information on the core topics, such that the comparison with the CAIE and NRW curricula can be made at a more equal level of detail.

3 Topic Maps

This paper presents topics maps for three educational standards. These maps are using the ACM computing classification system (CCS) as the baseline. It provides a hierarchy of 2113 categories and concepts, with 13 top-level categories and 84 level-two categories, up to 6 levels deep. The concept of *mutual exclusion*, for example, has been categorised as follows: *Software and its engineering > Software organisation and properties > Contextual software domains > Operating systems > Process management > Mutual exclusion.*

Figure 1 show the distribution of concept up to the level-two categories, which will be used in this paper. The most prominent top-level category is *Information systems*, followed by *Computing Methodologies*. The latter owes its prominent position because of *Machine Learning* and *Artificial Intelligence*. The distribution reflects how different research disciplines evolved over time, and cannot be used as such as a guide for which topics should be taught in school. It illustrates, however, that the educational standards make a biased choice from the topics in computer science, as neither of these topics is the most prominent topic in any of the three curricula, as the remainder will show.

When an educational standard mentions an identifiable topic it is mapped to a corresponding concept in the CCS. The CAIE for example states that a candidate should be able to "show understanding of how data for a bit-mapped image is encoded". This would be mapped to "Graphics file formats". The mapping considers only the topic and ignores for example that the verb "understanding" points to a certain cognitive domain in Bloom's taxonomy. The mapping uses concepts from level 2 or above in CCS; level 1 topics would give too little granularity. It is not always possible to map a topic to the CCS; there is for example no appropriate category for the topic of binary numbers. The CCS also does not mention audio or sound, while the CAIE syllabus does.

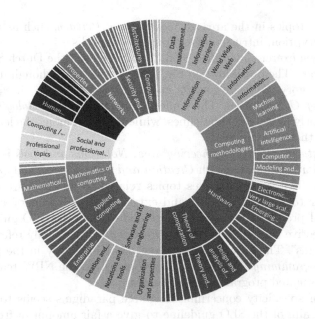

Fig. 1. Distribution of the first 2 levels in the ACM computing classification system.

For the NRW core teaching plan 71 different topics were identified. Figure 2 shows a breakdown of the first 2 levels of these topics. It is apparent that *Software and its engineering* is the most prominent category, followed by *Theory of Computation* and *Networks*. The most prominent sub-category *Notations and tools* includes sub-topics related to *syntax, semantics, compilers, interpreters* and *parsers*, but also topics such as *polymorphism, classes and objects, modules/packages, Unified Modeling Language (UML)* and *Object oriented frameworks*. Even topics that are associated with competence *modelling* are often related to modelling of object-oriented systems. Imperative programming, or any other language paradigm, is not mentioned once.

Within the CAIE syllabus 99 different topics were identified. As in the NRW teaching plan *Software and its engineering* is the most prominent category, as depicted in Fig. 3. However, *Networks* and *Security and Privacy* are more prominent, compared to the NRW plan. The same holds for the topic *Hardware* which is all but absent from the NRW plan. It mentions hardware only in relation to other topics such as networks. The topic *Theory of Computation* plays in contrast a less prominent role in the CAIE syllabus compared to the NRW curriculum.

The largest sub-category of *Software and its engineering* is *Notations and tools*. It contains topics related to parsing and compilation, like the NRW plan, but also topics such as imperative languages, declarative languages, and topics related to object-oriented programming. Object-oriented programming is mentioned throughout the syllabus but is always accompanied by mentions of other programming paradigms. The CAIE syllabus distinguishes itself also by mentioning specific topics in the area of *Security and Privacy*, such as asymmetric public-key encryption, intrusion detection, and firewalls.

The mapping exercise identified 81 different topics in the Dutch SLO examination guidelines. The breakdown in Fig. 4 shows that even though it is this still the largest category, *Software and its engineering* is more on an equal footing with *Theory of Computation*. The topic *Computation Methodologies* also features prominently in the SLO guidelines, while it ranks among the least featured topics in the other two curricula.

Within *Software and its engineering* area, *Notations and tools* is not largest sub-category, but comparable with *Creation and management*, and *Organization and properties*. The former includes topics related to the software design process, the latter topics to functional and extra-functional properties. The term object-oriented programming is not mentioned once in the SLO guideline. Not even in the elective theme *Programming Paradigms*, which only refers to "alternative paradigms". The only paradigm mentioned explicitly in the guideline is *Imperative Programming*. This is in sharp contrast to the NRW teaching plan, where object-oriented programming is the norm.

The lack of specificity concerning language paradigms seems to be related to the explicit aim of the SLO guideline to give a fair amount of freedom. The example specification provided by SLO, for example, states several times, that certain topics are not mandatory, something neither of the other curricula does. For example, when it discusses database query languages, it explicitly states that the language does not have to be SQL. The CAIE syllabus, in contrast, expects pupils to understand that SQL is the industry standard, with no qualification.

The SLO guidelines are also characterised by the fact that it covers more level 1 and level 2 topic areas than the CAIE or the NRW curricula. It is broader and less focused. This is largely due to the fact that it includes 12 elective themes. Students are only expected to select four themes, which means that they will not be exposed to the entire range of topics depicted in Fig. 4.

The comparison of the three curricula shows that certain topics have very different statuses in different curricula. The topic *Theory of Computation* plays a prominent role in the NRW and SLO curricula but is less prominent in the CAIE curriculum. *Computing methodology* plays a large role in the SLO curriculum, compared to the CAIE and NRW counterparts. The same holds for *Networks* and *Hardware*, which are fairly relevant in the CAIE syllabus, but almost absent from the NRW curriculum. But even within a topic area, the choice for sub-topics can diverge, as the question of language paradigms in the area *Software and its engineering* demonstrates.

This paper maps the different topics covered by the curricula, but it is beyond the scope to analyse the causes or effects of those choices. The next section, will, however, analyse a specific learning activity, which gives some indication of how research by individual research groups can influence covered topic areas.

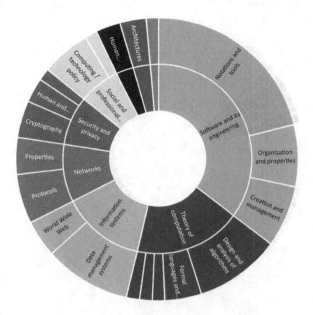

Fig. 2. Topic map for the NRW core teaching plan.

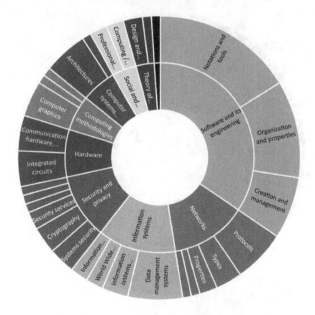

Fig. 3. Topic map for CAIE syllabus AS & A level.

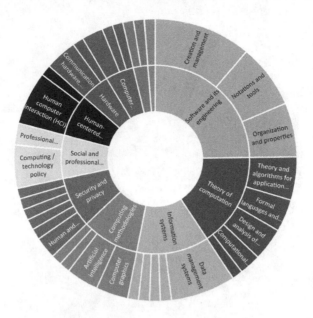

Fig. 4. Topic map for SLO examination guideline.

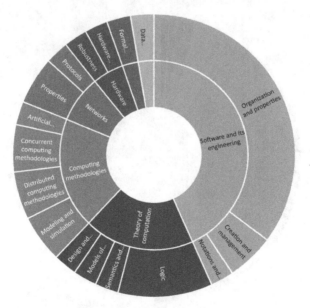

Fig. 5. Topic map for the *Informatica-Actief* model checking unit.

4 Model Checking Unit

Vaandrager et al. presented 2009 a model checking unit that was developed for a collaborative project between secondary schools and universities. The aim of that project was to review and revisit the content covered by ICT education, which covered at that time, as previously mentioned, mainly digital skills. Vaandrager et al. remarked that ICT education at that time failed to impart a sense of the fascinating fundamental questions that drive computer science research [19].

The unit used Uppaal to introduce students to a number of topics: mutual exclusion, data races, concurrency, leader election, and correctness. The unit covered a dozen examples that the pupils were asked to understand and solve, starting from models of automatic teller machines, train gate controllers, job-shop scheduling, and logic puzzles such as the goat-wolf-cabbage problem, to mutual exclusion protocols and leader election protocols such as Peterson algorithm. They observed that pupils were surprisingly capable to understand the problems, develop genuine solutions, and had a good grasp of correctness after completion of the unit [19].

This unit has been offered initially in the 2000s to pupils at about 30 schools in the Arnhem-Nijmegen region. The content has been adopted by Informatica-Actief [15], a content provider for computer science in *vwo* education. While it has been curated by editors of Informatica-Actief, the original content and setup are still intact as an integrated learning activity. It contributes to the elective theme *automata*, with as prerequisite familiarity with the core topic *foundations*, as defined in the 2019 SLO curriculum.

The topic mapping is based on the current 2022 version of the learning resource, as it is offered by Informatica-Actief. The activity distinguishes between an introductory section, which introduces Uppaal at the hand of custom-made examples and exercises, and an advanced section which considers protocols and algorithms from literature. For *vwo* pupils, it is recommended to complete both sections, and the topic map will be based on the entire learning activity.

The mapping was created similarly to the topic mapping for the curricula. Identifiable topics are mapped to the CCS, whether they were mentioned as part of the motivation, explicitly introduced as concepts or mentioned in the examples and exercises. For example, the learning activity names *distributed algorithms* explicitly in the introduction, introduces the concept later and gives examples and exercises illustrating the topic. This would be mapped to the CCS topic *Distributed algorithms*. The activity also discusses the importance of correctness in light of failing hardware, which is mapped to the hardware topic *Robustness*. The topic is not further expanded in the remainder of the resource. Both would be mapped to a single topic, even though they are covered differently. It is not the aim of the mapping to measure the frequency of a topic. However, once a topic is expanded on, like *Distributed algorithms*, it will usually be the case that other, related topics are touched upon, which will then appear in the topic map.

Figure 5 shows the topic map for the model checking learning activity. It is based on 37 different topics that are touched upon by the resource. This is surprisingly many, given that the resource itself slots it into only one elective theme of the curriculum, namely *automata*.

The most prominent topic area is *Software and its engineering*, just like it is in the curricula. However, the emphasis is different. The programming-related sub-category *Notations and tools* is mostly absent, while the topic area *Organization and properties* dominates. This contains the 11 sub-topics *Operating systems, Scheduling, Deadlocks, Mutual exclusion, Process synchronization, Correctness, Synchronization, Formal methods, Model checking, Software reliability,* and *Software safety*. All but *Operating systems* are recognisable as topics that were relevant at that time in Prof. Vaandrager's research group.

The two other topic areas that feature heavily in the learning resource are *Theory of Computation*, and *Computing Methodologies*. If we compare the topic map to the maps for the curricula, it becomes apparent that it resembles the SLO guidelines more than the CAIE or NRW curricula. The three most prominent topics of the model checking learning activity, feature also prominently in the SLO guideline. The NRW does not emphasize *Computing Methodologies*, while the CAIE curriculum emphasises neither *Computing Methodologies* nor *Theory of Computation*.

5   Discussion and Conclusion

Outcomes. This paper presents topic maps as a way to compare computer science curricula for secondary school. These maps are based on the ACM Computing Classification System, a hierarchy of concepts and categories used to categorise computer science research. The comparison shows a few commonalities, most notably that *Software and its engineering* is the most prominent topic area in all three curricula.

As interesting are the differences. Some topic areas feature prominently in one curriculum, but not in others. Even within the same topics area, differences can be significant, as was observed with the very different treatment of language paradigms. A particular question that arises from this comparison is whether the narrow focus in the NRW curriculum on object-oriented programming is justified, or whether avoiding guidance in this area, as it is done in the SLO guidelines is more appropriate. Even though the SLO guidelines and the NRW have a somewhat different purposes, in NRW it can be assumed that pupils will be exposed to object-oriented programming, maybe at the expense of exposing them to something else.

Although the topic maps have a limited scope, these observations can serve to inform the discussion of whether the curricula expose the pupils adequately to the field of computer science. It can help to identify topics that are overlooked, or too narrow, or whether the curriculum matches the profile and expectations of the tertiary institutions that want to recruit the pupils. Does the fact that none of the curricula has a prominent place for *Machine Learning* and *Artificial Intelligence* means that these topics are underrepresented, or does it mean that other topics are more relevant to achieving the aims of the curricula, such as the CAIE aim "to develop computational thinking"?

Even though this paper considered only one learning activity, it showed that a single activity can cover many topics, even if the activity is focused on one type of activity – in this case, the use of a model checker – and slotted into one theme within the curriculum – in this case *automata*. These activities can even be used to extend the scope set by the curricula. For example, one of the central topics of the model checking activity is concurrency; a topic that only the NRW curriculum mentions explicitly.

Limitations. There are some limitations to this study. The first limitation arises from the use of a subject classification, instead of a model curriculum as a baseline for the map. A model curriculum is presented by the ACM and IEEE report on *Computing Curricula 2020* which defines a list of 84 competencies for undergrad computer science [7]. The reason not to use such a model curriculum is that competencies defined in such a curriculum combine topic areas with skills and verbs that indicate a given cognitive domain in Bloom's taxonomy. To be useful for a topic mapping, the topics would first have to be extracted from these competencies, and the topics would still have been selected by educators, rather than the scientific community. The CSS offers an established hierarchy with 2113 topics that cover computer science, without mixing in educational concerns. A drawback, as well as a strength, is that these maps do not tell how prominent a topic will be in the classroom, or how well a pupil will master them. They only tell whether a topic is present.

Another limitation is that this paper compares educational standards that do not have the same purpose or institutional statute. The NRW teaching plan is set and developed by the state ministry of education. The Dutch Ministry of Education has tasked an external organisation, the SLO, to develop a framework for computing science examination. One is standard, the other a guideline, for the entire state or country. The situation in the UK is somewhat different, again, with a national curriculum that provides only general guidance. The accreditation providers use that freedom to develop a curriculum that is more specific and focused, while schools can then select an accreditation provider.

Outlook. This paper compared the topic map of three curricula and one learning activity. Selection of topics and whether they match expectations is only one problem that secondary school computer science faces. As a comparatively new subject computer science has to compete with other subjects. The *Gesellschaft für Informatik*, for example, recommended in 2015 that computer science should be treated equally to other science subjects [14]. However, it is still the case that in NRW computer science does not count toward the minimum requirements for STEM subjects [13]. Pupils can choose computer science in addition, but not instead of another science subject, which in practice discourages uptake.

As a subject that is still fairly new as a regular subject, and with significant changes to its curriculum, as discussed in this paper, schools also struggle to find qualified teachers [8,9]. There have been initiatives to train existing teachers or to attract professionals from ICT fields, but these efforts have been proven to be insufficient to meet demand. Related to this is a lack of diversity, both among teachers, but maybe even more concerning in the classroom. Selecting better topics will not be sufficient to address this problem.

Finally, teachers are still looking for quality content to meet the requirement set by the different curricula. This may be an opportunity for the research community to contribute and even have a chance to promote topics that are near to their heart, similarly to what was achieved with the model checking unit by Vaandrager et al.

Acknowledgement. Special thanks to Paul Bergervoet, editor of Informatica-Actief, for giving me access to the most current version of the model checking learning activity.

References

1. Arbeitskreis Bildungsstandards SII: Bildungsstandards Informatik für die Sekundarstufe II. Gesellschaft für Informatik (GI) e. V. (2016). https://informatikstandards.de/
2. Association for Computer Machinery: ACM Computing Classification System (2012). https://dl.acm.org/ccs
3. Barendsen, E., Grgurina, N., Tolboom, J.: A new informatics curriculum for secondary education in The Netherlands. In: Brodnik, A., Tort, F. (eds.) ISSEP 2016. LNCS, vol. 9973, pp. 105–117. Springer, Cham (2016). https://doi.org/10.1007/978-3-319-46747-4_9
4. Barendsen, E., Tolboom, J.: Advies examenprogramma informatica havo/vwo. Stichting Leerplanontwikkeling (SLO), Enschede (2016). https://www.slo.nl/publicaties/@4491/advies-0/
5. Buse, D., et al.: Dagstuhler Empfehlung zur Aufnahme des Fachs Informatik in den Pflichtbereich der Sekundarstufe II (1992). http://www.informatikdidaktik.de/HyFISCH/Informieren/politik/DagstuhlerEmpfehlung1992.htm
6. Cambridge Assessment International Education: Cambridge International AS & A Level Computer Science 9608. Cambridge Assessment International Education (2021). https://www.cambridgeinternational.org/programmes-and-qualifications/cambridge-international-as-and-a-level-computer-science-9608/
7. Clear, A., Parrish, A.: Computing curricula 2020 - paradigms for global computing education. ACM and IEEE (2020). https://www.acm.org/education/curricula-recommendations
8. Fowler, B., Vegas, E.: How England Implemented its Computer Science Education Program. Center for Universal Education at The Brookings Institution (2021). https://www.brookings.edu/research/how-england-implemented-its-computer-science-education-program/
9. Grgurina, N., Tolboom, J., Barendsen, E.: The second decade of informatics in Dutch secondary education. In: Pozdniakov, S.N., Dagienė, V. (eds.) ISSEP 2018. LNCS, vol. 11169, pp. 271–282. Springer, Cham (2018). https://doi.org/10.1007/978-3-030-02750-6_21
10. KNAW-Commissie Informatica: Digitale Geletterdheid In Het Voortgezet Onderwijs. Koninklijke Nederlandse Akademie van Wetenschappen (2012). https://www.knaw.nl/nl/actueel/publicaties/digitale-geletterdheid-in-het-voortgezet-onderwijs
11. Ministerium für Schule und Weiterbildung des Landes Nordrhein-Westfalen: Kernlehrplan für die Sekundarstufe II Gymnasium/Gesamtschule in Nordrhein-Westfalen. https://www.schulentwicklung.nrw.de/lehrplaene/lehrplannavigator-s-ii/gymnasiale-oberstufe/
12. Royal society: shut down or restart? the way forward for computing in UK schools. R. Acad. Eng. (2012). https://royalsociety.org/topics-policy/projects/computing-in-schools/report/

13. Schwarz, R., Hellmig, L., Friedrich, S.: Informatikunterricht in Deutschland – eine Übersicht. Informatik Spektrum **44**(2), 95–103 (2021). https://doi.org/10.1007/s00287-021-01349-9
14. Schöning, J., Gemulla, R., Martens, W., Schulte, C.: 3. Dagstuhl-Erklärung zur Informatischen Bildung in der Schule 2015 der Gesellschaft für Informatik e.V. (GI). Gesellschaft für Informatik e.V (2015). http://www.gi.de/fileadmin/redaktion/Download/GI-Dagstuhl-Erklaerung2015.pdf
15. Stichting Informatica-Actief: Informatica-Actief - Informatica lesmateriaal voor HAVO en VWO (2022). https://www.informatica-actief.nl
16. Tolboom, J.: Examenprogramma informatica havo/vwo. Stichting Leerplanontwikkeling (SLO) (2019). https://www.slo.nl/handreikingen/havo-vwo/handreiking-se-info-hv/examenprogramma/
17. Tolboom, J.: Handreiking SE Informatica - Het examenprogramma (2020). https://www.slo.nl/handreikingen/havo-vwo/handreiking-se-info-hv/examenprogramma/
18. UK Department for Education: GCE AS and A level subject content for computer science (2014). https://www.gov.uk/government/publications/gce-as-and-a-level-for-computer-science
19. Vaandrager, F., Jansen, D., Koopmans, E.: Een Module over Model Checking voor het VWO. In: Vodegel, F., Loots, M. (eds.) Proceedings NIOC 2009: Flexibel, adaptief, herbruikbaar. Utrecht : Hogeschool Utrecht (2009). http://hdl.handle.net/2066/75596

Tree-Based Adaptive Model Learning

Tiago Ferreira[1]([✉]) [iD], Gerco van Heerdt[1] [iD], and Alexandra Silva[1,2] [iD]

[1] University College London, London, UK
{t.ferreira,gerco.heerdt}@ucl.ac.uk
[2] Cornell University, Ithaca, USA
alexandra.silva@cornell.edu

A lot of the work the authors did in the last years on learning can be rooted back to learning from Frits. Gerco and Alexandra spent a few years in Nijmegen where Frits' enthusiasm for Angluin's algorithm infected them and made them want to keep learning. Later on, Tiago first learned about automata watching Frits' model learning video for CACM. On this landmark birthday, we thank Frits for his inspiration and wish him many happy returns!.

Abstract. We extend the Kearns–Vazirani learning algorithm to be able to handle systems that change over time. We present a new learning algorithm that can reuse and update previously learned behavior, implement it in the LearnLib library, and evaluate it on large examples, to which we make small adjustments between two runs of the algorithm. In these experiments our algorithm significantly outperforms both the classic Kearns–Vazirani learning algorithm and the current state-of-the-art adaptive algorithm.

1 Introduction

Formal methods have a long tradition and have had much success in critical applications, e.g. in the medical, space, and hardware industries. The last decade saw a rise in the use of formal methods in the software industry, with dedicated large teams in many companies, notably AWS and Facebook. This has caused a shift in focus to develop techniques that are helpful towards catching the most bugs as quickly as possible instead of performing complete verification [2].

The use of models to analyze system specifications, often pre-production, is common in certain domains, but requires expert knowledge to design the model and, throughout the system's life, update it. Motivated by the difficulties of building models, an automated technique called model learning [15] has been developed and used in the analysis of a range of (black-box system) implementations. One particularly successful application is that of network protocol implementations, e.g. TCP [6], SSH [7], and QUIC [5].

Classic active model learning algorithms like L* [1], Kearns–Vazirani [13], and TTT [10] exist for a number of automata types (deterministic, input-output,

---

Full implementation and experiment results available at https://github.com/UCL-PPLV/learnlib.

weighted, register) and have enabled analysis of numerous systems by providing faithful models to be used in model checking. However, these algorithms suffer from a common issue: systems often change faster than we can learn their models, as there is an inherent assumption that the learning process is running from scratch every time. As such, keeping a model up-to-date becomes quite challenging, often needing manual intervention from an expert. This does however introduce the chance of producing a model that is not actually correct, while being an extremely laborious task for any moderately sized complex system.

In this paper, we present an *incremental* model learning algorithm that can cope with evolving systems more effectively, and does not have to restart the learning process when a change occurs, providing a gain in efficiency when learning systems that undergo changes at known moments in time.

The work in the present paper can be seen as advancing the state of the art in *adaptive automata learning* [3,4,8,9,16]. Whereas previous work adapted the L* algorithm to reuse part of a data structure from a previous run, our adaptive algorithm is the first to use the more efficient Kearns–Vazirani algorithm. Although we focus on developing an algorithm for deterministic finite automata (DFAs), the techniques we developed can be transferred to other automata models. We expect this work and subsequent developments on adaptive learning will bring us closer to meet the specific needs of employing formal methods in fast moving environments commonly seen in the industry, and in large evolving systems.

The paper is organized as follows. After preliminary material on automata and learning (Sect. 2), in Sect. 3 we introduce and prove correctness of our incremental learning algorithm for DFAs, which targets evolving systems whose mutation points are known during learning. In Sect. 4 we benchmark and evaluate the efficiency of the algorithm, and we demonstrate its effectiveness in learning evolving systems. We conclude in Sect. 5 with a discussion of further directions on adaptive automata learning.

2   Preliminaries

Throughout this paper we will make use of standard notation from automata and learning theory. We define some of this notation below for the sake of clarity.

We fix a finite alphabet A and write A^* for the set of finite words over this alphabet. The empty word is ε and concatenation is written either by juxtaposition or with the operator $\cdot$. Given a word $w \in A^*$ we write $|w|$ for its length, and $w[i]$, $0 \leq i \leq |w|$, for the prefix of w of length i. A language over A^* is a set of strings such that $L \subseteq A^*$. We sometimes refer to the characteristic function $A^* \to 2 = \{\top, \bot\}$ of L also by L ($L(w) = \top$ if $w \in L$ and $L(w) = \bot$ if $w \notin L$).

The formal models generated by our algorithm are deterministic finite automata (DFAs). These are 4-tuples $\mathcal{A} = \langle Q, q_0, \delta, F \rangle$ where Q is a finite set of states, $q_0 \in Q$ is the initial state, $\delta \colon Q \times A \to Q$ is a transition function, and $F \subseteq Q$ is a set of final states. We define the usual reachability map $\mathsf{reach}_\mathcal{A} \colon A^* \to Q$ by $\mathsf{reach}_\mathcal{A}(\varepsilon) = q_0$ and $\mathsf{reach}_\mathcal{A}(ua) = \delta(\mathsf{reach}_\mathcal{A}(u), a)$. The language accepted by $\mathcal{A}$ is $\mathcal{L}_\mathcal{A} = \{u \in A^* \mid \mathsf{reach}_\mathcal{A}(u) \in F\}$. We write $A_\top$ for the minimal DFA accepting all of A^* and $A_\perp$ for the minimal DFA accepting the empty language $\emptyset$.

Our learner makes use of two types of oracles: *membership* and *equivalence* oracles. A membership oracle $\mathsf{mq} \colon A^* \to 2$ is able to answer whether a given input word is accepted in the target system; an equivalence oracle takes a DFA $\mathcal{A}$ and responds with $\mathsf{eq}(\mathcal{A}) \in A^* \cup \{null\}$, which represents either that the DFA is correct (*null*) or a word w such that $\mathcal{L}_\mathcal{A}(w) \neq \mathsf{mq}(w)$.

2.1   Learning with a Classification Tree

When designing a learning algorithm, one of the key aspects to consider is how we store the information we acquire over time. Learning then becomes a matter of being able to extend this structure with as little queries as possible, and transforming the data into a hypothesis automaton. The learning algorithm we introduce later, similarly to the classic Kearns–Vazirani algorithm, uses *classification trees* as its base data structure. Formally, the set of classification trees is given by the following grammar:

$$\mathsf{CT} ::= \mathsf{Node}\ A^*\ \mathsf{CT}\ \mathsf{CT}\ |\ \mathsf{Leaf}\ A^*$$

Here, a node contains a classifier $e \in A^*$, and $\perp$-child and $\top$-child subtrees, and a leaf contains a single access sequence $s \in A^*$. The child subtrees are named this way because of how the classifier e distinguishes access sequences $s_\perp$ and $s_\top$ present in the respective subtrees: $\mathsf{mq}(s_\perp \cdot e) = \perp$ and $\mathsf{mq}(s_\top \cdot e) = \top$. In particular, this holds for every pair of leaves and their *lowest common ancestor* node, the root node of the smallest subtree containing both leaves.

The classification tree is then able to classify every word $w \in A^*$ into a specific leaf of the tree, depending on how the target accepts or rejects w concatenated with specific classifiers e in the tree. This is done through *sifting* (Subroutine 1), where, starting from the root of the tree with classifier e, we pose the query $\mathsf{mq}(w \cdot e)$ and, depending on the result, proceed to the $\perp$-child or the $\top$-child of the node, from which we continue sifting, until we reach a leaf. The access sequence s of that leaf will then be deemed equivalent to w.

Subroutine 1: sift returns the leaf in a classification tree equivalent to a provided word w.r.t. the equivalence induced by the tree.

Data: Classification tree *tree*, membership oracle mq, word w.
Result: Equivalent leaf l in *tree*.
1 $n \leftarrow tree$;
2 **while** $n = \mathsf{Node}\ e\ left\ right$ **do**
3 $\quad |\quad n \leftarrow \mathsf{mq}(w \cdot e)\ ?\ right\ :\ left$;
4 **return** n;

The leaves of a classification tree represent the discovered states of the hypothesis, and sifting a word down the tree gives us the state this word should reach in the hypothesis. As such, one can easily retrieve the transitions of the hypothesis from the tree by, for each leaf with access sequence s sifting each extended word $s \cdot a$ to obtain the destination of the transition with symbol $a \in A$ from s. The initial state is simply the state we find by sifting the empty word ε, and the accepting states are the leaves in the $\top$-child subtree of the root node, which will have classifier ε. This logic is used by buildHyp (Subroutine 2) to extract the DFA represented by a classification tree.

Subroutine 2: buildHyp extracts a hypothesis DFA from a classification tree in the Classic KV algorithm.

Data: Classification tree *tree*
Result: Updated $\mathcal{H}$ w.r.t the current tree *tree*.

1   $q_o \leftarrow sift(tree, \text{mq}, \varepsilon)$; $Q \leftarrow \{q_0\}$; $F \leftarrow \varnothing$;
2   **for** $l \in leaves(tree)$ **do**
3     $Q \leftarrow Q \cup \{l\}$;
4   **if** $l \in leaves(child(tree, \top))$ **then**
5       $F \leftarrow F \cup \{l\}$;
6   **for** $l \in Q$ **do**
7   **for** $a \in \Sigma$ **do**
8       $\delta(l, a) \leftarrow sift(tree, \text{mq}, label(l) \cdot a)$;
9   **return** $\langle \Sigma, Q, q_0, F, \delta \rangle$;

With a hypothesis extracted from the classification tree, we can now pass this to an equivalence oracle to determine if the hypothesis is correct. If not, we will receive a counterexample word that we can use to improve the classification tree. The algorithm does this by understanding that, given that every hypothesis classifies the empty string ε correctly, and by definition the current hypothesis classifies the counterexample c incorrectly, there must be a prefix of c for which the classification first diverges. In terms of states, this then means that we are taking a transition into a state that is accepting in the hypothesis, and rejecting in the target, or vice-versa. This is fixed by realising that the state we take this transition from then must actually be two different states. The algorithm then uses this logic in updateTree (Subroutine 3) to split the state into two at the tree level, turning a leaf into a node with two leaves, one representing the new state discovered by the counterexample.

Subroutine 3: updateTree with a provided counterexample.

Data: Classification tree *tree*, counterexample $c \in A^*$.
Result: Updated *tree* taking into account c.

1   **for** $i \in [0 \cdots length(c) - 1]$ **do**
2     $s_i \leftarrow sift(tree, \text{mq}, c[i])$; $\hat{s}_i \leftarrow \text{reach}_{\mathcal{H}}(c[i])$;
3   **if** $s_i \neq \hat{s}_i$ **then**
4       $e \leftarrow c_i \cdot LCA(tree, s_i, \hat{s}_i)$;
5       $tree \leftarrow split(tree, s_{i-1}, c[i-1], e, \text{mq}(c[i-1] \cdot e))$;
6   **return** *tree*;

We provide the classic Kearns–Vazirani algorithm in Algorithm 4. This algorithm uses the `buildHyp` routine explained above to build a DFA from a classification tree, as well as `updateTree` (Subroutine 3) to extend the classification tree on receipt of a counterexample from an equivalence oracle.

Algorithm 4: Classic Kearns–Vazirani Algorithm

> **Data:** Alphabet A, membership oracle mq and equiv. oracle eq for language L.
> **Result:** The learned DFA $\mathcal{H}$ accepting L.
> 1 $init \leftarrow \mathsf{mq}(\varepsilon)$; $\mathcal{H} \leftarrow init$? $A_\top$: $A_\bot$; $s \leftarrow \mathsf{eq}(\mathcal{H})$;
> 2   **if** $s \neq null$ **then**
> 3 $tree \leftarrow init$? Node ε (Leaf s) (Leaf ε) : Node ε (Leaf ε) (Leaf s) ;
> 4 $\mathcal{H} \leftarrow \mathsf{buildHyp}(tree)$;
> 5 $cex \leftarrow \mathsf{eq}(\mathcal{H})$;
> 6   **while** $cex \neq null$ **do**
> 7 $tree \leftarrow \mathsf{updateTree}(tree, cex)$;
> 8 $\mathcal{H} \leftarrow \mathsf{buildHyp}(tree)$;
> 9 $cex \leftarrow \mathsf{eq}(\mathcal{H})$;
> 10 **return** $\mathcal{H}$;

---

3   Learning Evolving Systems Incrementally

We now develop a learning algorithm that is able to learn updates to a previous model without having to discard all behavior learned so far, and is also able to detect and remove behavior that no longer holds.

Classic algorithms are partially able to do this with equivalence oracles— they correct the current hypothesis based on a counterexample. *Adaptive model learners* are able to do this with the answers of both membership and equivalence oracles, even if the answer conflicts previous ones. Thus, they can deal with languages that mutate over time, adapting to changes by either trimming outdated behavior or distinguishing new behavior.

Our adaptive learning algorithm is targeted at systems with discrete changes, such as version controlled systems. Specifically, the system evolves at discrete known points, such as every version, forming a stream of target systems. Our *incremental learning algorithm* for DFAs, presented in Algorithm 6, is based on Kearns–Vazirani. As a first crucial difference, the incremental algorithm uses a previous learned model as its starting point. As such, it cannot just acquire new information; it also needs to be able to trim outdated behavior. This is done by `minimizeTree` (Subroutine 5), which prunes an initial tree by removing all leaves that are no longer represented by their reported access sequence. It achieves this by sifting every access sequence down the tree, removing leaves whose access sequences do not sift back into themselves.

This guarantees not only that the leaves left in our tree are correct in *a* correct automaton for this language, but that every leaf in the tree is unique w.r.t. the Myhill–Nerode congruence. If a pair of leaves were equivalent, then

---

Subroutine 5: `minimizeTree` trims the tree from redundant leaves.

Data: Classification tree *tree*, membership oracle mq.

Result: A minimized classification tree.

1   **for** $l \in$ *leaves*(*tree*) **do**

2     $s \leftarrow$ sift(*tree*, mq, label(l));

3   **if** $s \neq l$ **then**

4       $tree \leftarrow$ removeLeaf(*tree*, l);

5   **return** *tree*;

Algorithm 6: Incremental Algorithm

Data: Fixed alphabet A, optional previous classification tree *tree*, membership oracle mq and equivalence oracle eq w.r.t the language L.

Result: The learned DFA $\mathcal{H}$ equivalent to the language L.

1   *init* $\leftarrow$ mq(ε); $\mathcal{H} \leftarrow$ *init* ? $A_\top$: $A_\bot$; $s \leftarrow$ eq($\mathcal{H}$);

2   **if** $s \neq$ *null* **then**

3   **if** *tree* = *null* **then**

4   *tree* $\leftarrow$ *init* ? Node ε (Leaf s) (Leaf ε) : Node ε (Leaf ε) (Leaf s);

5   **else**

6   *tree* $\leftarrow$ minimizeTree(*tree*, mq);

7     $\mathcal{H} \leftarrow$ buildHyp(*tree*);

8   *cex* $\leftarrow$ eq($\mathcal{H}$);

9   **while** *cex* $\neq$ *null* **do**

10   *tree* $\leftarrow$ updateTree(*tree*, *cex*);

11       $\mathcal{H} \leftarrow$ buildHyp(*tree*);

12   *cex* $\leftarrow$ eq($\mathcal{H}$);

13 **return** $\mathcal{H}$;

---

both their access sequences would sift into only one of the nodes, leaving a leaf whose access sequence does not sift back into itself, and causing it to be removed.

While here we only present the relevant changes made to the classic Kearns–Vazirani algorithm to be able to adapt to changing behavior, we include the full algorithm with all its subroutines in Appendix A.

3.1 Correctness and Termination

As the algorithm only terminates with a hypothesis that is correct according to an equivalence query, correctness follows from termination. Termination of the original Kearns–Vazirani algorithm relies on the following key property: for every subtree of the form Node e *left right*, each leaf $s \in A^*$ of *left* satisfies $se \notin L$ and every leaf $s \in A^*$ of *right* satisfies $se \in L$. We note that this property also holds in our incremental algorithm as soon as we enter the main loop, as `minimizeTree` removes any leaf violating it.

When a counterexample *cex* is found, the procedure is the same as for the original Kearns–Vazirani algorithm, and can only be applied a finite number of times: By the property shown above every pair of leaves corresponds to a pair of distinct equivalence classes of the Myhill–Nerode congruence for $\mathcal{L}$, and therefore the leaves in the tree cannot exceed the number of equivalence classes. Furthermore, every counterexample of length at least 2 leads to an increase of the number of leaves (via `updateTree`, which preserves the above invariant).

4   Experiments

We evaluate the efficiency of our new learning algorithm by running experiments over random targets with different types of features. While we would like to evaluate it over a standard set of benchmarks [14], these currently only cover single target automata, and so are not fit for adaptive learners designed to learn automata that are *linked* due to small evolutions in their behavior. We designed two scenarios to benchmark this incremental algorithm. The first scenario takes an initial automaton and applies a series of random mutations: it randomly adds a state, removes a state, diverts a transition, and flips the acceptance of a state. Our second scenario simulates the common occurrence of adding a feature to an existing system. We do this by introducing a small *feature automaton* of 3 states to an original base automaton by diverting 3 random transitions into the start state of the feature automaton.

We perform these benchmarks on different automata of increasing number of states, while maintaining the number of mutations applied to them, and the size of the feature automaton. This way, we create different ratios of change, and simulate applying fixes, or adding features to different systems.

We call the first and second targets t_0 and t_1, respectively. For our adaptive learning algorithm, the target evolving system starts as t_0 and mutates to t_1 after 10000 queries. For the classic Kearns–Vazirani algorithm, as it cannot learn evolving systems at all, we have to run the algorithm twice, first targeting t_0, then from scratch targeting t_1. To ensure repeatable results, each benchmark in question has been run 300 times, each with fresh random inputs of the same parameters, and averaged. The graphs below represent the average run of both benchmarks, using that both have very similar results. Separate graphs per benchmark can be found in Appendix B.

We start by running the benchmark on the classic Kearns–Vazirani algorithm to set a baseline. These results can be seen in Fig. 1. The progress of each instance here is measured according to the following definition.

Definition 1. *Given* $\alpha \in [0, 1]$, *a stream* $(t_i)_{i \in \mathbb{N}}$ *of target automata, and a stream* $(h_i)_{i \in \mathbb{N}}$ *of hypothesis automata,*[1] *the* progress *is the stream* $(p_i)_{i \in \mathbb{N}}$, *with* $p_i \in [0, 1]$ *for all* $i \in \mathbb{N}$, *given by*

$$p_i = \sum_{u \in A^*, \mathcal{L}_{t_i}(u) = \mathcal{L}_{h_i}(u)} (1 - \alpha) \cdot \left(\frac{\alpha}{|A|} \right)^{|u|}.$$

---

[1] Finite streams may be turned into infinite ones by repeating the last element.

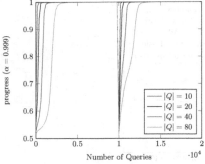
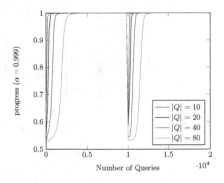

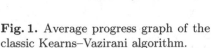

Fig. 1. Average progress graph of the classic Kearns–Vazirani algorithm.

Fig. 2. Average progress graph of the incremental algorithm.

As the learning curves show, the linear process of the classic algorithm for t_1 is very similar to the one for t_0. The two halves of the lines may not have the exact same gradients due to the targets being different, but we can see they follow a similar pattern, and more importantly, converge to 1.0 using a similar number of queries. This is because no knowledge is reused, and all states, even persisting ones, will have to be relearned.

We perform the same benchmark on the incremental algorithm: see results in Fig. 2. The incremental algorithm has a t_0 run very similar to the classic algorithm, due to the lack of previous knowledge. However, the t_1 segment is already very different. We immediately see that it does not start from such a low similarity value as the run of the classic algorithm. This is because while the classic algorithm always starts from a one state automaton, our incremental algorithm starts from the previous hypothesis, with outdated states pruned.

We can also see that it is not always the case that this line ascends immediately at the mutation point. This is because, as we are not starting from a widely dissimilar automaton, the equivalence oracle actually requires a number of queries to find a counterexample. This can be optimized by using more efficient equivalence oracles, but for the sake of simplicity and comparison all algorithms use the same random word search algorithm for equivalence testing.

These learning progress graph representations are great at demonstrating the overall behavior and approach of the learning algorithm, but we now want to evaluate whether this algorithm does indeed provide a benefit over learning systems classically, or with the current state-of-the-art adaptive algorithms, in terms of the number of queries it takes them to fully learn mutated targets. As such, we have computed and averaged the number of queries it takes to reach the final hypothesis while learning the t_1 on each run. We present the results as two ratios relative to the incremental algorithm: one comparing the classic Kearns–Vazirani algorithm, and another comparing the current state-of-the-art adaptive algorithm, Partial Dynamic L* [4]. We plot these in Fig. 3, and show how the ratio changes with the size of the state space of t_0.

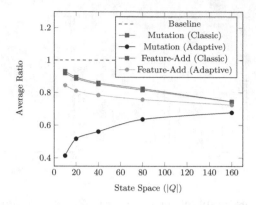

Fig. 3. Ratio of number of queries needed to learn the automata.

In this representation, a value of 1.0 would indicate that the incremental algorithm requires as many queries as the algorithm in comparison. Any value below indicates a benefit in running the incremental algorithm over such algorithm, and vice versa (the lower the ratio, the better the incremental algorithm).

As we can see, **the incremental algorithm consistently outperforms all other algorithms in all benchmarks,** even with small targets where a relatively big portion of the system has changed. When compared to the adaptive algorithm from the literature, we can see the incremental algorithm still consistently outperforms in terms of queries, with a tendency to plateau between a 0.75 and 0.7 ratio—a reduction by 25–30% in the number of queries.

5   Conclusion

We introduced a new state-of-the-art algorithm for *adaptive learning* which provides, to our knowledge, the most efficient adaptive learner to date, allowing us to learn systems that were before too big or evolved too quickly to be learned classically. We evaluated the fitness of this algorithm through a set of realistic experiments, demonstrating their benefit over classic and existing adaptive learners. Adaptive learning could provide a cooperative relationship between active and passive learning, due to its flexibility towards information that changes over time and becomes available at different stages. We want to explore this in future work, as well as developing a formal framework of adaptive learning, where other algorithms can be easily adapted, e.g. efficient classic algorithms such as TTT [11]. Finally, although our incremental algorithm allows us to learn systems that evolve at known points, this would not work in a true black-box scenario, where we cannot know if or when the system changes. In the future we would like to then develop a *continuous* learning algorithm for such evolving systems.

Related Work. Our algorithm contributes to the field of adaptive learning first introduced in [8], where information learned in previous models was used as guidance for which states to check first, instead of blindly looking for new ones. This was done by slightly modifying the L* algorithm to start from a previous set of access sequences. Chaki et al. [3] use a similar algorithm in combination with assume-guarantee reasoning [12] to provide a framework where model checking is used to find counterexamples in the model, and thus make progress in learning. Their algorithm, Dynamic L*, reuses not only the starting prefix/suffix sets, but also their computed values. However, these must still be validated on the new target. Finally, Damasceno et al. [4] introduce Partial Dynamic L*, which improves Dynamic L* by analysing the start prefix/suffix sets to trim them where possible, reducing the amount of information that needs to be validated.

These previous algorithms, however, suffer from using an observation table as their data structure, which increases the amount of redundant data to be acquired. As the tables grow, these redundancies significantly increase the number of queries that need to be asked.

A   Omitted Incremental Subroutines

Subroutine A.1: child returns the $(\bot/\top)$-child of a provided tree node.

Data: Tree node p, $b \in 2$
Result: b-child of p.
1 **if** $p = $ Node e *left right* **then**
2 $\quad$ **return** b ? *right* : *left*;
3 **return** *null*;

Subroutine A.2: children returns the children of a provided tree node.

Data: Tree node p.
Result: Set of children of p.
1 $C \leftarrow \varnothing$;
2 **if** $child(p, \bot) \neq null$ **then**
3 $\quad$ $C \leftarrow C \cup \{child(p, \bot)\}$;
4 **if** $child(p, \top) \neq null$ **then**
5 $\quad$ $C \leftarrow C \cup \{child(p, \top)\}$;
6 **return** C;

Subroutine A.3: setChild updates a child of a given inner node in a classification tree.

Data: Classification tree *tree*, parent node p, child outcome b, new child n.
Result: Updated classification tree *tree* where n is the b-child of p.

1 **if** *tree* = Node *e left right* **then**
2   **if** *tree* = p **then**
3   **if** b **then**
4   **return** Node *e left n*;
5   **else**
6   **return** Node *e n right*;
7   **return** Node *e setChild(left, p, b, n) setChild(right, p, b, n)*;
8 **return** *tree*;

Subroutine A.4: nodes returns the set of all nodes in a given tree.

Data: Classification tree *tree*.
Result: Set of nodes in *tree*.

1 **if** *tree* = Leaf *s* **then**
2   **return** {*tree*};
3 **return** *tree* $\cup$ *nodes(child(tree, $\bot$))* $\cup$ *nodes(child(tree, $\top$))*;

Subroutine A.5: leaves returns the set of leaves in a given tree.

Data: Classification tree *tree*.
Result: Set of leaves in *tree*.

1 **if** *tree* = Leaf *s* **then**
2   **return** {*tree*};
3 **return** *leaves(child(tree, $\bot$))* $\cup$ *leaves(child(tree, $\top$))*;

Subroutine A.6: label returns the label of a given node, be it a classifier or an access sequence.

Data: Node n.
Result: Label $\in A^*$.

1 **if** n = Leaf *s* **then**
2   **return** s;
3 **if** n = Node *e left right* **then**
4   **return** e;

Subroutine A.7: setLabel replaces the label in a specific leaf.

Data: Classification tree *tree*, leaf *l*, new label *w*.

Result: Updated classification tree *tree* with new label *w* in *l*.

1 **if** *tree* = *l* **then**
2 | **return** Leaf *w*;
3 **if** *tree* = Node *e left right* **then**
4 | **return** Node *e setLabel*(*left*, *l*, *w*) *setLabel*(*right*, *l*, *w*);
5 **return** *tree*;

Subroutine A.8: outcome returns whether a provided node *n* is a ⊥-child or a ⊤-child, or neither.

Data: Classification tree *tree*, provided node *n*

Result: ⊥, ⊤ or *null* if the node does not have a parent in *tree*

1 **if** *n* = *tree* **then**
2 | **return** *null*;
3 **return** *child*(*parent*(*tree*, *n*), ⊤) = *n*;

Subroutine A.9: parent returns the parent of a provided node in the classification tree.

Data: Classification tree *tree*, child leaf *l*.

Result: Parent node *p*.

1 $q \leftarrow Queue(tree)$;
2 **while** $|q| \neq 0$ **do**
3 | $p \leftarrow pop(q)$;
4 | **if** $l \in children(p)$ **then**
5 | | **return** *p*;
6 | **for** $c \in children(p)$ **do**
7 | | $q \leftarrow push(q, c)$;
8 **return** *null*;

Subroutine A.10: removeLeaf

Data: Classification tree *tree*, leaf $l \in$ **leaves**(*tree*) to be removed.

Result: A valid classification tree *tree* with *l* removed.

1 $node \leftarrow$ **parent**(*tree*, *l*);
2 $sibling \leftarrow$ **child**(*node*, ¬outcome(*tree*, *l*));
3 **return** setChild(*tree*, **parent**(*tree*, *node*), outcome(*tree*, *node*), *sibling*);

Subroutine A.11: LCA returns the lowest common ancestor node of two provided leaves in a classification tree.

Data: Classification tree *tree*, first leaf l_a, second leaf l_b.

Result: LCA node *n* in the classification tree *tree*.

1 $n \leftarrow l_a$;
2 **while** $l_b \notin leaves(n)$ **do**
3 | $n \leftarrow parent(tree, n)$;
4 **return** *n*;

Subroutine A.12: split splits a leaf in the tree into a node with 2 child leaves, one of them a new leaf introduced to the tree.

Data: Classification tree *tree*, current leaf *l* being split, label $w \in A^*$ for the new leaf, classifier $e \in A^*$ for the new node, $b \in 2$ indicating whether the new leaf is a $\top$-child.
Result: Updated classification tree *tree*.
1 *node* ← *b* ? Node *e l* (Leaf *w*) : Node *e* (Leaf *w*) *l*;
2 **return** *setChild*(*tree*, *parent*(*tree*, *l*), *outcome*(*tree*, *l*), *node*);

B   Additional Experiment Graphs

B.1   Mutation Benchmark

(See Figs. 4 and 5)

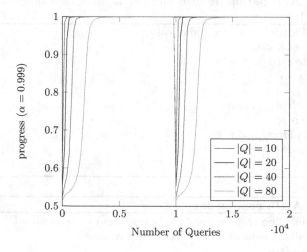

Fig. 4. Average progress graph of the classic Kearns–Vazirani algorithm.

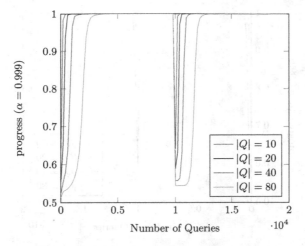

Fig. 5. Average progress graph of the incremental algorithm.

B.2   Feature-Add Benchmark

(See Figs. 6 and 7)

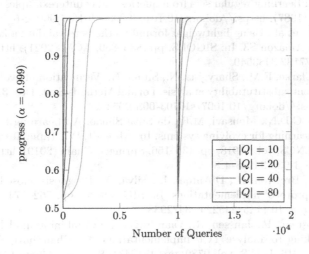

Fig. 6. Average progress graph of the classic Kearns–Vazirani algorithm.

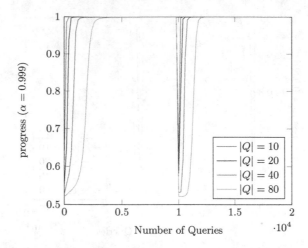

Fig. 7. Average progress graph of the incremental algorithm.

References

1. Angluin, D.: Learning regular sets from queries and counterexamples. Inf. Comput. **75**, 87–106 (1987). https://doi.org/10.1016/0890-5401(87)90052-6
2. Bornholt, J., et al.: Using lightweight formal methods to validate a key-value storage node in Amazon S3. In: SIGOPS, pp. 836–850. ACM (2021). https://doi.org/10.1145/3477132.3483540
3. Chaki, S., Clarke, E.M., Sharygina, N., Sinha, N.: Verification of evolving software via component substitutability analysis. Formal Methods Syst. Des. **32**(3), 235–266 (2008). https://doi.org/10.1007/s10703-008-0053-x
4. Damasceno, C.D.N., Mousavi, M.R., da Silva Simao, A.: Learning to reuse: adaptive model learning for evolving systems. In: Ahrendt, W., Tapia Tarifa, S.L. (eds.) IFM 2019. LNCS, vol. 11918, pp. 138–156. Springer, Cham (2019). https://doi.org/10.1007/978-3-030-34968-4_8
5. Ferreira, T., Brewton, H., D'Antoni, L., Silva, A.: Prognosis: closed-box analysis of network protocol implementations. In: SIGCOMM, pp. 762–774. ACM (2021). https://doi.org/10.1145/3452296.3472938
6. Fiterău-Broştean, P., Janssen, R., Vaandrager, F.: Combining model learning and model checking to analyze TCP implementations. In: Chaudhuri, S., Farzan, A. (eds.) CAV 2016. LNCS, vol. 9780, pp. 454–471. Springer, Cham (2016). https://doi.org/10.1007/978-3-319-41540-6_25
7. Fiterau-Brostean, P., Lenaerts, T., Poll, E., de Ruiter, J., Vaandrager, F.W., Verleg, P.: Model learning and model checking of SSH implementations. In: SPIN, pp. 142–151. ACM (2017). https://doi.org/10.1145/3092282.3092289
8. Groce, A., Peled, D., Yannakakis, M.: Adaptive model checking. In: Katoen, J.-P., Stevens, P. (eds.) TACAS 2002. LNCS, vol. 2280, pp. 357–370. Springer, Heidelberg (2002). https://doi.org/10.1007/3-540-46002-0_25

9. Huistra, D., Meijer, J., van de Pol, J.: Adaptive learning for learn-based regression testing. In: Howar, F., Barnat, J. (eds.) FMICS 2018. LNCS, vol. 11119, pp. 162–177. Springer, Cham (2018). https://doi.org/10.1007/978-3-030-00244-2_11
10. Isberner, M., Howar, F., Steffen, B.: The TTT algorithm: a redundancy-free approach to active automata learning. In: Bonakdarpour, B., Smolka, S.A. (eds.) RV 2014. LNCS, vol. 8734, pp. 307–322. Springer, Cham (2014). https://doi.org/10.1007/978-3-319-11164-3_26
11. Isberner, M., Howar, F., Steffen, B.: The open-source LearnLib. In: Kroening, D., Păsăreanu, C.S. (eds.) CAV 2015. LNCS, vol. 9206, pp. 487–495. Springer, Cham (2015). https://doi.org/10.1007/978-3-319-21690-4_32
12. Jones, C.B.: Tentative steps toward a development method for interfering programs. ACM Trans. Program. Lang. Syst. 5, 596–619 (1983). https://doi.org/10.1145/69575.69577
13. Kearns, M.J., Vazirani, U.V.: An Introduction to Computational Learning Theory. MIT Press, Cambridge (1994). https://mitpress.mit.edu/books/introduction-computational-learning-theory
14. Neider, D., Smetsers, R., Vaandrager, F., Kuppens, H.: Benchmarks for automata learning and conformance testing. In: Margaria, T., Graf, S., Larsen, K.G. (eds.) Models, Mindsets, Meta: The What, the How, and the Why Not? LNCS, vol. 11200, pp. 390–416. Springer, Cham (2019). https://doi.org/10.1007/978-3-030-22348-9_23
15. Vaandrager, F.W.: Model learning. Commun. ACM 60, 86–95 (2017). https://doi.org/10.1145/2967606
16. Windmüller, S., Neubauer, J., Steffen, B., Howar, F., Bauer, O.: Active continuous quality control. In: CBSE, pp. 111–120. ACM (2013). https://doi.org/10.1145/2465449.2465469

From Languages to Behaviors and Back

Markus Frohme[(✉)] and Bernhard Steffen

Chair of Programming Systems, Faculty of Computer Science,
TU Dortmund University, Dortmund, Germany
{markus.frohme,steffen}@cs.tu-dortmund.de

Abstract. We present two formalisms for describing behaviors of procedural systems, i.e., systems that consist of multiple procedures that can mutually call each other. Systems of procedural transition systems (SPTSs) provide a fine-grained formalism for the step-wise semantics of reactive systems whereas the equally expressive systems of behavioral automata (SBAs) provide a language-based characterization that can be used by active automata learning (AAL). Based on the concepts of our previous work on systems of procedural automata (SPAs), we present an AAL algorithm for SBAs and provide an open-source implementation of the algorithm that is publicly available for experimentation. In a synthetic benchmark evaluation, we show that our approach of learning behaviors can even out-perform our previous approaches for holistic system models.

Keywords: context-free languages · procedural systems · behavior · active automata learning · instrumentation

1 Introduction

In the last decades, active automata learning (AAL), originally intended to infer (regular) languages via querying, has been developed as a valuable means to infer models of software systems based on observations, i.e., via testing, or to support model-based testing without requiring any a priori model [14,21,24]. Already 20 years ago it has been observed that languages describing behaviors of software systems are by their nature prefix-closed. This observation and its practical impact has been refined by considering Mealy machines with output-deterministic behavior which can today be seen as the de facto standard when modeling reactive software systems [5,16]. An orthogonal development concerned generalization beyond regular systems, e.g., by considering infinite data domains [3,15,18,26] or introducing recursion [7,11,17]. Frits Vaandrager's work on such generalizations is characterized by its emphasis on mappers [1,2,4,9]: Dealing with realistic systems such as the telephony systems in [13] clearly requires a mapping between the abstract symbols known to the learner and the concrete system observations. Frits elaborated on the mapper concept in a way that allows one to reduce, e.g., the learning of register automata to a problem that can be solved via regular automata learning. In fact, the work presented in

© The Author(s), under exclusive license to Springer Nature Switzerland AG 2022
N. Jansen et al. (Eds.): Vaandrager Festschrift 2022, LNCS 13560, pp. 180–200, 2022.
https://doi.org/10.1007/978-3-031-15629-8_11

this paper is based on a similar reduction: Context-free systems are learned via orchestrated learning of regular automata over an extended alphabet [11].

In this paper we reconsider the impact of prefix-closure in particular under the perspective of procedural systems. Our previous work [11] introduces *systems of procedural automata (SPAs)* which describe instrumented, context-free languages via a set of independent procedures (represented by DFAs) that can mutually call each other. By nature, context-free languages enforce a notion of termination, or "empty stack" semantics, to describe valid words of the language.

In contrast, *behavior* often describes the step-wise actions that a system can perform. Formally, it is often represented via labeled transitions systems (LTSs), in which valid behavior is represented via transitions between nodes and invalid behavior is represented via the absence of transitions. While LTSs may support the notion of termination, e.g., via deadlock states, it is not mandatory. In the light of procedural systems, the step from regular to procedural behaviors can be regarded as a step from finite LTSs to sets of mutually recursive LTSs. In particular, with procedural behaviors, one is able to express concepts such as non-terminating procedures, which is not possible with the classic language-based interpretation.

For formalizing the notion of *procedural behavior*, we introduce the concept of *systems of procedural transition systems (SPTSs)* and present the notion of *systems of behavioral automata (SBAs)* to relate this concept to prefixes of SPA languages. We sketch an AAL algorithm for inferring SBAs and provide an open-source implementation[1] of this algorithm for public experimentation.

A particular interesting property of procedural behaviors (or equivalently, prefix-closed SPA languages) is that they *supersede* classic SPA languages. This leads to the idea of *reduction* which describes the process of removing all non-terminating behavior from a system model. Using reduction, we can *simulate* an SPA learner by inferring the behavior of a system first (via SBA inference) and then removing all non-terminating executions. In a set of synthetic benchmarks, we show that SBA-based learning has the potential to out-perform classic SPA learning and therefore, besides its semantic advantages, provide an even more efficient approach to the classic language-based learning process.

Outlook. In Sect. 2 we introduce preliminary concepts and notations for describing (regular) behavior and how it can be represented in the context of AAL. Section 3 lifts these concepts to the level of procedural systems. In Sect. 4 we present an AAL algorithm for inferring models described in Sect. 3. Sections 5 and 6 elaborate some qualitative properties of our approach and evaluate a set of benchmarks in order to explore some quantitative properties of behavioral systems in comparison to our previous work. Section 7 discusses related work and Sect. 8 summarizes the paper and discusses future research.

---

[1] https://github.com/LearnLib/learnlib-sba.

2   Preliminaries for Behavioral Systems

We introduce some general concepts and notation for describing the behavior of systems and present some background information about technical aspects of current technologies used in this paper.

2.1   A Semantic Point of View

For the foundation of behavioral systems we use the commonly known formalism of *labeled transition systems*.

Definition 1 (Labeled transition system (LTS)). *A* labeled transition system *is a tuple* $LTS = \langle S, I, \rightarrow, s_0 \rangle$, *where*

- *S denotes the (non-empty) set of states,*
- *I denotes the (non-empty) set of input labels,*
- $\rightarrow \subseteq (S \times I \times S)$ *denotes the transition relation and*
- $s_0 \in S$ *denotes the initial state.*

In this paper, we restrict ourselves to input-deterministic systems, i.e., $\forall s_1 \in S, i \in I: |\{(s_1, i, s_2) \in \rightarrow | s_2 \in S\}| \leq 1.$
    Let $w = i_1 \cdot \ldots \cdot i_n \in I^*$ *denote a sequence of input labels,* $|w| = n$ *denote the length of a sequence, and* $w[j] = i_j$ *denote the j-th element of a sequence for* $j \in \{1, \ldots, n\}$. *We define the* paths *of an LTS L as the concatenation of labels of all possible sequences of transitions of L, i.e.,*

$$P(L) = \{w \in I^* \mid (s_{i-1}, w[i], s_i) \in \rightarrow, \forall i \in \{1, \ldots, |w|\}, s_{i-1}, s_i \in S\}.$$

In an input-deterministic LTS, each "run" of a system starts at a designated initial state. For a given state and input label, there exists at most a single successor state which allows us to deterministically progress through the LTS when processing (input) actions. If at some point there does not exist a correspondingly labeled transition, we have encountered an unsupported behavior and the "execution" of the system stops. Therefore, the paths of a labeled transition system directly describe the valid behavior of the system and the step-wise semantics allow one to directly model and query the validity of each individual interaction. This allows LTSs to provide an intuitive formalism for modeling the behavior of a software or hardware system.

    With respect to learning behavioral systems, we assume that the systems we are going to investigate throughout this paper provide a similar step-wise mechanism for interacting with them.

2.2   A Technical Point of View

A popular field of research that deals with learning behaviors of (black-box) software and hardware systems is *active automata learning* (AAL). In AAL, system behavior is described by formal languages where words (sequences of input symbols) represent sequences of valid interactions with the system. The "language" of a system then describes the set of all valid interactions with the system. AAL often follows the MAT framework [8] which describes an iterative process where a *learner* initially poses *membership queries* (MQs) in order to explore the behavior of the *system under learning* (SUL), e.g., a software or hardware application. After the learner has constructed a tentative hypothesis from its observations, an *equivalence query* (EQ) is posed in order to validate the hypothesis. The answer to an EQ either indicates that the hypothesis conforms to the SUL or yields a *counterexample* (a sequence of input symbols) that exposes different behaviors of the hypothesis and the SUL, and is used to refine the hypothesis in a subsequent round of exploration. For a practical introduction see, e.g., [25].

In the following, we especially focus on DFA-based AAL.

Definition 2 (Deterministic finite acceptor (DFA)).   *A* deterministic finite acceptor *is a tuple* $A = \langle Q, I, \delta, q_0, Q_F \rangle$, *where*

- Q *denotes the finite, non-empty set of states,*
- I *denotes the finite, non-empty set of inputs,*
- $\delta \colon Q \times I \to Q$ *denotes the (total) transition function,*
- $q_0 \in Q$ *denotes the initial state and*
- $Q_F \subseteq Q$ *denotes the set of accepting states.*

Let $u \in I (v \in I^*)$ *denote a symbol of (word over)* I *and let* ε *denote the empty word. We generalize the transition function to words over* I *as follows:*

$$\delta(q, \varepsilon) = q$$
$$\delta(q, u \cdot v) = \delta(\delta(q, u), v)$$

We define the language *of a DFA* A *as the set of words that reach accepting states, i.e.,*

$$L(A) = \{w \in I^* \mid \delta(q_0, w) \in Q_F\}.$$

DFAs inherently describe system behavior holistically: given an input word, the verdict whether a word is accepted by the DFA is chosen after processing all input symbols of the word. In general, even accepted words may at some point traverse non-accepting states.

In order to align paths of LTSs with the languages of DFAs, we specifically look at *prefix-closed languages*, i.e., languages such that for every word w of a language, each prefix of w is also a member of the concerned language. This property allows us to establish a direct relation between paths of an (input-deterministic) LTS and words of a formal language. In fact, we can even directly translate between (finite-state) LTSs and DFAs that describe the same behavior. Given a finite LTS, the corresponding *prefix-closed DFA* is structurally similar to the LTS in the sense that every state of an LTS corresponds to an accepting state of the DFA and every transition defines the function value of the DFA's transition function. The fact that LTSs may represent partial behavior via undefined transitions can be easily compensated for by the DFA by adding a rejecting sink state that collects all transitions that are undefined in the LTS representation. Given that every (total) prefix-closed DFA necessarily contains such a sink as well, it is easy to see how the reverse translation can be implemented.

With prefix-closed languages, we are able to adequately represent the stepwise semantics of LTSs via formal languages. This enables us to use AAL-based techniques in order to infer behaviors of (LTS-based) systems in the following.

3   Systems of Procedural Transition Systems

We continue to lift the basic concepts of Sect. 2 to procedural systems and re-iterate some of the concepts of [11].

3.1   A Semantic Point of View

For modeling procedural systems, we use the well-known "copy-rule" semantics of context-free grammars: The global system consists of individual behavioral components (i.e., non-terminals or *procedures*) that can mutually call each other. The global system starts with an initial (or "main") procedure and may perform some local actions. Whenever a call to a procedure is encountered, execution is delegated to that procedure until termination where the execution returns to the call-site.

In order to make these systems learnable, we introduce an instrumentation that makes *calls to* and *returns from* procedures explicitly visible. To better distinguish between the roles of labels that signal entering and exiting procedures, let us introduce the notion of an *SPA alphabet*.

Definition 3 (SPA alphabet). *An* SPA alphabet $\Sigma = \Sigma_{call} \uplus \Sigma_{int} \uplus \{r\}$ *is the disjoint union of three finite sets, where Σ_{call} denotes the call alphabet, Σ_{int} denotes the internal alphabet and r denotes the return symbol.*

Given the specific roles of input labels, we can refine our previous notion for behavioral systems specifically for incorporating the semantics of procedures.

Definition 4 (Procedural transition system (PTS)). *Let Σ be an SPA alphabet and $c \in \Sigma_{call}$ denote a procedure. A procedural transition system for procedure c is a finite labeled transition system $LTS_{\mathcal{B}}^c = \langle S^c, \Sigma, \to^c, s_0^c \rangle$ (cf. Definition 1) such that*

$$(s_1, r, s_2) \in \to^c \Rightarrow (s_2, a, s_3) \notin \to^c$$

for all $s_1, s_2, s_3 \in S^c, a \in \Sigma$, i.e., return transitions are dead-ends.

The specific restriction to the transition relation accounts for the fact that upon returning from a procedure, no more actions should be possible as the procedure represented by the PTS has terminated. We can then describe a procedural system via an aggregation of individual PTSs for the involved procedures. To give an intuition for the structure of systems of procedural transition systems, Fig. 1 shows an exemplary system describing palindromes.

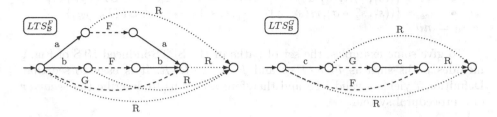

Fig. 1. A system of procedural transition systems over the SPA alphabet $\Sigma = \{F, G\} \uplus \{a, b, c\} \uplus \{R\}$ using two procedures for modeling palindromes over a, b, c.

Definition 5 (System of procedural transition systems (SPTS)). *Let Σ be an SPA alphabet with $\Sigma_{call} = \{c_1, \ldots, c_q\}$. A system of procedural transition systems $SPTS_\mathcal{B}$ over Σ is given by the tuple of procedural transition systems $(LTS_\mathcal{B}^{c_1}, \ldots, LTS_\mathcal{B}^{c_q})$ such that for each call symbol there exists a corresponding procedural transition system. We write $c_0 \in \Sigma_{call}$ to denote the initial procedure of $SPTS_\mathcal{B}$, i.e., one of the existing q procedures that is invoked first.*

SPTSs induce (potentially infinite-state) LTSs. Starting with the main procedure, each path of a PTS describes a procedural (sub-) path of a composed SPTS path. Whenever a PTS p traverses a call symbol-labeled transition, we switch to the initial state of the called procedure and return to the successor in p upon termination of the called procedure, which is indicated by an r-labeled transition.

In order to formally define the semantics of SPTSs, let us first introduce the notion of a stack in order to keep track of the correct return-successors in the induced LTS.

Definition 6 (SPTS stack domain/configuration). *Let Σ be an SPA alphabet and $SPTS_\mathcal{B}$ be an SPTS over Σ. We define $\Gamma_{SPTS} = N \uplus \{\bot\}$ as the stack domain with $N = \bigcup_{c \in \Sigma_{call}} S^c$ as the set of all states and $\bot$ as the unique bottom-of-stack symbol. We use $\bullet$ to denote the stacking of elements of Γ_{SPTS} where writing elements left-to-right displays the stack top-to-bottom and we write $ST(\Gamma_{SPTS})$ to denote the set of all possible stack configurations.*

Definition 7 (SPTS-induced LTS). *Let Σ be an SPA alphabet and $SPTS_\mathcal{B}$ be an SPTS over Σ. The $SPTS_\mathcal{B}$-induced LTS is an infinite-state LTS $LTS_{SPTS_\mathcal{B}} = \langle S, I, \rightarrow, s_0 \rangle$ such that*

- $S \subseteq \{init\} \uplus (N \times ST(\Gamma))$ with $N = \bigcup_{c \in \Sigma_{call}} S^c$,
- $I = \Sigma$,
- $\rightarrow = \rightarrow_{init} \uplus \rightarrow_{call} \uplus \rightarrow_{int} \uplus \rightarrow_{ret}$ *where*
  - $\rightarrow_{init} = \{(init, c_0, (s_0^{c_0}, \bot))\}$
  - $\rightarrow_{call} =$
    $\{((s_1^c, \sigma), i, (s_0^i, s_2^c \bullet \sigma)) \mid (s_1^c, i, s_2^c) \in \rightarrow^c, i \in \Sigma_{call}, \sigma \in ST(\Gamma_{SPTS})\}$

- $\rightarrow_{int} = \{((s_1^c,\sigma),i,(s_2^c,\sigma)) \mid (s_1^c,i,s_2^c) \in \rightarrow^c, i \in \Sigma_{int}, \sigma \in ST(\Gamma_{SPTS})\}$
- $\rightarrow_{ret} = \{((s_1^c,s_2^c \bullet \sigma),r,(s_2^c,\sigma)) \mid (s_1^c,r,s_3^c) \in \rightarrow^c, \sigma \in ST(\Gamma_{SPTS})\}$
- $s_0 = init$

To give some examples, the set of paths of the SPTS-induced LTS of Fig. 1 includes paths such as $F \cdot a \cdot F \cdot b$ and $F \cdot G \cdot c \cdot R \cdot R$. It is easy to see that Definition 7 yields a valid LTS and therefore allows us to describe the *behavior* of a procedural system.

3.2 A Technical Point of View

As discussed in Sect. 2.2, the characteristics of (finite, input-deterministic) LTS-based behavior can be equivalently described by (regular) prefix-closed languages. As SPTSs consists of individual (finite, input-deterministic) PTSs, we can define a language-equivalent formalism to SPTSs in order to establish a notion compatible with AAL.

For the language-based interpretation, we will often switch between a local, in-procedure interpretation of words, and a global, system-wide interpretation. In order to better differentiate between the two contexts of words, we use $\widehat{}$ to denote the procedural context and add (remove) this markup token when switching between the two contexts. Note that this token is only used for reasons of clarity and does not change or transform the actual input symbols.

We continue to introduce the language-based formalisms for representing behavior.

Definition 8 (Behavioral automaton (BA)). *Let Σ be an SPA alphabet and $c \in \Sigma_{call}$ denote a procedure. A behavioral automaton for procedure c is a prefix-closed DFA $P_{\mathcal{B}}^c$ over $\widehat{\Sigma}$ (cf. Definition 2).*

Definition 9 (System of behavioral automata (SBA)). *Let Σ be an SPA alphabet with $\Sigma_{call} = \{c_1, \ldots, c_q\}$. A system of behavioral automata $S_{\mathcal{B}}$ over Σ is given by the tuple of behavioral automata $(P_{\mathcal{B}}^{c_1}, \ldots, P_{\mathcal{B}}^{c_q})$ such that for each call symbol there exists a corresponding behavioral automaton. The initial procedure of $S_{\mathcal{B}}$ is denoted as $c_0 \in \Sigma_{call}$.*

We use *structural operational semantics* (SOS) [23] to formally define the language of SBAs. We write

$$\frac{guard}{(s_1,\sigma_1) \xrightarrow{o} (s_2,\sigma_2)}$$

for some states s_1, s_2 and some control components σ_1, σ_2 to denote that this transformation (if applicable) *emits* a symbol o. We generalize this notation to *sequences* by writing

$$(s_1,\sigma_1) \xrightarrow{w}{}^* (s_2,\sigma_2)$$

to denote that there exists a sequence of individual (applicable) transformations starting in configuration (s_1,σ_1) and ending in configuration (s_2,σ_2), whose concatenation of symbols yields w.

To formally define the semantics of SBAs by means of SOS rules, we first define a *stack* to model the control components of the SOS rules and then define the language of an SBA.

Definition 10 (SBA stack domain/configuration). *Let Σ be an SPA alphabet. We define $\Gamma_{SBA} = \widehat{\Sigma}^* \uplus \{\bot\}$ as the stack domain with $\bot$ as the unique bottom-of-stack symbol. We use $\bullet$ to denote the stacking of elements of Γ_{SBA} where writing elements left-to-right displays the stack top-to-bottom and we write $ST(\Gamma_{SBA})$ to denote the set of all possible stack configurations.*

Definition 11 (Language of an SBA). *Let Σ be an SPA alphabet and $S_{\mathcal{B}}$ be an SBA over Σ. Using tuples from $\widehat{\Sigma}^* \times ST(\Gamma)$ to denote a system configuration, we define three kinds of SOS transformation rules:*

1. *call-rules:*

$$\frac{\widehat{w} \in L(P_{\mathcal{B}}^c)}{(\widehat{c} \cdot \widehat{v}, \sigma) \xrightarrow{c} (\widehat{w}, \widehat{v} \bullet \sigma)}$$

   for all $\widehat{c} \in \widehat{\Sigma}_{call}$, $\widehat{v}, \widehat{w} \in \widehat{\Sigma}^*$, $\sigma \in ST(\Gamma_{SBA})$.

2. *int-rules:*

$$\frac{-}{(\widehat{i} \cdot \widehat{v}, \sigma) \xrightarrow{i} (\widehat{v}, \sigma)}$$

   for all $\widehat{i} \in \widehat{\Sigma}_{int}$, $\widehat{v} \in \widehat{\Sigma}^*$, $\sigma \in ST(\Gamma_{SBA})$.

3. *ret-rules:*

$$\frac{-}{(\widehat{r}, \widehat{v} \bullet \sigma) \xrightarrow{r} (\widehat{v}, \sigma)}$$

   for all $\widehat{v} \in \widehat{\Sigma}^*$, $\sigma \in ST(\Gamma_{SBA})$.

The language *of an SBA $S_{\mathcal{B}}$ is then defined as*

$$L(S_{\mathcal{B}}) = \{w \in \Sigma^* \mid \exists \sigma \in ST(\Gamma_{SBA}) \colon (\widehat{c}_0, \bot) \xrightarrow{w}{}^* (\varepsilon, \sigma)\}.$$

From Definitions 7 and 11 one can see how both formalisms incorporate the identical "copy-rule" semantics when expanding call symbols. Given the (finite) LTS-to-DFA translation discussed in Sect. 2.2, one can easily construct an SBA that yields a formal language describing the behavior of an SPTS. As a result, by developing an AAL algorithm for SBAs, we can provide a learning mechanism for procedural behavioral systems described by SPTSs.

In order to formulate a learning algorithm in Sect. 4, let us first introduce some essential properties of SBAs. Similar to the (non-prefix-closed) formalism of SPAs [11], the core idea will be to decompose the learning process of SBAs into a simultaneous inference of individual BAs. Therefore, let us re-iterate some formal definitions of [11].

Let $w = w_1 \cdot \ldots \cdot w_n \in \Sigma^*$. We write $w[i, j]$ to denote the sub-sequence of w starting at the symbol at position i and ending at position j (inclusive). We write $w[i,]$ ($w[, j]$) to denote the suffix starting at position i (prefix up to and including position j). For any $i > j$, $w[i, j]$ denotes the empty word ε. We call a word *well-matched* if every call symbol is at one point followed by a matching return symbol and there exist no unmatched call or return symbols. We call a word *return-matched* if every return symbol is at one point preceded by a matching call symbol. Note that in return-matched words, there may exist unmatched call symbols. We use $WM(\Sigma)$ to denote the set of well-matched words over Σ and $RM(\Sigma)$ to denote the set of return-matched words over Σ.

In order to determine the matching return-index of a call symbol, we use the *maximum well-matched suffix function*.

Definition 12 (Maximum well-matched suffix function). *Let Σ be an SPA alphabet and $w \in \Sigma^+$ non-empty. We define the* maximum well-matched *suffix function $\rho_w \colon \mathbb{N} \to \mathbb{N}$ as*

$$\rho_w(x) = \max\{i \in \mathbb{N} \mid w[x, i] \in WM(\Sigma)\}$$

Note that if there exists no well-matched suffix of $w[x,]$, e.g., if $w[x] = r$, $\rho_w(x)$ will return $x - 1$ as $w[x, x - 1] = \varepsilon \in WM(\Sigma)$.

For decomposing words of an SBA into runs of its involved BAs, we focus on the instances of procedural invocations and use a projection function to abstract from nested procedural invocations.

Definition 13 (Instances set). *Let Σ be an SPA alphabet and $w \in \Sigma^*$. We define the* instances set $Inst_w \subseteq \Sigma_{call} \times \mathbb{N}$ *as*

$$Inst_w = \{(c, i) \mid w[i] = c \in \Sigma_{call}\}$$

Definition 14 (Alpha projection). *Let Σ be an SPA alphabet. The* alpha projection $\alpha \colon WM(\Sigma) \to (\widehat{\Sigma}_{call} \uplus \widehat{\Sigma}_{int})^*$ *is defined as*

$$\alpha(\varepsilon) = \varepsilon$$

$$\alpha(u \cdot v) = \begin{cases} \widehat{u} \cdot \alpha(v) & \text{if } u \in \Sigma_{int} \\ \widehat{u} \cdot \alpha(v[\rho_v(1) + 1,]) & \text{if } u \in \Sigma_{call} \end{cases}$$

for all $u \in (\Sigma_{call} \uplus \Sigma_{int}), v \in \Sigma^*$.

With the above definitions, we can characterize the membership property of an SBA word equivalently via the membership property of the involved BAs.

Theorem 1 (Behavioral localization theorem). *Let Σ be an SPA alphabet and $S_{\mathcal{B}}$ be an SBA over Σ. Let $w \in RM(\Sigma)$ be a non-empty, return-matched word starting with c_0. Then we have*

$$w \in L(S_{\mathcal{B}}) \Leftrightarrow \forall (c, i) \in Inst_w \colon \alpha(u) \cdot \widehat{v} \in L(P_{\mathcal{B}}^c)$$

where $u = w[i + 1, j]$, $j = \rho_w(i + 1)$ and $\widehat{v} = \begin{cases} \varepsilon & \text{if } j = |w| \\ \widehat{w}[j + 1] & \text{otherwise} \end{cases}$

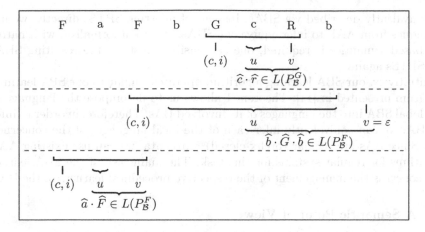

Fig. 2. Decomposition of the exemplary word $F \cdot a \cdot F \cdot b \cdot G \cdot c \cdot R \cdot b$ generated by the SBA of Fig. 1.

Proof. (Sketch) This equivalence is based on the fact that for every emitted call symbol c of an SBA, there needs to exist a corresponding word $\widehat{w} \in L(P_{\mathcal{B}}^c)$. One can verify this property for each call symbol by checking the membership of the projected, procedural trace in the language of the respective behavioral automata. Since procedural actions (return symbols, un-matched call symbols) are also decided by behavioral automata, we need to extend the trace-to-be-checked by this very action ($\widehat{v}$ in the equivalence). ☐

The main difference between the localization theorem of regular SPAs [11] and its behavioral version (Theorem 1) concerns the well-matchedness of regular SPA words. For well-matched words, every call symbol is at one point followed by a mandatory matching return symbol. As a result, we can restrict ourselves to only verify the projection of inner well-matched sub-sequences. For SBAs, the decision to return from a procedure is decided by the individual behavioral automata, and SBAs in general allow for un-matched call symbols (cf. Definition 11). Therefore, we encounter three different situations in which the behavioral automata need to verify

1. an additional call symbol (if the called procedure does not return),
2. an additional return symbol (if the current procedure returns) or
3. no symbol (if the current procedure stops mid-execution).

Figure 2 visualizes these three cases for an exemplary run of the SBA of Fig. 1.

4   Learning Systems of Procedural Transition Systems

This section presents an algorithmic approach to learning behaviors of procedural systems. Our approach is based on the discussions in Sect. 3 that SPTSs can be equivalently described via SBAs. Instead of inferring SPTSs directly, we use techniques from AAL to infer equivalent SBAs. In case a formalism with native LTS-based semantics is required, one can easily transform the resulting SBAs into SPTSs again.

Intuitively, our SBA learning algorithm operates similar to our SPA learning algorithm presented in [11]: Theorem 1 allows us to decompose the language of the global SBA into the languages of its involved BAs. Therefore, in order to infer an SBA, we can equivalently infer each of the local languages of the concerned BAs. Since BAs are regular (prefix-closed) automata, we can use existing AAL algorithms for regular systems for this task. The main task of the SBA learner then concerns the management of the respective procedural learners of the BAs.

4.1   A Semantic Point of View

Compared to our learning algorithm for SPAs [11], the prefix-closure of systems affects the inference process in numerous ways. In the following paragraphs we discuss two aspects that simplify the inference process and two aspects that require additional handling compared to classic SPA inference.

Simplifications. The first simplification is concerned with the analysis of counterexamples. Identifying a mis-behaving procedure in a counterexample for regular SPAs involves an intricate analysis process that requires specific properties on the current SPA hypothesis (*ts-conformance*) and potentially results in additional membership queries being posed. For SBAs, *reduced* counterexamples, i.e., counterexamples that expose an in-equivalence at the last symbol, allow one to directly find the violating procedure by simply determining the execution context of the last counterexample symbol. This can be done by simply traversing the counterexample back-to-front and searching for the first unmatched call symbol. This analysis requires no additional queries both in the case of positive or negative counterexamples. Especially for behavioral systems, one can easily construct reduced counterexamples because both the SBA hypothesis (via a prefix-closed language) and the (potentially LTS-based) SUL allow for direct step-wise feedback to detect mismatches as they occur. In monitor-based environments (e.g., in live-long learning setups [12]), this is even the natural way of detecting counterexamples.

The second simplification is concerned with the query expansion process. In order to explore the individual procedures, the DFA learners pose membership queries to the global system. For SPAs, this requires the procedural learners (or rather the membership oracles of the procedural learners) to embed queries in a context of access sequence and return sequence which ensure that the query of the procedural learner correctly enters and returns from the concerned procedure in the global system. Since the languages of SBAs are prefix-closed, one only needs a procedure's access sequence in order to guarantee observing the correct local behavior. Skipping return sequences during query expansion not only simplifies the translation but also improves the (symbol) query performance of the learner (cf. Sect. 6).

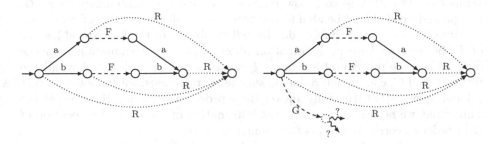

Fig. 3. A (PTS-based) hypothesis for LTS_B^F of Fig. 1 without any procedural G-transitions (left) and after incorporating the information of a positive counterexample $F \cdot G$ (right).

Adjustments. The first adjustment is related to the fact that behavioral automata are defined over the complete SPA alphabet, including the return symbol. When using learners for regular DFAs, this means that membership oracles of the procedural learners may pose queries that contain additional symbols after a return symbol. This essentially breaks out of the scope of a procedure (cf. Definition 11) and the observed behavior is generally non-deterministic as the response to the query depends on the access sequence used for embedding the local query. In order to tackle this issue and ensure that return transitions are dead-ends (cf. Definition 4), one can simply answer all procedural queries with "false" if their input sequence contains any symbols beyond the first occurrence of the return symbol. Additionally, the DFA hypotheses may violate this property after a refinement step. One can solve this issue by simply analyzing the procedural hypotheses for any accepted r-continuations after each refinement step and constructing a corresponding counterexamples if necessary. Note that in both situations (r-continuations in queries and hypotheses) no additional membership queries are necessary due to the prefix-closed properties of the concerned languages. Therefore, these adjustments come at zero (query) costs.

The second adjustment concerns the ability to incorporate information from counterexamples. For SPAs, positive counterexamples are well-matched, accepted words of the SUL and therefore yield truthful access sequences, terminating sequences and return sequences for each involved procedure. This allows us to structure the SPA inference process in an alphabet-incremental way: By initially rejecting words that contain "unknown" procedures, we enforce that counterexamples which contain these procedures are always positive. From these counterexamples, we can extract the necessary sequences, start new learner instances for the respective procedures, and add call symbols to the active learning alphabet of existing learner instances in order to incorporate the information from the counterexample.

For SBAs, this situation is different. Consider the situation depicted in Fig. 3. The left-hand side of Fig. 3 depicts a (PTS transformed) hypothesis of procedure F which resembles the corresponding procedure from Fig. 1 without the call symbol G. The SBA learner now receives the positive counterexample $F \cdot G$, i.e., procedure F should be able to perform a successful invocation of procedure G. However, we cannot simply add the call symbol $\widehat{G}$ to the procedural learner of F, because we have no information about a possible terminating sequence of G. When the procedural learner of F wants to explore behavior beyond the invocation of G, e.g., to determine its successor transitions, we cannot construct (global) queries that truthfully answer these procedural queries. However, at the same time, we need to incorporate the information of a successful invocation of G in order to correctly process the counterexample.

Semantically, such counterexamples introduce a "divergent" state, i.e., a state that represents actual system behavior but has unknown future behavior. The future behavior is unknown, because currently there is no evidence whether the invoked procedure does terminate, i.e., there exist successor states, or does not terminate, i.e., there exist no successor states. Both situations are equally possible. To resolve the divergence, it requires either an additional counterexample that continues beyond the procedural invocation, i.e., a counterexample that provides a terminating sequence for G, or the termination of the learning process which indicates that the procedure in fact does not terminate. In the following section, we propose a way to tackle this issue using alphabet extension.

4.2   A Technical Point of View

Divergent states are a problem in the context of AAL, because they may either represent (potentially temporary) sink states or coincide with existing states of the hypothesis. This may result in non-monotonic learning processes, i.e., states of the hypothesis may later have to be merged again, which can cause issues with termination and correctness properties of AAL algorithms. We tackle this issue by introducing two versions of call symbols: terminating and non-terminating ones. Similar to the concept of abstract alphabet refinement [15], this allows us to support multiple semantics for a single (abstract) call symbol throughout the learning process. In the following, we use $\widehat{\Sigma}_{call}$ to denote the set of terminating call symbols and $\widehat{\Sigma}'_{call}$ to denote the set of non-terminating call symbols.

Throughout the learning process of a procedure c we maintain a mapping $M^c : \Sigma_{call} \rightarrow (\widehat{\Sigma}_{call} \uplus \widehat{\Sigma}'_{call})$ that associates for each call symbol a representative that is used in the procedural hypothesis. When encountering a counterexample like in Fig. 3, we first add the non-terminating version of a call symbol to the procedural learning process. In case of Fig. 3, we would use $\widehat{G}'$.

Procedural queries that end with non-terminating call symbols such as $\widehat{G}'$ can still be expanded to global queries using the call symbol G. Due to the prefix-closure of behavioral systems, these (expanded) queries can also be answered truthfully. If the procedural learner poses a query that contains symbols beyond a non-terminating call symbol, the procedural membership oracle simply short-circuits these queries and answers them with "false" without actually delegating the query to the global system. This heuristic results in the divergent states materializing as accepting states that lead into a sink, irrespective of whether the corresponding call may eventually terminate.

Now, if the procedural learner receives a counterexample that provides an actual terminating sequence for a procedure, e.g., $F \cdot G \cdot c \cdot R$ in the context of Fig. 3, we add the terminating version of call symbol $\widehat{G}$ to the procedural learner and update the mapping $G \mapsto \widehat{G}$. For terminating call symbols, the procedural membership oracles can properly expand the procedural queries and the answers to these queries represent definitive behavior. Since the learning process is monotonic with regard to alphabet extension, introducing a new alphabet symbol does not cause any problems with potential state merges. On a procedural level, this approach results in behavioral automata being defined over the alphabet $\Sigma \uplus \Sigma'_{call}$. However, due to our mapping, we can easily provide an interface based on Σ alone which essentially "filters" out irrelevant transitions depending on whether we have found a terminating sequence or not. Furthermore, note that in case of counterexamples that directly introduce a terminating sequence, e.g., directly receiving $F \cdot G \cdot c \cdot R$ instead of $F \cdot G$, we can directly add $\widehat{G}$ to the learning alphabet and skip $\widehat{G}'$.

5   On Behaviors and Reductions to Well-Matched Languages

Having presented the intuitive and technical aspects of learning behaviors of procedural systems in the form of SBAs, we want to discuss in this section the impact of prefix-closure and its meaning for the model and inference process. Specifically, we want to contrast our prefix-closed approach to "classic" well-matched approaches such as SPAs [11].

SPAs have a direct correspondence to context-free grammars by modeling the production rules of non-terminals via procedural automata and defining the SPA language according to the well-known copy-rule semantics. In essence, the language of an SPA covers all derivations of the represented grammar. Necessary for the learnability of SPAs is an instrumentation that makes the start and end of a production rule visible. When implemented with a stack, SPAs enforce "empty-stack" semantics: For truthfully answering the membership question, a word must be well-matched, i.e., for every call symbol there must exist a matching return symbol.

While for certain applications domains, such as DTD learning [10], this property is natural, it can often times pose problems when integrating software systems or hardware systems in the learning process. Imagine a system that encounters erroneous behavior while running, e.g., an exception being thrown. In order to feed this information to an SPA learner, one would need to complete this erroneous run to an empty stack while making sure that the completion does not hide the actual observed error. In contrast to that, an SBA-based environment would allow one to directly construct a valid counterexample at the moment the error occurred.

The crux of this discrepancy is the question of which sensor is used to probe the system. An SPA sensor asks the question "What action is returnable in the system?" whereas an SBA sensor asks the question "What action is possible in the system right now?". Here, the prefix-closure of SBAs allow for a much more natural system exploration by breaking the connection between call symbols and return symbols forced by SPAs. Ultimately, this even allows for modeling non-terminating procedures, which is not possible with empty-stack semantics. SBAs enable a much more fine-grained representation of the system which is crucial when dealing with behavior.

These two views do not have to be mutually exclusive. For example, one can easily transform a behavioral automaton into a procedural automaton used by SPAs by

1. marking every state as rejecting,
2. marking every state with a (previously) accepting r-successor as accepting,
3. removing every r-transition.

On a global language level, this *reduction* corresponds to intersecting the SBA-language with the language of well-matched words, which exactly yields all SPA-languages. This allows one to *simulate* an SPA learner using an SBA-based kind of interaction which may be more convenient for system integration.

This alternate approach to SPA learning also impacts the learning process itself: SPA hypotheses are usually smaller because procedural automata ignore system states that cannot successfully return and consider fewer input symbols (cf. Sect. 4.2). This can potentially result in fewer queries necessary for infer-ring SPA models. However, since SPAs mandate empty-stack semantics, every expanded query requires appending a terminating sequence. For very nested systems, these sequences may become very long and therefore lower the symbol performance of the SPA learner. When using SBA semantics, this kind of expan-sion is not necessary. Section 6 shows that the savings of skipping the appended return sequences can outweigh the increased number of hypothesis states and overall boost the (symbol) query performance.

6   Evaluation

After discussing the qualitative aspects of SBAs, we want to investigate in this section the quantitative properties of SBAs—especially in comparison to SPAs in the context of active automata learning. Therefore, we conducted a series of benchmarks that evaluate the query and symbol performance of our SBA learner and present the results in the following. The benchmarks are available at https://github.com/LearnLib/learnlib-sba for reproducibility.

6.1   Benchmark Setup

For a single benchmark run, we first constructed a random SBA (see below) to use it as a SUL. We then instantiated the SBA learner with a specific reg-ular learner for its procedures and ran the learning loop (cf. Sect. 2.2) using a separating word-based equivalence oracle for constructing counterexamples (see below). For the comparison with the SPAs-based formalism, we used the generated SBA and reduced it as described in Sect. 5. The reduced SBA was then learned by the algorithm of [11] using the same procedural learner and counterexample generation technique.

Throughout the learning process, we counted for both approaches the number of membership queries as well as the cumulated number of symbols of these queries. In total, we ran 25 experiments and present in Sect. 6.2 the averaged results.

Random SBAs. For creating a random SBA, we first constructed an SPA alphabet of 5 call symbols, 10 internal symbols and the single return symbol. We considered two types of SBA systems.

Complete SBAs, i.e., SBAs where the transition function is totally defined, were constructed as follows:

1. For each call symbol $c \in \Sigma_{call}$, we generated a behavioral automaton P_B^c that initially consisted of $n - 2$ accepting states.
2. For each transition $(s, i) \in \{1, \ldots, n - 2\} \times (\widehat{\Sigma}_{call} \uplus \widehat{\Sigma}_{int})$ we selected a random successor from $\{1, \ldots, n - 2\}$ via a uniform distribution.
3. For each state s, we used a coin-flip to decide whether s should have an outgoing r-transition to a designated accepting "return" successor. This adds an additional accepting state to the behavioral automaton.
4. We made the behavioral automaton total by adding a rejecting sink state and letting every so-far undefined transition lead into this sink.

The *complete SBA* is then constructed by aggregating the individually generated random behavioral automata.

Partial SBAs, i.e., SBAs where the transition function is partially defined, were constructed identical to the "complete" case with the only difference being that step 2 introduces an additional coin-flip to decide whether a transition (s, i) should be undefined. If the coin-flip decided "yes", this transition would then lead into the rejecting sink by step 4.

For the parameter n we chose values from $\{10, 25, 50, 100\}$ which results in total SBA sizes of $50, 125, 250$ and 500 states, respectively.

Learner. For the procedural learner we used the TTT algorithm by Isberner et al. [19]. While the SBA learner can be parameterized with arbitrary learners for regular languages, we have observed similar results to our other research [11,12] in which the TTT algorithm yielded the best results. Therefore, we focus our analysis on the data of this setup.

Counterexamples. For generating counterexamples during the learning process, we sequentially compared the behavioral automata of the generated SBA with the current hypothesis model and checked whether there existed a separating word [22]. If such a word existed, we expanded the procedural counterexample to a valid SBA trace using previously computed, shortest access sequences and terminating sequences. While this construction of counterexample is not necessarily realistic, it allows us to emphasize the impact of SBAs as a structure, as there is no query overhead introduced by complex counterexample analysis.

6.2   Results

The results are shown in Fig. 4. In Fig. 4a we can see that for complete systems the SBA-based approach performs worse than the SPA-based approach regarding query performance. This was to be expected, because complete systems are "hard" systems in the context of SBAs: A lot of accepting states are interconnected, so there exist a lot of possible paths that eventually reach an accepting state via the return symbol. Here, the answers to "What is possible in the system?" and "What is returnable in the system?" hugely overlap. As a result, the SPA-based interpretation is more efficient because it can directly encode this information via the acceptance criterion of procedural automata. Compared to the SBA-based system, the reduced number of states and input symbols allows SPAs to out-perform the behavioral interpretation. However, regarding symbol performance, Fig. 4b shows the impact of the simplified query expansion. Despite the increased number of membership queries, the cumulated number of symbols of these queries is significantly lower than for the SPA-based interpretation.

For partial systems, we can see that the SBA-based approach significantly outperforms the SPA-based approach both query- and symbol-wise (cf. Figs. 4c and 4d). Here, the generated systems under learning contain more (procedural) paths that are executable but do not return. As a result, the SBA learner can exploit the prefix-closure of these systems and skip further exploration/queries when encountering such states. In contrast, the SPA-based learner needs to continue exploring beyond these states because in the holistic system interpretation, rejecting states may at some point still reach accepting states again. Consequently, the gap in symbol performance speaks even more in favor of the SBA formalism.

We argue that the quantitative benchmark results speak in favor of our newly developed formalism of SBAs. SBAs allow for a much more natural way to interact with SULs, which increases the applicability of AAL in practice, and they are capable of capturing behavioral properties that SPAs can not (cf. Sect. 5). These semantic improvements come at a (if any) moderate price which allow the SBA approach to remain competitive compared to the existing SPA approach. Even better, there also exist situations where this more intricate sensor for system behavior is able to *improve* learning performance as it allows to skip unnecessary exploration steps.

To get a better overview of which system structure impacts the learning process in which way, further analysis in future work is required. However, for the time being, the collected results give a promising impression for the potential of the SBA formalism.

7   Related Work

Our original work on SPAs [11] is related to the work on visibly push-down languages (VPLs) and visibly push-down automata (VPAs) by Alur et al. [6,7]. Similar to SPA languages and SBA languages, they utilize special symbols (call

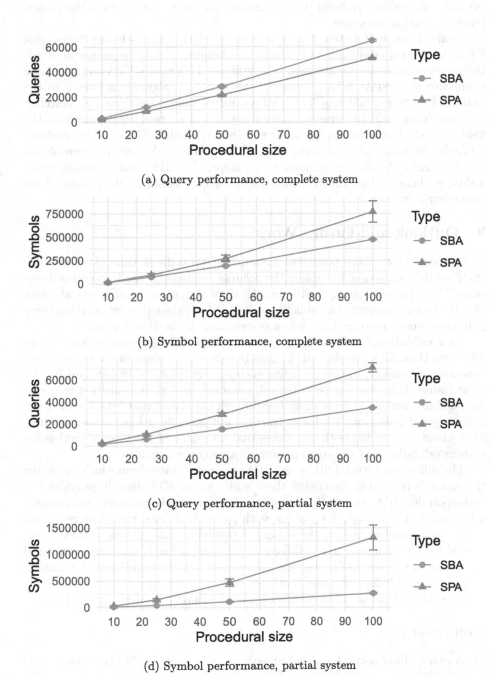

(a) Query performance, complete system

(b) Symbol performance, complete system

(c) Query performance, partial system

(d) Symbol performance, partial system

Fig. 4. Benchmark results

symbols and return symbols) that determine the stack operations of the underlying automaton structure.

Apart from well-matched and return-matched (prefix-closed) languages, VPAs in general even support call-matched languages, i.e., languages in which there exist words with un-matched call symbols. This makes VPAs strictly more expressive than SPAs/SBAs. However, the two AAL algorithms known to the authors [17,20] for inferring VPLs/VPAs only consider inferring well-matched systems. Therefore, the presented approach offers a novel contribution in the field of AAL. Furthermore, we have seen in [11,12] that SPAs can outperform VPAs by multiple orders of magnitude, which makes SPAs highly preferable for *practical* AAL. While this remains to be shown for SBAs and return-matched VPAs, we believe that similar results can be shown based on the results of our benchmarks in Sect. 6.

8   Outlook and Future Work

In this paper, we have presented systems of procedural transitions systems (SPTSs) that allows one to capture the *behavior* of instrumented, procedural systems. Using the equally expressive formalism of systems of behavioral automata (SBAs) we have presented a publicly available[2] AAL algorithm for inferring these behaviors from procedural black-box systems on the basis of testing.

As a validation technique for reactive systems, SBA learning is much more adequate than SPA learning, as it directly reflects the stepwise evolution of an execution. Moreover, states of reactive systems can typically be distinguished by their (immediate) interaction potential, meaning that their transition relations are partially defined. Our synthetic benchmark has shown that SBA learning significantly out-performs SPA-based learners for partially defined systems. Thus, SBA learning improves both the conceptual adequacy of the learned models for system validation and the corresponding learning performance.

The difference between SBAs and SPAs concerns states from which no return transition is reachable. Removing these states of an SBA directly provides the corresponding SPA. Thus, SBA-based learning can also be considered as an optimization of SPA learning for systems with partially defined transition relations.

As mentioned in Sect. 1, the notion of behaviors has—among others—been refined to capture input-output dialogs on the basis of Mealy machines. A natural extension for behaviors of procedural systems is given by a similar kind of (input-output-based) *dialogs* of procedural systems. We are currently working on a corresponding generalization covering systems of procedural Mealy machines.

References

1. Aarts, F., Fiterau-Brostean, P., Kuppens, H., Vaandrager, F.W.: Learning register automata with fresh value generation. In: Leucker, M., Rueda, C., Valencia, F.D. (eds.) ICTAC 2015. LNCS, vol. 9399, pp. 165–183. Springer, Cham (2015). https://doi.org/10.1007/978-3-319-25150-9_11

---

[2] https://github.com/LearnLib/learnlib-sba.

2. Aarts, F., Heidarian, F., Kuppens, H., Olsen, P., Vaandrager, F.: Automata learning through counterexample guided abstraction refinement. In: Giannakopoulou, D., Méry, D. (eds.) FM 2012. LNCS, vol. 7436, pp. 10–27. Springer, Heidelberg (2012). https://doi.org/10.1007/978-3-642-32759-9_4

3. Aarts, F., Howar, F., Kuppens, H., Vaandrager, F.W.: Algorithms for inferring register automata. In: Margaria, T., Steffen, B. (eds.) ISoLA 2014. LNCS, vol. 8802, pp. 202–219. Springer, Heidelberg (2014). https://doi.org/10.1007/978-3-662-45234-9_15

4. Aarts, F., Kuppens, H., Tretmans, J., Vaandrager, F.W., Verwer, S.: Learning and testing the bounded retransmission protocol. In: Heinz, J., de la Higuera, C., Oates, T. (eds.) Proceedings of the Eleventh International Conference on Grammatical Inference, ICGI 2012, University of Maryland, College Park, USA, 5–8 September 2012. JMLR Proceedings, vol. 21, pp. 4–18. JMLR.org (2012). http://proceedings.mlr.press/v21/aarts12a.html

5. Aarts, F., Vaandrager, F.: Learning I/O automata. In: Gastin, P., Laroussinie, F. (eds.) CONCUR 2010. LNCS, vol. 6269, pp. 71–85. Springer, Heidelberg (2010). https://doi.org/10.1007/978-3-642-15375-4_6

6. Alur, R., Kumar, V., Madhusudan, P., Viswanathan, M.: Congruences for visibly pushdown languages. In: Caires, L., Italiano, G.F., Monteiro, L., Palamidessi, C., Yung, M. (eds.) ICALP 2005. LNCS, vol. 3580, pp. 1102–1114. Springer, Heidelberg (2005). https://doi.org/10.1007/11523468_89

7. Alur, R., Madhusudan, P.: Visibly pushdown languages. In: Proceedings of the 36th Annual ACM Symposium on Theory of Computing, pp. 202–211. ACM (2004)

8. Angluin, D.: Learning regular sets from queries and counterexamples. Inf. Comput. **75**(2), 87–106 (1987)

9. Fiterău-Broştean, P., Janssen, R., Vaandrager, F.W.: Learning fragments of the TCP network protocol. In: Lang, F., Flammini, F. (eds.) FMICS 2014. LNCS, vol. 8718, pp. 78–93. Springer, Cham (2014). https://doi.org/10.1007/978-3-319-10702-8_6

10. Frohme, M., Steffen, B.: Active mining of document type definitions. In: Howar, F., Barnat, J. (eds.) FMICS 2018. LNCS, vol. 11119, pp. 147–161. Springer, Cham (2018). https://doi.org/10.1007/978-3-030-00244-2_10

11. Frohme, M., Steffen, B.: Compositional learning of mutually recursive procedural systems. Int. J. Softw. Tools Technol. Transf. **23**(4), 521–543 (2021). https://doi.org/10.1007/s10009-021-00634-y

12. Frohme, M., Steffen, B.: Never-stop context-free learning. In: Olderog, E.-R., Steffen, B., Yi, W. (eds.) Model Checking, Synthesis, and Learning. LNCS, vol. 13030, pp. 164–185. Springer, Cham (2021). https://doi.org/10.1007/978-3-030-91384-7_9

13. Hagerer, A., Hungar, H., Margaria, T., Niese, O., Steffen, B., Ide, H.-D.: Demonstration of an operational procedure for the model-based testing of CTI systems. In: Kutsche, R.-D., Weber, H. (eds.) FASE 2002. LNCS, vol. 2306, pp. 336–339. Springer, Heidelberg (2002). https://doi.org/10.1007/3-540-45923-5_25

14. Hagerer, A., Margaria, T., Niese, O., Steffen, B., Brune, G., Ide, H.D.: Efficient regression testing of CTI-systems: testing a complex call-center solution. Ann. Rev. Commun. Int. Eng. Consort. (IEC) **55**, 1033–1040 (2001)

15. Howar, F., Steffen, B., Merten, M.: Automata learning with automated alphabet abstraction refinement. In: Jhala, R., Schmidt, D. (eds.) VMCAI 2011. LNCS, vol. 6538, pp. 263–277. Springer, Heidelberg (2011). https://doi.org/10.1007/978-3-642-18275-4_19

16. Hungar, H., Niese, O., Steffen, B.: Domain-specific optimization in automata learning. In: Hunt, W.A., Somenzi, F. (eds.) CAV 2003. LNCS, vol. 2725, pp. 315–327. Springer, Heidelberg (2003). https://doi.org/10.1007/978-3-540-45069-6_31

17. Isberner, M.: Foundations of active automata learning: an algorithmic perspective. Ph.D. thesis, Technical University Dortmund, Germany (2015). http://hdl.handle.net/2003/34282

18. Isberner, M., Howar, F., Steffen, B.: Learning register automata: from languages to program structures. Mach. Learn. 1–34 (2013). https://doi.org/10.1007/s10994-013-5419-7

19. Isberner, M., Howar, F., Steffen, B.: The TTT algorithm: a redundancy-free approach to active automata learning. In: Bonakdarpour, B., Smolka, S.A. (eds.) RV 2014. LNCS, vol. 8734, pp. 307–322. Springer, Cham (2014). https://doi.org/10.1007/978-3-319-11164-3_26

20. Kumar, V., Madhusudan, P., Viswanathan, M.: Minimization, learning, and conformance testing of boolean programs. In: Baier, C., Hermanns, H. (eds.) CONCUR 2006. LNCS, vol. 4137, pp. 203–217. Springer, Heidelberg (2006). https://doi.org/10.1007/11817949_14

21. Merten, M., Howar, F., Steffen, B., Margaria, T.: Automata learning with on-the-fly direct hypothesis construction. In: Hähnle, R., Knoop, J., Margaria, T., Schreiner, D., Steffen, B. (eds.) ISoLA 2011. CCIS, pp. 248–260. Springer, Heidelberg (2012). https://doi.org/10.1007/978-3-642-34781-8_19

22. Moore, E.F.: Gedanken-experiments on sequential machines. Ann. Math. Stud. **34**, 129–153 (1956)

23. Plotkin, G.D.: A structural approach to operational semantics. Technical report, University of Aarhus (1981). dAIMI FN-19

24. Raffelt, H., Merten, M., Steffen, B., Margaria, T.: Dynamic testing via automata learning. Int. J. Softw. Tools Technol. Transf. (STTT) **11**(4), 307–324 (2009). https://doi.org/10.1007/s10009-009-0120-7

25. Steffen, B., Howar, F., Merten, M.: Introduction to active automata learning from a practical perspective. In: Bernardo, M., Issarny, V. (eds.) SFM 2011. LNCS, vol. 6659, pp. 256–296. Springer, Heidelberg (2011). https://doi.org/10.1007/978-3-642-21455-4_8

26. Vaandrager, F.W.: Active learning of extended finite state machines. In: Nielsen, B., Weise, C. (eds.) ICTSS 2012. LNCS, vol. 7641, pp. 5–7. Springer, Heidelberg (2012). https://doi.org/10.1007/978-3-642-34691-0_2

The Quest for an Adequate Semantic Basis of Dense-Time Metric Temporal Logic

Martin Fränzle(✉)(iD)

Department of Computing Science, Carl von Ossietzky Universität Oldenburg,
Ammerländer Heerstraße 114–118, 26129 Oldenburg, Germany
martin.fraenzle@uol.de

Abstract. The notoriously hard decidability problems of dense-time metric temporal logic have historically motivated investigations into means of removing extraneous expressiveness from these logics, both by confining their syntax such that certain constraints (e.g., punctuality) are no longer expressible and by confining the model class, i.e. the traces or trajectories they are interpreted about, in physically justifiable ways (e.g., bounding the number of state changes possible within a given time frame). In this note, we compare various of the latter semantic restrictions adopted in the formal methods community to the established notion of band limitation underlying digital signal processing. Exploiting the formal bridge between signals and timed traces or trajectories mediated by signal-based temporal logic, like Signal Temporal Logic [8], we base our investigation on exposing characteristic formulae that are able to distinguish between the various semantic models. The idea here is that indistinguishable pairs of restrictions, i.e. pair that do not feature a distinguishing formula in the temporal logic of interest, can be considered equivalent. Unfortunately, the results show that already simple fragments of signal-based metric-time temporal logic can distinguish the constraints on models hitherto suggested in the domain of metric temporal logic and band limitation, sparking a quest for additional investigations into an adequate semantic basis of dense-time metric temporal logic.

Keywords: Metric-time temporal logic · Variability constraints · Signals · Band limitation

1 Introduction

Dense-time metric variants of linear-time temporal logic, like Metric Interval Temporal Logic [2] or the Duration Calculus [3], pose notoriously hard decidability problems when interpreted over continuous time. Various means have been suggested to recover decidability, among them disallowing punctuality in specifications [1] as well as restricting the temporal dynamics and thus the set of traces

This research has received funding from Deutsche Forschungsgemeinschaft under grant No. DFG FR 2715/5-1.

or discrete-state signal trajectories the logic is interpreted upon [6,7,13,14]. The latter line of work builds on various notions of finitely bounded variability of timed traces or trajectories, like k-bounded variability (or k-variability for short) restricting (discrete-state) trajectory variability to at most k state changes within every unit interval of time, and has been motivated by considerations about concurrent programs as well as by the observation that actual embedded control systems are subject to band limitation in their inputs as well as outputs.

It does, however, seem that the exact relation between semantic restrictions on discrete-state abstractions, like confining temporal variability to be k-variable, and band-limitation of the continuous signals underlying these abstractions has never really been explored: while k-variability resembles band-limitation, it is not identical to the latter, as the conditions apply to different types of signals, namely discrete-state vs. continuous-state trajectories. Intuitively, the expected relation between the two types of trajectories is clear: the discrete-state trajectory is meant to be the image of the underlying continuous-time signal under observation through (idealized, delay- and inertia-free) threshold sensors, a notion made explicit in the semantics of Signal Temporal Logic [5]. But whether the set of discrete-state trajectories originating from observing band-limited signals of a certain bandwidth via a threshold sensor actually coincides to k-variability for a certain k (obviously dependent on the bandwidth) has not been explored hitherto. Such a coincidence would, however, constitute a necessary condition for giving (un-)decidability results of temporal logic fragments a precise physical interpretation, given that in- and outputs of embedded systems actually are (or at least ought be in a well-designed sampled system) band-limited.

In this note, we explore that problem by providing Duration Calculus (DC) [3] with a direct interpretation over continuous signals akin to STL [5]. This allows us to investigate the impact of various restrictions on signal dynamics on formula satisfaction. Such restrictions can either be imposed on the continuous signals (e.g., requiring Lipshitz continuity or band limitation) or indirectly enforced by imposing them to the discrete-state traces of such continuous signals w.r.t. state predicates (typical restrictions would then be finite variability or k-variability). This provides us with a basis for comparing such restrictions and exposing characteristic formulae that are able to distinguish between the various restrictions and, for parameterized notions like k-variability, their parameter values. The idea here is that indistinguishable pairs of restrictions, i.e. pair that do not feature a distinguishing formula in the temporal logic of interest, can be considered equivalent. The aforementioned intuitive correspondence between k-variability and band limitation would then imply non-existence of a distinguishing formula (for appropriate pairs (b, k) of band limit b and variability bound k). Unfortunately, the results show that already by a simple fragment of Duration Calculus featuring moderate expressiveness, the constraints on models hitherto suggested and band limitation are mutually distinguishable, sparking a quest for additional investigations into an adequate semantic basis of dense-time metric temporal logic.

The underlying mathematics applies equally well to any other metric-time temporal logic, like Metric Interval Temporal Logic [2] or Signal Temporal Logic [5], such that the particular constructions could easily be transferred. We chose to exemplify them on Duration Calculus as DC has been the issue of a scientific debate with Frits Vandraager back in my early career, with which Frits had enormous impact not only on my PhD thesis [6] and its analysis of DC over models featuring different forms of constrained variability, but far and beyond also on shaping my view of the domain of formal modeling and verification of embedded and hybrid control that I've since been working in. I am very grateful for that support.

2 Signal Duration Calculus

For the sake of our discussion, we introduce a version of Duration Calculus (DC) whose atomic predicates refer to values of real-valued continuous-time signals akin to Signal Temporal Logic (STL) [5]. In fact, this logic that we will subsequently call Signal Duration Calculus (SDC) provides the very same lifting of DC [3,4] to real-valued signals that STL [5] represents w.r.t. Metric Interval Temporal Logic (MITL) [2].

The syntax of the fragment of DC we consider is the $\{\lceil p \rceil, \ell \sim c\}$ fragment defined as follows:

Definition 1 (Syntax of SDC). *Formulae ϕ of Signal Duration Calculus are defined by the Backus-Naur form*

$$\phi ::= \lceil p \rceil \mid \ell \sim c \mid \neg\phi \mid \phi \vee \phi \mid \phi ^\frown \phi$$
$$p ::= g \sim c \mid \neg p \mid p \vee p$$
$$g := cx \mid cx + g$$
$$\sim ::= < \mid =$$
$$c ::\in \mathbb{Q}$$
$$x ::\in Var$$

where Var is a predefined set of signal names. We demand that $c \geq 0$ in $\ell \sim c$; the symbol ℓ denotes the length of the current observation interval. The operator $^\frown$, pronounced "chop", is the only modality of Duration Calculus; it splits the current observation interval into two adjacent subintervals on which the left and right, respectively, argument subformula have to hold. Figure 1 explains these operators by example.

The tautology $\top$, the antinomy $\bot$, other comparison operators than $<$ and $\leq$, further Boolean connectives like $\wedge$ or $\Rightarrow$, and further modalities $\Diamond\phi$ or $\Box\phi$ can be defined: for example, $g = c \equiv g \leq c \wedge \neg g < c$, $\phi \wedge \psi \equiv \neg(\neg\phi \vee \neg\psi)$, $\top \equiv \phi \vee \neg\phi$ with arbitrary ϕ, $\Diamond\phi \equiv \top ^\frown \phi ^\frown \top$, and $\Box\phi \equiv \neg\Diamond\phi$. Particularly useful is the leadsto operator $\phi \rightsquigarrow \lceil p \rceil \equiv \neg\Diamond(\phi ^\frown \lceil \neg p \rceil)$.

Note that the above definition confines state expressions g to be linear combinations of signals, in contrast to the standard definition [8] for STL, which permits more general state expressions. The reason for adopting this restriction is that we will later on consider band-limited signals, which are closed under linear combination, yet not under non-linear operators.

The semantics of SDC builds on the notion of a trajectory and an observation interval, as shown in Fig. 1:

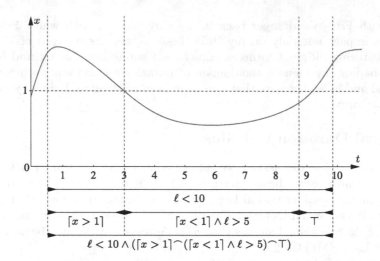

Fig. 1. SDC is interpreted over pairs of trajectories (depicted in green) and observation intervals (depicted underneath the t axis). A formula $\ell < c$ is satisfied iff the length of the current observation interval is less than c; $\ell > c$ respectively is satisfied if the duration of the observation interval exceeds c. A formula $\lceil p \rceil$ is satisfied iff state predicate p hold throughout the current observation interval (except perhaps its two endpoints). $\phi^\frown\psi$ is satisfied iff the current observation interval can be partitioned into two subintervals of which the left satisfies ϕ and the right satisfies ψ. (Color figure online)

Definition 2 (Semantics of SDC). *A state valuation σ is a mapping of signal names $x \in Var$ to real values, i.e., a function $\sigma : Var \to \mathbb{R}$. The set of all state valuations is denoted by Σ. A (continuous time) trajectory $traj : \mathbb{R} \to \Sigma$ is a mapping from time instants, where time is identified with the real numbers $\mathbb{R}$, to state valuations.*

An observation interval is a nonempty closed interval $[b, e] = \{x \in \mathbb{R} \mid a \le x \le b\}$ with $b \le e$ over the reals.

Satisfaction of an SDC formula ϕ by a *(discrete-time) trajectory $traj$ over an observation interval$[b, e]$, denoted as $traj, [b, e] \models \phi$, is defined recursively as*[1]

$traj, [b, e] \models \lceil p \rceil$ *iff $b < e$ and$\llbracket p \rrbracket(traj(m))$ holds for all$m \in]b, e[$,*
$traj, [b, e] \models \ell < c$ *iff $e - b < c$*
$traj, [b, e] \models \ell \le c$ *iff $e - b \le c$*
$traj, [b, e] \models \neg\phi$ *iff $traj, [b, e] \not\models \phi$,*
$traj, [b, e] \models \phi \vee \psi$ *iff $traj, [b, e] \models \phi$ or $traj, [b, e] \models \psi$,*
$traj, [b, e] \models \phi^\frown\psi$ *iff there is $m \in [b, e]$ s.t. $traj, [b, m] \models \psi$ and $traj, [m, e] \models \phi$.*

---

[1] The original version of DC derived the $\lceil \cdot \rceil$ operator from the accumulated duration operator by defining $\lceil p \rceil \equiv \int p = \ell \wedge \ell > 0$ such that $traj, [b, e] \models \lceil p \rceil$ iff $b < e$ and $\llbracket p \rrbracket(traj(m))$ holds for *almost* all $m \in]b, e[$. All formal results in this note are, however, insensitive to this detail.

Here, $[\![p]\!](\sigma)$ *denotes the natural interpretation of the state predicate p over state valuation* σ.

Following the standard definition, an SDC formula ϕ *is satisfied by a trajectory traj, denoted traj* $\models \phi$, *iff traj,* $[0, e] \models \phi$ *for all* $e \geq 0$. *We say that an SDC formula* ϕ *is satisfiable iff there exists some trajectory traj that satisfies* ϕ.

Satisfiability of an SDC formula ϕ obviously hinges on the shape of signals and thus the set of trajectories we admit. We consequently define different classes of trajectories that we will base our subsequent investigations on:

Definition 3. *The following classes of trajectories are characterized by different constraints on signal dynamics (also illustrated in Fig. 2).*

1. *A trajectory traj is called c-value-bounded, for* $c \in \mathbb{R}_{>0}$, *iff* $\forall t \in \mathbb{R} : \forall v \in Var : |traj(t)(v)| \leq c$, *i.e. iff it never takes values outside* $[-c, c]$. *The set of all c-value-bounded trajectories is denoted by* $Traj_{\leq c}$.
2. *A trajectory traj is called l-Lipshitz, for* $l \in \mathbb{R}_{>0}$, *iff the signal* $s_v : \mathbb{R} \to \mathbb{R}$ *given by* $s_v(t) = traj(t)(v)$ *is Lipshitz-continuous with Lipshitz constant l for each* $v \in Var$, *i.e. iff* $\forall t, t' \in \mathbb{R} : \forall v \in Var : |traj(t)(v) - traj(t')(v)| \leq l|t - t'|$. *The set of all l-Lipshitz trajectories is denoted by* $Traj_{Lip,l}$.
3. *A trajectory traj is called b-bandlimited, for* $b \in \mathbb{R}_{\geq 0}$, *iff the signal* $s_v : \mathbb{R} \to \mathbb{R}$ *given by* $s_v(t) = traj(t)(v)$ *is band-limited with band limit b for each* $v \in Var$. *The set of all b-bandlimited trajectories is denoted by* $Traj_{band,b}$.
4. *A trajectory traj is called finitely variable w.r.t. a set of state predicates P iff for each state predicate* $p \in P$, *the evaluation* $[\![p]\!](traj(t))$ *features finitely many changes in truth value over any finite time interval* $[b, e]$ *that t ranges over. That is, any such time interval* $[b, e]$ *can be partitioned into finitely many adjacent intervals* $[b_1, e_1], \ldots, [b_n, e_n]$ *with* $b_1 = b \wedge e_n = e \wedge \forall j \in \{1, n-1\} : e_j = b_{j+1}$ *such that* $\forall j \in \{1, n\} : \forall t, t' \in [b_j, e_j] : [\![p]\!](traj(t)) = [\![p]\!](traj(t'))$, *i.e. p has constant truth value over each* $[b_i, e_i]$. *The set of all finitely variable trajectories (w.r.t. P) is denoted by* $Traj_{fv,P}$. *We will drop the index P whenever it is understood, i.e., identical to the set of state predicates occurring in a formula under investigation.*
5. *A trajectory traj is called k-variable w.r.t. a set of state predicates P, for* $k \in \mathbb{N}_{>0}$, *iff for each state predicate* $p \in P$, *the evaluation* $[\![p]\!](traj(t))$ *features at most k changes in truth value over any unit time interval* $[b, b+1]$, $b \in \mathbb{R}^2$. *That is, any such time interval* $[b, b+1]$ *can be partitioned into k adjacent intervals* $[b_1, e_1], \ldots, [b_k, e_k]$ *with* $b_1 = b \wedge e_k = b+1 \wedge \forall j \in \{1, k-1\} : e_j = b_{j+1}$ *such that* $\forall j \in \{1, k\} : \forall t, t' \in [b_j, e_j] : [\![p]\!](traj(t)) = [\![p]\!](traj(t'))$. *The set of all k-variable trajectories (w.r.t. P) is denoted by* $Traj_{k,P}$. *Again, we will drop the index P whenever it is understood.*

Intersections of these classes can reasonably be built and are non-empty in general. For example, $Traj_{\leq c} \cap Traj_{band,b}$ *denotes the set of trajectories that are bounded in both values and spectral frequencies, with the respective bounds c and*

---

[2] Note that we constrain the number of truth-value changes per state predicate, not across all state predicates.

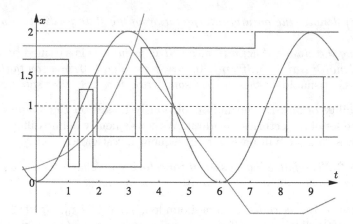

Fig. 2. Illustration of the trajectory classes: The red trajectory is 1.5-value-bounded, while all others are not. All but the exponential cyan trajectory, which is unbounded in value, are c-value-bounded for any $c \geq 2$. The green trajectory is l-Lipshitz for any $l \geq \frac{\pi}{3}$ and the magenta trajectory is l-Lipshitz for any $l \geq \frac{1}{2}$, while all other trajectories are not Lipshitz. The green trajectory is the only band-limited trajectory in the set, being b-bandlimited for any $b \geq \frac{1}{6}$. All trajectories depicted are finitely variable w.r.t. any set of predicates on x. All but the blue trajectory are 1-variable w.r.t. the singleton set $\{x > 1\}$ of state predicates. The blue trajectory is 3-variable w.r.t. $\{x > 1\}$ and it is 1-variable w.r.t. $\{x > 0.1, x \leq 1.5, x \geq 2\}$. Given an arbitrary set P of state predicates over x, the red, cyan, and magenta trajectories are 1-variable, the green is 2-variable, and the blue is 3-variable w.r.t. P. (Color figure online)

b. *Note that this particular combination actually defines a proper subset of the Lipshitz-continuous trajectories.*

Note that the notions of finite variability and of k-variability have extensively been investigated for metric real-time temporal logic over continuous time, with finite variability constituting the standard model [1–4] and k-variability (traditionally called k-boundedness, a term that we avoid here to avoid confusion with k-value-boundedness) providing additional decidability results [7,14]. Confinement to Lipshitz-continuous trajectories has been studied in connection with monitoring algorithms for Signal Temporal Logic [5,8], there providing means of guaranteed interpolation between sampling points. Band-limited signals in turn are the workhorses of digital signal processing [11] as well as of linear dynamic system theory.

Given the close relation between these fields, all of which provide formal descriptions of and underlying theories for embedded real-time computing, understanding the exact relation between their underlying model or trajectory classes is of utmost importance. Ideally, they would simply coincide. However, from Fig. 2 it becomes obvious that the trajectory classes defined in Definition 3 denote different sets of mathematical functions over time. Nevertheless, the various trajectory classes could constitute corresponding pairs (or viable abstractions of one another) in that they induce the same notion of satisfiability (or that satisfiability by one implies satisfiability by the other, resp.) on pertinent metric-time signal-based temporal logics like STL or SDC. This hope as historically been expressed concerning band-limitation and k-variability in particular.

In the following, we will show however that all these classes introduce subtly different notions of satisfiability and that in particular, the fundamental notion of band-limitation underlying all digital signal processing is not covered by any of the others, i.e., by none of the standard notions of variability employed throughout the theory of metric real-time temporal logic.

3   Formulae Differentiating Signal Classes

In order to rigorously show that satisfiability varies across the above trajectory classes and that no two of them coincide, we will state a set of formulae that differentiate between the different trajectory classes: each of the aforementioned classes will be uniquely characterized by rendering a particular subset of these formulae satisfiable. In fact, these characteristic formulae, as given in the subsequent Lemmata 1 to 4, will together even permit to determine the pertinent parameters of the parameterized model classes from Definition 3 up to the closest rational.

Lemma 1. *The SDC formula ϕ_1 defined as $\ell = 0 \vee \lceil x > 0 \rceil \vee (\lceil x > 0 \rceil \frown \lceil x = 0 \rceil)$ is unsatisfiable by band-limited signals, no matter how the band limit is. However, it is satisfiable by finitely variable trajectories, c-value-bounded trajectories (irrespective of the bound $c > 0$), l-Lipshitz trajectories (for arbitrary $l > 0$), and k-variable trajectories (for arbitrary $k \in \mathbb{N}_{>0}$).*

Proof. ϕ_1 defines a signal that is non-zero initially and for a finite duration, then continues being zero ad infinitum. That finitely variable, c-value bounded, l-Lipshitz, and k-variable trajectories of this type exist, is obvious, providing the positive satisfiability results.

However, no band-limited signal exists that is non-zero initially for a finite duration, then constantly zero. The reason is that finite support of a signal in the time domain and finite bandwidth in the frequency domain are mutually exclusive (except for the constant signal 0, which does not satisfy the formula) due to the uncertainty principle of signals processing.   □

Lemma 2. *The SDC formula $\phi_2(n, a)$ given, for $n \in \mathbb{N}_{>0}$ and $a \in \mathbb{Q}_{>0}$, as*

$$\left(0 < \ell \leq \frac{1}{n} \Rightarrow \lceil x = a \rceil \right)$$

$$\wedge \left(\lceil x = a \rceil \frown \ell = \frac{1}{n} \rightsquigarrow \lceil x = 0 \rceil \right)$$

$$\wedge \left(\lceil x = 0 \rceil \frown \ell = \frac{1}{n} \rightsquigarrow \lceil x = a \rceil \right),$$

where $\phi \rightsquigarrow \lceil p \rceil$ abbreviates $\neg(\top \frown \phi \frown \lceil \neg p \rceil \frown \top)$, defines a symmetric square-wave signal of pulse width $\frac{1}{n}$ and pulse height m. $\phi_2(n, a)$ consequently is satisfiable by finitely variable as well as over k-variable trajectories, for any $k \geq n$, yet neither satisfiable by a $< n$-variable model nor by any Lipshitz-continuous or band-limited trajectories, irrespective of the particular Lipshitz constant or the band limit. It is satisfiable by a c-value-bounded trajectory iff $c \geq a$.

Proof. Satisfiability of $\phi_2(n, a)$ by finitely variable and by appropriately k-variable as well as by c-bounded models is obvious, as is unsatisfiability by overconstrained $< n$-variable and $< m$-value-bounded models. Unsatisfiability by Lipshitz-continuous models is obvious, as the square-wave signal defined by ϕ_2 is discontinuous. Unsatisfiability by band-limited trajectories is implied by their continuity as well as by Gibb's phenomenon. □

Lemma 3. *The SDC formula $\phi_3(n, a)$ defined as, for any $n \in \mathbb{N}_{>0}$ and any $a \in \mathbb{Q}_{>0}$,*

$$\left(0 < \ell \leq \frac{1}{n} \Rightarrow \lceil x = a \rceil \right)$$

$$\wedge \left(\lceil x = a \rceil \frown \ell = \frac{1}{2n} \rightsquigarrow \lceil 0 < x < a \rceil \right)$$

$$\wedge \left(\lceil x = a \rceil \frown \lceil 0 < x < a \rceil \frown \ell = \frac{1}{2n} \rightsquigarrow \lceil x = 0 \rceil \right)$$

$$\wedge \left(\lceil x = 0 \rceil \frown \ell = \frac{1}{2n} \rightsquigarrow \lceil 0 < x < a \rceil \right)$$

$$\wedge \left(\lceil x = a \rceil \frown \lceil 0 < x < a \rceil \frown \ell = \frac{1}{2n} \rightsquigarrow \lceil x = a \rceil \right)$$

is satisfiable by finitely variable and by $\geq 2n$-variable trajectories as well as by l-Lipshitz-continuous trajectories with Lipshitz constant $l \geq 2n$ and by ≥ 1-value-bounded trajectories. It is unsatisfiable by any band-limited trajectory, no matter what the band limit is, as well as by $< 2n$-variable, < 1-value-bounded, and $< 2n$-Lipshitz trajectories.

Proof. Formula $\phi_3(n, a)$ defines a signal that holds constant value a at each time point $t \in \bigcup_{k \in \mathbb{N}}]2kn, 2kn + \frac{1}{2n}[$ and value 0 at each time point $t \in \bigcup_{k \in \mathbb{N}}]2kn + \frac{1}{n}, 2kn + \frac{3}{2n}[$. In between, the signal may take arbitrary values between 0 and a. The respective satisfiability and unsatisfiability results follow immediately for the cases of finitely variable, k-variable, c-bounded, and l-Lipshitz models. Unsatisfiability by any band-limited signal is implied by a variant of Gibb's phenomenon: a band-limited signal cannot become constant without overshoot, unless it is constant throughout or becomes only asymptotically constant. □

Table 1. Satisfiability of the characteristic formulae ϕ_1 to ϕ_4 over different model classes. • denotes satisfiability by the model class irrespective of the value of the parameter defining the model class. − denotes unsatisfiability irrespective of particular parameter values. Entries stating inequalities on parameters denote conditions on the parameters of the respective model class that are necessary and sufficient for satisfiability.

Formula	Constraint on dynamics / Trajectory class from Definition 3				
	c-value bounded	l-Lipshitz	b-bandlimited	finitely variable	k-variable
	$Traj_{\leq c}$	$Traj_{\text{Lip},\, l}$	$Traj_{\text{band},\, b}$	$Traj_{\text{fv}}$	$Traj_k$
ϕ_1	•	•	−	•	•
$\phi_2(n,a)$	$c \geq a$	−	−	•	$k \geq n$
$\phi_3(n,a)$	$c \geq a$	$l \geq 2an$	−	•	$k \geq 2n$
$\phi_4(a)$	•	•	$b \geq (2a)^{-1}$	•	$k \geq a^{-1}$

Lemma 4. *The SDC formula $\phi_4(a)$ defined as, for $a \in \mathbb{Q}_{>0}$,*

$$\left(0 < \ell < \frac{a}{\Rightarrow}\lceil x > 0\rceil\right)$$
$$\wedge\left(\lceil x > 0\rceil^\frown \ell = a \rightsquigarrow \lceil x < 0\rceil\right)$$
$$\wedge\left(\lceil x < 0\rceil^\frown \ell = a \rightsquigarrow \lceil x > 0\rceil\right)$$

is satisfiable by a band-limited trajectory iff the band limit is at least $\frac{1}{2a}$. Likewise, it is satisfiable by a k-variable model iff $k \geq \frac{1}{a}$. For finitely variable, l-Lipshitz, and c-value-bounded trajectories, ϕ_4 is satisfiable irrespective of the particular constants.

Proof. ϕ_4 defines a signal that has periodic a zero crossing every a time units. Generating such requires a model that is $> \frac{1}{a}$-variable or a $> \frac{1}{2a}$-band-limited model. As no constraints are given concerning the magnitude of the signal values between zero crossings, satisfiability is independent from value-bounding or Lipshitz bounds.   □

Altogether, these satisfiability results show that any two of the model classes defined in Definition 3 can be distinguished by characteristic SDC formulae, as becomes evident from Table 1 summarizing the above Lemmata. In fact, we can even identify the particular parametrization of the model classes:

Theorem 1. *For any pair of model classes from the set (a) finitely variable, (b) k-variable, (c) k'-variable with $k' \neq k$, (d) c-value bounded, (e) c'-value-bounded with $c' \neq c$, (f) l-Lipshitz, (g) l'-Lipshitz wirh $l' \neq l$, (h) b-bandlimited, and (i) b'-bandlimited with $b' \neq b$, there is an SDC formula that distinguishes the two classes in that it is satisfiable exactly one one of the two classes.*

Proof. Follows immediately from Lemmata 1 to 4 and the fact that the rational numbers are dense in the reals.   □

Corollary 1. *SDC can distinguish the standard model of band-limited signals generally underlying the theory of digital signal processing from any of the models traditionally investigated in the area of metric-time temporal logic.*

In particular, k-variable traces and band-limited trajectories induce differences in formula satisfiability such that k-variability does not constitute an adequate abstraction of band limitation.

The expectation that the semantic notion of k-variability would coincide, in the sense of providing a reasonable abstraction, with the physically justified notion of band limitation consequently is unjust. This is a negative result that ought spark fresh investigations into which model classes provide a reasonable semantic basis for metric-time temporal logic and the (un-)decidability results they imply. Unfortunately, the latter is not really understood for band-limited signals and may likely relate to fragments of arithmetic whose decidability is unknown due to a connection to Shanuel's conjecture [9], given the harmonic functions involved.

4   Conclusion

The past decades have seen an impressive broadening of the scope of formal methods in computer science: from correctness of sequential programs over concurrent programs, reactive and embedded systems to cyber-physical systems and systems of cyber-physical systems. Each of the advances has challenged the semantic foundations, exposing effects that could not be represented in the previous semantic models, yet were instrumental to the well-behavior of the mutually next class of systems. Input-output relations and pre-post-conditions reflecting these, as examples of pertinent models for sequential programs, could not cover concurrency and reactive behaviour, calling for a.o. qualitative-time temporal logic. Embedded systems called for relating to physical time and bore timed automata and metric-time temporal logic. Cyber-physical systems, finally, have to relate to physical systems, demanding a advance to (networks of) hybrid automata and signal-based temporal logic. Each of these progressions has built on the previous theories and tried to, as far as possible, provide conservative extensions, thereby inheriting properties of the previous formalization. Some of this inheritance has been deliberate, other accidental.

The latter implies a need for regularly checking the tacit assumptions underlying our semantic models. Within this note, we have pursued this w.r.t. the variability assumptions underlying the traces or trajectories employed as semantic basis of dense-time metric temporal logic, checking for consistency with the recent signal-based view induced by cyber-physical systems. Exposing distinguishing characteristic formulae, we have been able to show that even simple fragments of signal-based dense-time metric temporal logic can distinguish between the band-limited signals generally employed as a model in digital signal processing and any of the models suggested as semantic basis of dense-time metric temporal logic. This result points at an urgent need to investigate reasonable, in the sense of physically plausible, semantic bases for metric-time temporal logic and the (un-)decidability results they imply.

To the latter end, we plan to in future work exploit band limitation together with the Nyquist-Shannon sampling theorem for band-limited signals [10,12] and the corresponding exact reconstruction results for rigorously deriving an exact sampled-data semantics of SDC. An expected offspring would be exact monitoring algorithms for continuous-time DC based on discrete sequences of samples.

References

1. Alur, R., Feder, T., Henzinger, T.A.: The benefits of relaxing punctuality. In: Logrippo, L. (ed.) Proceedings of The Tenth Annual ACM Symposium on Principles of Distributed Computing, Montreal, Quebec, Canada, 19–21 August 1991, pp. 139–152. ACM (1991). https://doi.org/10.1145/112600.112613
2. Alur, R., Henzinger, T.A.: A really temporal logic. In: 30th Annual Symposium on Foundations of Computer Science, Research Triangle Park, North Carolina, USA, 30 October–1 November 1989, pp. 164–169. IEEE Computer Society (1989). https://doi.org/10.1109/SFCS.1989.63473
3. Chaochen, Z., Hansen, M.R.: Duration calculus-a formal approach to real-time systems. Monographs in Theoretical Computer Science. An EATCS Series, Springer (2004). https://doi.org/10.1007/978-3-662-06784-0
4. Chaochen, Z., Hoare, C., Ravn, A.P.: A calculus of durations. Inf. Process. Lett. **40**(5), 269–276 (1991). https://doi.org/10.1016/0020-0190(91)90122-X, https://www.sciencedirect.com/science/article/pii/002001909190122X
5. Donzé, A., Maler, O.: Robust satisfaction of temporal logic over real-valued signals. In: Chatterjee, K., Henzinger, T.A. (eds.) Formal Modeling and Analysis of Timed Systems - 8th International Conference, FORMATS 2010, Klosterneuburg, Austria, 8–10 September 2010. Proceedings. Lecture Notes in Computer Science, vol. 6246, pp. 92–106. Springer (2010). https://doi.org/10.1007/978-3-642-15297-9_9
6. Fränzle, M.: Controller design from temporal logic: undecidability need not matter. Ph.D. thesis, University of Kiel (1997). https://d-nb.info/951730746
7. Fränzle, M.: Model-checking dense-time duration calculus. Formal Aspects Comput. **16**(2), 121–139 (2004). https://doi.org/10.1007/s00165-004-0032-y
8. Maler, O., Nickovic, D.: Monitoring temporal properties of continuous signals. In: Lakhnech, Y., Yovine, S. (eds.) Formal Techniques, Modelling and Analysis of Timed and Fault-Tolerant Systems, Joint International Conferences on Formal Modelling and Analysis of Timed Systems, FORMATS 2004 and Formal Techniques in Real-Time and Fault-Tolerant Systems, FTRTFT 2004, Grenoble, France, 22–24 September 2004, Proceedings. Lecture Notes in Computer Science, vol. 3253, pp. 152–166. Springer (2004). https://doi.org/10.1007/978-3-540-30206-3_12
9. Marker, D.: Model theory and exponentiation. Not. AMS **43**(7), 753–759 (1996)
10. Nyquist, H.: Certain topics in telegraph transmission theory. Trans. Am. Inst. Electr. Eng. **47**(2), 617–644 (1928)
11. Orfanidis, S.J.: Introduction to Signal Processing. College Division, Prentice Hall, Upper Saddle River, NJ 07458 (1995)
12. Shannon, C.E.: Communication in the presence of noise. In: Proceeding IRE, vol. 37, no. (1) (1949)

13. Wilke, T.: Automaten und Logiken zur Beschreibung zeitabhängiger Systeme. Ph.D. thesis, University of Kiel, Germany (1994). https://d-nb.info/942315308
14. Wilke, T.: Specifying timed state sequences in powerful decidable logics and timed automata. In: Langmaack, H., de Roever, W.P., Vytopil, J. (eds.) Formal Techniques in Real-Time and Fault-Tolerant Systems, Third International Symposium Organized Jointly with the Working Group Provably Correct Systems - ProCoS, Lübeck, Germany, 19–23 September, Proceedings. Lecture Notes in Computer Science, vol. 863, pp. 694–715. Springer (1994). https://doi.org/10.1007/3-540-58468-4_191

Equivalence Checking 40 Years After: A Review of Bisimulation Tools

Hubert Garavel[(✉)] and Frédéric Lang[(✉)]

Univ. Grenoble Alpes, INRIA, CNRS, Grenoble INP, LIG, 38000 Grenoble, France
{hubert.garavel,frederic.lang}@inria.fr

Abstract. Equivalence checking is a formal verification approach that consists in proving that two programs or models are related modulo some equivalence relation, or that one is included in the other modulo some preorder relation. In the case of concurrent systems, which are often represented using labelled transition systems, the relations used for equivalence checking are bisimulations and their simulation preorders. In the case of probabilistic or stochastic systems, which are usually represented using Markov chains, the relations used for equivalence checking are lumpability, probabilistic and stochastic equivalences, and their associated preorders. The present article provides a synthetic overview of 40 years of research in the design of algorithms and software tools for equivalence checking.

1 Introduction

The present article was written in honor of Frits Vaandrager and included in a collective *Festschrift* book offered to him at the occasion of his 60th birthday.

Frits Vaandrager has published an impressive list of papers addressing very diverse topics in formal methods and concurrency theory, among which: operational semantics and SOS rules, process algebra, Petri nets, input-output automata, timed automata and real-time models, probabilistic automata, hybrid input-output automata and hybrid systems, action-based and state-based temporal logics, testing theory, automata learning, as well as formal modelling and verification of many industrial protocols. Among such a wealth of contributions, we have chosen to focus on bisimulations and equivalence checking, a topic that Frits Vaandrager contributed to advance significantly.

In formal methods, one never proves that a system (or a program) is correct *in itself*, but only that it is correct *with respect to* its specifications. Thus, formal verification does not consist in checking one artefact, but in comparing two artefacts one against the other, i.e., a system against its specifications that express desirable, expected properties. Depending on the formalism used for specifications, two cases need to be distinguished:

- If the system and its specifications are expressed in two different formalisms, one needs to prove that the system *satisfies* its specifications. A major approach is *model checking* [97], in which specifications are expressed in some temporal logic.

N. Jansen et al. (Eds.): Vaandrager Festschrift 2022, LNCS 13560, pp. 213–265, 2022.
https://doi.org/10.1007/978-3-031-15629-8_13

– If the system and its specifications are expressed in the same formalism, one needs to prove that the system is *equivalent* to its specifications or, in a weaker form, that the system *contains* or is *included* in its specifications. Such verification approaches are usually referred to as *equivalence checking* and, more often than not, the system is a much more complex artefact than its specifications, in which many low-level implementation details are abstracted away.

The present article presents a brief history of equivalence checking in the context of concurrent systems—leaving aside the widespread application of equivalence checking in the hardware-design industry to make sure that logic-synthesis tools preserve the intended behaviour of circuits.

The foundations of equivalence checking for concurrent systems have been laid in the 1970s. On the practical side, the protocol-engineering community developed verification techniques based on the systematic exploration of all reachable states of a concurrent system [378,397]. On the theoretical side, it became clear that the semantics of concurrent systems could be adequately represented using state-transition models, such as LTSs (Labelled Transition Systems) [274] or *Kripke structures* [287]—although alternative models, such as Petri nets, would also coexist.

Finding the right equivalence relation to compare two state-transition models describing two concurrent systems was a non-trivial problem, as the two main equivalence relations known at that time were not appropriate: on the one hand, *graph isomorphism* was too strong, requiring both models to be strictly identical modulo permutations, whereas both models often have different levels of abstraction; on the other hand, *language equivalence* was too weak, only checking that the sets of traces of both models are the same, thus failing to make distinctions such as $a.(b + c)$ vs $(a.b) + (a.c)$, which are essential as far as the semantics of concurrent systems is considered.

To address this problem, *behavioural* equivalences have been introduced. These are equivalence relations situated between graph isomorphism and language equivalence: they are coarser than the former and finer than the latter. Important examples of behavioural equivalence are *strong equivalence* and *observational equivalence* [345] (the latter being also called *weak equivalence*). A major breakthrough was made with the concept of *bisimulation* [362], which provides a conceptual framework for these equivalences—see [20] for an insightful account of these foundational steps of concurrency theory. In a nutshell, bisimulation identifies all states having the same future, i.e., all states from which one can execute the same (possibly infinite) trees of actions.

There exist many behavioural relations; an overview of them can be found in [190]. Each equivalence relation comes with its associated *preorder*. Therefore, equivalence checking consists in verifying that two systems are related modulo some equivalence relation, or that one system is included in the other modulo some preorder relation. Fortunately, not all of these relations are needed in practice: our experience shows that most real-life case studies can be addressed using only a handful of well-chosen relations.

In the case of probabilistic and stochastic systems, which are usually represented using Markov chains or models derived from Markov chains, bisimulation coincides with the concept of *lumpability* [275] and, thus, serves as a basis for the definition of probabilistic and stochastic equivalences on Markov chains.

The present article provides a retrospective account of 40 years of research in equivalence-checking techniques for concurrent systems. Compared to prior surveys on bisimulations [20,190], we focus here on the design of algorithms and software tools for the implementation of bisimulations on finite-state systems, leaving aside all aspects related to theorem proving—see [370] for a survey on bisimulation as a proof method. The article is organized chronologically: Sects. 2–5 present the main achievements done during the 1980s, 1990s, 2000s, and 2010s decades, respectively, and Sect. 6 gives a few concluding remarks.

2   Retrospective of the 1980s

2.1   Bisimulation Tools Based on Term Rewriting

The book of Robin Milner on CCS [345] and the seminal article of David Park providing a co-inductive definition of bisimulation [362], together with subsequent publications [346,347], laid the theoretical foundations for a deep research area, in which bisimulations are closely associated to process calculi. The definition of process calculi using either structural operational semantics [367–369] or algebraic semantics [27] initially led to consider term rewrite engines and theorem provers as natural approaches for implementing process calculi and bisimulations.

Among such early attempts, CIRCAL [342] was a tool that used algebraic laws to perform proofs of equivalence between two process-calculus programs.

ECRINS [320] was a tool for manipulating process calculi, the operators of which were defined using conditional rewrite rules. A semi-decision algorithm for strong bisimulation was implemented in ECRINS, and the tool was able to prove strong bisimulation automatically between CCS-like programs, without process recursion but with free process variables. Another use of ECRINS was to prove the correctness of semantic translation from one process calculus to another [134,135].

BIP (Bisimulation Prover) [84] was a verification tool for protocol specifications written in the ECCS language. This tool used an enhanced version of Sanderson's algorithm for bisimulation [383]; this enhanced version removes one limitation of Sanderson's by accepting the presence of nondeterminism and τ-transitions, i.e., internal (or silent, or non-observable) actions of an LTS.

CRLAB [121,124] was a tool that used term rewriting to compare processes written in CCS or basic LOTOS (i.e., the subset of LOTOS [259] without value passing) modulo observational equivalence.

2.2   Algorithms for Bisimulations on Finite-State Systems

However, alternative approaches to term rewriting quickly emerged. In these approaches, each program is first translated into a finite-state LTS, which is only possible if the program does not have an infinite number of states (e.g., does not handle unbounded data types nor infinitely many concurrent processes) and if the number of states is small enough to fit into the memory of available computers (i.e., does not face the well-known *state explosion* problem, which is a limiting factor for the verification of complex programs).

Assuming that an LTS has been successfully generated, one then executes a different, bisimulation-specific algorithm to *minimize* this LTS according to a chosen bisimulation (e.g., strong, observational, etc.); given that bisimulations are equivalence relations, such a minimal LTS always exists and is unique modulo a renaming of states. The same minimization algorithm can also be reused for *equivalence checking* purpose, i.e., to compare whether two LTSs are bisimilar or not: this is done by applying a minimization algorithm on the disjoint union of both LTSs and checking whether initial states are in the same equivalence class.

In a nutshell, these alternative approaches give up the generality of term rewriting (which can handle infinite-state programs but, in practice, is quite limited in the size of programs that can be handled) to adopt a less general approach (which only handles finite-state programs, but of a greater complexity that exceeds the capabilities of human reasoning). Finite-state approaches also have the advantage of being fully automated, meaning that bisimulation can be decided without human intervention.

In the 1980s, two key algorithms for computing bisimulation on finite LTSs have been proposed. In two articles [267, 268] that recently received the 2021 Dijkstra Prize, Paris Kanellakis and Scott Smolka proposed an algorithm for checking the equivalence of CCS processes. Their algorithm performs *relational coarsest partitioning* (also known as *coarsest partition refinement*): initially, all states are in the same set, which is progressively partitioned to separate states having different futures. The time and space complexities of their algorithm are $O(mn)$ and $O(m + n)$, respectively, where m is the number of transitions and n the number of states[1].

In a subsequent article [360], Robert Paige and Robert Tarjan proposed a more efficient algorithm for the same problem. Their algorithm only addresses strong bisimulation. Its time and space complexities are $O(m \log n)$ and $O(m + n)$, respectively.

2.3   Early Bisimulation Tools

The Kanellakis-Smolka and Paige-Tarjan algorithms aroused great interest and triggered the development of numerous software tools.

SCAN [353] was probably the first implementation of bisimulations. This tool could reduce and compare, with respect to strong or observational equivalence, networks of finite automata composed together using parallel operators and *filtering* (a combination of hiding and relabeling to abstract away the internal behaviour of composed automata).

---

[1] We use the same definitions of m and n throughout this article.

AUTO [66,67,321,390,410–412] was a tool for the analysis and manipulation of finite LTSs, which could be either specified using the MEIJE process calculus [17] or described graphically using the AUTOGRAPH editor and composed in parallel and connected together using synchronisation ports and communication wires. AUTO offered primitives to minimize an LTS modulo strong bisimulation, observational bisimulation, or trace language equivalence, to determinize an LTS, to compute the transitive closure of τ-transitions, and to eliminate τ-loops and single τ-transitions. It could also check the equivalence of two LTSs for strong or observational bisimulation.

VENUS [350,393] was a tool for minimizing and comparing CCS processes modulo strong or observational bisimulations. It also supported operations dedicated to τ-transitions, such as the elimination of τ-chains and τ-circuits.

TAV [53,54,194] was a tool that could check strong or observational equivalence between two CCS processes, and also check whether a CCS process satisfied a temporal-logic formula expressed in the Hennessy-Milner logic extended with recursion. A distinctive feature of TAV was the possibility to provide an *explanation* given as a Hennessy-Milner logic formula computed using a backtracking algorithm [245]. Another algorithm for providing a temporal-logical formula that differentiates two LTSs that are not strongly bisimilar was proposed in [98].

SQUIGGLES [49,50] was a tool that extended the Paige-Tarjan algorithm to compare LTSs or programs written in basic LOTOS with respect to strong equivalence, observational equivalence, or testing equivalence.

WINSTON [326] was a tool that could compare networks of finite-state processes using strong and observational equivalences implemented with the Kanellakis-Smolka algorithm.

ALDEBARAN [147–150] was a tool for minimizing and comparing LTSs according to strong bisimulation, observational equivalence, acceptance model equivalence, or safety equivalence; it could also display the equivalence class of each state of the LTS. Contrary to most other tools written in functional/declarative languages such as Lisp, Prolog, etc., ALDEBARAN was written in C and implemented an adaptation of the Paige-Tarjan algorithm. The simple file format used by ALDEBARAN for storing LTSs became popular and has been known since as the AUT format[2].

The ACP Bisimulation Tool [436] was a tool to compare programs written in the ACP_τ process calculus [28] modulo a weak relation called *bisimulation with τ-abstraction*. It computed a transitive closure of τ-transitions, followed by a relational coarsest partition algorithm.

PIPN [19] was a tool that could minimize, according to observational equivalence or trace equivalence, the labelled reachability graphs generated from Petri nets. PIPN was part of ESTIM [385], a simulation and verification tool for communicating state machines specified in the ESTELLE language [258].

CWB (Concurrency Workbench) [104,105] was an integrated tool for verifying networks of finite-state processes described in CCS, then converted to a state-transition model called *transition graphs*. Three kinds of analyses were

---

[2] https://cadp.inria.fr/man/aut.html.

supported by CWB: model checking (evaluation of temporal-logic formulas written in the propositional mu-calculus), equivalence checking (comparison of two transition graphs modulo C-bisimulation, a generic relation from which strong equivalence, observational equivalence, must equivalence, and testing failures equivalence can be derived), and preorder checking (comparison of two transition graphs modulo C-preorder, from which bisimulation divergence preorder, may preorder, must preorder, and testing preorders can be obtained). Equivalence checking was based on the Kanellakis-Smolka algorithm, while preorder checking was done using an ad hoc, less efficient algorithm. An early application of CWB to the analysis of mutual exclusion algorithms can be found in [418].

Most of the aforementioned tools performed at least two different tasks: (i) generate the LTSs corresponding to concurrent systems described either as networks of automata composed in parallel, or as process-calculi specifications; and (ii) minimize and/or compare these LTSs modulo various equivalence or preorder relations. Both tasks are subject to antagonistic implementation constraints: task (i) must store in memory the concrete contents of each state of the LTS being generated, while the transitions of the LTS can just be written to disk; conversely, task (ii) must store in memory all the transitions, and can ignore the concrete contents of states, which can just be treated like abstract numbers. It is thus difficult for the same tool to be optimally efficient in both tasks. One solution is to have separate tools, dedicated either to task (i) or to task (ii).

The first instance of a specialized tool for task (i) was CÆSAR [170,184], a tool for translating value-passing LOTOS specifications into LTSs encoded in the various file formats accepted by ALDEBARAN, AUTO, CWB, PIPN, SCAN, SQUIGGLES, etc. A distinctive feature of ALDEBARAN, CÆSAR, and their companion tools later integrated in the CADP toolbox [152] was to be plain, ordinary Unix commands that could be directly invoked from the shell with appropriate command-line options, and that communicated via files containing LTSs. Such an architectural design was a major departure from other bisimulation tools, most of which were built around custom command-line interpreters (with ad hoc primitives for, e.g., loading, generating, minimizing, and saving LTSs). It has been progressively adopted by other tools during the next decades.

3   Retrospective of the 1990s

3.1   New Algorithms for Bisimulations

The 1990s have been a very active decade, in which new equivalences, preorders, and algorithms have been invented and implemented in tools.

Testing equivalences [120], introduced in the 1980s, define that two models (typically a high-level specification and a lower-level implementation) are equivalent iff an observer interacting with them cannot distinguish one from the other by means of testing. Although these equivalences are weaker (i.e., less discriminative) than bisimulations, Cleaveland and Hennessy gave an algorithm [101] based on a characterization of these relations in terms of bisimulation. This algorithm was implemented in CWB.

Safety equivalence [56], named so because it preserves safety properties, is the equivalence relation obtained by the logical conjunction of two $\tau^*.a$ *preorders* [156] that abstract away τ-transitions. Algorithms for minimizing and comparing LTSs modulo safety equivalence were implemented in ALDEBARAN.

Branching bisimulation [191,192] was introduced by van Glabbeek and Weijland after observing that Milner's observational equivalence does not fully respect the branching structure of LTSs. To compute branching bisimulation, which is slightly stronger than observational equivalence, Groote and Vaandrager proposed an algorithm [206,207] for *relational coarsest partitioning with stuttering*. A key idea of the algorithm is the possibility to compress each strongly connected component of states connected by τ-transitions into a single state beforehand, using existing linear-time algorithms. This algorithm has a worst-case time complexity $O(mn)$ and a space complexity $O(m+n)$. Thus, branching bisimulation can be implemented more efficiently than observational equivalence, which has progressively been superseded by branching equivalence, except in the CCS community where observational equivalence remained popular, probably by fidelity to the foundations set by Milner. The Groote-Vaandrager algorithm was implemented in an efficient prototype named Branching Tool, as well as in other tools, among which ALDEBARAN and AUTO.

Groote and Vaandrager also proposed a format of Plotkin-style structural operational semantics rules [208] that guarantees, among other properties, that strong bisimulation is a congruence on the states of any transition system described using this format.

It was shown [371] that, for all equivalences between strong bisimulation and trace equivalences (i.e., almost all equivalences of practical interest), checking equivalence of two networks of LTSs is PSPACE-hard because, in the general case, one cannot avoid computing the product state space of each network.

De Nicola and Vaandrager investigated the logical characterization of branching bisimulation, and exhibited three logics such that two LTSs are branching bisimilar iff they exactly satisfy the same formulas of these logics [125,126].

There have been other attempts at computing bisimulations using model checkers, such as MEC [12] (later integrated in ALTARICA [13]) and SPIN [141, 142]. For instance, MEC did not implement dedicated algorithms for equivalence checking, but could define bisimulation as a concise formula in fix-point logic [11, 199], thus enabling bisimulation to be verified as a particular case of model checking.

3.2 Algorithms for On-the-Fly Verification

While the mainstream approach, so far, consisted in first generating LTSs before minimizing them or checking their equivalence, novel *on-the-fly* approaches emerged, where an LTS is *reduced* (i.e., partially minimized) while being generated, or where equivalence between two LTSs is checked while these LTSs are generated. Such approaches, which had already been experimented successfully for model checking, may avoid storing the entire set of states and/or transitions, especially when one does not need to fully explore both LTSs to decide that they are not equivalent.

An on-the-fly algorithm for equivalence checking was first proposed by Fernandez and Mounier [154,351]. Their algorithm was not based on partition refinement, which requires to compute the sets of states beforehand, but instead explored the states of the synchronous product of the LTSs under comparison, until a verdict can be given. Various adaptations of their algorithm to compute strong, branching, observational, and $\tau^*.a$ bisimulations, as well as safety equivalence and the corresponding preorders, have been implemented in ALDEBARAN [155]. A variant of their algorithm was later proposed, which does not store all states of the synchronous product, but only enough states so that the verification terminates [264].

A similar approach for on-the-fly equivalence checking modulo strong and observational bisimulations was implemented in the LOLA tool [354].

Lee and Yannakakis proposed another on-the-fly algorithm [306] for minimizing an LTS modulo strong bisimulation while this LTS is being generated.

A generic architecture, named OPEN/CÆSAR [172], was proposed for developing on-the-fly verification tools rationally. This architecture achieves a clear separation between, on the one hand, an LTS that is generated on-the-fly (e.g., from a process-calculus specification or a network of communicating automata) and, on the other hand, a verification algorithm that explores this LTS guided by a specific goal or property to be proven. One of the first applications of OPEN/CÆSAR was REDUCTOR [172], a tool that reduced LTSs on the fly modulo $\tau^*.a$ equivalence.

Partial-order reductions are techniques for reducing the size of the state space, by exploiting the independence of transitions to avoid unnecessary interleavings. Such techniques, provided they preserve a behavioural relation of interest, may be particularly useful when doing minimization or equivalence checking on the fly. Partial-order reductions were first studied in the context of linear-time semantics, then in the context of branching-time semantics to check branching bisimulation [186,408], strong bisimulation (between two LTSs having the same independent transitions) [249], and *failures refinement* [420].

3.3   Algorithms for Symbolic Verification

New algorithms were proposed, based on a symbolic representation of the system under verification in the form of a BDD (Binary Decision Diagram) [75].

An approach was proposed, in which CCS processes are translated to BDDs, thus allowing bisimulations (encoded as temporal logic formulas) to be computed on such a symbolic representation [140].

Bouali and De Simone proposed a symbolic algorithm [65] dedicated to the minimization of networks of LTSs according to strong bisimulation, as well as variants for observational and branching bisimulations.

Another symbolic algorithm [311] was proposed for comparing CCS processes modulo observational bisimulation, and compared, on a few benchmarks, to the equivalence-checking algorithm implemented in CWB.

Fisler and Vardi [159–161] implemented, using BDDs, three minimization algorithms in the setting of finite transition systems, the states of which are labelled with atomic propositions. Their experimental results indicate that BDDs are not a silver bullet for bisimulation minimization: the number of BDD nodes needed to compute the bisimulation relation grows quickly, outweighing the potential benefits of minimizing the global state space before performing symbolic model checking.

3.4 Algorithms for Compositional Verification

Given a concurrent system, e.g., a network of LTSs, compositional verification consists in generating a reduced (or even minimized) LTS for this system, modulo some behavioural relation of interest [147, 326, 379, 398, 399, 407, 428]. If this relation is a congruence for the operators of the network (typically, parallel composition and label hiding), which is the case of most bisimulations, then the generation can be done incrementally, by alternating operator applications and reductions of the intermediate LTSs.

However, while doing so, state explosion may happen in intermediate LTSs, due to the existence of transitions that are fireable locally, but not globally, as they could not meet the synchronization constraints in the entire network. Graf, Steffen, and Lüttgen proposed an approach to solve this problem, based on *interface specifications* (represented as LTSs) that cut off globally unfireable transitions [197, 198]. This approach was extended by Krimm and Mounier, and implemented in PROJECTOR [286], an on-the-fly tool developed using the OPEN/CÆSAR architecture.

A related approach, called *compositional reachability* [92], performs compositional reduction modulo observational equivalence while verifying a property represented as an LTS. This approach was implemented in the TRACTA tool [92], which also supported a variant [91] of Graf-Steffen-Lüttgen interface specifications.

A comprehensive survey on compositional verification, from the 1990s to the present, can be found in [181].

3.5 Enhanced Bisimulation Tools

Most bisimulation tools developed in the 1980s quickly became unavailable, due to lack of software maintenance at a time where processors, operating systems, and programming languages were rapidly evolving. There was, however, the notable exception of three tools (namely, ALDEBARAN, AUTO, and CWB), the development of which steadily progressed during the 1990s.

ALDEBARAN [156], so far mainly based on the Paige-Tarjan algorithm, was enhanced in four directions: counterexample generation algorithms, implementation of the Groote-Vaandrager algorithm for branching bisimulation, novel on-the-fly equivalence-checking algorithms [156,351], and symbolic verification algorithms based on BDDs [153,276,277]. ALDEBARAN was a key component of the CADP verification toolbox [71,151,152,171,174], which gathered a growing number of closely interconnected tools. Its synergy with CADP brought ALDEBARAN at least three benefits: the existence of an efficient LTS generator, the aforementioned compiler CÆSAR for LOTOS; the availability of BCG (*Binary Coded Graphs*), a compact file format[3] for storing large LTSs; and the integration within EUCALYPTUS, a graphical user interface that simplified the invocation of ALDEBARAN with command-line options.

ALDEBARAN, together with companion tools of CADP, has been used in numerous case studies[4] by scientists of many universities worldwide. Among the case studies involving equivalence checking, one can mention, in chronological order: a car overtaking protocol [143], dynamically changing communication structures [167], an ATM switch [158], a plain ordinary telephone service (starting from an existing specification [145]), a framework for groupware development [278], a trusted third-party protocol between video-on-demand service providers and customers [185,304], a railway signalling system [165], a bounded retransmission protocol [329,330] (starting from an existing specification [204]), the TCP Internet transport protocol [386], feature interactions in telephony systems [284], several variants of distributed leader election algorithms for unidirectional ring networks [183], a bus arbiter of a multiprocessor architecture [86], the link layer protocol of the IEEE-1394 serial bus [388], a departure clearance protocol for air traffic [260], testing of a distributed leader election algorithm [404,405], a flow-control protocol for a high-speed network [227], patterns for software architecture styles [221], an invoicing system [387,389], a protocol for road traffic control [421,422], asynchronous circuits [431–433], a reliable data-transfer service [318], an abstraction-display-controller model for user interfaces [327], a distributed cluster file system [364,365], an ISO high-speed transport protocol [25], highly reliable and reusable CORBA applications [285], a leader election protocol for home audio/video networks [374], synchronous hardware [218–220], a protocol for deploying intelligent telecommunication services [14–16], a handshake authentication protocol [305], a datalink system for air traffic control [380–382], a radio protocol for mobile telecommunications [315], a protection system against cloning of cellular phones [355,356], and hardware/software codesign [22,427]. Such an impressive list clearly indicates that formal verification should not be restricted to model checking only, and that equivalence checking and bisimulations also have a major role to play.

The evolution of AUTO and its associated graphical editor AUTOGRAPH also continued in the 1990s [323,324,376,377]. Companion tools were developed, among which: MAUTO, which extended AUTO to a large family of process calculi; FCTOOL [58], which implemented efficient partitioning algorithms (derived from the Groote-Vaandrager algorithm) for strong, branching, and observational bisimulations; and the FC2TOOLS set [61–64], which gathered a collection of

---

[3] https://cadp.inria.fr/man/bcg.html.
[4] http://cadp.inria.fr/case-studies.

tools offering both *explicit* and *implicit* (i.e., BDD-based) bisimulation algorithms, and designed around FC2, a dedicated file format for LTSs and networks of LTSs.

A few case studies were done using these tools, e.g., a bus instrumentation protocol specified in LOTOS [18], a sliding window protocol specified in LOTOS [322], a lift controller specified in ESTEREL [212], and a secure datagram protocol specified in LOTOS [193].

CWB also pursued its evolution during the 1990s. The performance of its LTS minimization algorithm was assessed in [144], the introduction of priorities was presented in [265], and an overall presentation of CWB can be found in [106]. Contrary to ALDEBARAN and AUTO, the development of which remained centralized in Grenoble and Sophia-Antipolis, respectively, CWB adopted a more decentralized approach: the original software was maintained in Edinburgh [348, 394][5] in collaboration with other universities (e.g., Sussex), while a new branch emerged in the United States under the successive names of Concurrency Factory [100, 102], NCSU Concurrency Workbench [108], Concurrency Workbench of North Carolina [107, 109], and Concurrency Workbench of the New Century [103, 110].

Besides the use of CWB by Swedish telecom companies to analyze parts of the GSM and ISDN protocols, other case studies used the equivalence-checking features of CWB, e.g., alternating bit protocol with lossy buffers [99], instruction pipelining and parallel memory models for the SPARC architecture [288], formalization in LOTOS of the GKS computer-graphics standard [373], and access monitoring for information flow security [162].

3.6 New Bisimulation Tools

Besides enhancements brought to already existing bisimulation tools, many new tools were developed during the 1990s.

PisaTool [254, 257] used term rewriting to compare CCS processes for strong, observational, or branching equivalences. Instead of relying on interleaving semantics, this tool took into account some aspects of true concurrency by introducing a parametric representation of finite-state systems and bisimulations.

SEVERO [83] was both an equivalence checker and a model checker for the ACTL temporal logic [122], applicable to finite-state processes that were converted to BDDs and reduced modulo observational equivalence using a symbolic minimization algorithm.

ARA (Advanced Reachability Analysis) [409] was a tool for minimization and equivalence checking of basic LOTOS processes modulo *CFFD equivalence* [406], a relation weaker than observational equivalence. ARA supported compositional LTS construction and partial-order reductions. It was used, e.g., to verify a small protocol for client-server communication [280] and, using compositional verification and in combination with CADP, a reliable data-transfer service [318].

---

[5] See also [395] and [396] for a reflection on the development of verification tools.

CCSTOOL2 [372] was a modular tool performing various computations on finite-state CCS descriptions, including minimization for strong and observational bisimulations.

JACK (Just Another Concurrency Kit) [60] was an integrated environment, with a graphical user interface, gathering verification tools designed around the FC2 file format. JACK supported model checking of ACTL logic formulas, as well as equivalence checking using CRLAB (term rewriting) and AUTO (algorithms for finite-state models). The equivalence-checking features of JACK have been used to verify hardware components [123], a railway interlocking system [30,31], and, in combination with CADP, an abstraction-display-controller model for user interfaces [327].

YAPV [36] was a research tool based on true concurrency, instead of interleaving semantics. It used a variant of the Kanellakis-Smolka algorithm to check bisimulation between processes.

BIDMIN [223] was a minimization tool written in Ada. It supported strong bisimulation, as well as variants of observational and branching bisimulations (e.g., rooted, divergence-preserving, etc.), these variants differing only in the definition of the initial partition of the LTS state set.

FDR2 [375] was a verification tool for the CSP process calculus [74]. It implemented strong bisimulation, as well as *failures* and *failures/divergences* equivalences, which were preferred to observational or branching bisimulation for checking equivalence and refinement (i.e., preorder inclusion) of CSP processes. FDR2 was used to formally verify STATEMATE statecharts [169].

ARC [361] was another formal verification tool for CSP, which had similar equivalence checking features as FDR2, but in which LTSs were represented symbolically using ordered BDDs.

XEVE [59] was a verification environment for ESTEREL specifications, which used the Bouali-De Simone algorithm to perform symbolic minimization modulo strong bisimulation.

ObjectGeode, an industrial environment for simulating and verifying SDL programs, was equipped with on-the-fly equivalence checking capabilities by a connection to CADP [279].

Getting an accurate panorama of bisimulation tools by reading publications is uneasy, as related work was not always cited properly. Fortunately, a few benchmarks and surveys exist, e.g., a gentle introduction [146] to the principles of bisimulation tools, followed by an overview of ALDEBARAN, AUTO, CWB, PVE, TAV, etc.; a comparative evaluation [283] of bisimulation techniques in ALDEBARAN, AUTO, CWB, TAV, WINSTON, etc.; an overview [319] of tools available in the early 1990s, among which ALDEBARAN, AUTO, CWB, ECRINS, FCTOOL, MAUTO, MEC, TAV, etc.; a study [222] of the respective performances of ALDEBARAN, BIDMIN, CWB, and FCTOOL/HOGGAR; and a survey [255, 256] of tools for the analysis of distributed systems specified using process calculi.

3.7 Bisimulation Tools for Timed and Hybrid Systems

There has been a variety of tools for modelling and analyzing real-time systems. First attempts used a discrete-time model, in which a special "tick" action represented the elapsing of one time unit. Since this approach did not scale to realistic systems, requiring too many transitions to model long delays, dense-time models supported by methods from continuous mathematics were progressively adopted, either as timed extensions of process calculi [118,200,307,308] or as *timed automata* [6], i.e., automata extended with real-valued clock variables. Tools for the analysis of timed systems often involved the generation of an untimed finite-state abstraction of the state space (e.g., a *region graph* [5]), that takes time constraints into account.

The first minimization algorithms for timed automata [3,4] generated a minimized region graph on the fly, by extending a prior algorithm [57] that directly generates a minimal LTS for strong bisimulation (rather than first generating an LTS that is minimized later).

VERSA [93,95,96] was a tool for the analysis of discrete-time systems with prioritized resources and events, described in a timed process calculus called ACSR (Algebra of Communicating Shared Resources). Besides checking equivalences by means of term rewriting, VERSA automatically translated ACSR processes with bounded delays to LTSs, and compared these (finite-state) LTSs modulo strong bisimulation and $\tau^*.a$ equivalence using the Kanellakis-Smolka algorithm. XVERSA [94] was an extension of VERSA with a graphical user interface.

TPWB (Timing and Probability Workbench) [166] was a tool for analyzing finite-state, discrete-time systems described in TPCCS [213,214], an extension of CCS with time and probabilities. It used an adaptation of the Kanellakis-Smolka algorithm with lumping of probabilities to perform minimization and equivalence checking on finite-state systems modulo strong bisimulation.

EPSILON [85,195,196] was an extension of TAV for analyzing dense-time systems described in TMS (Timed Modal Specifications), a formalism for timed networks inspired by TCCS [429] (a variant of CCS with a delay operator) extended with "may" and "must" modalities. EPSILON implemented equivalence and preorder checking for strong and observational bisimulations, as well as time-abstracted versions of these relations that gave finite representations of these networks. When the check was negative, EPSILON could generate, like TAV, a distinguishing formula in timed Hennessy-Milner logic. EPSILON was used to analyze a steam generator [289,290].

KRONOS [69,70,119,402,434] was a tool for minimization, equivalence checking, and preorder checking of timed automata. It used a time-abstracting bisimulation and linear constraints on the clocks of the timed automaton to generate an untimed abstraction of the state space. The resulting LTS could be minimized and checked using ALDEBARAN. KRONOS was used in many case studies, and also as a back-end [243] for the verification of systems described in ET-LOTOS [307,308], a timed extension of LOTOS. Later, Extended KRONOS (or OPEN/KRONOS) [401] enhanced KRONOS with a richer input language and on-the-fly verification capabilities based upon the OPEN/CÆSAR architecture.

TREAT (Timed Reachability Analysis Tool) [269] was a tool for timed automata. To fight the state explosion problem, TREAT generated untimed abstractions that preserved two behavioural relations named *history equivalence* and *transition bisimulation*.

RT-MEC [81], a component of PEP (Programming Environment based on Petri nets), was a tool for the analysis of systems modelled as Petri nets with dense time. It implemented equivalence checking modulo strong bisimulation and timed bisimulation, using partial-order reductions and on-the-fly techniques to generate a reduced region graph.

Hybrid automata are infinite-state models to describe digital programs interacting with an analog environment. Although hybrid automata encompass timed automata, there have been few tools implementing bisimulations on hybrid automata. A notable exception was HYTECH [225,226], which used bisimulations to reduce hybrid systems to finite LTSs. When such a reduction was possible, the hybrid automaton could be model checked.

A performance comparison between EPSILON, KRONOS, HYTECH, and the UPPAAL tool [24] (which does not use the concept of bisimulations) can be found in [301].

3.8   Bisimulation Tools for Probabilistic and Stochastic Systems

The advent of process calculi in the 1980s gave a new impulse to the study of Markovian models. In order to finely describe both the functional and performance aspects of concurrent systems, process calculi have been extended in various ways with non-functional concepts, such as probabilities and random durations, e.g., [238,247]. At a lower abstraction level, extended models have been proposed, combining LTSs, to model functional aspects, and DTMCs (Discrete-Time Markov Chains) or CTMCs (Continuous-Time Markov Chains), to model performance aspects.

To analyze such models, in addition to traditional techniques (steady-state and transient analyses, simulation, etc.) and novel quantitative model-checking approaches, various bisimulations have also been defined, such as probabilistic bisimulations [48,246,250,302,303,316,391] and Markovian/stochastic bisimulations [76,231,238,239]. These equivalences combine the concepts of bisimulation for the LTSs and of lumpability for the Markov chain aspects.

At first, such bisimulations were used for algebraic proofs of equivalence and performance calculations on simple models. But dedicated algorithms were progressively designed, e.g., [21], and implemented in already existing or novel software tools.

TIPPtool [237,281] was a tool for creating and analyzing concurrent systems described in the TIPP language, a stochastic process calculus based on LOTOS. Initiated in 1992, TIPPtool has been progressively extended with many features for functional and performance analyses. Bisimulations on LTSs and Markovian models played a major role in TIPPtool, especially for applying compositional minimization techniques [229,230,232,244] in order to contain state explosion.

Strong and observational bisimulations were implemented using the Kanellakis-Smolka algorithm, but an export to CADP's AUT format was also available; the Baier algorithm was used for Markovian bisimulations; symbolic algorithms based on BDDs were also developed for this purpose [240,241]. Various systems have been analyzed using TIPPtool, e.g., an alternating bit protocol [236], a communication protocol [163], a plain-old telephone system (tackled using TIPPtool in combination with CADP) [234], and an hospital communication system [230].

TwoTowers [34,35] was a tool for the functional and performance analysis of systems modelled in EMPA, a stochastic timed process calculus. TwoTowers combined two existing tools: the aforementioned Concurrency Workbench of North Carolina (for model checking, equivalence checking, and preorder checking) and MarCA (for steady-state and transient performance analysis); it also supported the strong extended Markovian reward bisimulation [33]. The equivalence-checking capabilities of TwoTowers have been used to analyze a randomized distributed algorithm for the dining philosophers problem [35] and a token ring protocol [32].

The APNN (Abstract Petri Net Notation) toolbox [23,77,78] was a set of tools for the functional and quantitative analysis of discrete-event dynamic systems. It offered many features, such as model checking, numerical analysis of Markov chains, and simulation, but also supported various kinds of bisimulations used to reduce, by means of compositional minimization techniques, the size of the generated state spaces.

3.9 Bisimulation Tools for Mobile Systems

Mobile process calculi, such as the π-calculus [343,344], enable the description of concurrent systems with potentially infinite state spaces, due to the dynamic creation of agents and communication channels. For such systems, verification approaches based on finite-state systems are hardly applicable, especially if they require an exhaustive exploration of the state space before verification can take place. For such problems, formal proofs (which are outside the scope of this survey) are the approach of choice [370]. Nevertheless, there have been attempts at developing automated equivalence-checking tools based on bisimulation theory for analyzing such systems.

MWB (Mobility Workbench) [413,414,416] was a tool for checking whether two π-calculus programs are equivalent with respect to open bisimulation [384]. MWB was based upon an on-the-fly algorithm (inspired from the Fernandez-Mounier approach) in which LTSs where generated on demand. MWB was later extended with an algorithm for checking symbolic hyperequivalence [363] for the fusion calculus [415, Chapter 7].

The π-environment [157] was a tool for checking (strong or observational) early and late bisimulations on finite-state processes specified in the π-calculus. This tool did not work on the fly, but relied on the aforementioned AUTO and JACK tools.

One can also mention algorithms for checking symbolic (strong or observational) bisimulations between value-passing LTSs extended with variables, inputs, and assignments [224,253,309,312,313]. These algorithms have been transposed to compute bisimulations for the π-calculus [310,314], but do not seem to have been implemented.

4   Retrospective of the 2000s

4.1   New Algorithm for Strong Bisimulation

A new *fast bisimulation* algorithm [137,138] for strong bisimulation was proposed, which extends the Paige-Tarjan algorithm with a notion of *state rank* defined as the maximum distance to a sink state (if any), not counting transitions which are internal to strongly connected components. Fast bisimulation is more efficient than the Paige-Tarjan algorithm on LTSs containing sink states, especially acyclic LTSs. It was implemented in the COPS checker [366] for security properties. A symbolic version of this algorithm was implemented using BDDs [136].

A survey on the complexity of some of the behavioural equivalences presented in [190], considering their application to finite- and infinite-state models, can be found in [349].

4.2   New Bisimulation Tools

In the 2000s, a new generation of bisimulation tools appeared, which progressively superseded the tools developed during the previous decades.

BCG_MIN [176] used the Kanellakis-Smolka and the Groote-Vaandrager algorithms to minimize LTSs modulo strong and branching bisimulations. BCG_MIN was released as a component of the CADP toolbox and used BCG as a native file format to represent LTSs compactly. Since BCG_MIN was globally more efficient than ALDEBARAN and could handle larger graphs, the original ALDEBARAN tool was replaced in 2005 by a backward-compatible shell script invoking BCG_MIN and other tools of CADP [178].

The μCRL toolset [38,39] used partition-refinement algorithms to perform equivalence checking and minimization of LTSs modulo strong and branching bisimulations. It generated LTSs in the AUT and BCG formats of CADP, and implemented the OPEN/CÆSAR interface, so that most tools of CADP could be used on μCRL specifications. It was succeeded by the mCRL2 toolset [203], which also supports equivalence checking based on bisimulations.

TVT (Tampere Verification Tool) [417], which succeeded the ARA tool, implemented strong bisimulation and CFFD equivalence.

CHISIGMA [55] was a tool environment that could minimize, modulo strong and branching bisimulations, LTSs generated from specifications written in the process language χ_σ.

ABC [72] checked the equivalence of π-calculus processes modulo open bisimulation.

TAPAS [82], which was developed for teaching purpose, implemented comparison and minimization of LTSs modulo strong, observational, and branching bisimulations.

LTSA (Labelled Transition System Analyser) [325] performed minimization modulo observational equivalence of LTSs generated from FSP (Finite-State Processes) specifications.

4.3 Bisimulation Tools Using On-the-Fly Verification

Significant advances in on-the-fly reduction and on-the-fly equivalence checking of LTSs have been made during the 2000s.

A key tool of CADP for on-the-fly verification is EXP.OPEN, which explores the state space of networks of LTSs composed together using synchronization vectors or parallel composition operators borrowed to various process calculi (CCS, CSP, LOTOS, LNT, or μCRL), as well as hiding, renaming, cutting, or priority operators. EXP.OPEN was enhanced with on-the-fly partial-order reductions that preserve strong, branching, or stochastic branching bisimulations [295].

The ARCATS tool [89, 90] implemented a different approach to on-the-fly reduction: it incrementally generated an LTS reduced for branching bisimulation, by alternating steps of partial LTS generation and steps of branching minimization of the partial LTS already generated.

A generic library, named CÆSAR_SOLVE [334], was developed, as part of CADP, for solving BESs (Boolean Equation Systems) [7, 332]. BESs are effective models in which both model-checking and equivalence-checking problems can be conveniently encoded. Given a BES, the CÆSAR_SOLVE library explores an LTS on the fly, using the features provided by OPEN/CÆSAR, in order to compute the truth value of certain BES variables.

To reduce an LTS partially, during its generation, one can apply the notion of τ-confluence [205], a form of partial-order reduction that analyzes τ-transitions and preserves branching bisimulation. Based on this idea, an algorithm was proposed [45] and implemented in the μCRL toolset, with the help of an automated theorem prover to identify τ-confluent transitions.

This idea was also implemented in CADP by enhancing the aforementioned REDUCTOR tool that performed $\tau^*.a$ reduction. The new version of REDUCTOR [333] supports many other reductions, among which τ-confluence, τ-closure (transitive reflexive closure over τ-transitions), τ-compression (collapsing of strongly connected components made of τ-transitions), safety reduction, etc. It uses OPEN/CÆSAR and CÆSAR_SOLVE to detect τ-confluent transitions on the fly.

The definition of τ-confluence was later generalized to visible actions [297], so as to enable better reductions in a compositional-verification setting.

CADP was also enriched with another tool, named BISIMULATOR [26, 336, 337], which checks whether two LTSs are equivalent modulo strong, branching, observational, or $\tau^*.a$ bisimulations, as well as safety equivalence. The comparison is expressed in terms of a BES, which is resolved on the fly using CÆSAR_SOLVE, one of the two LTSs being explored on demand using

OPEN/CÆSAR. This general approach based on BESs subsumes the dedicated Fernandez-Mounier algorithms for checking bisimulations on the fly. BISIMU-LATOR, REDUCTOR, and BCG_MIN have been used in many case studies, e.g., the verification of a plant unit for drilling of metal products [335].

Conversely, BESs (which can be seen as a particular form of LTSs) can be minimized using strong bisimulation and an extension of strong bisimulation called *idempotence-identifying bisimulation* [273]. Such minimization preserves the truth values and, if applied before solving the original BESs, may speed up the resolution.

Equivalence checking of infinite-state models can be expressed in terms of PBESs (Parameterized Boolean Equation Systems) [332], an extension of BESs designed for model checking value-passing temporal-logic formulas [331]. This problem was addressed in [88] for branching and observational bisimulations. In this approach, the comparison of two models (represented using linear process equations) is encoded as a PBES, which is generated automatically, but whose resolution cannot be fully automated and may thus require human intervention.

4.4   Bisimulation Tools Based on Compositional Verification

Compositional verification makes intensive use of bisimulations and requires different tools for, e.g., generating, minimizing, and composing LTSs in parallel.

To ease compositional verification, CADP was enriched with SVL [175, 294], which is both a scripting language and a compiler. SVL enables verification scenarios to be specified simply and executed efficiently, and thus offers an alternative to graphical user interfaces when dealing with complex, repetitive tasks. The SVL language has operators to generate, compose in parallel, minimize, and compare LTSs modulo various equivalence relations; LTSs can be either given in low-level formats (AUT, BCG, etc.) or specified using high-level languages (LOTOS, LNT [182], etc.); other operators support compositional-verification strategies and abstractions based on (handwritten or automatically generated [296]) interface specifications. The SVL compiler translates SVL scripts into shell scripts that invoke the appropriate CADP tools (BCG_MIN, EXP.OPEN, PROJEC-TOR, etc.), relieving users from taking care of command-line options and auxiliary files. SVL was used in several case studies [111, 338, 403].

4.5   Bisimulation Tools Based on Parallel/Distributed Computing

Blom and Orzan proposed both sequential and parallel/distributed algorithms for minimizing LTSs modulo strong bisimulation [40, 42–44] and branching bisimulation [41] (later improved in [46]). These algorithms, which are gathered in [358], are based on partition refinement and the novel concept of *signatures* (two states having different signatures cannot be bisimilar).

Although their sequential algorithms have worst-case time complexity $O(mn^2)$, which is higher than the best algorithms for strong and branching bisimulations, they exhibit more opportunities for parallelization.

Indeed, their parallel algorithms, which distribute an LTS across several machines, exhibit a linear speed-up, meaning that the time taken by these algorithms linearly decreases when the number of machines increases. A policy based on abstract interpretation for distributing the LTS across machines was proposed in [359].

4.6   Bisimulation Tools Based on Symbolic Verification

The SIGREF tool [426] implemented several equivalence relations (including strong, branching, observational, and *orthogonal* [29] bisimulations, as well as safety equivalence) using sequential algorithms combining Blom-Orzan signatures with a BDD representation of the LTS. Several papers were published, detailing an algorithm for branching bisimulation [424], optimization techniques for BDD-based bisimulation computation [425], and an efficient algorithm for Markov chains [423].

4.7   Bisimulation Tools for Timed Systems

Research on timed bisimulations, which was very active in the 1990s, has seemingly slowed down during the 2000s. This is most likely related to the decline of research on timed process calculi, progressively replaced by simpler models based on timed automata. As a consequence, timed bisimulations and timed modal μ-calculus have been replaced by more elementary analyses, such as reachability and safety properties computed on networks of timed automata. In this respect, the good performance of UPPAAL may have favored this evolution (see the related discussion in [430]). However, one can mention two advances in timed bisimulations during the 2000s.

A new bisimulation-based *faster-than* preorder [317] was proposed to compare asynchronous processes with respect to their worst-case timing behaviour.

A new equivalence-checking algorithm for timed branching bisimulation of communicating timed automata was designed and implemented in the RED tool [419], improving over prior algorithms for timed branching bisimulation.

4.8   Bisimulation Tools for Probabilistic and Stochastic Systems

The aforementioned BCG_MIN tool was designed to handle, not only LTSs, but also extended models combining normal transitions (labelled with an action), probabilistic transitions (whose label is a probability), and/or stochastic transitions (whose label is the rate parameter of an exponential distribution governing a random delay). Such models encompass DTMCs, which contain only probabilistic transitions, CTMCs, which contain only stochastic transitions, IMCs (Interactive Markov Chains) [73,228,235], which contain both normal and stochastic transitions, and IPCs (Interactive Probabilistic Chains) [112,114], which contain both normal and probabilistic transitions. BCG_MIN can minimize such models for various equivalences that combine strong or branching bisimulation with lumpability and, in the stochastic case, maximal progress. BCG_MIN, together with other tools for steady-state and transient analysis [233], has made CADP the actual successor of the TIPPtool [173] and has been used in several performance studies.

Version 4.0 of TwoTowers [2] implemented equivalence checking, for strong and observational Markovian equivalences, of architectural specifications written in a language named Æmilia. This tool was used to assess the securing strategy implemented in a trusted device for security architectures [1].

The PEPA workbench [187] was extended to support PEPA nets [188], a formalism that describes mobile agent systems using Petri nets in which mobile program code (expressed using the stochastic process calculus PEPA) moves across the places of the net. This workbench implemented *net bisimulation* [189], an equivalence relation for minimizing marking graphs of PEPA nets, and was used in many case studies.

Bisimulation algorithms for minimizing DTMCs and CTMCs have been proposed [128, 129]. These algorithms, which are based on symbolic representations and Blom-Orzan signatures, have been implemented in the SIGREF tool [423]. Independently, it has been evidenced that minimizing a DTMC or CTMC before analysis improves performance [271].

Symmetry reductions that preserve strong probabilistic bisimulation have been proposed [292], which may generate DTMCs, CTMCs, and MDPs (Markov Decision Processes) by several orders of magnitude smaller. These reductions have been implemented, using BDDs, in the PRISM model checker [293].

Finally, a minimization algorithm for observational bisimulation of acyclic IMCs with inputs and outputs was proposed, with an application to the analysis of DFTs (Dynamic Fault Trees) [116].

5   Retrospective of the 2010s

5.1   New Bisimulation Tools

The BCG_MIN tool of CADP was entirely rewritten in 2010. The new version 2.0 [179, 180] relies on the sequential Blom-Orzan algorithms for strong and branching bisimulations. Despite the worst-case time complexity $O(mn^2)$ of the Blom-Orzan algorithms is higher than the worst-case time complexity $O(mn)$ of the Groote-Vaandrager and Kanellakis-Smolka algorithms implemented in BCG_MIN 1.0, the new version of BCG_MIN is statistically faster, which seems to indicate that the worst cases for signature-based algorithms rarely occur in practice (crafted worst-case examples are given in [201, Section 8]).

BCG_CMP[6] uses the same algorithms as BCG_MIN 2.0 to check the equivalence of two LTSs modulo strong, branching, divergence-preserving branching, and observational bisimulations. When both LTSs are not equivalent, it generates an LTS explaining where and why bisimulation does not hold.

---

[6] http://cadp.inria.fr/man/bcg_cmp.html.

LTSMIN [47,270] is a comprehensive model-checking tool set, which also implements strong and branching bisimulations using the distributed Blom-Orzan algorithms. LTSMIN is used as a backend by, e.g., the mCRL2 toolset [115].

The aforementioned FDR2 toolset for analyzing CSP processes was extended with new features [10], among which minimization algorithms [68] for strong, observational, and delay bisimulations to reduce state spaces before verification.

RELTS [340,341] and T-BEG [282] are tools that implement strong bisimulation in terms of game theory. Another tool [79] defines various simulation relations in terms of an antagonistic two-player game. Also, game-theoretic definitions of branching and divergence-preserving branching bisimulations have been given in [168].

Educational motivation was behind the development of tools such as CAAL (Concurrency Workbench, Aalborg Edition) [9], which implements various strong or observational, timed or untimed, equivalences and preorders, and PSEUCO [37], which supports strong bisimulation. These tools exhibit fancy Web interfaces that help teaching concurrency theory in university courses.

One can also mention SMART [352], which implements strong and observational bisimulations using multiway decision diagrams, GREASE [164], which checks strong and observational bisimulations on-the-fly using syntactic criteria to try finding a counter-example as soon as possible, and an implementation of branching bisimulation dedicated to the reduction of BIP (Behaviour-Interaction-Priority) models [357].

5.2   Bisimulation Tools for Probabilistic and Stochastic Systems

Foundations were laid for strong and observational bisimulations and preorders on Markov automata, a combination of probabilistic automata and IMCs [139].

The aforementioned minimization tool BCG_MIN 2.0 was equipped with probabilistic and stochastic bisimulations [113]. For these relations (as well as for strong and branching bisimulations on LTSs), BCG_MIN 2.0 was found to use less memory and to be faster than BCG_MIN 1.0 [180]. Support for the same probabilistic and stochastic bisimulations was added in BCG_CMP too.

MRMC (Markov Reward Model Checker) [272,435] is a tool for verifying properties (expressed as CSL or PCTL temporal-logic formulas with their reward extensions) on probabilistic models. To alleviate state explosion, MRMC may minimize these models modulo strong bisimulation.

Polynomial algorithms for probabilistic observational bisimulation on probabilistic automata [216,242] and alternating probabilistic bisimulation on interval MDPs [217] were proposed and implemented. The latter relation was shown to be compositional [215].

An algorithm [127] for directly generating a DTMC minimized modulo probabilistic bisimulation from a probabilistic program described by guarded commands was proposed and implemented in the PRISM model checker using the SMT solver Z3. Another approach for generating, using PRISM, a DTMC from an RTL (Register Transfer Level) description and minimizing it, using SIGREF, modulo probabilistic bisimulation can be found in [87].

An approach was proposed [392] to accelerate the model checking of PCTL formulas on probabilistic automata, by iteratively refining an abstraction of a probabilistic automaton, using incrementally computed bisimulations and without resorting to any kind of counterexample analysis.

A fast algorithm for strong probabilistic bisimulation [209] was proposed and implemented in the mCRL2 toolset [80].

Another fast algorithm [263] was given to minimize, modulo branching bisimulation, DTMCs with labelled states.

Probabilistic bisimulation was also applied to infinite-state parameterized systems, i.e., systems with an arbitrary number of processes [248]. The approach was experimented in a prototype tool that was not made public.

5.3 Bisimulation Tools for Mobile Systems

Two new tools for analyzing extensions of the π-calculus were released during the 2010s.

PWB (Psi-Calculus Workbench) [51,52] was a generic tool for analyzing mobile processes by means of symbolic simulation and equivalence checking modulo symbolic (strong or observational) bisimulations [266].

SPEC [400] was an equivalence-checking tool for open bisimulation on security protocols specified in the spi-calculus.

5.4 Bisimulation Tools Based on Parallel/Distributed Computing

There have been commendable efforts to parallelize mainstream partition-refinement algorithms for minimizing LTSs modulo strong bisimulation. A parallel version of the Paige-Tarjan algorithm, in combination with Blom-Orzan signatures, was proposed in [291], and a parallel version of the Kanellakis-Smolka algorithm is given in [328].

Combinations of symbolic techniques and parallel algorithms have also been explored in the second half of the 2010s. SIGREFMC [130,133] was a bisimulation tool providing the same functionalities as SIGREF, but based on SYLVAN [131,132], a parallel implementation of BDDs on multi-core architectures.

While SIGREFMC encoded bisimulations as partitions of the state space, in the lineage of partition-refinement algorithms, a different approach was investigated in [251,252], where strong bisimulation was encoded directly as a relation, like in the Bouali-De Simone algorithm.

5.5 Bisimulation Tools Based on Compositional Verification

A new approach, called *smart reduction* [117], was proposed for the compositional minimization of networks of LTSs. Smart reduction analyzes the synchronizations between concurrent processes to infer a suitable order in which processes are composed and minimized. Such a heuristic, which tries to avoid state explosion by keeping the size of intermediate LTSs as small as possible, was implemented in the SVL scripting language of CADP [177].

A new family of equivalence relations, named *sharp bisimulations* [300], which combine strong bisimulation and divergence-preserving branching bisimulation [339], was defined. Sharp bisimulations provide effective reductions while preserving given temporal-logic formulas [299]. They have been implemented in the BCG_MIN and BCG_CMP tools of CADP, with user-friendly support in SVL.

Smart reduction and sharp bisimulations play a major role in modern approaches to compositional verification. Together with recent developments [298] around the idea of *partial model checking* [8], they enabled scientists from Grenoble and Pisa to solve nearly all the parallel problems of the RERS[7] verification challenge in 2019[8] and 2020[9].

5.6   Recent Results for Strong and Branching Bisimulations

An asymptotic lower bound $\Omega((m+n)\log n)$ on the time complexity of partition refinement algorithms was established [202].

A new (successively revised, improved, and simplified) minimization algorithm for branching bisimulation was proposed [201,210,211,261,262]. Its worst-case time complexity $O(m\log n)$ is lower than that of the Groote-Vaandrager algorithm, which has been the best-known algorithm since the early 1990s, and equal to that of the Paige-Tarjan algorithm, which is still the reference algorithm for strong bisimulation. This new algorithm has been implemented in the mCRL2 toolset.

6   Conclusion

Although model checking and equivalence checking have been discovered nearly at the same time in the early 1980s, model checking is now widespread in academia and industry, whereas equivalence checking plays a more discrete role. It nevertheless found numerous applications in the verification of communication protocols, hardware circuits, distributed systems, security systems, web services, etc. Actually, compared to model checking, equivalence checking presents several advantages:

- It is conceptually simpler, as it does not require learning another language (i.e., temporal logics) to express the properties under verification.
- It enables *visual checking*, an easy form of verification done by abstracting away certain observable actions of the system (i.e., by renaming them to τ-transitions), minimizing the resulting state space modulo some weak bisimulation, and visually inspecting the minimized state space if it is small enough.
- It may increase the effectiveness of model checking, as compositional state-space verification techniques based upon, e.g., congruence properties, smart reductions, and sharp bisimulations, are often capable of generating large state spaces that could not be explored otherwise.

---

[7] http://rers-challenge.org.
[8] http://cadp.inria.fr/news12.html.
[9] http://cadp.inria.fr/news13.html#section-3.

For these reasons, we believe that equivalence checking should play a growing role in the future, in close combination with model checking. This could resolve the longstanding dilemma between *state-based models* (in which information is attached to states, as in Kripke structures) and *action-based models* (in which information is attached to transitions, as in LTSs and Markov chains) by giving an advantage to the latter models. Model checking is equally applicable to both action- and state-based models (although with slightly different temporal logics [122]), but most bisimulation tools have been designed to operate on action-based models, which suggests that the latter models are more suitable where model checking and equivalence checking are to be used together.

During the last forty years, the development of algorithms and tools for checking bisimulations on finite- or infinite-state systems has steadily progressed. These essential achievements have been spanning over several decades, which is no surprise, keeping in mind how theoretically involved are these algorithms and how technically involved are these tools subject to severe performance requirements. A remarkable example of such long-lasting research and commitment is the Groote-Vaandrager algorithm for branching bisimulation [207], which has been gradually refined to lower its complexity [262].

It is worth noticing that most of the bisimulation tools developed for equivalence checking are no longer available today. Quite often, publications are the only remaining indication that such tools have existed; in some cases (e.g., for the promising BIDMIN tool), formal publications are even lacking. A counterexample is the CADP toolbox, the bisimulation tools of which have been, over several decades, constantly enhanced or replaced by better, backward-compatible tools.

Software tools get obsolete due to incompatible evolutions of programming languages and operating systems, but they also get abandoned when their authors leave academia or move from one university to another; this suggests that overemphasis on professional mobility may hamper long-term development of perennial software tools.

Finally, the development of bisimulation tools has probably suffered from additional factors, among which: (i) the lack of standard file formats agreed upon by the community, beyond the rather inefficient AUT format; (ii) the lack of benchmark examples, with the notable exception of VLTS[10], which plays the role of a de-facto test suite; and (iii) the lack of yearly software competitions dedicated to equivalence checking. We hope that the present survey will draw the attention to the past achievements and future promises of this research field.

Acknowledgements. We are grateful to Rance Cleaveland, Rocco De Nicola, Jan Friso Groote, Laurent Mounier, Elie Najm, and the anonymous referees for their valuable comments about this article. We also would like to thank the DBLP and Google Scholar teams, whose long-term undertaking made it possible to tackle such a comprehensive study.

---

[10] https://cadp.inria.fr/resources/vlts.

References

1. Aldini, A., Bernardo, M.: An integrated view of security analysis and performance evaluation: trading QoS with covert channel bandwidth. In: Heisel, M., Liggesmeyer, P., Wittmann, S. (eds.) SAFECOMP 2004. LNCS, vol. 3219, pp. 283–296. Springer, Heidelberg (2004). https://doi.org/10.1007/978-3-540-30138-7_24

2. Aldini, A., Bernardo, M.: TwoTowers 4.0: towards the integration of security analysis and performance evaluation. In: 1st International Conference on Quantitative Evaluation of Systems (QEST 2004), Enschede, The Netherlands, pp. 336–337. IEEE Computer Society, September 2004

3. Alur, R., Courcoubetis, C., Dill, D.L., Halbwachs, N., Wong-Toi, H.: An implementation of three algorithms for timing verification based on automata emptiness. In: Proceedings of the Real-Time Systems Symposium, Phoenix, Arizona, USA, December 1992, pp. 157–166. IEEE Computer Society (1992)

4. Alur, R., Courcoubetis, C., Halbwachs, N., Dill, D., Wong-Toi, H.: Minimization of timed transition systems. In: Cleaveland, W.R. (ed.) CONCUR 1992. LNCS, vol. 630, pp. 340–354. Springer, Heidelberg (1992). https://doi.org/10.1007/BFb0084802

5. Alur, R., Dill, D.: Automata for modeling real-time systems. In: Paterson, M.S. (ed.) ICALP 1990. LNCS, vol. 443, pp. 322–335. Springer, Heidelberg (1990). https://doi.org/10.1007/BFb0032042

6. Alur, R., Dill, D.L.: A theory of timed automata. Theor. Comput. Sci. **126**(2), 183–235 (1994)

7. Andersen, H.R.: Model checking and Boolean graphs. Theor. Comput. Sci. **126**(1), 3–30 (1994)

8. Andersen, H.R.: Partial model checking. In: Proceedings of the 10th Annual IEEE Symposium on Logic in Computer Science LICS (San Diego, California, USA), pp. 398–407. IEEE Computer Society Press, June 1995

9. Andersen, J.R., et al.: CAAL: Concurrency Workbench, Aalborg edition. In: Leucker, M., Rueda, C., Valencia, F.D. (eds.) ICTAC 2015. LNCS, vol. 9399, pp. 573–582. Springer, Cham (2015). https://doi.org/10.1007/978-3-319-25150-9_33

10. Armstrong, P., et al.: Recent developments in FDR. In: Madhusudan, P., Seshia, S.A. (eds.) CAV 2012. LNCS, vol. 7358, pp. 699–704. Springer, Heidelberg (2012). https://doi.org/10.1007/978-3-642-31424-7_52

11. Arnold, A.: Verification and comparison of transition systems. In: Gaudel, M.-C., Jouannaud, J.-P. (eds.) CAAP 1993. LNCS, vol. 668, pp. 121–135. Springer, Heidelberg (1993). https://doi.org/10.1007/3-540-56610-4_60

12. Arnold, A., Bégay, D., Crubillé, P.: Construction and Analysis of Transition Systems with MEC. AMAST Series in Computing, vol. 3. World Scientific (1994)

13. Arnold, A., Point, G., Griffault, A., Rauzy, A.: The AltaRica formalism for describing concurrent systems. Fundam. Informaticae **40**(2–3), 109–124 (1999)

14. Arts, T., van Langevelde, I.: Verifying a Smart Design of TCAP: A Synergetic Experience. Research Report SEN-R9910, CWI (1999)

15. Arts, T., van Langevelde, I.: How μCRL supported a smart redesign of a real-life protocol. In: Gnesi, S., Latella, D. (eds.) Proceedings of the 4th International ERCIM Workshop on Formal Methods for Industrial Critical Systems (Trento, Italy), pp. 31–53. ERCIM, CNR, July 1999

16. Arts, T., van Langevelde, I.: Correct performance of transaction capabilities. In: Valmari, A., Yakovlev, A. (eds.) Proceedings of the 2nd International Conference

on Application of Concurrency to System Design (ICACSD 2001), Newcastle upon Tyne, UK, pp. 35–42. IEEE Computer Society, June 2001

17. Austry, D., Boudol, G.: Algèbre de Processus et Synchronisation. Theor. Comput. Sci. **30**, 91–131 (1984)
18. Azema, P., Drira, K., Vernadat, F.: A bus instrumentation protocol specified in LOTOS. In: Quemada, J., Manas, J., Vázquez, E. (eds.) Proceedings of the 3rd International Conference on Formal Description Techniques FORTE 1990 (Madrid, Spain). North-Holland, November 1990
19. Azéma, P., Vernadat, F., Lloret, J.-C.: Requirement analysis for communication protocols. In: Sifakis, J. (ed.) CAV 1989. LNCS, vol. 407, pp. 286–293. Springer, Heidelberg (1990). https://doi.org/10.1007/3-540-52148-8_24
20. Baeten, J.C.M., Sangiorgi, D.: Concurrency theory: a historical perspective on coinduction and process calculi. In: Siekmann, J.H. (ed.) Computational Logic, Handbook of the History of Logic, vol. 9, pp. 399–442. Elsevier (2014)
21. Baier, C.: Polynomial time algorithms for testing probabilistic bisimulation and simulation. In: Alur, R., Henzinger, T.A. (eds.) CAV 1996. LNCS, vol. 1102, pp. 50–61. Springer, Heidelberg (1996). https://doi.org/10.1007/3-540-61474-5_57
22. Baray, F., Wodey, P.: Verification in the codesign process by means of LOTOS based model-checking. In: Gnesi, S., Schieferdecker, I., Rennoch, A. (eds.) Proceedings of the 5th International Workshop on Formal Methods for Industrial Critical Systems (FMICS 2000), Berlin, Germany, pp. 87–108. GMD Report 91, Berlin, April 2000
23. Bause, F., Buchholz, P., Kemper, P.: A toolbox for functional and quantitative analysis of DEDS. In: Puigjaner, R., Savino, N.N., Serra, B. (eds.) TOOLS 1998. LNCS, vol. 1469, pp. 356–359. Springer, Heidelberg (1998). https://doi.org/10.1007/3-540-68061-6_32
24. Bengtsson, J., Larsen, K., Larsson, F., Pettersson, P., Yi, W.: UPPAAL—a tool suite for automatic verification of real-time systems. In: Alur, R., Henzinger, T.A., Sontag, E.D. (eds.) HS 1995. LNCS, vol. 1066, pp. 232–243. Springer, Heidelberg (1996). https://doi.org/10.1007/BFb0020949
25. Benslimane, A., Abouaissa, A.: XTP specification and validation with LOTOS. In: Proceedings of the Western MultiConference WMC 1998, Communication Networks and Distributed Systems Modeling and Simulation CNDS 1998 (San Diego, California, USA). Society for Computer Simulation International, January 1998
26. Bergamini, D., Descoubes, N., Joubert, C., Mateescu, R.: BISIMULATOR: a modular tool for on-the-fly equivalence checking. In: Halbwachs, N., Zuck, L.D. (eds.) TACAS 2005. LNCS, vol. 3440, pp. 581–585. Springer, Heidelberg (2005). https://doi.org/10.1007/978-3-540-31980-1_42
27. Bergstra, J.A., Klop, J.W.: Process algebra for synchronous communication. Inf. Comput. **60**(1–3), 109–137 (1984)
28. Bergstra, J.A., Klop, J.W.: Algebra of communicating processes with abstraction. Theor. Comput. Sci. **37**, 77–121 (1985)
29. Bergstra, J.A., Ponse, A., van der Zwaag, M.: Branching time and orthogonal bisimulation equivalence. Theor. Comput. Sci. **309**(1–3), 313–355 (2003)
30. Bernardeschi, C., Fantechi, A., Gnesi, S.: An industrial application for the JACK environment. J. Syst. Softw. **39**(3), 249–264 (1997)
31. Bernardeschi, C., Fantechi, A., Gnesi, S., Larosa, S., Mongardi, G., Romano, D.: A formal verification environment for railway signaling system design. Formal Methods Syst. Des. **12**(2), 139–161 (1998)

32. Bernardo, M., Bravetti, M.: Functional and performance modeling and analysis of token ring using EMPA. In: Degano, P., Vaccaro, U., Pirillo, G. (eds.) Proceedings of the 6th Italian Conference on Theoretical Computer Science (1998)

33. Bernardo, M.: An algebra-based method to associate rewards with EMPA terms. In: Degano, P., Gorrieri, R., Marchetti-Spaccamela, A. (eds.) ICALP 1997. LNCS, vol. 1256, pp. 358–368. Springer, Heidelberg (1997). https://doi.org/10.1007/3-540-63165-8_192

34. Bernardo, M.: Implementing symbolic models for value passing in TwoTowers. In: Haverkort, B.R., Bohnenkamp, H.C., Smith, C.U. (eds.) TOOLS 2000. LNCS, vol. 1786, pp. 370–373. Springer, Heidelberg (2000). https://doi.org/10.1007/3-540-46429-8_34

35. Bernardo, M., Cleaveland, R., Sims, S., Stewart, W.: TwoTowers: a tool integrating functional and performance analysis of concurrent systems. In: Budkowski, S., Cavalli, A.R., Najm, E. (eds.) Formal Description Techniques and Protocol Specification, Testing and Verification, FORTE XI/PSTV XVIII 1998, IFIP TC6 WG6.1 Joint International Conference on Formal Description Techniques for Distributed Systems and Communication Protocols (FORTE XI) and Protocol Specification, Testing and Verification (PSTV XVIII), Paris, France. IFIP Conference Proceedings, vol. 135, pp. 457–467. Kluwer, November 1998

36. Bianchi, A., Coluccini, S., Degano, P., Priami, C.: An efficient verifier of truly concurrent properties. In: Malyshkin, V. (ed.) PaCT 1995. LNCS, vol. 964, pp. 36–50. Springer, Heidelberg (1995). https://doi.org/10.1007/3-540-60222-4_95

37. Biewer, S., Freiberger, F., Held, P.L., Hermanns, H.: Teaching academic concurrency to amazing students. In: Aceto, L., Bacci, G., Bacci, G., Ingólfsdóttir, A., Legay, A., Mardare, R. (eds.) Models, Algorithms, Logics and Tools. LNCS, vol. 10460, pp. 170–195. Springer, Cham (2017). https://doi.org/10.1007/978-3-319-63121-9_9

38. Blom, S., Fokkink, W., Groote, J.F., van Langevelde, I., Lisser, B., van de Pol, J.: μCRL: a toolset for analysing algebraic specifications. In: Berry, G., Comon, H., Finkel, A. (eds.) CAV 2001. LNCS, vol. 2102, pp. 250–254. Springer, Heidelberg (2001). https://doi.org/10.1007/3-540-44585-4_23

39. Blom, S., Groote, J.F., van Langevelde, I., Lisser, B., van de Pol, J.: New developments around the mCRL tool set. Electron. Notes Theor. Comput. Sci. **80**, 284–288 (2003)

40. Blom, S., Orzan, S.: A distributed algorithm for strong bisimulation reduction of state spaces. Electron. Notes Theor. Comput. Sci. **68**(4), 523–538 (2002)

41. Blom, S., Orzan, S.: Distributed branching bisimulation reduction of state spaces. Electron. Notes Theor. Comput. Sci. **89**(1), 99–113 (2003)

42. Blom, S., Orzan, S.: Distributed state space minimization. Electron. Notes Theor. Comput. Sci. **80**, 109–123 (2003)

43. Blom, S., Orzan, S.: A distributed algorithm for strong bisimulation reduction of state spaces. Softw. Tools Technol. Transfer **7**(1), 74–86 (2005)

44. Blom, S., Orzan, S.: Distributed state space minimization. Softw. Tools Technol. Transfer **7**(3), 280–291 (2005)

45. Blom, S., van de Pol, J.: State space reduction by proving confluence. In: Brinksma, E., Larsen, K.G. (eds.) CAV 2002. LNCS, vol. 2404, pp. 596–609. Springer, Heidelberg (2002). https://doi.org/10.1007/3-540-45657-0_50

46. Blom, S., van de Pol, J.: Distributed branching bisimulation minimization by inductive signatures. In: Brim, L., van de Pol, J. (eds.) Proceedings 8th International Workshop on Parallel and Distributed Methods in Verification (PDMC 2009), Eindhoven, The Netherlands. EPTCS, vol. 14, pp. 32–46, November 2009

47. Blom, S., van de Pol, J., Weber, M.: LTSMIN: distributed and symbolic reachability. In: Touili, T., Cook, B., Jackson, P. (eds.) CAV 2010. LNCS, vol. 6174, pp. 354–359. Springer, Heidelberg (2010). https://doi.org/10.1007/978-3-642-14295-6_31

48. Blute, R., Desharnais, J., Edalat, A., Panangaden, P.: Bisimulation for labelled Markov processes. In: Proceedings of the 12th Annual IEEE Symposium on Logic in Computer Science, Warsaw, Poland, pp. 149–158. IEEE Computer Society, June 1997

49. Bolognesi, T., Caneve, M.: SQUIGGLES: a tool for the analysis of LOTOS specifications. In: Turner, K.J. (ed.) Proceedings of the 1st International Conference on Formal Description Techniques (FORTE 1988), Stirling, Scotland, pp. 201–216. North-Holland, September 1988

50. Bolognesi, T., Caneve, M.: Equivalence verification: theory, algorithms, and a tool. In: van Eijk, P., Vissers, C.A., Diaz, M. (eds.) The Formal Description Technique LOTOS, pp. 303–326. North-Holland (1989)

51. Borgström, J., Gutkovas, R., Rodhe, I., Victor, B.: A parametric tool for applied process calculi. In: Carmona, J., Lazarescu, M.T., Pietkiewicz-Koutny, M. (eds.) 13th International Conference on Application of Concurrency to System Design, ACSD 2013, Barcelona, Spain, pp. 180–185. IEEE Computer Society, July 2013

52. Borgström, J., Gutkovas, R., Rodhe, I., Victor, B.: The psi-calculi workbench: a generic tool for applied process calculi. ACM Trans. Embed. Comput. Syst. **14**(1), 9:1–9:25 (2015)

53. Børjesson, A., Larsen, K.G., Skou, A.: Generality in design and compositional verification using TAV. In: Diaz, M., Groz, R. (eds.) Proceedings of the IFIP TC6/WG6.1 5th International Conference on Formal Description Techniques for Distributed Systems and Communication Protocols (FORTE 1992), Perros-Guirec, France, 13–16 October 1992. IFIP Transactions, vol. C-10, pp. 449–464. North-Holland, September 1992

54. Børjesson, A., Larsen, K.G., Skou, A.: Generality in design and compositional verification using TAV. Formal Methods Syst. Des. **6**(3), 239–258 (1995)

55. Bos, V.: ChiSigma Manual (2002). ResearchGate

56. Bouajjani, A., Fernandez, J.C., Graf, S., Rodriguez, C., Sifakis, J.: Safety for branching time semantics. In: Albert, J.L., Monien, B., Artalejo, M.R. (eds.) ICALP 1991. LNCS, vol. 510, pp. 76–92. Springer, Heidelberg (1991). https://doi.org/10.1007/3-540-54233-7_126

57. Bouajjani, A., Fernandez, J.-C., Halbwachs, N.: Minimal model generation. In: Clarke, E.M., Kurshan, R.P. (eds.) CAV 1990. LNCS, vol. 531, pp. 197–203. Springer, Heidelberg (1991). https://doi.org/10.1007/BFb0023733

58. Bouali, A.: Weak and Branching Bisimulation in FcTool. Research Report 1575, INRIA (1992)

59. Bouali, A.: XEVE: An ESTEREL Verification Environment (Version v1.3). Technical Report 214, INRIA (1997)

60. Bouali, A., Gnesi, S., Larosa, S.: The Integration Project for the JACK Environment. Research Report CS-R9443, CWI (1994)

61. Bouali, A., Ressouche, A., Roy, V., de Simone, R.: The FC2TOOLS set. In: Alur, R., Henzinger, T.A. (eds.) CAV 1996. LNCS, vol. 1102, pp. 441–445. Springer, Heidelberg (1996). https://doi.org/10.1007/3-540-61474-5_98

62. Bouali, A., Ressouche, A., Roy, V., de Simone, R.: The FC2TOOLS set. In: Wirsing, M., Nivat, M. (eds.) AMAST 1996. LNCS, vol. 1101, pp. 595–598. Springer, Heidelberg (1996). https://doi.org/10.1007/BFb0014350

63. Bouali, A., Ressouche, A., Roy, V., de Simone, R.: The FC2TOOLS set (tool demonstration). In: Margaria, T., Steffen, B. (eds.) TACAS 1996. LNCS, vol. 1055, p. 396. Springer, Heidelberg (1996). https://doi.org/10.1007/3-540-61042-1_57

64. Bouali, A., Ressouche, A., Roy, V., de Simone, R.: The FCTOOLS User Manual (Version 1.0). Technical Report RT-0191, INRIA, June 1996

65. Bouali, A., de Simone, R.: Symbolic bisimulation minimisation. In: von Bochmann, G., Probst, D.K. (eds.) CAV 1992. LNCS, vol. 663, pp. 96–108. Springer, Heidelberg (1993). https://doi.org/10.1007/3-540-56496-9_9

66. Boudol, G., Roy, V., de Simone, R., Vergamini, D.: Process calculi, from theory to practice: verification tools. In: Sifakis, J. (ed.) CAV 1989. LNCS, vol. 407, pp. 1–10. Springer, Heidelberg (1990). https://doi.org/10.1007/3-540-52148-8_1

67. Boudol, G., de Simone, R., Vergamini, D.: Experiment with AUTO and AUTO-GRAPH on a simple case of sliding window protocol. Research Report 870, INRIA (1988)

68. Boulgakov, A., Gibson-Robinson, T., Roscoe, A.W.: Computing maximal weak and other bisimulations. Formal Aspects Comput. **28**(3), 381–407 (2016)

69. Bozga, M., Daws, C., Maler, O., Olivero, A., Tripakis, S., Yovine, S.: KRONOS: a model-checking tool for real-time systems. In: Hu, A.J., Vardi, M.Y. (eds.) CAV 1998. LNCS, vol. 1427, pp. 546–550. Springer, Heidelberg (1998). https://doi.org/10.1007/BFb0028779

70. Bozga, M., Daws, C., Maler, O., Olivero, A., Tripakis, S., Yovine, S.: KRONOS: a model-checking tool for real-time systems. In: Ravn, A.P., Rischel, H. (eds.) FTRTFT 1998. LNCS, vol. 1486, pp. 298–302. Springer, Heidelberg (1998). https://doi.org/10.1007/BFb0055357

71. Bozga, M., Fernandez, J.C., Kerbrat, A., Mounier, L.: Protocol verification with the ALDEBARAN toolset. Int. J. Softw. Tools Technol. Transf. **1**(1–2), 166–184 (1997)

72. Briais, S.: ABC User's Guide (2005). http://sbriais.free.fr/tools/abc/abc_ug.ps

73. Brinksma, E., Hermanns, H.: Process algebra and Markov chains. In: Brinksma, E., Hermanns, H., Katoen, J.-P. (eds.) EEF School 2000. LNCS, vol. 2090, pp. 183–231. Springer, Heidelberg (2001). https://doi.org/10.1007/3-540-44667-2_5

74. Brookes, S.D., Hoare, C.A.R., Roscoe, A.W.: A theory of communicating sequential processes. J. ACM **31**(3), 560–599 (1984)

75. Bryant, R.E.: Graph-based algorithms for Boolean function manipulation. IEEE Trans. Comput. **C-35**(8) (1986)

76. Buchholz, P.: Equivalence relations for stochastic automata networks. In: Stewart, W.J. (ed.) Computation with Markov Chains: Proceedings of the 2nd International Workshop on the Numerical Solution of Markov Chains, pp. 197–216. Kluwer (1995)

77. Buchholz, P., Kemper, P.: A toolbox for the analysis of discrete event dynamic systems. In: Halbwachs, N., Peled, D. (eds.) CAV 1999. LNCS, vol. 1633, pp. 483–486. Springer, Heidelberg (1999). https://doi.org/10.1007/3-540-48683-6_41

78. Buchholz, P., Kemper, P.: Modular state level analysis of distributed systems techniques and tool support. In: Cleaveland, W.R. (ed.) TACAS 1999. LNCS, vol. 1579, pp. 420–434. Springer, Heidelberg (1999). https://doi.org/10.1007/3-540-49059-0_29

79. Bulychev, P.E.: Game-theoretic simulation checking tool. Program. Comput. Softw. **37**(4), 200–209 (2011)

80. Bunte, O., et al.: The mCRL2 toolset for analysing concurrent systems. In: Vojnar, T., Zhang, L. (eds.) TACAS 2019. LNCS, vol. 11428, pp. 21–39. Springer, Cham (2019). https://doi.org/10.1007/978-3-030-17465-1_2

81. Bystrov, A.V., Virbitskaite, I.B.: Implementing model checking and equivalence checking for time petri nets by the RT-MEC tool. In: Malyshkin, V. (ed.) PaCT 1999. LNCS, vol. 1662, pp. 194–199. Springer, Heidelberg (1999). https://doi.org/10.1007/3-540-48387-X_20

82. Calzolai, F., De Nicola, R., Loreti, M., Tiezzi, F.: TAPAs: a tool for the analysis of process algebras. Trans. Petri Nets Other Model. Concurr. **1**, 54–70 (2008)

83. Camurati, P., Corno, F., Prinetto, P.: An efficient tool for system-level verification of behaviors and temporal properties. In: Proceedings of the European Design Automation Conference (EURO-DAC 1993), Hamburg, Germany, pp. 124–129. IEEE Computer Society, September 1993

84. Carchiolo, V., Faro, A.: A tool for the automated verification of ECCS specifications of OSI protocols. In: Varaiya, P., Kurzhanski, A.B. (eds.) Discrete Event Systems: Models and Applications. LNCIS, pp. 57–68. Springer, Heidelberg (1987). https://doi.org/10.1007/BFb0042304

85. Cerans, K., Godskesen, J.C., Larsen, K.G.: Timed Modal Specification - Theory and Tools. Research Report RS-97-11, BRICS (1997)

86. Chehaibar, G., Garavel, H., Mounier, L., Tawbi, N., Zulian, F.: Specification and verification of the PowerScale bus arbitration protocol: an industrial experiment with LOTOS. In: Gotzhein, R., Bredereke, J. (eds.) Proceedings of the IFIP Joint International Conference on Formal Description Techniques for Distributed Systems and Communication Protocols, and Protocol Specification, Testing, and Verification (FORTE/PSTV 1996), Kaiserslautern, Germany, pp. 435–450. Chapman & Hall, October 1996. Full version available as INRIA Research Report RR-2958

87. Chen, L., Ebrahimi, M., Tahoori, M.B.: Quantitative evaluation of register vulnerabilities in RTL control paths. In: Natale, G.D. (ed.) Proceedings of the 19th IEEE European Test Symposium (ETS 2014), Paderborn, Germany, pp. 1–2. IEEE, May 2014

88. Chen, T., Ploeger, B., van de Pol, J., Willemse, T.A.C.: Equivalence checking for infinite systems using parameterized Boolean equation systems. In: Caires, L., Vasconcelos, V.T. (eds.) CONCUR 2007. LNCS, vol. 4703, pp. 120–135. Springer, Heidelberg (2007). https://doi.org/10.1007/978-3-540-74407-8_9

89. Cheng, Y.P., Cheng, Y.R., Wang, H.Y.: ARCATS: a scalable compositional analysis tool suite. In: Haddad, H. (ed.) Proceedings of the 2006 ACM Symposium on Applied Computing (SAC 2006), Dijon, France, pp. 1852–1853. ACM, April 2006

90. Cheng, Y.-P., Wang, H.-Y., Cheng, Y.-R.: On-the-fly branching bisimulation minimization for compositional analysis. In: Ibarra, O.H., Yen, H.-C. (eds.) CIAA 2006. LNCS, vol. 4094, pp. 219–229. Springer, Heidelberg (2006). https://doi.org/10.1007/11812128_21

91. Cheung, S.C., Kramer, J.: Enhancing compositional reachability analysis with context constraints. In: Proceedings of the 1st ACM SIGSOFT International Symposium on the Foundations of Software Engineering (Los Angeles, CA, USA), pp. 115–125. ACM Press, December 1993

92. Cheung, S.C., Giannakopoulou, D., Kramer, J.: Verification of liveness properties using compositional reachability analysis. In: Jazayeri, M., Schauer, H. (eds.) ESEC/SIGSOFT FSE 1997. LNCS, vol. 1301, pp. 227–243. Springer, Heidelberg (1997). https://doi.org/10.1007/3-540-63531-9_17

93. Clarke, D.: VERSA: Verification, Execution and Rewrite System for ASCR. Technical Report MS-CIS-95-34, University of Pennsylvania (1995)
94. Clarke, D., Ben-Abdallah, H., Lee, I., Xie, H.-L., Sokolsky, O.: XVERSA: an integrated graphical and textual toolset for the specification and analysis of resource-bound real-time systems. In: Alur, R., Henzinger, T.A. (eds.) CAV 1996. LNCS, vol. 1102, pp. 402–405. Springer, Heidelberg (1996). https://doi.org/10.1007/3-540-61474-5_89
95. Clarke, D., Lee, I.: VERSA: a tool for analyzing resource-bound real-time systems. J. Comput. Softw. Eng. 3(2) (1995)
96. Clarke, D., Lee, I., Xie, H.L.: VERSA: A Tool for the Specification and Analysis of Resource-Bound Real-Time Systems. Technical Report MS-CIS-93-77, University of Pennsylvania (1993)
97. Clarke, E.M., Emerson, E.A., Sifakis, J.: Model checking: algorithmic verification and debugging. Commun. ACM 52(11), 74–84 (2009)
98. Cleaveland, R.: On automatically explaining bisimulation inequivalence. In: Clarke, E.M., Kurshan, R.P. (eds.) CAV 1990. LNCS, vol. 531, pp. 364–372. Springer, Heidelberg (1991). https://doi.org/10.1007/BFb0023750
99. Cleaveland, R.: Analyzing concurrent systems using the Concurrency Workbench. In: Lauer, P.E. (ed.) Functional Programming, Concurrency, Simulation and Automated Reasoning. LNCS, vol. 693, pp. 129–144. Springer, Heidelberg (1993). https://doi.org/10.1007/3-540-56883-2_8
100. Cleaveland, R., Gada, J.N., Lewis, P.M., Smolka, S.A., Sokolsky, O., Zhang, S.: The Concurrency Factory - practical tools for specification, simulation, verification, and implementation of concurrent systems. In: Blelloch, G.E., Chandy, K.M., Jagannathan, S. (eds.) Proceedings of the DIMACS Workshop on Specification of Parallel Algorithms, Princeton, New Jersey, USA. DIMACS Series in Discrete Mathematics and Theoretical Computer Science, vol. 18, pp. 75–89. DIMACS/AMS, May 1994
101. Cleaveland, R., Hennessy, M.: Testing equivalence as a bisimulation equivalence. In: Sifakis, J. (ed.) CAV 1989. LNCS, vol. 407, pp. 11–23. Springer, Heidelberg (1990). https://doi.org/10.1007/3-540-52148-8_2
102. Cleaveland, R., Lewis, P.M., Smolka, S.A., Sokolsky, O.: The Concurrency Factory: a development environment for concurrent systems. In: Alur, R., Henzinger, T.A. (eds.) CAV 1996. LNCS, vol. 1102, pp. 398–401. Springer, Heidelberg (1996). https://doi.org/10.1007/3-540-61474-5_88
103. Cleaveland, R., Li, T., Sims, S.: The Concurrency Workbench of the New Century (Version 1.2) - User's Manual, July 2000. State University of New York at Stony Brook
104. Cleaveland, R., Parrow, J., Steffen, B.: A semantics based verification tool for finite state systems. In: Brinksma, E., Scollo, G., Vissers, C.A. (eds.) Proceedings of the 9th International Symposium on Protocol Specification, Testing and Verification (PSTV 1989), Enschede, The Netherlands, pp. 287–302. North-Holland (1989)
105. Cleaveland, R., Parrow, J., Steffen, B.: The Concurrency Workbench. In: Sifakis, J. (ed.) CAV 1989. LNCS, vol. 407, pp. 24–37. Springer, Heidelberg (1990). https://doi.org/10.1007/3-540-52148-8_3
106. Cleaveland, R., Parrow, J., Steffen, B.: The Concurrency Workbench: a semantics-based tool for the verification of concurrent systems. ACM Trans. Program. Lang. Syst. 15(1), 36–72 (1993)
107. Cleaveland, R., Sims, S.: The Concurrency Workbench of North Carolina User's manual (version 1.0) (1996)

108. Cleaveland, R., Sims, S.: The NCSU Concurrency Workbench. In: Alur, R., Henzinger, T.A. (eds.) CAV 1996. LNCS, vol. 1102, pp. 394–397. Springer, Heidelberg (1996). https://doi.org/10.1007/3-540-61474-5_87

109. Cleaveland, R., Sims, S.: Generic tools for verifying concurrent systems. In: Proceedings of the 1998 ARO/ONR/NSF/DARPA Monterey Workshop on Engineering Automation for Computer Based Systems, pp. 38–46 (1999)

110. Cleaveland, R., Sims, S.: Generic tools for verifying concurrent systems. Sci. Comput. Program. 42(1), 39–47 (2002)

111. Cornejo, M.A., Garavel, H., Mateescu, R., de Palma, N.: Specification and verification of a dynamic reconfiguration protocol for agent-based applications. In: Laurentowski, A., Kosinski, J., Mossurska, Z., Ruchala, R. (eds.) Proceedings of the 3rd IFIP WG 6.1 International Working Conference on Distributed Applications and Interoperable Systems (DAIS 2001), Krakow, Poland, pp. 229–242. Kluwer Academic Publishers, September 2001. Full version available as INRIA Research Report RR-4222

112. Coste, N.: Vers la prédiction de performance de modèles compositionnels dans les architectures GALS. Ph.D. thesis, Université de Grenoble, June 2010

113. Coste, N., Garavel, H., Hermanns, H., Lang, F., Mateescu, R., Serwe, W.: Ten years of performance evaluation for concurrent systems using CADP. In: Margaria, T., Steffen, B. (eds.) ISoLA 2010. LNCS, vol. 6416, pp. 128–142. Springer, Heidelberg (2010). https://doi.org/10.1007/978-3-642-16561-0_18

114. Coste, N., Hermanns, H., Lantreibecq, E., Serwe, W.: Towards performance prediction of compositional models in industrial GALS designs. In: Bouajjani, A., Maler, O. (eds.) CAV 2009. LNCS, vol. 5643, pp. 204–218. Springer, Heidelberg (2009). https://doi.org/10.1007/978-3-642-02658-4_18

115. Cranen, S., et al.: An overview of the mCRL2 toolset and its recent advances. In: Piterman, N., Smolka, S.A. (eds.) TACAS 2013. LNCS, vol. 7795, pp. 199–213. Springer, Heidelberg (2013). https://doi.org/10.1007/978-3-642-36742-7_15

116. Crouzen, P., Hermanns, H., Zhang, L.: On the minimisation of acyclic models. In: van Breugel, F., Chechik, M. (eds.) CONCUR 2008. LNCS, vol. 5201, pp. 295–309. Springer, Heidelberg (2008). https://doi.org/10.1007/978-3-540-85361-9_25

117. Crouzen, P., Lang, F.: Smart reduction. In: Giannakopoulou, D., Orejas, F. (eds.) FASE 2011. LNCS, vol. 6603, pp. 111–126. Springer, Heidelberg (2011). https://doi.org/10.1007/978-3-642-19811-3_9

118. Davies, J.W., Schneider, S.A.: A brief history of timed CSP. Theor. Comput. Sci. 138(2), 243–271 (1995)

119. Daws, C., Olivero, A., Tripakis, S., Yovine, S.: The tool KRONOS. In: Alur, R., Henzinger, T.A., Sontag, E.D. (eds.) HS 1995. LNCS, vol. 1066, pp. 208–219. Springer, Heidelberg (1996). https://doi.org/10.1007/BFb0020947

120. De Nicola, R., Hennessy, M.C.B.: Testing equivalences for processes. Theor. Comput. Sci. 34, 83–133 (1984)

121. De Nicola, R., Inverardi, P., Nesi, M.: Equational reasoning about LOTOS specifications: a rewriting approach. In: Proceedings of the 6th International Workshop on Software Specification and Design, pp. 148–155 (1991)

122. De Nicola, R., Vaandrager, F.: Action versus state based logics for transition systems. In: Guessarian, I. (ed.) LITP 1990. LNCS, vol. 469, pp. 407–419. Springer, Heidelberg (1990). https://doi.org/10.1007/3-540-53479-2_17

123. De Nicola, R., Fantechi, A., Gnesi, S., Larosa, S., Ristori, G.: Verifying hardware components with JACK. In: Camurati, P.E., Eveking, H. (eds.) CHARME 1995.

LNCS, vol. 987, pp. 246–260. Springer, Heidelberg (1995). https://doi.org/10.1007/3-540-60385-9_15

124. De Nicola, R., Inverardi, P., Nesi, M.: Using the axiomatic presentation of behavioural equivalences for manipulating CCS specifications. In: Sifakis, J. (ed.) CAV 1989. LNCS, vol. 407, pp. 54–67. Springer, Heidelberg (1990). https://doi.org/10.1007/3-540-52148-8_5

125. De Nicola, R., Vaandrager, F.W.: Three logics for branching bisimulation (extended abstract). In: Proceedings of the 4th Annual Symposium on Logic in Computer Science (LICS 1989), Pacific Grove, California, USA, pp. 118–129. IEEE Computer Society (1990)

126. De Nicola, R., Vaandrager, F.W.: Three logics for branching bisimulation. J. ACM 42(2), 458–487 (1995)

127. Dehnert, C., Katoen, J.-P., Parker, D.: SMT-based bisimulation minimisation of Markov models. In: Giacobazzi, R., Berdine, J., Mastroeni, I. (eds.) VMCAI 2013. LNCS, vol. 7737, pp. 28–47. Springer, Heidelberg (2013). https://doi.org/10.1007/978-3-642-35873-9_5

128. Derisavi, S.: A symbolic algorithm for optimal Markov chain lumping. In: Grumberg, O., Huth, M. (eds.) TACAS 2007. LNCS, vol. 4424, pp. 139–154. Springer, Heidelberg (2007). https://doi.org/10.1007/978-3-540-71209-1_13

129. Derisavi, S.: Signature-based symbolic algorithm for optimal Markov chain lumping. In: Proceedings of the 4th International Conference on the Quantitative Evaluation of Systems (QEST 2007), Edinburgh, Scotland, UK, pp. 141–150. IEEE Computer Society, September 2007

130. van Dijk, T., van de Pol, J.: Multi-core symbolic bisimulation minimisation. In: Chechik, M., Raskin, J.-F. (eds.) TACAS 2016. LNCS, vol. 9636, pp. 332–348. Springer, Heidelberg (2016). https://doi.org/10.1007/978-3-662-49674-9_19

131. van Dijk, T., van de Pol, J.: SYLVAN: multi-core framework for decision diagrams. Int. J. Softw. Tools Technol. Transf. 19(6), 675–696 (2017)

132. van Dijk, T., van de Pol, J.: Multi-core decision diagrams. In: Hamadi, Y., Sais, L. (eds.) Handbook of Parallel Constraint Reasoning, pp. 509–545. Springer, Cham (2018). https://doi.org/10.1007/978-3-319-63516-3_13

133. van Dijk, T., van de Pol, J.: Multi-core symbolic bisimulation minimisation. Int. J. Softw. Tools Technol. Transf. 20(2), 157–177 (2018)

134. Doumenc, G., Madelaine, E.: Une traduction de PLOTOS en MEIJE. Research Report RR-0938, INRIA (1988)

135. Doumenc, G., Madelaine, E., De Simone, R.: Proving Process Calculi Translations in ECRINS: The pureLOTOS -> MEIJE Example. Research Report RR-1192, INRIA (1990)

136. Dovier, A., Gentilini, R., Piazza, C., Policriti, A.: Rank-based symbolic bisimulation (and model checking). Electron. Notes Theor. Comput. Sci. 67, 166–183 (2002)

137. Dovier, A., Piazza, C., Policriti, A.: A fast bisimulation algorithm. In: Berry, G., Comon, H., Finkel, A. (eds.) CAV 2001. LNCS, vol. 2102, pp. 79–90. Springer, Heidelberg (2001). https://doi.org/10.1007/3-540-44585-4_8

138. Dovier, A., Piazza, C., Policriti, A.: An efficient algorithm for computing bisimulation equivalence. Theor. Comput. Sci. 311(1–3), 221–256 (2004)

139. Eisentraut, C., Hermanns, H., Zhang, L.: Concurrency and composition in a stochastic world. In: Gastin, P., Laroussinie, F. (eds.) CONCUR 2010. LNCS, vol. 6269, pp. 21–39. Springer, Heidelberg (2010). https://doi.org/10.1007/978-3-642-15375-4_3

140. Enders, R., Filkorn, T., Taubner, D.: Generating BDDs for symbolic model checking in CCS. In: Larsen, K.G., Skou, A. (eds.) CAV 1991. LNCS, vol. 575, pp. 203–213. Springer, Heidelberg (1992). https://doi.org/10.1007/3-540-55179-4_20

141. Erdogmus, H.: Verifying semantic relations in SPIN. In: Proceedings of the 1st SPIN Workshop (Montréal, Québec) (1995)

142. Erdogmus, H., de B. Johnston, R., Cleary, C.: Formal verification based on relation checking in SPIN: a case study. In: Proceedings of the 1st Workshop on Formal Methods in Software Practice (San Diego, California, USA) (1995)

143. Ernberg, P., Fredlund, L., Jonsson, B.: Specification and Validation of a Simple Overtaking Protocol using LOTOS. T 90006, Swedish Institute of Computer Science, Kista, Sweden, October 1990

144. Ernberg, P., Fredlund, L.A.: Identifying Some Bottlenecks of the Concurrency Workbench. Research Report T90/9002, SICS (1990)

145. Ernberg, P., Hovander, T., Monfort, F.: Specification and implementation of an ISDN telephone system using LOTOS. In: Diaz, M., Groz, R. (eds.) Proceedings of the IFIP TC6/WG6.1 5th International Conference on Formal Description Techniques for Distributed Systems and Communication Protocols (FORTE 1992), Perros-Guirec, France. IFIP Transactions, vol. C-10, pp. 171–186. North-Holland, October 1992

146. Estenfeld, K., Schneider, H.A., Taubner, D., Tidén, E.: Computer aided verification of parallel processes. In: Pfitzmann, A., Raubold, E. (eds.) VIS 1991, vol. 271, pp. 208–226. Springer, Heidelberg (1991). https://doi.org/10.1007/978-3-642-76562-9_13

147. Fernandez, J.C.: ALDEBARAN: Un système de vérification par réduction de processus communicants. Ph.D. thesis, Université Joseph Fourier (Grenoble), May 1988

148. Fernandez, J.C.: ALDEBARAN: A Tool for Verification of Communicating Processes. Rapport SPECTRE C14, Laboratoire de Génie Informatique - Institut IMAG, Grenoble, September 1989

149. Fernandez, J.C.: ALDEBARAN: User's Manual. Laboratoire de Génie Informatique – Institut IMAG, Grenoble, January 1989

150. Fernandez, J.C.: An implementation of an efficient algorithm for bisimulation equivalence. Sci. Comput. Program. **13**(2–3), 219–236 (1990)

151. Fernandez, J.-C., Garavel, H., Kerbrat, A., Mounier, L., Mateescu, R., Sighireanu, M.: CADP (CÆSAR/ALDEBARAN Development Package): a protocol validation and verification toolbox. In: Alur, R., Henzinger, T.A. (eds.) CAV 1996. LNCS, vol. 1102, pp. 437–440. Springer, Heidelberg (1996). https://doi.org/10.1007/3-540-61474-5_97

152. Fernandez, J.C., Garavel, H., Mounier, L., Rasse, A., Rodríguez, C., Sifakis, J.: A toolbox for the verification of LOTOS programs. In: Clarke, L.A. (ed.) Proceedings of the 14th International Conference on Software Engineering (ICSE 2014), Melbourne, Australia, pp. 246–259. ACM, May 1992

153. Fernandez, J.C., Kerbrat, A., Mounier, L.: Symbolic equivalence checking. In: Courcoubetis, C. (ed.) CAV 1993. LNCS, vol. 697, pp. 85–96. Springer, Heidelberg (1993). https://doi.org/10.1007/3-540-56922-7_8

154. Fernandez, J.C., Mounier, L.: Verifying bisimulations "On the Fly". In: Quemada, J., Manas, J., Vázquez, E. (eds.) Proceedings of the 3rd International Conference on Formal Description Techniques (FORTE 1990), Madrid, Spain. North-Holland, November 1990

155. Fernandez, J.C., Mounier, L.: A tool set for deciding behavioral equivalences. In: Proceedings of CONCUR 1991, Amsterdam, The Netherlands, August 1991

156. Fernandez, J.-C., Mounier, L.: "On the fly" verification of behavioural equivalences and preorders. In: Larsen, K.G., Skou, A. (eds.) CAV 1991. LNCS, vol. 575, pp. 181–191. Springer, Heidelberg (1992). https://doi.org/10.1007/3-540-55179-4_18

157. Ferrari, G., Modoni, G., Quaglia, P.: Towards a semantic-based verification environment for the π-calculus. In: De Santis, A. (ed.) Proceedings of the 5th Italian Conference on Theoretical Computer Science (1995)

158. Février, A., Najm, E., Prost, N., Robles, F.: Verifying an ATM switch with Formal Methods (1994). http://cadp.inria.fr/ftp/publications/others/Fevrier-Najm-Prost-Robles-94.pdf

159. Fisler, K., Vardi, M.Y.: Bisimulation minimization in an automata-theoretic verification framework. In: Gopalakrishnan, G., Windley, P. (eds.) FMCAD 1998. LNCS, vol. 1522, pp. 115–132. Springer, Heidelberg (1998). https://doi.org/10.1007/3-540-49519-3_9

160. Fisler, K., Vardi, M.Y.: Bisimulation and model checking. In: Pierre, L., Kropf, T. (eds.) CHARME 1999. LNCS, vol. 1703, pp. 338–342. Springer, Heidelberg (1999). https://doi.org/10.1007/3-540-48153-2_29

161. Fisler, K., Vardi, M.Y.: Bisimulation minimization and symbolic model checking. Formal Methods Syst. Des. **21**(1), 39–78 (2002)

162. Focardi, R., Gorrieri, R.: The compositional security checker: a tool for the verification of information flow security properties. IEEE Trans. Softw. Eng. **23**(9), 550–571 (1997)

163. Franceschinis, G., Ribaudo, M.: Symmetric and behavioural aggregation in a simple protocol example. In: Proceedings of the 6th International Workshop on Process Algebra and Performance Modelling (PAPM 1998), Nice, France (1998)

164. Francesco, N.D., Lettieri, G., Santone, A., Vaglini, G.: GreASE: a tool for efficient "Nonequivalence" checking. ACM Trans. Softw. Eng. Methodol. **23**(3), 24:1–24:26 (2014)

165. Fredlund, L., Orava, F.: An experiment in formalizing and analysing railyard configurations. In: Brezočnik, Z., Kapus, T. (eds.) Proceedings of COST 247 International Workshop on Applied Formal Methods in System Design (Maribor, Slovenia), pp. 51–60. University of Maribor, Slovenia, June 1996

166. Fredlund, L.A.: The Timing and Probability Workbench: A tool for Analysing Timed Processes (1994). CiteSeer

167. Fredlund, L.A., Orava, F.: Modelling dynamic communication structures in LOTOS. In: Parker, K.R., Rose, G.A. (eds.) Proceedings of the IFIP TC6/WG6.1 4th International Conference on Formal Description Techniques for Distributed Systems and Communication Protocols (FORTE 1991), Sydney, Australia. IFIP Transactions, vol. C-2, pp. 185–200. North-Holland, November 1991

168. de Frutos Escrig, D., Keiren, J.J.A., Willemse, T.A.C.: Branching bisimulation games. In: Albert, E., Lanese, I. (eds.) FORTE 2016. LNCS, vol. 9688, pp. 142–157. Springer, Cham (2016). https://doi.org/10.1007/978-3-319-39570-8_10

169. Fuhrmann, K., Hiemer, J.: Formal verification of statemate-statecharts. In: Berghammer, R., Lakhnech, Y. (eds.) Tool Support for System Specification, Development and Verification. ACS, pp. 92–107. Springer, Heidelberg (1998). https://doi.org/10.1007/978-3-7091-6355-9_7

170. Garavel, H.: Compilation et vérification de programmes LOTOS. Ph.D. thesis, Université Joseph Fourier (Grenoble), November 1989

171. Garavel, H.: An overview of the Eucalyptus toolbox. In: Brezočnik, Z., Kapus, T. (eds.) Proceedings of the COST 247 International Workshop on Applied Formal

Methods in System Design (Maribor, Slovenia), pp. 76–88. University of Maribor, Slovenia, June 1996

172. Garavel, H.: OPEN/CÆSAR: an open software architecture for verification, simulation, and testing. In: Steffen, B. (ed.) TACAS 1998. LNCS, vol. 1384, pp. 68–84. Springer, Heidelberg (1998). https://doi.org/10.1007/BFb0054165

173. Garavel, H., Hermanns, H.: On combining functional verification and performance evaluation using CADP. In: Eriksson, L.-H., Lindsay, P.A. (eds.) FME 2002. LNCS, vol. 2391, pp. 410–429. Springer, Heidelberg (2002). https://doi.org/10. 1007/3-540-45614-7_23 Full version available as INRIA Research Report 4492

174. Garavel, H., Jorgensen, M., Mateescu, R., Pecheur, C., Sighireanu, M., Vivien, B.: CADP'97 - status, applications and perspectives. In: Lovrek, I. (ed.) Proceedings of the 2nd COST 247 International Workshop on Applied Formal Methods in System Design (Zagreb, Croatia), June 1997

175. Garavel, H., Lang, F.: SVL: a scripting language for compositional verification. In: Kim, M., Chin, B., Kang, S., Lee, D. (eds.) Proceedings of the 21st IFIP WG 6.1 International Conference on Formal Techniques for Networked and Distributed Systems (FORTE 2001), Cheju Island, Korea, pp. 377–392. Kluwer Academic Publishers, August 2001. Full version available as INRIA Research Report RR-4223

176. Garavel, H., Lang, F., Mateescu, R.: An Overview of CADP 2001. European Association for Software Science and Technology (EASST) Newsletter 4, 13–24 (Aug 2002), also available as INRIA Technical Report RT-0254, December 2001

177. Garavel, H., Lang, F., Mateescu, R.: Compositional verification of asynchronous concurrent systems using CADP. Acta Informatica 52(4), 337–392 (2015)

178. Garavel, H., Mateescu, R., Lang, F., Serwe, W.: CADP 2006: a toolbox for the construction and analysis of distributed processes. In: Damm, W., Hermanns, H. (eds.) CAV 2007. LNCS, vol. 4590, pp. 158–163. Springer, Heidelberg (2007). https://doi.org/10.1007/978-3-540-73368-3_18

179. Garavel, H., Lang, F., Mateescu, R., Serwe, W.: CADP 2010: a toolbox for the construction and analysis of distributed processes. In: Abdulla, P.A., Leino, K.R.M. (eds.) TACAS 2011. LNCS, vol. 6605, pp. 372–387. Springer, Heidelberg (2011). https://doi.org/10.1007/978-3-642-19835-9_33

180. Garavel, H., Lang, F., Mateescu, R., Serwe, W.: CADP 2011: a toolbox for the construction and analysis of distributed processes. Int. J. Softw. Tools Technol. Transfer (STTT) 15(2), 89–107 (2013)

181. Garavel, H., Lang, F., Mounier, L.: Compositional verification in action. In: Howar, F., Barnat, J. (eds.) FMICS 2018. LNCS, vol. 11119, pp. 189–210. Springer, Cham (2018). https://doi.org/10.1007/978-3-030-00244-2_13

182. Garavel, H., Lang, F., Serwe, W.: From LOTOS to LNT. In: Katoen, J.-P., Langerak, R., Rensink, A. (eds.) ModelEd, TestEd, TrustEd. LNCS, vol. 10500, pp. 3–26. Springer, Cham (2017). https://doi.org/10.1007/978-3-319-68270-9_1

183. Garavel, H., Mounier, L.: Specification and verification of various distributed leader election algorithms for unidirectional ring networks. Sci. Comput. Program. 29(1–2), 171–197 (1997). Special issue on Industrially Relevant Applications of Formal Analysis Techniques. Full version available as INRIA Research Report RR-2986

184. Garavel, H., Sifakis, J.: Compilation and verification of LOTOS specifications. In: Logrippo, L., Probert, R.L., Ural, H. (eds.) Proceedings of the 10th IFIP International Symposium on Protocol Specification, Testing and Verification (PSTV 1990), Ottawa, Canada, pp. 379–394. North-Holland, June 1990

185. Germeau, F., Leduc, G.: Model-based design and verification of security protocols using LOTOS. In: Orman, H., Meadows, C. (eds.) Proceedings of the DIMACS Workshop on Design and Formal Verification of Security Protocols (Rutgers University, New Jersey, USA), September 1997

186. Gerth, R., Kuiper, R., Peled, D.A., Penczek, W.: A partial order approach to branching time logic model checking. Inf. Comput. **150**(2), 132–152 (1999)

187. Gilmore, S., Hillston, J.: The PEPA workbench: a tool to support a process algebra-based approach to performance modelling. In: Haring, G., Kotsis, G. (eds.) TOOLS 1994. LNCS, vol. 794, pp. 353–368. Springer, Heidelberg (1994). https://doi.org/10.1007/3-540-58021-2_20

188. Gilmore, S., Hillston, J., Kloul, L.: PEPA nets. In: Calzarossa, M.C., Gelenbe, E. (eds.) MASCOTS 2003. LNCS, vol. 2965, pp. 311–335. Springer, Heidelberg (2004). https://doi.org/10.1007/978-3-540-24663-3_15

189. Gilmore, S., Hillston, J., Kloul, L., Ribaudo, M.: PEPA nets: a structured performance modelling formalism. Perform. Eval. **54**(2), 79–104 (2003)

190. van Glabbeek, R.J.: The linear time - branching time spectrum I. In: Bergstra, J.A., Ponse, A., Smolka, S.A. (eds.) Handbook of Process Algebra, pp. 3–99. North-Holland/Elsevier (2001)

191. van Glabbeek, R.J., Weijland, W.P.: Branching-time and abstraction in bisimulation semantics (extended abstract). CS R8911, Centrum voor Wiskunde en Informatica, Amsterdam (1989). Also in Proceedings of IFIP 11th World Computer Congress, San Francisco (1989)

192. van Glabbeek, R.J., Weijland, W.P.: Branching time and abstraction in bisimulation semantics. J. ACM **43**(3), 555–600 (1996)

193. Gnesi, S., Madelaine, E., Ristori, G.: An exercise in protocol verification, pp. 255–279. Kluwer (1995)

194. Godskesen, J.C., Larsen, K.G., Zeeberg, M.: TAV (tools for automatic verification). In: Sifakis, J. (ed.) Proceedings of the 1st International Workshop on Automatic Verification Methods for Finite State Systems (CAV 1989), Grenoble, France, June 1989. Article present only in the participants proceedings, not in the LNCS 407 post-proceedings volume

195. Godskesen, J.C., Larsen, K.G.: User's Manual for Epsilon (Draft), available from CiteSeer

196. Godskesen, J.C., Larsen, K.G., Skou, A.: Automatic verification of real-time systems using Epsilon. In: Vuong, S.T., Chanson, S.T. (eds.) Protocol Specification, Testing and Verification XIV, Proceedings of the 14th IFIP WG6.1 International Symposium on Protocol Specification, Testing and Verification, Vancouver, BC, Canada. IFIP Conference Proceedings, vol. 1, pp. 323–330. Chapman & Hall (1994)

197. Graf, S., Steffen, B.: Compositional minimization of finite state systems. In: Clarke, E.M., Kurshan, R.P. (eds.) CAV 1990. LNCS, vol. 531, pp. 186–196. Springer, Heidelberg (1991). https://doi.org/10.1007/BFb0023732

198. Graf, S., Steffen, B., Lüttgen, G.: Compositional minimization of finite state systems using interface specifications. Formal Aspects Comput. **8**(5), 607–616 (1996)

199. Griffault, A., Vincent, A.: The Mec 5 model-checker. In: Alur, R., Peled, D.A. (eds.) CAV 2004. LNCS, vol. 3114, pp. 488–491. Springer, Heidelberg (2004). https://doi.org/10.1007/978-3-540-27813-9_43

200. Groote, J.: The Syntax and Semantics of Timed μCRL. Technical Report SEN-R9709, CWI, Amsterdam, The Netherlands, June 1997

201. Groote, J.F., Jansen, D.N., Keiren, J.J.A., Wijs, A.: An $O(m \log n)$ algorithm for computing stuttering equivalence and branching bisimulation. ACM Trans. Comput. Log. **18**(2), 13:1–13:34 (2017)

202. Groote, J.F., Martens, J., de Vink, E.P.: Bisimulation by partitioning is $\Omega((m + n) \log n)$. In: Haddad, S., Varacca, D. (eds.) 32nd International Conference on Concurrency Theory (CONCUR 2021), Virtual Conference. LIPIcs, vol. 203, pp. 31:1–31:16. Schloss Dagstuhl - Leibniz-Zentrum für Informatik, August 2021

203. Groote, J.F., Mathijssen, A., van Weerdenburg, M., Usenko, Y.S.: From μCRL to mCRL2: motivation and outline. Electron. Notes Theor. Comput. Sci. **162**, 191–196 (2006)

204. Groote, J.F., van de Pol, J.: A bounded retransmission protocol for large data packets. In: Wirsing, M., Nivat, M. (eds.) AMAST 1996. LNCS, vol. 1101, pp. 536–550. Springer, Heidelberg (1996). https://doi.org/10.1007/BFb0014338

205. Groote, J.F., Sellink, M.P.A.: Confluence for process verification. Theor. Comput. Sci. **170**(1–2), 47–81 (1996)

206. Groote, J., Vaandrager, F.: An Efficient Algorithm for Branching Bisimulation and Stuttering Equivalence. CS-R 9001, Centrum voor Wiskunde en Informatica, Amsterdam, January 1990

207. Groote, J.F., Vaandrager, F.: An efficient algorithm for branching bisimulation and stuttering equivalence. In: Paterson, M.S. (ed.) ICALP 1990. LNCS, vol. 443, pp. 626–638. Springer, Heidelberg (1990). https://doi.org/10.1007/BFb0032063

208. Groote, J.F., Vaandrager, F.W.: Structured operational semantics and bisimulation as a congruence. Inf. Comput. **100**(2), 202–260 (1992)

209. Groote, J.F., Verduzco, J.R., de Vink, E.P.: An efficient algorithm to determine probabilistic bisimulation. Algorithms **11**(9), 131 (2018)

210. Groote, J.F., Wijs, A.: An $O(m \log n)$ algorithm for stuttering equivalence and branching bisimulation. In: Chechik, M., Raskin, J.-F. (eds.) TACAS 2016. LNCS, vol. 9636, pp. 607–624. Springer, Heidelberg (2016). https://doi.org/10.1007/978-3-662-49674-9_40

211. Groote, J.F., Wijs, A.: An $O(m \log n)$ algorithm for stuttering equivalence and branching bisimulation. CoRR abs/1601.01478 (2016)

212. Halbwachs, N.: Using Auto for Esterel program verification. In: Halbwachs, N. (ed.) Synchronous Programming of Reactive Systems, vol. 215, pp. 149–155. Springer, Boston (1993). https://doi.org/10.1007/978-1-4757-2231-4_10

213. Hansson, H.A.: Time and probability in formal design of distributed systems. Ph.d. thesis, University Uppsala, Sweden (1991)

214. Hansson, H.A.: Time and Probability in Formal Design of Distributed Systems. Elsevier (1994)

215. Hashemi, V., Hermanns, H., Song, L., Subramani, K., Turrini, A., Wojciechowski, P.: Compositional bisimulation minimization for interval Markov decision processes. In: Dediu, A.-H., Janoušek, J., Martín-Vide, C., Truthe, B. (eds.) LATA 2016. LNCS, vol. 9618, pp. 114–126. Springer, Cham (2016). https://doi.org/10.1007/978-3-319-30000-9_9

216. Hashemi, V., Hermanns, H., Turrini, A.: On the efficiency of deciding probabilistic automata weak bisimulation. Electron. Commun. Eur. Assoc. Softw. Sci. Technol. **66** (2013)

217. Hashemi, V., Turrini, A., Hahn, E.M., Hermanns, H., Elbassioni, K.: Polynomial-time alternating probabilistic bisimulation for interval MDPs. In: Larsen, K.G., Sokolsky, O., Wang, J. (eds.) SETTA 2017. LNCS, vol. 10606, pp. 25–41. Springer, Cham (2017). https://doi.org/10.1007/978-3-319-69483-2_2

218. He, J., Turner, K.J.: Modelling and Verifying Synchronous Circuits in DILL. Technical Report CSM-152, Department of Computing Science and Mathematics, University of Stirling (1999)

219. He, J., Turner, K.J.: Protocol-inspired hardware testing. In: Csopaki, G., Dibuz, S., Tarnay, K. (eds.) Proceedings of the IFIP 12th International Workshop on Testing of Communicating Systems (IWTCS 1999), Budapest, Hungary, pp. 131–147. Kluwer Academic, September 1999

220. He, J., Turner, K.J.: Specification and verification of synchronous hardware using LOTOS. In: Wu, J., Chanson, S.T., Gao, Q. (eds.) Proceedings of the IFIP Joint International Conference on Formal Description Techniques for Distributed Systems and Communication Protocols and Protocol Specification, Testing, and Verification (FORTE/PSTV 1999), Beijing, China, pp. 295–312. Kluwer Academic Publishers, October 1999

221. Heisel, M., Lévy, N.: Using LOTOS patterns to characterize architectural styles. In: Bidoit, M., Dauchet, M. (eds.) CAAP 1997. LNCS, vol. 1214, pp. 818–832. Springer, Heidelberg (1997). https://doi.org/10.1007/BFb0030643

222. Hellgren, V.: Performance Evaluation of Four Verification Tools: ALDEBARAN, BIDMIN, Concurrency Workbench and HOGGAR. Technical report, University of Helsinki, Department of Computer Science, p. 4, August 1995

223. Hellgren, V.: User's Manual: BIDMIN Version 1.2. Technical report, University of Helsinki, Department of Computer Science, p. 10, August 1995

224. Hennessy, M., Lin, H.: Symbolic bisimulations. Theor. Comput. Sci. **138**(2), 353–389 (1995)

225. Henzinger, M.R., Henzinger, T.A., Kopke, P.W.: Computing simulations on finite and infinite graphs. In: 36th Annual Symposium on Foundations of Computer Science, Milwaukee, Wisconsin, USA, 23–25 October 1995, pp. 453–462. IEEE Computer Society (1995)

226. Henzinger, T.A.: Hybrid automata with finite bisimulations. In: Fülöp, Z., Gécseg, F. (eds.) ICALP 1995. LNCS, vol. 944, pp. 324–335. Springer, Heidelberg (1995). https://doi.org/10.1007/3-540-60084-1_85

227. Herbert, M.: Evaluation de performances et spécification formelle sur un réseau de stations haut débit. Master's thesis, Institut National des Télécommunications, Laboratoire pour les hautes performances en calcul (Lyon, France), December 1997

228. Hermanns, H.: Interactive Markov Chains: The Quest for Quantified Quality. LNCS, vol. 2428. Springer, Heidelberg (2002). https://doi.org/10.1007/3-540-45804-2

229. Hermanns, H., Herzog, U., Klehmet, U., Mertsiotakis, V., Siegle, M.: Compositional performance modelling with the TIPPtool. In: Puigjaner, R., Savino, N.N., Serra, B. (eds.) TOOLS 1998. LNCS, vol. 1469, pp. 51–62. Springer, Heidelberg (1998). https://doi.org/10.1007/3-540-68061-6_5

230. Hermanns, H., Herzog, U., Klehmet, U., Mertsiotakis, V., Siegle, M.: Compositional performance modelling with the TIPPtool. Perform. Eval. **39**(1–4), 5–35 (2000)

231. Hermanns, H., Herzog, U., Mertsiotakis, V.: Stochastic process algebras as a tool for performance and dependability modelling. In: Proceedings of the 1995 International Computer Performance and Dependability Symposium, pp. 102–111. IEEE (1995)

232. Hermanns, H., Herzog, U., Mertsiotakis, V.: Stochastic process algebras - between LOTOS and Markov chains. Comput. Netw. **30**(9–10), 901–924 (1998)

233. Hermanns, H., Joubert, C.: A set of performance and dependability analysis components for CADP. In: Garavel, H., Hatcliff, J. (eds.) TACAS 2003. LNCS, vol. 2619, pp. 425–430. Springer, Heidelberg (2003). https://doi.org/10.1007/3-540-36577-X_30

234. Hermanns, H., Katoen, J.P.: Automated compositional Markov chain generation for a plain-old telephone system. Sci. Comput. Program. **36**, 97–127 (2000)

235. Hermanns, H., Katoen, J.-P.: The how and why of interactive Markov chains. In: de Boer, F.S., Bonsangue, M.M., Hallerstede, S., Leuschel, M. (eds.) FMCO 2009. LNCS, vol. 6286, pp. 311–337. Springer, Heidelberg (2010). https://doi.org/10.1007/978-3-642-17071-3_16

236. Hermanns, H., Mertsiotakis, V., Rettelbach, M.: Performance analysis of distributed systems using TIPP—a case study. In: Proceedings of the 10th U.K. Performance Engineering Workshop for Computer and Telecommunication Systems, Edinburgh, Scotland, United Kingdom. Edinburgh University Press, September 1994

237. Hermanns, H., Mertsiotakis, V., Siegle, M.: TIPPtool: compositional specification and analysis of Markovian performance models. In: Halbwachs, N., Peled, D. (eds.) CAV 1999. LNCS, vol. 1633, pp. 487–490. Springer, Heidelberg (1999). https://doi.org/10.1007/3-540-48683-6_42

238. Hermanns, H., Rettelbach, M.: Syntax, semantics, equivalences, and axioms for MTIPP. In: Herzog, U., Rettelbach, M. (eds.) Proceedings of the 2nd Workshop on Process Algebras and Performance Modelling (PAPM 1994), Erlangen, Germany. Lecture Notes in Computer Science, vol. 1601, pp. 71–88. University of Erlangen-Nürnberg, Germany, July 1994

239. Hermanns, H., Rettelbach, M., Weiss, T.: Formal characterisation of immediate actions in SPA with nondeterministic branching. Comput. J. **38**(7), 530–541 (1995)

240. Hermanns, H., Siegle, M.: Bisimulation algorithms for stochastic process algebras and their BDD-based implementation. In: Katoen, J.-P. (ed.) ARTS 1999. LNCS, vol. 1601, pp. 244–264. Springer, Heidelberg (1999). https://doi.org/10.1007/3-540-48778-6_15

241. Hermanns, H., Siegle, M.: Symbolic minimisation of stochastic process algebra models. In: Spies, K., Schätz, B. (eds.) Formale Beschreibungstechniken für verteilte Systeme, 9. GI/ITG-Fachgespräch, München, Juni 1999, pp. 73–82. Herbert Utz Verlag (1999)

242. Hermanns, H., Turrini, A.: Deciding probabilistic automata weak bisimulation in polynomial time. In: D'Souza, D., Kavitha, T., Radhakrishnan, J. (eds.) IARCS Annual Conference on Foundations of Software Technology and Theoretical Computer Science, FSTTCS 2012, Hyderabad, India, 15–17 December 2012. LIPIcs, vol. 18, pp. 435–447. Schloss Dagstuhl - Leibniz-Zentrum für Informatik (2012)

243. Hernalsteen, C.: A timed automaton model for ET-LOTOS verification. In: Togashi, A., Mizuno, T., Shiratori, N., Higashino, T. (eds.) Formal Description Techniques and Protocol Specification, Testing and Verification, FORTE X/PSTV XVII 1997, IFIP TC6 WG6.1 Joint International Conference on Formal Description Techniques for Distributed Systems and Communication Protocols (FORTE X) and Protocol Specification, Testing and Verification (PSTV XVII), Osaka, Japan, 18–21 November 1997. IFIP Conference Proceedings, vol. 107, pp. 193–204. Chapman & Hall (1997)

244. Herzog, U., Mertsiotakis, V.: Stochastic process algebras applied to failure modelling. In: Herzog, U., Rettelbach, M. (eds.) Proceedings of the 2nd Workshop

on Process Algebras and Performance Modelling, Regensberg, Germany. Arbeits-berichte des IMMD, Universität Erlangen-Nürnberg, Germany, July 1994

245. Hillerström, M.: Verification of CCS-processes. Master's thesis, Computer Science Department, Aalborg University (1987)

246. Hillston, J.: A compositional approach to performance modelling. Ph.D. thesis, University of Edinburgh, December 1994

247. Hillston, J., Hermanns, Herzog, U., Mertsiotakis, V., Rettelbach, M.: Stochastic Process Algebras: Integrating Qualitative and Quantitative Modelling. Technical report, IMMD VII, University of Erlangen-Nürnberg, Germany (1994)

248. Hong, C.-D., Lin, A.W., Majumdar, R., Rümmer, P.: Probabilistic bisimulation for parameterized systems. In: Dillig, I., Tasiran, S. (eds.) CAV 2019. LNCS, vol. 11561, pp. 455–474. Springer, Cham (2019). https://doi.org/10.1007/978-3-030-25540-4_27

249. Huhn, M., Niebert, P., Wehrheim, H.: Partial order reductions for bisimula-tion checking. In: Arvind, V., Ramanujam, R. (eds.) FSTTCS 1998. LNCS, vol. 1530, pp. 271–282. Springer, Heidelberg (1998). https://doi.org/10.1007/978-3-540-49382-2_26

250. Huth, M., Kwiatkowska, M.: On Probabilistic Model Checking (1996). CiteSeer

251. Huybers, R.: A parallel relation-based algorithm for symbolic bisimulation mini-mization. Ph.D. thesis, Leiden University (2018)

252. Huybers, R., Laarman, A.: A parallel relation-based algorithm for symbolic bisim-ulation minimization. In: Enea, C., Piskac, R. (eds.) VMCAI 2019. LNCS, vol. 11388, pp. 535–554. Springer, Cham (2019). https://doi.org/10.1007/978-3-030-11245-5_25

253. Ingólfsdóttir, A., Lin, H.: A symbolic approach to value-passing processes. In: Bergstra, J.A., Ponse, A., Smolka, S.A. (eds.) Handbook of Process Algebra, pp. 427–478. North-Holland/Elsevier (2001)

254. Inverardi, P., Priami, C., Yankelevich, D.: Verification of concurrent systems in SML. In: Proceedings of ACM SIGPLAN Workshop on ML and its Applications, pp. 169–174 (1992)

255. Inverardi, P., Priami, C.: Evaluation of tools for the analysis of communicating systems. Bull. Eur. Assoc. Theor. Comput. Sci. (EATCS) **45**, 158–185 (1991)

256. Inverardi, P., Priami, C.: Automatic verification of distributed systems: the pro-cess algebra approach. Formal Methods Syst. Des. **8**(1), 7–38 (1996)

257. Inverardi, P., Priami, C., Yankelevich, D.: Automatizing parametric reasoning on distributed concurrent systems. Formal Aspects Comput. **6**(6), 676–695 (1994). https://doi.org/10.1007/BF03259392

258. ISO/IEC: ESTELLE - A Formal Description Technique Based on an Extended State Transition Model. International Standard 9074, International Organization for Standardization - Information Processing Systems - Open Systems Intercon-nection, Geneva, September 1988

259. ISO/IEC: LOTOS - A Formal Description Technique Based on the Temporal Ordering of Observational Behaviour. International Standard 8807, International Organization for Standardization - Information Processing Systems - Open Sys-tems Interconnection, Geneva, September 1989

260. de Jacquier, A., Massart, T., Hernalsteen, C.: Vérification et correction d'un pro-tocole de contrôle aérien. Technical report 363, Université Libre de Bruxelles, May 1997

261. Jansen, D.N., Groote, J.F., Keiren, J.J.A., Wijs, A.: A simpler $O(m \log n)$ algorithm for branching bisimilarity on labelled transition systems. CoRR abs/1909.10824 (2019)

262. Jansen, D.N., Groote, J.F., Keiren, J.J.A., Wijs, A.: An $O(m \log n)$ algorithm for branching bisimilarity on labelled transition systems. In: Biere, A., Parker, D. (eds.) TACAS 2020. LNCS, vol. 12079, pp. 3–20. Springer, Cham (2020). https://doi.org/10.1007/978-3-030-45237-7_1

263. Jansen, D.N., Groote, J.F., Timmers, F., Yang, P.: A near-linear-time algorithm for weak bisimilarity on Markov chains. In: Konnov, I., Kovács, L. (eds.) 31st International Conference on Concurrency Theory, CONCUR 2020, Vienna, Austria, 1–4 September 2020 (Virtual Conference). LIPIcs, vol. 171, pp. 8:1–8:20. Schloss Dagstuhl - Leibniz-Zentrum für Informatik (2020)

264. Jard, C., Jéron, T., Fernandez, J.C., Mounier, L.: On-the-Fly Verification of Finite Transition Systems. Research Report 1861, INRIA (1993)

265. Jensen, C.T.: The Concurrency Workbench with priorities. In: Larsen, K.G., Skou, A. (eds.) CAV 1991. LNCS, vol. 575, pp. 147–157. Springer, Heidelberg (1992). https://doi.org/10.1007/3-540-55179-4_15

266. Johansson, M., Victor, B., Parrow, J.: Computing strong and weak bisimulations for psi-calculi. J. Log. Algebraic Methods Program. **81**(3), 162–180 (2012)

267. Kanellakis, P.C., Smolka, S.A.: CCS expressions, finite state processes, and three problems of equivalence. Inf. Comput. **86**(1), 43–68 (1990)

268. Kanellakis, P.C., Smolka, S.A.: CCS expressions, finite state processes, and three problems of equivalence. In: Probert, R.L., Lynch, N.A., Santoro, N. (eds.) Proceedings of the 2nd Annual ACM SIGACT-SIGOPS Symposium on Principles of Distributed Computing, Montreal, Quebec, Canada, pp. 228–240. ACM, August 1983

269. Kang, I., Lee, I., Kim, Y.S.: A state minimization technique for timed automata. In: Proceedings of International Workshop on Verification of Infinite State Systems INFINITY 1996 (1996)

270. Kant, G., Laarman, A., Meijer, J., van de Pol, J., Blom, S., van Dijk, T.: LTSmin: high-performance language-independent model checking. In: Baier, C., Tinelli, C. (eds.) TACAS 2015. LNCS, vol. 9035, pp. 692–707. Springer, Heidelberg (2015). https://doi.org/10.1007/978-3-662-46681-0_61

271. Katoen, J.-P., Kemna, T., Zapreev, I., Jansen, D.N.: Bisimulation minimisation mostly speeds up probabilistic model checking. In: Grumberg, O., Huth, M. (eds.) TACAS 2007. LNCS, vol. 4424, pp. 87–101. Springer, Heidelberg (2007). https://doi.org/10.1007/978-3-540-71209-1_9

272. Katoen, J., Zapreev, I.S., Hahn, E.M., Hermanns, H., Jansen, D.N.: The ins and outs of the probabilistic model checker MRMC. Perform. Eval. **68**(2), 90–104 (2011)

273. Keiren, J.J.A., Willemse, T.A.C.: Bisimulation minimisations for Boolean equation systems. In: Namjoshi, K., Zeller, A., Ziv, A. (eds.) HVC 2009. LNCS, vol. 6405, pp. 102–116. Springer, Heidelberg (2011). https://doi.org/10.1007/978-3-642-19237-1_12

274. Keller, R.M.: Formal verification of parallel programs. Commun. ACM **19**(7), 371–384 (1976)

275. Kemeny, J.G., Snell, J.L.: Finite Markov Chains. Undergraduate Texts in Mathematic, Springer, Heidelberg (1976)

276. Kerbrat, A.: Méthodes symboliques pour la vérification de processus communicants: Etude et mise en œuvre. Ph.D. thesis, Université Joseph Fourier (Grenoble), November 1994

277. Kerbrat, A.: Reachable state space analysis of LOTOS programs. In: Hogrefe, D., Leue, S. (eds.) Proceedings of the 7th International Conference on Formal

Description Techniques for Distributed Systems and Communication Protocols FORTE 1994 (Bern, Switzerland), October 1994

278. Kerbrat, A., Ben Atallah, S.: Formal specification of a framework for groupware development. In: FORTE 1995. IAICT, pp. 303–310. Springer, Boston (1996). https://doi.org/10.1007/978-0-387-34945-9_22

279. Kerbrat, A., Rodriguez, C., Lejeune, Y.: Interconnecting the ObjectGEODE and CÆSAR/ALDEBARAN toolsets. In: Cavalli, A., Sarma, A. (eds.) Proceedings of the 8th SDL Forum (Evry, France), September 1997

280. Kervinen, A., Valmari, A., Järnström, R.: Debugging a real-life protocol with CFFD-based verification tools. In: Gnesi, S., Ultes-Nitsche, U. (eds.) Proceedings of the 6th International Workshop on Formal Methods for Industrial Critical Systems (FMICS 2001), Paris, France, pp. 13–27. Université Paris 7 - LIAFA and INRIA Rhône-Alpes, July 2001

281. Klehmet, U., Mertsiotakis, V.: TIPPtool: Timed Processes and Performability Evaluation (User's Guide-Version 2.3) (1998). CiteSeer

282. König, B., Mika-Michalski, C., Schröder, L.: User Manual T-Beg: A Tool for Behavioural Equivalence Games (2002). http://www.ti.inf.uni-due.de/fileadmin/public/tools/tbeg/manual.pdf

283. Korver, H.P.: The Current State of Bisimulation Tools. P 9101, Centrum voor Wiskunde en Informatica, Amsterdam, January 1991

284. Korver, H.: Detecting feature interactions with Cæsar/Aldebaran. Sci. Comput. Program. **29**(1–2), 259–278 (1997). Special issue on Industrially Relevant Applications of Formal Analysis Techniques

285. Krämer, B.J., Völker, N., Lichtenecker, R., Kötter, H.: Deriving CORBA applications from formal specifications. J. Syst. Integr. **8**(2), 143–158 (1998)

286. Krimm, J.-P., Mounier, L.: Compositional state space generation from LOTOS programs. In: Brinksma, E. (ed.) TACAS 1997. LNCS, vol. 1217, pp. 239–258. Springer, Heidelberg (1997). https://doi.org/10.1007/BFb0035392 Extended version with proofs available as Research Report VERIMAG RR97-01

287. Kripke, S.: Semantical considerations on modal logic. Acta Philosophica Fennica **16**, 83–94 (1963)

288. Krishnan, P.: A case study in specifying and testing architectural features. Microprocess. Microsyst. **18**(3), 123–130 (1994)

289. Kristensen, C., Andersen, J., Skou, A.: Specification and automated verification of real-time behaviour: a case study. In: Proceedings of the 3rd IFAC/IFIP Workshop on Algorithms and Architectures for Real-Time Control (AARTC 1995), Ostend, Belgium (1995)

290. Kristensen, C., Andersen, J., Skou, A.: Specification and automated verification of real-time behaviour: a case study. Annu. Rev. Control. **20**, 55–70 (1996)

291. Kulakowski, K.: Concurrent bisimulation algorithm. CoRR abs/1311.7635 (2013)

292. Kwiatkowska, M., Norman, G., Parker, D.: Symmetry reduction for probabilistic model checking. In: Ball, T., Jones, R.B. (eds.) CAV 2006. LNCS, vol. 4144, pp. 234–248. Springer, Heidelberg (2006). https://doi.org/10.1007/11817963_23

293. Kwiatkowska, M., Norman, G., Parker, D.: PRISM 4.0: verification of probabilistic real-time systems. In: Gopalakrishnan, G., Qadeer, S. (eds.) CAV 2011. LNCS, vol. 6806, pp. 585–591. Springer, Heidelberg (2011). https://doi.org/10.1007/978-3-642-22110-1_47

294. Lang, F.: Compositional verification using SVL scripts. In: Katoen, J.-P., Stevens, P. (eds.) TACAS 2002. LNCS, vol. 2280, pp. 465–469. Springer, Heidelberg (2002). https://doi.org/10.1007/3-540-46002-0_33

295. Lang, F.: Exp.Open 2.0: a flexible tool integrating partial order, compositional, and on-the-fly verification methods. In: Romijn, J., Smith, G., van de Pol, J. (eds.) IFM 2005. LNCS, vol. 3771, pp. 70–88. Springer, Heidelberg (2005). https://doi.org/10.1007/11589976_6 Full version available as INRIA Research Report RR-5673

296. Lang, F.: Refined interfaces for compositional verification. In: Najm, E., Pradat-Peyre, J.-F., Viguié Donzeau-Gouge, V. (eds.) FORTE 2006. LNCS, vol. 4229, pp. 159–174. Springer, Heidelberg (2006). https://doi.org/10.1007/11888116_13 Full version available as INRIA Research Report RR-5996

297. Lang, F., Mateescu, R.: Partial order reductions using compositional confluence detection. In: Cavalcanti, A., Dams, D.R. (eds.) FM 2009. LNCS, vol. 5850, pp. 157–172. Springer, Heidelberg (2009). https://doi.org/10.1007/978-3-642-05089-3_11

298. Lang, F., Mateescu, R.: Partial model checking using networks of labelled transition systems and Boolean equation systems. Logical Methods Comput. Sci. 9(4), 1–32 (2013)

299. Lang, F., Mateescu, R., Mazzanti, F.: Compositional verification of concurrent systems by combining bisimulations. In: ter Beek, M.H., McIver, A., Oliveira, J.N. (eds.) FM 2019. LNCS, vol. 11800, pp. 196–213. Springer, Cham (2019). https://doi.org/10.1007/978-3-030-30942-8_13

300. Lang, F., Mateescu, R., Mazzanti, F.: Sharp congruences adequate with temporal logics combining weak and strong modalities. In: Biere, A., Parker, D. (eds.) TACAS 2020. LNCS, vol. 12079, pp. 57–76. Springer, Cham (2020). https://doi.org/10.1007/978-3-030-45237-7_4

301. Larsen, K.G., Pettersson, P., Yi, W.: Model-checking for real-time systems. In: Reichel, H. (ed.) FCT 1995. LNCS, vol. 965, pp. 62–88. Springer, Heidelberg (1995). https://doi.org/10.1007/3-540-60249-6_41

302. Larsen, K.G., Skou, A.: Bisimulation through probabilistic testing. In: Conference Record of the 16th Annual ACM Symposium on Principles of Programming Languages, Austin, Texas, USA, 11–13 January 1989, pp. 344–352. ACM Press (1989)

303. Larsen, K.G., Skou, A.: Bisimulation through probabilistic testing. Inf. Comput. 94(1), 1–28 (1991)

304. Leduc, G., Bonaventure, O., Koerner, E., Léonard, L., Pecheur, C., Zanetti, D.: Specification and verification of a TTP protocol for the conditional access to services. In: Proceedings of the 12th Jacques Cartier Workshop on "Formal Methods and their Applications: Telecommunications, VLSI and Real-Time Computerized Control System", Montréal, Canada, October 1996

305. Leduc, G.: Verification of two versions of the challenge handshake authentication protocol (CHAP). Ann. Telecommun. 55(1–2), 18–30 (2000)

306. Lee, D., Yannakakis, M.: Online minimization of transition systems (extended abstract). In: Kosaraju, S.R., Fellows, M., Wigderson, A., Ellis, J.A. (eds.) Proceedings of the 24th Annual ACM Symposium on Theory of Computing, Victoria, British Columbia, Canada, 4–6 May 1992, pp. 264–274. ACM (1992)

307. Léonard, L., Leduc, G.: An introduction to ET-LOTOS for the description of time-sensitive systems. Comput. Netw. ISDN Syst. 29(3), 271–292 (1997)

308. Léonard, L., Leduc, G.: A formal definition of time in LOTOS. Formal Aspects Comput. 10(3), 248–266 (1998). https://doi.org/10.1007/s001650050015

309. Li, Z., Chen, H.: Computing strong/weak bisimulation equivalences and observation congruence for value-passing processes. In: Cleaveland, W.R. (ed.) TACAS

1999. LNCS, vol. 1579, pp. 300–314. Springer, Heidelberg (1999). https://doi.org/10.1007/3-540-49059-0_21

310. Li, Z., Chen, H., Wang, B.: Symbolic transition graph and its early bisimulation checking algorithms for the π-calculus. Sci. China Ser. E: Technol. Sci. **42**(4), 342–353 (1999)

311. Lichtenecker, R., Gotthardt, K., Zalewski, J.: Automated verifications of communication protocols using CCS and BDDs. In: Rolim, J. (ed.) IPPS 1998. LNCS, vol. 1388, pp. 1057–1066. Springer, Heidelberg (1998). https://doi.org/10.1007/3-540-64359-1_771

312. Lin, H.: A verification tool for value-passing processes. In: Danthine, A.A.S., Leduc, G., Wolper, P. (eds.) Proceedings of the IFIP TC6/WG6.1 13th International Symposium on Protocol Specification, Testing and Verification (PSTV 1993), Liège, Belgium. IFIP Transactions, vol. C-16, pp. 79–92. North-Holland, May 1993

313. Lin, H.: Symbolic transition graph with assignment. In: Montanari, U., Sassone, V. (eds.) CONCUR 1996. LNCS, vol. 1119, pp. 50–65. Springer, Heidelberg (1996). https://doi.org/10.1007/3-540-61604-7_47

314. Lin, H.: Computing bisimulations for finite-control pi-calculus. J. Comput. Sci. Technol. **15**(1), 1–9 (2000)

315. Logrippo, L., Andriantsiferana, L., Ghribi, B.: Prototyping and formal requirement validation of GPRS: a mobile data packet radio service for GSM. In: Weinstock, C.B., Rushby, J. (eds.) Proceedings of the 7th IFIP International Working Conference on Dependable Computing for Critical Applications (DCCA-7), San Jose, CA, USA, January 1999

316. López, N., Núñez, M.: An overview of probabilistic process algebras and their equivalences. In: Baier, C., Haverkort, B.R., Hermanns, H., Katoen, J.-P., Siegle, M. (eds.) Validation of Stochastic Systems. LNCS, vol. 2925, pp. 89–123. Springer, Heidelberg (2004). https://doi.org/10.1007/978-3-540-24611-4_3

317. Lüttgen, G., Vogler, W.: Bisimulation on speed: worst-case efficiency. Inf. Comput. **191**(2), 105–144 (2004)

318. Luukkainen, M., Ahtiainen, A.: Compositional verification of large SDL systems. In: Proceedings of the 1st Workshop of the SDL Forum Society on SDL and MSC (SAM 1998), Berlin, Germany, June 1998

319. Madelaine, E.: Verification tools from the CONCUR project. EATCS Bull. **47**, 110–120 (1992)

320. Madelaine, E., Simone, R.: ECRINS: un laboratoire de preuve pour les calculs de processus. Rapport de recherche 672, INRIA, May 1987

321. Madelaine, E., Vergamini, D.: AUTO: a verification tool for distributed systems using reduction of finite automata networks. In: Vuong, S.T. (ed.) Proceedings of the 2nd IFIP International Conference on Formal Description Techniques for Distributed Systems and Communication Protocols (FORTE'89), Vancouver, BC, Canada, pp. 61–66. North-Holland, December 1989

322. Madelaine, E., Vergamini, D.: Specification and verification of a sliding window protocol in LOTOS. In: Parker, K.R., Rose, G.A. (eds.) Formal Description Techniques, IV, Proceedings of the IFIP TC6/WG6.1 4th International Conference on Formal Description Techniques for Distributed Systems and Communication Protocols (FORTE 1991), Sydney, Australia. IFIP Transactions, vol. C-2, pp. 495–510. North-Holland, November 1991

323. Madelaine, E., Vergamini, D.: Tool demonstration: tools for process algebras. In: Parker, K.R., Rose, G.A. (eds.) Formal Description Techniques, IV, Proceedings of

the IFIP TC6/WG6.1 4th International Conference on Formal Description Techniques for Distributed Systems and Communication Protocols (FORTE 1991), Sydney, Australia. IFIP Transactions, vol. C-2, pp. 463–466. North-Holland, November 1991

324. Madelaine, E., Vergamini, D.: Verification of communicating processes by means of automata reduction and abstraction. In: Finkel, A., Jantzen, M. (eds.) STACS 1992. LNCS, vol. 577, pp. 613–614. Springer, Heidelberg (1992). https://doi.org/10.1007/3-540-55210-3_221

325. Magee, J., Kramer, J.: Concurrency: State Models and Java Programs. Wiley, Hoboken (1999)

326. Malhotra, J., Smolka, S.A., Giacalone, A., Shapiro, R.: A tool for hierarchical design and simulation of concurrent systems. In: Proceedings of the BCS-FACS Workshop on Specification and Verification of Concurrent Systems, Stirling, Scotland, UK, pp. 140–152. British Computer Society, July 1988

327. Markopoulos, P., Rowson, J., Johnson, P.: Dialogue modelling in the framework of an interactor model. In: Bodart, F., Vanderdonckt, J. (eds.) Proceedings of the 3rd International Workshop on Design, Specification, and Verification of Interactive Systems DSV-IS 1996 (Namur, Belgium). University of Namur, June 1996

328. Martens, J., Groote, J.F., van den Haak, L., Hijma, P., Wijs, A.: A linear parallel algorithm to compute bisimulation and relational coarsest partitions. In: Salaün, G., Wijs, A. (eds.) FACS 2021. LNCS, vol. 13077, pp. 115–133. Springer, Cham (2021). https://doi.org/10.1007/978-3-030-90636-8_7

329. Mateescu, R.: Formal description and analysis of a bounded retransmission protocol. In: Brezočnik, Z., Kapus, T. (eds.) Proceedings of the COST 247 International Workshop on Applied Formal Methods in System Design (Maribor, Slovenia), pp. 98–113. University of Maribor, Slovenia, June 1996. Also available as INRIA Research Report RR-2965

330. Mateescu, R.: Vérification de systèmes répartis: l'exemple du protocole BRP. Technique et Science Informatiques **16**(6), 725–751 (1997)

331. Mateescu, R.: Local model-checking of an alternation-free value-based modal mu-calculus. In: Bossi, A., Cortesi, A., Levi, F. (eds.) Proceedings of the 2nd International Workshop on Verification, Model Checking and Abstract Interpretation (VMCAI 1998), Pisa, Italy. University Ca' Foscari of Venice, September 1998

332. Mateescu, R.: Vérification des propriétés temporelles des programmes parallèles. Ph.D. thesis, Institut National Polytechnique de Grenoble, April 1998

333. Mateescu, R.: On-the-fly state space reductions for weak equivalences. In: Margaria, T., Massink, M. (eds.) Proceedings of the 10th International Workshop on Formal Methods for Industrial Critical Systems (FMICS 2005), Lisbon, Portugal, pp. 80–89. ERCIM, ACM Computer Society Press, September 2005

334. Mateescu, R.: CAESAR_SOLVE: a generic library for on-the-fly resolution of alternation-free Boolean equation systems. Int. J. Softw. Tools Technol. Transfer (STTT) **8**(1), 37–56 (2006). Full version available as INRIA Research Report RR-5948, July 2006

335. Mateescu, R.: Specification and analysis of asynchronous systems using CADP. In: Merz, S., Navet, N. (eds.) Modeling and Verification of Real-Time Systems - Formalisms and Software Tools, chap. 5, pp. 141–170. ISTE Publishing/Wiley (2008)

336. Mateescu, R., Oudot, E.: Bisimulator 2.0: an on-the-fly equivalence checker based on Boolean equation systems. In: Proceedings of the 6th ACM-IEEE International Conference on Formal Methods and Models for Codesign (MEMOCODE 2008), Anaheim, CA, USA, pp. 73–74. IEEE Computer Society Press, June 2008

337. Mateescu, R., Oudot, E.: Improved on-the-fly equivalence checking using Boolean equation systems. In: Havelund, K., Majumdar, R., Palsberg, J. (eds.) SPIN 2008. LNCS, vol. 5156, pp. 196–213. Springer, Heidelberg (2008). https://doi.org/10. 1007/978-3-540-85114-1_15 Full version available as INRIA Research Report RR-6777

338. Mateescu, R., Poizat, P., Salaün, G.: Adaptation of service protocols using process algebra and on-the-fly reduction techniques. In: Bouguettaya, A., Krueger, I., Margaria, T. (eds.) ICSOC 2008. LNCS, vol. 5364, pp. 84–99. Springer, Heidelberg (2008). https://doi.org/10.1007/978-3-540-89652-4_10

339. Mateescu, R., Wijs, A.: Property-dependent reductions adequate with divergence-sensitive branching bisimilarity. Sci. Comput. Program. **96**(3), 354–376 (2014)

340. Mehta, M., Guha, S.: ReLTS 1.0 User Manual (2014). http://airbornemihir. github.io/lts_reltool/manual.pdf

341. Mehta, M., Guha, S., Arun-Kumar, S.: ReLTS: A Tool for Checking Generalized Behavioural Relations over LTSs (2014). http://airbornemihir.github.io/lts_reltool/NFM.pdf

342. Milne, G.J.: CIRCAL and the representation of communication, concurrency, and time. ACM Trans. Progr. Lang. Syst. **7**(2), 270–298 (1985)

343. Milner, R., Parrow, J., Walker, D.: A calculus of mobile processes I. Inf. Comput. **100**(1), 1–40 (1992)

344. Milner, R., Parrow, J., Walker, D.: A calculus of mobile processes II. Inf. Comput. **100**(1), 41–77 (1992)

345. Milner, R.: A Calculus of Communicating Systems. LNCS, vol. 92. Springer, Heidelberg (1980). https://doi.org/10.1007/3-540-10235-3

346. Milner, R.: Calculi for synchrony and asynchrony. Theor. Comput. Sci. **25**, 267–310 (1983)

347. Milner, R.: Communication and Concurrency. Prentice-Hall (1989)

348. Moller, F.: The Edinburgh Concurrency Workbench (Version 6.1). User manual, Laboratory for the Foundations of Computer Science, University of Edinburgh (1992)

349. Moller, F., Smolka, S.A., Srba, J.: On the computational complexity of bisimulation. Redux. Inf. Comput. **194**(2), 129–143 (2004)

350. Montes, A.S.: VENUS: un outil d'aide à la vérification des systèmes communicants. Ph.D. thesis, Institut National Polytechnique de Grenoble, January 1987

351. Mounier, L.: Méthodes de vérification de spécifications comportementales: étude et mise en œuvre. Ph.D. thesis, Université Joseph Fourier (Grenoble), January 1992

352. Mumme, M., Ciardo, G.: An efficient fully symbolic bisimulation algorithm for non-deterministic systems. Int. J. Found. Comput. Sci. **24**(2), 263–282 (2013)

353. Najm, E., Budkowski, S., Gilot, T., Lumbroso, L.: General presentation of SCAN - a distributed systems modelling and validation tool. In: Diaz, M. (ed.) Proceedings of the 5th IFIP International Workshop on Protocol Specification, Testing, and Verification (PSTV 1985), Moissac, France, pp. 103–118. North-Holland, June 1985

354. Nistal, M.L., Quemada, J., Iglesias, M.J.F.: Direct verification of bisimulations. In: Gotzhein, R., Bredereke, J. (eds.) Formal Description Techniques IX: Theory, application and tools, IFIP TC6 WG6.1 International Conference on Formal Description Techniques IX/Protocol Specification, Testing and Verification XVI, Kaiserslautern, Germany, 8–11 October 1996. IFIP Conference Proceedings, vol. 69, pp. 349–363. Chapman & Hall (1996)

355. Notare, M.S.M.A., da Silva Cruz, F.A., Riso, B.G., Westphall, C.B.: Wireless communications: security management against cloned cellular phones. In: Proceedings of the IEEE Wireless Communications and Networking Conference WCNC 1999 (New Orleans, LA, USA), pp. 1412–1416. IEEE, September 1999

356. Notare, M., Boukerche, A., Cruz, F., Riso, B., Westphall, C.: Security management against cloning mobile phones. In: Seamless Interconnection for Universal Services, Global Telecommunications Conference, GLOBECOM 1999 (Cat. No.99CH37042), vol. 3, pp. 1969–1973 (1999)

357. Noureddine, M., Jaber, M., Bliudze, S., Zaraket, F.A.: Reduction and abstraction techniques for BIP. In: Lanese, I., Madelaine, E. (eds.) FACS 2014. LNCS, vol. 8997, pp. 288–305. Springer, Cham (2015). https://doi.org/10.1007/978-3-319-15317-9_18

358. Orzan, S.: On distributed verification and verified distribution. Ph.D. thesis, Vrije Universiteit Amsterdam (2004)

359. Orzan, S., van de Pol, J., Espada, M.V.: A state space distribution policy based on abstract interpretation. Electron. Notes Theor. Comput. Sci. **128**(3), 35–45 (2005)

360. Paige, R., Tarjan, R.E.: Three partition refinement algorithms. SIAM J. Comput. **16**(6), 973–989 (1987)

361. Parashkevov, A.N., Yantchev, J.: ARC - a verification tool for concurrent systems. In: Proceedings of the 3rd Australasian Parallel and Real-Time Conference (1996)

362. Park, D.: Concurrency and automata on infinite sequences. In: Deussen, P. (ed.) GI-TCS 1981. LNCS, vol. 104, pp. 167–183. Springer, Heidelberg (1981). https://doi.org/10.1007/BFb0017309

363. Parrow, J., Victor, B.: The fusion calculus: expressiveness and symmetry in mobile processes. In: 13th Annual IEEE Symposium on Logic in Computer Science, Indianapolis, Indiana, USA, 21–24 June 1998, pp. 176–185. IEEE Computer Society (1998)

364. Pecheur, C.: Advanced Modelling and Verification Techniques Applied to a Cluster File System. Research Report RR-3416, INRIA, Grenoble, May 1998

365. Pecheur, C.: Advanced modelling and verification techniques applied to a cluster file system. In: Hall, R.J., Tyugu, E. (eds.) Proceedings of the 14th IEEE International Conference on Automated Software Engineering (ASE 1999), Cocoa Beach, Florida, USA. IEEE Computer Society, October 1999. Extended version available as INRIA Research Report RR-3416

366. Piazza, C., Pivato, E., Rossi, S.: CoPS – checker of persistent security. In: Jensen, K., Podelski, A. (eds.) TACAS 2004. LNCS, vol. 2988, pp. 144–152. Springer, Heidelberg (2004). https://doi.org/10.1007/978-3-540-24730-2_11

367. Plotkin, G.: A Structural Approach to Operational Semantics. Technical Report DAIMI FN-19, Computer Science Department, Aarhus University, Denmark (1981)

368. Plotkin, G.D.: A structural approach to operational semantics. J. Logic Algebraic Program. **60–61**, 17–139 (2004)

369. Plotkin, G.D.: The origins of structural operational semantics. J. Logic Algebraic Program. **60–61**, 3–15 (2004)

370. Pous, D., Sangiorgi, D.: Bisimulation and coinduction enhancements: a historical perspective. Formal Aspects of Comput. **31**(6), 733–749 (2019)

371. Rabinovich, A.: Checking equivalences between concurrent systems of finite agents (extended abstract). In: Kuich, W. (ed.) ICALP 1992. LNCS, vol. 623, pp. 696–707. Springer, Heidelberg (1992). https://doi.org/10.1007/3-540-55719-9_115

372. van Rangelrooij, A., Voeten, J.P.M.: CCSTOOL2: An Expansion, Minimization and Verification Tool for Finite State CCS Descriptions. Research Report 94-E-284, Eindhoven University of Technology (1994)

373. Reade, C.: Process algebra in the specification of graphics standards. Comput. Standards Interfaces **17**, 277–290 (1995)

374. Romijn, J.: Analysing industrial protocols with formal methods. Ph.D. thesis, University of Twente, The Netherlands, September 1999

375. Roscoe, A.W.: The Theory and Practice of Concurrency. Prentice Hall (1998)

376. Roy, V., de Simone, R.: Auto/Autograph. In: Kurshan, R.P., Clarke, E.M. (eds.) Proceedings of the 2nd Workshop on Computer-Aided Verification (Rutgers, New Jersey, USA). DIMACS Series in Discrete Mathematics and Theoretical Computer Science, vol. 3, pp. 477–491. AMS-ACM, June 1990

377. Roy, V., de Simone, R.: Auto/Autograph. Formal Methods Syst. Des. **1**(2/3), 239–249 (1992)

378. Rudin, H., West, C.H., Zafiropulo, P.: Automated protocol validation: one chain of development. Comput. Netw. **2**, 373–380 (1978)

379. Sabnani, K.K., Lapone, A.M., Ümit Uyar, M.: An algorithmic procedure for checking safety properties of protocols. IEEE Trans. Commun. **37**(9), 940–948 (1989)

380. Sage, M., Johnson, C.W.: A declarative prototyping environment for the development of multi-user safety-critical systems. In: Proceedings of the 17th International System Safety Conference (ISSC 1999), Orlando, Florida, USA. System Safety Society, August 1999

381. Sage, M., Johnson, C.W.: Formally verified rapid prototyping for air traffic control. In: Proceedings of the 3rd Workshop on Human Error, Safety and Systems Development, Liege, Belgium (1999)

382. Sage, M., Johnson, C.W.: Formally verified rapid prototyping for air traffic control. Reliab. Eng. Syst. Saf. **75**(2), 121–132 (2002)

383. Sanderson, M.T.: Proof Techniques for CCS. Internal Report CST-19-82, University of Edinburgh (1982)

384. Sangiorgi, D.: A theory of bisimulation for the π-calculus. In: Best, E. (ed.) CONCUR 1993. LNCS, vol. 715, pp. 127–142. Springer, Heidelberg (1993). https://doi.org/10.1007/3-540-57208-2_10

385. Saqui-Sannes, P., Courtiat, J.P.: From the simulation to the verification of ESTELLE* specifications. In: Vuong, S.T. (ed.) Proceedings of the 2nd International Conference on Formal Description Techniques FORTE 1989 (Vancouver B.C., Canada). North-Holland, December 1989

386. Schieferdecker, I.: Abruptly-terminated connections in TCP - a verification example. In: Brezočnik, Z., Kapus, T. (eds.) Proceedings of the COST 247 International Workshop on Applied Formal Methods in System Design, Maribor, Slovenia, pp. 136–145. University of Maribor, Slovenia, June 1996

387. Sighireanu, M.: Model-checking validation of the LOTOS descriptions of the invoicing case study. In: Habrias, H. (ed.) Proceedings of the International Workshop on Comparing System Specification Techniques (Nantes, France), March 1998

388. Sighireanu, M., Mateescu, R.: Validation of the link layer protocol of the IEEE-1394 serial bus ("FireWire"): an experiment with E-LOTOS. In: Lovrek, I. (ed.) Proceedings of the 2nd COST 247 International Workshop on Applied Formal Methods in System Design (Zagreb, Croatia), June 1997. Full version available as INRIA Research Report RR-3172

389. Sighireanu, M., Turner, K.: Requirement Capture, Formal Description and Verification of an Invoicing System. Research Report RR-3575, INRIA, Grenoble, December 1998

390. de Simone, R., Vergamini, D.: Aboard AUTO. Technical Report 111, INRIA (1989)

391. Sokolova, A., de Vink, E.P.: Probabilistic automata: system types, parallel composition and comparison. In: Baier, C., Haverkort, B.R., Hermanns, H., Katoen, J.-P., Siegle, M. (eds.) Validation of Stochastic Systems. LNCS, vol. 2925, pp. 1–43. Springer, Heidelberg (2004). https://doi.org/10.1007/978-3-540-24611-4_1

392. Song, L., Zhang, L., Hermanns, H., Godskesen, J.C.: Incremental bisimulation abstraction refinement. ACM Trans. Embed. Comput. Syst. **13**(4s), 142:1–142:23 (2014)

393. Soriano, A.: Prototype de Venus: Un Outil d'Aide à la Vérification de Systèmes Communicants. In: Cori, R., Wirsing, M. (eds.) STACS 1988. LNCS, vol. 294, pp. 401–402. Springer, Heidelberg (1988). https://doi.org/10.1007/BFb0035867

394. Stevens, P.: The Edinburgh Concurrency Workbench (Version 7.1). User manual, Laboratory for the Foundations of Computer Science, University of Edinburgh (1997)

395. Stevens, P.: A verification tool developer's Vade Mecum. Int. J. Softw. Tools Technol. Transfer (STTT) **2**(2), 89–94 (1998)

396. Stevens, P.: Some issues in the software engineering of verification tools. In: Cleaveland, W.R. (ed.) TACAS 1999. LNCS, vol. 1579, pp. 435–438. Springer, Heidelberg (1999). https://doi.org/10.1007/3-540-49059-0_30

397. Sunshine, C.A.: Survey of protocol definition and verification techniques. Comput. Netw. **2**(4–5), 346–350 (1978)

398. Tai, K.C., Koppol, P.V.: An incremental approach to reachability analysis of distributed programs. In: Proceedings of the 7th International Workshop on Software Specification and Design, Los Angeles, CA, USA, pp. 141–150. IEEE Press, Piscataway, December 1993

399. Tai, K.C., Koppol, P.V.: Hierarchy-based incremental reachability analysis of communication protocols. In: Proceedings of the IEEE International Conference on Network Protocols, San Francisco, CA, USA, pp. 318–325. IEEE Press, Piscataway, October 1993

400. Tiu, A., Nguyen, N., Horne, R.: SPEC: an equivalence checker for security protocols. In: Igarashi, A. (ed.) APLAS 2016. LNCS, vol. 10017, pp. 87–95. Springer, Cham (2016). https://doi.org/10.1007/978-3-319-47958-3_5

401. Tripakis, S.: Extended KRONOS/CADP Tool: Minimization, On-the-Fly Verification and Compositionality. Technical Report T226, VERIMAG, Grenoble, France, April 1999

402. Tripakis, S., Yovine, S.: Analysis of timed systems based on time-abstracting bisimulations. In: Alur, R., Henzinger, T.A. (eds.) CAV 1996. LNCS, vol. 1102, pp. 232–243. Springer, Heidelberg (1996). https://doi.org/10.1007/3-540-61474-5_72

403. Tronel, F., Lang, F., Garavel, H.: Compositional verification using CADP of the ScalAgent deployment protocol for software components. In: Najm, E., Nestmann, U., Stevens, P. (eds.) FMOODS 2003. LNCS, vol. 2884, pp. 244–260. Springer, Heidelberg (2003). https://doi.org/10.1007/978-3-540-39958-2_17 Full version available as INRIA Research Report RR-5012

404. Ulrich, A.: A description model to support test suite derivation for concurrent systems. In: Zitterbart, M. (ed.) KiVS 1997, pp. 151–166. Springer, Heidelberg (1997). https://doi.org/10.1007/978-3-642-60729-5_11

405. Ulrich, A., König, H.: Specification-based testing of concurrent systems. In: Higashino, T., Togashi, A. (eds.) Proceedings of the IFIP Joint International Conference on Formal Description Techniques and Protocol Specification, Testing, and Verification (FORTE/PSTV 1997), Ozaka, Japan. Chapman & Hall, November 1997

406. Valmari, A., Tienari, M.: An improved failure equivalence for finite-state systems with a reduction algorithm. In: Jonsson, B., Parrow, J., Pehrson, B. (eds.) Proceedings of the 11th IFIP International Workshop on Protocol Specification, Testing and Verification (Stockholm, Sweden). North-Holland, June 1991

407. Valmari, A.: Compositional state space generation. In: Rozenberg, G. (ed.) ICATPN 1991. LNCS, vol. 674, pp. 427–457. Springer, Heidelberg (1993). https://doi.org/10.1007/3-540-56689-9_54

408. Valmari, A.: Stubborn set methods for process algebras. In: Peled, D.A., Pratt, V.R., Holzmann, G.J. (eds.) Proceedings of the DIMACS Workshop on Partial Order Methods in Verification, Princeton, New Jersey, USA. DIMACS Series in Discrete Mathematics and Theoretical Computer Science, vol. 29, pp. 213–231. DIMACS/AMS, July 1996

409. Valmari, A., Kemppainen, J., Clegg, M., Levanto, M.: Putting advanced reachability analysis techniques together: The "ARA" tool. In: Woodcock, J.C.P., Larsen, P.G. (eds.) FME 1993. LNCS, vol. 670, pp. 597–616. Springer, Heidelberg (1993). https://doi.org/10.1007/BFb0024669

410. Vergamini, D.: Verification by Means of Observational Equivalence on Automata. Research Report 0501, INRIA (1986)

411. Vergamini, D.: Vérification de réseaux d'automates finis par équivalences observationnelles: le système AUTO. Ph.D. thesis, Université de Nice (1987)

412. Vergamini, D.: Verification of distributed systems: an experiment. In: Pin, J.E. (ed.) LITP 1988. LNCS, vol. 386, pp. 249–259. Springer, Heidelberg (1989). https://doi.org/10.1007/BFb0013124

413. Victor, B.: A verification tool for the polyadic π-calculus. Licentiate thesis, Department of Computer Systems, Uppsala University, Sweden, May 1994. Available as report DoCS 94/50

414. Victor, B.: The Mobility Workbench User's Guide, Polyadic version 3.122 (1995)

415. Victor, B.: The fusion calculus: expressiveness and symmetry in mobile processes. Ph.D. thesis, Department of Computer Systems, Uppsala University, Sweden, June 1998. Available as report DoCS 98/98

416. Victor, B., Moller, F.: The Mobility Workbench—a tool for the π-calculus. In: Dill, D.L. (ed.) CAV 1994. LNCS, vol. 818, pp. 428–440. Springer, Heidelberg (1994). https://doi.org/10.1007/3-540-58179-0_73

417. Virtanen, H., Hansen, H., Valmari, A., Nieminen, J., Erkkilä, T.: Tampere verification tool. In: Jensen, K., Podelski, A. (eds.) TACAS 2004. LNCS, vol. 2988, pp. 153–157. Springer, Heidelberg (2004). https://doi.org/10.1007/978-3-540-24730-2_12

418. Walker, D.: Automated Analysis of Mutual Exclusion Algorithms using CCS. Research Report ECS-LFCS-89-91, Laboratory for Foundations of Computer Science, Department of Computer Science, University of Edinburg (1989)

419. Wang, F.: Symbolic branching bisimulation-checking of dense-time systems in an environment. In: Majumdar, R., Tabuada, P. (eds.) HSCC 2009. LNCS, vol. 5469, pp. 485–489. Springer, Heidelberg (2009). https://doi.org/10.1007/978-3-642-00602-9_40

420. Wehrheim, H.: Partial order reductions for failures refinement. In: Castellani, I., Victor, B. (eds.) 6th International Workshop on Expressiveness in Concurrency (EXPRESS 1999), Eindhoven, The Netherlands. Electronic Notes in Theoretical Computer Science, vol. 27, pp. 71–84. Elsevier, August 1999

421. Willemse, T., Tretmans, J., Klomp, A.: A case study in formal methods: specification and validation of the OM/RR protocol. In: Gnesi, S., Schieferdecker, I., Rennoch, A. (eds.) Proceedings of the 5th International Workshop on Formal Methods for Industrial Critical Systems (FMICS 2000), Berlin, Germany, pp. 331–344. GMD Report 91, Berlin, April 2000

422. Willemse, T.A.: The specification and validation of the OM/RR-protocol. Master's thesis, Department of Mathematics and Computing Science, Eindhoven University of Technology, Eindhoven, The Netherlands, June 1998

423. Wimmer, R., Derisavi, S., Hermanns, H.: Symbolic partition refinement with dynamic balancing of time and space. In: Proceedings of the 5th International Conference on the Quantitative Evaluation of Systems (QEST 2008), Saint-Malo, France, pp. 65–74. IEEE Computer Society, September 2008

424. Wimmer, R., Herbstritt, M., Becker, B.: Minimization of large state spaces using symbolic branching bisimulation. In: Reorda, M.S., et al. (eds.) Proceedings of the 9th IEEE Workshop on Design & Diagnostics of Electronic Circuits & Systems (DDECS 2006), Prague, Czech Republic, pp. 9–14. IEEE Computer Society, April 2006

425. Wimmer, R., Herbstritt, M., Becker, B.: Optimization techniques for BDD-based bisimulation computation. In: Zhou, H., Macii, E., Yan, Z., Massoud, Y. (eds.) Proceedings of the 17th ACM Great Lakes Symposium on VLSI, Stresa, Lago Maggiore, pp. 405–410. ACM, March 2007

426. Wimmer, R., Herbstritt, M., Hermanns, H., Strampp, K., Becker, B.: SIGREF – a symbolic bisimulation tool box. In: Graf, S., Zhang, W. (eds.) ATVA 2006. LNCS, vol. 4218, pp. 477–492. Springer, Heidelberg (2006). https://doi.org/10.1007/11901914_35

427. Wodey, P., Baray, F.: Linking codesign and verification by means of E-LOTOS FDT. In: Józwiak, L. (ed.) Proceedings of the Euromicro Workshop on Digital System Design: Architectures, Methods and Tools (Milano, Italy). IEEE, September 1999

428. Yeh, W.J., Young, M.: Compositional reachability analysis using process algebra. In: Proceedings of the ACM SIGSOFT Symposium on Testing, Analysis, and Verification (SIGSOFT 1991), Victoria, British Columbia, Canada, pp. 49–59. ACM Press, October 1991

429. Wang, Y.: Real-time behaviour of asynchronous agents. In: Baeten, J.C.M., Klop, J.W. (eds.) CONCUR 1990. LNCS, vol. 458, pp. 502–520. Springer, Heidelberg (1990). https://doi.org/10.1007/BFb0039080

430. Yi, W.: A Tool Environment for the Development of Embedded Systems (1999)

431. Yoeli, M.: Modulo-3 Transition Counter: A Case Study in LOTOS-Based Verification. Technical Report TR CS0950, Technion, Computer Science Department, Haifa, Israel, February 1998

432. Yoeli, M.: Examples of LOTOS-Based Verification of Asynchronous Circuits. Technical Report TR CS-2001-08, Technion, Computer Science Department, Haifa, Israel, February 2001

433. Yoeli, M., Ginzburg, A.: LOTOS/CADP-Based Verification of Asynchronous Circuits. Technical Report TR CS-2001-09, Technion, Computer Science Department, Haifa, Israel, March 2001

434. Yovine, S.: KRONOS: a verification tool for real-time systems. Int. J. Softw. Tools Technol. Transfer (STTT) **1**(1/2), 123–133 (1997)

435. Zapreev, I., Jansen, C.: MRMC Test Suite - Version 1.4.1 (2009). http://www.mrmc-tool.org/downloads/MRMC/Specs/TS_Manual_1.4.1.pdf

436. Zuidweg, H.: Verification by abstraction and bisimulation. In: Sifakis, J. (ed.) CAV 1989. LNCS, vol. 407, pp. 105–116. Springer, Heidelberg (1990). https://doi.org/10.1007/3-540-52148-8_10

Apartness and Distinguishing Formulas in Hennessy-Milner Logic

Herman Geuvers[1,2(✉)]

[1] ICIS, Radboud University Nijmegen, Nijmegen, The Netherlands
herman@cs.ru.nl
[2] Faculty of Mathematics and Computer Science, Technical University Eindhoven, Eindhoven, The Netherlands

Abstract. For Labelled Transition Systems, an important question is when two states in such a system are bisimilar. Here we study the dual, in the sense of logical opposite, of bisimilarity, known as "apartness". This gives a positive way of distinguishing two states (stating that they are not bisimilar). In [3] we have studied apartness (and bisimilarity) in general co-algebraic terms. As opposed to bisimilarity, which is co-inductive, apartness is an inductive notion and we have given and studied proof systems for deriving that two states are apart. In the present paper we continue the study of apartness in the light of Hennessy-Milner theorems that establish an equivalence between bisimulation and validity of (modal) formulas: two states are bisimilar if and only if they satisfy the same set of formulas. Using the apartness view, this can be dualized: two states are apart if and only there is a formula that distinguishes them. We work this out for three situations: bisimulation for labelled transition systems (LTSs), weak bisimulation for LTSs with silent (τ) steps and branching bisimulation for LTSs with silent (τ) steps. We study the equivalences with the well-known variants of Hennessy-Milner logic and show how an apartness proof gives rise to a distinguishing formula.

1 Introduction

The standard way of looking at equality of states in a Labeled Transition Systems (LTS) is indistinguishability, which is captured via the notion of bisimulation. States are observed through "destructors", which in an LTS are the transition-steps. A bisimulation is a relation that satisfies the "transfer principle": if two states are related, and we take a transition-step, then we get two new related states. Two states are bisimilar if and only if they are observationally indistinguishable, i.e. there is a bisimulation that relates them. The coinduction principle states that two states that are bisimilar (have the same observations) are equal.

In previous work [3], we have described apartness as the dual of bisimulation for systems that are defined as co-algebras. Categorically, bisimulation is described in the category of relations **Rel**, and apartness in the "fibred opposite" of **Rel**. Here, we take a more pedestrian approach and use apartness to provide a new look on some concrete known results about various forms of bisimulation. The basic idea is that two states are apart in case they are observationally distinguishable: there is a sequence of observations that can be made on one state but not on the other. Apartness is a positive notion: two states are apart if there is a positive way to distinguish them, and being apart is the negation of being bisimilar. Bisimilarity is co-inductive: it is the union of all bisimulation relations and therefore the largest bisimulation relation (and a final co-algebra). Apartness is inductive: it is the intersection of all apartness relations and therefore the smallest apartness relation (and an initial algebra). As apartness is inductive, there is a proof system with derivation rules to derive that two states are apart.

In the present paper, we study the proof systems for deriving apartness for some concrete cases. First we look into well-known non-deterministic LTSs, where we have transitions of the form $q \rightarrow_a q'$, with q, q' states and a a label. The non-determinism means that from a state q there are multiple a-transitions possible (or none). The apartness we get here is the dual, in the sense of the logical opposite, of standard bisimulation. Then we add silent (τ) steps, which we study modulo weak bisimulation (giving rise to its dual 'weak apartness') and modulo branching bisimulation (giving rise to its dual 'branching apartness'). For each case, we give the deduction rules for deriving that two states are apart.

To argue that apartness is a fruitful way of looking at distinguishability, we establish for each of these cases a Hennessy-Milner connection with a modal logic. This is a very well-known connection between bisimulation and logic [2,6] that we now re-establish via apartness. In bisimulation terms, the Hennessy-Milner Theorem says that two states are bisimilar if and only if the same modal formulas hold in these states, where of course the notion of bisimulation and the logic for formulas depends on the type of systems under study. In terms of apartness, the Hennessy-Milner Theorem gets a more "positive flavor" saying that two states are apart if and only if there is a modal formula that distinguishes them (i.e. that holds in one state, but not in the other). So, from a proof of the apartness of two states q and p, we can derive a formula φ such that φ holds for q and $\neg\varphi$ holds for p: the formula φ gives a positive 'witness', an explanation, for the fact that q and p are distinguishable. We illustrate this with some examples.

As a matter of fact, the present paper can be seen as an "apartness footnote" [3] to the original papers by Hennessy and Milner [6], De Nicola and Vaandrager [2] and Van Glabbeek and Weijland [4], where bisimulation has been studied in various forms for various systems with motivating examples, and its properties have been established, also in terms of modal logic.

Special Thanks

We dedicate this article to Frits Vaandrager on the occasion of his 60th birthday. I have known Frits for a long time as a very respectable researcher and colleague at Radboud University. We have met for the first time at the LiCS conference of 1992 at Santa Cruz, but that was only a very brief encounter. It is nice to see that much of Frits' earlier work, on branching bisimulation for LTSs, I have recently started appreciating much more after looking at the "apartness view" of co-algebraically defined systems. It is even nicer to see that this apartness view has been inspiring for Frits and others to study algorithms for automata learning [10]. Thanks Frits for all the nice co-operations!

2 Bisimulation and Apartness for LTSs

We start from labeled transition systems over a set of actions A, and study the well-known notion of bisimulation and the (less well-known) notion of apartness for these systems.

Definition 1. *Let A be a fixed set of actions. A labelled transition system over A or LTS over A, is a pair $(S, \rightarrow)$ where S is a set of states and $\rightarrow \subseteq S \times A \times S$. For $(q, a, p) \in \rightarrow$, we write $q \rightarrow_a p$ and we call the LTS image finite in case the set $\{p \mid q \rightarrow_a p\}$ is finite for each q, a. On an LTS we define the notions of bisimulation and apartness*

1. *A relation $R \subseteq S \times S$ is a* bisimulation *if it is symmetric and it satisfies the following transfer property*

$$\frac{q_1 \rightarrow_a q_2 \qquad R(q_1, p_1)}{\exists p_2 (p_1 \rightarrow_a p_2 \wedge R(q_2, p_2))} (\leftrightarrow)$$

   Two states $q, p \in S$ are bisimilar, *notation $q \leftrightarrow p$, is defined by*

$$q \leftrightarrow p := \exists R \subseteq S \times S \, (R \text{ is a bisimulation and } R(q, p)).$$

2. *A relation $Q \subseteq S \times S$ is an* apartness *if it is symmetric and satisfies the following rule*

$$\frac{q_1 \rightarrow_a q_2 \qquad \forall p_2 \in S(p_1 \rightarrow_a p_2 \implies Q(q_2, p_2))}{Q(q_1, p_1)} (\text{in}_{\#})$$

   Two states $q, p \in S$ are apart, *notation $q \mathrel{\#} p$, is defined by*

$$q \mathrel{\#} p := \forall Q \subseteq S \times S \, (\text{if } Q \text{ is an apartness, then } Q(q, p)).$$

As an immediate consequence of the definition, $q \mathrel{\#} p$ if and only if (q, p) is in the intersection of all apartness relations, and $\#$ is the smallest apartness relation. It is standard that in an LTS, two states are bisimilar if and only if they are not apart, so we have

$$q \leftrightarrow p \qquad \Longleftrightarrow \qquad \neg(q \mathrel{\#} p).$$

Also, apartness is an inductive notion, and so we can equivalently define q and p to be apart, $q \mathrel{\#} p$, if this can be *derived* using the deduction rules in Fig. reffig.aptrules. So, we can use the rules that define what an apartness relation is as the deduction rules for a proof system to derive $q \mathrel{\#} p$.

It should be noted that in case the LTS is image-finite, the rule above can also be written with a finite set of hypotheses:

$$\frac{q_1 \rightarrow_a q_2 \qquad \bigwedge_{\{p_2 \in S \mid p_1 \rightarrow_a p_2\}} q_2 \mathrel{\#} p_2}{q_1 \mathrel{\#} p_1} (\text{in}_{\#})$$

Before moving to formulas that distinguish states, we first give an example to see what a proof of apartness looks like concretely.

$$\frac{q_1 \rightarrow_a q_2 \qquad \forall p_2 \in S(p_1 \rightarrow_a p_2 \implies q_2 \mathbin{\#} p_2)}{q_1 \mathbin{\#} p_1} \text{(in}_\#)$$

$$\frac{p \mathbin{\#} q}{q \mathbin{\#} p} \text{(symm)}$$

Fig. 1. The deduction system for deriving $q \mathbin{\#} p$

Example 1. We consider the LTS with actions $\{a, b, c\}$ and states and transitions as indicated in the figure.

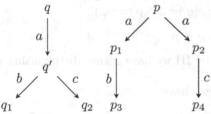

It is well-known that q and p are not bismilar. They can be shown to be apart using the following derivation

$$\frac{q \rightarrow_a q' \qquad \dfrac{\dfrac{q' \rightarrow_c q_2 \quad \checkmark}{q' \mathbin{\#} p_1} \qquad \dfrac{q' \rightarrow_b q_1 \quad \checkmark}{q' \mathbin{\#} p_2}}{\forall p'(p \rightarrow_a p' \implies q' \mathbin{\#} p')}}{q \mathbin{\#} p}$$

Note that the apartness $q' \mathbin{\#} p_1$ holds because $q' \rightarrow_c q_2$ and there is no c-transition from p_1, expressed by the check-mark. So the universal quantification $\forall p''(p_1 \rightarrow_c p'' \implies \dots)$ is empty, and therefore holds. These are the "base cases" of the inductive definition of apartness: where we can do some transition from q but not from p, and therefore $q \mathbin{\#} p$.

2.1 Hennessy-Milner Logic for Bisimulation

We now introduce the well-known modal logic that captures bisimulation logically and we prove the well-known Hennessy-Milner theorem using apartness.

Definition 2. *Given a set of actions A, we define the Hennessy-Milner logic for A, HML_A by the following set of formulas φ, where $a \in A$.*

$$\varphi ::= \top \mid \neg\varphi \mid \varphi_1 \wedge \varphi_2 \mid \langle a \rangle \varphi.$$

Let $(S, \rightarrow)$ be an LTS over A. For $q \in S$ and φ a formula of HML_A, we define the notion φ holds in state q, notation $q \models \varphi$, as follows, by induction on φ.

- $q \models \top$ *always holds.*
- $q \models \neg\varphi$ *if* $q \not\models \varphi$.
- $q \models \varphi_1 \wedge \varphi_2$ *if* $q \models \varphi_1$ *and* $q \models \varphi_2$.
- $q \models \langle a \rangle \varphi$ *if there is a* q' *such that* $q \to_a q'$ *and* $q' \models \varphi$.

For $(S, \to)$ *an LTS over* A, $q, p \in S$, *and* $\varphi \in HML_A$, *we say that* φ *distinguishes* q, p *if* $q \models \varphi$ *and* $p \models \neg\varphi$.

The well-known Hennessy-Milner theorem [2,6] states that $q \leftrightarrow p$ if and only if $\forall\varphi(q \models \varphi \Leftrightarrow p \models \varphi)$. We prove the apartness analogon of this, where we compute a *distinguishing formula* from an apartness proof.

Proposition 1. *Given an image-finite LTS* $(S, \to)$ *over* A, *and* $q, p \in S$, *we have*

$$q \mathrel{\#} p \qquad \Longleftrightarrow \qquad \exists\varphi(q \models \varphi \wedge p \models \neg\varphi).$$

Proof. ($\Rightarrow$) by induction on the proof of $q \mathrel{\#} p$.

- If the last applied rule is symm, then by IH we have φ that distinguishes p, q, and therefore $\neg\varphi$ distinguishes q, p.
- If the last applied rule is $(\mathrm{in}_{\#})$, then we have

$$\frac{q \to_a q' \qquad \bigwedge_{\{p' \in S | p \to_a p'\}} q' \mathrel{\#} p'}{q \mathrel{\#} p} \; (\mathrm{in}_{\#})$$

where the conjunction is over a finite set of formulas, say $\{p' \in S \mid p \to_a p'\} = \{p_1, \ldots, p_n\}$. By IH we have φ_i $(1 \leq i \leq n)$ such that φ_i distinguishes q', p_i. Now we take $\varphi := \langle a \rangle \bigwedge_{1 \leq i \leq n} \varphi_i$ and we have
  1. $q \models \varphi$: $q \to_a q'$ with $q' \models \varphi_i$ for every i, so $q \models \langle a \rangle \bigwedge_{1 \leq i \leq n} \varphi_i$.
  2. $p \models \neg\varphi$: for each p' with $p \to_a p'$ there is an i with $p' \models \neg\varphi_i$, and therefore $p' \models \neg \bigwedge_{1 \leq i \leq n} \varphi_i$. So $p \models \neg\langle a \rangle \bigwedge_{1 \leq i \leq n} \varphi_i$.

($\Leftarrow$) by induction on φ, where $q \models \varphi$ and $p \models \neg\varphi$.

- $\varphi = \top$ cannot occur, because $p \models \neg\top$ never holds.
- $\varphi = \neg\psi$. Then $p \models \psi$ and $q \models \neg\psi$, so by induction we have a derivation of $p \mathrel{\#} q$. By rule (symm) we have a derivation of $q \mathrel{\#} p$.
- $\varphi = \varphi_1 \wedge \varphi_2$. Then $q \models \varphi_1$ and $q \models \varphi_2$, and also $p \models \neg\varphi_1$ or $p \models \neg\varphi_2$. In case $p \models \neg\varphi_1$ we have, by induction, a derivation of $q \mathrel{\#} p$, and similarly in case $p \models \neg\varphi_2$, so we are done.
- $\varphi = \langle a \rangle \psi$. We know $q \models \langle a \rangle \psi$, so let q' be such that $q \to_a q'$ and $q' \models \psi$. Also $p \models \neg\langle a \rangle \psi$, so for all p' with $p \to_a p'$ we have $p' \models \neg\psi$. By induction hypothesis we have derivations of $q' \mathrel{\#} p'$ for all p' with $p \to_a p'$, so we have the following derivation of $q \mathrel{\#} p$, using rule $(\mathrm{in}_{\#})$

$$\frac{q \to_a q' \qquad \forall p' \in S(p \to_a p' \implies q' \mathrel{\#} p')}{q \mathrel{\#} p} \; (\mathrm{in}_{\#})$$

$\square$

It is well-known ([6]) that image finiteness is needed for Proposition 1 to hold. This can also be observed from the proof of ($\Rightarrow$), where the image finiteness guarantees that the generated distinguishing formula contains finitely many conjunctions. So the implication ($\Rightarrow$) only holds for image finite systems, while the implication ($\Leftarrow$) holds in general.

Example 2. We continue Example 1 by giving the formula that distinguishes states q and p. It can be derived from the derivation of $q \mathrel{\#} p$, by following the steps in the proof of Proposition 1. The distinguishing formula is

$$\varphi := \langle a\rangle(\langle c\rangle\top \wedge \langle b\rangle\top),$$

which can be read as saying: "we can do an a-step such that after that we can do both a b-step and a c-step".

Example 3. As another example we show how we can use apartness for nondeterministic finite automata, which have also been discussed in [3]. In this example we use a special step, a c-transition (ending up in state q_f) to mimic that a state is final.

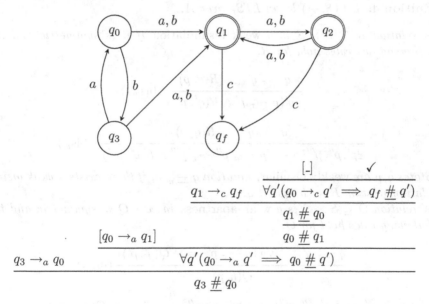

It can be shown that $q_3 \mathrel{\#} q_0$ by the derivation given above. In the derivation, we indicate between [...] all possible transitions that we need to prove a universal hypothesis of the form $\forall q'(\ldots \to q' \implies \ldots)$. Note that $q_0 \to_a q_1$ is the only a-step from q_0. The check-mark denotes the empty side-hypothesis that vacuously holds, as there is no c-step possible from q_0. The distinguishing formula computed from this derivation is $\langle a\rangle\neg\langle c\rangle\top$, saying that from q_3 one can do an a-step to a state where one cannot do a c-step, while for q_0 this is not the case.

3   Weak Bisimulation and Apartness for LTSs

We now add silent steps, or τ-steps to labeled transition systems and we study the (well-known) notion of weak bisimulation and the (less well-known) notion of weak apartness for LTSs with τ.

Definition 3. *Let A be a fixed set of basic actions. We denote by $A_\tau := A \cup \{\tau\}$ the set of all actions, which includes the silent action τ. We let α (and $\beta, \gamma, \ldots$) range over A_τ and a (and $b, c, \ldots$) range over A. A labelled transition system with τ-steps over A or LTS_τ, is a pair $(S, \to)$ where S is a set of states and $\to \subset S \times A_\tau \times S$. For $(q, \alpha, p) \in \to$, we write $q \to_\alpha p$.*

We will be interested in the transitive reflexive closure of $\to_\tau$, which we denote by $\twoheadrightarrow_\tau$. We call the LTS_τ image finite in case the set $\{q' \mid \exists q_1, q_2 (q \twoheadrightarrow_\tau q_1 \to_\alpha q_2 \twoheadrightarrow_\tau q')\}$ is finite for each q, α.

On an LTS_τ, we define the notions of weak bisimulation [2,6] and weak apartness. The first is well-known and the second is its dual and has been discussed in [3].

Definition 4. *Let $(S, \to)$ be an LTS_τ over A.*

1. *A relation $R \subseteq S \times S$ is a weak bisimulation if it is symmetric and the following two rules hold for R.*

$$\frac{q \to_\tau q' \qquad R(q,p)}{\exists p'(p \twoheadrightarrow_\tau p' \wedge R(q',p'))} \ (\text{bis}_{w\tau})$$

$$\frac{q \to_a q' \qquad R(q,p)}{\exists p', p'', p'''(p \twoheadrightarrow_\tau p' \to_a p'' \twoheadrightarrow_\tau p''' \wedge R(q',p'''))} \ (\text{bis}_w)$$

   States q, p are weakly bismilar, notation $q \underline{\leftrightarrow}_w p$, if there exists a weak bisimulation relation R such that $R(q,p)$.

2. *A relation $Q \subseteq S \times S$ is a weak apartness in case Q is symmetric and the following rules hold for Q.*

$$\frac{q \to_\tau q' \qquad \forall p'(p \twoheadrightarrow_\tau p' \implies Q(q',p'))}{Q(q,p)} \ (\text{in}_{w\tau})$$

$$\frac{q \to_a q' \qquad \forall p', p'', p'''(p \twoheadrightarrow_\tau p' \to_a p'' \twoheadrightarrow_\tau p''' \implies Q(q',p'''))}{Q(q,p)} \ (\text{in}_w)$$

   The states q and p are weakly apart, notation $q \underline{\#}_w p$, if for all weak apartness relations Q, we have $Q(q,p)$.

Again, as an immediate consequence of the definition, $q \underline{\#}_w p$ if and only if (q,p) is in the intersection of all weak apartness relations, and $\underline{\#}_w$ is the smallest weak apartness relation.

Just as in LTSs, for LTS_τs we also have that two states are weakly bisimilar if and only if they are not weakly apart, so we have

$$q \underline{\leftrightarrow}_w p \quad \Leftrightarrow \quad \neg(q \mathrel{\underline{\#}}_w p).$$

Weak apartness is an inductive notion, and so also in this case, we have a derivation system for proving $q \mathrel{\underline{\#}}_w p$, using the three deduction rules of Fig. 2.

$$\frac{q \rightarrow_\tau q' \qquad \forall p'(p \twoheadrightarrow_\tau p' \implies q' \mathrel{\underline{\#}}_w p')}{q \mathrel{\underline{\#}}_w p} \;(\mathrm{in}_{w\tau})$$

$$\frac{q \rightarrow_a q' \qquad \forall p',p'',p'''(p \twoheadrightarrow_\tau p' \rightarrow_a p'' \twoheadrightarrow_\tau p''' \implies q' \mathrel{\underline{\#}}_w p''')}{q \mathrel{\underline{\#}}_w p} \;(\mathrm{in}_w)$$

$$\frac{p \mathrel{\underline{\#}}_w q}{q \mathrel{\underline{\#}}_w p} \;(\mathrm{symm})$$

Fig. 2. The deduction system for deriving $q \mathrel{\underline{\#}}_w p$

In case the LTS_τ is image-finite, the rules above can be written with a finite set of hypotheses:

$$\frac{q \rightarrow_\tau q' \qquad \bigwedge_{\{p' \mid p \twoheadrightarrow_\tau p'\}} q' \mathrel{\underline{\#}}_w p'}{q \mathrel{\underline{\#}}_w p} \;(\mathrm{in}_{w\tau})$$

$$\frac{q \rightarrow_a q' \qquad \bigwedge_{\{p''' \mid \exists p',p''(p \twoheadrightarrow_\tau p' \rightarrow_a p'' \twoheadrightarrow_\tau p''')\}} q' \mathrel{\underline{\#}}_w p'''}{q \mathrel{\underline{\#}}_w p} \;(\mathrm{in}_w)$$

3.1 Hennessy-Milner Logic for Weak Bisimulation

We now introduce the well-known modal logic that captures weak bisimulation logically and we prove the well-known Hennessy-Milner theorem [2] using weak apartness.

Definition 5. *We adapt the formulas of the logic of Definition 2 by just adding τ in the modality, so we have, given a set of actions A, the formulas of $HML\tau_A$ given by the following set, where $\alpha \in A_\tau$.*

$$\varphi ::= \top \mid \neg\varphi \mid \varphi_1 \wedge \varphi_2 \mid \langle \alpha \rangle \varphi.$$

Let $(S, \rightarrow)$ be an LTS_τ over A. For $q \in S$ and φ a formula of $HML\tau_A$, we define the notion φ holds in state q, notation $q \models_w \varphi$, as follows, by induction on φ.

- $q \models_w \top$ *always holds.*
- $q \models_w \neg\varphi$ *if* $q \not\models_w \varphi$.
- $q \models_w \varphi_1 \wedge \varphi_2$ *if* $q \models_w \varphi_1$ *and* $q \models_w \varphi_2$.
- $q \models_w \langle a \rangle \varphi$ *if* $\exists q_1, q_2, q_3 (q \twoheadrightarrow_\tau q_1 \rightarrow_a q_2 \twoheadrightarrow_\tau q_3 \wedge q_3 \models_w \varphi)$.
- $q \models_w \langle \tau \rangle \varphi$ *if* $\exists q' (q \twoheadrightarrow_\tau q' \wedge q' \models_w \varphi)$.

For $q, p \in S$, *and* $\varphi \in HML\tau_A$, *we say that* φ *distinguishes* q, p *if* $q \models_w \varphi$ *and* $p \models_w \neg\varphi$.

Again, the well-known Hennessy-Milner theorem states that $q \underline{\leftrightarrow}_w p$ if and only if $\forall \varphi \in HML\tau_A (q \models_w \varphi \Leftrightarrow p \models_w \varphi)$. We prove the apartness analogon of this, where we compute a *distinguishing formula* from an apartness proof. For this it is useful to adapt the derivation rules for $\#_w$ a bit. This adaptation is borrowed from the "bisimulation side", where it is easily shown to be equivalent.

The rules $(bis_{w\tau})$ and (bis_w) for weak bisimulation can easily seen to be equivalent to the following ones, where we replace a one-step transition by a multiple step transition. (The equivalence is standard, e.g. from [2].)

$$\frac{q \twoheadrightarrow_\tau q' \qquad R(q,p)}{\exists p' (p \twoheadrightarrow_\tau p' \wedge R(q',p'))} \ (bis'_{w\tau})$$

$$\frac{q \twoheadrightarrow_\tau q_1 \rightarrow_a q_2 \twoheadrightarrow_\tau q' \qquad R(q,p)}{\exists p', p'', p''' (p \twoheadrightarrow_\tau p' \rightarrow_a p'' \twoheadrightarrow_\tau p''' \wedge R(q',p'''))} \ (bis'_w)$$

Therefore, by duality, taking the logical opposite, we also have the following equivalent set of rules for weak apartness.

Lemma 1. *Weak apartness, as defined in Definition 4 can equivalently be captured using the following derivation rules (where we use the set notation, as that's the one we will be using later, when we restrict to image-finite systems).*

$$\frac{q \twoheadrightarrow_\tau q' \qquad \bigwedge_{\{p' | p \twoheadrightarrow_\tau p'\}} q' \mathbin{\#_w} p'}{q \mathbin{\#_w} p} \ (in'_{w\tau})$$

$$\frac{q \twoheadrightarrow_\tau q_1 \rightarrow_a q_2 \twoheadrightarrow_\tau q' \qquad \bigwedge_{\{p''' | \exists p', p'' (p \twoheadrightarrow_\tau p' \rightarrow_a p'' \twoheadrightarrow_\tau p''')\}} q' \mathbin{\#_w} p'''}{q \mathbin{\#_w} p} \ (in'_w)$$

$$\frac{p \mathbin{\#_w} q}{q \mathbin{\#_w} p} \ (symm)$$

Proposition 2. *Given* $(S, \rightarrow)$, *an image-finite* LTS_τ *over* A, *and* $q, p \in S$, *we have*

$$q \mathbin{\#} p \quad \Longleftrightarrow \quad \exists \varphi \in HML\tau_A (q \models_w \varphi \wedge p \models_w \neg\varphi).$$

Proof. ($\Rightarrow$) by induction on the proof of $q \mathbin{\#} p$.

- If the last applied rule is symm, then by IH we have φ that distinguishes p, q, and therefore $\neg\varphi$ distinguishes q, p.
- If the last applied rule is $(\text{in}'_{w\tau})$, we have

$$\frac{q \rightarrow_\tau q' \qquad \bigwedge_{\{p' \mid p \twoheadrightarrow_\tau p'\}} q' \mathbin{\#_w} p'}{q \mathbin{\#_w} p} \ (\text{in}'_{w\tau})$$

Say $\{p' \mid p \twoheadrightarrow_\tau p'\} = \{p_1, \ldots, p_n\}$. By induction hypothesis we have $\varphi_1, \ldots, \varphi_n$ with $q' \models_w \varphi_i$ and $p_i \models_w \neg\varphi_i$ for all i $(1 \leq i \leq n)$. Now take $\varphi := \langle \tau \rangle (\varphi_1 \wedge \ldots \wedge \varphi_n)$. Then $q \models_w \varphi$ and $p \models_w \neg\varphi$.

- If the last applied rule is (in'_w), we have

$$\frac{q \twoheadrightarrow_\tau q_1 \rightarrow_a q_2 \twoheadrightarrow_\tau q' \qquad \bigwedge_{\{p''' \mid \exists p', p'' (p \twoheadrightarrow_\tau p' \rightarrow_a p'' \twoheadrightarrow_\tau p''')\}} q' \mathbin{\#_w} p'''}{q \mathbin{\#_w} p} \ (\text{in}'_w)$$

Say $\{p''' \mid \exists p', p'' (p \twoheadrightarrow_\tau p' \rightarrow_a p'' \twoheadrightarrow_\tau p''')\} = \{p_1, \ldots, p_n\}$. By induction hypothesis we have $\varphi_1, \ldots, \varphi_n$ with $q' \models_w \varphi_i$ and $p_i \models_w \neg\varphi_i$ for all i $(1 \leq i \leq n)$. Now take $\varphi := \langle a \rangle (\varphi_1 \wedge \ldots \wedge \varphi_n)$. Then $q \models_w \varphi$ and $p \models_w \neg\varphi$.

($\Leftarrow$) by induction on φ, where $q \models_w \varphi$ and $p \models_w \neg\varphi$.

- The case $\varphi = \top$, $\varphi = \neg\psi$ and $\varphi = \varphi_1 \wedge \varphi_2$ are exactly the same as in the proof of Proposition 1.
- $\varphi = \langle \tau \rangle \psi$. We know $q \models_w \langle \tau \rangle \psi$, so let q' be such that $q \rightarrow_\tau q'$ and $q' \models_w \psi$. Also $p \models_w \neg\langle a \rangle \psi$, so for all p' with $p \twoheadrightarrow_\tau p'$ we have $p' \models_w \neg\psi$. By induction hypothesis we have derivations of $q' \mathbin{\#} p'$ for all p' for which $p \twoheadrightarrow_\tau p'$, so we have the following derivation of $q \mathbin{\#} p$, using rule $(\text{in}'_{w\tau})$

$$\frac{q \rightarrow_\tau q' \qquad \bigwedge_{\{p' \mid p \twoheadrightarrow_\tau p'\}} q' \mathbin{\#_w} p'}{q \mathbin{\#_w} p} \ (\text{in}'_{w\tau})$$

- $\varphi = \langle a \rangle \psi$. We know $q \models_w \langle a \rangle \psi$, so let q_1, q_2, q_3 be such that $q \twoheadrightarrow_\tau q_1 \rightarrow_a q_2 \twoheadrightarrow_\tau q_3$ and $q_3 \models_w \psi$. Also $p \models_w \neg\langle a \rangle \psi$, so for all p_1, p_2, p_3 with $p \twoheadrightarrow_\tau p_1 \rightarrow_a p_2 \twoheadrightarrow_\tau p_3$ we have $p_3 \models_w \neg\psi$. By induction hypothesis we have derivations of $q' \mathbin{\#} p_3$ for all $p_3 \in \{p''' \mid \exists p', p'' (p \twoheadrightarrow_\tau p' \rightarrow_a p'' \twoheadrightarrow_\tau p''')\}$, so we have the following derivation of $q \mathbin{\#} p$, using rule (in'_w)

$$\frac{q \twoheadrightarrow_\tau q_1 \rightarrow_a q_2 \twoheadrightarrow_\tau q' \qquad \bigwedge_{\{p''' \mid \exists p', p'' (p \twoheadrightarrow_\tau p' \rightarrow_a p'' \twoheadrightarrow_\tau p''')\}} q' \mathbin{\#_w} p'''}{q \mathbin{\#_w} p} \ (\text{in}'_w)$$

$\square$

4   Branching Bisimulation and Apartness for LTSs

We now study the notions of branching bisimulation and branching apartness on Labelled Transition Systems with τ-steps. So the systems we consider are still the LTS_τ systems of Definition 3, but now with a different notion of equivalence, branching bisimulation, that takes the branching structure due to the τ-steps into account. It is well-known that weak bisimulation is really weaker than branching bisimulation (if $s \underline{\leftrightarrow}_b t$, then $s \underline{\leftrightarrow}_w t$, but in general not the other way around) and similarly, weak apartness is really stronger than branching apartness (if $s \underline{\#}_w t$, then $s \underline{\#}_b t$, but in general not the other way around).

On an LTS_τ, we define the notions of branching bisimulation [2,4] and branching apartness. The first is well-known and the second is its dual and has been discussed in [3].

Definition 6. *Given* $(S, \rightarrow)$, *an* LTS_τ *over* A *(see Definition 3), a relation* $R \subseteq S \times S$ *is a* branching bisimulation relation *if the following rules hold for* R.

$$\frac{q \rightarrow_\tau q' \qquad R(q,p)}{R(q',p) \vee \exists p',p''(p \twoheadrightarrow_\tau p' \rightarrow_\tau p'' \wedge R(q,p') \wedge R(q',p''))} \; (\text{bis}_{b\tau})$$

$$\frac{q \rightarrow_a q' \qquad R(q,p)}{\exists p',p''(p \twoheadrightarrow_\tau p' \rightarrow_a p'' \wedge R(q,p') \wedge R(q',p''))} \; (\text{bis}_b)$$

$$\frac{R(q,p)}{R(p,q)} \; (\text{symm})$$

The states q,p *are* branching bisimilar, *notation* $q \underline{\leftrightarrow}_b p$ *if and only if there exists a branching bisimulation relation* R *such that* $R(q,p)$.

We say that $Q \subseteq S \times S$ *is a* branching apartness *in case the following rules hold for* Q.

$$\frac{q \rightarrow_\tau q' \qquad Q(q',p) \qquad \forall p',p''(p \twoheadrightarrow_\tau p' \rightarrow_\tau p'' \implies Q(q,p') \vee Q(q',p''))}{Q(q,p)} \; (\text{in}_{b\tau})$$

$$\frac{q \rightarrow_a q' \qquad \forall p',p''(p \twoheadrightarrow_\tau p' \rightarrow_a p'' \implies Q(q,p') \vee Q(q',p''))}{Q(q,p)} \; (\text{in}_b)$$

$$\frac{Q(p,q)}{Q(q,p)} \; (\text{symm})$$

The states q *and* p *are* branching apart, *notation* $q \underline{\#}_b p$, *if for all branching apartness relations* Q, *we have* $Q(q,p)$.

Again, as an immediate consequence of the definition, $q \underline{\#}_b p$ if and only if (q,p) is in the intersection of all branching apartness relations, and $\underline{\#}_b$ is the smallest branching apartness relation.

Just as for weak bisimulation and weak apartness we also have that two states are branching bisimilar if and only if they are not branching apart, so we have

$$q \underline{\leftrightarrow}_b p \qquad \Longleftrightarrow \qquad \neg(q \mathrel{\#_b} p).$$

Being branching apart is the smallest branching apartness relation, so is an inductive definition that we can define using a derivation system. We can capture $q \mathrel{\#_b} p$ using the derivation rules of Fig. 3, where we use a conjunction because in the following we will be studying branching apartness for image-finite systems.

$$\frac{q \rightarrow_\tau q' \qquad q' \mathrel{\#_b} p \qquad \bigwedge_{\{p,p'' \mid p \twoheadrightarrow_\tau p' \rightarrow_\tau p''\}} q \mathrel{\#_b} p' \vee q' \mathrel{\#_b} p''}{q \mathrel{\#_b} p} \; (\text{in}_{b\tau})$$

$$\frac{q \rightarrow_a q' \qquad \bigwedge_{\{p',p'' \mid p \twoheadrightarrow_\tau p' \rightarrow_a p''\}} q \mathrel{\#_b} p' \vee q' \mathrel{\#_b} p''}{q \mathrel{\#_b} p} \; (\text{in}_b)$$

$$\frac{p \mathrel{\#_b} q}{q \mathrel{\#_b} p} \; (\text{symm})$$

Fig. 3. The deduction system for deriving $q \mathrel{\#_b} p$

4.1 Hennessy-Milner Logic for Branching Bisimulation

We now introduce the modal logic that captures branching bisimulation. The logic is an adaptation of the logic $\text{HML}\tau_A$ with an "until" operator instead of a simple unary modality. We also state the well-known Hennessy-Milner theorem using apartness:

$$q \mathrel{\#_b} p \Longleftrightarrow \exists \varphi (q \models_b \varphi \wedge p \models_b \neg\varphi),$$

of which we only prove the ($\Rightarrow$) case, which produces a distinguishing formula from an apartness proof. We will illustrate this with some examples.

Of course the ($\Leftarrow$) implication above also holds, and it can be proven by contra-position, by proving $q \underline{\leftrightarrow}_b p \Longrightarrow \forall \varphi (q \models_b \varphi \Longrightarrow p \models_b \varphi)$, a proof of which can be found e.g. in [2]. It would be nice to prove it directly, by induction on φ, similar to the proofs of Propositions 1 and 2, but that turns out to be difficult, and we have not yet been able to establish a direct proof.

Definition 7. *We define HMLτb_A by the following set of formulas, given a set of actions A (where $\alpha \in A_\tau$):*

$$\varphi ::= \top \mid \neg\varphi \mid \varphi_1 \wedge \varphi_2 \mid \varphi_1 \langle \alpha \rangle \varphi_2.$$

Let $(S, \rightarrow)$ be an LTS_τ over A. For $q \in S$ and φ a formula of $HML\tau b_A$, we define the notion φ holds in state q, notation $q \models_b \varphi$, as follows, by induction on φ.

- $q \models_b \top$ always holds.
- $q \models_b \neg\varphi$ if $q \not\models \varphi$.
- $q \models_b \varphi_1 \wedge \varphi_2$ if $q \models \varphi_1$ and $q \models \varphi_2$.
- $q \models_b \varphi\langle a\rangle\psi$ if there are states $q_1, \ldots, q_n, q_{n+1}$ such that
  $q = q_1 \rightarrow_\tau \cdots \rightarrow_\tau q_n \rightarrow_a q_{n+1} \wedge \forall i(1 \leq i \leq n) \; q_i \models \varphi \wedge q_{n+1} \models \psi$.
- $q \models_b \varphi\langle\tau\rangle\psi$ if $q \models \psi$ or there are states $q_1, \ldots, q_n, q_{n+1}$ such that
  $q = q_1 \rightarrow_\tau \cdots \rightarrow_\tau q_n \rightarrow_\tau q_{n+1} \wedge \forall i(1 \leq i \leq n) \; q_i \models \varphi \wedge q_{n+1} \models \psi$.

For $q, p \in S$, and $\varphi \in HML\tau b_A$, we say that φ distinguishes q, p if $q \models_b \varphi$ and $p \models_b \neg\varphi$.

Again, the well-known Hennessy-Milner theorem states that $q \underleftrightarrow{}_b p$ if and only if $\forall\varphi \in HML\tau b_A(q \models_b \varphi \Leftrightarrow p \models_b \varphi)$. We state the apartness analogon of this, where we compute a *distinguishing formula* from an apartness proof.

Proposition 3. *Given* $(S, \rightarrow)$, *an image-finite* LTS_τ *over* A, *and* $q, p \in S$, *we have*

$$q \mathrel{\#}_b p \quad \Longleftrightarrow \quad \exists\varphi \in HML\tau b_A(q \models_b \varphi \wedge p \models_b \neg\varphi).$$

Proof. The Proposition is of course a corollary of the bisimulation version, which is just the contra-positive, and which is proved, e.g. in [2]. We only prove ($\Rightarrow$) by induction on the proof of $q \mathrel{\#}_b p$.

- If the last applied rule is symm, then by IH we have φ that distinguishes p, q, and therefore $\neg\varphi$ distinguishes q, p.
- If the last applied rule is (in$_b$), then we have

$$\frac{q \rightarrow_a q' \qquad \bigwedge_{\{p', p'' \mid p \twoheadrightarrow_\tau p' \rightarrow_a p''\}} q \mathrel{\#}_b p' \vee q' \mathrel{\#}_b p''}{q \mathrel{\#}_b p} \; (\text{in}_b)$$

where the conjunction is over a finite set of formulas, say that $\{(p', p'') \mid p \twoheadrightarrow_\tau p' \rightarrow_a p''\} = \{(p_1, r_1) \ldots, (p_m, r_m)\}$, so the pairs (p_j, r_j) are the states for which we have $p \twoheadrightarrow_\tau p_j \rightarrow_a r_j$. By IH we have for each j ($1 \leq j \leq m$) a φ_j such that φ_j distinguishes q and p_j ($q \models_b \varphi_j$, $p_j \models_b \neg\varphi_j$), or a ψ_j such that ψ_j distinguishes q' and r_j ($q' \models_b \psi_j$, $r_j \models_b \neg\psi_j$). Now we take

$$\Phi := \bigwedge_{1 \leq j \leq m} \varphi_j,$$

$$\Psi := \bigwedge_{1 \leq j \leq m} \psi_j,$$

$$\varphi := \Phi\langle a\rangle\Psi.$$

We have

1. $q \models_b \varphi$: For $q \to_a q'$ we have $q \models \Phi$ and $q' \models_b \Psi$.
2. $p \models_b \neg\varphi$: let $p_1, \ldots, p_n, p_{n+1}$ be such that $p = p_1 \to_\tau \ldots \to_\tau p_n \to_a p_{n+1}$. We know by induction hypothesis that for some j, $p_n \models_b \neg\varphi_j$ (and then $p_n \models_b \neg\Phi$) or $p_{n+1} \models_b \neg\psi_j$ (and then $p_{n+1} \models_b \neg\Psi$). So $\exists i \leq n (p_i \models_b \neg\Phi)$ or $p_{n+1} \models_b \neg\Psi$, which what we needed to prove.

– If the last applied rule is $(\mathrm{in}_{b\tau})$, then we have

$$\frac{q \to_\tau q' \qquad q' \, \underline{\#}_b \, p \qquad \bigwedge_{\{p, p'' \mid p \twoheadrightarrow_\tau p' \to_\tau p''\}} q \, \underline{\#}_b \, p' \vee q' \, \underline{\#}_b \, p''}{q \, \underline{\#}_b \, p} \ (\mathrm{in}_{b\tau})$$

where the conjunction is over a finite set of formulas, say that $\{(p', p'') \mid p \twoheadrightarrow_\tau p' \to_\tau p''\} = \{(p_1, r_1) \ldots, (p_m, r_m)\}$, so the pairs (p_j, r_j) are the states for which we have $p \twoheadrightarrow_\tau p_j \to_\tau r_j$. By IH we have a φ_0 for which $q' \models_b \varphi_0$ and $p \models_b \neg\varphi_0$. Also by IH we have for each j $(1 \leq j \leq m)$ a φ_j such that $q \models_b \varphi_j$ and $p_j \models_b \neg\varphi_j$, or a ψ_j such that $q' \models_b \psi_j$ and $r_j \models_b \neg\psi_j$. Now we take

$$\Phi := \bigwedge_{1 \leq j \leq m} \varphi_j,$$

$$\Psi := \varphi_0 \wedge \bigwedge_{1 \leq j \leq m} \psi_j,$$

$$\varphi := \Phi\langle\tau\rangle\Psi.$$

We have

1. $q \models_b \varphi$: For $q \to_\tau q'$ we have $q \models \Phi$ and $q' \models_b \Psi$.
2. $p \models_b \neg\varphi$: $p \models_b \neg\Psi$ (by $p \models_b \neg\varphi_0$) and for $p_1, \ldots, p_n, p_{n+1}$ with $p = p_1 \to_\tau \ldots \to_\tau p_n \to_a p_{n+1}$ we know by induction hypothesis that for some j: $p_n \models_b \neg\varphi_j$ (and then $p_n \models_b \neg\Phi$) or $p_{n+1} \models_b \neg\psi_j$ (and then $p_{n+1} \models_b \neg\Psi$). So $\exists i \leq n(p_i \models_b \neg\Phi)$ or $p_{n+1} \models_b \neg\Psi$, which what we needed to prove. □

4.2 Examples

We now give some examples of how to compute a distinguishing formula from an apartness proof.

Example 4. The first example is a well-known LTS_τ with two states that are not branching bisimilar and we give the proof of their branching apartness and compute the distinguishing formula from that proof.

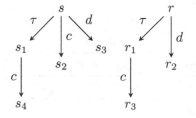

We give a derivation of $s \mathrel{\#_b} r$, where we indicate between [...] all possible transitions that we need to prove a hypothesis for (just one in the case of the c-step; none in the case of the d-step).

$$
\cfrac{s \to_d s_3 \quad \cfrac{\overset{[\_]\ \checkmark}{\forall r', r''(r_1 \twoheadrightarrow_\tau r' \to_d r'' \implies s \mathrel{\#_b} r' \lor s_3 \mathrel{\#_b} r'')}}{s \mathrel{\#_b} r_1}}{\cfrac{\cfrac{s \mathrel{\#_b} r_1 \lor s_2 \mathrel{\#_b} r_3}{[r \to_\tau r_1 \to_c r_3] \qquad \forall r', r''(r \twoheadrightarrow_\tau r' \to_c r'' \implies s \mathrel{\#_b} r' \lor s_2 \mathrel{\#_b} r'')}}{s \mathrel{\#_b} r}}
$$

The distinguishing formula that we compute from this derivation, following the proof of Proposition 3 is

$$(\top \langle d \rangle \top)\langle c \rangle \top,$$

which holds in state s and expresses that there is a τ-path to a state where a c-step is possible, and in all states along that τ-path, a d-step is possible.

Example 5. We have the LTS given below, for which we have $q_0 \mathrel{\#_b} p_0$, which we prove and then compute the distinguishing formula.

A derivation of $q_0 \mathrel{\#_b} p_0$ is the following, where for space reasons, we singled out the sub-derivation of $q_0 \mathrel{\#_b} p_2$, which we call Σ. Again, we indicate between [...] all possible transitions that we need to prove a hypothesis for.

$$
\cfrac{q_0 \to_d q_2 \quad \cfrac{[p_0 \to_d p_1]\ \cfrac{\cfrac{\cfrac{p_1 \to_e p_0}{p_1 \mathrel{\#_b} q_2}}{q_2 \mathrel{\#_b} p_1}}{q_0 \mathrel{\#_b} p_0 \lor q_2 \mathrel{\#_b} p_1}\quad [p_0 \twoheadrightarrow_\tau p_2 \to_d p_3]\ \cfrac{\Sigma}{q_0 \mathrel{\#_b} p_2 \lor q_2 \mathrel{\#_b} p_3}}{\forall p', p''(p_0 \twoheadrightarrow_\tau p' \to_d p'' \implies q_0 \mathrel{\#_b} p' \lor q_2 \mathrel{\#_b} p'')}}{q_0 \mathrel{\#_b} p_0}
$$

And here is the sub-derivation Σ of $q_0 \mathrel{\#_b} p_2$:

$$
\Sigma := \cfrac{q_0 \to_d q_1 \quad [p_2 \twoheadrightarrow_\tau p_2 \to_d p_3]\ \cfrac{\cfrac{\cfrac{q_1 \to_e q_0}{q_1 \mathrel{\#_b} p_3}}{q_0 \mathrel{\#_b} p_2 \lor q_1 \mathrel{\#_b} p_3}}{\forall p', p''(p_2 \twoheadrightarrow_\tau p' \to_d p'' \implies q_0 \mathrel{\#_b} p' \lor q_1 \mathrel{\#_b} p'')}}{q_0 \mathrel{\#_b} p_2}
$$

The distinguishing formula that we compute from Σ is $\top \langle d \rangle (\top \langle e \rangle \top)$. The distinguishing formula for $q_0 \mathrel{\underline{\#}}_b p_0$ is

$$\Phi := (\top \langle d \rangle (\top \langle e \rangle \top)) \langle d \rangle \neg (\top \langle e \rangle \top)$$

We have $q_0 \models_b \Phi$ and $p_0 \models_b \neg\Phi$.

Example 6. We can also use the proof system for $\mathrel{\underline{\#}}_b$ to establish that $q \mathrel{\underline{\leftrightarrow}}_b p$. Here is a simple example to illustrate this.

If $q \mathrel{\underline{\#}}_b p$, then there is a *shortest derivation* of $q \mathrel{\underline{\#}}_b p$, and we notice that it doesn't exist. Therefore we can conclude that $\neg q \mathrel{\underline{\#}}_b p$ and so $q \mathrel{\underline{\leftrightarrow}}_b p$. In our search for a derivation of $q \mathrel{\underline{\#}}_b p$ we have to keep track of goals that we have already encountered; the search would proceed as follows:

$$\cfrac{q \to_a q' \quad \cfrac{q' \to_a q \quad \cfrac{\text{fail}}{q' \mathrel{\underline{\#}}_b p \vee q \mathrel{\underline{\#}}_b p}}{q' \mathrel{\underline{\#}}_b p}}{\cfrac{q \mathrel{\underline{\#}}_b p \vee q' \mathrel{\underline{\#}}_b p}{q \mathrel{\underline{\#}}_b p}}$$

4.3 Related and Further Work

Of course, the concept of observations is well-known and tightly related to bisimulation. Korver [8] presents an algorithm that, if two states are not branching bisimilar, produces a formula in Hennessy-Milner [6] logic with until operator that distinguishes the two states. This work implicitly uses the notion of apartness without singling out its proof rules. Another work is Chow [1] on testing equivalence of states in finite state machines and more recent work is by Smetsers et al. [9], where an efficient algorithm is presented for finding a minimal separating sequence for a pair of in-equivalent states in a finite state machine. It would be interesting to see whether this work, and the idea of finding such a separating sequence, can be formulated in terms of apartness, and if the algorithms can be improved using that approach. In general it would be interesting to understand the various efficient algorithms for checking branching bisimulation [5,7] in terms of apartness. A first concrete application of apartness for studying systems has been made by Vaandrager and colleagues [10] in the development of a new automata learning algorithm.

For the meta-theoretic study of bisimulation, it sometimes pays off to go to the "dual view" of apartness, for one because apartness is an inductive notion, so we have an induction principle. There are examples of that in [3]. Also, sometime, the apartness view just gives a different, fresh, angle on bisimulation which might be fruitful. We have also seen examples where the bisimulation view works much better than the apartness view, e.g. in the proof of the reverse implication of Proposition 3, which we have not been able to establish directly (without first going from the apartness-view to the bisimulation-view). It is interesting to understand why this is the case.

Finally, we believe that apartness and the proof system for apartness may provide useful in studying more quantitative or qualitative notions of distinguishability: how "different" are two states and in which points do they differ? The latter is already established by the Hennessy-Milner formula, but one can also think of this in a more "directed sense", by studying a notion of "directed apartness" (as a dual to simulation?) and witnesses establishing that states are not simulated by others.

References

1. Chow, T.S.: Testing software design modeled by finite-state machines. IEEE Trans. Softw. Eng. **4**(3), 178–187 (1978)
2. De Nicola, R., Vaandrager, F.W.: Three logics for branching bisimulation. J. ACM **42**(2), 458–487 (1995)
3. Geuvers, H., Jacobs, B.: Relating apartness and bisimulation. Logical Meth. Comput. Sci. 17(3) (2021)
4. Van Glabbeek, R., Weijland, P.: Branching time and abstraction in bisimulation semantics. J. ACM **43**, 613–618 (1996)
5. Groote, J.F., Vaandrager, F.: An efficient algorithm for branching bisimulation and stuttering equivalence. In: Paterson, M.S. (ed.) ICALP 1990. LNCS, vol. 443, pp. 626–638. Springer, Heidelberg (1990). https://doi.org/10.1007/BFb0032063
6. Hennessy, M., Milner, R.: Algebraic laws for nondeterminism and concurrency. J. ACM **32**(1), 137–161 (1985)
7. Jansen, D.N., Groote, J.F., Keiren, J.J.A., Wijs, A.: An $O(m \log n)$ algorithm for branching bisimilarity on labelled transition systems. In: TACAS 2020. LNCS, vol. 12079, pp. 3–20. Springer, Cham (2020). https://doi.org/10.1007/978-3-030-45237-7_1
8. Korver, H.: Computing distinguishing formulas for branching bisimulation. In: Larsen, K.G., Skou, A. (eds.) CAV 1991. LNCS, vol. 575, pp. 13–23. Springer, Heidelberg (1992). https://doi.org/10.1007/3-540-55179-4_3
9. Smetsers, R., Moerman, J., Jansen, D.N.: Minimal separating sequences for all pairs of states. In: Dediu, A.-H., Janoušek, J., Martín-Vide, C., Truthe, B. (eds.) LATA 2016. LNCS, vol. 9618, pp. 181–193. Springer, Cham (2016). https://doi.org/10.1007/978-3-319-30000-9_14
10. Vaandrager, F., Garhewal, B., Rot, J., Wißmann, T.: A new approach for active automata learning based on apartness. In: Fisman, D., Rosu, G. (eds.) Tools and Algorithms for the Construction and Analysis of Systems, pp. 223–243, Cham. Springer International Publishing (2022). https://doi.org/10.1007/978-3-030-99524-9_12

Playing Wordle with Uppaal Stratego

Peter G. Jensen, Kim G. Larsen, and Marius Mikučionis[✉]

Computer Science, Aalborg University, Aalborg, Denmark
{pgj,kgl,marius}@cs.aau.dk

Abstract. In this paper we model and solve the popular game Wordle using Uppaal Stratego. We model three different game-modes in terms of POMDPs, with more than 12,000 controllable actions. These constitute by far the largest models ever presented to Uppaal Stratego. Our experimental evaluation is encouraging: e.g. in the hard game-mode the partitioning-refinement learning method of Uppaal Stratego reduces the expected number of guesses from a baseline of 7.67 to 4.40 using 1 million training episodes. To better understand the convergence properties of our learning method we also study reduced versions of Wordle.

1 Introduction

Frits Vaandrager has for many years been one of the most faithful Uppaal users. Having in 1994 verified the tolerance on clock accuracy of the Philips Audio protocol using linear hybrid automata [6], Frits became aware of the new tool Uppaal (first release in 1995) and sent his Master thesis student David Griffioen to Aalborg in order to apply Uppaal to the automatic verification of an extended version with two senders and bus collision [5]. Since then Frits Vaandrager has been using Uppaal in several applications:

- In 2006 [11] Frits and co-authors used Uppaal to model and analyze formally model parts of Zeroconf, a protocol for dynamic configuration of IPv4 link-local addresses that has been defined in RFC 3927 of the IETF.
- Also in 2006 [28] Frits and co-authors modelled and analysed the biphase mark protocol – a convention for representing both a string of bits and clock edges in square waves. Uppaal was used to derive maximal tolerances on clock rates, for different instances of the protocol, and to support the general parametric verification carried out using the proof assistant PVS.
- For a case-study of a wafer scanner from the semiconductor industry Frits and co-authors used Uppaal in combination with the symbolic model checker SMV to compute (1) a simple yet optimal deadlock avoidance policy, and (2) an infinite schedule that optimizes throughput [14].
- Within the European project QUASIMODO Frits and co-authors [26] developed a detailed timed automata model of the clock synchronization algorithm being used in a wireless sensor network under development by the Dutch company Chess. Using Uppaal Frits discovered that in certain cases a static, fully synchronized network may eventually become unsynchronized if the current algorithm is used, even in a setting with infinitesimal clock drifts.

© The Author(s), under exclusive license to Springer Nature Switzerland AG 2022
N. Jansen et al. (Eds.): Vaandrager Festschrift 2022, LNCS 13560, pp. 283–305, 2022.
https://doi.org/10.1007/978-3-031-15629-8_15

- Using UPPAAL in combination with colored Petri nets Frits and co-authors modelled a challenging industrial case involving an existing state-of-the-art image processing pipeline within professional digital document printers [17, 18]. The modelling effort was used to derive schedules for multiple concurrent jobs in the presence of limited resources (CPUs, memory, USB bandwidth, ..).

Besides applying UPPAAL, Frits Vaandrager has also been actively involved in development of the tool over the years. Here we mention:

- In 2003, Frits contributed to a prototype extension of UPPAAL with symmetry reduction [13]. For several examples the prototype demonstrated drastic reduction both in computation time and memory usage.
- Around 2000 Frits was coordinator of the European project AMETIST, with participation of several Dutch, French, German and Danish partners. During the project a strong request was made by the involved participants from control theory (more specifically by Professor Sebastian Engel from Dortmund): in addition to constraints and optimization with respect time they were even more interested in optimization with respect to energy. This lead to the extension of *priced* timed automata, and very quickly highly efficient implementation in UPPAAL CORA [3].
- In 2000 Frits, with Thomas Hune and Gerd Behrmann from Aalborg, developed, implemented and evaluated the a distributed verification engine for timed automata [4].
- In 2001, Frits, with Thomas Hune, Judi Romijn and Marielle Stoelinga, developed an extension of UPPAAL capable of synthesizing linear constraints for the correctness of parametric timed automata [16].

Moreover, Frits has been using UPPAAL in his teaching. Here we mention:

- with Roelof Hamberg, Frits Vaandrager have used the UPPAAL model checker in an introductory course on operating systems for first-year computer science students at the Radboud University Nijmegen. Using UPPAAL, their students have found mistakes in purported solutions to concurrency-control problems presented by Allen Downey in his popular textbook *The Little Book of Semaphores* [9].
- The unpublished note by Frits "A first Introduction to UPPAAL" [27] has for several years been part of the material used in first lectures on UPPAAL at Aalborg University. The note also shows that Frits has an affinity to games – in particular the note introduces the puzzle of "Gossiping Girls", which is regularly used as a mini-project exercise.

Since the early days of UPPAAL, considerable effort is now invested in the development of the branch UPPAAL STRATEGO, which uses combination of symbolic and machine learning techniques for generating safe and near-optimal strategies from Timed or even Hybrid Markov Decision processes. In this paper, we celebrate Frits Vaandrager's 60'th birthday by describing how the extremely popular game WORDLE may be modelled and solved using UPPAAL STRATEGO. We hope that he will find enjoyment in this and become as an enthusiastic user of UPPAAL STRATEGO as he has been of UPPAAL.

The outline of the paper is as follows: in Sect. 2 we give a brief description of WORDLE. In Sect. 3 we give a short presentation of UPPAAL STRATEGO and its partition-based Q-learning method based on the well-known Monty Hall Problem. We also present an extended 4-door version of this problem illustrating the need for memory-full strategies. In Sect. 4 we model three different game-modes of WORDLE, including the so-called *hard mode*. As POMDPs the models are orders of magnitude larger than any other model previously presented to UPPAAL STRATEGO. The models have more than 12,000 controllable actions – i.e. all the 5-letter English words – to be selected based on observation of a knowledge memorizing data-structure. Finally in Sect. 5 we apply UPPAAL STRATEGO as a solver for WORDLE, while studying the impact of (combination of) game-mode(s), training budget and the impact of our partitioning-refinement technique. Our results are encouraging: e.g. for the hard game-mode UPPAAL STRATEGO reduces the expected number of guesses from a baseline of 7.67^1 to 4.40 after 1 million training episodes. For the largely unrestricted permissive game-mode, UPPAAL STRATEGO also makes a significant reduction from 14.33 expected guesses to 10.55. This is still far away from the maximum 6 guesses allowed in WORDLE, so a substantial increase of the training budget is required. To better understand the convergence of our UPPAAL STRATEGO encodings we also consider reduced version of WORDLE. E.g. reduction by a factor of 128 makes all game-modes converge to an average of 2.21 guesses with the permissive mode starting from a baseline of 12.78 guesses. In all the experiments the use of our partition-refinement based Q-learning method clearly demonstrates its advantage over a traditional, fully explicit Q-learning approach.

2 WORDLE

WORDLE is a web-based word game created and developed by Welsh software engineer Josh Wardle, and owned and published by The New York Times Company since 2022 [29]. The game has gained a large amount of popularity after Wardle added the ability for players to copy their daily results as emoji squares around December 2021, which were widely shared on Twitter. Many clones and variations of the game were also created, as were versions in languages besides English.

In WORDLE a Player has six attempts to guess a five-letter word selected by an Opponent. After each guess the Opponent will provide, with feedback in the form of colored tiles indicating when letters match or occupy the correct position.

---

[1] i.e. when choosing legal words uniformly random.

More precisely, as illustrated in Fig. 1 after each guess, the letters which are not in the word are highlighted in grey, the letters which are in the word, but are in the wrong place are highlighted in yellow, and the letters which are in the correct spot in the word are highlighted green. If a guess contains repeated letters, but there is only one instance of that letter in the word, the second instance of the letter is marked grey.

Now the guess/feedback-interaction between the Player and the Opponent may be viewed as a decision tree, e.g. Fig. 2 is part of the decision tree in the setting of just 7 words. In the figure only a single guess is shown at each node, but the full decision tree contains all (up to) 7 choices along with their respective sub-trees.

Fig. 1. WORDLE screenshot.

More formally, WORDLE is a *game* between the Opponent and the Player. In one setting, the Opponent is *antagonistic* and will non-deterministically select one of the 12,972 legal 5-letter English words in order to maximize the minimum number of guesses required by the Player. In the second setting – to be pursued in this paper – the Opponent uses a probability distribution to select the 5-letter word to be guessed. Here the objective of the Player is to find a strategy that will minimize the expected number of guesses needed to reveal the selected word. In both cases, the word selected by the Opponent is obviously not visible to the Player. In the probabilistic case the game at hand is thus formally a POMDP (Partially observable Markov decision process). In the following we shall demonstrate how the POMPD of WORDLE may be easily expressed using the rich modelling formalism of UPPAAL STRATEGO, and subsequently used for learning and analysis of a (near-) optimal strategy for the Player.

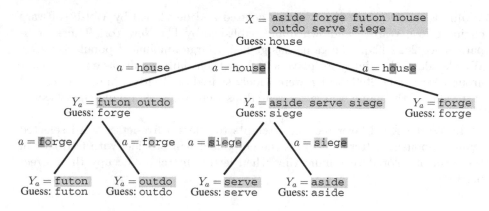

Fig. 2. (Partial) Decision Tree for Wordle (with 7 words).

Research Related to WORDLE. Internet and popular press is buzzing with many speculations about the best opening guesses[2,3,4] and algorithms to minimize maximum and average number of guesses[5,6]. However the bad news is that WORDLE has been shown to be *NP-hard* [24] and *NP-complete* [25] and therefore require a lot of resources to compute absolute optimal solutions.

Reinforcement learning has been applied to find optimal human strategy using maximum correct letter probabilities [2]. They implement the game in Python and explore various score functions to come up with optimal 1-, 2-, 3-, 4-, 5-guess sequences out of 2,315 curated words to help the human to play more efficiently.

The game has been implemented in Matlab toolbox and has been applied to evaluate the probability of winning when employing 6 strategies including *active learning* with hard mode and knowledge [7].

3 UPPAAL STRATEGO

UPPAAL STRATEGO [8] is the newest branch of the UPPAAL Tool Suite using symbolic model checking and reinforcement learning to obtain safe and (near-optimal) strategies for Markov Decision Processes (MDP). The MPDs considered are infinite state, being based on either timed automata [1] (Timed MDPs) or hybrid automata [15] (Continuous-Space MDPs). Using symbolic techniques from model checking – and abstracting a given MDP $\mathcal{M}$ into a two-player timed game – a most permissive strategy σ_S for a given safety objective S is synthesized. Now, applying various versions of reinforcement learning [19], (still safe) sub-strategies σ_O optimizing a given optimization criteria O are obtained. Finally, UPPAAL STRATEGO may provide obtained strategies in terms of explainable decision trees, and furthermore supports synthesis of strategies taking partial observability into account, so-called POMDPS. So far UPPAAL STRATEGO has been applied successfully within a number of application domains including heating systems [21], adaptive cruise control [23], maneuvers of train in railway stations [22], swarm robotics [22], storm-water detention ponds [12], and traffic control [10].

Monty Hall Problem and Strategies. To illustrate the use of UPPAAL STRATEGO for learning optimal strategies of POMDPs we consider a variant of the well-known Monty Hall Problem. Here a host ("Monty") provides a player with three doors, one containing a valuable prize and the other two containing a "gag", valueless prize. The contestant is offered a choice of one of the doors without knowledge of the content behind them. "Monty", who knows which door

---

[2] https://www.3blue1brown.com/lessons/wordle2.

[3] https://jonathanolson.net/experiments/optimal-wordle-solutions.

[4] http://sonorouschocolate.com/notes/index.php/The_best_strategies_for_Wordle.

[5] https://www.poirrier.ca/notes/wordle-optimal/.

[6] https://github.com/TylerGlaiel/wordlebot.

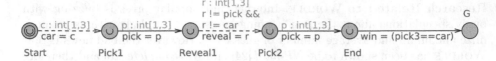

Fig. 3. UPPAAL STRATEGO model for the original 3-door Monty Hall Problem.

has the prize, opens a door that the player did not select that has a gag prize, and then offers the player the option to switch from their choice to the other remaining unopened door. The probability problem arises from asking if the player should switch to the unrevealed door.

In Fig. 3 an MDP model of the original Monty Hall Problem in UPPAAL STRATEGO is given. The MDP has 6 locations, with the choices of the host indicated by dashed edges and the choices by the player indicated by full edges. In Start the host (uniformly) randomly selects the door behind which the car is placed. In Pick1 the player makes the initial choice of a door. In Reveal the host reveals opens a door not selected by the player and without the car. Now in Pick2 the player makes the final choice of a door which, which in End will determine the value of win. The objective is to now to find a strategy sp of the player that will maximize the expected value of win when reaching Hall.G. Clearly the strategy will not be allowed to observe the value of the variable car, effectively making the model a POMDP.

In UPPAAL STRATEGO synthesis of optimal strategies under partial observability is specified using optimization queries of the following form:

```
strategy Name = minE(Cost) [Bound]
             { ExprList1 } -> { ExprList2 } : <> Goal
```

where:

Name is the name associated with the strategy, which can be later used to refer to the strategy when saving it to a file or examining its properties in other SMC queries.

minE(Cost) asks the tool to minimize the expected cost defined by Cost expression. One can replace this entry with maxE(Gain) to maximize the expected gain defined by Gain expression.

Bound defines a length of a stochastic simulation run, which can be described in terms of number of discrete transitions, absolute time or a limit on some variable in general.

Goal is a state predicate defining the goal state, which also terminates the stochastic simulation run and marks it as "winning".

ExprList1 and ExprList2 are comma-separated expressions over the locations and variables defining the parts of the system state to be observed by the strategy.

Now, UPPAAL STRATEGO uses the Q-learning algorithm from [19] to learn an approximator for the function $\mathcal{Q}^*$, that for any value (E_1, E_2) of the expression-lists ExprList1 and ExprList2 and for any decision action a returns the minimal expected cost $\mathcal{Q}^*(E_1, E_2)(a)$ of reaching the Goal from (E_1, E_2) by choosing a. More precisely, for each decision action a and value E_1 of ExprList1 the algorithm maintains a cost-function approximator of $\lambda E_2.\mathcal{Q}^*(E_1, E_2)(a)$ mapping values E_2 of ExprList2 to the expected cost $\mathcal{Q}^*(E_1, E_2)(a)$. This approximator itself is maintained by a partition refinement method. Experience has indicated that it is preferable that the set of ExprList1 values are discrete and relatively small (e.g. integer expressions, Boolean predicates over variables, distinct floating point values), where even a small change in value requires a different cost function altogether. In contrast, the set of ExprList2 values can be large, represented by integers, clocks and floating point expressions, whenever small changes in value have small effects on cost. We shall later see the effect of placing expressions to be observed in either ExprList1 or ExprList2 in our experience with learning strategies for WORDLE.

Now returning to the Monty Hall Problem we pose the following query in UPPAAL STRATEGO:

```
strategy sp = maxE(win) [<=1]
        { Hall.location, pick, reveal } -> {}: <> Hall.G
```

The set-annotation Hall.location, pick, reveal restricts the strategy of the player to only depend on the locations of Hall and the values of pick and reveal. In particular, the value of the variable of car is not observable. Now, the value of the learned strategy sp is obtained by the following query:

```
E[<=1;1000] (max:win) under sp
```

returning 0.641 ± 0.029783 as a 95% confidence interval after 1000 runs. Further examination of the strategy reveals that in sp the player always opt for switching from the initial choice to the remaining unopened door.

A part of the computed strategy is seen in Listing 1.1. In the observed vector (3,3,1), corresponding to being in Pick2 having pick=3 and reveal=1, we can see that action 2 has the highest computed Q-value of 0.7044. Here 2 denotes the action to switch and 0.7044 is an estimator of the expected win-ratio under the strategy. Conversely we can see that UPPAAL STRATEGO has learned that picking 1 after 1 was revealed by the host comes with zero reward.

4-Door Monty Hall Problem & Memory-Full Strategies. In general optimal strategies for POMDPs require memory. This was not required in the simple POMDP of the Monty Hall Problem. To address the need for memory-full strategies and see how this can be handled in UPPAAL STRATEGO we consider in Fig. 4(a) an extended version of the Monty Hall Problem now with 4 doors, and an extra exchange between the host and the player. In all the moves of the player (full edges), the player may pick any of the four doors. The door selected in the

Listing 1.1. A snippet of the computed strategy for the 3-door Monty Hall Problem when in the observed state (Pick2,pick=3,reveal=1). Action indexes have been re-indexed for readability.

```
1  {...,"regressors":
2          "(3,3,1)": {...,"regressor": {
3                  "3" : 0.3690...,
4                  "2" : 0.7044...,
5                  "1" : 0}, ...
6              }
7  }
```

final pick Pick3 is the final choice of the player. As for the host, the first door revealed in Reveal1 is (as in the 3-door version) a randomly chosen door with no car and different from the first door selected by the player. In the second round, the door revealed by the host in Reveal2 is randomly chosen among the doors with no car, and different from the second pick of the player, and different from the first door reveal by the host. Now the learning query of UPPAAL STRATEGO

```
strategy sp4 = maxE(win) [<=1]
    { Hall.location, pick, reveal } -> {}: <> Hall.G
```

gives a strategy sp4 with expected winning probability 66%. Examining the learned strategy it is found (perhaps not surprisingly) that the final picked door must be different from the second door picked as well as different from the last door revealed by the host.

However in the above strategy sp4 is memoryless. In particular, in the last round the player is not allowed to take into account knowledge from the first round, e.g. what was the first door picked and the first door revealed. To allow for the strategy of the player to take information from all the past moves into account, Fig. 4(b) presents an extended model with round-numbered versions of the variables pick and reveal having been added. Clearly a principle that may be added to all acyclic POMDPs. Now the learning query:

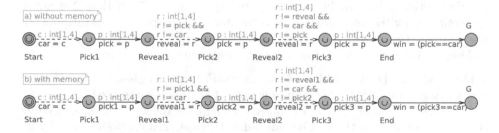

Fig. 4. Models for 4-door Monty Hall Problem: without memory and with.

```
strategy sp4h = maxE(win) [<=1] {
        Hall.location, pick1, reveal1, pick2, reveal2
    } -> {}: <> Hall.G
```

will learn a strategy for the player that may depend on the value of `pick` and `reveal` from all rounds, but of course still not the position of the `car`. Now the query `E[<=1;1000] (max:win) under sp4h` returns 0.744 ± 0.0270956 as a 95% confidence interval for the expected probability of winning under `sp4h`, a significant improvement compared to `sp4` that did not use memory. Finally, the probability estimation query:

```
Pr[<=1](<> Hall.G
        && !(pick3==pick2) && !(pick3==pick1)
        && (pick2==pick1) && !(pick3==reveal1)
        && !(pick3==reveal2) && !(pick2==reveal1)) under sp4h
```

returns ≈ 1, revealing interesting information about the strategy `sp4h`, e.g. that the door picked in the first and second round of the player should be *the same*, and that the door picked in the final round should be *different* from that.

We leave it to the interested reader (including Frits Vaandrager) to further investigate optimal strategies of N-door generalizations of the Monty Hall Problem using UPPAAL STRATEGO.

4   WORDLE in UPPAAL STRATEGO

Figure 5 shows the UPPAAL STRAT-EGO model of the POMDP for the WORDLE puzzle, where the *Player* repeatedly makes (controllable) decisions against a stochastic *Opponent*. The model follows the flow of the normal WORDLE game – although with several book-keeping steps of the Player allowing us to experiment with different game-modes such as the WORDLE hard-mode. Each word in the dictionary of valid words receives an index ranging from 0 to 12,972, captured by the constant NWORDS, of which the first 2,315 words can appear as solutions, captured by the constant CURATED. For convenience, WORDLE is extended to a timed-game in which each guess takes exactly one time-unit (tracked by the

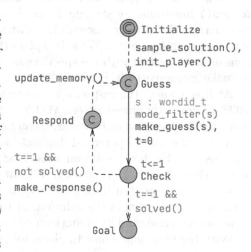

Fig. 5. UPPAAL STRATEGO model of WORDLE where a global clock guesses (not shown) keeps track of the total elapsed time, effectively measuring the number of guesses.

clock t) allowing us to track the total progression of time using the clock `guesses` which is never reset. Here is the general flow of the game:

In `Initialize` location the Opponent must select a word from the curated solution-set by picking a word-index 0 and `CURATED`, this is done by the `sample_solution()` function. Meanwhile the `init_player()` function initializes the book-keeping memory of the player.

In `Guess` the Player may select the next guess `s : wordid_t`, with `wordid_t` defined as `int[0,NWORDS]`, that is valid with the current game-mode (checked by `mode_filter(s)`), like hard-mode which limits the guesses according to the specified game mode (e.g. hard-mode). The call to `make_guess(s)` effectively stores the guess of the player. Notice that this is the only location where the Player has decision (denoted by solid edges) whereas all other edges are under the control of the Opponent.

`Check` forces the Opponent to either validate that the guess is correct (checked by `solved()`) or that the guess was incorrect (`not solved()`), in which case a response is computed (`make_response()`). Notice that the invariant `t<=1` forces the opponent to reside in `Check` for at most 1 time unit, while the guards on the outgoing edges (`t==1`) enforces delay of exactly one time unit per guess.

`Goal` is the final location, denoting that the word proposed initially by the Opponent was found by the Player.

`Respond` allows for the Player to update the internal book-keeping memory.

The objective of the game is to reach `Goal` with the minimum expected value of the `guesses` clock.

While the `sample_solution()`, `init_player()`, `make_guess(s)` and `solved()` functions are straight forward, in that they simply copy, check and clear arrays, the `make_response()`, `update_memory()` and `mode_filter(s)` are of a more complex nature. We will explain the latter two in the following subsections as they are tied with the specific game mode employed. Let us first explain the `make_response()` in Listing 1.2.

At first glance, the response computation seems straight forward: respond `GREEN` on correctly placed letters, `YELLOW` if the letter appears in a different position, and `GRAY` otherwise. However, the *actual* feedback computation of WORDLE is more subtle due to potential duplicate letters. For example, the word `hello` contains two '1's. If the solution word is `afoul` (with a single '1' present), then only a single letter '1' is marked `YELLOW` and another '1' is `GRAY`. Thus the response is computed in three passes: 1) to determine the number of occurrences of the different letters in the solution, 2) to mark `GREEN` responses (and deduct spent occurrences), and 3) to mark an adequate amount of characters as `YELLOW`.

With the main game flow in place, we can now discuss various game modes.

Game-Modes and Memory. We experiment with three different game modes, that is, limitations for the Player guesses implemented by the `mode_filter(s)` guard in accordance with the (condensed) history of the guesses and responses:

1. *Hard mode*, where any prior hints of yellow and green must be respected in subsequent guesses,

Listing 1.2. Computes response (hint) based on guess and solution.

```
1   void make_response() {
2       int[0,NPOS] counts[letter_t];
3       // mark correct positions and count unmarked letters:
4       for (p : pos_t)
5           if (guess[p] == solution[p])
6               response[p] = GREEN;
7           else {
8               response[p] = GRAY;
9               ++counts[solution[p]];
10          }
11      // mark out of place letters:
12      for (p : pos_t) {
13          if (response[p] != GREEN) {
14              if (counts[guess[p]] > 0) {
15                  response[p] = YELLOW;
16                  --counts[guess[p]];
17              }
18          }
19      }
20  }
```

2. *Conservative mode*, where any prior hints of gray (i.e. non-existence of letter in the solution) must be respected s.t. any subsequent guess is delimited from using such letters, and
3. *Permissive mode*, where any new guess must change the internal knowledge structure.

The model uses a notion of memory to enforce the rules of the game mode which generic across all three modes and is represented by the following two data structures:

1. knowledge: an integer array of $|pos\_t| \times |letter\_t|$ size (i.e. 5×26) taking the value MAYBE (default) for "no knowledge", SURELY_NOT for GRAY hints (implying the letter can not be present at the given position) and SURELY for GREEN hints (implying that the letter must be present at the position), and
2. counts: an integer array of $|letter\_t|$ size (0-initialized) to keep track of the maximal number of occurrences for each letter observed in a single word (e.g. getting YELLOW and GREEN hint on the l's of hello would set the 12th position to 2).

Listing 1.3 shows update_memory() procedure to update the memory according to the rules above and the chosen STRATEGY_TYPE: conservative strategy (value STRATEGY_PERMISSIVE) or the permissive or combined strategy (values STRATEGY_PERMISSIVE and STRATEGY_CONS_PERM respectively).

Listing 1.3. The memory update function.

```
1   void update_memory() {
2       update_count();
3       update_hints();
4       if (STRATEGY_TYPE == STRATEGY_CONSERVATIVE)
5           update_conservative();
6       if (STRATEGY_TYPE == STRATEGY_PERMISSIVE ||
7           STRATEGY_TYPE == STRATEGY_CONS_PERM)
8           update_permissive();
9       if (HARDMODE)
10          update_hard();
11  }
12
13  void update_count() {
14      int local_counts[letter_t];
15      for (p : pos_t)
16          if (response[p] != GRAY)
17              local_counts[guess[p]] += 1;
18      for (c : letter_t)
19          counts[c] = max(counts[c], local_counts[c]);
20  }
21
22  void update_conservative() {
23      for (p : pos_t) {
24          if (response[p] == GREEN) {
25              for (l : letter_t)
26                  knowledge[p][l] = SURELY_NOT;
27              knowledge[p][guess[p]] = SURELY;
28          } else if (response[p] == YELLOW) {
29              knowledge[p][guess[p]] = SURELY_NOT;
30          } else if (response[p] == GRAY) {
31              if (counts[guess[p]] == 0) { // absent
32                  for (q : pos_t)
33                      knowledge[q][guess[p]] = SURELY_NOT;
34              } else {
35                  knowledge[p][guess[p]] = SURELY_NOT;
36                  if (forall(q : pos_t)
37                          guess[q] != guess[p] ||
38                          response[q] != YELLOW)
39                  {   // all are correctly placed
40                      for (q : pos_t)
41                          if (guess[q] != guess[p] ||
42                              response[q] != GREEN)
43                              knowledge[q][guess[p]] = SURELY_NOT;
44                  }
45              }
46          }
47      }
48  }
49
50  void update_permissive() {
51      update_conservative();
```

```
52        check_sums();
53    }
54
55    void check_sums() {
56        int letter_sum;
57        letter_t letter;
58        int local_counts[letter_t];
59        bool changed = true;
60        while (changed) {
61            changed = false;
62            local_counts = counts;
63            // check if only one unknown letter left
64            for (p : pos_t) {
65                letter_sum = 0;
66                for (l : letter_t)
67                    if (knowledge[p][l] != SURELY_NOT) {
68                        letter = l;
69                        letter_sum += 1;
70                    }
71                // new information?
72                if (letter_sum = 1 &&
73                        knowledge[p][letter] != SURELY) {
74                    knowledge[p][letter] = SURELY;
75                    changed = true;
76                }
77                if (letter_sum == 1)
78                    --local_counts[letter];
79            }
80            if ((sum(l : letter_t) counts[l]) == NPOS)
81                // remove all inconsistent with the 5 known letters
82                for (p : pos_t)
83                    for (l : letter_t)
84                        if (knowledge[p][l] != SURELY &&
85                                counts[l] == 0)
86                            knowledge[p][l] = SURELY_NOT;
87        }
88    }
```

Let us discuss the functions in order:

update_count() updates the count-array by first computing the sum of occurrences of letters in the guessed word for which the feedback was either green or yellow. In the end, this is aggregated into the count array by keeping only the largest value; the target word will not change during a single execution.

update_conservative() has three cases for each letter/response position:

1. if the response is GREEN, update the row corresponding to the position to SURELY_NOT and then mark the correct GREEN letter with the value SURELY,

2. if the response is YELLOW, update the single position/letter entry to the value SURELY_NOT, and

3. if the response is GRAY, either the target word contains no such letter
   (first sub-case) and we can update across the knowledge rows with the
   value SURELY_NOT. Alternatively we check whether, in the current guess,
   all other occurrences of the letter are correctly placed – in which case we
   can achieve a similar effect, and otherwise we limit ourselves to updating
   the single cell of the position/letter in the knowledge to SURELY_NOT.

update_permissive() calls first the update_conservative() function and then
   attempts to deduce even more values via a call to check_sums().

check_sums() checks, if at a given position, only a single letter is possible, and
   then updates the knowledge array accordingly. If all 5 letters are known (but
   their positions not), the function will furthermore remove all non-valid letters
   from the knowledge array by marking them with the SURELY_NOT value.

We can now introduce the action-filtering code behind the different modes
in Listing 1.4.

Listing 1.4. Game-mode filtering of actions.

```
1   bool mode_filter(wordid_t solution) {
2       if(HARDMODE && !hard[solution]) return false;
3       if (STRATEGY_TYPE == STRATEGY_CONSERVATIVE)
4           return conservative_strategy(solution);
5       else if (STRATEGY_TYPE == STRATEGY_PERMISSIVE)
6           return permissive_strategy(solution);
7       else if(STRATEGY_TYPE == STRATEGY_CONS_PERM)
8           return combined_strategy(solution);
9       else return true;
10  }
11
12  bool is_hard(wordid_t solution) {
13      int local_counts[letter_t];
14      bool ok_green;
15      bool used_hints;
16      ok_green = forall(p : pos_t)
17                      knowledge[p][words[solution][p]] == SURELY ||
18                      (not exists(l : letter_t)
19                          knowledge[p][l] == SURELY);
20      local_counts = counts;
21      for(p : pos_t) --local_counts[words[solution][p]];
22      used_hints = forall(p : pos_t) local_counts[p] <= 0;
23      return ok_green && used_hints;
24  }
25
26  bool conservative_strategy(wordid_t solution) {
27      return not exists(p : pos_t)
             knowledge[p][words[solution][p]] == SURELY_NOT;
28  }
29
```

```
30   bool permissive_strategy(wordid_t solution) {
31       if (forall(p : pos_t)
32               knowledge[p][words[solution][p]] == SURELY)
33           return true;
34       // anything that feasibly improves the knowledge is allowed
35       return exists(p : pos_t)
36           knowledge[p][words[solution][p]] == MAYBE;
37   }
38
39   bool combined_strategy(wordid_t solution) {
40       if (forall(p : pos_t)
41               knowledge[p][words[solution][p]] == SURELY)
42           return true;
43       // anything that feasibly improves the knowledge is allowed
44       // also must not use characters shown to be useless
45       return exists(p : pos_t)
46           knowledge[p][words[solution][p]] == MAYBE &&
47               forall(p : pos_t)
48                   knowledge[p][words[solution][p]] != SURELY_NOT;
49   }
```

The mode_filter(s) function checks if the word with index s is valid guess based on the game mode – HARDMODE or particular STRATEGY_TYPE, which effectively filters the actions of the Player based on the different heuristics described.

Hard mode checks firstly that if GREEN hint was ever given, then the proposed word *must* contain the said letter in the said position. Secondly we validate that the sum of occurrences of letters matches with YELLOW and GREEN hints given prior.

Conservative mode is instead concerned with GRAY (absence) hints and strictly disallows any word where GRAY hint has been given. This generalizes to disallowing any word where the value of the knowledge for any letter of the word is SURELY_NOT (must be absent).

Permissive mode instead attempts to be as liberal as possible, but ensuring the progress. The mode disallows any word (except for the solution-word), which will not yield an update to the knowledge-array. This is done by requiring at least the presence of a single MAYBE in the knowledge vector, for a letter/position-combination of the proposed word.

Furthermore, we conjecture the following:

- the projection state of WORDLE on the POMDP with the observable state of the knowledge and counts arrays is sufficient to compute optimal strategies, and
- the optimal solution to the permissive game mode is also optimal in the original WORDLE.

Here optimality should be understood as the expected number of guesses, assuming that the Opponent uses a uniform random choice to select the solution word.

Partial Observable WORDLE. Similar to the Monty Hall Problem presented in Sect. 3, we employ partial observability to correctly capture the nature of WORDLE. To follow our conjecture, we assume that it is sufficient for the strategy to depend on the `knowledge` and `count` arrays as observable entities. We thus construct the following query to synthesize near-optimal strategies:

```
strategy S = minE(guesses) [<=MAXG] {
    Play.counts[0], ..., Play.counts[25],
    Play.knowledge[0][0], ..., Play.knowledge[0][25],
    ...
    Play.knowledge[4][0], ..., Play.knowledge[4][25]
} -> {}: <> Play.Goal
```

Here `MAXG` is a sufficiently high bound on time, i.e., the number of guesses within which the game is expected to be completed. For all practical purposes and the proposed game modes, a value of 100 suffices, as witnessed in the experiments (See Fig. 8).

However, 6×26 memory variables can take three different values ($\{0, 1, 2\}$ for `counts`, `SURELY_NOT`, `MAYBE` and `SURELY` for the `knowledge`), the hypothetical number of combinations is astronomically high and cannot be visited exhaustively. Therefore we also experiment with the partition refinement technique of UPPAAL STRATEGO to automatically deduce a sufficient partitioning of the state-space. This is reflected in the following query:

```
strategy S = minE(guesses) [<=MAXG] {
    Play.counts[0], ..., Play.counts[25]
} -> {
    Play.knowledge[0][0], ..., Play.knowledge[0][25],
    ...
    Play.knowledge[4][0], ..., Play.knowledge[4][25]
}: <> Play.Goal
```

Here we retain that each unique assignment to `counts` must lead to a different partition, i.e. a pre-partitioning of the observed state-space, while assignment to the `knowledge`-array can be aggregated at will of the learning-algorithm.

Informally, the learning algorithms *can* chose to lump together different assignments of the `knowledge` array, but *must* consider assignments of `counts` as being radically different.

The choice of placement of these observable variables is not arbitrary. The expected actual assignments to the `counts` array is expected to be small, and on the other hand, different assignments to this array is expected to have very different optimal strategies; i.e. best next word. On the other hand, the `knowledge` array is expected to have a huge domain of possible assignments where minor differences in assignment will have little effect on the optimal next word. Again we refer the reader to the work of M. Jaeger et al. [19] for the details of the partition refinement procedure.

5 Evaluation

We experiment with using UPPAAL STRATEGO as a solver for the POMDP induced by the encoding of the WORDLE game presented in the previous section and we study the impact of:

1. increasing the training budget,
2. the different game modes, and
3. the partition-refinement technique of UPPAAL STRATEGO (denoted PT).

As the game modes presented in Sect. 4 can be combined, we experiment not only with the individual game-modes but also combinations. In particular we consider as basis *CONS*, the conservative mode, *PERM*, the permissive mode, *COMB* the combined mode of *CONS* and *PERM*. These three game-modes are then further combined with the hard-mode (denoted *HM*). For each of such a combination we denote by the *baseline* the random strategy under the given game mode. That is, in a given state, the strategy picks uniformly among all actions (words) allowed by the game mode. We refrain from experimenting with *HM* directly as experiments demonstrated a low probability of winning the game under the baseline strategy within a reasonable number of guesses.

All experiments are conducted on dis-homogeneous hardware and we thus refrain from commenting explicitly on running-times. We note that 1000 simulations on an Intel i7-1165G7 takes roughly 90 s, and that training times can be extrapolated to within a factor of two from this measure. Furthermore, to reduce the simulation time, we have modeled various caching techniques and in addition utilize the external C-library linking to offload the updates of the `knowledge` and `count` arrays.

Models, strategies, and an interactive tool for using the produced strategies in a game of WORDLE is available in a repeatability package [20].

Evaluation: We experiment with the learning-algorithms in UPPAAL STRATEGO over the 6 different strategy profiles and for each profile use either the explicit observation vectors or the partition-refinement technique (*PT*). Specifically we here also study the impact of increasing the training budget and we configure UPPAAL STRATEGO to utilize the full learning-budget and restrict the tool to only evaluate the quality of the strategy when the learning budget is exhausted. To evaluate the quality of a strategy S, we execute the query:

```
E[#<=MAXS;23150](max:guesses) under S
```

Notice that this evaluation allows for each word in the selected set of curated word set to be picked (on average) 10 times. Each experimental configuration is repeated 5 times and we report the best solution found for each configuration. We conduct three series of experiments; one with the full word-set of WORDLE and one where it is reduced by a factor of 64 and 128 denoted as WORDLE/64 and WORDLE/128 respectively. Let us first study the reduced versions of WORDLE.

WORDLE/{64,128}: In Fig. 6a we see the gradual improvement in performance of the learning algorithm of UPPAAL STRATEGO when playing the WORDLE/128 game (reduced by a factor 128). We observe that all methods converge to strategies delivering on average 2.21 guesses. In the case of *COMB-HM* (black, dashed), the reduction from the baseline of 2.95 is modest while the game mode *PERM* (red, solid) has the largest improvement, having a baseline of 12.78 guesses. We can observe that the larger search-space of the permissive game mode (red) has a negative impact on the needed budget for convergence and without the game mode providing any benefit compared to the more restrictive game modes. In general all the tested configurations have converged with a budget of 4.096 million episodes.

We observe similar tendencies in WORDLE/64 (Fig. 6b) with all modes converging on a performance of 2.27 guesses, however with the permissive game (red lines) modes not reaching a plateau and thus still with potential to improve beyond this limit. The *PERM* game mode (red, solid) here enjoys a drop from a baseline of 13.49 to 2.38 but also under the *COMB-HM* game mode the result is improved from a baseline of 3.94 to 2.27. Furthermore we see the partition refinement algorithm (annotated by x in the plot) generally appears to improve on the rate of learning initially, but is eventually, after enough episodes, overtaken by an explicit representation of the states (annotated by box in the plot). This indicates that the learning algorithm initially can exploit grouping large sets of states together under the same sub-strategy, and thus accumulate more information for this aggregate sub-strategy per episode. However, with enough samples, the partition-refinement scheme is overtaken when this same aggregation needs to be sub-partitioned, at which point the explicit representation has been trained sufficiently. Comparing Fig. 6a and Fig. 6b we can see that at least a 16 times larger training set is needed (2^4) for the learning methods to reach a plateau, indicating a radical growth in the total search space. Studying both plots we can also observe that an exponential increase in the learning budget (x-axis is in $\log_2$) leads to a less than linear improvement in the performance (y-axis is in $\log_{10}$). We hypothesize that this is due to the large action and sample space combined with the dampening of the updates of the Q-values when applying Q-learning.

Full WORDLE: As witnessed by Fig. 7a, UPPAAL STRATEGO is challenged more by the full version of WORDLE, however the tool still manages to produce a strategy yielding 4.01 guesses on average under the *COMB-HM* (black, dashed). This is a significant improvement compared to the 4.8 guesses on average when comparing to playing in the same game mode but using the baseline strategy. Given the astronomically large search space of WORDLE, having more than 20 million configurations after the first guess ($2,315$ possible "words of the day" times $12,972$ possible initial guesses), finding an optimal solution is not expected.

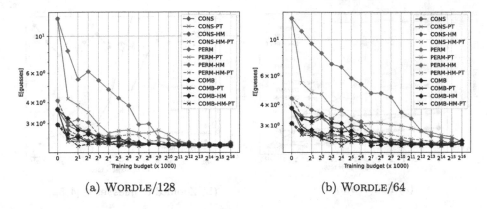

(a) WORDLE/128   (b) WORDLE/64

Fig. 6. Improvement of training using UPPAAL STRATEGO under different observability patterns and different strategies for the WORDLE model reduced by a factor of 128 (left) or 64 (right). The y-axis is given in $\log_{10}$ and the x-axis in $\log_2$. The 0-point on the x-axis represents the baseline (a training budget of 0 episodes).

Similar to the reduced WORDLE games the *PERM* game mode (red) enjoys large improvements, dropping from a baseline of 7.67 guesses on average to 4.40 under hard-mode (red, dashed) and from 14.33 to 10.55 without hard-mode (red, solid) when using partitioning (PT). Comparing Fig. 7a and Fig. 7b where y-axis interval of $[4, 5]$ is in focus, it becomes apparent that a plateau has not yet been reached. We can observe that the best performing game modes slowly improve, in an oscillating fashion, hinting that additional training episodes can lead to improved strategies. Contrary to what was observed in the WORDLE/128 and WORDLE/64 experiments, the explicit memory representation (annotated by squares) achieve little to no improvement when the number of training episodes is increased, although they still manage to outperform the random strategy. We can also see that the hard-mode (dashed lines) has a much higher impact. Comparing the *PERM-HM-PT* (red, dashed) with *PERM-PT* (red, solid) under the partition refinement (x annotated), we observe that the *PERM-HM-PT* has a significantly lower starting-point and also achieves radical improvements from 1.024 to 2.048 million episodes. It remains to be seen whether the *PERM-PT* exhibits the same behavior as the experiments have yet to complete at the time of writing.

In Fig. 8 we can see that the different game-modes presented are effected vastly differently by training in terms of reduction in the expected number of guesses. Using the permissive game-mode yields a performance improvement from 14.33 guesses on average to 7.67 when hard mode is enabled as well. Playing according to the conservative mode leads to 5.93 guesses on average (4.87 under hard-mode) while the combined game-mode lands on average of 5.69 guesses (4.88 under hard-mode) (Table 1).

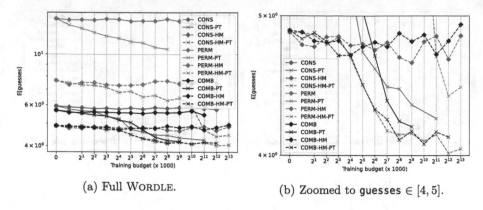

(a) Full WORDLE.   (b) Zoomed to guesses $\in [4,5]$.

Fig. 7. Improvement of training using UPPAAL STRATEGO under different observability patterns and different strategies for the full WORDLE game. The y-axis is given in $\log_{10}$ and the x-axis in $\log_2$. The 0-point on the x-axis represents the baseline (a training budget of 0 episodes).

Table 1. Quality of the best obtained strategy for full WORDLE using partitioning (PT) or explicit memory representation in different modes. The Baseline row indicate the performance under a random strategy.

Game Mode	CONS	CONS-HM	PERM	PERM-HM	COMB	COMB-HM
Baseline	5.93	4.87	14.33	7.67	5.69	4.88
Explicit	5.76	4.64	13.60	7.30	5.44	4.69
PT	4.24	4.01	10.55	4.40	4.19	4.07

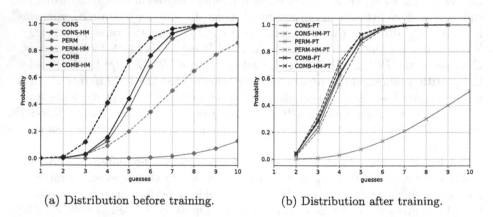

(a) Distribution before training.   (b) Distribution after training.

Fig. 8. Comparison of random plays under the permissive (red), conservative (green) and combined (black) strategies. The dashed lines indicate hard-mode enabled where solid lines indicate normal mode. (Color figure online)

6 Conclusion

In this paper we have modelled and solved the popular game WORDLE using the tool UPPAAL STRATEGO constituting by orders of magnitude the largest POMDP ever presented to the tool. The experimental evaluation are encouraging: our partitioning-refinement Q-learning method reduces significantly the expected number of guesses, e.g. from 7.67 to 4.40 guesses for the hard game-mode. In all our experiments, the partitioning-refinement method performs better than traditional, explicit Q-learning. Future research include learning directly from the feedback-history rather than from observation of the manually maintained knowledge and count data structures.

References

1. Alur, R., Dill, D.L.: A theory of timed automata. Theor. Comput. Sci. **126**(2), 183–235 (1994)
2. Anderson, B.J., Meyer, J.G.: Finding the optimal human strategy for wordle using maximum correct letter probabilities and reinforcement learning (2022)
3. Behrmann, G., et al.: Minimum-cost reachability for priced time automata. In: Di Benedetto, M.D., Sangiovanni-Vincentelli, A. (eds.) HSCC 2001. LNCS, vol. 2034, pp. 147–161. Springer, Heidelberg (2001). https://doi.org/10.1007/3-540-45351-2_15
4. Behrmann, G., Hune, T., Vaandrager, F.: Distributing timed model checking—how the search order matters. In: Emerson, E.A., Sistla, A.P. (eds.) CAV 2000. LNCS, vol. 1855, pp. 216–231. Springer, Heidelberg (2000). https://doi.org/10.1007/10722167_19
5. Bengtsson, J., et al.: Verification of an audio protocol with bus collision using UPPAAL. In: Alur, R., Henzinger, T.A. (eds.) CAV 1996. LNCS, vol. 1102, pp. 244–256. Springer, Heidelberg (1996). https://doi.org/10.1007/3-540-61474-5_73
6. Bosscher, D., Polak, I., Vaandrager, F.: Verification of an audio control protocol. In: Langmaack, H., de Roever, W.-P., Vytopil, J. (eds.) FTRTFT 1994. LNCS, vol. 863, pp. 170–192. Springer, Heidelberg (1994). https://doi.org/10.1007/3-540-58468-4_165
7. Brown, K.A.: MODEL, GUESS, CHECK: wordle as a primer on active learning for materials research. NPJ Comput. Mater. **8**(97), 1–3 (2022)
8. David, A., Jensen, P.G., Larsen, K.G., Mikučionis, M., Taankvist, J.H.: UPPAAL STRATEGO. In: Baier, C., Tinelli, C. (eds.) TACAS 2015. LNCS, vol. 9035, pp. 206–211. Springer, Heidelberg (2015). https://doi.org/10.1007/978-3-662-46681-0_16
9. Downey, A.B.: The Little Book of Semaphores, 2nd edn. The Ins and Outs of Concurrency Control and Common Mistakes. Createspace (2009)
10. Eriksen, A., et al.: UPPAAL stratego for intelligent traffic lights. In: 12th ITS European Congress. ERTICO - ITS Europe, 2017. 12th ITS European Congress: ITS Beyond Borders, 19–22 June 2017 (2017)
11. Gebremichael, B., Vaandrager, F.W., Zhang, M.: Analysis of the Zeroconf protocol using UPPAAL. In: Min, S.L., Yi, W. (eds.) Proceedings of the 6th ACM & IEEE International Conference on Embedded Software, EMSOFT 2006, Seoul, Korea, 22–25 October 2006, pp. 242–251. ACM (2006)

12. Goorden, M.A., Larsen, K.G., Nielsen, J.E., Nielsen, T.D., Rasmussen, M.R., Srba, J.: Learning safe and optimal control strategies for storm water detention ponds. In: Jungers, R.M., Ozay, N., Abate, A. (eds.) 7th IFAC Conference on Analysis and Design of Hybrid Systems, ADHS 2021. IFAC-PapersOnLine, Brussels, Belgium, 7–9 July 2021, vol. 54, pp. 13–18. Elsevier (2021)

13. Hendriks, M., Behrmann, G., Larsen, K., Niebert, P., Vaandrager, F.: Adding symmetry reduction to UPPAAL. In: Larsen, K.G., Niebert, P. (eds.) FORMATS 2003. LNCS, vol. 2791, pp. 46–59. Springer, Heidelberg (2004). https://doi.org/10.1007/978-3-540-40903-8_5

14. Hendriks, M., van den Nieuwelaar, B., Vaandrager, F.W.: Model checker aided design of a controller for a wafer scanner. Int. J. Softw. Tools Technol. Transf. 8(6), 633–647 (2006)

15. Henzinger, T.A.: The theory of hybrid automata. In: Proceedings of the 11th Annual IEEE Symposium on Logic in Computer Science, New Brunswick, New Jersey, USA, 27–30 July 1996, pp. 278–292. IEEE Computer Society (1996)

16. Hune, T., Romijn, J., Stoelinga, M., Vaandrager, F.: Linear parametric model checking of timed automata. In: Margaria, T., Yi, W. (eds.) TACAS 2001. LNCS, vol. 2031, pp. 189–203. Springer, Heidelberg (2001). https://doi.org/10.1007/3-540-45319-9_14

17. Igna, G., et al.: Formal modeling and scheduling of datapaths of digital document printers. In: Cassez, F., Jard, C. (eds.) FORMATS 2008. LNCS, vol. 5215, pp. 170–187. Springer, Heidelberg (2008). https://doi.org/10.1007/978-3-540-85778-5_13

18. Igna, G., Vaandrager, F.: Verification of printer datapaths using timed automata. In: Margaria, T., Steffen, B. (eds.) ISoLA 2010. LNCS, vol. 6416, pp. 412–423. Springer, Heidelberg (2010). https://doi.org/10.1007/978-3-642-16561-0_38

19. Jaeger, M., Jensen, P.G., Guldstrand Larsen, K., Legay, A., Sedwards, S., Taankvist, J.H.: Teaching stratego to play ball: optimal synthesis for continuous space MDPs. In: Chen, Y.-F., Cheng, C.-H., Esparza, J. (eds.) ATVA 2019. LNCS, vol. 11781, pp. 81–97. Springer, Cham (2019). https://doi.org/10.1007/978-3-030-31784-3_5

20. Jensen, P.G., Larsen, K.G., Mikucionis, M.: Artefact for "Playing Wordle with Uppaal Stratego", June 2022. https://doi.org/10.5281/zenodo.6703959

21. Jensen, P.G., Larsen, K.G., Srba, J.: Real-time strategy synthesis for timed-arc Petri net games via discretization. In: Bošnački, D., Wijs, A. (eds.) SPIN 2016. LNCS, vol. 9641, pp. 129–146. Springer, Cham (2016). https://doi.org/10.1007/978-3-319-32582-8_9

22. Karra, S.L., Larsen, K.G., Lorber, F., Srba, J.: Safe and time-optimal control for railway games. In: Collart-Dutilleul, S., Lecomte, T., Romanovsky, A. (eds.) RSSRail 2019. LNCS, vol. 11495, pp. 106–122. Springer, Cham (2019). https://doi.org/10.1007/978-3-030-18744-6_7

23. Larsen, K.G., Mikučionis, M., Taankvist, J.H.: Safe and optimal adaptive cruise control. In: Meyer, R., Platzer, A., Wehrheim, H. (eds.) Correct System Design. LNCS, vol. 9360, pp. 260–277. Springer, Cham (2015). https://doi.org/10.1007/978-3-319-23506-6_17

24. Lokshtanov, D., Subercaseaux, B.: Wordle is NP-hard (2022)

25. Rosenbaum, W.: Finding a winning strategy for wordle is NP-complete (2022)

26. Schuts, M., Zhu, F., Heidarian, F., Vaandrager, F.W.: Modelling clock synchronization in the chess gMAC WSN protocol. In: Andova, S., et al. (eds.) Proceedings First Workshop on Quantitative Formal Methods: Theory and Applications, QFM

2009, EPTCS. Eindhoven, The Netherlands, 3rd November 2009, vol. 13, pp. 41–54 (2009)

27. Vaandrager, F.: A first introduction to Uppaal. Deliverable no.: D5. 12 Title of Deliverable: Industrial Handbook, vol. 18 (2011)

28. Vaandrager, F.W., de Groot, A.: Analysis of a biphase mark protocol with Uppaal and PVS. Formal Aspects Comput. **18**(4), 433–458 (2006)

29. Wikipedia. Wordle – Wikipedia, the free encyclopedia (2022). http://en.wikipedia.org/w/index.php?title=Wordle&oldid=1093753215. Accessed 19 June 2022

Using the Parallel ATerm Library for Parallel Model Checking and State Space Generation

Jan Friso Groote$^{(\boxtimes)}$, Kevin H. J. Jilissen , Maurice Laveaux ,
P. H. M. van Spaendonck , and Tim A. C. Willemse

Department of Mathematics and Computer Science, Eindhoven University
of Technology, Eindhoven, The Netherlands
{J.F.Groote,M.Laveaux,P.H.M.v.Spaendonck,T.A.C.Willemse}@tue.nl,
K.H.J.Jilissen@student.tue.nl

Abstract. Process algebras are used to study the behaviour of parallel systems. The mCRL2 toolset has been designed to analyse process
algebraic models of such systems. Given that almost any contemporary
desktop computer has multiple processors on board it seems natural that
a toolset to analyse parallel behaviour now also employs parallelism.

This paper gives a compact account of the recently developed parallel
term library [13]; terms are used to represent almost any main concept
in the mCRL2 toolset. It subsequently reports on how the library is used
to make parallel implementations of the generation of state spaces and
the instantiation of Parameterised Boolean Equation Systems (PBES).
We show that a gain of an order of magnitude is possible using parallel
processing on contemporary hardware.

Keywords: The mCRL2 toolset · A parallel ATerm library · Parallel
state space generation · Parallel model checking

1 Introduction

A long time ago, Frits Vaandrager[1] was part of the European SPECS project.
The goal of the project was to make tools for various specification languages. The
'brilliant' idea was that instead of making n tools for m languages, which requires
$m \times n$ effort, it is far better to make an intermediate *Common Representation
Language (CRL)*. Then it is only needed to translate the m languages to CRL,
and make n different tools for CRL. This would simplify matters a lot, as only
$n + m$ effort would be required.

Some of the specification languages in existence were LOTOS [1], Chill [37],
SDL [36] and PSF [31], but the framework should be generic enough to "support

---

[1] Henri Korver, Wan Fokkink and Jan Friso Groote participated also.

Partially supported by the projects 612.001.751 (NWO, AVVA) and 00795160 (TTW,
MASCOT).

N. Jansen et al. (Eds.): Vaandrager Festschrift 2022, LNCS 13560, pp. 306–320, 2022.
https://doi.org/10.1007/978-3-031-15629-8_16

any software specification language to be invented". The process specification constructs and data types of these languages were very different, and as the language CRL had to support them all, CRL became a draconic beast for which the members of SPECS still carefully tried to define a full formal semantics. But when the project went on, formulating the semantics became harder and harder. Moreover, it became obvious that writing tools to support this Hydra was an impossible task, making CRL unsuitable for the higher goals of the SPECS project.

Taking the SPECS project very seriously, the conclusion was inevitable that this was the wrong way to go. Hence, it was decided to define μCRL, a very concise micro Common Specification Language. This language consisted of process algebraic behavioural specifications and equational data types [16]. Later it was succeeded by mCRL2 [14,15]. The essential differences between μCRL and mCRL2 in the datatypes are that the latter made a distinction between constructors and functions, allowed conditional equations, and added predefined data types including functions, sets and bags. For processes the conditional operator (μCRL: $p \triangleleft c \triangleright q$) was replaced (mCRL2: $c \rightarrow p \diamond q$), multi-actions were introduced as first class citizen allowing to replace the global communication function γ by an operator Γ_C. Also the semantics of time was changed, not to allow multiple consecutive actions to take place at the same time. Later probabilities were added to mCRL2.

In the early days, analysis of process specifications was performed by hand, based on the axioms of process algebra and the equations of the data specification [15,17]. But manual analysis for realistic systems is not doable as these systems quickly become too sizeable. The software of the KidCom, a gaming device targeted at girls, with a touchscreen and infrared communication was modelled extensively [9]. The models stretched over dozens of pages, and clearly tool support is essential to be able to check properties and get some confidence in models of this size. Actually, by model based testing of KidCom software, it was detected that the models contained unintended and unexpected deadlocks. This was the direct reason to start with the μCRL/mCRL2 toolset.

The toolset initially focussed on generating a state space and reduce it modulo various process equivalences, and check simple properties such as deadlock freedom or the presence or absence of certain actions. But it was realised that this was not enough as there is a desire to verify more complex properties on behaviour. This led to the development of the modal μ-calculus with time and data. The question of whether a modal formula holds for a process is translated to a Parameterised Boolean Equation System (PBES) [19–21,30]. Solving the PBES answers this question.

There were several attempts to make the toolset parallel. Most notably, Jaco van de Pol c.s., worked on distributed solutions to generate and reduce state spaces on multiple computers [2,3]. The primary motivation was that the limit of 4GByte imposed by 32-bits machines was circumvented and larger state spaces could be generated using multiple computers.

The core of the toolset is the ATerm library [4] which provides functionality to manipulate terms. Processes, data expressions, equations, states, modal formulas and PBESs are all stored as terms in memory. Virtually any operation in the toolset consists of inspecting, creating and destroying terms. Therefore, a natural approach to make the toolset parallel, is to make the ATerm library parallel. There were a few attempts [10,11,22] to design the algorithmic ingredients where intriguing wait free algorithms were developed. But the overhead of the necessary parallel programming constructs, generally nullified the benefits of a few extra processors, stopping any attempt to make the whole toolset parallel dead in its tracks.

Still, giving the development of cramping more processors in a single computer, and with increased hardware and software support for parallelism, it was decided to try once again to make the ATerm library parallel. But the approach differed from earlier attempts in the sense that no generic wait free algorithms were developed, but a dedicated minimal protocol was developed that optimally uses the hardware structure of modern computers [13]. This protocol is the busy-forbidden mutual exclusion protocol that allows for shared- and exclusive mutual access, and that is optimal if exclusive mutual access is rarely required. The parallel ATerm library is built on top of this algorithm.

It is noteworthy that we designed the busy-forbidden protocol and the parallel ATerm library first in mCRL2 and proved their correctness using model checking for finite parallel instances. This was very effective in the sense that we neither spent time on endless debugging of faulty protocols, nor spent the, often discouragingly large, effort in manually proving the correctness.

This paper sketches how with the availability of the parallel ATerm library we managed to generate state spaces and verify modal formulas via PBESs in parallel in a rather straightforward manner obtaining very substantial gains in the time required to perform these tasks. As most data structures used for verification purposes in the toolset are naturally formulated as terms, the potential for further parallelisation is tantamount.

2   ATerm Library

The ATerm library was developed by Paul Klint c.s. [4] to provide easy manipulation of basic term data structures. This library was originally intended for language workbenches to build translators between various languages. A program in a language would essentially be represented as a term.

The original term format is quite unwieldy. We are using a more concise variant:

Definition 2.1. Given an arbitrary set F of function symbols. A *term* is either a 64-bit number n, or given terms $t_1, \ldots, t_n$, a function symbol f applied to these terms, denoted as $f(t_1, \ldots, t_n)$, or a list of these terms, denoted by $[t_1, \ldots, t_n]$.

Terms are stored in memory in a shared way. For function symbols f and g, the term $f(g, g)$ only contains one occurrence of g in memory. This has the advantage that to determine whether two terms t and t' are equal, it only needs to be determined that t and t' are stored at the same address in memory.

The operations on terms are the following:

- **Inspect a term.** If a term is a number, get this number. If a term has the shape $f(t_1, \ldots, t_n)$, retrieve the function symbol or one of its arguments, and if a term is a list, obtain its head or tail.
- **Create a term.** Given a value, a function symbol and/or sub-terms, create a term of the shape n, $f(t_1, \ldots, t_n)$ or $[t_1, \ldots, t_n]$. Due to maximal sharing only a new term is created in memory, if this term was not already in existence.
- **Compare terms.** Check whether two terms are equal.
- **Copy and move terms.** Terms can be copied and moved to other memory locations. Note that this means that only references to terms are copied and moved. The terms themselves remain static in memory.

With the new term library the above operations can be carried out fully in parallel in one single term repository in which all terms that are in use are stored. Terms that are not in use anymore, are garbage collected. For this *term protection sets* are used, as in the initial ATerm library. Each location in memory where a term can be stored must be protected explicitly by putting this location in a protection set. In languages such as C++ that use constructors and destructors this does not lead to any programming overhead. An alternative approach is to protect terms using reference counting. Although this is widely used for sequential ATerm libraries, this does not scale well in a parallel context.

When garbage collection is being carried out, it is not possible to create or move terms. For this we use the busy-forbidden protocol [13], which is a mutual exclusion protocol which allows for shared and exclusive access, in exactly the same way as in a reader-writer lock. Garbage collection requires exclusive access to the ATerm data structures, while creating, moving and copying requires shared access. The busy-forbidden protocol is designed such that it is very efficient to access the shared section and it is computationally expensive to access the exclusive section. This is exactly what we need, as garbage collection occurs rarely.

Inspecting and comparing terms can be performed without restriction, which is a very nice feature of the ATerm structure. We want to stress that the new term library has exactly the same interface as the sequential one, meaning that all existing sequential software can use it without any extra effort.

The busy-forbidden protocol and the parallel ATerm library have been developed by first making models in mCRL2. These were model checked against the desired mutual exclusion and liveness properties. We found no correctness issues when implementing, making this way of working very effective and efficient, indeed. This cannot be said about performance, which required a substantial knowledge of modern processor and compiler technology, as well as some fiddling around, to get it within acceptable bounds.

3   State Space Generation

Generating a state space from a specification takes two steps. First an mCRL2 specification is transformed to a linear process specification [38]. In essence this boils down to eliminating parallel behaviour and transforming the processes to a simple list of condition-action-effect triples.

Definition 3.1. A linear process equation is a process of the following form [15]:

$$P(d) = \sum_{i \in I} \sum_{e_i:E_i} c_i(d, e_i) \rightarrow a_i(f_i(d, e_i)) \cdot P(g_i(d, e_i)).$$

The state of the process is represented by d, which in general consists of a sequence of typed data variables. The set I is a finite index set, indicating that for each $i \in I$ there is a condition-action-effect triple, often referred to as a summand. For each summand i and all values e_i from a data domain E_i if condition $c_i(d, e_i)$ holds, then action $a_i(f(d, e_i))$ can be executed ending in the state characterised by $g_i(d, e_i)$. As a transition this can typically be written as

$$d \xrightarrow{a_i(f_i(d,e_i))} g_i(d, e_i).$$

A simple example of a linear process is a Boolean queue of size N that can *read* and *deliver* Booleans.

$$P(q{:}List(\mathbb{B})) = \sum_{b:\mathbb{B}} (\#q < N) \rightarrow read(b) \cdot P(b \triangleright q) +$$
$$(q \not\approx []) \rightarrow deliver(rhead(q)) \cdot P(rtail(q)).$$

It has two summands, so the index set I has size 2. In the first summand the condition is $\#q < N$, asserting that list q is of length less than N. In the second summand the sum operator is trivial and therefore left out.

The data types that are used in a specification are defined using conditional equations. Term rewriters are used to evaluate or simplify a data expression, i.e., for a rewriter R and a term t the normal form of t is denoted as $R(t)$. There are several rewriters of which the most important are the just in time interpreting rewriter (jitty) and the just in time compiling rewriter (jittyc). Just in time compilation is a depth first rewriting strategy where rewriting of terms is postponed as long as possible [35]. For instance in an expression $if(c_{cond}, e_{then}, e_{else})$ the condition is evaluated first, and the then- and else-part are only rewritten if they are needed.

Generating a state space in parallel follows the straightforward description in Algorithm 1. The algorithm explores the state space of a linear process P with initial state e_{init} and rewriter R. Note that each state is just a sequence of data expressions, or more precisely a balanced tree of data expressions. These balanced trees are ATerms, which are maximally shared, leading to a very small memory footprint to store the states.

There are two main data structures globally accessible by all threads. The set *discovered* contains all states that have been detected by the algorithm. The set *todo* contains those states in *discovered* of which the outgoing transitions have not yet been explored. As it stands, only one thread can have access to the sets *discovered* and *todo* at any time, and therefore they are surrounded with a mutex variable, with lock and unlock operations.

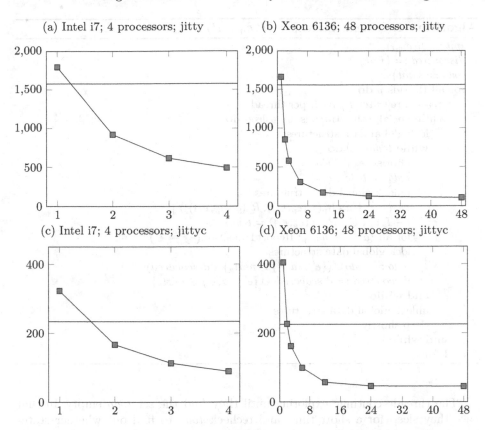

Fig. 1. State space generation for the IEEE 1394 firewire protocol with 10 data elements. The x-axis shows the number of threads. The y-axis shows the required wall clock time in seconds. At the left one Intel i7 and at the right Xeon 6136 processors are used. The upper diagrams use the interpreting jitty rewriter. The lower use the compiling jittyc rewriter without the compile time. The straight line shows the performance of sequential state space generation.

With the basis data structures in place, any desired number of threads can be started to explore the state space. Each thread has its own rewriter R_p to evaluate conditions and data expressions. But note that all rewriters operate on the common ATerm term repository. Every newly created data expression is stored exactly once in this repository.

Each thread p obtains a non explored state (i.e., sequence/tree of data expressions) e_p from the set *todo* and then uses the linear process P and the rewriter R_p to calculate $next_p$ containing all states reachable from e_p. Note that the linear process P is also an ATerm, shared among all threads. Calculating $next_p$ is relatively time consuming and can be done by all threads in parallel. The new transitions are reported, either to be inspected or stored, and the found states are put in *discovered* and *todo*.

Algorithm 1. GenerateStateSpace(P, e_{init}, R)

$init := R(e_{init})$
$discovered := \{init\}$
$todo := \{init\}$
for all threads p **do**
    create a rewriter $R_p := R$ per thread
    while not all other threads are asleep **do**
        lock global data structures
        while $todo \neq \emptyset$ **do**
            choose $e_p \in todo$
            $todo := todo \setminus \{e_p\}$
            unlock global data structures
            $next_p = \{\langle a_i(R_p(f_i(e_p, e_i)), R_p(g_i(e_p, e_i)))\rangle \mid$
            $i \in I, e_i : E_i \quad R_p(c_i(e_p, e_i)) = true\}$
            for all $\langle a, e' \rangle \in next_p$: ReportTransition($e_p \xrightarrow{a} e'$)
            lock global data structures
            $todo := todo \cup (\{e' \mid \langle a, e' \rangle \in next_p\} \setminus discovered)$
            $discovered := discovered \cup \{e' \mid \langle a, e' \rangle \in next_p\}$
        end while
        unlock global data structures
        sleep shortly
    end while
end for

The threads continue exploring until they find the set $todo$ empty. In that case they sleep for a short time, and recheck $todo$ to find out whether states became available in the mean time. If the state space exploration is done, this means all processes will soon be sleeping. If more work needs to be done, the sleeping threads will quickly rejoin the exploration fray.

The parallel state space exploration works remarkably well. We show experiments on an iMac (27 in., 2017, 4.2Ghz Quad-Core Intel i7 7700K, clang 13) and a multicore machine with 48 processors (Intel(R) Xeon(R) Gold 6136 CPU @ 3.00GH, clang 10).

We observed that the nature of the explored process is very relevant for the obtained performance. When there are only a few easy conditions in the linear process, calculating $next_p$ is relatively easy, and accessing the global data structures becomes more of a bottleneck, hampering parallel progress. However, we typically see the behaviour as depicted in Fig. 1, showing that more threads lead to shorter state space generation time.

For the experiment we use the IEEE 1394 firewire protocol [28] with 10 data elements, having 7.2M states and 16M transitions. For comparison, we also show the time for sequential state space generation as a horizontal line, which uses the same algorithm where the use of parallel safe guarding mechanisms such as mutexes and the busy-forbidden protocol is switched off. We want to stress that for the generation of this benchmark we do not use any optimisation features available within the mCRL2 toolset, such as caching data or optimising the structure of the linear process, which by itself can have a huge impact on the exploration time and even the size of the state space. The reason is that including optimisations in the benchmarks gives a less clear picture of what we are precisely measuring. For the exploration of large state spaces, one should of course use the tools with all effective optimisations and employ multiple processors.

Figure 1 clearly shows that having more processors available is beneficial, and in many cases doubling the number of processors reduces generation time almost by half. The compiling jittyc rewriter is much faster than jitty rewriter. The relatively poorer parallel speedup when using the jittyc rewriter is most likely due to increased contention in sequentially accessing the data structures *todo* and *discovered*, which is a natural candidate to be investigated and improved next.

4   Model Checking via Boolean Equation Systems

Most specifications give rise to state spaces that are too large and complex to assess their correctness by means of simulation or a visual inspection. Instead, the correctness of a specification can be established using model checking, a technique that automatically and exhaustively scrutinises the state space and assesses whether or not desired functional requirements of the specification hold true. Such requirements are typically given as expressions of some temporal logic; in mCRL2, the first-order modal μ-calculus [20] is used as a requirement language.

In mCRL2, the model checking problem is converted to the problem of solving a Parameterised Boolean Equation System (PBES) [21]. A PBES is obtained by combining a linear process specification and a temporal formula into a single system of fixed point equations; for details we refer to [15, 20, 34]. Formally, a PBES is a system of fixed point equations of the following form:

$$(\sigma_1 X_1(d_1{:}D_1) = \phi_1) \ldots (\sigma_n X_n(d_n{:}D_n) = \phi_n).$$

The left-hand side of each equation has a fixed point sign $\sigma_i \in \{\mu, \nu\}$, a unique predicate variable X_i, and a (possibly empty) vector of data parameters d_i of type D_i; the length of this vector indicates the arity of the predicate variable. Each right-hand side is a formula built from the usual first-order language constructs and *predicate variable instantiations*: predicate variables with expressions as arguments. We only consider right-hand side formulae in which each predicate variable instantiation occurs under an even number of negations, and all predicate variable instantiations refer to predicate variables occurring at the left-hand side of *some* equation in the PBES. Moreover, we assume that all (non-predicate) variables that occur in the right-hand side of an equation are those that occur in the data parameter list at the left-hand side of the equation or are bound in a quantifier.

A PBES is said to be a *Boolean Equation System* (BES) exactly if the predicate variables occurring at the left-hand side of an equation have arity 0, and all right-hand side formulae consist only of conjunctions, disjunctions, constants *true* and *false*, and (0-arity) predicate variables.

Consider the following requirement for the linear process modelling the finite queue of Sect. 3, asserting that invariantly, every Boolean value b that is added to the queue is inevitably delivered:

$$\nu Y. \; ([true]Y \wedge \forall b{:}\mathbb{B}.[read(b)]\mu Z. \; ([\neg deliver(b)]Z \wedge \langle true\rangle true)).$$

Note that this requirement holds true, simply because once the queue is full, the only option is to deliver the values stored in the queue. The PBES that is obtained by translating the linear process modelling the finite queue and the above requirement is as follows:

$$
\begin{aligned}
(\nu \bar{Y}(q{:}List(\mathbb{B})) \quad &= (\forall b{:}\mathbb{B}. \; (\#q < N) \Rightarrow \bar{Y}(b{\triangleright}q)) \\
&\wedge (q \not\approx [] \Rightarrow \bar{Y}(rtail(q))) \\
&\wedge (\forall b{:}\mathbb{B}. \; (\#q < N) \Rightarrow \bar{Z}(b{\triangleright}q, b))), \\
(\mu \bar{Z}(q{:}List(\mathbb{B}), b{:}\mathbb{B}) &= (\forall b'{:}\mathbb{B}. \; (\#q < N) \Rightarrow \bar{Z}(b'{\triangleright}q, b)) \\
&\wedge ((q \not\approx [] \wedge b \not\approx rhead(q)) \Rightarrow \bar{Z}(rtail(q), b))) \\
&\wedge (\#q < N \vee q \neq []).
\end{aligned}
$$

The linear process $X(q)$ satisfies the above requirement if and only if the solution to $\bar{Y}(q)$ is *true*.

Solving a PBES, and thereby the encoded model checking problem, can be done in many ways, but a straightforward one proceeds in two steps: (1) extracting a (representation of a) BES from the PBES, and (2) solving the resulting BES. The first step is analogous to exploring a state space from a linear process specification, see [8,34]; for the second step, a variety of algorithms are available, ranging from Gauß elimination [29] and proof systems [26] to translating it to the problem of parity game solving using one of the many algorithms for this problem [5,12,23,40]. Other techniques for solving a PBES include symbolic approximations [20], SMT solving fragments [25,32], quotienting [33] and pattern matching [21]; these techniques do not require extracting a BES from a PBES.

We use the example PBES to illustrate the extraction of a BES from a PBES. Assume, for the sake of argument, that $N > 0$ and that we are interested in the truth value of $\bar{Y}([])$. Filling in the value $[]$ for parameter q in the right-hand side formula associated with the equation of $\bar{Y}$, and subsequently rewriting the resulting expression, yields the following Boolean equation for $\bar{Y}([])$:

$$\nu \bar{Y}([]) = \bar{Y}([false]) \wedge \bar{Y}([true]) \wedge \bar{Z}([false], false) \wedge \bar{Z}([true], true)$$

This means that the truth value of $\bar{Y}([])$ depends on the truth values of $\bar{Y}([false])$, $\bar{Y}([true])$, $\bar{Z}([false], false)$ and $\bar{Z}([true], true)$. In order to compute the truth value of $\bar{Y}([])$, the extraction procedure must therefore also compute the Boolean equations for $\bar{Y}([false])$, $\bar{Y}([true])$, and so on, until all dependencies have been computed.

We represent the Boolean equations extracted from a PBES as a *structure graph* [24]. See Fig. 2 for the fragment of the structure graph representing the equation above. Apart from the dependencies between the predicate variables (and their arguments), these graphs also record whether a given (sub)formula is conjunctive or disjunctive (by annotating vertices with ▲ or ▼, respectively). Moreover, whether equations are least or greatest fixed point equations is recorded by annotating vertices with a number encoding the alternation depth of the associated equation. This information suffices to recreate the essence of a Boolean equation system from a structure graph.

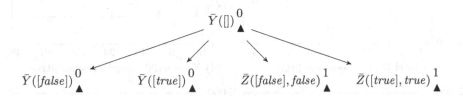

Fig. 2. Example of part of a structure graph representing a Boolean equation resulting from an instantiation of a PBES.

In some cases, on-the-fly solving the BES while it is being extracted from a PBES can significantly speed-up the entire process by preventing the exploration of many unnecessary equations [27]. When the solution is not as expected (for instance, a requirement which was expected to hold true of a system turns out not to hold), a counterexample can be extracted using a *proof graph* [7] of the PBES, see [39]. A counterexample, and, dually, a witness, is a subgraph of the linear process specification that allows for reconstructing the solution to the original PBES. This notion of counterexample is based on [6].

The algorithm for extracting (a structure graph representation of) a BES from a PBES is, as the above example suggests, essentially the same as the algorithm of Sect. 3 for extracting a transition system from a linear process specification. The main difference is that in this setting, the "successor states" are the instantiated predicate variables occurring in a formula φ which are extracted from φ using the function $occ(\varphi)$.

Parallelism can be used in a similar way to speed up the entire process, see Algorithm 2. This algorithm takes a PBES $\mathcal{E}$ as input, along with a designated predicate variable X_{init} and argument e_{init} which we assume to be a closed expression, and a data rewriter R. For ease of notation, we assume that each equation in $\mathcal{E}$ is of the form $(\sigma_i X_i(d_i : D_i) = \varphi_i)$. As in Algorithm 1 we use the subscript p to stress that certain variables are local for the thread p.

To illustrate the performance gains of Algorithm 2, we show the performance of our implementation on the problem of deadlock detection in the IEEE 1394 firewire protocol we also considered in the previous section. Absence of deadlock is expressed in the first-order modal μ-calculus by the formula $\nu X.([true]X \wedge \langle true \rangle true)$. Extracting the BES from the PBES is the most time-consuming part in solving the PBES that encodes this problem. As can be seen, parallelism speeds-up the entire process significantly, see Fig. 3.

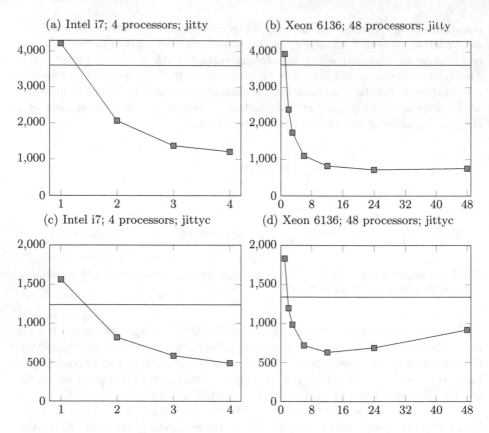

Fig. 3. Solving a deadlock freedom formula on the IEEE 1394 firewire protocol with 10 data elements. The x-axis shows the number of threads. The y-axis shows the required wall clock time in seconds. At the left the Intel i7 and at the right Xeon 6136 processors are used. The upper diagrams use the interpreting jitty rewriter. The lower uses the compiling jittyc rewriter without the compile time. The straight line shows the performance of sequential formula solving.

But we also observe that especially when using the compiling jittyc rewriter, performance deteriorates when the number of of threads exceeds 16. With so many PBES equations being processed in parallel, the bottleneck becomes to maintain the data structures *todo* and *discovered*, which are accessed in a mutual exclusive way. Especially, when a thread is halted when passing a lock, it tends to use a lot of additional computational time, for instance to reload its data back in the cache when it can continue processing.

Algorithm 2. InstantiateGraph($\mathcal{E}$, $X_{init}(e_{init})$, R)

$init := R(X_{init}(e_{init}))$
$todo := \{init\}$
$discovered := \{init\}$
create an empty structure graph G
for all threads p **do**
    create a rewriter $R_p := R$ per thread
    while not all other threads are asleep **do**
        lock global data structures
        while $todo \neq \emptyset$ **do**
            choose $X_k(e_p) \in todo$
            $todo := todo \setminus \{X_k(e_p)\}$
            unlock global data structures
            $\psi_p := R_p(\varphi_k[d_k := e_p])$
            lock global data structures
            integrate equation $\sigma_k X_k(e_p) = \psi_p$ in structure graph G
            $todo := todo \cup (\mathrm{occ}(\psi_p) \setminus discovered)$
            $discovered := discovered \cup \mathrm{occ}(\psi_p)$
        end while
        unlock global data structures
        sleep shortly
    end while
end for
solve BES represented by G

---

5   Conclusion

We saw that the availability of a parallel ATerm library makes it possible to implement the parallel generation of state spaces and the parallel instantiation of Parameterised Boolean Equation Systems in a pretty straightforward way. But the parallel term library is so versatile that it can easily be used to make parallel implementations of other structures such as binary decision diagrams. These are widely used, for instance in our symbolic state space generation tools [27]. Other potential application are parallel confluence checking [18] or the parallel elimination of constant parameters in linear processes and PBESs, both of which can be quite time consuming operations.

References

1. ISO 8807:1989. Information processing systems - Open Systems Interconnection - LOTOS - A formal description technique based on the temporal ordering of observational behaviour (1989). ISO/IECJTC1/SC7
2. Blom, S., Lisser, B., van de Pol, J., Weber, M.: A database approach to distributed state space generation. Electron. Notes Theor. Comput. Sci. **198**(1), 17–32 (2008)

3. Blom, S., van de Pol, J.: Distributed branching bisimulation minimization by inductive signatures. In: Brim, L., van de Pol, J. (eds.) Proceedings 8th International Workshop on Parallel and Distributed Methods in verifiCation, PDMC 2009, Eindhoven, The Netherlands, 4th November 2009, volume 14 of EPTCS, pp. 32–46 (2009)

4. van den Brand, M.G., de Jong, H.A., Klint, P., Olivier, P.A.: Efficient annotated terms. Softw. Pract. Experience **30**(3), 259–291 (2000)

5. Calude, C.S., Jain, S., Khoussainov, B., Li, W., Stephan, F.: Deciding parity games in quasipolynomial time. In: STOC, pp. 252–263. ACM (2017)

6. Cranen, S., Luttik, B., Willemse, T.A.C.: Proof graphs for parameterised Boolean equation systems. In: D'Argenio, P.R., Melgratti, H. (eds.) CONCUR 2013. LNCS, vol. 8052, pp. 470–484. Springer, Heidelberg (2013). https://doi.org/10.1007/978-3-642-40184-8_33

7. Cranen, S., Luttik, B., Willemse, T.A.: Evidence for fixpoint logic. In: CSL, Volume 41 of LIPIcs, pp. 78–93 (2015). Schloss Dagstuhl - Leibniz-Zentrum für Informatik

8. van Dam, A., Ploeger, B., Willemse, T.A.C.: Instantiation for parameterised Boolean equation systems. In: Fitzgerald, J.S., Haxthausen, A.E., Yenigun, H. (eds.) ICTAC 2008. LNCS, vol. 5160, pp. 440–454. Springer, Heidelberg (2008). https://doi.org/10.1007/978-3-540-85762-4_30

9. Engel, A.J.P.M., Feijs, L.M.G., Groote, J.F., van de Pol, J.C., Springintveld, J.: Specification, design and simulation of services and protocols for a PDA using the infra red medium. Technical report RWB-510-re-95012, Information and Software Technology, Philips research. confidential (1995)

10. Gao, H., Groote, J.F., Hesselink, W.H.: Lock-free dynamic hash tables with open addressing. Distrib. Comput. **18**(1), 21–42 (2005). https://doi.org/10.1007/s00446-004-0115-2

11. Gao, H., Groote, J.F., Hesselink, W.H.: Lock-free parallel and concurrent garbage collection by mark&sweep. Sci. Comput. Program. **64**(3), 341–374 (2007)

12. Gazda, M., Willemse, T.A.: Zielonka's recursive algorithm: dull, weak and solitaire games and tighter bounds. In: GandALF, Volume 119 of EPTCS, pp. 7–20 (2013)

13. Groote, J.F., Laveaux, M., van Spaendonck, P.H.M.: A thread-safe term library. arXiv preprint arXiv:2111.02706 (2021)

14. Groote, J.F., Mathijssen, A., Van Weerdenburg, M., Usenko, Y.: From μCRL to mCRL2: motivation and outline. Electron. Notes Theor. Comput. Sci. **162**, 191–196 (2006)

15. Groote, J.F., Mousavi, M.R.: Modeling and Analysis of Communicating Systems. MIT Press, Cambridge (2014)

16. Groote, J.F., Ponse, A.: The syntax and semantics of μCRL. Technical report CS-R9076, CWI, Amsterdam (1990)

17. Groote, J.F., Ponse, A.: Proof theory for μCRL: a language for processes with data. In: Andrews, D.J., Groote, J.F., Middelburg, C.A. (eds.) Semantics of Specification Languages (SoSL). WC, pp. 232–251. Springer, London (1994). https://doi.org/10.1007/978-1-4471-3229-5_13

18. Groote, J.F., Sellink, M.P.A.: Confluence for process verification. Theor. Comput. Sci. **170**(1–2), 47–81 (1996)

19. Groote, J.F., Willemse, T.A.C.: A checker for modal formulae for processes with data. In: de Boer, F.S., Bonsangue, M.M., Graf, S., de Roever, W.-P. (eds.) FMCO 2003. LNCS, vol. 3188, pp. 223–239. Springer, Heidelberg (2004). https://doi.org/10.1007/978-3-540-30101-1_10

20. Groote, J.F., Willemse, T.A.: Model-checking processes with data. Sci. Comput. Program. **56**(3), 251–273 (2005)
21. Groote, J.F., Willemse, T.A.: Parameterised Boolean equation systems. Theor. Comput. Sci. **343**(3), 332–369 (2005)
22. Hesselink, W.H., Groote, J.F.: Wait-free concurrent memory management by create and read until deletion (carud). Distrib. Comput. **14**(1), 31–39 (2001). https://doi. org/10.1007/PL00008924
23. Jurdziński, M.: Small progress measures for solving parity games. In: Reichel, H., Tison, S. (eds.) STACS 2000. LNCS, vol. 1770, pp. 290–301. Springer, Heidelberg (2000). https://doi.org/10.1007/3-540-46541-3_24
24. Keiren, J.J., Reniers, M.A., Willemse, T.A.: Structural analysis of Boolean equation systems. ACM Trans. Comput. Logic (TOCL) **13**(1), 1–35 (2012)
25. Koolen, R.P.J., Willemse, T.A.C., Zantema, H.: Using SMT for solving fragments of parameterised Boolean equation systems. In: Finkbeiner, B., Pu, G., Zhang, L. (eds.) ATVA 2015. LNCS, vol. 9364, pp. 14–30. Springer, Cham (2015). https:// doi.org/10.1007/978-3-319-24953-7_3
26. Larsen, K.G.: Efficient local correctness checking. In: von Bochmann, G., Probst, D.K. (eds.) CAV 1992. LNCS, vol. 663, pp. 30–43. Springer, Heidelberg (1993). https://doi.org/10.1007/3-540-56496-9_4
27. Laveaux, M., Wesselink, W., Willemse, T.A.C.: On-the-fly solving for symbolic parity games. In: Fisman, D., Rosu, G. (eds.) TACAS 2022. Lecture Notes in Computer Science, vol. 13244, pp. 137–155. Springer, Cham (2022). https://doi. org/10.1007/978-3-030-99527-0_8
28. Luttik., B.: Description and formal specification of the link layer of P1394. In: International Workshop on Applied Formal Methods in System Design, pp. 43–56 (1997)
29. Mader, A.: Verification of modal properties using Boolean equation systems. Ph.D. thesis, Technical University Munich (1997)
30. Mateescu, R.: Vérification des propriétés temporelles des programmes parallèles. Ph.D thesis, Institut National Polytechnique de Grenoble (1998)
31. Mauw, S., Veltink, G.: A process specification formalism. Fundamenta Informaticae **13**, 85–139 (1990)
32. Nagae, Y., Sakai, M.: Reduced dependency spaces for existential parameterised Boolean equation systems (2018). arXiv preprint arXiv:1802.06496
33. Neele, T., Willemse, T.A.C., Groote, J.F.: Solving parameterised boolean equation systems with infinite data through quotienting. In: Bae, K., Ölveczky, P.C. (eds.) FACS 2018. LNCS, vol. 11222, pp. 216–236. Springer, Cham (2018). https://doi. org/10.1007/978-3-030-02146-7_11
34. Ploeger, B., Wesselink, J.W., Willemse, T.A.: Verification of reactive systems via instantiation of parameterised Boolean equation systems. Inf. Comput. **209**(4), 637–663 (2011)
35. Pol, J.: JITty: a rewriter with strategy annotations. In: Tison, S. (ed.) RTA 2002. LNCS, vol. 2378, pp. 367–370. Springer, Heidelberg (2002). https://doi.org/10. 1007/3-540-45610-4_26
36. Rockström, A., Saracco, R.: SDL-CCITT specification and description language. IEEE Trans. Commun. **30**(6), 1310–1318 (1982)
37. ITU-T Telecommunication standardisation sector of ITU. CHILL - The ITU-T programming language. ITU-T recommendation Z.200. Technical report, International Telecommunication Union (1999)

38. Usenko, Y.: Linearisation in μCRL. Ph. D thesis, Eindhoven University of Technology (2002)
39. Wesselink, W., Willemse, T.A.C.: Evidence extraction from parameterised Boolean equation systems. In ARQNL@IJCAR, volume 2095 of CEUR Workshop Proceedings, pp. 86–100. CEUR-WS.org (2018)
40. Zielonka, W.: Infinite games on finitely coloured graphs with applications to automata on infinite trees. Theor. Comput. Sci. **200**(1–2), 135–183 (1998)

Active Automata Learning as Black-Box Search and Lazy Partition Refinement

Falk Howar[(✉)] and Bernhard Steffen

TU Dortmund University, Dortmund, Germany
{falk.howar,bernhard.steffen}@tu-dortmund.de

Abstract. We present a unifying formalization of active automata learning algorithms in the MAT model, including a new, efficient, and simple technique for the analysis of counterexamples during learning: L^λ is the first active automata learning algorithm that does not add substrings of counterexamples to the underlying data structure for observations but instead performs black-box search and partition refinement. We analyze the worst case complexity in terms of membership queries and equivalence queries and evaluate the presented learning algorithm on benchmark instances from the *Automata Wiki*, comparing its performance against efficient implementations of some learning algorithms from LEARNLIB.

Keywords: Model Learning · Active Automata Learning · Minimally Adequate Teacher

1   Introduction

Active automata learning has gained a lot of traction as a formal analysis method for black-box models in the previous decade [19]. We provide a detailed account of the first half of the decade in a dedicated survey paper [8]. The second half of the decade saw extensions to new automata models, e.g. to symbolic automata [4] and one-timer automata [20], applications, e.g., in model checking network protocols [5], and algorithmic advances, e.g., an SMT-based learning algorithm [17]. We cannot do the development of the field adequate justice in a couple of paragraphs, and hence will not even attempt to.

What has remained elusive for a long time is a simple and generic formalization of active automata learning and a lower bound result. Frits Vaandrager and coauthors have recently presented active automata learning in the framework of apartness [21], providing a nice formalization of the long established intuition that active automata learning is about distinguishing states.

We continue in this vein and show that it is sufficient to remember which states to distinguish while disregarding the concrete evidence for their apartness: In this paper on the occasion of Frits Vaandrager's 60th birthday, we present a unifying formalization of active automata learning algorithms in the MAT model for finite state acceptors, Moore machines, and Mealy machines and develop a

© The Author(s), under exclusive license to Springer Nature Switzerland AG 2022
N. Jansen et al. (Eds.): Vaandrager Festschrift 2022, LNCS 13560, pp. 321–338, 2022.
https://doi.org/10.1007/978-3-031-15629-8_17

new, efficient, and simple technique for the analysis of counterexamples during learning. The L^λ (λ for lazy) algorithm is—to the best of our knowledge— the first active automata learning algorithm that does not add sub-strings of counterexamples to the underlying data structure for observations but instead performs black-box search and lazy partition refinement, based on information extracted from a counterexample.

We establish the correctness of the presented framework in a series of straight-forward lemmas. The presented proofs do not rely on concrete underlying data structures, which will hopefully facilitate easy adaptation of the algorithmic ideas to other (richer) classes of models. We analyze the worst case complexity in terms of membership queries and equivalence queries and evaluate the presented learning algorithm on benchmark instances from the *Automata Wiki*[1], comparing its performance against efficient implementations of some learning algorithms from LEARNLIB [11]. We still cannot provide a lower bound but we certainly hope that the L^λ is one step on the way to such a bound.

Outline. The remainder of the paper is structured as follows. We present a unifying view on regular languages, finite state acceptors, and Mealy machines in the next section, before recapitulating the MAT learning model and existing learning algorithms in Sect. 3. Our main contribution, the L^λ learning algorithm, is presented in Sect. 4 and demonstrated in Sect. 5. Results of the performance evaluation are discussed in Sect. 6.

2   Regular Languages and Automata

We start with a brief unifying recapitulation of different finite automata models. For some fix finite alphabet Σ, we usually use a to denote a symbol from that alphabet, and u, v, w for words in Σ^*. For empty word ϵ, let $\Sigma^+ = \Sigma^* \setminus \{\epsilon\}$. We use symbols like words in concatenation uv (or $u \cdot v$ for emphasis) where $uv = u_1 \cdots u_m \cdot v_1 \cdots v_n$ for $u = u_1 \cdots u_m$ and $v = v_1 \cdots v_n$. Finally, we use $u_{[i,j]}$ for $1 \le i \le j \le |u|$ as a shorthand for the sub-word $u_i \cdots u_j$ of u.

Definition 1. *A Deterministic Finite Automaton (DFA) is a tuple $\langle Q, q_0, \Sigma, \delta \rangle$ where Q is a finite nonempty set of states, $q_0 \in Q$ is the initial state, Σ is a finite alphabet, and $\delta : Q \times \Sigma \to Q$ is the transition function.*

We extend δ to words in the natural way by defining $\delta(q, \epsilon) = q$ for the empty word ϵ and $\delta(q, ua) = \delta(\delta(q, u), a)$ for $u \in \Sigma^*$ and $a \in \Sigma$.

We can generally distinguish automata that associate output or acceptance with states (i.e., finite state acceptors and Moore machines) from those that associate output with transitions (i.e., Mealy machines).

Definition 2. *A Moore machine is a tuple $\langle Q, q_0, \Sigma, \Omega, \delta, \lambda \rangle$ where $\langle Q, q_0, \Sigma, \delta \rangle$ is a DFA, Ω is a finite set of outputs, and $\lambda : Q \to \Omega$ is the state output function.*

---

[1] Automata Wiki: ru.nl and [13].

A Moore machine $M = \langle Q, q_0, \Sigma, \Omega, \delta, \lambda \rangle$ maps words $w \in \Sigma^*$ to outputs $o \in \Omega$ through the *semantic function* $S_A^* : \Sigma^* \to \Omega$, which we define as $S_M^* =_{def} \lambda \circ \delta$.

Definition 3. *A finite state acceptor (FSA) is a tuple $\langle Q, q_0, \Sigma, \delta, F \rangle$ defining a Moore machine $\langle Q, q_0, \Sigma, \{0, 1\}, \delta, \lambda \rangle$ in which $\lambda : Q \to \{0, 1\}$ marks the set of accepting states $(\lambda(q) = 1$ iff $q \in F)$.*

An FSA $F = \langle Q, q_0, \Sigma, \delta, \lambda \rangle$ accepts a regular language $L_F \subseteq \Sigma^*$: for $w \in \Sigma^*$ let $w \in L_F$ iff $S_F^*(w) = 1$, i.e., if $\delta(w) \in F$.

Definition 4. *A Mealy machine is a tuple $\langle Q, q_0, \Sigma, \Omega, \delta, \lambda \rangle$ where $\langle Q, q_0, \Sigma, \delta \rangle$ is a DFA, Ω is a finite set of outputs, and $\lambda : Q \times \Sigma \to \Omega$ is the transition output function.*

A Mealy machine $M = \langle Q, q_0, \Sigma, \Omega, \delta, \lambda \rangle$ maps words $w \in \Sigma^+$ to outputs $o \in \Omega$ through the semantic function $S_M^+ : \Sigma^+ \to \Omega$, which we define as $S_M^+(ua) =_{def} \lambda(\delta(u), a)$ for $u \in \Sigma^*$ and $a \in \Sigma$.

Residuals and Congruences. For some DFA $A = \langle Q, q_0, \Sigma, \delta \rangle$ and state $q \in Q$, the *q-residual* DFA $A|q$ is the automaton $\langle Q, q, \Sigma, \delta \rangle$, in which we make q the initial state. The automaton $A|q$ represents the behavior of A after reaching state q.

The concept of residuals extends to regular languages and semantic functions: For a Moore machine $M = \langle Q, q_0, \Sigma, \{0, 1\}, \delta, \lambda \rangle$ and some word $u \in \Sigma^*$, let $q = \delta(u)$ and $M|q$ with semantic function $S_{M|q}^*$. As $S_{M|q}^*(w) = S_M^*(u \cdot w)$ for $w \in \Sigma^*$, we omit $M|q$ and write $u^{-1}S_M^*$ for the *residual semantic function* of S_M^* after u. We can then define a congruence relation $\equiv_S$ on the set Σ^* of words: for words $u, v \in \Sigma^*$ let $u \equiv_S v$ iff $u^{-1}S_M^* = v^{-1}S_M^*$. For regular languages, this congruence is the well-known Nerode-relation [14]. For a Mealy machine M, we can make an analogous construction using its semantic function S_M^+ and the set of words Σ^+ [18].

Canonical Automata. Congruence relations are the basis for constructing canonical automata models. A semantic function S^* can be represented as a finite automaton if $\equiv_S$ is of finite index. The canonical automaton for any such S over some alphabet Σ is the automaton $A_S = \langle Q, q_0, \Sigma, \delta \rangle$ with one state in Q for every class of $\equiv_S$ and q_0 the state for ϵ. The transition function is defined using the congruence as $\delta([u]_S, a) = [ua]_S$ for $u \in \Sigma^*$, $a \in \Sigma$, where $[u]_S$ denotes the class of u in $\equiv_S$. For a semantic function $S^* : \Sigma^* \to \Omega$, the canonical Moore machine M_S (or FSA in the case of $\Omega = \{0, 1\}$) is the automaton $\langle Q, q_0, \Sigma, \Omega, \delta, \lambda \rangle$ with $\langle Q, q_0, \Sigma, \delta \rangle$ as above and $\lambda([u]) =_{def} S^*(u)$ for $u \in \Sigma^*$. For a semantic function $S^+ : \Sigma^* \to \Omega$, the canonical Mealy machine M_S is the automaton $\langle Q, q_0, \Sigma, \Omega, \delta, \lambda \rangle$ with $\langle Q, q_0, \Sigma, \delta \rangle$ as above and $\lambda([u], a) =_{def} S^+(ua)$ for $u \in \Sigma^*$ and $a \in \Sigma$.

3 MAT Learning

Active automata learning [2] is concerned with the problem of inferring an automaton model for an unknown semantic function $\mathcal{L}$ over some alphabet Σ.

	From Observations	One Prefix of CE	All Prefixes of CE
From Observations	L^λ MQ: $O(kn^2 + n^2 log\, m)$ IS: $O(kn^3 + n^2 m\, log\, m)$ TTT [10]	Kearns/Vazirani [12] MQ: $O(kn^2 + n^2 m)$ IS: $O(kn^2 m + n^2 m^2)$	L^* [2] MQ: $O(kn^2 m)$ IS: $O(kn^2 m^2)$
One Suffix of CE	Rivest/Shapire [16], Packs [7], $L^\#$ [21] MQ: $O(kn^2 + n\, log\, m)$ IS: $O(kn^2 m + nm\, log\, m)$		
All Suffixes of CE	Maler/Pnueli [15] MQ: $O(kn^2 m)$ IS: $O(kn^2 m^2)$		

Fig. 1. Active Automata Learning Algorithms. Cells (One Suffix of CE) and (One Prefix of CE) contain more algorithms than shown. For (One Prefix of CE): complexities pertain to Kearns/Vazirani not to cell. We compare number of membership queries (MQ) and number of input symbols (IS).

MAT Model. Active learning is often formulated as a cooperative game between a learner and a teacher. The task of the learner is to learn a model of some unknown semantic function $\mathcal{L}$. The teacher assists the learner by answering two kinds of queries:

Membership queries ask for the value of $\mathcal{L}$ for a single word $w \in \Sigma^*$. The teacher answers these queries with $\mathcal{L}(w)$.

Equivalence queries ask if a candidate function, represented as a finite *hypothesis* automaton $\mathcal{H}$, is equal to $\mathcal{L}$. If $\mathcal{H}$ is not equal to $\mathcal{L}$, the teacher will provide a counterexample: a word w for which $\mathcal{H}(w) \neq \mathcal{L}(w)$.

The teacher in this model is called a *minimally adequate teacher* (MAT) and the learning model is hence often referred to as MAT learning.

Dana Angluin originally presented the MAT learning model along with a first learning algorithm [2]. With the MAT learning model, she introduced an abstraction that enabled the separation of concerns (constructing stable preliminary models and checking the correctness of these models). This enabled an algorithmic pattern that allowed the formulation and optimization of learning algorithms. The L^* learning algorithm for regular languages and corresponding sequence of lemmas showing the correctness of the algorithms have served as a basis for learning algorithms inferring more complex classes of concepts, e.g., symbolic automata [4] and register automata [1,9]. The L^* algorithms and all other MAT learning algorithms that have been discovered subsequently mimic the construction of canonic automata, using a finite set $Sp \subset \Sigma^*$ of *short prefixes* for representing classes of $\equiv_S$ and a set $V \subset \Sigma^*$ (resp. $V \subset \Sigma^+$ for Mealy machines) of suffixes for distinguishing classes of $\equiv_\mathcal{L}$: for all $u, u' \in \Sigma^*$ with $u \not\equiv_\mathcal{L} u'$ exists $v \in \Sigma^*$ (resp. $v \in \Sigma^+$ for Mealy machines) with $\mathcal{L}(uv) \neq \mathcal{L}(u'v)$. Membership queries and equivalence queries are used for finding new short prefixes and distinguishing suffixes.

All known active learning algorithms fall into one of two classes, as is shown in Fig. 1: The first class comprises algorithms that search for new short prefixes and construct new suffixes incrementally through observable *inconsistencies* between residual semantic functions of prefixes [2,12], relying on the following observation.

Proposition 1 (New short prefix [2,12]). *Every counterexample w has a prefix w' for which $w' \equiv_\mathcal{H} u$ for some $u \in Sp$ while $w'a \not\equiv_\mathcal{H} ua$ for some $a \in \Sigma$, proven by some $v \in V$ for which $\mathcal{L}(w'av) \neq \mathcal{L}(uav)$.*

In algorithms of this class, the word w' is used as a new short prefix and a av will subsequently (while refining the current hypothesis) be constructed as a new suffix, documenting $w' \not\equiv_\mathcal{H} u$.

The second group of algorithms searches for new suffixes and identifies new short prefixes through corresponding observable differences (so-called *unclosedness*) [7,15,16,18,21].

Proposition 2 (New suffix [16]). *A counterexample w has a suffix v that distinguishes two words $ua \equiv_\mathcal{H} u'$ with $u, u' \in Sp$ and $a \in \Sigma$ through $\mathcal{L}(uav) \neq \mathcal{L}(u'v)$.*

The suffix v of the counterexample is used as a new distinguishing suffix and ua will subsequently become a new short prefix.

Algorithms in the first group produce a suffix-closed set of suffixes but are prone to adding unnecessarily long prefixes of counterexamples as short prefixes. Algorithms in the second group produce a prefix-closed set of short prefixes but are generally vulnerable to using unnecessarily long distinguishing suffixes.

Both groups can be further sub-divided into algorithms that add one prefix (or suffix) of a counterexample to the observations and ones that use all prefixes and suffixes. As can be seen in Fig. 1, moving toward the left or to the top in the groups, improves the worst-case number of membership queries and symbol complexity of algorithms. We could further subdivide the left cell in the middle row to distinguish by underlying data structure, which does not have an impact on the worst case but in practice has a significant impact.

The TTT algorithm [10], though belonging to the second group, is the first algorithm that produces a prefix-closed set of short prefixes and a suffix-closed set of suffixes, albeit, at the expense of using long suffixes as preliminary distinguishing suffixes in cases where incremental construction of a new suffix is not immediately possible.

The L^λ algorithm that we present in the next section extends upon ideas from both classes of algorithms: it constructs a prefix-closed set of short prefixes and a suffix-closed set of suffixes without any intermediate artifacts. It is thus the first algorithm that belongs to the top left group in Fig. 1.

```
begin
    Sp ← Sp ∪ {w}
    for wa ∈ ({w} · Σ) do
        if B ∈ ℬ and u ∈ Sp ∩ B with ℒ(wa · v) = ℒ(u · v) for all v ∈ V_B then
            B ← B ∪ {wa}
        else
            Let B̄ = {wa}
            Let V_B̄ s.t. for B ∈ ℬ, u ∈ Sp ∩ B exists v ∈ V_B̄ ∩ V_B with
                ℒ(wa · v) ≠ ℒ(u · v)
            ℬ ← ℬ ∪ {B̄}
            Expand(wa)
        end
    end
end
```

Procedure Expand(w).

4 The L^λ Algorithm

We present the L^λ learning algorithm in the unifying framework of semantic functions and without using a concrete data structure. The idea of an abstract data structure that unifies arguments for implementations based on observation tables and for implementations based on discrimination trees is inspired by partition refinement and was also used by Balcázar et al. [3] as a basis for their unified overview of active automata learning algorithms for FSAs.

Abstract Data Structure. The learner maintains a prefix-closed set $Sp \subset \Sigma^*$ of words (so-called *short prefixes*) to represent equivalence classes of $\equiv_S$. In order to mimic the definition of the transition function in the construction of the canonic automaton, she will maintain a set $U = Sp \cup Sp \cdot \Sigma$ of *prefixes* that cover transitions between equivalence classes. She also maintains a partitioning of U into a *pack* of *components* $\mathcal{B} = \{B_0, B_1, \ldots\}$, i.e., such that $U =_{def} \bigcup_{B \in \mathcal{B}}(B)$, ensuring that, every time she submits a hypothesis $\mathcal{H}$ to an equivalence query, each component contains *exactly one* short prefix.

Two prefixes $u, u' \in U$ are equivalent w.r.t. $\mathcal{B}$, denoted by $u \equiv_\mathcal{B} u'$ iff they are in the same component. For every component B, the learner maintains a set V_B of suffixes such that prefixes $u, u' \in B$ are not distinguished by V_B, i.e., such that $S(uv) = S(u'v)$ for $v \in V_B$. For $u \in B$ and $u \not\equiv_\mathcal{B} u'$, on the other hand, the set V_B contains at least one suffix v for which $S(uv) \neq S(u'v)$, distinguishing $[u]$ from $[u']$ in $\equiv_S$ and the components of u and u' in $\mathcal{B}$. She initializes the observation pack $\mathcal{B}$ with a single component $B^\epsilon = \{\epsilon\}$ and an empty set of $Sp = \emptyset$. The initial set of suffixes V_B^ϵ is initialized as $\{\epsilon\}$ when inferring Moore machine models or finite state acceptors and as Σ when inferring Mealy machine models—reflecting how residuals are defined for semantic functions $\mathcal{L}^*$ and $\mathcal{L}^+$.

The learner performs the following two main operations, detailed in Procedure Expand and Procedure Refine, on this data structure.

begin
    For $o \in \Omega$ let $B^\circ = \{w \in B \mid \mathcal{L}(w \cdot v) = o\}$
    $\mathcal{B} \leftarrow (\mathcal{B} \setminus B) \cup \{B^\circ \neq \emptyset \mid o \in \Omega\}$
    $V_{B^\circ} = V_B \cup \{v\}$ for all new components and discard of V_B
    if $B^\circ \cap Sp = \emptyset$ *for a new component* **then**
       | Expand(u) for some $u \in B^\circ$
    end
end

Procedure Refine(B, v).

Expand. Similar to a search on the states of an automaton, the learner will expand the set Sp of short prefixes with a word u from the set $U \setminus Sp$ of prefixes whenever she can prove that u belongs to an equivalence class of $\equiv_S$ which is not yet represented in Sp. The set U is extended accordingly and a new set of suffixes is introduced in such a case.

Refine. Similar to partition refinement, the learner will refine a class B of $\mathcal{B}$ whenever she finds that two short prefixes $u', u'' \in B$ do not belong to the same class of $\equiv_S$. This is the case if for some $a \in \Sigma$ she has already established that $u'a \not\equiv_B u''a$. The learner can then identify a suffix v that distinguishes $u'a$ from $u''a$ and she uses av to distinguish u' from u''.

Conjectures and Equivalence Queries. At certain points during learning, the learner computes a conjecture $\mathcal{H} = \langle Q, q_0, \Sigma, \Omega, \delta_{\mathcal{H}}, \lambda_{\mathcal{H}} \rangle$ where

- Q contains a state q_B for every class B of $\mathcal{B}$,
- $q_0 = q_{B^\epsilon}$ is the initial state,
- $\delta_{\mathcal{H}}(q_B, a) = q_{B'}$ for $Sp \cap B = \{u\}$, $a \in \Sigma$, and $B' \ni ua$,
- Ω is the set of observed outputs, and

in the case of an unknown semantic function $\mathcal{L}^*$, the output function is defined as $\lambda_{\mathcal{H}}(q_B) = \mathcal{L}^*(u)$ for $Sp \cap B = \{u\}$. In the case of an unknown semantic function $\mathcal{L}^+$, the output function is defined as $\lambda_{\mathcal{H}}(q_B, a) = \mathcal{L}^+(ua)$ for $Sp \cap B = \{u\}$ and $a \in \Sigma$.[2]

Conjectured automata are well-defined as they are only constructed when every component contains exactly one short prefix as we will show below and since ϵ is an element (resp. Σ is a subset) of every set of suffixes. The conjecture $\mathcal{H}$ is then submitted to an equivalence query. In case $\mathcal{H}$ equals $\mathcal{L}$, the teacher acknowledges this and learning ends with the correct model. Otherwise, the learner receives a counterexample w for which $\mathcal{L}(w) \neq \mathcal{H}(w)$.

Analyzing Counterexamples. Counterexamples are used to find prefixes in the set U from equivalence classes of $\equiv_S$ that are not represented in the set of short prefixes yet. As long as the hypothesis is not equivalent to $\mathcal{L}$, the set U

---

[2] The L^λ algorithm may (where possible) use its underlying data structure for determining output values or resort to membership queries and a cache.

begin

    $B^\epsilon = \{\epsilon\}$, $\mathcal{B} = \{B^\epsilon\}$, $V_{B^\epsilon} = \{\epsilon\}$ (resp. $V_{B^\epsilon} = \emptyset$ for Mealy), and $Sp = \emptyset$

    Expand(ϵ)

    $\mathcal{H} \leftarrow$ Conjecture(Sp, $\mathcal{B}$)

    while *find counterexample* $w \in \Sigma^+$ *with* $\mathcal{H}(w) \neq \mathcal{L}(w)$ **do**

        $C = \{w\}$

        while *exists* $w \in C$ *with* $\mathcal{H}(w) \neq \mathcal{L}(w)$ **do**

            // *Analyze Counterexample*

            Let i s.t. $w = w_{[1,i]}av$ with $\mathcal{H}(ua \cdot v) \neq \mathcal{L}(ua \cdot v)$ for $u \in As(w_{[1,i]})$

                                while $\mathcal{H}(u' \cdot v) = \mathcal{L}(u' \cdot v)$ for all $u' \in As(w_{[1,i+1]})$

            $C \leftarrow C \cup \{uav, u'v\}$

            Expand(ua)

            // *Lazy Refinement*

            for $u, u' \in Sp$ *with* $u \equiv_{\mathcal{B}} u'$ *but* $ua \not\equiv_{\mathcal{B}} u'a$ *for some* $a \in \Sigma$

            or $\mathcal{L}^+(ua) \neq \mathcal{L}^+(u'a)$ *in the case of Mealy machines* **do**

                Let $B \ni ua$ and $v \in V_B \cup \{\epsilon\}$ with $\mathcal{L}(ua \cdot v) \neq \mathcal{L}(u'a \cdot v)$

                Refine(B', av) for $B' \ni u$

            end

            $\mathcal{H} \leftarrow$ Conjecture(Sp, $\mathcal{B}$)

        end

    end

    Return $\mathcal{H}$ as final model

end

Algorithm 1: The abstract L^λ algorithm.

must contain a word $ua \in B \setminus Sp$ such that for some suffix $v \in \Sigma^+$ and a short prefix $u' \in B \cap Sp$ it holds that $\mathcal{L}(ua \cdot v) \neq \mathcal{L}(u' \cdot v)$. The algorithms find such a ua by binary search on the counterexample and adds ua to the set of short prefixes.

For longer v, adding ua to the short prefixes may not immediately lead to an inconsistency with corresponding new suffix, and subsequent refinement. Intuitively, more steps ahead may be required until the difference in behavior becomes detectable with the current sets of distinguishing suffixes. In such cases, multiple new short prefixes can be derived from a counterexample and one of the two words uav and $u'v$ is a guaranteed counterexamples until ua and u' are refined into two different components, as we will show.

The Learning Algorithm. The abstract L^λ algorithm is shown in Algorithm 1. The algorithms starts by initializing the set of prefixes with ϵ, the access sequence of the initial state. The set of suffixes is initialized to $\{\epsilon\}$ in the case of FSAs or Moore machines, distinguishing states by their associated output, and to the empty set in the case of Mealy machines. The observations are initialized by expanding ϵ as the basis for an initial conjecture. Then the algorithm proceeds by searching for counterexamples. As long as a counterexample w exists, the algorithm initializes a set of candidate counterexamples with w and iterates the following steps until exhausted. First, a new short prefix and two new candi-

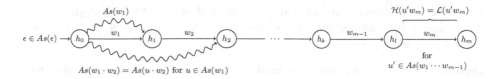

Fig. 2. Replacing prefixes of a counterexamples with short prefixes. For semantic function $\mathcal{L}$ and hypothesis $\mathcal{H}$ it is guaranteed that for symbol w_m of the counterexample the conjecture is correct by the definition of the output function λ.

date counterexamples are generated from one of the candidate counterexamples. Then, consistency of observations is checked. Inconsistent observations for two short prefixes lead to a new suffix and refinement.

While the abstract L^λ algorithm can be presented without assuming details about the underlying data structure, we have to specify special cases for inferring Mealy machine models in two lines of the algorithm: when initializing the set of suffixes, and when checking consistency. Since it is not guaranteed that a symbol $a \in \Sigma$ is in the set of suffixes, we have to add corresponding consistency checks. On the other hand, this (to the best of our knowledge) manifests the first active automata learning algorithm for Mealy machines that can use an observation table as a data structure and does not add all alphabet symbols as suffixes to the table.

Correctness and Complexity. We present technical details and arguments for the correctness of the approach in the following two lemmas where we use $As(w)$ as a shorthand for the set $B \cap Sp$ of short prefixes in $B \in \mathcal{B}$ corresponding to state $q_B = \delta_{\mathcal{H}}(w)$, reached by w in $\mathcal{H}$.

Lemma 1. *A counterexample w of length m has a prefix $w_1 \ldots w_{i-1}$ with $i < m$ such that for some $u \in As(w_1 \cdots w_i)$ and it holds that*

1. *uw_{i+1} is not a short-prefix, i.e., $uw_{i+1} \notin Sp$, and*
2. *uw_{i+1} should become a short-prefix since $uw_{i+1} \not\equiv_S u'$, as witnessed by $\mathcal{L}(uw_{i+1} \cdot w_{i+2} \cdots w_m) \neq \mathcal{L}(u' \cdot w_{i+2} \cdots w_m)$, for all $u' \in As(u \cdot w_{i+1})$.*

Proof. The argument is almost identical to the one presented by Rivest and Schapire in their proof of the existence of a distinguishing suffix in a counterexample [16]. The idea of the argument is visualized in Fig. 2. We analyze decompositions $w = w_{[1,i]} \cdot w_{[i+1,m]}$ of the counterexample where $w_{[i,j]} = w_i \cdots w_j$ for $0 \leq i \leq j \leq m$ and with $w_{[0,0]} = \epsilon$. Since w is a counterexample, it must hold that

$$\mathcal{L}(\epsilon \cdot w_{[1,m]}) = \mathcal{L}(w) \neq \mathcal{H}(w) = \mathcal{L}(u' \cdot w_{[m,m]})$$

for all $u' \in As(w_{[1,m-1]})$. As a consequence, there must be some index $1 \leq i < m$ at which for some $u \in As(w_{[0,i-1]})$ and all $u' \in As(w_{[0,i]})$

$$\mathcal{L}(u \cdot w_{[i,m]}) \neq \mathcal{L}(u' \cdot w_{[i+1,m]}).$$

The word uw_i is obviously not a short-prefix but should be a short-prefix: the stated inequality implies $uw_i \not\equiv_{\mathcal{L}} u'$ since $u \cdot w_{[i,m]} = uw_i \cdot w_{i+1} \cdots w_m$ and $u'w_{[i+1,m]} = u' \cdot w_{i+1} \cdots w_m$. $\qquad\square$

Lemma 2. *Analyzing a counterexample leads to refinement and after the analysis every component has one short prefix.*

Proof. We perform a case analysis. A counterexample w leads to new word ua at index i and witnesses $uav, u'v$ for $u' \in As(ua)$. Suffix v proves that ua is not $\equiv_{\mathcal{L}}$-equivalent to any u'. We can distinguish two basic cases:

1) **Immediate Refinement.** Short prefix ua leads to immediate refinement. There is one short prefix per component.
2) **No Immediate Refinement.** If no refinement happens, then $\mathcal{H}$ does not change and w is still counterexample. Still, there is progress: w cannot be split again at index i since ua was added to Sp. Moreover, we obtain witnesses $uav, u'v$, one of which will be a counterexample until ua and u' are refined into different components.

As a consequence, we have one access sequence per component after processing a counterexample. $\qquad\square$

After the lemmas we have proven, correctness of L^λ is trivial: Every counterexample will lead to at least one new short prefix for which it can be proven that it is not $\equiv_{\mathcal{L}}$-equivalent to any existing short prefix. Hypothesis construction guarantees that $\mathcal{H}(w) = \mathcal{L}(w)$ for $ua \in U$, that $|As(ua)| = 1$, and (at least for the final model) that for $u' \in As(ua)$ it holds that $ua \equiv_{\mathcal{L}} u'$—this generalizes to Σ^* or Σ^+ by induction.

As for query complexity and symbol complexity, for a target $\mathcal{L}$ with k input symbols, n states in the canonic automaton for L, and counterexamples of length m or shorter L^λ uses $O(kn)$ prefixes and $O(n)$ suffixes in the observations. The algorithm performs a binary search on counterexamples, and during processing of counterexamples, components may have more than one access sequence, requiring $O(n)$ tests per analyzed index of the counterexample in the worst case. This yields the following theorem.

Theorem 1. *Algorithm L^λ learns $\mathcal{L}^*$ with $O(kn^2 + n^2 log(m))$ membership queries and $O(n)$ equivalence queries.* $\qquad\square$

Since words in the observations are of length in $O(n)$, we obtain the following corollary on the symbol complexity of L^λ.

Corollary 1. *The symbol complexity of Algorithm L^λ is $O(kn^3 + n^2 m \, log(m))$.* $\qquad\square$

Comparing the obtained worst-case complexities with the results displayed in Fig. 1, relying on refinements can increase the queries for analyzing counterexamples in cases when refinement does not occur immediately. While we construct such a case in the next section, we were not able to observe delayed

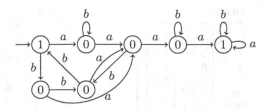

Fig. 3. Canonical FSA of target language.

refinement in any of the experiments on models of real systems reported in Sect. 6. On the other hand, the symbol complexity associated with observations used for constructing hypothesis automata does not depend on the length of counterexamples for L^λ, which can be observed in experiments.

5   Demonstration

For the sake of simplicity, we assume an observation table as a data structure in the presentation of this demonstration example.[3] Rows of an observation table are labeled with prefixes from U, columns are labeled with suffixes. We use a single big set V that distinguishes all components pairwisely. The cell in row u and column v holds the value of $S(u \cdot v)$. We demonstrate how the learning algorithm infers the canonical FSA for a target language shown in Fig. 3.

The learning algorithm starts by expanding ϵ, adding it to the set of short prefixes (depicted as the upper set of rows in the table) and adds prefixes a and b. As $S(a \cdot \epsilon) \neq S(\epsilon \cdot \epsilon)$, prefix a becomes a short prefix as well and is expanded by adding prefixes aa and ab. Now the observations become stable. The corresponding observation table resulting hypothesis are shown in Fig. 4, marked as *Obs 1* and *Hyp 1*.

Now, let us assume that the counterexample find the counterexample $bbbabbaaa$, which is in the target language but not accepted by the hypothesis. The learner discovers that she can split the counterexample as $\epsilon b \cdot bbabbaaa$, which is still a counterexample, but when she replaces prefix ϵb by its only access sequence a, the word $a \cdot bbabbaaa$ is not a counterexample. Hence, she expands b and adds words $bbbabbaaa$ and $abbabbaaa$ to the pool of potential counterexamples.

The expansion does not lead to a refinement. Another analysis of the counterexample yields the split $aa \cdot aa$, where short prefix a is one access sequence of the prefix $bbbabb$ of the counterexample. While $aa \cdot aa$ is still a counterexample, none ob the words in $\{a,b\} \cdot \{aa\}$ are. Expanding aa (and the set of candidate counterexamples) still does not lead to a refinement. The next analysis results in the split $aaa \cdot a$ (aa now being one of the access sequences for the prefix $bbbabba$) of the counterexample. Since none of the words in $\{a,b,aa\} \cdot \{a\}$ is a

---

[3] A more efficient tree-based version of is used in the evaluation. Both variants are implemented in LEARNLIB for reference.

Obs 1:

	ε
ε	1
a	0
b	0
aa	0
ab	0

Obs 2:

	ε	a	aa	aaa
ε	1	0	0	0
a	0	0	0	1
b	0	0	0	1
aa	0	0	1	1
aaa	0	1	1	1
aaaa	1	1	1	1
ba	0	0	1	1
bb	0	0	0	1
ab	0	0	0	1
aab	0	0	1	1
aaab	0	1	1	1
aaaaa	1	1	1	1
aaaab	1	1	1	1

Obs 3:

	ε	a	aa	aaa	baaa	bbaaa
ε	1	0	0	0	1	1
a	0	0	0	1	1	1
b	0	0	0	1	1	0
aa	0	0	1	1	1	0
aaa	0	1	1	1	1	1
aab	0	0	0	1	0	1
aaaa	1	1	1	1	1	1
ba	0	0	1	1	1	0
bb	0	0	0	1	0	1
ab	0	0	0	1	1	1
aaba	0	0	1	1	1	0
aabb	1	0	0	0	1	1
aaab	0	1	1	1	1	1
aaaaa	1	1	1	1	1	1
aaaab	1	1	1	1	1	1

Hyp 1:

Hyp 2:

Fig. 4. Observation table and hypothesis at time of first equivalence query (no. 1), when *bbbabbaaa* is no longer a counterexample (no. 2), and final observation table (no. 3).

counterexample, prefix *aaa* is expanded (along with the set of candidate counterexamples), finally leading to a sequence of refinements, adding suffixes *a*, *aa*, and *aaa* and generating components for *aa*, *aaa* and *aaaa*. The corresponding observation table and hypothesis are shown as *Obs 2* and *Hyp 2* in Fig. 4.

At this point, the word *bbbabbaaa* stops being a counterexample but candidate word *abbabbaaa* has become a counterexample. Analyzing this new counterexample, the learner splits it into *aab · baaa*, which is a counterexample (*abba* has access sequence *aa*). For the next index *aa · baaa* is not a counterexample. Expanding *aab* yields refinements, adding suffixes *baaa* and *bbaaa*, generating the remaining components and resulting in observation table *Obs 3*, which is equivalent to the canonical DFA.

We can observe the two particular features discussed in the previous section. First: in a round of learning, all expansions eventually lead to refinements. Second: when analyzing counterexamples, components may contain a growing number of short prefixes until all refinements are performed.

6   Evaluation

We evaluate the performance of the presented algorithm in three series of experiments on the benchmark set from the *Automata Wiki* [13]. We implemented four versions of the new algorithm in LEARNLIB, two based on an observation table (for FSAs and for Mealy Machines), and two based on a discrimination tree. We use the Mealy variants, denoted L_{DT}^λ and L_{Obs}^λ in our experiments and compare these variants against Mealy variants of learning algorithms implemented in LEARNLIB [11], namely TTT [10], Observation Packs [7], ADT [6], Kearns/Vazirani [12], Rivest/Schapire [16], and L^* [2].

In the first series of experiments, we evaluate all algorithms on the $m106.dot$ model from the *Automata Wiki* and vary the length of counterexamples, enabling a basic comparison of algorithms of the different groups shown in Fig. 1. Counterexamples are generated using a heuristic that tries to find counterexamples of a certain length cannot be shortened trivially (i.e., such that prefixes of a counterexample are not counterexamples).

In the second series, we compare the subset of the most efficient learning algorithms (TTT, Observation Packs, and L_{DT}^λ) on several benchmarks instances from the *Automata Wiki*, namely:

$$learnresult\_new\_Rand\_500\_10 - 15\_MC\_fix.dot \qquad (R500),$$
$$mosquitto\_two\_client\_will\_retain.dot \qquad (Mosq),$$
$$OpenSSH.dot \qquad (SSH),$$
$$TCP\_Windows8\_Server.dot \qquad (TCP),$$
$$m95.dot \qquad (M95).$$

As a third series of experiments, we reproduce the results presented by Frits and his coauthors in their TACAS 2022 [21] paper and add the new L_{DT}^λ learning algorithm to the analysis. We also replace Rivest and Schapire's learning algorithm by ObservationPacks to generate data on the effect of using adaptive distinguishing sequences: The ADT algorithm, the first learning algorithm that used adaptive distinguishing sequences [6], is algorithmically closest related to ObservationPacks. This lets us compare the two pairs $L^\#$, $L_{ADS}^\#$ and ObservationPacks, ADT.

All experiments were computed on a $3, 2$ GHz 6-Core Intel Core $i7$ Mac mini (2018) with 32 GB of RAM. LEARNLIB is executed in a JAVA virtual machine with 32 GB heap memory. We report averages and standard deviations from 10 executions of every experiment.

Figure 5 shows the results from the first series of experiments. We report membership queries, equivalence queries, actual length of generated counterexamples, and number of input symbols used in membership queries.

The data shows that L^* and the algorithm by Kearns and Vazirani are impacted by the length of counterexamples with respect to membership queries and input symbols. L^* adds all prefixes of counterexamples to the observation table. Kearns and Vazirani perform a linear forward search over a counterexample. Moreover, we can observe that in relation to the other algorithms L_{DT}^λ, TTT, and ObservationPacks use virtually equally many membership queries and input symbols (we take a closer look in the second series of experiments) and that on this benchmark instance not adding all alphabet symbols to the set of

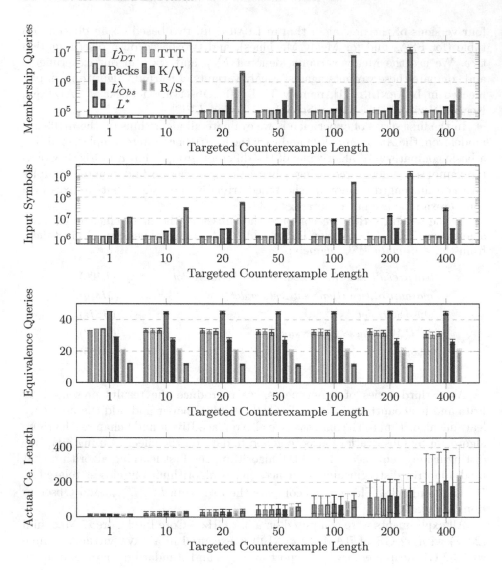

Fig. 5. Membership queries, input symbols used in membership queries, equivalence queries, and actual length of generated counterexamples for learning *m*106.*dot* from the *Automata Wiki* with different learning algorithms and different counterexample lengths. L^* did not terminate successfully in most cases for a targeted counterexample length of 400.

suffixes leads to a significant reduction in membership queries and symbols for L^λ_{Obs} compared to Rivest and Schapire's algorithm.

For equivalence queries we observe that in our limited experiments all algorithms are invariant to the length of counterexamples. The L^* algorithm that

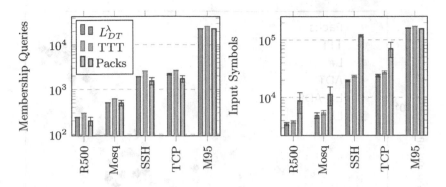

Fig. 6. Membership queries and input symbols for L_{DT}^{λ}, TTT, and ObservationPacks on several systems from the *Automata Wiki*.

adds all prefixes of counterexamples to the observation table needs the fewest number of equivalence queries, followed by Rivest and Schapire's algorithm that uses an observation table, too (and hence uses found distinguishing suffixes globally), and the L_{Obs}^{λ} algorithm, which uses an observation table but initializes the set of suffixes as $\emptyset$, leading to more equivalence queries than the other two algorithms require. Among the algorithms that are based on decision trees, the algorithm of Kearns and Vazirani uses more equivalence than the other algorithms consistently since it is the only algorithm that (in it's original version) will not analyze counterexamples exhaustively. The fact that ObservationPacks, TTT, and L_{DT}^{λ} use virtually the same number of equivalence queries seems to indicate that the additional witnesses used by L_{DT}^{λ} do not provide an advantage on this benchmark instance.

The actual length of counterexamples shows that the target length rather serves as an upper bound over the length of experiment—likely since it is hard for our randomized implementation to find long counterexamples for early (small) hypothesis models.

Figure 6 shows the results from the second series of experiments. We report membership queries and number of input symbols used in membership queries for L_{DT}^{λ}, TTT, and ObservationPacks on five benchmark instances from the *Automata Wiki* for counterexamples of (targeted) length 100. ObservationPacks and L_{DT}^{λ} use fewer membership queries than TTT, which exchanges long suffixes during learning by shorter ones, resulting in additional queries (we observe 10% to 30% overhead compared to L_{DT}^{λ}). ObservationPacks in many cases uses significantly fewer membership queries than the other two algorithms. This can be explained by the fact that in LEARNLIB, in contrast to our presentation here, Mealy machines semantics is modeled as $\Sigma^{+} \mapsto \Omega^{+}$ making long suffixes more likely to distinguish many prefixes. Considering the number of input symbols, the ObservationPacks algorithm is influenced most by long counterexamples as the algorithm uses suffixes of counterexamples directly. L_{DT}^{λ} and TTT use a

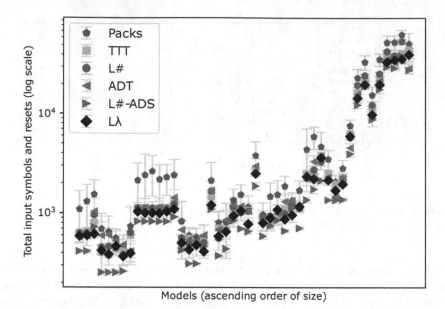

Fig. 7. Input Symbols and resets for L_{DT}^λ, TTT, ObservationPacks, ADT, $L^\#$, and $L_{ADS}^\#$ on experiments from TACAS 2022 [21].

significantly smaller amount of input symbols on most examples, with a visible edge for L_{DT}^λ which (in contrast to TTT) does not rely on intermediate suffixes.

Figure 7 shows the results from the third series of experiments.[4] The L_{DT}^λ narrowly but consistently outperforms the other learning algorithms that do not use adaptive distinguishing sequences. As in the second series of experiments, the ObservationPacks performs worst since it uses long suffixes of counterexamples in the observations. The two learning algorithms that use adaptive distinguishing sequences improve significantly upon the corresponding variants without adaptive distinguishing sequences (ADT vs. ObservationPacks and $L_{ADS}^\#$ vs. $L^\#$), yielding the question if similar improvements could be realized for TTT and L_{DT}^λ. A detailed account of the integration of distinguishing sequences is beyond the scope of this paper. We refer readers to [21] instead.

7 Conclusion

We have presented the abstract L^λ learning algorithm along with four implementations (for finite state acceptors and Mealy machines, as well as based on an observation table, and based on a decision tree). The defining characteristic of the L^λ algorithm is that no sub-strings of counterexamples are used in

---

[4] Replicating results from a recent paper by Frits and coauthors [21], we count input symbols and resets instead of inputs symbols in this series.

the algorithm's main data structure, resulting in new worst-case complexities for membership queries and input symbols. We show that, though the obtained worst-case complexities are slightly worse than the lowest existing worst-case complexities, the algorithm seems to outperform existing learning algorithms in practice.

References

1. Aarts, F., Fiterau-Brostean, P., Kuppens, H., Vaandrager, F.W.: Learning register automata with fresh value generation. In: Leucker, M., Rueda, C., Valencia, F.D. (eds.) ICTAC 2015. LNCS, vol. 9399, pp. 165–183. Springer, Cham (2015). https://doi.org/10.1007/978-3-319-25150-9_11
2. Angluin, D.: Learning regular sets from queries and counterexamples. Inf. Comput. **75**(2), 87–106 (1987)
3. Balcázar, J.L., Díaz, J., Gavaldà, R.: Algorithms for learning finite automata from queries: a unified view. In: Du, D.Z., Ko, K.I. (eds.) Advances in Algorithms. Languages, and Complexity, pp. 53–72. Springer, Heidelberg (1997). https://doi.org/10.1007/978-1-4613-3394-4_2
4. Drews, S., D'Antoni, L.: Learning symbolic automata. In: Legay, A., Margaria, T. (eds.) TACAS 2017, Part I. LNCS, vol. 10205, pp. 173–189. Springer, Heidelberg (2017). https://doi.org/10.1007/978-3-662-54577-5_10
5. Fiterau-Brostean, P., Lenaerts, T., Poll, E., de Ruiter, J., Vaandrager, F.W., Verleg, P.: Model learning and model checking of SSH implementations. In: Erdogmus, H., Havelund, K. (eds.) Proceedings of the 24th ACM SIGSOFT International SPIN Symposium on Model Checking of Software, Santa Barbara, CA, USA, 10–14 July 2017, pp. 142–151. ACM (2017)
6. Frohme, M.T.: Active automata learning with adaptive distinguishing sequences. CoRR, abs/1902.01139 (2019)
7. Howar, F.: Active learning of interface programs. Ph.D. thesis, Dortmund University of Technology (2012)
8. Howar, F., Steffen, B.: Active automata learning in practice. In: Bennaceur, A., Hähnle, R., Meinke, K. (eds.) Machine Learning for Dynamic Software Analysis: Potentials and Limits. LNCS, vol. 11026, pp. 123–148. Springer, Cham (2018). https://doi.org/10.1007/978-3-319-96562-8_5
9. Howar, F., Steffen, B., Jonsson, B., Cassel, S.: Inferring canonical register automata. In: Kuncak, V., Rybalchenko, A. (eds.) VMCAI 2012. LNCS, vol. 7148, pp. 251–266. Springer, Heidelberg (2012). https://doi.org/10.1007/978-3-642-27940-9_17
10. Isberner, M., Howar, F., Steffen, B.: The TTT algorithm: a redundancy-free approach to active automata learning. In: Bonakdarpour, B., Smolka, S.A. (eds.) RV 2014. LNCS, vol. 8734, pp. 307–322. Springer, Cham (2014). https://doi.org/10.1007/978-3-319-11164-3_26
11. Isberner, M., Howar, F., Steffen, B.: The open-source LearnLib. In: Kroening, D., Păsăreanu, C.S. (eds.) CAV 2015, Part I. LNCS, vol. 9206, pp. 487–495. Springer, Cham (2015). https://doi.org/10.1007/978-3-319-21690-4_32
12. Kearns, M.J., Vazirani, U.V.: An Introduction to Computational Learning Theory. MIT Press, Cambridge (1994)

13. Neider, D., Smetsers, R., Vaandrager, F.W., Kuppens, H.: Benchmarks for automata learning and conformance testing. In: Margaria, T., Graf, S., Larsen, K.G. (eds.) Models, Mindsets, Meta: The What, the How, and the Why Not? LNCS, vol. 11200, pp. 390–416. Springer, Cham (2019). https://doi.org/10.1007/978-3-030-22348-9_23
14. Nerode, A.: Linear automaton transformations. Proc. Am. Math. Soc. **9**(4), 541–544 (1958)
15. Maler, O., Pnueli, A.: On the learnability of infinitary regular sets. Inf. Comput. **118**(2), 316–326 (1995)
16. Rivest, R.L., Schapire, R.E.: Inference of finite automata using homing sequences. Inf. Comput. **103**(2), 299–347 (1993)
17. Smetsers, R., Fiterău-Broștean, P., Vaandrager, F.W.: Model learning as a satisfiability modulo theories problem. In: Klein, S.T., Martín-Vide, C., Shapira, D. (eds.) LATA 2018. LNCS, vol. 10792, pp. 182–194. Springer, Cham (2018). https://doi.org/10.1007/978-3-319-77313-1_14
18. Steffen, B., Howar, F., Merten, M.: Introduction to active automata learning from a practical perspective. In: Bernardo, M., Issarny, V. (eds.) SFM 2011. LNCS, vol. 6659, pp. 256–296. Springer, Heidelberg (2011). https://doi.org/10.1007/978-3-642-21455-4_8
19. Vaandrager, F.W.: Model learning. Commun. ACM **60**(2), 86–95 (2017)
20. Vaandrager, F.W., Bloem, R., Ebrahimi, M.: Learning mealy machines with one timer. In: Leporati, A., Martín-Vide, C., Shapira, D., Zandron, C. (eds.) LATA 2021. LNCS, vol. 12638, pp. 157–170. Springer, Cham (2021). https://doi.org/10.1007/978-3-030-68195-1_13
21. Vaandrager, F.W., Garhewal, B., Rot, J., Wißmann, T.: A new approach for active automata learning based on apartness. In: Fisman, D., Rosu, G. (eds.) TACAS 2022, Part I. LNCS, vol. 13243, pp. 223–243. Springer, Cham (2022). https://doi.org/10.1007/978-3-030-99524-9_12

A Reconstruction of Ewens' Sampling Formula via Lists of Coins

Bart Jacobs[✉]

Institute for Computing and Information Sciences, Radboud University,
Nijmegen, The Netherlands
bart@cs.ru.nl

Abstract. This overview paper starts from an elementary fact about lists of numbers (coins) for which a simple arithmetical proof is lacking. The paper does provide a proof, but via probabilistic reasoning, using iterations of probabilistic functions (channels), or equivalently, using iteration of transitions in a probabilistic automaton. The formulas involved capture mutations, with a rate parameter, as developed some fifty years ago in population biology by Warren Ewens. Here, this formula is reconstructed, in a theoretical computer science setting, first for lists and then also for multisets—like in the original work. The methods for describing such mutations have wider significance, beyond biology, for instance in machine learning, when the number of clusters in a classification problem may grow.

1 Introduction

A good part of Frits Vaandrager's academic work has involved probabilities, esp. in automata, for testing and model checking, see *e.g.* [4,8,20]. Moreover, being a mathematician by training, he appreciates formal arguments in computer science. Therefore, hopefully, this paper is to his liking.

The starting point below is an elementary arithmetical result about sums, products and factorials, see Theorem 2. A simple proof is lacking—as far as I know. A proof will be provided, but it is not so simple. The nice thing about this proof, however, is that it leads us into probabilistic territory, in particular, into an area that has been explored some fifty years ago by researchers in population biology [10,11,18,19]. They looked at the evolution of genes and sought to capture mutations of such genes via probabilistic formulas. An important outcome is Ewens' famous sampling formula. This work is being rediscovered in computer science, esp. in machine learning, *e.g.* in (probabilistic) clustering problems where the number of clusters is not fixed and may grow during the analysis, via a form of mutation, using Dirichlet, Poisson-Dirichlet, or Pitman-Yor processes, *e.g.* [9,21–23]. There is also a personal interest in the mathematical structures underlying these mutations, see [15,16].

This paper has an expository nature and does not contain novel research results. Its contribution lies in the way that it presents older results from mathematical biology in a

---

Dedicated to my dear colleague Frits Vaandrager, on the occasion of his 60th birthday.

© The Author(s), under exclusive license to Springer Nature Switzerland AG 2022
N. Jansen et al. (Eds.): Vaandrager Festschrift 2022, LNCS 13560, pp. 339–357, 2022.
https://doi.org/10.1007/978-3-031-15629-8_18

more modern setting of (theoretical) computer science, together with explicit proofs—which are not always present in the original sources. The paper provides an elementary account that leads via several generalisation steps to Ewens' formula, in Proposition 14. This account does not use genes as motivating example, but lists of coins. A key question is how to transform a list of coins with sum N into lists with sum $N + 1$. This may happen by incrementing the value of one of the coins in the list, or by adding a coin with value one—which constitutes a mutation. Each of these transitions will have a probability; these transitions will be iterated. This is the topic of Sect. 3.

In a next step the probabilities of mutations will be governed by a mutation rate parameter. This extension is in Sect. 4. It makes the approach more general, but does not fundamentally change the setting.

The lengths of lists of coins that sum to N varies from length 1, for the singleton list $\langle N \rangle$ with one coin of value N, to length N, for the list $\langle 1, \ldots, 1 \rangle$ of coins with value 1. Once there is a distribution on lists of coins, one can look at the distribution of lengths of such lists. In this new distribution the so-called Stirling numbers (of the first kind) show up. Moreover, this length is a sufficient statistic. Informally this means, that once we know the length of lists, the mutation rate parameter becomes irrelevant. All this is described in Sect. 5.

Ewens' sampling formula assigns probabilities, not to lists, but to multisets of numbers—called partitions, see [2, 15]. Informally, a multiset is a subset in which elements may occur multiple time, or a list in which the order of elements is irrelevant. There is a basic 'accumulation' function from lists to multisets. It is used in Sect. 6 to produce Ewens' distribution, via accumulation, from the coin list distribution. This is a non-standard way to arrive at Ewens' formula.

The paper uses a minimum of category theory, simply because category theory provides an appropriate language to capture the relevant phenomena—also in probability theory. The required concepts will be explained along the way, in the form of 'excursions'.

2   The Challenge

Let $\mathbb{N} = \{0, 1, 2, \ldots\}$ be the set of natural numbers, and $\mathbb{N}_{>0} = \{1, 2, 3, \ldots\} \subseteq \mathbb{N}$ the set of non-negative/positive numbers. Let's write $\mathcal{L}(\mathbb{N}_{>0}) = (\mathbb{N}_{>0})^*$ for the set of finite lists of such positive numbers. I will use the sum and product of a list of numbers in the obvious way:

$$\begin{aligned}
\mathrm{sum}(\langle n_1, \ldots, n_k \rangle) &:= n_1 + \cdots + n_k = \textstyle\sum_i n_i \\
\mathrm{prod}(\langle n_1, \ldots, n_k \rangle) &:= n_1 \cdot \ldots \cdot n_k = \textstyle\prod_i n_i.
\end{aligned} \tag{1}$$

For a list $\ell \in \mathcal{L}(\mathbb{N}_{>0})$ I will write $\|\ell\|$ for the length, that is, for its number of elements.

Let's look at the following issue. Suppose I have arbitrarily many coins for each value $i \in \mathbb{N}$. Given an 'amount' $N \in \mathbb{N}_{>0}$, I wish to consider the lists $\ell \in \mathcal{L}(\mathbb{N}_{>0})$ with $\mathrm{sum}(\ell) = N$. Such a list is a sequence of coins that make up the amount N. For instance for $N = 4$ we have the lists:

$$\langle 1, 1, 1, 1 \rangle \quad \langle 1, 1, 2 \rangle \quad \langle 1, 2, 1 \rangle \quad \langle 2, 1, 1 \rangle \quad \langle 2, 2 \rangle \quad \langle 1, 3 \rangle \quad \langle 3, 1 \rangle \quad \langle 4 \rangle. \tag{2}$$

These lists are in the inverse image:

$$sum^{-1}(N) := \{\ell \in \mathcal{L}(\mathbb{N}_{>0}) \mid sum(\ell) = N\}.$$

Here is a first result. The proof is skipped and left as an (easy) exercise, as warming up. Induction on N works.

Lemma 1. *For $N \in \mathbb{N}_{>0}$, the subset $sum^{-1}(N) \subseteq \mathcal{L}(\mathbb{N}_{>0})$ has 2^{N-1} elements.* ☐

Indeed, in (2) we have $8 = 2^3 = 2^{N-1}$ lists, for $N = 4$.

The next result is the starting point of this paper. It is an elementary number-theoretic fact, involving sums, products and factorials of natural numbers. I am not aware of an earlier statement of the result in this elementary form.

Theorem 2. *For each $N \in \mathbb{N}$,*

$$\sum_{\ell \in sum^{-1}(N)} \frac{1}{\|\ell\|! \cdot prod(\ell)} = 1. \tag{3}$$

The obvious thing is to try and prove this result by induction on N, using some basic arithmetic properties. That fails—at least when I try. A less elementary proof is presented in the next section—see ultimately in Corrolary 6. It takes quite a detour. In the end, it does involve an inductive reconstruction of the formula (3).

Here is an illustration of Theorem 2, for $N = 4$, using the lists in (2). The associated probabilities and their sum (3) are illustrated below.

$\langle 1,1,1,1 \rangle$	$\langle 1,1,2 \rangle$	$\langle 1,2,1 \rangle$	$\langle 2,1,1 \rangle$	$\langle 2,2 \rangle$	$\langle 1,3 \rangle$	$\langle 3,1 \rangle$	$\langle 4 \rangle$
↧	↧	↧	↧	↧	↧	↧	↧
$\frac{1}{4!\cdot 1}$	$\frac{1}{3!\cdot 2}$	$\frac{1}{3!\cdot 2}$	$\frac{1}{3!\cdot 2}$	$\frac{1}{2!\cdot 4}$	$\frac{1}{2!\cdot 3}$	$\frac{1}{2!\cdot 3}$	$\frac{1}{1!\cdot 4}$
‖	‖	‖	‖	‖	‖	‖	‖
$\frac{1}{24}$	$\frac{1}{12}$	$\frac{1}{12}$	$\frac{1}{12}$	$\frac{1}{8}$	$\frac{1}{6}$	$\frac{1}{6}$	$\frac{1}{4}$

with sum: 1

When you feel challenged to try and find yourself an elementary proof of Theorem 2, pause here and do not read on.

3 Going Probabilistic

One can view the expression on the left-hand-side in (3) as a sum of probabilities, specifically as a sum that adds up to one. Thus, there is a probability distribution at play.

So what is a probability distribution? It is an expression of the form:

$$\tfrac{1}{3}|R\rangle + \tfrac{1}{2}|G\rangle + \tfrac{1}{6}|B\rangle.$$

This describes a mixture of three colours red (R), green (G) and blue (B), each with an associated probability, where all probabilities add up to one. The 'ket' brackets $| - \rangle$

have no meaning but are used only to separate probabilities from elements. This notation is borrowed from quantum theory.

Thus we can view Theorem 2 as justification for the definition of a distribution, called *CLD* for coin list distribution. Explicitly, with parameter $N \geq 1$,

$$CLD[N] := \sum_{\ell \in sum^{-1}(N)} \frac{1}{\|\ell\|! \cdot prod(\ell)} |\ell\rangle. \tag{4}$$

For instance, as we have seen, at the end of Sect. 2:

$$CLD[4] = \tfrac{1}{24}|1,1,1,1\rangle + \tfrac{1}{12}|1,1,2\rangle + \tfrac{1}{12}|1,2,1\rangle + \tfrac{1}{12}|2,1,1\rangle \\ + \tfrac{1}{8}|2,2\rangle + \tfrac{1}{6}|1,3\rangle + \tfrac{1}{6}|3,1\rangle + \tfrac{1}{4}|4\rangle. \tag{5}$$

The main idea is to obtain these expressions $CLD[N]$ inductively, starting from the (obvious) distribution $CLD[1] = 1|1\rangle$, via a construction transforming $CLD[N]$ into $CLD[N + 1]$. This transformation should work in such a way that if $CLD[N]$ is a distribution—with probabilities adding up to one—then so is $CLD[N + 1]$. This will then prove Theorem 2.

Thus, the question becomes: how to move from $CLD[N]$ to $CLD[N+1]$. Intuitively, we can think about it as follows. Suppose we have a list $\ell \in \mathcal{L}(\mathbb{N}_{>0})$ of coins with $sum(\ell) = N$. Can we transform ℓ into a list of coins with sum $N + 1$? Sure, there are many ways to do so.

(a) We can pick a coin (item) n in the list ℓ and replace it with a coin $n + 1$ with incremented value, while keeping the rest of ℓ unchanged. The resulting list has sum $N + 1$. This increment can be done for each of the $\|\ell\|$-many coins in ℓ, which can each be incremented separately. Doing so does not change the length of ℓ.

(b) We can add a single coin with value 1 to the list ℓ. There are many places to do so. In fact, there are $\|\ell\| + 1$ many places, since the new coin 1 can be inserted at any position in ℓ, including at the front and at the end. In this way we increment the length of the list, by one, but we do not change any of the (existing) coin values. $\qquad(6)$

For instance, for a list $\ell = \langle 1, 2, 3\rangle$ with sum 6, these two approaches give the following lists with sum 7.

(a) Via increasing one of the elements: $\langle 2, 2, 3\rangle$, $\langle 1, 3, 3\rangle$, $\langle 1, 2, 4\rangle$;
(b) Via insterting a single coin 1 at all possible places: $\langle 1, 1, 2, 3\rangle$, $\langle 1, 1, 2, 3\rangle$, $\langle 1, 2, 1, 3\rangle$, $\langle 1, 2, 3, 1\rangle$.

Notice that the different methods may yield the same outcome.

People with a background in automata—like Frits Vaandrager—may recognise a (probabilistic) automaton in these transitions. That makes sense, but it still has to be determined what the appropriate transition probabilities are. My own background is in category theory and so I will proceed from a slightly different angle. This requires some basic definitions—where I will suppress the categorical technicalities—but I'm going to exploit that probability distributions form a 'monad', with an associated form of 'Kleisli' extension $\gg\!\!=$ and composition $\odot$.

Excursion 3. *For a set A, I will write $\mathcal{D}(A)$ for the set of (discrete) probability distributions over A. These are finite formal sums of the form $\sum_i r_i | a_i \rangle$, where $a_i \in A$, and $r_i \in [0, 1]$ satisfy $\sum_i r_i = 1$. Such an expression $\omega \in \mathcal{D}(A)$ can be identified with a function $\omega \colon A \to [0, 1]$ with finite support $\operatorname{supp}(\omega) := \{ a \in A \mid \omega(a) \neq 0 \}$ and satisfying $\sum_{a \in A} \omega(a) = 1$. I will switch back-and-forth between the ket-notation and the function-notation, whenever convenient.*

Thus, to recall, the aim is to prove membership:

$$CLD[N] \in \mathcal{D}\Big(\operatorname{sum}^{-1}(N) \Big).$$

It is well known in functional programming—via a 'map-list' operation—that functions f can be applied to lists, say $\langle u, v, w \rangle$, via element-wise application, giving: $\langle f(u), f(v), f(w) \rangle$. The same 'functoriality' exists for distributions: each function $f \colon A \to B$ can be turned into a function $\mathcal{D}(f) \colon \mathcal{D}(A) \to \mathcal{D}(B)$ via:

$$\mathcal{D}(f)\Big(\sum_i r_i | a_i \rangle \Big) := \sum_i r_i | f(a_i) \rangle. \tag{7}$$

One then has $\mathcal{D}(g \circ f) = \mathcal{D}(g) \circ \mathcal{D}(f)$ and also $\mathcal{D}(\operatorname{id}) = \operatorname{id}$, where id is the identity function.

I call a function of the form $f \colon A \to \mathcal{D}(B)$ a channel *and write it with a special arrow as $f \colon A \rightsquigarrow B$. These channels will be used as probabilistic functions/computations. They are known and used in the literature under various names, such as: conditional probability, stochastic matrix, probabilistic classifier, Markov kernel, statistical model, conditional probability table (in Bayesian network), and finally as Kleisli map (in category theory). The latter categorical perspecitive emphasises that such channels can be composed sequentially and in parallel, and thus that they form a symmetric monoidal category.*

What we need is transformation *of distributions* along *a channel. Given a distribution $\omega \in \mathcal{D}(A)$ and a channel $f \colon A \rightsquigarrow B$ one can form a 'push forward' distribution on B, written as $f \mathbin{>\!\!\!=} \omega$. This is called 'bind' in the functional programming language Haskell. Explicitly:*

$$f \mathbin{>\!\!\!=} \Big(\sum_i r_i | a_i \rangle \Big) := \sum_i r_i \cdot f(a_i) = \sum_{b \in B} \Big(\sum_i r_i \cdot f(a_i)(b) \Big) | b \rangle. \tag{8}$$

The assumption is that $\sum_i r_i = 1$. The right-hand-side of (8) is then a distribution again, with probabilities adding up to one:

$$\sum_{b \in B} \Big(\sum_i r_i \cdot f(a_i)(b) \Big) = \sum_i r_i \cdot \sum_{b \in B} f(a_i)(b) = \sum_i r_i \cdot 1 = 1.$$

Via this transformation $\mathbin{>\!\!\!=}$ one can define sequential composition of channels, written as $\circ$. It turns two composable channels $f \colon A \rightsquigarrow B$ and $g \colon B \rightsquigarrow C$ into a new channel $g \circ f \colon A \rightsquigarrow C$ via:

$$(g \circ f)(a) := g \mathbin{>\!\!\!=} f(a) = \sum_{c \in C} \Big(\sum_{b \in B} f(a)(b) \cdot g(b)(c) \Big) | c \rangle. \tag{9}$$

This composition ⊚ is associative and has the channel $a \mapsto 1|a\rangle$ as identity. This gives a category of channels, incorporating discrete probabilistic computation.

The next step is to define a 'coin addition' channel; it will play a crucial role in the proof of Theorem 2. For a list of numbers $\ell = \langle n_0, \ldots, n_{k-1} \rangle \in \mathcal{L}(\mathbb{N}_{>0})$ of length $\|\ell\| = k$ the following Python-style notation will be used.

- $\ell[i]$ is the i-th element n_i in the list, where $0 \leq i < k$;
- $\ell[:i]$ is the sublist $\langle n_0, \ldots, n_{i-1} \rangle$ with the i elements up to position i;
- $\ell[i:]$ is the sublist $\langle n_i, \ldots, n_{k-1} \rangle$ with the elements from position i onwards;
- $+$ is concatenation of lists.

This is used to introduce additional notation for incrementing an entry at position $i < \|\ell\|$ in list ℓ, and for adding an element (coin) 1 at position $j \leq \|\ell\|$, namely:

$$
\begin{aligned}
\ell[i] + \!\!+ &:= \ell[:i] + \langle \ell[i] + 1 \rangle + \ell[(i+1):] \\
\ell + \!\!+_j &:= \ell[:j] + \langle 1 \rangle + \ell[j:].
\end{aligned}
\tag{10}
$$

Below, in the proof of Proposition 5 (2) it is used that the set of lists k with $sum(k) = N + 1$ can be obtained via these two constructions, $\ell[i] + \!\!+$ and $\ell + \!\!+_j$, for lists ℓ with $sum(\ell) = N$ and suitable i and j. These two cases also show up in the following coin addition channel.

Definition 4. *The coin addition channel:*

$$
\mathcal{L}(\mathbb{N}_{>0}) \xrightarrow{\;\;ca\;\;} \mathcal{D}\Big(\mathcal{L}(\mathbb{N}_{>0})\Big)
$$

is defined as:

$$
\begin{aligned}
ca(\ell) := &\sum_{0 \leq i < \|\ell\|} \frac{\ell[i]}{sum(\ell) + 1} \Big| \ell[i] + \!\!+ \Big\rangle \\
+ &\sum_{0 \leq j \leq \|\ell\|} \frac{1}{(sum(\ell)+1)(\|\ell\|+1)} \Big| \ell + \!\!+_j \Big\rangle.
\end{aligned}
\tag{11}
$$

These two sums correspond to the steps (a) and (b) in (6): increment by one in ℓ at each position $i < \|\ell\|$, and add a coin 1 at each $j \leq \|\ell\|$, see (10).

Let's elaborate how the coin addition channel acts on the coin sequence $\langle 1, 2, 3 \rangle$ with sum 6. This concretely shows the increments by one and the additions of one.

$$
\begin{aligned}
ca(\langle 1, 2, 3 \rangle) = &\tfrac{1}{7}|2, 2, 3\rangle + \tfrac{2}{7}|1, 3, 3\rangle + \tfrac{3}{7}|1, 2, 4\rangle \\
&+ \tfrac{1}{28}|1, 1, 2, 3\rangle + \tfrac{1}{28}|1, 1, 2, 3\rangle + \tfrac{1}{28}|1, 2, 1, 3\rangle + \tfrac{1}{28}|1, 2, 3, 1\rangle \\
= &\tfrac{1}{7}|2, 2, 3\rangle + \tfrac{2}{7}|1, 3, 3\rangle + \tfrac{3}{7}|1, 2, 4\rangle \\
&+ \tfrac{1}{14}|1, 1, 2, 3\rangle + \tfrac{1}{28}|1, 2, 1, 3\rangle + \tfrac{1}{28}|1, 2, 3, 1\rangle.
\end{aligned}
$$

It still needs to be checked that $ca(\ell)$ in (12) is well-defined: its probabilities add up to one since:

$$\sum_{0 \le i < \|\ell\|} \frac{\ell[i]}{sum(\ell) + 1} + \sum_{0 \le j \le \|\ell\|} \frac{1}{(sum(\ell) + 1)(\|\ell\| + 1)}$$

$$= \frac{\sum_{0 \le i < \|\ell\|} \ell[i]}{sum(\ell) + 1} + \frac{\sum_{0 \le j \le \|\ell\|} 1}{(sum(\ell) + 1)(\|\ell\| + 1)}$$

$$= \frac{sum(\ell)}{sum(\ell) + 1} + \frac{\|\ell\| + 1}{(sum(\ell) + 1)(\|\ell\| + 1)}$$

$$= \frac{sum(\ell)}{sum(\ell) + 1} + \frac{1}{sum(\ell) + 1}$$

$$= 1.$$

If you like to think in terms of probabilistic automata—or coalgebras—then you can read the above definition of the coin addition channel ca as giving an automaton with lists in $\mathcal{L}(\mathbb{N}_{>0})$ as positions and with probabilistic transitions between them of the form:

$$\ell \xrightarrow{\ r\ } \ell' \qquad \text{iff} \qquad ca(\ell)(\ell') = r \in [0, 1].$$

This is finitely branching, since for each ℓ there are finitely many ℓ' with $\ell \xrightarrow{\ r\ } \ell'$, namely those ℓ' with an incremented entry or with an extra 1. The aim is to prove that the coin list expression $CLD[N]$ in (4) arises via N transition steps, starting from the singleton sequence $\langle 1 \rangle$.

There is some logic behind the probabilities of the coin addition channel ca in (12). For instance, the probability of the increment $\ell[i]{+}{+}$ is determined by the number of occurrences $\ell[i]$. A link to biological mutations is given in Remark 7 below. First, I describe the main, intended properties of coin addition.

Proposition 5. *Let* $N \in \mathbb{N}_{>0}$.

1. *The coin addition channel ca from Definition 4 restricts to a channel:*

$$sum^{-1}(N) \xrightarrow{\ ca\ } \mathcal{D}\Big(sum^{-1}(N + 1)\Big)$$

2. *The transformation along the coin addition channel preserves the coin distributions* (4):

$$ca \gg\!= CLD[N] = CLD[N + 1].$$

Proof. The first item holds by construction, so I concentrate on the second one. There:

$$ca \gg= CLD[N]$$

$$= \sum_{\ell \in sum^{-1}(N)} CLD[N](\ell) \cdot ca(\ell)$$

$$= \sum_{\ell \in sum^{-1}(N)} \sum_{0 \le i < \|\ell\|} \frac{1}{\|\ell\|! \cdot prod(\ell)} \cdot \frac{\ell[i]}{sum(\ell)+1} \left| \ell[i]\!+\!+ \right\rangle$$
$$+ \sum_{0 \le j \le \|\ell\|} \frac{1}{\|\ell\|! \cdot prod(\ell)} \cdot \frac{1}{(sum(\ell)+1)(\|\ell\|+1)} \left| \ell\!+\!+_j \right\rangle$$

$$= \sum_{\ell \in sum^{-1}(N)} \sum_{0 \le i < \|\ell\|} \frac{1}{\|\ell[i]\!+\!+ \|! \cdot prod(\ell[i]\!+\!+)} \cdot \frac{\ell[i]+1}{N+1} \left| \ell[i]\!+\!+ \right\rangle$$
$$+ \sum_{0 \le j \le \|\ell\|} \frac{1}{\|\ell\!+\!+_j \|! \cdot prod(\ell\!+\!+_j)} \cdot \frac{1}{N+1} \left| \ell\!+\!+_j \right\rangle$$

$$= \sum_{\ell \in sum^{-1}(N)} \sum_{0 \le i < \|\ell[i]\!+\!+\|} \frac{1}{\|\ell[i]\!+\!+ \|! \cdot prod(\ell[i]\!+\!+)} \cdot \frac{(\ell[i]\!+\!+)[i]}{N+1} \left| \ell[i]\!+\!+ \right\rangle$$
$$+ \sum_{0 \le j < \|\ell\!+\!+_j\|} \frac{1}{\|\ell\!+\!+_j \|! \cdot prod(\ell\!+\!+_j)} \cdot \frac{(\ell\!+\!+_j)[j]}{N+1} \left| \ell\!+\!+_j \right\rangle$$

$$= \sum_{k \in sum^{-1}(N+1)} \sum_{0 \le i < \|k\|} \frac{1}{\|k\|! \cdot prod(k)} \cdot \frac{k[i]}{N+1} \left| k \right\rangle$$

$$= \sum_{k \in sum^{-1}(N+1)} \frac{1}{\|k\|! \cdot prod(k)} \left| k \right\rangle \qquad \text{since} \sum_{0 \le i < \|k\|} k[i] = N+1$$

$$= CLD[N+1]. \qquad \qquad \square$$

Corollary 6. *The description of CLD*$[N]$ *in* (4) *yields a well-defined distribution, with its probabilities adding up to one, since* $CLD[1] = 1|1\rangle$ *trivially is a distribution, and* $CLD[N+1] = ca \gg= CLD[N]$ *is a distribution too.*

Hence, Theorem 2 holds. $\qquad \square$

Remark 7. I promised to say a bit more about the probabilities in the coin addition channel *ca* in (12). There is a biological and a gastronomical account.

1. Distributions on lists of numbers, like in (4), emerged in population biology. A list of numbers $\langle n_0, n_1, \ldots, n_{k-1} \rangle$ can be used as *type* that captures the numbers of occurrences of certain features (like alleles, variants of genes). These numbers may increase over time, with a probability that is proportional to their existing number. This explains the occurrence of the number $\ell[i]$, of occurrences of the i-th feature, in the first sum in the coin addition description (12). But also, new features may emerge, as a mutation. These mutations are captured by the second sum in (12), where a new 1 is added, somewhere in the sequence. The total probability for such a mutation is $\frac{1}{N+1}$. Since in our list description the addition may happen at any of the possible $\|\ell\| + 1$ positions in a list ℓ, the probability of each individual mutation is $\frac{1}{(N+1)(\|\ell\|+1)}$.

In fact, the descriptions in population biology differ in two ways from the above account.

- The mutation rate is not fixed, but governed by a parameter θ; this will be included in the next section.
- The numbers of features are not captured as lists, with an ordering of the numbers, but as multisets (called partitions), without such ordering, see Sect. 6 below.

This probabilistic description of (parameterised) mutation first appeared in the work of Warren Ewens [10] from 1972. It formed the starting point for much subsequent further research, see *e.g.* [17–19], or [9] for a more recent overview. The sum formula for lists (3) that is central in the current account does not occur in this earlier line of work—simply because lists are not used at all. But it is very much in the same spirit.

2. Another description of the situation in this paper is known as the *Chinese restaurant process*, see [3] for an old (original) account, or [1, §11.19] and [9, §3.1 and §4.5]. This process is standardly described in terms of multisets, but below I will reformulate it in the current setting with lists. It is unclear to me why the restaurant is called Chinese.

Assume a restaurant has arbitrarily many tables, arranged in one line, at which arbitrarily many people can sit. The situation in the restaurant, at a particular point in time, is determined by a list $\langle n_0, n_1, \ldots, n_{k-1} \rangle$ of non-negative numbers, where n_i is the number of people sitting at the i-th table. When a new customer arrives several things may happen, with certain probabilities.

(a) The new customer can join an existing (occupied) table, say i, with probability proportional to the number n_i of people already sitting at that table.

(b) The new customer can start a new table, which will then have this new customer as sole occupant. This new table may be inserted at any position in the existing line-up of tables.

It may be clear that these two options correspond to the ones from (6). The second case with the new customer starting a new table is the mutation case.

4   Adding a Mutation Rate Parameter

As already mentioned in Remark 7 (1) biologists have already looked, a long time ago, at the probabilistic mutations that are inherent in the channel-based transitions that we used so far. In this section we integrate these mutations in a more flexible manner, via a mutation parameter $\theta > 0$. It will be incorporated in a parameterised version of the coin addition channel.

Definition 8. *Let $\theta \in \mathbb{R}_{>0}$ be a mutation parameter. The coin addition channel from Definition 4 will be modified to a parameterised channel:*

$$\mathcal{L}(\mathbb{N}_{>0}) \xrightarrow{\ ca(\theta)\ } \mathcal{D}\Big(\mathcal{L}(\mathbb{N}_{>0})\Big)$$

The earlier definition is adapted to:

$$ca(\theta)(\ell) := \sum_{0 \le i < \|\ell\|} \frac{\ell[i]}{sum(\ell) + \theta} \Big| \ell[i]++ \Big\rangle$$

$$+ \sum_{0 \le j \le \|\ell\|} \frac{\theta}{(sum(\ell) + \theta)(\|\ell\| + 1)} \Big| \ell++_j \Big\rangle. \tag{12}$$

The first, unparametrised description ca *in Definition 4 corresponds to the special case where* $\theta = 1$. *Thus,* ca = ca(1).

It is not hard to see that the probabilities in $ca(\theta)(\ell)$ add up to one and that coin addition restricts to a channel $ca(\theta) \colon sum^{-1}(N) \rightarrow sum^{-1}(N+1)$, for each $\theta \in \mathbb{R}_{>0}$ and $N \in \mathbb{N}_{>0}$.

Given these channels, one can apply them iteratively to the singleton sequence in $sum^{-1}(1)$. I use the same notation as in (4), but now with a parameter t in:

$$CLD[N](\theta) := ca(\theta)^{N-1}(\langle 1 \rangle)$$
$$= \Big(ca(\theta) \circ \cdots \circ ca(\theta) \Big)(\langle 1 \rangle) \qquad (N-1 \text{ times}) \tag{13}$$
$$= ca(\theta) \gg \Big(ca(\theta) \gg \cdots \gg ca(\theta)(\langle 1 \rangle) \Big) \in \mathcal{D}\Big(sum^{-1}(N) \Big).$$

The formula (14) below is a 'list' version of the famous *Ewens sampling formula*, after [10]; the original 'multiset' version appears in the next Section, in Proposition 14. The proof of (14) works like for Proposition 5 (2) and is left to the interested reader.

Proposition 9. *Let* $\theta \in \mathbb{R}_{>0}$ *and* $N \in \mathbb{N}_{>0}$. *The parameterised coin list distribution in* (13) *can be described via the explicit formula:*

$$CLD[N](\theta) = \sum_{\ell \in sum^{-1}(N)} \frac{N! \cdot \theta^{\|\ell\|}}{\|\ell\|! \cdot prod(\ell) \cdot \prod_{i<N} \theta + i} \Big| \ell \Big\rangle. \tag{14}$$

When θ *is a (positive) natural number, this becomes:*

$$CLD[N](\theta) = \sum_{\ell \in sum^{-1}(N)} \frac{\theta^{\|\ell\|}}{\|\ell\|! \cdot prod(\ell) \cdot \left(\binom{\theta}{N} \right)} \Big| \ell \Big\rangle.$$

The latter expression involves the multichoose *coefficient:*

$$\left(\binom{\theta}{N} \right) := \binom{\theta + N - 1}{N} = \frac{(\theta + N - 1)!}{(t-1)! \cdot N!}. \qquad \Box$$

This result implicitly involves a strengthening of Theorem 2 in the form of an equation:

$$\sum_{\ell \in sum^{-1}(N)} \frac{\theta^{\|\ell\|}}{\|\ell\|! \cdot prod(\ell)} = \frac{\prod_{i<N} \theta + i}{N!}$$
$$= \left(\binom{\theta}{N} \right) \qquad \text{when } \theta \in \mathbb{N}_{>0}.$$

Theorem 2 is a special case, for $\theta = 1$. Thus the original challenge turns out to be an instance of a more general, parameterised summation formula.

5   The Lengths of Coin Sequences

This section first introduces the distribution of lengths of coin sequences, with a fixed sum. Somewhat remarkably, in this distribution Stirling numbers show up. They are used in combinatorics to count cycles of permutations. Next, this section shows how this lengths forms a so-called *sufficient statistic* and thus captures a key property of coin list distributions.

One may have noticed that the lengths of lists $\ell \in sum^{-1}(N)$, with a fixed sum N, varies considerably, from length 1, for $\ell = \langle N \rangle$ to length N, for $\ell = \langle 1, 1, \ldots, 1 \rangle$. Thus one can ask what the distribution of lengths is, given the distribution of lists (14). For instance, for the lists with sum 4 in (2) we have seen the distribution $CLD[4] = CLD[4](1)$ in (5). Applying the length function $\| - \|$ to the lists inside the ket-brackets can be expressed via the functoriality (7) of $\mathcal{D}$, see Excursion 3:

$$\mathcal{D}(\| - \|)\Big(CLD[4]\Big)$$
$$= \tfrac{1}{24}\big|\,\|1,1,1,1\|\,\big\rangle + \tfrac{1}{12}\big|\,\|1,1,2\|\,\big\rangle + \tfrac{1}{12}\big|\,\|1,2,1\|\,\big\rangle + \tfrac{1}{12}\big|\,\|2,1,1\|\,\big\rangle$$
$$+ \tfrac{1}{8}\big|\,\|2,2\|\,\big\rangle + \tfrac{1}{6}\big|\,\|1,3\|\,\big\rangle + \tfrac{1}{6}\big|\,\|3,1\|\,\big\rangle + \tfrac{1}{4}\big|\,\|4\|\,\big\rangle \qquad (15)$$
$$= \tfrac{1}{24}\big|4\big\rangle + \big(\tfrac{1}{12} + \tfrac{1}{12} + \tfrac{1}{12}\big)\big|3\big\rangle + \big(\tfrac{1}{8} + \tfrac{1}{6} + \tfrac{1}{6}\big)\big|2\big\rangle + \tfrac{1}{4}\big|1\big\rangle$$
$$= \tfrac{1}{24}\big|4\big\rangle + \tfrac{1}{4}\big|3\big\rangle + \tfrac{11}{24}\big|2\big\rangle + \tfrac{1}{4}\big|1\big\rangle.$$

Interestingly, these distributions $\mathcal{D}(\| - \|)\big(CLD[N](\theta)\big)$ of lengths can be described in terms of *Stirling numbers*. They are fundamental in combinatorics, in the study of permutations. There are Stirling numbers 'of the first kind' and 'of the second kind'. The ones of the first kind are relevant here, and will simply be called Stirling numbers. See *e.g.* [13] for more information.

Excursion 10. *For numbers $n, k \in \mathbb{N}$ the defining property of the Stirling number $\left[{n \atop k}\right]$ is:*

$$\begin{bmatrix} n \\ k \end{bmatrix} = \begin{cases} \text{the number of permutations of } n \text{ elements with } k \text{ disjoint cycles} & \text{if } k \leq n \\ 0 & \text{if } k > n \end{cases}$$

The following basic properties are useful in calculations. For $n \in \mathbb{N}$ and $k \in \mathbb{N}_{>0}$,

$$\begin{bmatrix} 0 \\ 0 \end{bmatrix} = 1 \qquad \begin{bmatrix} 0 \\ k \end{bmatrix} = \begin{bmatrix} k \\ 0 \end{bmatrix} = 0 \qquad \begin{bmatrix} n + 1 \\ k \end{bmatrix} = n \cdot \begin{bmatrix} n \\ k \end{bmatrix} + \begin{bmatrix} n \\ k-1 \end{bmatrix}. \qquad (16)$$

One can then prove further identities like:

$$\begin{bmatrix} n \\ n \end{bmatrix} = 1 \qquad \begin{bmatrix} n + 1 \\ 1 \end{bmatrix} = n!. \qquad (17)$$

The next equation will be used to make a connection between Stirling numbers and sums of lists. For $N \in \mathbb{N}_{>0}$ and $\theta > 0$,

$$\sum_{1 \leq k \leq N} \begin{bmatrix} N \\ k \end{bmatrix} \cdot \theta^k = \prod_{0 \leq i < N} \theta + i \qquad (18)$$

It is easy to derive, by induction on N.

This last Eq. (18) can be used to define what is called here the *Stirling distribution* on $\{1, \ldots, N\}$.

$$SD[N](\theta) := \sum_{1 \le k \le N} \begin{bmatrix} N \\ k \end{bmatrix} \cdot \frac{\theta^k}{\prod_{0 \le i < N} \theta + i} \, |k\rangle. \tag{19}$$

For instance,

$$SD[4](1) = \tfrac{1}{24}|1\rangle + \tfrac{11}{24}|2\rangle + \tfrac{1}{4}|3\rangle + \tfrac{1}{4}|4\rangle \qquad \text{as in (15)}$$

$$SD[5](2) = \tfrac{1}{15}|1\rangle + \tfrac{5}{18}|2\rangle + \tfrac{7}{18}|3\rangle + \tfrac{2}{9}|4\rangle + \tfrac{2}{45}|5\rangle.$$

The next result is known in the setting of Ewens distributions, see *e.g.* [9, §2.2], but there it is formulated for multisets/partitions (and without proof). The version below is formulated for lists.

Proposition 11. *For each $N \ge 1$ the channels of coin list distributions $CLD[N]$ and Stirling distributions $SD[N]$ are connected via lengths of lists $\| - \|$ in the following commuting diagram.*

$$
\begin{array}{ccc}
\mathcal{D}\big(sum^{-1}(N)\big) & \xrightarrow{\;\; \mathcal{D}(\| - \|) \;\;} & \mathcal{D}(\{1, \ldots, N\}) \\
& \nwarrow \quad \nearrow & \\
CLD[N] & \mathbb{R}_{>0} & SD[N]
\end{array}
$$

This means that for each $\theta \in \mathbb{N}_{>0}$,

$$\sum_{\ell \in sum^{-1}(N)} \frac{N! \cdot \theta^{\|\ell\|}}{\|\ell\|! \cdot prod(\ell) \cdot \prod_{i<N} \theta + i} \, \big| \|\ell\| \big\rangle = \mathcal{D}(\| - \|)\big(CLD[N](\theta)\big)$$

$$= SD[N](\theta)$$

$$= \sum_{1 \le k \le N} \begin{bmatrix} N \\ k \end{bmatrix} \cdot \frac{\theta^k}{\prod_{0 \le i < N} \theta + i} \, |k\rangle.$$

Proof. By induction on $N \ge 1$. When $N = 1$, only $\langle 1 \rangle$ is in $sum^{-1}(N)$, so:

$$\sum_{\ell \in sum^{-1}(1)} \frac{1! \cdot \theta^{\|\ell\|}}{\|\ell\|! \cdot prod(\ell) \cdot \prod_{i<1} \theta + i} \, \big| \|\ell\| \big\rangle = \frac{\theta^1}{1! \cdot 1 \cdot \prod_{i<1} \theta + i} \, |1\rangle$$

$$= \begin{bmatrix} 1 \\ 1 \end{bmatrix} \cdot \frac{\theta^1}{\prod_{i<1} \theta + i} \, |1\rangle$$

$$= \sum_{1 \le k \le 1} \begin{bmatrix} 1 \\ k \end{bmatrix} \cdot \frac{\theta^k}{\prod_{i<1} \theta + i} \, |k\rangle.$$

The induction step is more involved.

$$\mathcal{D}(\|-\|)\Big(CLD[N+1](\theta)\Big)$$

$$= \sum_{k \in sum^{-1}(N+1)} CLD[N+1](\theta)(k)\,\big|\|k\|\big\rangle$$

$$= \sum_{k \in sum^{-1}(N+1)} \Big(ca[N](\theta) \succcurlyeq CLD[N](\theta)\Big)(k)\,\big|\|k\|\big\rangle$$

$$= \sum_{k \in sum^{-1}(N+1),\,\ell \in sum^{-1}(N)} CLD[N](\theta)(\ell) \cdot ca[N](\theta)(\ell)(k)\,\big|\|k\|\big\rangle$$

$$= \sum_{\ell \in sum^{-1}(N)} \sum_{0 \le i < \|\ell\|} \frac{N! \cdot \theta^{\|\ell\|}}{\|\ell\|! \cdot prod(\ell) \cdot \prod_{i<N} \theta + i} \cdot \frac{\ell[i]}{sum(\ell)+\theta}\,\big|\|\ell[i]{+}{+}\|\big\rangle$$

$$+ \sum_{0 \le j \le \|\ell\|} \frac{N! \cdot \theta^{\|\ell\|}}{\|\ell\|! \cdot prod(\ell) \cdot \prod_{i<N} \theta + i} \cdot \frac{\theta}{(sum(\ell)+\theta)(\|\ell\|+1)}\,\big|\|\ell{+}{+}_j\|\big\rangle$$

$$= \sum_{\ell \in sum^{-1}(N)} \frac{N! \cdot \theta^{\|\ell\|}}{\|\ell\|! \cdot prod(\ell) \cdot \prod_{i<N} \theta + i} \cdot \frac{N}{N+\theta}\,\big|\|\ell\|\big\rangle$$

$$+ \sum_{\ell \in sum^{-1}(N)} \frac{N! \cdot \theta^{\|\ell\|}}{\|\ell\|! \cdot prod(\ell) \cdot \prod_{i<N} \theta + i} \cdot \frac{\theta}{N+\theta}\,\big|\|\ell\|+1\big\rangle.$$

$$\overset{(IH)}{=} \sum_{1 \le k \le N} \begin{bmatrix} N \\ k \end{bmatrix} \cdot \frac{\theta^k}{\prod_{i<N} \theta + i} \cdot \frac{N}{N+\theta}\,|k\rangle$$

$$+ \frac{\theta}{N+\theta} \cdot \mathcal{D}(-{+}1)\left(\sum_{\ell \in sum^{-1}(N)} \frac{N! \cdot \theta^{\|\ell\|}}{\|\ell\|! \cdot prod(\ell) \cdot \prod_{i<N} \theta + i}\,\big|\|\ell\|\big\rangle\right)$$

$$\overset{(IH)}{=} \frac{N}{N+\theta} \cdot \sum_{1 \le k \le N} \begin{bmatrix} N \\ k \end{bmatrix} \cdot \frac{\theta^k}{\prod_{i<N} \theta + i}\,|k\rangle$$

$$+ \frac{\theta}{N+\theta} \cdot \mathcal{D}(-{+}1)\left(\sum_{1 \le k \le N} \begin{bmatrix} N \\ k \end{bmatrix} \cdot \frac{\theta^k}{\prod_{i<N} \theta + i}\,|k\rangle\right)$$

$$= \sum_{1 \le k \le N} N \cdot \begin{bmatrix} N \\ k \end{bmatrix} \cdot \frac{\theta^k}{\prod_{i<N+1} \theta + i}\,|k\rangle + \sum_{1 \le k \le N} \begin{bmatrix} N \\ k \end{bmatrix} \cdot \frac{\theta^{k+1}}{\prod_{i<N+1} \theta + i}\,|k+1\rangle$$

$$= \frac{1}{\prod_{i<N+1} \theta + i} \cdot \left(N \cdot \begin{bmatrix} N \\ 1 \end{bmatrix} \cdot \theta^1\,|1\rangle + \left(N \cdot \begin{bmatrix} N \\ 2 \end{bmatrix} + \begin{bmatrix} N \\ 1 \end{bmatrix}\right) \cdot \theta^2\,|2\rangle + \cdots + \right.$$

$$\left. \left(N \cdot \begin{bmatrix} N \\ N \end{bmatrix} + \begin{bmatrix} N \\ N-1 \end{bmatrix}\right) \cdot \theta^N\,|N\rangle + \begin{bmatrix} N \\ N \end{bmatrix} \cdot \theta^{N+1}\,|N+1\rangle\right)$$

$$\overset{(16)}{=} \frac{1}{\prod_{i<N+1} \theta + i} \cdot \left(\begin{bmatrix} N+1 \\ 1 \end{bmatrix} \cdot \theta^1\,|1\rangle + \begin{bmatrix} N+1 \\ 2 \end{bmatrix} \cdot \theta^2\,|2\rangle + \cdots + \right.$$

$$\left. \begin{bmatrix} N+1 \\ N \end{bmatrix} \cdot \theta^N\,|N\rangle + \begin{bmatrix} N+1 \\ N+1 \end{bmatrix} \cdot \theta^{N+1}\,|N+1\rangle\right)$$

$$= \sum_{1 \le k \le N+1} \begin{bmatrix} N+1 \\ k \end{bmatrix} \cdot \frac{\theta^k}{\prod_{i<N+1} \theta + i}\,|k\rangle.$$

$\square$

There is more to say. If we consider a coin list distribution $CLD[N](\theta)$ and we condition on a fixed length $k \in \{1, \ldots, N\}$, the mutation rate θ drops out—like in the Fisher-Neyman factorisation theorem. This indicates that length is a sufficient statistic, see *e.g.* [5–7]. I avoid the notion of conditioning and will instead use the string-diagrammatic description of sufficient statistics developed in [12]—and elaborated in [16]. These string diagrams are a modern intuitive graphical language for computations via channels in (quantum) probability theory. The remainder of this section describes the situation at hand, without developing a wider picture. The interested reader is referred to [12, 16] for further information.

For a fixed number N, taking the length $\| - \|$ of coin lists forms a function $\| - \|$: $sum^{-1}(N) \to \{1, \ldots, N\}$. It turns out to have a 'dagger', in the form of a channel $\| - \|^{\dagger} \colon \{1, \ldots, N\} \to \mathcal{D}(sum^{-1}(N))$ in the opposite direction. It assigns to a number $1 \le k \le N$ a distribution over lists in $sum^{-1}(N)$ of length k. This can be described as follows.

$$\|k\|^{\dagger} = \sum_{\ell \in sum^{-1}(N),\, \|\ell\| = k} \frac{CLD[N](1)(\ell)}{SD[N](1)(k)} \, |\ell\rangle. \tag{20}$$

This is a well-defined distribution by Proposition 11. The following result summarises the situation and includes Proposition 11 (by discarding the left wire). The proof is a rehearsel of what has already been done.

Theorem 12. *Length* $\| - \|$ *is a sufficient statistic for the coin list distribution CLD, as expressed by the following equality of string diagrams.*

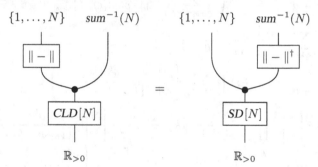

The flow in the diagram works upward. The equality expresses that for $N \in \mathbb{N}_{>0}$ *and* $\theta \in \mathbb{R}_{>0}$ *the following two joint distributions on* $\{1, \ldots, N\} \times sum^{-1}(N)$ *are equal:*

$$\sum_{k \in \{1, \ldots, N\}} \sum_{\ell \in sum^{-1}(N),\, \|\ell\| = k} CLD[N](\theta)(\ell) \, \Big| k, \ell \Big\rangle$$

$$= \sum_{k \in \{1, \ldots, N\}} \sum_{\ell \in sum^{-1}(N),\, \|\ell\| = k} SD[N](\theta)(k) \cdot \|k\|^{\dagger}(\ell) \, \Big| k, \ell \Big\rangle. \qquad \square$$

The essence of this theorem occurs in [9, §2.2], but without the dagger of the length and the formulation as string diagram.

6   Multisets Instead of Lists

So far I have used *lists* of coins, with a certain sum N. That gives rise to a decent theory, but there are good reasons to use *multisets* instead of lists. Recall that a multiset—sometimes also called 'bag'—is a 'subset' in which elements may occur multiple times. Alternatively, multisets are 'lists' in which the order does not matter. The ket notation will be used not only for distributions, but also for multisets. Thus, $3|R\rangle + 4|G\rangle + 5|B\rangle$ describes a multiset with the element R occurring 3 times, G occuring 4 times, and B 5 times.

Why use multisets? There are two reasons.

- In the beginning, this paper discussed lists of coins that sum up to a certain value, like in (2), where the order of the coins is relevant. This is not what happens practice when people consider coin values. They usually say things like: I use two coins of 1 and one of 3 to get the amount 5. In that case they use the multiset $2|1\rangle + 1|3\rangle$, without worrying about the order of the coins. Instead of lists summing to 4, as in (2) one can use the following multisets.

$$4|1\rangle \qquad 2|1\rangle + 1|2\rangle \qquad 2|2\rangle \qquad 1|1\rangle + 1|3\rangle \qquad 1|4\rangle. \qquad (21)$$

- When we reconsider the big horizontal brace, at the end of Sect. 2, we see that lists whose elements are permuted, like $\langle 1, 1, 2\rangle$, $\langle 1, 2, 1\rangle$ and $\langle 2, 1, 1\rangle$ have the same probability. These lists correspond to the same multiset $2|1\rangle + 1|2\rangle$. This is an indication that multisets are the more appropriate data type. This suspicion is confirmed when we take a closer look at the coin list distribution $CLD[N]$ in (4) and (14): The probability of list ℓ is expressed via the length $\|\ell\|$ and the multiplication $prod(\ell)$ of its elements. Both operations are invariant under permutations of the elements in the list.

Excursion 13. *A (finite) multiset over a set A is a formal finite sum $\sum_i n_i|a_i\rangle$ of elements $a_i \in A$ with multiplicity $n_i \in \mathbb{N}$. Alternatively, it is a function $\varphi: A \to \mathbb{N}$ with finite support, where $\varphi(a)$ is the multiplicity of the element a.*

The size $\|\varphi\|$ of a multiset φ over A is its number of elements, where multiplicities are counted. Thus, $\|\varphi\| = \sum_{a \in A} \varphi(a)$. The set of multisets over A is written as $\mathcal{M}(A)$, and the set of multisets of a fixed size K is the subset $\mathcal{M}[K](A) \subseteq \mathcal{M}(A)$.

One can turn a list over A into a multiset over A via what I call accumulation, *written as* acc, *see [14]. Thus, for example,*

$$\mathrm{acc}(b, a, c, a, b, a, b) = 3|a\rangle + 3|b\rangle + 1|c\rangle.$$

More abstractly, accumulation is a function acc: $\mathcal{L}(A) \to \mathcal{M}(A)$, *defined as:*

$$\mathrm{acc}(\langle a_0, \ldots, a_{k-1}\rangle) := \sum_i 1|a_i\rangle.$$

It restricts to acc: $A^K \to \mathcal{M}[K](A)$, *for each $K \in \mathbb{N}$. This works, since $\|\mathrm{acc}(\ell)\| = \|\ell\|$, for a list ℓ.*

For a fixed multiset $\varphi = \sum_i n_i | a_i \rangle \in \mathcal{M}(A)$ the number of lists $\ell \in \mathcal{L}(A)$ with acc$(\ell) = \varphi$ *is given by the* multinomial coefficient:

$$(\varphi) := \frac{(\sum_i n_i)!}{\prod_i n_i!} = \frac{\|\varphi\|!}{\prod_i n_i!}. \tag{22}$$

Let set A have $n \geq 1$ elements. Then:

$$\binom{n}{K} = \text{the number of subsets of } A \text{ of size } K \leq n$$
$$\left(\binom{n}{K}\right) = \text{the number of multisets over } A \text{ of size } K. \tag{23}$$

Recall the latter multichoose from Proposition 9.

Earlier, sums and products (1) played an important role for lists over $\mathbb{N}_{>0}$. They will be used for multiset over $\mathbb{N}_{>0}$ too, in such a way that both sides of the following diagram commute.

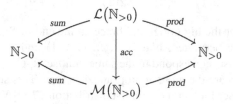

These analogues for multisets are defined as:

$$\text{sum}\left(\sum_i n_i | k_i \rangle\right) := \sum_i n_i \cdot k_i \quad \text{prod}\left(\sum_i n_i | k_i \rangle\right) := \prod_i k_i^{n_i}. \tag{24}$$

The set $\mathfrak{P}(N)$ of *partitions*, see [2, 15], with sum $N \geq 1$ is written as:

$$\mathfrak{P}(N) := \{\sigma \in \mathcal{M}(\mathbb{N}_{>0}) \mid \text{sum}(\sigma) = N\}.$$

The elements of the set $\mathfrak{P}(4)$ have already been described, in (21). It is not hard to see that accumulation of lists to multisets restricts to a function:

$$\text{sum}^{-1}(N) \xrightarrow{\quad \text{acc} \quad} \mathfrak{P}(N)$$

The *Ewens distribution* $EW[N](\theta) \in \mathcal{D}(\mathfrak{P}(N))$ can now be defined as by translating the coin list distribution to a distribution on partitions, via accumulation:

$$EW[N](\theta) := \mathcal{D}(\text{acc})\left(CLD[N](\theta)\right) \in \mathcal{D}(\mathfrak{P}(N)). \tag{25}$$

This yields Ewens' sampling formula, now reformulated as convex formal sum using ket's.

Proposition 14. *For $N \in \mathbb{N}_{>0}$ and $\theta \in \mathbb{R}_{>0}$, Ewens's sampling formula (25) is:*

$$EW[N](\theta) = \sum_{\sigma \in \mathfrak{P}(N)} \frac{N! \cdot \theta^{\|\sigma\|}}{\|\sigma\|! \cdot prod(\sigma) \cdot \prod_{i<N} \theta + i} \,|\sigma\rangle$$

$$= \sum_{\sigma \in \mathfrak{P}(N)} \frac{N! \cdot \theta^{\|\sigma\|}}{\prod_i \sigma(i)! \cdot i^{\sigma(i)} \cdot (\theta + i)} \,|\sigma\rangle.$$

Proof. Since:

$$EW[N](\theta) = \mathcal{D}(acc)\Big(CLD[N](\theta)\Big)$$

$$= \sum_{\ell \in sum^{-1}(N)} \frac{N! \cdot \theta^{\|\ell\|}}{\|\ell\|! \cdot prod(\ell) \cdot \prod_{i<N} \theta + i} \,|acc(\ell)\rangle$$

$$= \sum_{\ell \in sum^{-1}(N)} \frac{N! \cdot \theta^{\|acc(\ell)\|}}{\|acc(\ell)\|! \cdot prod(acc(\ell)) \cdot \prod_{i<N} \theta + i} \,|acc(\ell)\rangle$$

$$= \sum_{\sigma \in \mathfrak{P}(N)} \sum_{\ell \in acc^{-1}(\sigma)} \frac{N! \cdot \theta^{\|acc(\ell)\|}}{\|acc(\ell)\|! \cdot prod(acc(\ell)) \cdot \prod_{i<N} \theta + i} \,|acc(\ell)\rangle$$

$$\stackrel{(22)}{=} \sum_{\sigma \in \mathfrak{P}(N)} \frac{(\sigma) \cdot N! \cdot \theta^{\|\sigma\|}}{\|\sigma\|! \cdot prod(\sigma) \cdot \prod_{i<N} \theta + i} \,|\sigma\rangle$$

$$= \sum_{\sigma \in \mathfrak{P}(N)} \frac{N! \cdot \theta^{\|\sigma\|}}{\prod_{1 \leq i \leq N} \sigma(i)! \cdot i^{\sigma(i)} \cdot (\theta + i - 1)} \,|\sigma\rangle. \qquad \square$$

Finally, here are some examples. The first one is a multiset version of (5).

$$EW[4](1) = \tfrac{1}{24}|4|1\rangle\rangle + \tfrac{1}{4}|2|1\rangle + 1|2\rangle\rangle + \tfrac{1}{8}|2|2\rangle\rangle + \tfrac{1}{3}|1|1\rangle + 1|3\rangle\rangle + \tfrac{1}{4}|1|4\rangle\rangle$$

$$EW[5](2) = \tfrac{2}{45}|5|1\rangle\rangle + \tfrac{2}{9}|3|1\rangle + 1|2\rangle\rangle + \tfrac{1}{6}|1|1\rangle + 2|2\rangle\rangle + \tfrac{2}{9}|2|1\rangle + 1|3\rangle\rangle$$
$$+ \tfrac{1}{9}|1|2\rangle + 1|3\rangle\rangle + \tfrac{1}{6}|1|1\rangle + 1|4\rangle\rangle + \tfrac{1}{15}|1|5\rangle\rangle$$

The probability of 'ones only', that is of the multisets $4|1\rangle$ and $5|1\rangle$ that arise via multiple mutations, is (relatively) higher in the second distribution $EW[5](2)$, because it involves a higher mutation rate (2 versus 1).

In combination with Proposition 11 there is the following (standard) result, stating that the sizes of multisets in Ewens' distribution are (also) described by the Stirling distribution $SD[N](\theta)$ from (19).

Corollary 15. *For each $N \geq 1$ the following diagram commutes.*

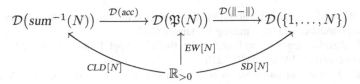

By functoriality, $\mathcal{D}(\| - \|) \circ \mathcal{D}(acc) = \mathcal{D}(\| - \| \circ acc) = \mathcal{D}(\| - \|)$, so that for each $\theta \in \mathbb{N}_{>0}$,

$$\mathcal{D}(\| - \|)\Big(EW[N](\theta)\Big) = SD[N](\theta). \qquad \square$$

Acknowledgements. Thanks are due to Ceel Pierik for helpful discussion on the material in Sect. 5.

References

1. Aldous, D.J.: Exchangeability and related topics. In: Hennequin, P.L. (ed.) École d'Été de Probabilités de Saint-Flour XIII—1983. LNM, vol. 1117, pp. 1–198. Springer, Heidelberg (1985). https://doi.org/10.1007/BFb0099421
2. Andrews, G.: The Theory of Partitions. Cambridge University Press, Cambridge (1998)
3. Antoniak, C.: Mixtures of Dirichlet processes with applications to Bayesian non-parametric problems. Ann. Stat. **2**, 1152–1174 (1974). https://doi.org/10.1214/aos/1176342871
4. Berendsen, J., Jansen, D., Vaandrager, F.: Fortuna: model checking priced probabilistic timed automata. In: Quantitative Evaluation of Systems (QEST), pp. 273–281. IEEE Computer Society (2010). https://doi.org/10.1109/QEST.2010.41
5. Bernardo, J., Smith, A.: Bayesian Theory. Wiley, Hoboken (2000). https://onlinelibrary. wiley.com/doi/book/10.1002/9780470316870, https://doi.org/10.1002/9780470316870
6. Billingsley, P.: Probability and Measure. Wiley-Interscience, New York (1995)
7. Bishop, C.: Pattern Recognition and Machine Learning. Information Science and Statistics. Springer, Heidelberg (2006)
8. Cheung, L., Stoelinga, M., Vaandrager, F.: A testing scenario for probabilistic processes. J. ACM **54**(6), 29 (2007). https://doi.org/10.1145/1314690.1314693
9. Crane, H.: The ubiquitous Ewens sampling formula. Stat. Sci. **31**(1), 1–19 (2016). https:// doi.org/10.1214/15-STS529
10. Ewens, W.: The sampling theory of selectively neutral alleles. Theoret. Popul. Biol. **3**, 87–112 (1972). https://doi.org/10.1016/0040-5809(72)90035-4
11. Ferguson, T.: A Bayesian analysis of some nonparametric problems. Ann. Stat. **1**(2), 209–230 (1973). https://doi.org/10.1214/aos/1176342360
12. Fritz, T.: A synthetic approach to Markov kernels, conditional independence, and theorems on sufficient statistics. Adv. Math. **370**, 107239 (2020). https://doi.org/10.1016/J.AIM.2020. 107239
13. Guichard, D.: Combinatorics and graph theory (2022). https://www.whitman.edu/ mathematics/cgt_online/book/
14. Jacobs, B.: From multisets over distributions to distributions over multisets. In: Logic in Computer Science. IEEE, Computer Science Press (2021). https://doi.org/10.1109/ lics52264.2021.9470678
15. Jacobs, B.: Partitions and Ewens distributions in element-free probability theory. In: Logic in Computer Science. IEEE, Computer Science Press (2022). https://doi.org/10.1145/3531130. 3532419
16. Jacobs, B.: Sufficient statistics and split idempotents in discrete probability theory. In: Mathematical Foundation of Programming Semantics (2022)
17. Joyce, P.: Partition structures and sufficient statistics. J. Appl. Probab. **35**(3), 622–632 (1998). https://doi.org/10.1239/jap/1032265210
18. Kingman, J.: Random partitions in population genetics. Proc. R. Soc. Ser. A **361**, 1–20 (1978). https://doi.org/10.1098/rspa.1978.0089

19. Kingman, J.: The representation of partition structures. J. London Math. Soc. **18**(2), 374–380 (1978). https://doi.org/10.1112/jlms/s2-18.2.374
20. Lynch, N., Segala, R., Vaandrager, F.: Compositionality for probabilistic automata. In: Amadio, R., Lugiez, D. (eds.) CONCUR 2003. LNCS, vol. 2761, pp. 208–221. Springer, Heidelberg (2003). https://doi.org/10.1007/978-3-540-45187-7_14
21. McCullagh, P., Yang, J.: How many clusters? Bayesian Anal. **3**(1), 101–120 (2008). https://doi.org/10.1214/08-BA304
22. Pitman, J.: Random discrete distributions invariant under size-biased permutation. Adv. Appl. Probab. **28**(2), 525–539 (1995). https://doi.org/10.2307/1428070
23. Pitman, J., Yor, M.: The two-parameter Poisson-Dirichlet distribution derived from a stable subordinator. Ann. Probab. **25**(2), 855–900 (1997). https://doi.org/10.1214/aop/1024404422

Rooted Divergence-Preserving Branching Bisimilarity is a Congruence: A Simpler Proof

David N. Jansen[1,2]([✉]) [iD] and Xinxin Liu[1,2,3]([✉])

[1] State Key Laboratory of Computer Science, Institute of Software, Chinese Academy of Sciences, Beijing, China
{dnjansen,xinxin}@ios.ac.cn
[2] University of Chinese Academy of Sciences, Beijing, China
[3] Southwest University, Chongqing, China

Abstract. Van Glabbeek, Luttik and Spanink proved in 2020 [3] that rooted divergence-preserving branching bisimilarity is a congruence for the process specification language consisting of inaction, action prefix, choice, and recursion. In this article we show the same result by using an alternative characterization of bisimulation, so that the heavy notion of bisimulation up to can be spared and a shorter proof obtained.

Keywords: Branching bisimulation · Divergence preservation · Congruence

1 Introduction

Already in the first publication mentioned on his webpage [13], Vaandrager included an extensive discussion of *fairness* in process algebra. He defines this notion as "a certain option is not discarded infinitely often." In particular, this holds for probabilistic choice: if a discrete random experiment is started infinitely often, almost surely every outcome is chosen. In the publication, this was used to prove progress properties of a certain communication protocol where failures occur with a (low but not further specified) probability. Vaandrager admitted that "in reality certain choices are fair, other choices are unfair" (for example, non-probabilistic choices) but decided to postpone the introduction of unfairness. In this article, we are looking at one consequence of unfairness, namely divergence.

We are working on the basis of Milner's CCS to describe and compare behaviours of interacting processes [10]. We mainly consider the subset of *finite-state* processes. They are composed from actions by action prefix, choice and recursion. Full CCS also includes parallel composition and two operators supporting the latter (restriction and relabelling). The recursion operator uses process variables to describe a behaviour X satisfying $X = E$, where X may appear in the process expression E again.

While CCS differs from ACP, the process algebra used by Vaandrager in several publications including [13], we are confident that the superficial differences are less important than the "close relationships between the various process algebras" in terms of the "semantical reality" (using Vaandrager's words from [5]).

N. Jansen et al. (Eds.): Vaandrager Festschrift 2022, LNCS 13560, pp. 358–370, 2022.
https://doi.org/10.1007/978-3-031-15629-8_19

Often, processes are compared by means of bisimilarities, notions to find processes that have equivalent behaviours. For process expressions considered in this paper, bisimilarities can be defined in two ways: an *algebraic* definition defines bisimilarity on expressions that do not contain free process variables first and then extends to all expressions through substitutions; an *operational* definition defines bisimilarity directly on all expressions, including process variables. Generally, the two definitions lead to the same relation, and we find both definitions in the literature, depending on what is easier to use in the context.

In branching and weak bisimulation, it is agreed that internal activity (denoted with the special action symbol τ in CCS) should be regarded as invisible to the behaviour comparison; but what about divergent internal activity $\tau.\tau.\tau\ldots$? Depending on the property that the process is required to satisfy, divergence may be a relevant distinction or not: divergent behaviour—if we do not assume fairness—may delay a required visible behaviour or termination indefinitely.

Branching and weak bisimilarity differ slightly in how they treat internal choice; we will concentrate on branching bisimilarity, like Vaandrager [6] did. Branching and weak bisimilarity are not congruences for the CCS operators. One normally corrects that by a rootedness condition: an *initial* invisible step is inequivalent to doing nothing. The resulting relations are called branching (behaviour) congruence and weak (behaviour) congruence, respectively. The advantage is: it is much easier to reason about a congruence using an equational axiomatisation. Several sound and complete axiomatisations for these congruences (and their divergence-preserving variants) exist [2,7,8,11].

However, in order to do so, one needs to prove that this rootedness condition actually suffices to turn bisimilarity into a congruence. Milner [10] already proved that rooted weak bisimilarity is a congruence using the algebraic definition of weak bisimilarity. Van Glabbeek [2] claims that the proof for branching bisimilarity proceeds similarly. These proofs have to proceed in two steps, following the algebraic definition: first, congruence is proven for all closed processes, and then the proof is extended to the open processes. The divergence-preserving variants were proven congruences later: For rooted divergence-preserving weak bisimilarity, a proof along these lines is found in [8]. A detailed proof that rooted divergence-preserving branching bisimilarity is a congruence has recently appeared as [3]. In all the proofs mentioned above, a general technique called bisimulation up to was used, whose soundness often needs lengthy justification.

This contribution shows that using the operational definition of rooted divergence-preserving branching bisimilarity, one can achieve a shorter proof without resorting to bisimulation up to.

2   Finite-State CCS and Branching Bisimulation

Let $\mathcal{V}$ be an infinite set of *variables,* $\mathcal{A}$ an infinite set of *visible actions,* τ the *invisible action* or *silent move* ($\tau \notin \mathcal{A}$). We write $\mathcal{A}_\tau$ for $\mathcal{A} \cup \{\tau\}$. The *(finite-state process) expressions* are defined by the BNF grammar (for $a \in \mathcal{A}_\tau$ and $X \in \mathcal{V}$):

$$E \quad ::= \quad \mathbf{0} \mid X \mid a.E \mid E + E \mid \mu X.E$$

We denote the set of expressions with $\mathcal{E}$. Informally, the expressions mean:

Inaction: **0** is not capable of any action.
Prefix: $a.E$ first performs action a and afterwards behaves as E.
Non-deterministic Choice: $E + F$ can behave either as E or as F.
Recursion: $\mu X.E$ behaves as E, except that whenever X is reached in an execution, then it behaves as $\mu X.E$ again.

We define the *free variables* of an expression as follows:

$$fv(\mathbf{0}) = \varnothing \qquad fv(X) = \{X\} \qquad fv(a.E) = fv(E)$$
$$fv(E + F) = fv(E) \cup fv(F) \qquad fv(\mu X.E) = fv(E) \setminus \{X\}$$

A *closed expression* or *process* is an expression $P \in \mathcal{E}$ with $fv(P) = \varnothing$. The set of all closed expressions is denoted $\mathcal{P}$, and we use P to range over $\mathcal{P}$.

We write $E\{F/X\}$ for the expression obtained by capture-free substitution of F for free occurrences of X in E. We write $E \equiv F$ when E and F are syntactically identical.

We define the semantics of expressions operationally by a transition relation $\longrightarrow$ and a binary relation $\triangleright$ between expressions and variables.

Definition 1. *The transition relation* $\longrightarrow \subseteq \mathcal{E} \times \mathcal{A}_\tau \times \mathcal{E}$ *(written* $E \xrightarrow{a} E'$*) is the smallest relation that satisfies:*

1. $a.E \xrightarrow{a} E$.
2. *If* $E \xrightarrow{a} E'$ *then* $E + F \xrightarrow{a} E'$ *and* $F + E \xrightarrow{a} E'$.
3. *If* $E\{\mu X.E/X\} \xrightarrow{a} E'$ *then* $\mu X.E \xrightarrow{a} E'$.

We also write $\Longrightarrow$ *for* $(\xrightarrow{\tau})^*$ *(the transitive-reflexive closure of* $\xrightarrow{\tau}$*) and* $\xRightarrow{a}$ *for* $\Longrightarrow \xrightarrow{a} \Longrightarrow$.

The relation $\triangleright \subseteq \mathcal{E} \times \mathcal{V}$ *(written* $E \triangleright X$*) is the smallest relation that satisfies:*

1. $X \triangleright X$.
2. *If* $E \triangleright X$ *then* $E + F \triangleright X$ *and* $F + E \triangleright X$.
3. *If* $E\{\mu Y.E/Y\} \triangleright X$ *then* $\mu Y.E \triangleright X$.

Lemma 2. *Let* $E, F, H \in \mathcal{E}$, $a \in \mathcal{A}_\tau$, *and* $X \in \mathcal{V}$. *Then*

1. *If* $H \triangleright X$ *and* $E \xrightarrow{a} F$ *then* $H\{E/X\} \xrightarrow{a} F$.
2. *If* $H \xrightarrow{a} H'$, *then* $H\{E/X\} \xrightarrow{a} H'\{E/X\}$.
3. *If* $H\{E/X\} \xrightarrow{a} F$, *then either* $H \triangleright X$ *and* $E \xrightarrow{a} F$, *or there is* H' *such that* $H \xrightarrow{a} H'$ *and* $F \equiv H'\{E/X\}$.
4. *If* $H\{E/X\} \triangleright Y$, *then either* $H \triangleright X$ *and* $E \triangleright Y$, *or* $H \triangleright Y$.

Proof. This is Lemma 4 in [2], adapted to our notation. $\square$

Lemma 3. *Let $E, F \in \mathcal{E}$, $a \in \mathcal{A}_\tau$, and $X, W \in \mathcal{V}$.*

1. *$\mu X.E \xrightarrow{a} F$ iff there is $E' \in \mathcal{E}$ such that $F \equiv E'\{\mu X.E/X\}$ and $E \xrightarrow{a} E'$.*
2. *$\mu X.E \triangleright W$ iff $E \triangleright W$ and $W \neq X$.*

Proof. Claim 1 is Lemma 6 in [8]. The proof of Claim 2 is straightforward. □

The following way to define bisimulation is modelled after [11].

Definition 4 (Operational Definition). *A binary relation $R \subseteq \mathcal{E} \times \mathcal{E}$ is a divergence-preserving branching bisimulation if R is symmetric and satisfies the following conditions, for every $\langle E, F \rangle \in R$:*

1. ***Simulation of Actions:*** *Whenever $E \xrightarrow{a} E'$, then either $a = \tau$ and there exists F' such that $F \Longrightarrow F'$ and $\langle E, F' \rangle \in R$ and $\langle E', F' \rangle \in R$, or there exist F', F'' such that $F \Longrightarrow F' \xrightarrow{a} F''$ and $\langle E, F' \rangle \in R$ and $\langle E', F'' \rangle \in R$.*
2. ***Simulation of Variables:*** *Whenever $E \triangleright X$, then there exists F' such that $F \Longrightarrow F' \triangleright X$ and $\langle E, F' \rangle \in R$.*
3. ***Simulation of Divergence:*** *Whenever $E \xrightarrow{\tau} E_1 \xrightarrow{\tau} E_2 \xrightarrow{\tau} \cdots$ is an infinite τ-run from E, then there exist E_i on the τ-run and F' such that $F \Longrightarrow F'$ and $\langle E_i, F' \rangle \in R$.*

Two expressions $E, F \in \mathcal{E}$ are divergence-preserving branching bisimilar *(written $E \approx_b^\Delta F$) if there exists a divergence-preserving branching bisimulation containing the pair $\langle E, F \rangle$.*

Definition 2.1 of [3] defines divergence-preserving branching bisimulation for closed expressions only and uses a different clause, denoted (D), instead of our Clause 3 in Definition 4. The two clauses are equivalent for closed expressions according to Proposition 3.1 in [4]. In other words, when applied to processes, Definition 4 results in the same divergence-preserving bisimilarity as Definition 2.1 in [3]. Finally, [4] also proves that $\approx_b^\Delta$ is an equivalence relation, and that it is the largest divergence-preserving branching bisimulation.

3   Congruence for Finite-State Processes

As mentioned earlier, branching bisimulation is not a congruence for the CCS operators. In particular, $a.\mathbf{0} \approx_b^\Delta \tau.a.\mathbf{0}$ but $a.\mathbf{0} + b.\mathbf{0} \not\approx_b^\Delta \tau.a.\mathbf{0} + b.\mathbf{0}$. One normally corrects that by a rootedness condition: an initial invisible step is inequivalent to doing nothing. The resulting relation is called a branching (behaviour) congruence. The advantage is: it is much easier to reason about a congruence using an equational axiomatisation.

Definition 5. *Two process expressions $E, F \in \mathcal{E}$ are* rooted divergence-preserving branching bisimilar *or* divergence-preserving branching congruent *(written $E =_b^\Delta F$) if they satisfy:*

1. **Simulation of Actions:** *Whenever* $E \xrightarrow{a} E'$, *then there exists* F' *such that* $F \xrightarrow{a} F'$ *and* $E' \approx_b^\Delta F'$; *whenever* $F \xrightarrow{a} F'$, *then there exists* E' *such that* $E \xrightarrow{a} E'$ *and* $E' \approx_b^\Delta F'$.
2. **Simulation of Variables:** $E \rhd X$ *if and only if* $F \rhd X$.

Lemma 6. *Let* $E \in \mathcal{E}$, $X \in \mathcal{V}$. *Then* $\mu X.E =_b^\Delta E\{\mu X.E/X\}$.

Proof. Immediately follows from the operational semantics of Definition 1.   □

Lemma 7. *Let* E_0, E, F_0, F *be expressions,* X *and* Y *be variables. If* $E_0 \approx_b^\Delta F_0$ *and* $E =_b^\Delta F$, *then* $E_0\{\mu X.E/Y\} \approx_b^\Delta F_0\{\mu X.F/Y\}$.

Proof. For the given E, F with $E =_b^\Delta F$, construct the binary relation S:

$$S = \{\langle G\{\mu X.E/Z\}, H\{\mu X.F/Z\}\rangle \mid G, H \in \mathcal{E}, Z \in \mathcal{V}, \text{ and } G \approx_b^\Delta H\}.$$

We show that $S \cup S^{-1}$ is a divergence-preserving branching bisimulation. When this is done, since $E_0 \approx_b^\Delta F_0$, so $\langle E_0\{\mu X.E/Y\}, F_0\{\mu X.F/Y\}\rangle \in S$, we obtain $E_0\{\mu X.E/Y\} \approx_b^\Delta F_0\{\mu X.F/Y\}$.

It is obvious that $S \cup S^{-1}$ is symmetric. To show that $S \cup S^{-1}$ is a divergence-preserving branching bisimulation, let $\langle C, D \rangle \in S \cup S^{-1}$. We need to check the conditions of Definition 4. If $\langle C, D \rangle \in S$, then according to the construction of S, there exist $G \approx_b^\Delta H$ such that $C \equiv G\{\mu X.E/Z\}$ and $D \equiv H\{\mu X.F/Z\}$.

1. **Simulation of Actions.**
   Suppose that $G\{\mu X.E/Z\} \xrightarrow{a} G'$. We distinguish cases following Lemma 2, Claim 3:
   Case 1.1: $G \xrightarrow{a} G_1$ with $G' \equiv G_1\{\mu X.E/Z\}$.
     We further distinguish cases on how H simulates transition $G \xrightarrow{a} G_1$:
     Case 1.1.1: $a = \tau$, there is H_1 with $H \Longrightarrow H_1$ and $G \approx_b^\Delta H_1 \approx_b^\Delta G_1$.
       Then $H\{\mu X.F/Z\} \Longrightarrow H_1\{\mu X.F/Z\}$, and by the definition S contains the two pairs $\langle G\{\mu X.E/Z\}, H_1\{\mu X.F/Z\}\rangle$ and $\langle G_1\{\mu X.E/Z\}, H_1\{\mu X.F/Z\}\rangle$.
     Case 1.1.2: There are H_1, H_2 with $H \Longrightarrow H_1 \xrightarrow{a} H_2$ and $G \approx_b^\Delta H_1$, $G_1 \approx_b^\Delta H_2$.
       Then $H\{\mu X.F/Z\} \Longrightarrow H_1\{\mu X.F/Z\} \xrightarrow{a} H_2\{\mu X.F/Z\}$, and by the definition S contains the two pairs $\langle G\{\mu X.E/Z\}, H_1\{\mu X.F/Z\}\rangle$ and $\langle G_1\{\mu X.E/Z\}, H_2\{\mu X.F/Z\}\rangle$.
   Case 1.2: $G \rhd Z$ and $\mu X.E \xrightarrow{a} G'$.
     According to Claim 1 of Lemma 3, there is E_1 such that $E \xrightarrow{a} E_1$ and $G' \equiv E_1\{\mu X.E/X\}$. Since $E =_b^\Delta F$, there exists F_1 with $F \xrightarrow{a} F_1$ and $E_1 \approx_b^\Delta F_1$, thus by Claim 2 of Lemma 2 $F\{\mu X.F/X\} \xrightarrow{a} F_1\{\mu X.F/X\}$ and $\langle E_1\{\mu X.E/X\}, F_1\{\mu X.F/X\}\rangle \in S$. On the other hand, since $\approx_b^\Delta$ is a divergence-preserving branching bisimulation, there is H_1 such that $H \Longrightarrow H_1 \rhd Z$ and $G \approx_b^\Delta H_1$. Thus $H\{\mu X.F/Z\} \Longrightarrow H_1\{\mu X.F/Z\} \xrightarrow{a} F_1\{\mu X.F/X\}$ and $\langle G\{\mu X.E/X\}, H_1\{\mu X.F/X\}\rangle \in S$.
   In all cases, we have found a matching transition for $G\{\mu X.E/X\} \xrightarrow{a} G'$.

2. **Simulation of Variables.**
   Suppose $G\{\mu X.E/Z\} \rhd W$. Then according to Lemma 2, Claim 4, either $G \rhd Z$ and $\mu X.E \rhd W$, or $G \rhd W$, and it is routine to show that in both cases there is H_1 with $H\{\mu X.F/Z\} \Longrightarrow H_1\{\mu X.F/Z\} \rhd W$ and $\langle G\{\mu X.E/Z\}, H_1\{\mu X.F/Z\}\rangle \in S$.
3. **Simulation of Divergence.**
   Suppose $G\{\mu X.E/Z\} \equiv G_0 \xrightarrow{\tau} G_1 \xrightarrow{\tau} G_2 \xrightarrow{\tau} \cdots$ is an infinite τ-run from $G\{\mu X.E/Z\}$. Then we distinguish cases by Lemma 2, Claim 3, according to whether $\mu X.E$ ever participates in this infinite τ-run.

   Case 3.1: $\mu X.E$ does not participate in the infinite τ-run.
   Then there is an infinite τ-run $G \xrightarrow{\tau} G'_1 \xrightarrow{\tau} G'_2 \xrightarrow{\tau} \cdots$ such that $G_i \equiv G'_i\{\mu X.E/Z\}$ for $i = 1, 2, \ldots$. Since $\approx_b^\Delta$ is a divergence-preserving branching bisimulation, with $G \approx_b^\Delta H$ there must be H' and m such that $H \Longrightarrow H'$ and $G'_m \approx_b^\Delta H'$, thus $H\{\mu X.F/Z\} \Longrightarrow H'\{\mu X.F/Z\}$ and $\langle G'_m\{\mu X.E/Z\}, H'\{\mu X.F/Z\}\rangle \in S$.

   Case 3.2: $\mu X.E$ does participate in the infinite τ-run.
   Then we can find the smallest k such that $G_i \equiv G'_i\{\mu X.E/Z\}$ for $i = 0, \ldots, k$ and $G'_k \rhd Z$ and $\mu X.E \xrightarrow{\tau} G_{k+1}$. By Claim 1 of Lemma 3 there is E' such that $E \xrightarrow{\tau} E'$ and $G_{k+1} \equiv E'\{\mu X.E/X\}$. Then, since $E =_b^\Delta F$ there is F' such that $F \xrightarrow{\tau} F'$ with $E' \approx_b^\Delta F'$. So $F\{\mu X.F/X\} \xrightarrow{\tau} F'\{\mu X.F/X\}$ and $\langle E'\{\mu X.E/X\}, F'\{\mu X.F/X\}\rangle \in S$. On the other hand we have $G \approx_b^\Delta H$, and for the τ-run from G to G'_k, there must be H_1 such that $H \Longrightarrow H_1$ and $G'_k \approx_b^\Delta H_1$. Since $G'_k \rhd Z$ there must be H' such that $H_1 \Longrightarrow H' \rhd Z$ and $G'_k \approx_b^\Delta H'$. Thus we get $H\{\mu X.F/Z\} \Longrightarrow H'\{\mu X.F/Z\} \xrightarrow{\tau} F'\{\mu X.F/X\}$, and so we have found $F'\{\mu X.F/X\}$ such that $H\{\mu X.F/X\} \Longrightarrow F'\{\mu X.F/X\}$ and $\langle G_{k+1}, F'\{\mu X.F/X\}\rangle \in S$.

If $\langle C, D\rangle \in S^{-1}$, then $\langle D, C\rangle \in S$, and according to the construction of S, there exist $G \approx_b^\Delta H$ such that $D \equiv G\{\mu X.E/Z\}$ and $C \equiv H\{\mu X.F/Z\}$. We can reason as above to show that $\langle C, D\rangle$ also satisfies the conditions of simulation of actions, variables and divergence. This establishes that $S \cup S^{-1}$ is a divergence-preserving branching bisimulation.   □

Note that in the proof (Case 3.2), we require congruence $E =_b^\Delta F$ (and not only $E \approx_b^\Delta F$) to ensure that if E_0 has an infinite run involving $\mu X.E$, then F_0 can take at least one τ-step using $\mu X.F$. This avoids the wrong conclusion from $\tau.X \approx_b^\Delta X$ to $\mu X.\tau.X \overset{?}{\approx_b^\Delta} \mu X.X$.

With the preparation of Lemma 7, we are in the position to present our main result, which is to provide a more direct proof of the congruence of $=_b^\Delta$.

Theorem 8. $=_b^\Delta$ *is a congruence on* $\mathcal{E}$, *i.e. if* $E =_b^\Delta F$ *then* $a.E =_b^\Delta a.F$, $E + D =_b^\Delta F + D$, $D + E =_b^\Delta D + F$, *and* $\mu X.E =_b^\Delta \mu X.F$ *for arbitrary* $a \in \mathcal{A}_\tau$, $D \in \mathcal{E}$, *and* $X \in \mathcal{V}$.

Proof. We assume $E =_b^\Delta F$ and prove $\mu X.E =_b^\Delta \mu X.F$, all other constructions are simple.

Assume $\mu X.E \xrightarrow{a} E'$. We need to prove that this transition can be simulated by some strong transition $\mu X.F \xrightarrow{a} F'$. By Claim 1 of Lemma 3, there exists E'' such that $E \xrightarrow{a} E''$ and $E' \equiv E''\{\mu X.E/X\}$. Because $E =_{\mathsf{b}}^{\triangle} F$, there also exists F'' such that $F \xrightarrow{a} F''$ and $E'' \approx_{\mathsf{b}}^{\triangle} F''$, and by Lemma 7 we then get $E''\{\mu X.E/X\} \approx_{\mathsf{b}}^{\triangle} F''\{\mu X.F/X\}$. Therefore, $\mu X.F \xrightarrow{a} F''\{\mu X.F/X\}$ is the transition simulating $\mu X.E \xrightarrow{a} E'$. The converse statement (a transition $\mu X.F \xrightarrow{a} F'$ can be simulated by $\mu X.E$) is proven analogously.

Clause 2 of Definition 5 is proven similarly, using Claim 2 of Lemma 3.   □

Now we have arrived at the conclusion that $=_{\mathsf{b}}^{\triangle}$ is a congruence. But since we used an operational definition of $=_{\mathsf{b}}^{\triangle}$, we need to argue that it is the same relation discussed in [3]. We will make such an argument in the next section. In the rest of this section we will prove some properties of $\approx_{\mathsf{b}}^{\triangle}$ and $=_{\mathsf{b}}^{\triangle}$ which will be used to support the argument in the next section.

Lemma 9. *Let* $E, F, G \in \mathcal{E}$ *be expressions,* X *be a variable. If* $E =_{\mathsf{b}}^{\triangle} F$*, then*

1. $G\{E/X\} =_{\mathsf{b}}^{\triangle} G\{F/X\}$;
2. $E\{G/X\} =_{\mathsf{b}}^{\triangle} F\{G/X\}$.

Proof. $G\{E/X\} =_{\mathsf{b}}^{\triangle} G\{F/X\}$ is easily proved by routine induction on the structure of G, using Theorem 8.

To prove $E\{G/X\} =_{\mathsf{b}}^{\triangle} F\{G/X\}$, we first prove the following fact: If K, H are expressions such that $K \approx_{\mathsf{b}}^{\triangle} H$, then $K\{G/X\} \approx_{\mathsf{b}}^{\triangle} H\{G/X\}$. To see the fact, let Y be a variable such that $Y \notin fv(G)$, by Lemma 6 $\mu Y.G =_{\mathsf{b}}^{\triangle} G\{\mu Y.G/Y\}$, and $G\{\mu Y.G/Y\} \equiv G$ since Y does not occur freely in G. Then

$$
\begin{aligned}
K\{G/X\} &=_{\mathsf{b}}^{\triangle} K\{\mu Y.G/X\} &&\text{(Claim 1 above)} \\
&\approx_{\mathsf{b}}^{\triangle} H\{\mu Y.G/X\} &&\text{(Lemma 7)} \\
&=_{\mathsf{b}}^{\triangle} H\{G/X\} &&\text{(Claim 1 above)}
\end{aligned}
$$

With this fact, suppose $E =_{\mathsf{b}}^{\triangle} F$, it is easy to prove that $E\{G/X\} =_{\mathsf{b}}^{\triangle} F\{G/X\}$ by analysing the transitions from $E\{G/X\}$ and $F\{G/X\}$ using Lemma 2.   □

We define the *sort* (of visible actions) of a process expression as follows:

$$
\begin{aligned}
sort(\mathbf{0}) &= \varnothing & sort(E + F) &= sort(E) \cup sort(F) \\
sort(X) &= \varnothing & sort(\mu X.E) &= sort(E) \\
sort(\tau.E) &= sort(E) & sort(a.E) &= sort(E) \cup \{a\} \quad (\text{if } a \neq \tau)
\end{aligned}
$$

We will write $sort(E, F)$ for $sort(E) \cup sort(F)$.

The following lemma is formally very similar to Lemma 20 in [8], but as that paper uses the algebraic definition and concerns (variants of) weak bisimulation, we cannot copy their proof.

Lemma 10. *Let* $E, F \in \mathcal{E}$ *be expressions,* X *be a variable,* a *be a visible action,* $a \notin sort(E, F)$. *If* $E\{a.\mathbf{0}/X\} =_{\mathsf{b}}^{\triangle} F\{a.\mathbf{0}/X\}$ *then* $E =_{\mathsf{b}}^{\triangle} F$.

Proof. First we construct the following binary relation S:

$$S = \{\langle G, H\rangle \mid G, H \in \mathcal{E}, a \notin sort(G, H), \text{ and } G\{a.\mathbf{0}/X\} \approx_b^\Delta H\{a.\mathbf{0}/X\}\}.$$

It is routine to show that S is a divergence-preserving branching bisimulation (note that S is symmetric).

Now suppose E, F be expressions, X be a variable, a be a visible action, $a \notin sort(E, F)$, and $E\{a.\mathbf{0}/X\} =_b^\Delta F\{a.\mathbf{0}/X\}$. To prove that $E =_b^\Delta F$, assume $E \xrightarrow{b} E'$. We need to show that this transition can be simulated by a strong transition $F \xrightarrow{b} F'$. Note that by Claim 2 of Lemma 2, $E \xrightarrow{b} E'$ implies $E\{a.\mathbf{0}/X\} \xrightarrow{b} E'\{a.\mathbf{0}/X\}$, since $E\{a.\mathbf{0}/X\} =_b^\Delta F\{a.\mathbf{0}/X\}$, it follows that there is F'' such that $F\{a.\mathbf{0}/X\} \xrightarrow{b} F''$ and $E'\{a.\mathbf{0}/X\} \approx_b^\Delta F''$, then by Claim 3 of Lemma 2 there exists F' such that $F \xrightarrow{b} F'$ and $F'' \equiv F'\{a.\mathbf{0}/X\}$ (since $a \notin sort(E, F)$, b cannot be a), so $\langle E', F'\rangle \in S$, thus $E' \approx_b^\Delta F'$. Therefore, $F \xrightarrow{a} F'$ is the transition simulating $E \xrightarrow{b} E'$. Clause 2 of Definition 5 is proven similarly, using Claim 4 of Lemma 2. □

Theorem 11. *Let $E, F \in \mathcal{E}$ be expressions, $\{X_1, \ldots, X_n\}$ be a set of variables. Then $E =_b^\Delta F$ if and only if for arbitrary processes $P_1, \ldots, P_n \in \mathcal{P}$ it holds that $E\{P_1/X_1, \ldots, P_n/X_n\} =_b^\Delta F\{P_1/X_1, \ldots, P_n/X_n\}$.*

Proof. We prove the theorem by induction on n. If $n = 0$, then it holds vacuously. Assume the claim holds for n, i.e. $E' =_b^\Delta F'$ if and only if for arbitrary processes $P_1, \ldots, P_n \in \mathcal{P}$ we have $E'\{P_1/X_1, \ldots, P_n/X_n\} =_b^\Delta F'\{P_1/X_1, \ldots, P_n/X_n\}$. We prove that the claim holds for $n + 1$. For the only if direction, suppose $E =_b^\Delta F$ and $P_1, \ldots, P_{n+1} \in \mathcal{P}$, we will show

$$E\{P_1/X_1, \ldots, P_{n+1}/X_{n+1}\} =_b^\Delta F\{P_1/X_1, \ldots, P_{n+1}/X_{n+1}\}.$$

In this case, since $E =_b^\Delta F$, by Claim 2 of Lemma 9 $E\{P_{n+1}/X_{n+1}\} =_b^\Delta F\{P_{n+1}/X_{n+1}\}$, then by the ind. hyp. $E\{P_{n+1}/X_{n+1}\}\{P_1/X_1, \ldots, P_n/X_n\} =_b^\Delta F\{P_{n+1}/X_{n+1}\}\{P_1/X_1, \ldots, P_n/X_n\}$, so

$$
\begin{aligned}
E\{P_1/X_1, \ldots, P_{n+1}/X_{n+1}\} &\equiv E\{P_{n+1}/X_{n+1}\}\{P_1/X_1, \ldots, P_n/X_n\} \\
&=_b^\Delta F\{P_{n+1}/X_{n+1}\}\{P_1/X_1, \ldots, P_n/X_n\} \quad \text{(IH)} \\
&\equiv F\{P_1/X_1, \ldots, P_{n+1}/X_{n+1}\}.
\end{aligned}
$$

Hence the only if direction. For the if direction, we will prove $E =_b^\Delta F$ under the assumption that $E\{P_1/X_1, \ldots, P_{n+1}/X_{n+1}\} =_b^\Delta F\{P_1/X_1, \ldots, P_{n+1}/X_{n+1}\}$ for all $P_1, \ldots, P_{n+1} \in \mathcal{P}$. In this case, choose $a \notin sort(E, F)$, then for all $P_1, \ldots, P_n \in \mathcal{P}$ we have

$$
\begin{aligned}
E\{a.\mathbf{0}/X_{n+1}\}\{P_1/X_1, \ldots, P_n/X_n\} &\equiv E\{P_1/X_1, \ldots, P_n/X_n, a.\mathbf{0}/X_{n+1}\} \\
&=_b^\Delta F\{P_1/X_1, \ldots, P_n/X_n, a.\mathbf{0}/X_{n+1}\} \\
&\equiv F\{a.\mathbf{0}/X_{n+1}\}\{P_1/X_1, \ldots, P_n/X_n\}.
\end{aligned}
$$

Then by the induction hypothesis $E\{a.\mathbf{0}/X_{n+1}\} =_b^\Delta F\{a.\mathbf{0}/X_{n+1}\}$. Now by Lemma 10 $E =_b^\Delta F$. □

4   Comparison with the Congruence Proof for a Traditional Definition

Here, we compare our proof with the recent proof by Glabbeek, Luttik and Spanink [3], who define divergence-preserving branching bisimulation on closed process expressions only and extend it to open process expressions through substitutions. This more traditional approach is often used to prove that some rooted bisimilarity is a congruence; it follows the basic idea of Milner [9,10]. He was the first to use the so-called "up-to technique": A relation R is called a *weak bisimulation up to* $\approx$ if $P \, R \, Q$ and $P \stackrel{a}{\Longrightarrow} P'$ imply that there exists some Q' with $Q \stackrel{a}{\Longrightarrow} Q'$ and $P' \approx R \approx Q'$. It can be shown that if R is a weak bisimulation up to $\approx$ then $\approx R \approx$ is a weak bisimulation.

The important step to prove that some behavioural congruence $=$ is a congruence under recursion, i.e. $E = F$ implies $\mu X.E = \mu X.F$, is: one shows that the symmetric closure of relation $R_{E,F} = \{\langle G\{\mu X.E/X\}, G\{\mu X.F/X\}\rangle \mid G \in \mathcal{E}$ and $fv(G) \subseteq \{X\}\}$ is a bisimulation up to $\approx$ (or, sometimes, a slighty stronger relation).

Glabbeek, in [2], stated that the proof of [10] can be adapted to (non-divergence-preserving) branching bisimilarity. However, the case of divergence-preserving branching bisimilarity was only handled by Glabbeek et al. [3] recently. The latter paper used the bisimulation-up-to technique to prove that rooted divergence-preserving branching bisimilarity is a congruence. They had to vary the relation $R_{E,F}$ for the proof.

More in detail, rooted (divergence-preserving) weak or branching bisimilarity is defined in [3,8,10] by applying Definition 5 only to closed process expressions. for open process expressions, [3] sets:

Definition 12 (Algebraic Definition of Divergence-Preserving Branching Congruence). *Given two expressions $E, F \in \mathcal{E}$ and a vector of variables $\langle X_1, \ldots, X_n\rangle$ that covers their free variables (i.e. $fv(E) \cup fv(F) \subseteq \{X_1, \ldots, X_n\}$), E and F are algebraically rooted divergence-preserving branching bisimilar or algebraically divergence-preserving branching congruent (written $E =_a^\Delta F$) if for arbitrary processes $P_1, \ldots, P_n \in \mathcal{P}$ we have*

$$E\{P_1/X_1, \ldots, P_n/X_n\} =_b^\Delta F\{P_1/X_1, \ldots, P_n/X_n\}.$$

The two definitions lead to the same relation on finite-state expressions, i.e. for two expressions E, F it holds that $E =_a^\Delta F$ if and only if $E =_b^\Delta F$. Here is a direct proof using Theorem 11: Let $E, F \in \mathcal{E}$ and $fv(E) \cup fv(E) = \{X_1, \ldots, X_n\}$, then $E =_a^\Delta F$ iff (by Definition 12) for arbitrary processes $P_1, \ldots, P_n \in \mathcal{P}$, we have $E\{P_1/X_1, \ldots, P_n/X_n\} =_b^\Delta F\{P_1/X_1, \ldots, P_n/X_n\}$ iff (by Theorem 11) $E =_b^\Delta F$. Similar proofs are found e.g. in [2] as Propositions 2[1] and 3. Van Glabbeek writes, however, "defining $\approx_b^\Delta$ on open process expressions ... does not carry over to full CCS."

Then, [3] introduces their variant of "bisimulation up to $\approx_b^\Delta$":

---

[1] Proposition 2 in [2] claims more than we need. An error in another part of the proof has been pointed out and corrected in [1].

Definition 13 ([3], Definition 3.10). *The symmetric relation R on $\mathcal{P}$ is a rooted divergence-preserving branching bisimulation up to $\approx_b^\Delta$ if it satisfies the conditions:*

1. **Root Condition:** *If $P \xrightarrow{a} P'$, then there exists Q' such that $Q \xrightarrow{a} Q'$ and $P' \approx_b^\Delta R \approx_b^\Delta Q'$.*

2. **Simulation of Actions:** *If $P \Longrightarrow P'' \xrightarrow{\hat{a}} P'$, then there exist Q'' and Q such that $Q \Longrightarrow Q'' \xrightarrow{\hat{a}} Q'$ and $P'' \approx_b^\Delta R \approx_b^\Delta Q''$ and $P' \approx_b^\Delta R \approx_b^\Delta Q'$. (Here, $P'' \xrightarrow{\hat{a}} P'$ means: either $P'' \xrightarrow{a} P'$, or $a = \tau$ and $P'' \equiv P'$.)*

3. **Simulation of Divergence:** *If there exists an infinite sequence of closed process expressions $(P_k)_{k \in \omega}$ such that $P = P_0$ and $P_k \xrightarrow{\tau} P_{k+1}$ for all $k \in \omega$, then there also exists an infinite sequence of closed process expressions $(Q_\ell)_{\ell \in \omega}$ and a mapping $\sigma : \omega \to \omega$ such that $Q = Q_0$ and $Q_\ell \xrightarrow{\tau} Q_{\ell+1}$ and $P_{\sigma(\ell)} \approx_b^\Delta R \approx_b^\Delta Q_\ell$ for all $\ell \in \omega$.*

While they define simulation of divergence differently, it can be shown that this condition is equivalent to our usual condition (see the explanation after Definition 4). Also note that $\approx_b^\Delta$ is only used to relate closed expressions, where there is no difference between an operational and an algebraic definition.

They then go on to prove that if R is a rooted divergence-preserving branching bisimulation up to $\approx_b^\Delta$ then $R \subseteq =_b^\Delta$ (note that all the relations are between processes). Then comes the hardest part: they spend almost three pages to prove that the relation $R_{E,F}$ is a rooted divergence-preserving branching bisimulation up to $\approx_b^\Delta$ if $fv(E) \cup fv(F) \subseteq \{X\}$. After that, they can use this property to prove quickly that $=_a^\Delta$ is indeed a congruence under $\mu X.\_$ for all process expressions.

In comparison, our proof is much shorter. Still, the hard work of [3] is not completely lost: we will see shortly that our method does not extend to further CCS operators. The reason that we can achieve a shorter proof is that the operational definition of bisimulation (Definition 4) allows us to discuss operational behaviour directly on expressions containing free variables, so that we can construct the relation

$$S = \{\langle G\{\mu X.E/Z\}, H\{\mu X.F/Z\}\rangle \mid G, H \in \mathcal{E}, Z \in \mathcal{V}, \text{ and } G \approx_b^\Delta H\}$$

in the proof of Lemma 7 and prove $S \cup S^{-1}$ to be a divergence-preserving branching bisimulation, instead of constructing the less powerful (more strict)

$$R_{E,F} = \{\langle G\{\mu X.E/X\}, G\{\mu X.F/X\}\rangle \mid G \in \mathcal{E} \text{ and } fv(G) \subseteq \{X\}\}$$

and then having to use the bisimulation-up-to technique. In this way we successfully avoided the complication relating to this technique. It is interesting to note the similarities and differences between the constructions of S and $R_{E,F}$. In fact, [3] already used a construction similar to S in the proof of Lemma 3.6, which corresponds to Claim 2 of Lemma 9 of this paper. In other words, following the idea of this paper, the proof of Lemma 3.6 in [3] can be generalized to a proof that $\mu X.\_$ preserves $=_a^\Delta$, thus avoiding the use of the bisimulation-up-to technique altogether.

5   Extending the Proof to Full CCS?

Thus far we did only look at finite-state CCS; however, there are operators for parallelism as well. Full CCS has the following grammar:

$$E \quad ::= \quad \mathbf{0} \mid X \mid a.E \mid E + E \mid \mu X.E \mid E|F \mid E\backslash H \mid E[f]$$

where $a \in Act := \mathcal{A} \cup \overline{\mathcal{A}} \cup \{\tau\}$, $X \in \mathcal{V}$ as above, $H \subseteq \mathcal{A}$, and $f : \mathcal{A} \to Act$. We denote the set of process expressions in full CCS with $\mathcal{E}_{\mathrm{par}}$. Informally, the new expressions mean:

Actions with Overline $\overline{a}$: Actions a and $\overline{a}$ can synchronize in parallel processes. We set $\overline{\overline{a}} = a$ and $\overline{\tau} = \tau$.

Parallel Composition: $E|F$ interleaves the behaviours of E and F. Additionally, if $E \xrightarrow{a} E'$ and $F \xrightarrow{\overline{a}} F'$ for some $a \in \mathcal{A} \cup \overline{\mathcal{A}}$, the parallel composition has the behaviour $E|F \xrightarrow{\tau} E'|F'$. This models a synchronisation between the processes.

Restriction: $E\backslash H$ can do all behaviours of E except the actions in H. This operator is used to forbid $E|F$ from taking certain steps without synchronisation.

Relabelling: Whenever E can do action a or $\overline{a}$, then $E[f]$ can do action $f(a)$ or $\overline{f(a)}$, respectively, instead.

The transition relation, which is the first part of Definition 1, can easily be extended to include these constructs:

Definition 14. *The transition relation* $\longrightarrow \subseteq \mathcal{E}_{par} \times Act \times \mathcal{E}_{par}$ *(written* $E \xrightarrow{a} E'$*) is the smallest relation that satisfies the clauses given in Definition 1 and:*

1. *If* $E \xrightarrow{a} E'$*, then* $E|F \xrightarrow{a} E'|F$ *and* $F|E \xrightarrow{a} F|E'$*.*
2. *If* $E \xrightarrow{a} E'$ *and* $F \xrightarrow{\overline{a}} F'$ *for some* $a \in \mathcal{A} \cup \overline{\mathcal{A}}$*, then* $E|F \xrightarrow{\tau} E'|F'$*.*
3. *If* $E \xrightarrow{a} E'$ *and* $a, \overline{a} \notin H$*, then* $E\backslash H \xrightarrow{a} E'\backslash H$*.*
4. *If* $E \xrightarrow{a} E'$*, then* $E[f] \xrightarrow{f(a)} E'[f]$*. If* $E \xrightarrow{\overline{a}} E'$*, then* $E[f] \xrightarrow{\overline{f(a)}} E'[f]$*. If* $E \xrightarrow{\tau} E'$*, then* $E[f] \xrightarrow{\tau} E'[f]$*.*

However, the relation $\rhd$, which is the second part of Definition 1, does not convey enough information to form the basis of a correct operational definition of bisimulation. In particular, one would like to define $X|X \rhd X$, but how can this relation then distinguish expression $X \in \mathcal{E}$ from $X|X \in \mathcal{E}_{\mathrm{par}}$? Perhaps van Glabbeek's notation of [2,3] can help; they write $E \xrightarrow{X} \mathbf{0}$ instead of our $E \rhd X$, and this notation could be extended to something like $E|E \xrightarrow{X} E|\mathbf{0} \xrightarrow{X} \mathbf{0}|\mathbf{0}$. In any case, this would also require extending Claim 3 of Lemma 2: The expression $E = a.X|X$ cannot do a τ step, but $E\{\overline{a}.\mathbf{0}/X\}$ can. Similarly, E is not divergent, but $E\{\mu Z.\overline{a}.a.Z/X\}$ is, even though neither E nor $\mu Z.\overline{a}.a.Z$ can do τ steps. The proof of our central Lemma 7 would need a corresponding extension.

Even if that may be possible, other difficulties remain: van Glabbeek's notation is not informative enough to describe a restriction like $X \backslash \{a\} | \bar{a}.0$ or a relabelling like $X[a \mapsto \bar{a}] | X$. We could not find an obvious extension of the above proof method to full CCS. We are working on an extension [12], using the bisimulation-up-to technique.

Weak bisimulation (not divergence-preserving) has been shown to be a congruence for all operators except $+$, and rooted weak bisimulation is a congruence for all operators [10]. However, these proofs use the bisimulation-up-to technique.

We assume that Robin Milner was aware of (some of) these difficulties and therefore chose to switch between the two definitions and the two methods: in 1986 [9] he used what we called the algebraic definition to prove congruence for full CCS, while his article [11] used the operational definition with the smaller set of operators (to prove the completeness of his axiomatisation of rooted weak bisimilarity). The remark of van Glabbeek, cited above on page 9, also suggests that van Glabbeek was aware of the discrepancies. Perhaps the long-term goal of proving the congruence property for all CCS operators motivated him and the other authors of [3] to pursue the longer path.

References

1. Basten, T.: Branching bisimilarity is an equivalence indeed! Inf. Proc. Lett. **58**(3), 141–147 (1996). https://doi.org/10.1016/0020-0190(96)00034-8
2. van Glabbeek, R.J.: A complete axiomatization for branching bisimulation congruence of finite-state behaviours. In: Borzyszkowski, A.M., Sokołowski, S. (eds.) Mathematical Foundations of Computer Science 1993. LNCS, vol. 711, pp. 473–484. Springer, Berlin (1993). https://doi.org/10.1007/3-540-57182-5_39
3. van Glabbeek, R., Luttik, B., Spaninks, L.: Rooted divergence-preserving branching bisimilarity is a congruence. Log. Meth. Comput. Sci. **16**(3), 14:1–14:16 (2020). https://doi.org/10.23638/LMCS-16(3:14)2020
4. van Glabbeek, R., Luttik, B., Trčka, N.: Branching bisimilarity with explicit divergence. Fundam. Inform. **93**(4), 371–392 (2009). https://doi.org/10.3233/FI-2009-109
5. van Glabbeek, R., Vaandrager, F.: Modular specification of process algebras. Theor. Comput. Sci. **113**(2), 293–348 (1993). https://doi.org/10.1016/0304-3975(93)90006-F
6. Groote, J.F., Vaandrager, F.: An efficient algorithm for branching bisimulation and stuttering equivalence. In: Paterson, M.S. (ed.) Automata, Languages and Programming. LNCS, vol. 443, pp. 626–638. Springer, New York (1990). https://doi.org/10.1007/BFb0032063
7. Liu, X., Yu, T.: A complete axiomatisation for divergence preserving branching congruence of finite-state behaviours. In: 2021 36th Annual ACM/IEEE Symposium on Logic in Computer Science (LICS), pp. 1–13. IEEE, [s.l.] (2021). https://doi.org/10.1109/LICS52264.2021.9470647
8. Lohrey, M., D'Argenio, P.R., Hermanns, H.: Axiomatising divergence. Inf. Comput. **203**(2), 115–144 (2005). https://doi.org/10.1016/j.ic.2005.05.007
9. Milner, R.: Lectures on a calculus for communicating systems. In: Broy, M. (ed.) Control Flow and Data Flow: Concepts of Distributed Programming, pp. 205–228. Springer, Berlin (1986). https://doi.org/10.1007/978-3-642-82921-5_5

10. Milner, R.: Communication and Concurrency. Prentice-Hall, New York (1989)
11. Milner, R.: A complete axiomatisation for observational congruence of finite-state behaviours. Inf. Comput. **81**(2), 227–247 (1989). https://doi.org/10.1016/0890-5401(89)90070-9
12. Sun, Q., Jansen, D.N., Liu, X., Zhang, W.: Divergence-preserving congruences for CCS. Manuscript under submission (2022)
13. Vaandrager, F.W.: Verification of two communication protocols by means of process algebra. Report CS-R6808, CWI, Amsterdam (1986). https://ir.cwi.nl/pub/6298

Learning Language Intersections

Sebastian Junges and Jurriaan Rot$^{(\boxtimes)}$

Institute for Computing and Information Sciences, Radboud University,
Nijmegen, The Netherlands
{sjunges,jrot}@cs.ru.nl

Abstract. We study active automata learning, where the target language is given as the intersection of n regular languages. We assume membership oracles for the individual languages, and various forms of equivalence queries, implemented as usual via conformance testing. These oracles can be used by several different learning strategies. In this paper, we propose these strategies and compare them experimentally.

Keywords: automata learning · intersection · regular language · conformance testing · active learning

1 Introduction

Active automata learning is a popular research topic in the last decades, featuring an intriguing combination of elegant theory with proven potential for applications in analysing correctness of software and hardware systems. Since the seminal work of Angluin, who proposed the L^* learning algorithm [1], there have been numerous results on optimisations and efficient algorithms, extensions to various different models, and practical case studies [4,9].

We assume a setting in which there are n machines, whose behaviour is represented by regular languages $L_1, \ldots, L_n$ over a common alphabet. Our aim is to learn an automaton which represents the target language

$$L_1 \cap \ldots \cap L_n.$$

To this end, we assume membership and equivalence queries for each of the individual machines. As usual in automata learning, equivalence queries are implemented by conformance testing.

What is the most effective strategy of learning such a target language? Of course, one can simply ignore the intersection structure altogether, and use any of the existing algorithms for active learning. However, there are several other natural strategies for learning such languages; for instance by learning one component at a time, and perhaps reusing information gathered from learning previous components to speed up learning of the remainder.

This problem is motivated by a practical problem well known to most researchers, and certainly familiar to the recipient of this festschrift: how to get coffee. More specifically, how to obtain coffee in a dynamic academic

N. Jansen et al. (Eds.): Vaandrager Festschrift 2022, LNCS 13560, pp. 371–381, 2022.
https://doi.org/10.1007/978-3-031-15629-8_20

environment, where at every corner of the building there is a slightly different coffee machine (let alone the different coffee machines an academic needs to
deal with on their travels). The problem here is to learn a language of interaction
sequences that results in coffee, regardless of the exact model of coffee machine
used[1]. Slightly more seriously, the problem of learning intersection languages can
be relevant if our task is to learn the safe system interactions in a set of environments: if an autonomous robot has to operate in a number of similar, but
slightly different environments, it may be important to know the language of
interactions that are safe in all environments. Yet another example could be the
problem of learning all sequences of inputs that lead to a successful recalibration
of a set of industrial printers.

In this paper we identify and compare three basic strategies for learning
intersections of regular languages, as described above. The paper starts with a
description of three natural strategies (Sect. 2). We then briefly describe our prototype implementation Lcap with several relevant design choices (Sect. 3). Subsequently we present an empirical evaluation using this prototype implementation,
with examples that favor the different strategies (Sect. 4). We measure *symbol complexity*: the total number of input letters provided both in membership
queries and equivalence queries (that is, during conformance testing). Finally,
we describe a range of research challenges that arise in our setting (Sect. 5).

2   Strategies

As described in the introduction, the problem is to learn a minimal automaton
for the intersection

$$\bigcap_{i \leq n} L_n$$

of a finite family of regular languages $L_1, \ldots, L_n$ over a common alphabet Σ,
in the style of active automata learning: we assume access to an oracle/teacher
answering membership and equivalence queries. In this section we describe several strategies for this task. We refer to the collection of these strategies as $L^\cap$.
These strategies are formulated on top of an active learning algorithm, such as
$L^\star$ [1], TTT [5], $L^\sharp$ [10], etc.—the strategies are independent of the choice of algorithm. Explaining how these algorithms work is beyond the scope of this paper;
it suffices for the reader to know that can effectively learn minimal automata
using a polynomial number of membership and equivalence queries.

The precise assumptions about the oracle—which kinds of queries do they
answer—differ slightly among the strategies. Each of these strategies relies on
access to membership queries for individual languages, given by

$$\mathcal{M}_i(w) = [w \in L_i]$$

for each $i \leq n$ and $w \in \Sigma^*$. This returns true if $w \in L_i$, and false otherwise.

---

[1] This might also involve a careful choice of alphabet, perhaps allowing for actions
such as kicking the machine [3].

Further, we assume access to an equivalence query

$$\mathcal{E}_i(L_?) = [L_? = L_i]$$

for each of the languages L_i; this returns true iff $L_? = L_i$. In active learning algorithms, the argument of the query is typically presented in terms of an automaton, referred to as a *hypothesis*. It is standard to implement equivalence queries using black-box testing techniques.

For some of the strategies, we also assume an equivalence query of the form $\mathcal{E}_{1...i}(L_?) = [L_? = \bigcap_{1 \leq j \leq i} L_i]$.

2.1   The Word-by-Word Strategy

The first approach, which we refer to as the *word-by-word* strategy, is to ignore the structure of the target language $\bigcap_{i \leq n} L_n$ altogether, and just use any active learning algorithm to learn it. This requires access to the relevant queries for the intersection language:

– membership queries for the entire intersection, $\mathcal{M}_!(w) = \bigwedge_i [w \in L_i]$; and
– equivalence queries for the entire intersection, $\mathcal{E}_!(L_?) = [L_? = \bigcap_i L_i]$.

These membership queries can be expressed in terms of membership queries w.r.t. the individual languages, that is, $\mathcal{M}_!(w) = \bigwedge_i \mathcal{M}_i(w)$. It makes sense to use lazy evaluation: compute $\mathcal{M}_1(w), \ldots, \mathcal{M}_n(w)$ in order, and return `false` whenever one of the queries returns `false`.

The equivalence query $\mathcal{E}_!$ for the intersection can not be encoded in this way by individual equivalence queries, and indeed this is a non-trivial assumption. However, just like for individual equivalence queries, the equivalence query $\mathcal{E}_!$ can be implemented naturally via conformance testing; it just means testing words on multiple machines. Note that we can again use a lazy evaluation strategy in such an implementation, as with membership queries.

2.2   The Independent Strategy

The next strategy is referred to as *independent learning*. Here, we learn automata for each of the languages $L_1, \ldots, L_n$, compute an automaton for the intersection using the product construction, and finally minimise. This just requires membership queries $\mathcal{M}_i$ and equivalence queries $\mathcal{E}_i$ for the individual languages. The independent learning strategy is the most basic one: it simply calls an active learning algorithm for each of the languages.

The word-by-word strategy and the independent learning strategy are, in a sense, complementary: where in the independent strategy the intersection is taken *after* learning, by the learner, in the word-by-word strategy the intersection takes place *before* learning, by the teacher.

2.3   The Machine-by-Machine Strategy

The two previous strategies, word-by-word and independent, can be viewed as realising two extremes: either view the intersection as a single language and ignore the components (word-by-word), or learn the languages entirely separately (independent). We now turn to a somewhat more refined strategy, which iteratively learns partial intersections $L_{\leq i} = L_1 \cap \ldots \cap L_i$, for increasing i, making use of previous results as a filter. To this end, we assume access to membership queries $\mathcal{M}_{1\ldots i}$ and equivalence queries $\mathcal{E}_{1\ldots i}$ for $L_{\leq i}$.

More precisely, the *machine-by-machine* strategy is as follows. It starts by simply learning L_1. Now, suppose we learned an automaton which recognises $L_{\leq i}$: This language is the *filter*. We then learn $L_{\leq i+1}$, which requires membership and equivalence queries for the intersection language $L_{\leq i+1}$. The key idea is that, whenever we do an membership query with word w, we first check whether $w \in L_{\leq i}$, and only if the answer is `true`, we query L_{i+1}. Similarly, whenever we do an equivalence query, we first check whether the language of the hypothesis is a subset of $L_{\leq i}$. In case it is, we proceed with an actual equivalence query; in case it is not, this gives us a counterexample without having to perform any queries. Checking subset inclusion here can be done with standard automata-theoretic techniques, as we access to both models (that is, no queries required).

Note that the machine-by-machine strategy never learns the individual machines, except for the first language L_1; it only learns partial intersections, which are increasingly close to the target language. Further note that the order could matter quite a bit in this strategy. This is emphasised by our empirical evaluation in Sect. 4.

3   Prototype Implementation

We implemented the $L^\cap$-flavours in a python library `Lcap` that serves as a playground for investigating the different strategies[2]. `Lcap` takes as input a set of DFAs and then runs the different learning strategies as described in the previous section. `Lcap` uses other libraries based on their ease-of-use: We use the `dfa` library [11] for DFA operations, in particular for construction and taking the intersection. We use the L^* implementation and equivalence oracles in `aalpy` [8].

The implementation of the $L^\cap$ strategies presents some challenges that required adapting existing learning algorithms as the APIs did not allow the required modifications from the outside.

3.1   The Membership Oracle Signature

While the theory for DFA learning typically presents a membership oracle as a function $M\colon \Sigma^* \to \{0,1\}$, a Mealy-machine view on DFA learning leads to a membership oracle $M_{\mathrm{seq}}\colon \Sigma^* \to \{0,1\}^*$ with $|M_{\mathrm{seq}}(w)| = |w|$ and $M_{\mathrm{seq}}(w)_i =$

---

[2] `Lcap` is available on https://github.com/sjunges/Lcap and https://doi.org/10.5281/zenodo.6685973.

$M(w[..i])$. Such an oracle matches a realistic assumption that the teacher can tell us for any sequence of inputs to a system it is learning whether it is an accepting state or not and adheres to the natural rule that we should share as much of the available information with the learner, but it does complicate lazy evaluation and filtering. We provide the following two solutions: Either we disable caching or we use up-to-evaluation. Furthermore, we can use system caching to recover from the lack of cache.

Up-to-Evaluation. To ensure that the cache works as intended, we construct the query for M_{seq} on w as follows. We analyze the first word (on the filter or the first automaton) completely with the corresponding M_{seq} oracle. We search for the last position on which the response yields a positive answer, say on position j, and take the prefix of the word $w[..j]$. At this point, we know that the correct response is the response to $M_{\text{seq}}(w)$ must be of the form $M_{\text{seq}}(w[..j]) \cdot 0^{|w|-j}$. Since we are after intersection languages, on subsequent machines we can shorten the query by omitting the trailing $0^{|w|-j}$.

Machine Caching. The idea behind system caching is to put the cache on the level of the individual machines. That is, one does not cache in the learner, but rather in the oracle for each machine independently. This does yield additional overhead in the implementation and in the runtime and it potentially prevents the learner from inspecting the cache. In terms of the symbol complexity, this solution is equivalent to having a cache.

3.2   An Adequate Equivalence Oracle

We support the off-the-shelf oracles in `aalpy` and use the `RandomWMethodEq`-oracle in our experiments[3], which combines random tests with a characterisation set for the hypothesis. The construction of the tests is thus not influenced by the problem structure (that is, its presentation as an intersection). However, it is good to note the following: The length – or similarly, the expected maximum size of an automaton – should be sufficient to cover the states of the automaton. In Mod(30), the intersection of the Mod(2), Mod(3), and Mod(5) languages outlined above, a path of length say 50 often does not suffice to find the accepting state.

Practically, this conformance oracle does not query individual words, but interfaces with a `step(letter)` interface that conceptually iterates over the output of the M_{seq}-oracle defined above. The advantage of this oracle is that it determines violations of equality early on. For the lazy word-by-word strategy and the machine-by-machine strategy, we therefore cache steps that we do not require for determining the result. Concretely, for the machine-by-machine, we keep a FIFO buffer with the tokens. In every step, we first evaluate the step on the hypothesis. If we do *not* transition to an accepting state, we add the token to the buffer and return false. Otherwise, if we transition to an accepting state, we first replay the buffer to the system under learning and then return whether the

---

[3] Using `walks_per_state=10`, `walk_len=100`.

system under learning is currently in an system under learning. Similarly, when doing lazy evaluation in the word-by-word strategy, we hold n FIFO buffers. We first put the token in all buffer and then iterate over the languages, for each language we empty the buffer and either return false if we are not in an accepting state or continue with the next language.

4   Empirical Evaluation

We discuss the prototype on a limited collection of benchmarks. We briefly discuss the setup, the main takeaways, and then discuss some results in more detail[4].

4.1   Setup

We discuss the merits of the different strategies on some handcrafted examples, using our prototype implementation. In particular, we consider independent learning, word-by-word evaluation with lazy evaluation, and machine-by-machine evaluation. We disabled the cache on the learner and instead cache on the level of the machines. We do not use up-to-evaluation. All experiments are executed via Python 3.9 on a Macbook Pro; the individual experiments run in a matter of seconds and a memory limit of 1 GB is never exceeded.

We collect the following essential data: The number of membership- and equivalence-queries posed by the oracle ($\sharp$MQ, $\sharp$EQ respectively) and the symbol complexity for answering both methods, denoted $\mathrm{SC_{MQ}}$ and $\mathrm{SC_{EQ}}$. Notice that we measure symbol complexity as the number of symbols/inputs simulated on any machine/language. For independent learning, all these values are the sum of the individual invocations. In an (eager) word-by-word fashion, answering the membership query for a word $|w|$ has symbol-complexity $n \cdot w$. In the machine-by-machine approach, querying a learned automaton for $L_1 \cap \ldots L_j$ has no symbol-complexity: we assume that executing these actions on an automaton known to the learner, rather than on a remote machine, has insignificant cost. As the algorithm is randomized, all this data is collected as averages over 20 runs and rounded to the nearest integer.

4.2   Summary

Before we consider details, we summarize our main observations based on the limited set of benchmarks. First, each of the strategies can be drastically more efficient than the others in its use of membership queries and the associated symbol complexity. This statement is witnessed, e.g., by the IMOD(2, 3, 5), IMOD(10, 8, 2) and MOD(8, 16, 32) benchmarks as detailed below. Different benchmarks also vary significantly in the symbol complexity for equivalence queries, but the difference is not as stark. Second, generally, independent learning is the best whenever the intersection requires a DFA that is larger than

---

[4] The source code, log files, and experiments are all available via https://doi.org/10.5281/zenodo.6685973.

the individual DFAs, whereas the contrary is true for the word-by-word strategy. The situation for machine-by-machine learning is slightly differently, but it is generally good to quickly learn the target language as this yields a rather efficient filter.

4.3 Detailed Results

The MOD Languages. Consider the following language over $\Sigma = \{0,1\} \subseteq \mathbb{N}$.

$$\mathrm{MOD}(x) = \{w \in \Sigma^* \mid |w| \bmod x = 0\},$$

where $|w|$ denotes the length (number of alphabet letters) of a word w. The minimal DFA for this language has x states. These $\mathrm{MOD}(x)$ languages are closed under intersection. We use $\mathrm{MOD}(x_1, \ldots, x_n)$ to denote $\mathrm{MOD}(x_1) \cap \ldots \cap \mathrm{MOD}(x_n)$ and consider learning these languages with the three strategies outlined above. For details regarding the implementation we use, we refer to Sect. 3. Despite the simplicity of this setup, we can make plenty of observations based on the data shown in Table 1. First, above the first horizontal line, we are always learning the MOD(30) language. Between the first and the second line, we are learning MOD(24). We make the following observations for MOD(30) and remark that similar statements hold for MOD(24).

- In the first line, this language is the intersection of just MOD(30); in this case, all algorithms indeed behave equivalently.
- In the second line, we learn the intersection of three languages. In this case, independent learning performs very well: We must learn a two-state, a three-state and a five-state automaton. Neither the symbol complexity for the membership nor for the equivalence queries is high in this case. For the word-by-word approach, we are still learning the same automaton. In the eager case, this would require three times as many membership queries and a symbol complexity three times higher (because every step and every query must now be executed on three machines). However, as this is the lazy case, we do not observe this three-times increase. Finally, for the machine-by-machine case, we first learn MOD(2), then MOD(6) assuming MOD(2), and then MOD(30) assuming MOD(6). For this, we require indeed less queries than independently learning MOD(2), MOD(6), and MOD(30).
- Generally, as the following lines show, the independent approach suffers in terms of membership queries and the associated symbol complexity from having to learn on more machines whereas for the other approaches, the additional cost often alleviates. On the other hand, the equivalence queries remain expensive as the conformance test scales with the number of states and the number of machines.
- In the word-by-word approach, after having obtained the correct response for MOD(30) by querying MOD(2), MOD(3) and MOD(5), only 56 queries are evaluated on MOD(30) or $2 \cdot 56$ queries on MOD(6) and MOD(10). These queries are the queries that ask about words in MOD(30); lazy evaluation cannot avoid that these queries are executed on all machines.

Table 1. Learning Modulo-languages

	Independent				Word-By-Word				Machine-By-Machine			
	$\sharp$MQ	SC$_{\text{MQ}}$	$\sharp$EQ	SC$_{\text{EQ}}$	$\sharp$MQ	SC$_{\text{MQ}}$	$\sharp$EQ	SC$_{\text{EQ}}$	$\sharp$MQ	SC$_{\text{MQ}}$	$\sharp$EQ	SC$_{\text{EQ}}$
MOD(30)	1480	68236	2	27644	1480	68236	2	27644	1480	68236	2	27644
MOD(2, 3, 5)	51	270	5	5303	2496	114306	2	81613	303	12556	5	30758
MOD(2, 3, 5, 6, 10)	234	2727	9	14771	2608	118986	2	121179	417	17441	9	69739
MOD(2, 3, 5, 30)	1573	70632	7	32937	2552	116646	2	101396	360	15034	7	50086
MOD(2, 3, 5, 6, 10, 15, 30)	2125	81825	13	53038	2719	123666	2	160745	535	22576	13	108676
MOD(30, 15, 10, 6, 5, 3, 2)	2062	79452	13	52989	1815	82276	2	146342	1825	83054	14	144862
MOD(15, 10, 6, 5, 3, 2)	617	12072	11	25551	1812	82252	2	130818	711	24203	12	113431
MOD(24)	899	32867	2	19876	899	32867	2	19876	899	32867	2	19876
MOD(3, 8)	101	1092	4	6254	1213	44077	2	39476	342	12009	4	21147
MOD(3, 8, 24)	1101	39485	6	26346	1257	45491	2	54544	388	13610	6	36127
MOD(2, 3, 8)	111	1236	5	7304	1526	55250	2	58668	195	6105	5	23082
MOD(2, 3, 6, 8, 12, 24)	1339	41716	11	38397	1774	63707	2	107840	301	9470	11	56047
MOD(24, 12, 8, 6, 3, 2)	1273	38644	11	38467	1116	39936	2	95214	1128	40686	12	94515
MOD(12, 8, 2, 6, 3)	358	5458	9	18710	1113	39940	2	82817	431	11657	10	70271
MOD(32)	1734	84019	2	30184	1734	84019	2	30184	1734	84019	2	30184
MOD(32, 16, 8)	2262	96594	6	46523	1853	89373	2	72833	1858	89737	6	72847
MOD(8, 16, 32)	2241	100253	6	46657	2079	100074	2	84481	260	8047	6	41438
MOD(32, 16, 8, 4, 2)	2286	96694	9	49646	1973	94726	2	115481	1976	95018	10	115214
MOD(2, 4, 8, 16, 32)	2329	100324	9	49827	3402	163621	2	143979	228	7461	9	44245

- Similarly, in the machine-by-machine approach, the filter after handling MOD(2), MOD(3) and MOD(5) is MOD(30), thus only words in MOD(30) are queried to the further machines.

The situation is a bit different when learning MOD(32). Here, we observe that this setting allows for very efficient filtering in the machine-by-machine approach, accelerating the learning.

The Inverse of the MOD Languages. We consider the inverse of these languages, that is

$$\text{IMOD}(x) = \{w \in \Sigma^* \mid |w| \bmod x \neq 0\}.$$

The minimal DFA for this language has x states. We display some results in Table 2. We distinguish two cases here: Above the first line, we are again learning IMOD(30) from individual languages that admit smaller representations. Additionally, compared to MOD(30), the language (as a set) is much larger. This means that lazy evaluation and filtering is less efficient. In some sense, this setting yields the worst-case for word-by-word and machine-by-machine learning.

Below the first line, and in stark contrast to the situation before, the target language is smaller than the individual languages. Such a situation plays to the strength of the word-by-word approach. Furthermore, if correctly ordered, the machine-by-machine approach also avoids creating a large intermediate automaton.

Table 2. Learning Not-modulo-languages

	Independent				Word-By-Word				Machine-By-Machine			
	$\sharp$MQ	SC$_{MQ}$	$\sharp$EQ	SC$_{EQ}$	$\sharp$MQ	SC$_{MQ}$	$\sharp$EQ	SC$_{EQ}$	$\sharp$MQ	SC$_{MQ}$	$\sharp$EQ	SC$_{EQ}$
IMOD(30)	1480	68236	2	27644	1480	68236	2	27644	1480	68236	2	27644
IMOD(2, 3, 5)	51	270	5	5303	1975	54835	5	67017	429	11187	10	26764
IMOD(2, 3, 5, 6, 10)	234	2727	9	14771	2601	71609	5	110570	632	16277	18	69780
IMOD(2, 3, 5, 6, 10, 15, 30)	2125	81825	13	53038	3227	88383	5	154124	852	21788	26	112759
IMOD(30, 15, 10, 6, 5, 3, 2)	2062	79452	13	52989	6003	168201	5	157321	2760	103784	24	135103
IMOD(15, 10, 6, 5, 3, 2)	617	12072	11	25551	5003	140364	5	134784	1661	45854	22	107856
IMOD(8)	83	1070	2	4721	83	1070	2	4721	83	1070	2	4721
IMOD(16, 8)	499	11482	4	16403	165	2140	2	9439	428	10595	4	16520
IMOD(8, 16)	467	10808	4	16142	157	2037	2	9432	108	1273	4	9322
IMOD(32, 24, 16, 8)	3245	134373	8	66514	328	4279	2	18874	8133	556202	12	201424
IMOD(8, 16, 24, 32)	3262	139417	8	66632	306	3969	2	18855	158	1679	8	18434
IMOD(2)	5	6	1	1044	5	6	1	1044	5	6	1	1044
IMOD(8, 4, 2)	106	1163	5	7913	11	16	1	3117	99	1152	5	7927
IMOD(2, 4, 8)	124	1417	5	7959	9	12	1	3089	9	12	3	2996
IMOD(32, 16, 8, 4, 2)	2286	96694	9	49646	17	26	1	5202	1827	85853	9	49781
IMOD(2, 4, 8, 16, 32)	2329	100324	9	49827	13	18	1	5134	13	18	5	4983
IMOD(2, 10, 20)	843	24655	5	22862	9	12	1	3089	9	12	3	2996
IMOD(20, 10, 2)	801	22362	5	22609	11	16	1	3127	676	20359	5	22658

5   Conclusion and Outlook

In this paper, we discussed a straightforward question: What is a natural way to implement active learning of an intersection of languages. We introduced Lcap, a prototype implementation of three strategies towards this learning problem. The empirical evaluation shows that each of these strategies have their strengths and weaknesses. The problem of learning intersections is an interesting playground, with plenty of conceptual questions and further room for research[5]. We identify several challenges below, divided into three entangled categories.

Conceptual Improvements. The strategies that we considered in this paper are independent of the underlying algorithm. But one could think of strategies that re-use the internal data structures that arise during learning (e.g., a table in L^* and many of its decendants, or an observation tree as in $L^{\sharp}$). For instance, in the machine-by-machine strategy one could start learning the next intersection language $L_1 \cap \ldots \cap L_{i+1}$ starting not from an empty table (or tree), but from the one that led to the final hypothesis for the previous intersection language $L_1 \cap \ldots \cap L_i$. This table/tree should perhaps then be checked against the current language via membership queries. Such a strategy might work relatively well if the languages in question are close.

In a similar spirit, the proposed machine-by-machine strategy learns languages in well-defined steps. There is room for adapting the equivalence queries and loosening this strict stepwise approach. Instead of investing a similar effort

---

[5] Perhaps by the *Festgegenstand*!

on the equivalence queries for intermediate results, one may arguably assume that an equivalence query passes and only at the very end do a proper effort to execute the equivalence query. The risk here is that one assumes an incorrect intersection of $L_1 \cap \ldots L_j$; however, one may detect this mistake in the final equivalence query and roll back.

Practical Considerations. The elephant in the room is which type of intersections is most relevant in real life. We think that the application of these algorithms to industrial case studies would be most interesting.

While the strategies may be implemented on top of existing frameworks, it would be best if learning frameworks actively support the required interfaces, see also the conceptual improvements above. This would additionally allow for some more practical improvements: The different characteristics we observe in our empirical evaluation hint at room for hybrid strategies that combine different aspects. For example, one may group languages, learn their intersection using a word-by-word approach, and then apply machine-by-machine or independent learning over those intersections. Alternatively, even in a machine-by-machine or independent setup, one can query (short) words on additional machines.

Finally, languages are currently statically ordered as provided by the user. The experiments show that the order has a significant influence on the performance. Developing strategies that adapt the order based on the word being queried or based on a sample of words may significantly reduce the dependence on the user-provided order.

Extensions. In the current paper we focused on DFA learning. A natural extension is to treat Mealy (and Moore) machines; this would require some kind of algebraic structure on the outputs, generalising conjunction (with Booleans as output) which we considered here. A related question is whether there is a connection to the problem of learning product automata, as considered in [7]. Beyond DFAs, different modular setups for learning with a focus on the consequences for the complexity of the problem are discussed in [2]. Orthogonally to the problem in this paper, one may assume that the target language is the intersection of individual languages but that we do not have oracle-access to these individual languages. A similar problem is studied for passive learning in [6].

In this paper, we measured the uniform symbol complexity. This may be unrealistic: For example, not all (coffee) machines are equally expensive to access: A machine located in your house is cheaper to test on than a machine one does not own. The evaluation of words may depend on the execution speed of a machine: A digital twin may be much quicker to evaluate on than on a physical machine. This list is not exhaustive; e.g., some machines have high access cost (walking to the coffee machine on a different floor) but executing multiple queries is cheap. The addition of a cost model may open room for more interesting combinations.

References

1. Angluin, D.: Learning regular sets from queries and counterexamples. Inf. Comput. **75**(2), 87–106 (1987)
2. Caulfield, B., Seshia, S.A.: Modularity in query-based concept learning. CoRR, abs/1911.02714 (2019)
3. Fiterau-Brostean, P.: Active Model Learning for the Analysis of Network Protocols. Ph.D thesis, Radboud University, April (2018)
4. Howar, F., Steffen, B.: Active automata learning in practice. In: Bennaceur, A., Hähnle, R., Meinke, K. (eds.) Machine Learning for Dynamic Software Analysis: Potentials and Limits. LNCS, vol. 11026, pp. 123–148. Springer, Cham (2018). https://doi.org/10.1007/978-3-319-96562-8_5
5. Isberner, M., Howar, F., Steffen, B.: The TTT algorithm: a redundancy-free approach to active automata learning. In: Bonakdarpour, B., Smolka, S.A. (eds.) RV 2014. LNCS, vol. 8734, pp. 307–322. Springer, Cham (2014). https://doi.org/10.1007/978-3-319-11164-3_26
6. Lauffer, N., Yalcinkaya, B., Vazquez-Chanlatte, M., Shah, A., Seshia, S.A.: Learning deterministic finite automata decompositions from examples and demonstrations. CoRR, abs/2205.13013 (2022)
7. Moerman, J.: Learning product automata. In: ICGI, volume 93 of Proceedings of Machine Learning Research, pp. 54–66. PMLR (2018)
8. Muškardin, E., Aichernig, B.K., Pill, I., Pferscher, A., Tappler, M.: AALpy: an active automata learning library. In: Hou, Z., Ganesh, V. (eds.) ATVA 2021. LNCS, vol. 12971, pp. 67–73. Springer, Cham (2021). https://doi.org/10.1007/978-3-030-88885-5_5
9. Vaandrager, F.: Model learning. Commun. ACM **60**(2), 86–95 (2017)
10. Vaandrager, F., Garhewal, B., Rot, J., Wißmann, T.: A new approach for active automata learning based on apartness. In: TACAS, volume 13243 of LNCS, pp. 223–243. Springer (2022). https://doi.org/10.1007/978-3-030-99524-9_12
11. Marcell Vazquez-Chanlatte. dfa: A python library for deterministic finite automata. https://github.com/mvcisback/dfa

Runtime Verification of Compound Components with ComMA

Ivan Kurtev[1,2](✉) and Jozef Hooman[3]

[1] Capgemini Engineering, Eindhoven, The Netherlands
ivan.kurtev@capgemini.com
[2] Eindhoven University of Technology, Eindhoven, The Netherlands
[3] ESI (TNO), Eindhoven, The Netherlands
jozef.hooman@tno.nl

Abstract. The ComMA language has been developed to specify interfaces of software components, including protocol state machines, time and data constraints, and constraints on relations between events of multiple interfaces. The language has been devised in close collaboration with an industrial partner where it has been used to model a large number of interfaces. Based on a ComMA model, a number of artefacts can be generated such as documentation and test cases. Important is the generation of a monitor which is used to check if an implementation conforms to the specified model. This paper describes the ComMA monitoring algorithms. They are based on runtime verification techniques which have been extended to deal with the expressive ComMA language.

Keywords: Interface modeling · Runtime Verification · Component-based development

1 Introduction

Modern high-tech systems are complex entities consisting of multiple interacting components, typically supplied by different vendors. The lack of precise and explicit specifications of component interfaces often leads to problems during the integration of components. Component updates in already deployed systems may also lead to issues caused, for example, by unexpected changes in the interaction protocol and the time behavior. To address these issues, the ComMA (Component Modeling and Analysis) method and tool have been developed to support precise modeling of components and their interfaces.

ComMA provides a number of domain-specific languages for specifying client-server interfaces and component models in which multiple interfaces are used together. The interface language allows definitions of custom types, interface signatures in terms of messages exchanged between a client and server, behavior that specifies the allowed order of messages, and constraints on timing and data parameters. The component language allows modeling of simple and compound components (containing multiple parts) that use several interfaces together.

© The Author(s), under exclusive license to Springer Nature Switzerland AG 2022
N. Jansen et al. (Eds.): Vaandrager Festschrift 2022, LNCS 13560, pp. 382–402, 2022.
https://doi.org/10.1007/978-3-031-15629-8_21

Figure 1 shows a simple *Control* component that provides interface *IControl* to its clients via the provided *iControlPort3* port and uses the interfaces *ITemperature*, *IVacuum* and *ISource* via its required ports shown as dashed squares. Furthermore, component models support definition of constraints on the input/output relation of a component in the view of its interfaces and their interactions.

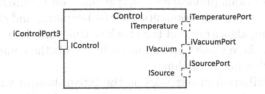

Fig. 1. Example simple ComMA component

The ComMA tool facilitates a number of engineering tasks by automatically generating artefacts from models. Figure 2 shows the main generators. Using models as a single source, the generators create UML diagrams of models, documentation based on a predefined MS Word template, monitoring infrastructure and test cases among others. The ability to monitor interfaces and components is a powerful feature of ComMA. It is used to check if an implementation conforms to an interface and/or component model. The automatically generated monitor checks if an execution trace that contains messages observed during component executions adheres to the behavior model and the time and data constraints. The output of the monitor is conveniently shown in a dashboard that summarizes the discovered issues along with other useful diagnostic information.

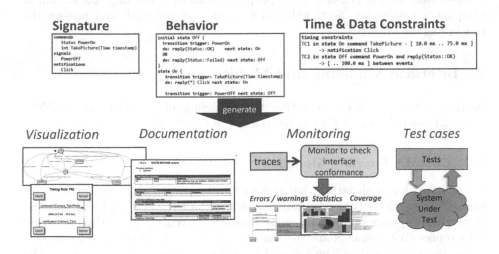

Fig. 2. Overview of ComMA generators

One of the main goals of ComMA is to allow easy application by industrial users. The modeling languages use familiar engineering notations such as state-based specification of the behavioral aspects, commonly found patterns for timing properties, and software architecture description concepts for component models. The languages have been developed iteratively respecting the requests and the feedback from the industrial users.

A number of previous publications [6, 7] focused on ComMA interface specifications giving the syntax and semantics of the language, and elaborated on the interface monitoring algorithm and the check of time and data constraints. This paper builds upon these results and explains in details the component modeling language and monitoring algorithm.

The main contribution of our work is the integration of various theoretical results from the runtime verification body of knowledge into a framework that bridges the gap between the formal specification languages and the notations used by engineers, supports automation and integration of engineering tasks. The proposed specification language constructs do not introduce new logic, they focus on specifying constraints at the level of abstraction of the engineering models, handling components with multiple clients, and achieving compact specifications by refering to interface states. We are currently not aware of other component monitoring frameworks that utilize commonly used modeling notations to the degree that ComMA does.

The ComMA tooling is available via the open source Eclipse CommaSuite project[1]. The example used in the paper is included in the distribution.

Section 2 is an overview of ComMA interface models and monitoring, highlighting the features that are later used for the purpose of component modeling. Section 3 introduces the component modeling language on the basis of an example of a simple component. Section 4 follows with the presentation of compound components. Section 5 discusses the purpose, challenges and implementation of component monitoring. Sections 6 and 7 discuss related work and present the concluding remarks.

2   Interface Modeling and Monitoring

In this section we briefly describe the modeling of interfaces in ComMA (Sect. 2.1) and the monitoring of interfaces (Sect. 2.2).

2.1   ComMA Interface Modeling

An interface has a signature that defines synchronous and asynchronous calls from client to server (named commands and signals respectively) and notifications which are asynchronous messages from server to client. These three together with replies to commands are the messages that can be exchanged between a client and server and will be referred to as interface events or messages. The

---

[1] https://www.eclipse.org/comma/.

events may carry parameters. The signature of a simple interface called *IVacuum*, for managing vacuum in a system is shown in the next listing.

```
signature IVacuum
commands
    void VacuumOn
    void VacuumOff
notifications
    VacuumOK
```

In ComMA, the allowed order of interface events is captured in an interface behavior model which is defined as a protocol state machine. In addition, an interface defines time and data constraints. Time constraints specify allowed time intervals between events. Time and data constraints have been reported in [6] and are out of scope of this paper. As an example, the state machine of interface *IVacuum* is listed.

```
interface IVacuum
machine VacuumMachine {
    initial state NoVacuum {
            transition trigger: VacuumOn
                do: reply
                next state: Evacuating
    }
    state Evacuating {
            transition
                do: VacuumOK
                next state: Vacuum
    }
    state Vacuum {
            transition trigger: VacuumOff
                do: reply
                next state: NoVacuum }
}
```

The state machine describes a client-server interface from the viewpoint of a server, that is, transitions are triggered by client calls of a command or a signal. The *do* part of a transition contains a sequence of actions of the server, which may include assignments to variables, a reply to a command, if-then-else statements, and notification patterns. A notification pattern specifies the occurrence of notifications; a special case is the *any order* construct to specify that events may happen in any order. Moreover, the language allows non-determinism, e.g., after a client call there may be multiple possible transitions by the server, possibly leading to different responses and states.

2.2 Interface Monitoring

Interface monitoring is the process of checking if a trace of observed events between client and server conforms to the interface definition. The following is an example of the ComMA trace format (apart from this, JSON format is also supported):

components
Control ctrl
Vacuum vacuum

events

command 0.0 ctrl iVacuumPort vacuum iVacuumPort
          IVacuum VacuumOn
End

reply 0.11 vacuum iVacuumPort ctrl iVacuumPort
          IVacuum VacuumOn
End

notification 1.2 vacuum iVacuumPort ctrl iVacuumPort
          IVacuum VacuumOK
End

A trace starts with declarations of component instances (elaborated later when the component language is explained). They interact by sending messages to each other. Each message has a timestamp, a source instance and port (ports are explained in Sect. 3), a target instance and port, and contains the event and the interface it belongs to. The first message in the example is the command *VacuumOn* with timestamp 0.0 sent from component *ctrl* and its port *iVacuumPort* to component *vacuum*.

In ComMA, an interface monitor is a Java program that is automatically generated from the interface model. The ComMA monitor starts from the initial state of the state machine and consumes the events from the trace one by one. As soon as the monitor detects that an event in the trace does not conform to the state machine, it reports an error with some diagnostic info and stops monitoring.

Interface Events Augmented with State Information. As will be described in Sect. 3, component constraints may refer to states of interface descriptions. To allow checking of such constraints, the interface monitor augments interface events with the current state of the interface model. If an event is accepted by the monitor, it is annotated with the state in which it has been observed (known as *observation state*) and with the state that will be the current state when the next event is observed (known as *post-observation state*).

Since interface models allow non-determinism, multiple transitions for an event may be possible leading to potentially different observation and post-observations states. Consider Fig. 3: after observing notification *n1*, two transitions can be taken leading to different post-observations states: *S1* and *S3* respectively. The interface monitor explores all possible traversal paths. If for a given path, the observed event is not allowed in the current state, the path is discarded. If all traversal paths are discarded then an interface monitoring error is detected. If in our example, signal s is observed after $n1$ then the path which contains the transition to $S2$ will be discarded since there notification $n2$ is expected.

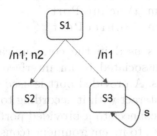

Fig. 3. Example state machine with non-determinism

The interface monitor maintains a list with *traversal path descriptions*. A description contains an identifier of the path, observation and post-observation states. At the start of monitoring only one path exists, assume its identifier is p. If a path leads to branching due to multiple possible transitions, each branch is uniquely numbered. The identifiers of the new paths are formed by concatenating the identifier of the parent path with the branch number. For example, if path with identifier $p122$ leads to two new branches their identifiers will be $p1221$ and $p1222$. A path p is a branch of q if the identifier of q is a prefix of the identifier of p.

After checking an event, the interface monitor provides a list of descriptions of all active traversal paths. In Sect. 5, we show how these path descriptions are used in the component monitoring process.

3   Component Models

We present the language constructs to specify components with constraints in Sect. 3.1 and to capture the identity of communication partners in Sect. 3.2.

3.1   Components with Functional Constraints

Interface specifications define the allowed order of events when a client uses an interface. Multiple interfaces are usually used together in the context of a single software unit that interacts with its environment. ComMA uses component models to define the allowed order of events from multiple interfaces and from multiple clients of the same interface.

As an example, we consider the *Control* component in Fig. 1 that provides interface *IControl* to its clients and uses services from other components via three interfaces. The textual syntax of component models in ComMA is as follows:

component Control

provided port IControl iControlPort3
required port ITemperature iTemperaturePort
required port IVacuum iVacuumPort
required port ISource iSourcePort

Ports are connection points used in the communication between component instances and are always associated to an interface. We distinguish between provided and required ports. A provided port is used by the clients of the component to connect to and interact with it according to the port's interface. Multiple clients are allowed to connect to a provided port. Required ports are used by the component to connect to its environment (consisting of other component instances).

The main purpose of a component model is to define constraints on the order of events observable in the context of the model (sent to or from the component ports). The construct used to specify this order is called *functional constraint*. A functional constraint captures an aspect of the complete behavior of the component and is usually restricted to a small subset of the observable events. Component models are not intended to define the complete component behavior in terms of reactions to all possible events in different states. In other words, component models are not design specifications that are used to derive a complete component implementation. An implementation is expected to satisfy all the functional constraints defined in a component model. In addition, a component model may define time and data constraints (not covered in this paper).

Functional constraints have two forms: state-based specification (known as state-based functional constraint) and an expression that has to evaluate to true for every observed event in the component context (called predicate functional constraint). The information about the current state of the interface associated to a port can be used in functional constraints.

As an example, the Control component handles requests for image acquisition and controls the vacuum and temperature in the system. A requirement for the control logic is that image acquisition is only possible if vacuum is present, and a certain temperature is reached. In terms of allowed message sequences, the command *AcquireImage* must be observed after the notifications about the correct state of vacuum and temperature, and only then the acquisition can be started. The following (simplified) constraint captures this requirement.

use events
command iControlPort3 :: AcquireImage
command iSourcePort :: StartAcquisition

```
initial state Ready {
        // if vacuum and temperature OK start acquisition
        command iControlPort3 :: AcquireImage
            where iVacuumPort in Vacuum and
                  iTemperaturePort in TemperatureSet
        command iSourcePort :: StartAcquisition
        next state: Ready
}
```

The constraint uses only two events listed in the section *use events*. The *use events* sections can also specify event patterns that denote more than one event such as all commands observed at a given port, all messages at a given port and so on. The allowed order of the specified events is given in a state machine similarly to the interface protocol state machines. Events that do not belong to the set defined in *use events* are not restricted.

In the example, the machine is very simple, consisting of one state and a single transition. The transition is triggered when command *AcquireImage* is observed at port *iControlPort3*. The pattern *command iControlPort3::AcquireImage* is a subject of a condition: a Boolean expression after the *where* keyword. *iVacuumPort in Vacuum* evaluates to true if the sequence of messages at *iVacuumPort* until the observation of *AcquireImage* has led to state *Vacuum*. Here *Vacuum* is a state in the *IVacuum* interface as shown in Sect. 2.1.

The pattern match is successful only if the condition is true. In terms of our example: *AcquireImage* is allowed to occur only if the vacuum and temperature ports are in the right state. This access to interface state information of ports is extremely handy. Without it, the functional constraint needs to replicate the sequence of the messages on the two ports that lead to the indicated interface states, information that is already present in the interface specifications. This way, code duplication is avoided and the size of the constraint is reduced.

In general, transitions in functional constraints are sequences of actions where the first action is a *message pattern*: an indication that a message of a given kind is expected to be observed. The other supported actions are assignment and if-then-else. Informally, a state-based functional constraint determines a set of message traces that conform to it. A trace in this set is such that (i) for every port, the projection of the trace on this port (i.e. the trace obtained by keeping only the messages on this port) conforms to the port interface; (ii) the trace obtained by keeping all the used events conforms to the constraint state machine. Here 'conforms' means that starting from the initial state and the first event in the trace, there is at least one transition traversal path that accepts the trace.

3.2   Using the Identity of Communication Partners

In a trace, every message has a source and a target, which are identifiers of component instances, and source and target ports. The component language provides a construct to capture the identity of the communication party for a message observed at a component port. For example, when a command is received at a provided port, the identifier of the client can be obtained. Similarly, when a command is sent from a required port of a component, the identifier of the component can be obtained. This is illustrated by an example of a shared resource with multiple clients.

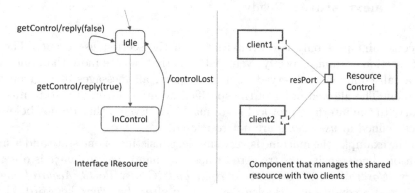

Fig. 4. Example interface and component models for managing shared resource

Assume that a component is providing access to a shared resource via a single provided port named *resPort* associated to interface *IResource* (see Fig. 4). Multiple clients can request control over this resource and the component is responsible for the policy of sharing it. The requirement is that at most one client is allowed to control the resource at a given moment. The following is a snippet from the corresponding functional constraint.

```
use events
resPort :: reply to command getControl
notification resPort :: controlLost

variables
id c
id c1

initial state ResourceFree {
    <c> resPort :: reply(true) to command getControl
    next state: ResourceTaken

    resPort :: reply(false) to command getControl
    next state: ResourceFree
}

state ResourceTaken {
    notification <c1>resPort :: controlLost where c == c1
```

next state: ResourceFree

resPort :: **reply**(false) **to command** getControl
next state: ResourceTaken
}

If in the initial state, called *ResourceFree*, a reply to command *getControl* with argument *true* is observed then the identifier of the client who receives the reply is bound to the variable c. Note that the type of the variable is *id*. This is a predefined primitive type that allows only identity comparison operations. If a client receives a positive reply to *getControl*, the state *ResourceTaken* becomes the current state. In *ResourceTaken* no more positive replies to control requests are allowed. The control over the resource can be released only if the component decides to send notification *controlLost* to the client which currently has the control. Observe the usage of the variable *c1* that takes as value the identifier of the receiver of the notification. It is used in the condition that ensures the client which is currently in control receives the notification.

This example can be formulated more compactly as a *predicate* functional constraint. A predicate constraint is an expression preceded with the keyword *always*:

always $[0-1]$ **connections at** portRes **in** InControl

The constraint states that at most one client connected to *portRes* is in interface state *InControl*. The expression uses a quantifier over the port connections (zero or one connection satisfies a condition). Note that for every client/connection of a provided port, a separate instance of the interface state machine is created, each with its own current state. This example shows how component functional constraints can restrict the order of events over the connections of a single port. In contrast, the first example (about control, vacuum and temperature) involves multiple ports and interfaces.

The interface state of the client at the moment of observing a message may be different from the state assumed after the observation (recall the difference between observation and post-observation states explained in Sect. 2.2). As an illustration, consider two consecutive actions in a functional constraint in the context of our current example:

<c> resPort :: **reply**(true) **to command** getControl
    where c **at** resPort **in** Idle

b := (c **at** resPort **in** Idle)

The first action is a pattern that matches replies to *getControl* with parameter true. If it matches the currently observed message, variable c takes a value (the identifier of the receiver of the reply) and then the *where* clause is evaluated. Assume that its value is true (indeed, such a reply can only be observed in state *Idle*).

In the second action, however, the same expression evaluates to false since after observing the reply, the transition to *InControl* is taken and the interface changes its state (see Fig. 4). Variable b will be assigned with false. This subtlety affects how the expressions that use the current interface state of a connection are evaluated. If they are used in the context of a message pattern, the state at the moment of observing the message is used for the corresponding connection, otherwise the post-observation state for the last observed message for this connection is used.

4   Compound Components

Component models may also define the internal component structure: its subcomponents (parts) and their interactions.

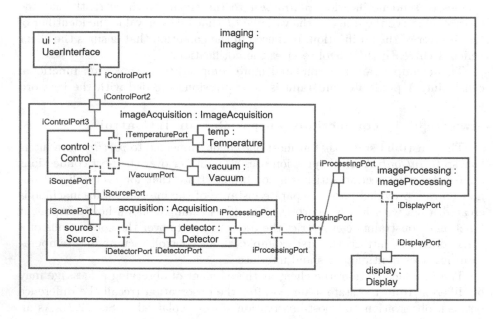

Fig. 5. Example compound component model

Figure 5 shows an example of a non-trivial component model called *Imaging*. It represents a system that captures images of some specimen. The model has four parts that are instances of other component models: *ui*, *imageAcquisiton*, *imageProcessing* and *display*. These component models may have their own internal structure as can be seen from the figure. The process of image acquisition requires vacuum in the system and a certain temperature level. The image is produced by a beam, generated by a source, going through the material and captured by a detector. The detector sends the data for further processing, storage and possibly visualization at a display. The *imageAcquisition.control* part is responsible for orchestrating the process: first ensuring vacuum and correct temperature and then starting the acquisition process. The type of *imageAcqui-sition.control* is the *Control* component introduced in the previous section.

Components are connected via their ports; in Fig. 5 provided ports are shown as a solid square and required ports as a dashed square. Messages originating from the required port *ui.iControlPort1* are transmitted via a connection to the provided port *imageAcquisition.iControlPort2*. The connection between the latter and *control.iControlPort3* means that the messages will be further transmitted to the part *control*. In this way, a chain of connections defines a full path for message transmission. A more complex path can be observed between *detector.iProcessingPort* and *imageProcessing.iProcessingPort*.

As an example of the textual syntax of compound components, the next listing shows the specification of the *ImageAcquisition* component.

component ImageAcquisition

provided port IControl iControlPort2
required port IProcessing iProcessingPort

parts
Control control
Temperature temperature
Vacuum vacuum
Acquisition acquisition

connections
iControlPort2 <-> control::iControlPort3
control::iTemperaturePort <-> temperature::iTemperaturePort
control::iVacuumPort <-> vacuum::iVacuumPort
control::iSourcePort <-> acquisition::iSourcePort
acquisition::iProcessingPort <-> iProcessingPort

Note that a compound component contains *parts* which are named instances of component models. The parts have all the ports defined in their model. We will call such ports *part ports* and will refer to the ports defined by the component model as *boundary ports*. Within a component model, parts can interact with other parts by using connections between their ports. A connection of this kind is defined between a pair of provided and required ports of the same interface. Furthermore, a boundary port may be connected to a part port with the same kind (provided or required) and of the same interface. A connection indicates a channel for transmitting messages between the ports. For example, a message observed at a boundary port is redirected to the connected port of one of its parts. The ports do not perform any computation. A connection between a boundary port and a part port is just an indication of a path to the message's destination. The boundary port does not create a new message that is forwarded over the connection.

For a compound component, functional constraints can be used to relate events of interfaces of different components. For instance, such a constraint may express that an *AcquireImage* event on port *iControlPort1* of component *ui* alternates with event *DisplayImage* on port *iDisplayPort* of component *display*. Moreover, also end-to-end time constraints can be expressed, e.g. to express that the *DisplayImage* event should happen within a certain amount of time after the *AcquireImage* event.

5   Component Monitoring

Component monitoring is performed for a given trace and component model. It checks if the trace satisfies: (i) the functional constraints in the model; (ii) the interface models associated to the component ports. Furthermore, if the component model has parts, the trace is checked against their models too.

The monitor for a trace has the following logical structure: *trace processor* that reads the trace, identifies the component instances to be monitored, and invokes *component and interface monitors*. A component monitor contains *functional constraint monitors*.

We first briefly explain how component instances are specified in the traces, an elaboration of the information previously given in Sect. 2.2.

5.1   Traces with Messages Between Component Instances

A trace starts with a declaration of all component instances and their models. The part-whole relation between the instances is encoded in their identifiers.

```
Imaging imaging
UserInterface imaging.ui
ImageAcquisition imaging.imageAcquisition
```

In this declaration, there is one instance of the *Imaging* model, called *imaging*, and two parts of *imaging* which are named with a compound name where the prefix is the name of the containing instance and the last segment is the simple name given in the component model.

Messages cannot cross the boundaries of the containing components for its source and target. For example, a message from *imaging.ui* can only be sent to the parts at the same level of nesting, that is, to *imaging.imageAcquisition*. Observe that *imageAcquisition.iControlPort2* is connected to *control.iControlPort3* (Fig. 5) so the messages received at the former will be further directed to the latter port. Regardless of the connection, it is not allowed to specify a message from *imaging.ui.iControlPort1* to *imaging.imageAcquisition.control.iControlPort3* because it crosses the boundary of the enclosing *imageAcquisition* component.

5.2   Algorithm for Monitoring a Trace

For a given trace and a component model, all instances of the component model are monitored. Note that a trace may have instances of different models. Only the instances of the given model are considered. An instance behaves according to its model if the sequence of the messages relevant to this instance satisfies the constraints in the model and in the models of its direct or indirect parts. A direct part is contained immediately in the instance, an indirect part is contained further down in the containment tree induced by the part-whole relation among components. A message is relevant for a component instance if it is observed at one of its boundary ports or is exchanged between two of its direct or indirect parts. When a component instance is monitored all its direct and indirect parts are monitored too.

Due to the possibility of connections between ports, a given message can be checked against more than one component model. One of the tasks of the monitoring algorithm is for a given message to determine a sequence of checks against the relevant component models. Assume that we monitor the instance *imaging* (see the example in previous section) and *imaging.imageAcquisition* receives a message at *iControlPort2* from *imaging.ui*. Let's denote this message as *(ui, iControlPort1, imageAcquisition, iControlPort2)* abstracting away the message kind and possible parameters. This is a message between parts of the component being monitored, it is visible in the context of component model *Imaging* and therefore it has to be checked against the *Imaging* constraints. Furthermore, the message is observed at the boundary ports of two parts thus posing the need to check it against their models (*UserInterface* and *ImageAcquisition*).

When the message is received at *imageAcquisition.iControlPort2*, the connection to *control.iControlPort3* is followed and the message is ultimately received by the *control* part. The message needs to be checked against the *Control* model as well. In summary, the considered message will be checked against the following component models: *Imaging*, *UserInterface*, *ImageAcquisition*, and *Control*.

The constraints in *Control* model will refer to messages observed at *Control* instances and their boundary ports. Because of this, before checking the message against the constraints defined in *Control*, the destination of the message is changed to *(ui, iControlPort1, imageAcquisition.control, iControlPort3)*.

In summary, for every message relevant to the monitored instance, a list of (component instance, port) pairs is determined, where the presence of port is optional. For every element in the list, the message will be checked by the component monitor for the instance. Both the instance and the port will be used if one of the message ends needs renaming. In our example the list of pairs is *(imaging, _), (userInterface, _), (imageAcquisition, _), (control, iControlPort3)*.

Generally, the list is formed in the following way: (i) for a message at component boundary port, the instances are the ones reachable following the chain of port connections towards the component parts; (ii) for a message between parts, the instances are the ones reachable following the connections from the source and target message ports plus the immediate parent of the parts. Our example falls under the second case.

Before the check of functional constraints, interface monitoring is performed. Every relevant message is exchanged in a pair of client and server components and an interface monitor will be created for this pair. In our example, an interface monitor will be created for the connection between *ui.iControlPort1* and *imageAcquisition.iControlPort2*. It will provide interface state information shared among three ports: the two mentioned above and *control.iControlPort3* (note the connection between *imageAcquisition.iControlPort2* and *control.iControlPort3*).

A sketch of the algorithm that processes and monitors a trace is given in procedure *MonitorComponentInstances* that takes as input a component model *cModel* and a trace. Recall that the trace contains information about the component instances and the messages among them. Monitoring is performed on all messages from the trace that are relevant for the instances of *cModel*. All instances of *cModel* can be obtained from the component declarations part in trace (line 2). As explained before, a relevant message is observed at a boundary port or between two (direct or indirect) parts of some instance (lines 9–11). If a relevant message is found, it is first checked by its interface monitor (created for the connection between the message's sender and receiver). The interface monitor is treated as an object: it can be created, stored and it has behavior and internal state (line 18). Interface monitoring of a relevant message is always performed as long as no interface error has been detected for this connection. If at least one interface error is found for a given component instance on some of its ports, the check against the component model is not performed anymore. The map *interfaceErrorStatus* (line 6) keeps track if an interface error has been observed for an instance (see lines 24 and 42 where the map is used and updated). If the interface monitor accepts the message the next step is to perform the check against the relevant component models (which further leads to checking of their functional constraints). Traversal path descriptions that will be used in functional constraint checks are obtained from the interface monitor (line 27). The pairs of component instance and port (as explained previously) are determined and then iterated (lines 31–40). For every component instance in the pairs, a component monitor is obtained (line 36, created once on demand, then stored and used later when the same instance is monitored for another message).

```
1   MonitorComponentInstances(cModel, trace)
2     instances <- instances of cModel from trace
3
4     //indicates if interface monitoring error occurred
5     //for an instance; initialized with false
6     interfaceErrorStatus <- map from instances to Boolean
7     While trace has unprocessed messages Do
8         msg <- read next message from trace
9         If (msg at boundary port of some i in instances)
10            Or
11            (msg between parts of some i in instances)
12        Then
13            i <- the instance that satisfies the
14                 condition in lines 9-11
15            //interface monitor is instantiated once on
16            //demand for each pair (client, server),
17            //stored and used when needed
```

```
18              interfaceMonitor <- obtain interface monitor
19                             for msg
20          If interfaceMonitor already gave error Then
21              Continue
22          End If
23          If msg is accepted by interfaceMonitor Then
24              If interfaceErrorStatus at i is true Then
25                  Continue
26              End If
27              pathDescriptions <- obtain traversal path
28                      descriptions from interfaceMonitor
29              pairsInstancePort <- list of (instance, port)
30                             for cModel and i
31              For Each pair in pairsInstancePort Do
32                  change the relevant message end for pair
33
34                  //component monitor instantiated on
35                  //demand and stored
36                  componentMonitor <- obtain component
37                         monitor for pair.instance
38                  MonitorComponentInstance(componentMonitor,
39                             msg, pathDescriptions)
40              End For
41          Else
42              set interfaceErrorStatus at i to true
43          End If
44      End If
45  End While
46  collect and print results from all interface and
47  component monitors
48 End
```

The monitoring of a component instance is sketched in procedure *MonitorComponentInstance*. A component monitor contains a list of functional constraint monitors (line 4, *componentMonitor.fcMonitors*). The input message is checked by every functional constraint monitor for which no error has previously been detected.

```
1   MonitorComponentInstance(componentMonitor,
2                               msg,
3                               pathDescriptions)
4       For Each fcMonitor in componentMonitor.fcMonitors Do
5           If fcMonitor has not previously detected error
6           Then
7               MonitorFunctionalConstraint(fcMonitor, msg,
8                                       pathDescriptions)
9           End If
10      End For
11  End
```

The implementation of functional constraint monitors and the usage of the traversal path descriptions is explained in the next section.

5.3   Checking Functional Constraints

We will first discuss how expressions that use interface states at ports are evaluated using the information in the traversal path descriptions, and then will outline the implementation of functional constraint monitors.

Different traversal paths in an interface state machine may lead to different states. In functional constraints, the expressions that refer to port states may produce different results for different paths ultimately causing a constraint to fail for some paths and succeed for others. Furthermore, multiple ports with multiple interface monitors can exist in the context of a component instance, each monitor possibly having multiple traversal paths. This means that for a given component instance, all combinations of traversal paths from all monitors on all ports need to be formed and functional constraints have to be evaluated for every combination. When forming the combinations we take into account that connected ports share an interface monitor and therefore share traversal paths in a single combination.

In the following explanation we assume that for each functional constraint there is an implementation in some programming language. Such an implementation may be based on some of the well known ways to implement state machine specifications in a general purpose programming language. We also assume that the implementation is parameterized with a constraint execution context. The context contains the current state of the machine, the values of the variables, and the states of the interface monitors associated to the component ports (as explained previously). The implementation can be configured with a given context and provides a function called *consume* that receives a message as input. This function, based on the current machine state, searches for transitions that match the message. For such a transition, all actions are executed thus leading to new execution context. If more than one transition exists, all are explored leading to multiple new execution contexts. The function returns the list of these new execution contexts. If the list is empty, then the functional constraint fails for the observed message in the given execution context.

At conceptual level, a functional constraint monitor is a data structure that contains the implementation of the constraint, a set of tuples with the traversal path descriptions per interface monitor on the ports (referred to as *portsStates*), and for every such tuple a set of constraint execution contexts.

The next procedure sketches the check of a functional constraint on a given message. The idea here is to check the functional constraint for every tuple with ports states. The functional constraint monitor is responsible for initializing and updating the set with these tuples. Since a functional constraint may have multiple execution contexts, a given tuple with ports states is associated to a set of execution contexts.

```
1    MonitorFunctionalConstraint(fcMonitor,
2                                msg,
3                                pathDescriptions)
4        update fcMonitor.portsStates for the given msg
5            with info from pathDescriptions
6        If fcMonitor.portsStates is empty Then
7            register functional constraint error
8            Return
9        End If
10       If msg not used by the functional constraint Then
11           Return
12       End If
13       newPortsStates <- empty list
14       For Each portsStateTuple in fcMonitor.portsStates Do
15           set current ports states in fcMonitor
16           to portsStateTuple
17           newFCExecutionContexts <- empty list
18           For Each fcContext in portsStateTuple.fcContexts
19           Do
20               set current context in fcMonitor to fcContext
21               newContexts <- fcMonitor.consume(msg)
22               add newContexts to newFCExecutionContexts
23           End For
24           If newFCExecutionContexts is not empty Then
25               portsStateTuple.fcContexts <-
26                   newFCExecutionContexts
27               add portsStateTuple to newPortsStates
28           End If
29       End For
30       If newPortsStates is empty Then
31           register functional constraint error
32           Return
33       Else
34           fcMonitor.portsStates <- newPortsStates
35       End If
36   End
```

The first operation in the procedure updates the tuples of ports states with the info from the path descriptions provided by the interface monitor (line 4). If in a given tuple the path identifier at the port on which the message is observed is not a prefix for any path in *pathDescriptions* this means that the path has been discarded by the interface monitor after the check of the message. The tuple is discarded as well. If the path identifier is a prefix of some paths in *pathDescriptions*, the tuple is replicated for every such path and state information is updated. It is possible that after this update, all tuples are discarded. This is treated as functional constraint violation: there are no traversal paths in the interface monitor that satisfy the functional constraint (lines 6–9). Observe also that this update is done for every message even if it is not used by the functional constraint (not listed in *use events* section).

After the update of the ports states, and the check if the message is used by the constraint (lines 10–12), the logic is straightforward: the outer loop (starting in line 14) iterates over each tuple of ports states, the inner loop (line 18–23) iterates over the functional constraint execution contexts for this tuple. The functional constraint instance is configured with a pair of ports states and context and then function *consume* is called. The result is a list of new execution contexts (line 21). If for a given tuple and all its contexts no transition in the functional constraint is found for the message (manifested by empty list of new contexts) the tuple is discarded. If all tuples are discarded, a functional constraint error is registered (lines 30–32).

The set of tuples with port states may become very large. In practice this hardly happens: multiple traversal paths in an interface are usually reduced to one after observing a few events.

The monitoring algorithms presented here serve as a base for the implementation of the component monitoring tool (done in Java and available in the Eclipse CommaSuite project). The trace processor, component and functional constraint monitors, and the functional constraints are completely generated from component and interface models.

6 Related Work

The component modeling approach presented in this paper uses the concepts of component, interface, port and connector. They are known from software architecture and system modeling languages such as UML, SysML, AADL among others. This is a conscious choice based on the observation that these concepts are familiar to the practitioners. Monitoring of systems with complex component architecture has been addressed in [4,13]. Falcone et al. [4] propose a runtime verification framework for component-based systems modeled with similar constructs where behavior is modeled with finite state machines. The ports in this approach accept simple values whereas in ComMA, ports are associated to interfaces with signatures that may use complex structures. Stockmann et al. [13] execute monitoring on traces obtained from simulating a software architecture specified in an executable modeling language. In our approach, traces are observations on the implementation.

There is a large variety of languages for specifying properties to be monitored. Their theoretical underpinnings are usually in formal logics. Dwyer et al. [3] identify patterns for properties observed in practice. These patterns have been used in property specification languages to achieve more compact and intuitive syntax. ParTraP [2] is a recent work based on this idea. Time and data constraints in ComMA are derived from common patterns observed in industrial practice, like periodicity, response time and others. We have considered using the patterns identified in [3] for functional constraints but opted for state-based specifications, already used in the interface definition language.

RML [1] is a domain-specific language for runtime verification. ComMA constructs like *any order* and event patterns have their counterparts in this language.

An interesting possibility is to treat ComMA specifications as syntactic sugar and investigate how they can be translated to RML primitives.

There exist approaches that weave the monitor's code into the system under monitoring (e.g. the language LIME and its monitoring infrastructure [5]). In our work the monitor is executed separately from the monitored system, often in offline mode after collecting the observations. This is beneficial in cases where the system implementation cannot be altered and instrumented.

ComMA compound components may represent distributed systems. This opens the possibility for distributed monitoring. Currently, the component monitor is monolithic, executed on a single node and working with traces that unite all (possibly distributed) observations. Performing distributed monitoring is a possible future direction, whose importance is recognized in a recent survey [10].

7 Conclusions

We presented the ComMA language that allows modeling component-based systems and specifying properties that are monitored during system execution. Monitors are automatically generated from component specifications. This work extends our previous work on specification and monitoring of component interfaces in industrial context. It brings a new application scope by allowing multiple interfaces to be used together in a single component and specifying interacting components at system level.

As mentioned in earlier publications [6,7,11], ComMA has been developed driven by user needs in close collaboration with Philips, following the industry-as-laboratory approach [8]. Hence, the languages use concepts and notations that are familiar to engineers and aim at rapid industrial adoption. Currently, the ComMA tooling is actively used at Philips to model and monitor of a number of industrial components, see for instance [9,12]. Future work will focus on applications in more complex cases where monitoring the order and timing of component interaction is a primary focus.

Acknowledgements. We would like to thanks our colleague Dennis Dams and the anonymous reviewers for many useful suggestions for improvements.

References

1. Ancona, D., Franceschini, L., Ferrando, A., Mascardi, V.: RML: theory and practice of a domain specific language for runtime verification. Sci. Comput. Program. **205**, 102610 (2021). https://doi.org/10.1016/j.scico.2021.102610
2. Blein, Y.: ParTraP: a language for the specification and runtime verification of parametric properties. (ParTraP: Un langage pour la spécification et vérification à l'exécution de propriétés paramétriques). Ph.D. thesis, Grenoble Alpes University, France (2019). https://tel.archives-ouvertes.fr/tel-02269062
3. Dwyer, M.B., Avrunin, G.S., Corbett, J.C.: Patterns in property specifications for finite-state verification. In: Boehm, B.W., Garlan, D., Kramer, J. (eds.) Proceedings of the 1999 International Conference on Software Engineering, ICSE 1999, Los

Angeles, CA, USA, 16–22 May 1999, pp. 411–420. ACM (1999). https://doi.org/10.1145/302405.302672

4. Falcone, Y., Jaber, M., Nguyen, T.-H., Bozga, M., Bensalem, S.: Runtime verification of component-based systems in the BIP framework with formally-proved sound and complete instrumentation. Softw. Syst. Model. **14**(1), 173–199 (2013). https://doi.org/10.1007/s10270-013-0323-y

5. Kähkönen, K., Lampinen, J., Heljanko, K., Niemelä, I.: The LIME interface specification language and runtime monitoring tool. In: Bensalem, S., Peled, D.A. (eds.) RV 2009. LNCS, vol. 5779, pp. 93–100. Springer, Heidelberg (2009). https://doi.org/10.1007/978-3-642-04694-0_7

6. Kurtev, I., Hooman, J., Schuts, M.: Runtime monitoring based on interface specifications. In: Katoen, J.-P., Langerak, R., Rensink, A. (eds.) ModelEd, TestEd, TrustEd. LNCS, vol. 10500, pp. 335–356. Springer, Cham (2017). https://doi.org/10.1007/978-3-319-68270-9_17

7. Kurtev, I., Schuts, M., Hooman, J., Swagerman, D.J.: Integrating interface modeling and analysis in an industrial setting. In: Proceedings of 5th International Conference on Model-Driven Engineering and Software Development (MODELSWARD 2017), pp. 345–352 (2017)

8. Potts, C.: Software-engineering research revisited. IEEE Softw. **19**(9), 19–28 (1993)

9. Roos, N.: ComMA interfaces open the door to reliable high-tech systems. Bits & Chips, 8 September 2020. https://bits-chips.nl/artikel/comma-interfaces-open-the-door-to-reliable-high-tech-systems/

10. Sánchez, C., et al.: A survey of challenges for runtime verification from advanced application domains (beyond software). Formal Methods Syst. Des. **54**(3), 279–335 (2019). https://doi.org/10.1007/s10703-019-00337-w

11. Schuts, M., Hooman, J., Kurtev, I., Swagerman, D.J.: Reverse engineering of legacy software interfaces to a model-based approach. In: Proceedings of the 2018 Federated Conference on Computer Science and Information Systems (FedCSIS 2018). Annals of Computer Science and Information Systems (ACSIS), vol. 15, pp. 867–876 (2018)

12. Schuts, M., Swagerman, D.J., Kurtev, I., Hooman, J.: Improving interface specifications with ComMA. Bits & Chips, 14 September 2017. https://bits-chips.nl/artikel/improving-interface-specifications-with-comma/

13. Stockmann, L., Laux, S., Bodden, E.: Architectural runtime verification. In: IEEE International Conference on Software Architecture Companion, ICSA Companion 2019, Hamburg, Germany, 25–26 March 2019, pp. 77–84. IEEE (2019). https://doi.org/10.1109/ICSA-C.2019.00021

A Basic Compositional Model for Spiking Neural Networks

Nancy Lynch[1(✉)] and Cameron Musco[2]

[1] Department of Electrical Engineering and Computer Science,
Massachusetts Institute of Technology, Cambridge, USA
lynch@csail.mit.edu
[2] Department of Computer Science, University of Massachusetts, Amherst, USA

Abstract. We present a formal, mathematical foundation for modeling and reasoning about the behavior of *synchronous, stochastic Spiking Neural Networks (SNNs)*, which have been widely used in studies of neural computation. Our approach follows paradigms established in the field of concurrency theory.

Our SNN model is based on directed graphs of neurons, classified as input, output, and internal neurons. We focus here on basic SNNs, in which a neuron's only state is a Boolean value indicating whether or not the neuron is currently firing. We also define the *external behavior* of an SNN, in terms of probability distributions on its external firing patterns. We define two operators on SNNs: a *composition operator*, which supports modeling of SNNs as combinations of smaller SNNs, and a *hiding operator*, which reclassifies some output behavior of an SNN as internal. We prove results showing how the external behavior of a network built using these operators is related to the external behavior of its component networks. Finally, we definition the notion of a *problem* to be solved by an SNN, and show how the composition and hiding operators affect the problems that are solved by the networks.

We illustrate our definitions with three examples: a Boolean circuit constructed from gates, an *Attention* network constructed from a *Winner-Take-All* network and a *Filter* network, and a toy example involving combining two networks in a cyclic fashion.

Keywords: Spiking Neural Networks · Composition of networks · Compositionality

1 Introduction

Understanding computation in biological neural networks like the human brain is a central challenge of modern neuroscience and artificial intelligence. One

This work was supported by NSF awards CCF-1810758, CCF-2139936, CCF-2003830, CCF-2046235, and CCF-1763618. Musco was also partially supported by an Adobe Research grant.

N. Jansen et al. (Eds.): Vaandrager Festschrift 2022, LNCS 13560, pp. 403–449, 2022.
https://doi.org/10.1007/978-3-031-15629-8_22

approach to this challenge uses algorithmic methods from theoretical computer science. That means defining formal computational models for brain networks, identifying abstract problems that can be solved by such networks, and defining and analyzing algorithms that solve these problems. Work along these general lines includes that of Valiant, Navlakha, Papadimitriou, and their collaborators (see, for example, [3,31,38]).

For the past few years, we and our collaborators have been working on an algorithmic theory of brain networks, based on *synchronous, stochastic Spiking Neural Network (SNN) models*. SNNs are a model for neural computation that includes many important biologically-plausible features, yet is still simple enough to study theoretically. An SNN is a directed graph of neurons, in which each neuron fires in discrete spikes, in response to a sufficiently high membrane potential. The potential is induced by spikes from neighboring neurons, which can be either excitatory or inhibitory, increasing or decreasing the incoming potential. In our SNNs, the neurons operate in synchronous rounds, and make firing decisions stochastically. Inspired by tasks that are solved in actual brains, we have been defining and studying abstract problems to be solved by our SNNs. So far, we have developed models and networks for the *Winner-Take-All* problem from computational neuroscience [15,17,30,34], problems of neural coding and similarity detection [6,16], problems of spatial representation of temporal information [7,40], and problems involving learning [1,2,14,39]. We are continuing to study many other problems and networks, including both static networks and networks that learn.

In our work so far, we have defined formal models in each paper, as needed. Here we define a more general computational model for SNNs that we hope will provide a useful foundation for formal modeling of many networks and formal reasoning about their behavior. Note that this model is not the most general one that will be needed, but we believe that it will prove to be a useful first step. In particular, in the basic version of the SNN model defined here, a neuron's only state is a Boolean value indicating whether or not the neuron is currently firing. This is sufficient to model some algorithms, such as the simple two-inhibitor Winner-Take-All network in [17]. Other algorithmic work uses variants of the basic model with more elaborate state such as limited local history, or flags that enable certain behavior such as learning [14,34]; we expect that the results of this paper should be extendable to these variants as well, but this remains to be worked out. We also define an *external behavior notion* for SNNs, in terms of probability distributions on its external firing patterns. This can be used for stating requirements to be satisfied by the networks.

We then define a *composition operator* for SNNs, which supports modeling of SNNs as combinations of smaller SNNs. We prove that our external behavior notion is *compositional*, in the sense that the external behavior of a composed network depends only on the external behaviors of the component networks and not their internal operation. We also define a *hiding operator* that reclassifies some output behavior of an SNN as internal, and show that the behavior of a network obtained by hiding depends only on that of the original network.

A common use of hiding is after composition, when some of the interactions between the composed networks might be suppressed in the external behavior.

Finally, we give a formal definition of a *problem* to be solved by an SNN, and give basic results showing how the composition and hiding operators affect the problems that are solved by the networks. We illustrate our definitions with three examples: a Boolean circuit constructed from neurons that act as logical gates, an *Attention* network constructed from a *Winner-Take-All* network and a *Filter* network, and a toy example involving combining two networks in a cyclic fashion.

Related Work: The general approach of this paper—defining formal models and operators and proving that the operators respect network behavior—is based on the paradigms of the research area of *concurrency theory* [5]. Our particular definitions are inspired by prior work on Input/Output Automata models [8, 18–23, 33], including timed, hybrid and probabilistic variants.

Our focus on SNNs was partly inspired by research of Maass, et al. [24–26] on the computational power of SNNs. Maass explored how features like randomness [27], temporal coding [28], and dynamic edge weights [11] affect the computational power and efficiency of neural network models. Maass's work differs from ours in that he mostly considers asynchronous models that allow fine-grained control of spike timing—models with significantly different computing power from ours.

An early synchronous neural network model is the *perceptron model*, based on a neuron model invented by McCulloch and Pitts [29]. The neurons are modeled as deterministic linear threshold elements, without any stochastic behavior as in our neurons. These elements are assembled into feedforward, layered networks, whereas our networks are arbitrary directed graphs. Another difference with respect to our basic model is that, in perceptron networks, real values can be passed along edges between layers, whereas we use a binary activation function. Perceptron networks are generally used to implement supervised algorithms for learning to recognize patterns.

Work by Valiant, Navlakha, Papadimitriou, and collaborators [3,31,38], is based on a variety of synchronous neural network models. These models are not presented as general compositional models in the style of concurrency theory. However, they appear to be compatible with (extended versions of) our model. Some differences between these models and our basic model are: Valiant [38] includes elaborate state changes, rather than just simple binary firing decisions; Papadimitriou [31] and Navlakha [3] assume built-in Winner-Take-All mechanisms; and Valiant and Papadimitriou focus on learning.

In recent work, Berggren and his group are developing a hardware implementation of a Spiking Neural Network model using nanowires [35,36]. They have developed a simulator for their implementation, based on the basic SNN model presented in this paper [12].

Paper Organization: Section 2 contains our definitions for Spiking Neural Networks and their external behavior. Section 3 contains our definitions for the composition operator for SNNs. Section 4 focuses on the special case of acyclic composition, in which connections between SNNs go in only one direction; we prove a compositionality theory for this case. Section 5 extends these ideas to the more general case of composition that allows connections in both directions. Section 6 introduces the hiding operator for SNNs. Section 7 introduces our notion of a problem to be solved by an SNN. We conclude in Sect. 8.

2 The Spiking Neural Network Model

Here we present our model definitions. We first specify the structure of our networks—the neurons and connections between them. Then we describe how the networks execute; this involves defining individual (non-probabilistic) executions and then defining probabilistic behavior. Next we define the external behavior of a network. We illustrate with two fundamental examples: a Boolean circuit and a Winner-Take-All network.

2.1 Network Structure

Assume a universal set U of neuron names. A *firing pattern* for a set $V \subseteq U$ of neuron names is a mapping from V to $\{0, 1\}$. Here, 1 represents "firing" and 0 represents "not firing".

A *Spiking Neural Network*, which we generally refer to as just a *network*, $\mathcal{N}$, consists of:

- N, a subset of U, partitioned into input neurons N_{in}, output neurons N_{out}, and internal neurons N_{int}. We sometimes write N_{ext} as shorthand for $N_{in} \cup N_{out}$, and N_{lc} as shorthand for $N_{out} \cup N_{int}$. (Here, lc stands for "locally controlled", which means "not input"). Each neuron $u \in N_{lc}$ has an associated *bias*, $bias(u) \in \mathbb{R}$; this can be any real number, positive, negative, or 0.
- E, a set of ordered pairs of neurons, i.e., directed edges between neurons, representing synapses. We permit self-loops. Each edge $e = (u, v)$ has a *weight*, $weight(e) = weight(u, v)$, which is a nonzero (positive or negative) real number.
- F_0, an initial firing pattern for the set N_{lc} of non-input neurons; that is, $F_0 : N_{lc} \rightarrow \{0, 1\}$.

We assume that input neurons have no incoming edges, not even self-loops. Output neurons may have incoming or outgoing edges, or both.

Example: Consider the Winner-Take-All network in Fig. 2. The set N of neuron names consists of $N_{in} = \{x_1, \ldots, x_n\}$, $N_{out} = \{y_1, \ldots, y_n\}$, and $N_{int} = \{a_1, a_2\}$. We have $bias(a_1) = .5\gamma$, $bias(a_2) = 1.5\gamma$, and for every i, $bias(y_i) = 3\gamma$, for some positive real γ. E includes an edge from each x_i to its corresponding y_i, an edge in each direction between every a neuron and every y neuron, and a self-loop on each y neuron. Weights of the edges are as depicted in the figure. The initial firing pattern F_0 gives arbitrary Boolean values for the a and y

neurons (technically, each F_0 yields a different network). The initial values of the x neurons are unspecified, indicating that this network can be used with any inputs.

2.2   Executions and Probabilistic Executions

We describe how a network operates, beginning with its ordinary, non-probabilistic executions and then adding probabilistic considerations.

Executions and Traces. We begin by defining a "configuration" of a network, which describes the current states of all neurons. Namely, a *configuration* of a neural network $\mathcal{N}$ is a firing pattern for N, the set of all the neurons in the network. We consider several related definitions:

- An *input configuration* is a firing pattern for the input neurons, N_{in}.
- An *output configuration* is a firing pattern for the output neurons, N_{out}.
- An *internal configuration* is a firing pattern for the internal neurons, N_{int}.
- An *external configuration* is a firing pattern for the input and output neurons, N_{ext}.
- A *non-input configuration* is a firing pattern for the internal and output neurons, N_{lc}.

We define projections of configurations onto subsets of N. Thus, if C is a configuration and M is any subset of N, then $C{\restriction}M$ is the firing pattern for M obtained by projecting C onto the neurons in M. In particular, we have $C{\restriction}N_{in}$ for the projection of C on the input neurons, $C{\restriction}N_{out}$ for the output neurons, $C{\restriction}N_{int}$ for the internal neurons, $C{\restriction}N_{ext}$ for the external neurons, and $C{\restriction}N_{lc}$ for the non-input neurons. More generally, we can define the projection of any firing pattern F for a set $M \subseteq N$ of neurons onto any subset $M' \subseteq M$.

An *initial configuration* is a configuration C such that $C{\restriction}N_{lc} = F_0$. That is, the values for the locally-controlled neurons are as specified by the given initial firing pattern. The values for the input neurons are arbitrary. We consider them to be controlled somehow, from outside the network. For example, they may be output neurons of another network, or may represent sensory inputs to the network.

Now we define formally how a network $\mathcal{N}$ executes; we assume that it operates in synchronous rounds. Namely, an *execution* α of $\mathcal{N}$ is a (finite or infinite) sequence of configurations, $C_0, C_1, \ldots$, where C_0 is an initial configuration.[1] We define the *length* of a finite execution $\alpha = C_0, C_1, \ldots, C_t$, $length(\alpha)$, to be t. As a special case, if α consists of just the initial configuration C_0, then $length(\alpha) = 0$. The *length* of an infinite execution is defined to be ∞.

We define projections of executions onto subsets of the neurons of $\mathcal{N}$. Namely, if $\alpha = C_0, C_1, \ldots$ is an execution of $\mathcal{N}$ and M is any subset of N, then $\alpha{\restriction}M$

---

[1] We place no other restrictions on the general notion of an execution because our basic model does not impose any restriction on possible transitions.

is defined to be the sequence $C_0 \lceil M, C_1 \lceil M, \ldots$. We define an M-execution of $\mathcal{N}$ to be $\alpha \lceil M$ for any execution α of $\mathcal{N}$. We define an *input execution* to be an M-execution where $M = N_{in}$, and similarly for *output execution, internal execution, external execution,* and *locally-controlled execution (or lc-execution)*.

To focus on the external behavior of the network, we define the notion of a "trace". Namely, for an execution α, we write $trace(\alpha)$ as an alternative notation for $\alpha \lceil N_{ext}$, the projection of α on the external neurons. We define a *trace* of $\mathcal{N}$ to be the trace of any execution α of $\mathcal{N}$.

Example: Again, consider the Winner-Take-All network. Suppose that F_0, the initial firing pattern, assigns 0 to all the a neurons and y neurons, that is, none of these fire initially. Then the executions of the network are just all the sequences of configurations in which the starting configuration has values of 0 for all the a and y neurons. The values of the x neurons are arbitrary.

Probabilistic Executions. We define a unique "probabilistic execution" for any particular infinite input execution β_{in}. First, we say that an infinite execution α of the network is *consistent with* β_{in} provided that $\alpha \lceil N_{in} = \beta_{in}$. Also, a finite execution α is *consistent with* β_{in} provided that $\alpha \lceil N_{in}$ is a prefix of β_{in}. Note that all of the (finite and infinite) executions that are consistent with β_{in} have the same initial configuration C_0. This configuration is constructed from the first configuration of β_{in} and the initial non-input firing pattern for the network, F_0.

The probabilistic execution for β_{in} is defined as a probability distribution P on the sample space Ω of infinite executions that are consistent with β_{in}. The σ-algebra of measurable sets is generated from the "cones", each of which is the set of infinite executions in Ω that extend a particular finite execution. Formally, if α is a finite execution that is consistent with β_{in}, then $A(\alpha)$, the *cone of* α, is the set of infinite executions that are consistent with β_{in} and extend α. The other measurable sets in the σ-algebra are obtained by starting with these cones and closing under countable union, countable intersection, and complement.

Now we define the probabilities for the measurable sets. We start by explicitly defining the probabilities for the cones, $P(A(\alpha))$. Based on these, we can derive the probabilities of the other measurable sets in a unique way, using general measure extension theorems. For example, Segala presents a similar construction for probabilistic executions in his PhD thesis, Chapter 4 [32].

We compute the probabilities $P(A(\alpha))$ recursively based on the length of α (we assume here that α is consistent with β_{in}):

1. α is of length 0.
   Then α consists of just the initial configuration C_0; define $P(A(\alpha)) = 1$.
2. α is of length t, $t > 0$.
   Let α' be the length-$(t - 1)$ prefix of α. We determine the probability q of extending α' to α. Then the probability $P(A(\alpha))$ is simply $P(A(\alpha')) \times q$.
   Let C be the final configuration of α and C' the final configuration of α'.
   Then for each neuron $u \in N_{lc}$ separately, we use C' and the weights of u's

incoming edges to compute a potential and then a firing probability for neuron u. Specifically, for each u, we first calculate a *potential*, pot_u, defined as

$$pot_u = \sum_{(v,u) \in E} C'(v) weight(v, u) - bias(u).$$

We then convert pot_u to a firing probability p_u using a standard sigmoid function:

$$p_u = \frac{1}{1 + e^{-pot_u/\lambda}},$$

where λ is a positive real number "temperature" parameter.[2] We combine all those probabilities to compute the probability of generating C from C': for each $u \in N_{lc}$ such that $C(u) = 1$, use the calculated probability p_u, and for each $u \in N_{lc}$ for which $C(u) = 0$, use $1 - p_u$. The product

$$\prod_{u \in N_{lc}:C(u)=1} p_u \times \prod_{u \in N_{lc}:C(u)=0} (1 - p_u)$$

is the probability of generating C from C', which is the probability q of extending α' to α.

Example: Continuing with the Winner-Take-All network in Fig. 2, suppose again that F_0 assigns 0 to all the non-input neurons. Consider this network with the input configuration that assigns 1 to x_1 and 0 to all the other x_i neurons. Suppose that $\gamma = \lambda = 1$. We compute the probability that y_1 fires. The potential for neuron y_1 is $1 \times 3 - 3 = 0$, and the firing probability calculated from this using the standard sigmoid function is .50. For any other y neurons, we get potential $0 \times 3 - 3 = -3$, yielding a firing probability of .05.

We will often consider conditional probabilities of the form $P(A(\alpha_1)|A(\alpha_2))$. Because we use a sigmoid function, we know that $P(A(\alpha_2))$ cannot be 0, and so this conditional probability is well-defined.[3] The following lemma is straightforward.

Lemma 1. *Let α_1 and α_2 be finite executions of $\mathcal{N}$ that are consistent with β_{in}.*

1. *If neither α_1 nor α_2 is an extension of the other, that is, if they are incomparable, then $P(A(\alpha_1)|A(\alpha_2)) = 0$.*
2. *If α_1 is an extension of α_2, then $P(A(\alpha_1)|A(\alpha_2)) = \frac{P(A(\alpha_1))}{P(A(\alpha_2))}$.*

Lemma 1 shows how we can compute the conditional probabilities from the absolute probabilities. Conversely, we can compute the absolute probabilities from the conditional ones, as follows.

---

[2] This function is called the sigmoid function because of its S-shape, monotonically mapping the real line to the interval $[0, 1]$. Although we assume a standard sigmoid function, the results of this paper would also work with other S-shaped functions.

[3] One useful property of standard sigmoid functions is that the probabilities are never exactly 0 or 1, so we don't need to worry about 0-probability sets when conditioning.

Lemma 2. *Let α be a length-t execution of $\mathcal{N}$, $t > 0$, and suppose that α is consistent with β_{in}. Let α_i, $0 \leq i \leq t$ be the successive prefixes of α (so that α_0 consists of the initial configuration C_0 and $\alpha_t = \alpha$). Then*

$$P(A(\alpha)) = P(A(\alpha_1)|A(\alpha_0)) \times P(A(\alpha_2)|A(\alpha_1)) \cdots \times P(A(\alpha_t)|A(\alpha_{t-1})).$$

Notice in the above expression, we did not start with a term for $P(A(\alpha_0))$. This is not needed because we are considering only executions in which α_0 is obtained from β_{in} and the initial assignment F_0. So $P(A(\alpha_0)) = 1$. Also note that each of the conditional terms is simply a one-step transition probability, which can be calculated using the potential as described above.

Since we can compute the conditional and absolute probabilities from each other, either can be used to characterize the probabilistic execution.

Tree Representation: The probabilistic execution for β_{in} can be visualized as an infinite tree of configurations, where the tree nodes at level t represent the configurations that might occur at time t (with the given input execution β_{in}). The configuration at the root of the tree is the initial configuration C_0. Each infinite branch of the tree represents an infinite execution of the network, and finite initial portions of branches represent finite executions. Note that the same configuration can appear many times at different vertices of the tree.

If α is a finite branch in the tree, then $P(A(\alpha))$ is the probability that an infinite execution will be in the "cone" of executions that begin with α. We can associate the probability $P(A(\alpha))$ with the node at the end of the finite branch—this is simply the probability of reaching the node during probabilistic operation of the network, using the inputs from β_{in}.

Probabilities for Projected Executions. We extend the $A(\alpha)$ notation so that it applies to projections of finite executions, not just complete finite executions. Namely, suppose that M is any subset of the neurons N of $\mathcal{N}$, and γ is a finite M-execution of $\mathcal{N}$. Then we say that γ is *consistent with* β_{in} provided that $\gamma \lceil M \cap N_{in} = \beta_{in} \lceil M \cap N_{in}$. (This definition is equivalent to our earlier definition of consistency in Sect. 2.2, for the special case where $M = N$.) In this case, we write $A(\gamma)$ for the set consisting of all infinite executions α of $\mathcal{N}$ that are consistent with β_{in} such that γ is a prefix of $\alpha \lceil M$. We have:

Lemma 3. *Let M be any subset of the neurons N of $\mathcal{N}$, and let γ be a finite M-execution of $\mathcal{N}$ that is consistent with β_{in}. Then, letting α range over the set of finite executions that are consistent with β_{in} and such that $\alpha \lceil M = \gamma$:*

1.

$$A(\gamma) = \bigcup_\alpha A(\alpha).$$

2.

$$P(A(\gamma)) = \sum_\alpha P(A(\alpha)).$$

As an important special case, we consider $M = N_{ext}$, so that γ is specialized to a finite external execution β of $\mathcal{N}$; that is, we consider projections on the external neurons. Then our definition says that β is *consistent with* β_{in} provided that $\beta \lceil N_{in} = \beta_{in}$. In this case, we get:

Lemma 4. *Let β be a finite trace of $\mathcal{N}$ that is consistent with β_{in}. Then, letting α range over the set of finite executions that are consistent with β_{in} and such that $trace(\alpha) = \beta$:*

1.
$$A(\beta) = \bigcup_\alpha A(\alpha).$$

2.
$$P(A(\beta)) = \sum_\alpha P(A(\alpha)).$$

We remark that the probabilities for finite executions and traces depend only on their projections on the locally-controlled neurons, since the input execution is always β_{in}.

Lemma 5. *1. Suppose that α is a finite execution of $\mathcal{N}$ that is consistent with β_{in}. Then $A(\alpha) = A(\alpha \lceil N_{lc})$ and $P(A(\alpha)) = P(A(\alpha \lceil N_{lc}))$.*
2. Suppose that β is a finite trace of $\mathcal{N}$ that is consistent with β_{in}. Then $A(\beta) = A(\beta \lceil N_{out})$ and $P(A(\beta)) = P(A(\beta \lceil N_{out}))$.

Now we give some simple lemmas involving the probabilities for finite executions and related finite traces. In the following lemma, the conditional probability statements follow directly from the subset statements.

Lemma 6. *Let α be a finite execution of $\mathcal{N}$ that is consistent with β_{in}. Suppose that α' is a prefix of α. Let $\beta = trace(\alpha) = \alpha \lceil N_{ext}$ and $\beta' = trace(\alpha') = \alpha' \lceil N_{ext}$. Then α', β, and β' are also consistent with β_{in}, and*

1. $A(\alpha) \subseteq A(\beta)$, and $P(A(\alpha)|A(\beta)) = \frac{P(A(\alpha))}{P(A(\beta))}$.
2. $A(\alpha) \subseteq A(\alpha')$, and $P(A(\alpha)|A(\alpha')) = \frac{P(A(\alpha))}{P(A(\alpha'))}$.
3. $A(\alpha) \subseteq A(\beta')$, and $P(A(\alpha)|A(\beta')) = \frac{P(A(\alpha))}{P(A(\beta'))}$.
4. $A(\alpha') \subseteq A(\beta')$, and $P(A(\alpha')|A(\beta')) = \frac{P(A(\alpha'))}{P(A(\beta'))}$.
5. $A(\beta) \subseteq A(\beta')$, and $P(A(\beta)|A(\beta')) = \frac{P(A(\beta))}{P(A(\beta'))}$.

Consequences of the previous lemmas include the following, which is used in Sect. 5.2.

Lemma 7. *Let α, α', β, and β' be as in Lemma 6. Then*

1. $P(A(\alpha)|A(\beta')) = P(A(\alpha)|A(\beta)) \times P(A(\beta)|A(\beta'))$.
2. $P(A(\alpha)|A(\beta')) = P(A(\alpha)|A(\alpha')) \times P(A(\alpha')|A(\beta'))$.

We also give a lemma about repeated conditioning, as for probabilistic executions:

Lemma 8. *Let β be a length-t trace of $\mathcal{N}$, $t > 0$, and suppose that β is consistent with β_{in}. Let β_i, $0 \le i \le t$, be the successive prefixes of β (so that β_0 consists of the initial configuration C_0 projected on N_{ext} and $\beta_t = \beta$). Then*

$$P(A(\beta)) = P(A(\beta_1)|A(\beta_0)) \times P(A(\beta_2)|A(\beta_1)) \cdots \times P(A(\beta_t)|A(\beta_{t-1})).$$

As before, we do not need a separate term for $P(A(\beta_0))$, because we are considering only traces in which β_0 is obtained from β_{in} and the initial assignment F_0. So $P(A(\beta_0)) = 1$.

Probabilistic Traces. The previous definitions allow us to define a unique "probabilistic trace" for any particular infinite input execution β_{in}. The *probabilistic trace* for β_{in} is defined as a new probability distribution Q, this one on the sample space Ω' of infinite traces β that are consistent with β_{in}. All of these traces have the same initial configuration, constructed from the first configuration of β_{in} and the initial output firing pattern for the network, $F_0 \lceil N_{out}$.

The basic measurable sets are the sets of infinite traces in Ω' that extend a particular finite trace. Formally, if β is a particular finite trace that is consistent with β_{in}, then $B(\beta)$, the "cone" of β, is the set of infinite traces β that are consistent with β_{in} and extend β. Equivalently, $B(\beta)$ is just the set $traces(A(\beta))$. Again, the other measurable sets in the σ-algebra are obtained by starting with these cones and closing under countable union, countable intersection, and complement.

We define the probabilities for the cones, $Q(B(\beta))$, based on the corresponding probabilities for the probabilistic execution for β_{in}. Namely, if β is a finite trace of $\mathcal{N}$ that is consistent with β_{in}, then we define $Q(B(\beta))$ to be simply $P(A(\beta))$. As before, we can use these probabilities to derive the probabilities of the other measurable sets in a unique way, using general measure extension theorems as in [32].

2.3   External Behavior of a Network

So far we have talked about individual probabilistic traces, each of which depends on a fixed input execution β_{in}. Now we define a notion of *external behavior* of a network, which is intended to capture its visible behavior for all possible inputs. In Sects. 4 and 5, we will show that our notion of external behavior is *compositional*, which means that the external behavior of the composition of two networks, $\mathcal{N}^1 \times \mathcal{N}^2$, is uniquely determined by the external behavior of $\mathcal{N}^1$ and the external behavior of $\mathcal{N}^2$.

Our definition of external behavior is based on the entire collection of probabilities for the cones of all finite traces. Namely, the external behavior $Beh(\mathcal{N})$ is the mapping f that maps each infinite input execution β_{in} of $\mathcal{N}$ to the collection of probabilities $\{P(A(\beta))\}$ determined by the probabilistic execution for

β_{in}. Here, β ranges over the set of finite traces of $\mathcal{N}$ that are consistent with β_{in}.[4] In terms of probabilistic traces, this is the same as the collection $\{Q(B(\beta))\}$, where β has the same range.

Alternative Behavior Definitions: Other definitions of external behavior are possible. Any such definition would have to assign some "behavior object" to each network $\mathcal{N}$.

In general, we define two external behavior notions Beh_1 and Beh_2 to be *equivalent* provided that the following holds. Suppose that $\mathcal{N}$ and $\mathcal{N}'$ are two networks with the same input neurons and the same output neurons. Then $Beh_1(\mathcal{N}) = Beh_1(\mathcal{N}')$ if and only if $Beh_2(\mathcal{N}) = Beh_2(\mathcal{N}')$.

Here we define one alternative behavior notion, based on one-step conditional probabilities. This will be useful in our proofs for compositionality in Sect. 5. Namely, we define $Beh_2(\mathcal{N})$ to be the mapping f_2 that maps each infinite input execution β_{in} to the collection of conditional probabilities $\{P(A(\beta)|A(\beta'))\}$ based on the probabilistic execution for β_{in}. Here, β ranges over the set of finite traces of $\mathcal{N}$ with length > 0 that are consistent with β_{in}, and β' is the one-step prefix of β.

Lemma 9. *The two behavior notions Beh and Beh_2 are equivalent.*

Proof. Suppose that $\mathcal{N}$ and $\mathcal{N}'$ are two networks with the same input neurons and the same output neurons. We show that Beh and Beh_2 are equivalent by arguing the two directions separately:

1. If $Beh(\mathcal{N}) = Beh(\mathcal{N}')$ then $Beh_2(\mathcal{N}) = Beh_2(\mathcal{N}')$.
   This follows because the conditional probability $P(A(\beta)|A(\beta'))$ is determined by the unconditional probabilities $P(A(\beta))$ and $P(A(\beta'))$; see Lemma 6.
2. If $Beh_2(\mathcal{N}) = Beh_2(\mathcal{N}')$ then $Beh(\mathcal{N}) = Beh(\mathcal{N}')$.
   This follows because the unconditional probability $P(A(\beta))$ is determined by the conditional probabilities, see Lemma 8.   □

2.4   Examples

In this subsection we give two fundamental examples to illustrate our definitions so far: some simple Boolean gate networks, and a network implementing the "Winner-Take-All" mechanism from computational neuroscience [9,10,37].

Simple Boolean Gate Networks. Figure 1 depicts the structure of simple Spiking Neural Networks in our model that represent and-gates, or-gates, and not-gates. For completeness, we also include an SNN representing the identity computation.

---

[4] Formally, this "collection" is the mapping from finite traces β that are consistent with β_{in} to the probabilities $P(A(\beta))$. Thus, in terms of data types, $Beh(\mathcal{N})$ is a nested mapping: a mapping from the set of input executions to the set of mappings from the set of finite traces consistent with β_{in} to the set $[0, 1]$.

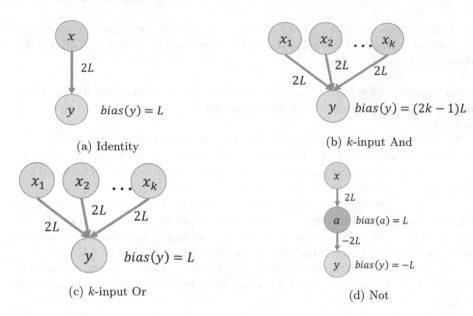

Fig. 1. Networks representing simple Boolean gates; here $L = \lambda \ln(\frac{1-\delta}{\delta})$, where δ is the error probability.

We describe the operation of each of these types of networks, in turn. Fix a positive real number λ for the temperature parameter of the sigmoid function. Fix an error probability δ, $0 < \delta < 1$. For each network below, let the initial firing pattern F_0 assign 0 to each locally controlled neuron.

Throughout this section, we use the abbreviation L for the quantity $\lambda \ln(\frac{1-\delta}{\delta})$; note that L may be any real number, but we focus on the case where $\delta \leq \frac{1}{2}$, which makes L non-negative. We use the following identities repeatedly:

$$e^{L/\lambda} = \frac{1-\delta}{\delta}, \frac{1}{1+e^{L/\lambda}} = \delta, \text{ and } \frac{1}{1+e^{-L/\lambda}} = 1-\delta.$$

Identity Network: The Identity network has one input neuron x and one output neuron y, connected by an edge with weight w. The output neuron y has bias b. Here we define $b = L$ and $w = 2L$.

With these settings, we get potential $w - b = 2L - L = L$ and (expanding L, plugging into the sigmoid function, and using the calculations above) output firing probability $1 - \delta$, in the case where the input fires. Similarly, we get potential $-b = -L$ and output firing probability δ, in the case where the input does not fire. Combining these two claims, consider the firing state of x at time 0. Whether it is 0 or 1, the probability that y's firing state at time 1 is the same as x's firing state at time 0 is exactly $1 - \delta$.

Now consider what happens with an arbitrary infinite input execution β_{in}, rather than just one input, that is, consider the probabilistic execution for β_{in}. Let β be a finite trace of length $t \geq 1$ that is consistent with β_{in}; by our assumption about F_0, β must include an initial firing state of 0 for the output neuron y. Suppose further that β has the property that, for every t', $1 \leq t' \leq t$, the firing state of y at time t' is equal to the firing state of x at time $t' - 1$. Then by repeated use of the argument above, we get that $P(A(\beta)) = (1 - \delta)^t$.

Now suppose, as above, that β is a length t trace, $t \geq 1$, that is consistent with β_{in}. But now suppose that, in β, the firing state of y at time t is equal to the firing state of x at time $t - 1$, but the firing states of y for all earlier times are arbitrary. Let β' denote the one-step prefix of β. Then we can show that $P(A(\beta)|A(\beta')) = 1 - \delta$. It follows that, for every time $t \geq 1$, the probability that the firing state of y at time t is equal to the firing state of x at time $t - 1$ is $1 - \delta$. This uses the law of Total Probability, considering all the possible length $t - 1$ traces that are consistent with β_{in}.

We also describe the external behavior Beh for this network. Namely, for each β_{in}, we must specify the collection of probabilities $P(A(\beta))$, where β ranges over the set of finite traces of the network that are consistent with β_{in}. In this case, for each such β of length t, the probability $P(A(\beta))$ is simply $(1-\delta)^a \delta^{t-a}$, where a is the number of positions t', $1 \leq t' \leq t$, for which y's firing state in β at time t' is equal to x's firing state in β at time $t' - 1$.

k-*Input And Network:* The And network has k input neurons, $x_1, x_2, \ldots, x_k$, and one output neuron y. Each input neuron is connected to the output neuron by an edge with weight w. The output neuron has bias b. The Identity network is a special case of this network, where $k = 1$.

The idea here is to treat this as a threshold problem, and set b and w so that being over or under the threshold gives output firing state 1 or 0, respectively, in each case with probability at least $1 - \delta$. For a k-input And network, the output neuron y should fire with probability at least $1 - \delta$ if all k input neurons fire, and with probability at most δ if at most $k - 1$ input neurons fire.

The settings for b and w generalize those for the Identity network. Namely, define $b = (2k - 1)L$ and $w = \frac{2b}{2k-1} = 2L$. When all k input neurons fire, the potential is $kw - b = L$, and (expanding L and plugging into the sigmoid function) the output firing probability is $1 - \delta$. When $k - 1$ input neurons fire, the potential is $(k - 1)w - b = -L$, and the output firing probability is δ. If fewer than $k - 1$ fire, the potential and the output firing probability are smaller. Similar claims about the external behavior Beh for multi-round computations to those we argued for the Identity network also hold for the And network.

k-*Input Or Network:* The Or network has the same structure as the And network. The Or network also generalizes the Identity network, which is the same as the 1-input Or network. Now the output neuron y should fire with probability at least $1 - \delta$ if at least one of the input neurons fires, and with probability at most δ if no input neurons fire. This time we set $b = L$ and $w = 2L$. When one input neuron fires, the potential is $w - b = L$ and the output firing probability is $1 - \delta$. When more than one fire, then the potential and the firing probability are greater. When no input neurons fire, the potential is $-b = -L$, and the output firing probability is δ. Again, similar claims about the external behavior for multi-round computations hold for the Or network.

Not Network: The Not network has one input x, one output y, and one internal neuron a, which acts as an inhibitor for the output neuron.[5] The network contains two edges, one from x to a with weight w, and one from a to y with weight w'. The internal neuron a has bias b and the output neuron y has bias b'.

The assembly consisting of the input and internal neurons acts like the Identity network, with settings of b and w as before: $b = L$ and $w = 2L$. So, for example, if we consider just x's firing state at time 0, the probability that a's firing state at time 1 is the same is exactly $1 - \delta$.

Let b', the bias of the output neuron, be $-L$, and let w', the weight of the outgoing edge of the inhibitor, be $-2L$. Then if the internal neuron a fires at time 1, then the output neuron y fires at time 2 with probability δ, and if a does not fire at time 1, then y fires at time 2 with probability $1 - \delta$. This yields probability $1 - \delta$ of correct inhibition, which then yields probability at least $(1 - \delta)^2$ that the output at time 2 gives the correct answer for the Not network.

Similar claims about multi-round computations as before also hold for the Not network, except that the Not network has a delay of 2 instead of 1. More precisely, consider an arbitrary infinite input execution β_{in}, and consider the probabilistic execution for β_{in}. Let β be a finite trace of length $t \geq 2$ that is consistent with β_{in}. Then we know that β must begin with a firing state of 0 for y; suppose also that the firing state of y at time 1 is 1. Suppose further that β has the property that, for every t', $2 \leq t' \leq t$, the firing state of y at time t' is unequal to the firing state of x at time $t' - 2$. Then we claim that $P(A(\beta)) \geq (1 - \delta)^{2(t-1)+1} = (1 - \delta)^{2t-1}$. This is because, with probability $1 - \delta$, the firing state of y at time 1 is equal to 1, and for each of the following times t', $2 \leq t' \leq t$, with probability at least $(1 - \delta)^2$, the firing state of y at time t' is unequal to the firing state of x at time $t' - 2$.

Winner-Take-All Network. Our next example is a simple *Winner-Take-All (WTA)* network for n inputs and n corresponding outputs. It is based on a network presented in [17]. Assume that some nonempty subset of the input neurons fire, in a stable manner. The output firing behavior is supposed to converge to a configuration in which exactly one of the outputs, corresponding to one of the firing inputs, fires. We would like this convergence to occur quickly, in some fairly short time t_c. And we would like the resulting configuration to remain stable for a fairly long time t_s. Figure 2 depicts the structure of the network. There should be edges between every pair (x_i, y_i) with weight 3γ, but these would be messy to draw.

In terms of the notation in this paper, consider any infinite input execution β_{in} in which all the input configurations are the same and at least one input neuron is firing. Consider the probabilistic execution for β_{in}. In [17], we prove that, in this probabilistic execution, for certain values of t_c and t_s, the probability

---

[5] We often classify neurons into two categories: *excitatory neurons*, all of whose outgoing edges have positive weights, and *inhibitory neurons*, whose outgoing edges have negative weights. However, this classification is not needed for the results in this paper.

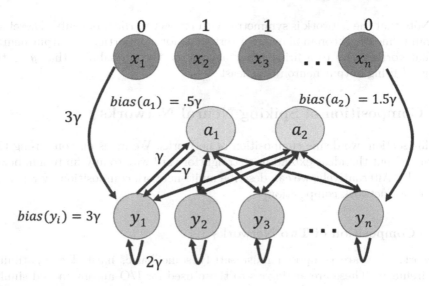

Fig. 2. A basic Winner-Take-All network.

of convergence within time t_c to an output configuration that remains stable for time t_s is at least $1 - \delta$.

The formal theorem statement is as follows. Here, γ is the weighting factor used in the biases and edge weights in the network, δ is a bound on the failure probability, and c_1 and c_2 are particular small constants.

Theorem 1. *Assume* $\gamma \geq c_1 \log(\frac{n t_s}{\delta})$. *Then starting from any configuration, with probability* $\geq 1 - \delta$, *the network converges, within time* $t_c \leq c_2 \log n \log(\frac{1}{\delta})$, *to a single firing output corresponding to a firing input, and remains stable for time* t_s. c_1 *and* c_2 *are universal constants, independent of* n, t_s, *and* δ.

In terms of our model, the desirable executions are determined by what happens in their prefixes ending with time $t_c + t_s - 1$. The correctness condition is that, within this prefix, there is a consecutive sequence of t_s times in which the output neurons exhibit an unchanging firing pattern in which exactly one output y_i fires, and we have $x_i = 1$ in the input configuration. Note that this is a statement about external behavior (traces) only. Correctness can be expressed formally in terms of the probabilities of the cones starting with these desirable traces.

The proof appears in [17]. The basic idea is that, when more than one output is firing, both inhibitors are triggered to fire. When they both fire, they cause each firing output to continue firing with probability $\frac{1}{2}$. This serves to reduce the number of firing outputs at a predictable rate. Once only a single output fires, only one inhibitor continues to fire; its effect is sufficient to prevent other non-firing outputs from beginning to fire, but not sufficient to stop the firing output from firing. All this, of course, is probabilistic.

Note that the network is symmetric with respect to the n outputs. Therefore, we can refine the theorem above to assert that, for any particular output neuron y_i that corresponds to a firing input neuron x_i, the probability that y_i is the eventual firing output neuron is at least $\frac{1-\delta}{n}$.

3   Composition of Spiking Neural Networks

In this section, we define composition of networks. We focus on composing two networks, but the ideas extend in a straightforward way to any finite number of networks. Alternatively, we can describe multi-network composition by repeated use of two-network composition.

3.1   Composition of Two Networks

Networks that are composed must satisfy some basic, natural compatibility requirements. These are analogous to those used for I/O automata and similar models [8,13,23], except that instead of input and output actions, we consider input and output neurons. Namely, two networks $\mathcal{N}^1$ and $\mathcal{N}^2$ are said to be *compatible* provided that:

1. No internal neuron of $\mathcal{N}^1$ is a neuron of $\mathcal{N}^2$.
2. No internal neuron of $\mathcal{N}^2$ is a neuron of $\mathcal{N}^1$.
3. No neuron is an output neuron of both $\mathcal{N}^1$ and $\mathcal{N}^2$.

On the other hand, the two networks may have common input neurons, and output neurons of one network may also be input neurons of the other network.[6]

Lemma 10. *If $\mathcal{N}^1$ and $\mathcal{N}^2$ are compatible, then they do not have any edges in common.*

Proof. Suppose for contradiction that they have a common edge, from a neuron u to a neuron v. Then both u and v belong to both networks. Since v is shared, it must be an input neuron of at least one of the networks, by compatibility. But then that network has an edge leading to one of its input neurons, which is forbidden by our network definition.   □

Assuming $\mathcal{N}^1$ and $\mathcal{N}^2$ are compatible, we define their composition $\mathcal{N} = \mathcal{N}^1 \times \mathcal{N}^2$ as follows:

- N, the set of neurons of $\mathcal{N}$, is the union of N^1 and N^2, which are the sets of neurons of $\mathcal{N}^1$ and $\mathcal{N}^2$ respectively. Note that common neurons are included only once in the set N.
  In network $\mathcal{N}$, each neuron retains its classification as input/output/internal from its sub-network, except that a neuron that is an input of one sub-network

---

[6] In the brain setting, common input neurons for two different networks seem to make sense: a neuron might have two different sets of outgoing edges (synapses), leading to different sets of neurons in the two networks.

and output of the other gets classified as an output neuron of $\mathcal{N}$. In particular, an output neuron of one sub-network that is also an input neuron of the other sub-network remains an output neuron of $\mathcal{N}$.[7]

Each non-input neuron in $\mathcal{N}$ inherits its *bias* from its original sub-network. This definition of bias is unambiguous: if a neuron belongs to both sub-networks, it must be an input of at least one of them, and input neurons do not have biases.

- E, the set of edges of $\mathcal{N}$, is defined as follows. If e is an edge from neuron u to neuron v in either $\mathcal{N}^1$ or $\mathcal{N}^2$, then we include e also in $\mathcal{N}$; these are the only edges in $\mathcal{N}$.

Each edge inherits its weight from its original sub-network. This definition of weight is unambiguous, by Lemma 10.

Thus, if the source neuron u is an input of both sub-networks, then in $\mathcal{N}$, u has edges to all the nodes to which it has edges in $\mathcal{N}^1$ and $\mathcal{N}^2$. If u is an output of one sub-network, say $\mathcal{N}^1$, and an input of the other, $\mathcal{N}^2$, then in $\mathcal{N}$, it has all the incoming and outgoing edges it has in $\mathcal{N}^1$ as well as the outgoing edges it has in $\mathcal{N}^2$.

On the other hand, the target neuron v cannot be an input of both networks since it has an incoming edge in one of them. So v must be an output of one, say $\mathcal{N}^1$, and an input of the other, $\mathcal{N}^2$. Then in $\mathcal{N}$, v has all the incoming and outgoing edges it had in $\mathcal{N}^1$ as well as the outgoing edges it has in $\mathcal{N}^2$.

- F_0, the initial non-input firing pattern of $\mathcal{N}$, gets inherited directly from the two sub-networks' initial non-input firing patterns. Since the two sub-networks have no non-input neurons in common, this is well-defined.

The probabilistic executions and probabilistic traces of the new network $\mathcal{N}$ are defined in the usual way, as in Sect. 2. In Sects. 4 and 5, we show how to relate these to the probabilistic executions and probabilistic traces of $\mathcal{N}^1$ and $\mathcal{N}^2$.

Here are some basic lemmas analogous to those in Sect. 2.2. For these lemmas, fix $\mathcal{N} = \mathcal{N}^1 \times \mathcal{N}^2$ and a particular input execution β_{in} of $\mathcal{N}$, which yields a particular probabilistic execution P. Recall that we use the notation N^j for the set of neurons of $\mathcal{N}^j$, $j \in \{1,2\}$.

Lemma 11. *Let α be a finite execution of $\mathcal{N}$ that is consistent with β_{in}. Suppose that α' is a prefix of α. Let $\beta = trace(\alpha) = \alpha \lceil N_{ext}$ and $\beta' = trace(\alpha') = \alpha' \lceil N_{ext}$.*

Let $j \in \{1,2\}$. Let $\alpha^j = \alpha \lceil N^j$, $\alpha'^j = \alpha' \lceil N^j$, $\beta^j = \beta \lceil N^j$, and $\beta'^j = \beta' \lceil N^j$. Then α^j, α'^j, β^j, and β'^j are also consistent with β_{in}, and

1. *$A(\alpha^j) \subseteq A(\beta^j)$, and $P(A(\alpha^j)|A(\beta^j)) = \frac{P(A(\alpha^j))}{P(A(\beta^j))}$.*
2. *$A(\alpha^j) \subseteq A(\alpha'^j)$, and $P(A(\alpha^j)|A(\alpha'^j)) = \frac{P(A(\alpha^j))}{P(A(\alpha'^j))}$.*
3. *$A(\alpha^j) \subseteq A(\beta'^j)$, and $P(A(\alpha^j)|A(\beta'^j)) = \frac{P(A(\alpha^j))}{P(A(\beta'^j))}$.*

---

[7] In Sect. 6, we will introduce a hiding operator that reclassifies some output neurons as internal neurons.

4. $A(\alpha'^j) \subseteq A(\beta'^j)$, and $P(A(\alpha'^j)|A(\beta'^j)) = \frac{P(A(\alpha'^j))}{P(A(\beta'^j))}$.

5. $A(\beta^j) \subseteq A(\beta'^j)$, and $P(A(\beta^j)|A(\beta'^j)) = \frac{P(A(\beta^j))}{P(A(\beta'^j))}$.

As before, the previous lemmas directly imply other properties, such as:

Lemma 12. *Let α^j, α'^j, β^j, and β'^j be as in Lemma 11. Then*

1. $P(A(\alpha^j)|A(\beta'^j)) = P(A(\alpha^j)|A(\beta^j)) \times P(A(\beta^j)|A(\beta'^j))$.

2. $P(A(\alpha^j)|A(\beta'^j)) = P(A(\alpha^j)|A(\alpha'^j)) \times P(A(\alpha'^j)|A(\beta'^j))$.

Now we consider projections on the locally-controlled neurons of one of the networks. We have:

Lemma 13. *Let α be a finite execution of $\mathcal{N}$ that is consistent with β_{in}. Let α' be a prefix of α and $\beta' = trace(\alpha')$. Let $j \in \{1,2\}$. Then*

1. $P(A(\alpha\lceil N_{lc}^j)|A(\alpha'\lceil N^j)) = \frac{P(A(\alpha\lceil N_{lc}^j) \cap A(\alpha'\lceil N^j))}{P(A(\alpha'\lceil N^j))}$.

2. $P(A(\alpha\lceil N_{lc}^j)|A(\beta'\lceil N^j)) = \frac{P(A(\alpha\lceil N_{lc}^j) \cap A(\beta'\lceil N^j))}{P(A(\beta'\lceil N^j))}$.

3. $P(A(\alpha\lceil N_{lc}^j)|A(\beta'\lceil N^j)) = P(A(\alpha\lceil N_{lc}^j)|A(\alpha'\lceil N^j)) \times P(A(\alpha'\lceil N^j)|A(\beta'\lceil N^j))$.

Proof. Parts 1 and 2 are just the definitions of conditional probability, specialized to these sets. For Part 3, note that $A(\alpha\lceil N_{lc}^j) \cap A(\beta'\lceil N^j) = A(\alpha\lceil N_{lc}^j) \cap A(\alpha'\lceil N^j)$, because $\alpha'\lceil N^j$ already determines all the firing states for neurons in N_{lc}^j. Thus, we have that

$$P(A(\alpha\lceil N_{lc}^j)|A(\beta'\lceil N^j)) = \frac{P(A(\alpha\lceil N_{lc}^j) \cap A(\beta'\lceil N^j))}{P(A(\beta'\lceil N^j))}$$

by Part 2, which is equal to

$$\frac{P(A(\alpha\lceil N_{lc}^j) \cap A(\alpha'\lceil N^j))}{P(A(\beta'\lceil N^j))},$$

which is in turn equal to

$$\frac{P(A(\alpha\lceil N_{lc}^j) \cap A(\alpha'\lceil N^j))}{P(A(\alpha'\lceil N^j))} \times \frac{P(A(\alpha'\lceil N^j))}{P(A(\beta'\lceil N^j))}.$$

Part 1 and Lemma 11 then imply that this is equal to

$$P(A(\alpha\lceil N_{lc}^j)|A(\alpha'\lceil N^j)) \times P(A(\alpha'\lceil N^j)|A(\beta'\lceil N^j)),$$

as needed. $\square$

A Special Case: Acyclic Composition: An important special case of composition is acyclic composition, in which edges connect in only one direction, say from network $\mathcal{N}^1$ to network $\mathcal{N}^2$. Formally, we say that a composition is *acyclic* provided that it satisfies the additional compatibility restriction $N_{in}^1 \cap N_{out}^2 = \emptyset$, that is, output neurons of $\mathcal{N}^2$ cannot be input neurons of $\mathcal{N}^1$.

Thus, $\mathcal{N}^1$ may have inputs only from the "outside world", whereas its outputs can connect to $\mathcal{N}^1$, $\mathcal{N}^2$, and the outside world. $\mathcal{N}^2$ may have inputs from the outside world and from $\mathcal{N}^1$, and its outputs can connect only to $\mathcal{N}^2$ and the outside world.

3.2 Examples

Here we give three examples. The first two use acyclic composition, and the third is a toy example that involves cycles.

Boolean Circuits. Figure 3 contains a circuit that is a composition of four Boolean gate circuits of the types described in Sect. 2.4: two And networks, one Or network, and a Not network. We compose these networks into a larger network that is intended to compute an Xor function.

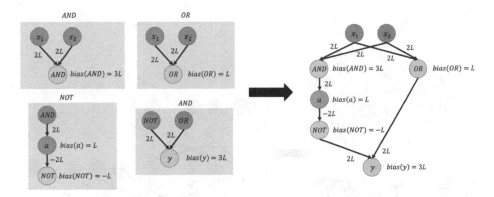

Fig. 3. Composing four Boolean gate circuits into an Xor network

In terms of the binary composition operator, we can compose the four networks in three stages:

1. Compose one of the And networks and the Not network to get a network with two input neurons, two output neurons, and one internal neuron, by identifying the output neuron of the And network with the input neuron of the Not network. Note that the composed network has two output neurons because the And neuron remains an output—the composition operator does not reclassify it as an internal neuron. The composed network is intended to compute the Nand of the two inputs (as well as the And).
2. Compose the network produced in Stage 1 with the Or network to get a 2-input-neuron, 3-output-neuron, 1-internal-neuron network, by identifying the corresponding inputs in the two networks. The resulting network has output neurons corresponding to the Nand and the Or of the two inputs (in addition to the And output neuron).
3. Finally, compose the Nand network and the Or network with the second And network, by identifying the Nand output neuron and the Or output neuron with the two input neurons of the And network. The resulting network has an output neuron corresponding to the Xor of the two original inputs (in addition to outputs for the first And, the Nand, and the Or networks).

To state a simple guarantee for this composed circuit, let us assume that the inputs fire consistently, in an unchanged firing pattern. Then, working from the previously-shown guarantees of the individual networks, we can say that the probability that the final output neuron y produces its required Xor value at time 4 is at least $(1 - \delta)^5$. We revisit this example later, in Sect. 4.2.

Attention Using Winner-Take-All. Figure 4 depicts the composition of our WTA network from Sect. 2.4 with a $2n$-input n output $Filter$ network. The $Filter$ network is, in turn, a composition of n disjoint And gates. The composition is acyclic since information can flow from WTA to $Filter$ but not vice versa.

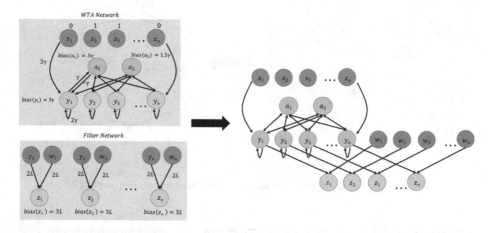

Fig. 4. An *Attention* network built from a WTA network and a $Filter$ network

The $Filter$ network is designed to fire any of its outputs, z_i, right after the corresponding w_i input fires, provided that its y_i input (which is an output of the WTA network) also fires. In this way, the WTA network is used to select particular outputs of the $Filter$ network to fire—those that are "reinforced" by the inputs from the WTA.

Assume that the WTA and $Filter$ networks are composed, and the WTA inputs fire stably, with at least one input firing. Then, as we described in Sect. 2.4, with probability at least $1 - \delta$, the WTA network soon stabilizes to an output configuration with a single firing output y_i, which is equally likely to be any of the n outputs whose corresponding input is firing. That output configuration should persist for a long time. (Specific bounds are given in Theorem 1.)

After the WTA stabilizes, it reinforces only a particular input w_i for the $Filter$. From that point on, the $Filter$'s z_i outputs should mirror its w_i inputs, and no other z outputs should fire. The probability of such mirroring should be at least $(1-\delta')^{nt_s}$, if δ' denotes the failure probability for an And gate. (Recall from Example 2.4 that t_s is the length of the stable period for the WTA's outputs.) In this way, the composition can be viewed as an *Attention* circuit, which pays attention to just a single input stream.

Note that the composed network behaves on two different time scales: the WTA takes some time to converge, but after that, the responses to the selected intput stream will be essentially immediate.

A Toy Example for Cyclic Composition. Now we give a toy example, consisting of two networks, $\mathcal{N}^1$ and $\mathcal{N}^2$, that affect each other's behavior. Throughout this section, we use the abbreviation L for the quantity $\lambda \ln(\frac{1-\delta}{\delta})$, as in Sect. 2.4. We assume that δ is "sufficiently small".

Figure 5 shows a network $\mathcal{N}^1$ with one input neuron x_1, one output neuron x_2, and one internal neuron a_1. It has edges from x_1 to a_1, from a_1 to x_2, and from x_2 to itself (a self-loop). The biases of a_1 and x_2 are L and the weights on all edges are $2L$.

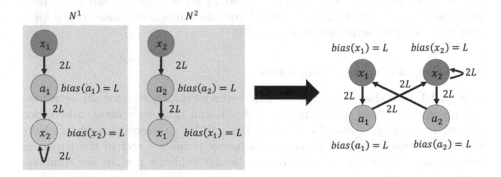

Fig. 5. A cyclic composition

Network $\mathcal{N}^1$ behaves so that, at any time $t \geq 1$, the firing probability for the internal neuron a_1 is exactly $1 - \delta$ if x_1 fires at time $t - 1$, and is exactly δ if x_1 does not fire at time $t - 1$. This is the same as for the output neuron of the Identity network in Sect. 2.4. The firing probability of the output neuron x_2 of $\mathcal{N}^1$ depends on the firing states of both a_1 and x_2 at time $t - 1$. This probability is:

- δ, if neither a_1 nor x_2 fires at time $t - 1$.
- $1 - \delta$, if exactly one of a_1 and x_2 fires at time $t - 1$.
- $1 - \frac{\delta^3}{(1-\delta)^3 + \delta^3}$ if both a_1 and x_2 fire at time $t - 1$.

It follows that, if input x_1 fires at some time t, then output x_2 is likely to fire at time $t + 2$ (with probability at least $(1 - \delta)^2$). Without any additional input firing, and ignoring the low-likelihood spurious firing of a_1, the firing of x_2 is sustained only by the self-loop. This means that the firing probability of x_2 decreases steadily over time, by a factor of $(1 - \delta)$ at each time. Eventually, the firing should "die out".

Network $\mathcal{N}^2$ is similar, replacing x_1, a_1, and x_2 by x_2, a_2, and x_1, respectively. However, we omit the self-loop edge on x_1. The biases are L and the weights on the two edges are $2L$. Network $\mathcal{N}^2$ behaves so that, at any time $t \geq 1$, the firing probability for the internal neuron a_2 is exactly $1 - \delta$ if x_2 fires at time $t - 1$, and is exactly δ if x_2 does not fire at time $t - 1$. Likewise, the firing probability for the output neuron x_1 is exactly $1 - \delta$ if a_2 fires at time $t - 1$ and δ if a_2 does not fire. Thus, if input x_2 fires at some time t, then output x_1 is likely to fire at time $t + 2$ (with probability at least $(1 - \delta)^2$). However, in this case, the firing of x_1 is not sustained.

Now consider the composition $\mathcal{N} = \mathcal{N}^1 \times \mathcal{N}^2$, identifying the output x_2 of $\mathcal{N}^1$ with the input x_2 of $\mathcal{N}^2$, and the output x_1 of $\mathcal{N}^2$ with the input x_1 of $\mathcal{N}^1$. The behavior of $\mathcal{N}$ depends on the initial firing pattern. Assume that neither a_1 nor a_2 fires initially; we consider the behavior for the various starting firing patterns for x_1 and x_2. We consider two cases: If neither x_1 nor x_2 fires at time 0, then with "high probability", none of the four neurons will fire for a long time. On the other hand, If one or both of x_1 and x_2 fire at time 0, then with "high probability", they will trigger all the neurons to fire and continue to fire for a long time. We give some details in Sect. 5.4.

3.3 Compositionality Definitions

In Sect. 2.3, we defined a specific external behavior notion Beh for our networks, and an equivalent alternative notion Beh_2. Recall that, in general, a behavior definition B assigns some "behavior object" $B(\mathcal{N})$ to every network $\mathcal{N}$. Here we define compositionality for general behavior notions. Later in the paper, in Sects. 4 and 5, we will prove that our particular behavior notions are compositional.

In general, we define an external behavior notion B to be *compositional* provided that the following holds: Consider any four networks $\mathcal{N}^1$, $\mathcal{N}^2$, $\mathcal{N}'^1$, and $\mathcal{N}'^2$, where $\mathcal{N}^1$ and $\mathcal{N}'^1$ have the same sets of input and output neurons, $\mathcal{N}^2$ and $\mathcal{N}'^2$ have the same sets of input and output neurons, $\mathcal{N}^1$ and $\mathcal{N}^2$ are compatible, and $\mathcal{N}'^1$ and $\mathcal{N}'^2$ are compatible. Suppose that $B(\mathcal{N}^1) = B(\mathcal{N}'^1)$ and $B(\mathcal{N}^2) = B(\mathcal{N}'^2)$. Then $B(\mathcal{N}^1 \times \mathcal{N}^2) = B(\mathcal{N}'^1 \times \mathcal{N}'^2)$. Said another way:

Lemma 14. *An external behavior notion B is compositional if and only if, for all compatible pairs of networks $\mathcal{N}^1$ and $\mathcal{N}^2$, $B(\mathcal{N}^1 \times \mathcal{N}^2)$ is uniquely determined by $B(\mathcal{N}^1)$ and $B(\mathcal{N}^2)$.*

Now we show that, in general, if two external behavior notions are equivalent and one is compositional, then so is the other. This will provide us with a method that will be helpful in Sect. 5 for showing compositionality.

Theorem 2. *If B and B' are two equivalent external behavior notions for spiking neural networks, and B is compositional, then also B' is compositional.*

Proof. Suppose that B and B' are two external behavior notions and B is compositional. We show that B' is compositional. For this, consider any four networks $\mathcal{N}^1$, $\mathcal{N}^2$, $\mathcal{N}'^1$, and $\mathcal{N}'^2$, where $\mathcal{N}^1$ and $\mathcal{N}'^1$ have the same sets of input and output neurons, $\mathcal{N}^2$ and $\mathcal{N}'^2$ have the same sets of input and output neurons, $\mathcal{N}^1$ and $\mathcal{N}^2$ are compatible, and $\mathcal{N}'^1$ and $\mathcal{N}'^2$ are compatible. Suppose that $B'(\mathcal{N}^1) = B'(\mathcal{N}'^1)$ and $B'(\mathcal{N}^2) = B'(\mathcal{N}'^2)$. We must show that $B'(\mathcal{N}^1 \times \mathcal{N}^2) = B'(\mathcal{N}'^1 \times \mathcal{N}'^2)$.

Since B and B' are equivalent and $B'(\mathcal{N}^1) = B'(\mathcal{N}'^1)$, we have that $B(\mathcal{N}^1) = B(\mathcal{N}'^1)$. Likewise, since $B'(\mathcal{N}^2) = B'(\mathcal{N}'^2)$, we have that $B(\mathcal{N}^2) = B(\mathcal{N}'^2)$. Since B is assumed to be compositional, this implies that $B(\mathcal{N}^1 \times \mathcal{N}^2) = B(\mathcal{N}'^1 \times \mathcal{N}'^2)$. Then since B and B' are equivalent, we get that $B'(\mathcal{N}^1 \times \mathcal{N}^2) = B'(\mathcal{N}'^1 \times \mathcal{N}'^2)$, as needed. □

4 Theorems for Acyclic Composition

Our general composition results appear in Sect. 5. Those are a bit complicated, mainly because of the possibility of connections in both directions between the sub-networks. Acyclic composition is an important special case of general composition; many interesting examples satisfy the acyclic restriction. Since this case can be analyzed more easily, we present this first.

Throughout this section, we fix the notation $\mathcal{N} = \mathcal{N}^1 \times \mathcal{N}^2$, and assume that $N_{in}^1 \cap N_{out}^2 = \emptyset$, that is, there are no edges from $\mathcal{N}^2$ to $\mathcal{N}^1$.

In this section, and from now on in the paper, we will generally avoid writing the cone notation $A()$. Thus, we will abbreviate $P(A(\alpha))$ and $P(A(\beta))$ as just $P(\alpha)$ and $P(\beta)$. We hope that this makes it easier to read complex formulas and does not cause any confusion.

4.1 Compositionality

We have not formally defined "compositionality" for the special case of acyclic composition. So here, we will simply show (Lemma 17) how to express $Beh(\mathcal{N})$ as a function of $Beh(\mathcal{N}^1)$ and $Beh(\mathcal{N}^2)$. Thus (Theorem 3), $Beh(\mathcal{N})$ is uniquely determined by $Beh(\mathcal{N}^1)$ and $Beh(\mathcal{N}^2)$.

Specifically, we fix any particular input execution β_{in} of $\mathcal{N}$, which generates a particular probability distribution P on infinite executions of $\mathcal{N}$. We consider an arbitrary finite trace β of $\mathcal{N}$ that is consistent with β_{in}. We show how to express $P(\beta)$ in terms of probability distributions P^1 and P^2 on infinite executions of $\mathcal{N}^1$ and $\mathcal{N}^2$, respectively. These distributions P^1 and P^2 are defined from certain input executions of $\mathcal{N}^1$ and $\mathcal{N}^2$, respectively.

We begin by deriving a simple expression for $P(\beta)$, for an arbitrary finite trace β of $\mathcal{N}$ that is consistent with β_{in}, in terms of the same probability distribution P on projections of β.

Lemma 15. Let β be a finite trace of $\mathcal{N}$ that is consistent with β_{in}. Then

$$P(\beta) = P(\beta \lceil N_{out}^1) \times P((\beta \lceil N_{out}^2)|(\beta \lceil N_{in}^2)).$$

Proof. Since $\beta \lceil N_{in}$ is fixed, we have that

$$P(\beta) = P(\beta \lceil N_{out}) = P((\beta \lceil (N_{out}^1 \cup N_{out}^2)).$$

This last expression is equal to

$$P(\beta \lceil N_{out}^1) \times P((\beta \lceil N_{out}^2) | (\beta \lceil N_{out}^1))$$

by basic conditional probability reasoning. We have that

$$P((\beta \lceil N_{out}^2) | (\beta \lceil N_{out}^1)) = P((\beta \lceil N_{out}^2) | (\beta \lceil (N_{out}^1 \cap N_{in}^2))),$$

because the behavior of $\mathcal{N}^2$ does not depend on the firing states of neurons in $N_{out}^1 - N_{in}^2$. (That is, the firing behavior of the neurons in N_{out}^2 is independent of the behavior of the neurons in $N_{out}^1 - N_{in}^2$, conditioned on the behavior of the neurons in $N_{out}^1 \cap N_{in}^2$). The right-hand side of this equation is equal to

$$P((\beta \lceil N_{out}^2) | (\beta \lceil (N_{in}^2)))$$

because N_{in}^2 consists of $N_{out}^1 \cap N_{in}^2$ plus some neurons in N_{in}, whose firing states are fixed in β_{in}. Substituting yields

$$P(\beta) = P(\beta \lceil N_{out}^1) \times P((\beta \lceil N_{out}^2) | (\beta \lceil N_{in}^2)),$$

as needed.   □

Thus, Lemma 15 assumes an arbitrary input execution β_{in} of $\mathcal{N}$, which generates a probability distribution P. This lemma expresses $P(\beta)$, for an arbitrary β, in terms of the P-probabilities of other finite traces. However, we are not quite there: Our main goal here is to express $P(\beta)$ in terms of probability distributions P^1 and P^2 that are generated by $\mathcal{N}^1$ and $\mathcal{N}^2$, respectively, from particular infinite input executions for those respective sub-networks. We define these input executions and distributions as follows.

- Input execution β_{in}^1 and distribution P^1 for $\mathcal{N}^1$:
  Define the infinite input execution β_{in}^1 of $\mathcal{N}^1$ to be $\beta_{in} \lceil N_{in}^1$, that is, the projection of the given input execution on the inputs of $\mathcal{N}^1$. Then define P^1 to be the probability distribution that is generated by $\mathcal{N}^1$ from input execution β_{in}^1.
- Input execution β_{in}^2 and distribution P^2 for $\mathcal{N}^2$:
  This is more complicated, since the input to $\mathcal{N}^2$ depends not only on the external input β_{in}, but also on the output produced by $\mathcal{N}^1$. Define the infinite input execution β_{in}^2 of $\mathcal{N}^2$ as follows. First, note that $N_{in}^2 \subseteq N_{in} \cup N_{out}^1$, that is, every input of $\mathcal{N}^2$ is either an input of $\mathcal{N}$ or an output of $\mathcal{N}^1$. Define the firing patterns of the neurons in $N_{in}^2 \cap N_{in}$ using β_{in}, that is, define $\beta_{in}^2 \lceil (N_{in}^2 \cap N_{in}) = \beta_{in} \lceil N_{in}^2$. And for the firing patterns of the neurons in $N_{in}^2 \cap N_{out}^1$, use β, that is, define $\beta_{in}^2 \lceil (N_{in}^2 \cap N_{out}^1) = \beta \lceil (N_{in}^2 \cap N_{out}^1)$ for times $0, \ldots, length(\beta)$ and the default 0 for all later times. (This choice for later times is arbitrary—we just chose 0s to be concrete.) Then define P^2 to be the probability distribution that is generated by $\mathcal{N}^2$ from input execution β_{in}^2.

Note that, in the second case above, the choice of the input execution β_{in}^2 depends on the particular trace β for which we are trying to express the P-probability. This is allowed because the external behavior $Beh(\mathcal{N}^2)$ is defined to specify a probability distribution for *every* individual infinite input execution of $\mathcal{N}^2$.[8]

The next lemma restates the result of Lemma 15 in terms of the new probability distributions P^1 and P^2. The key idea is that the probability P^2 is essentially a conditional probability distribution, giving probabilities for $\mathcal{N}^2$'s outputs, conditioned on its inputs being consistent with β.

Lemma 16. *Let β be a finite trace of $\mathcal{N}$ that is consistent with β_{in}. Then*

$$P(\beta) = P^1(\beta\lceil N_{out}^1) \times P^2(\beta\lceil N_{out}^2).$$

Proof. Fix β, a finite trace of of $\mathcal{N}$ that is consistent with β_{in}. By Lemma 15, we know that:

$$P(\beta) = P(\beta\lceil N_{out}^1) \times P((\beta\lceil N_{out}^2)|(\beta\lceil N_{in}^2)).$$

It suffices to show that these two terms are equal to the corresponding terms in this lemma, that is, that

$$P(\beta\lceil N_{out}^1) = P^1(\beta\lceil N_{out}^1)$$

and

$$P((\beta\lceil N_{out}^2)|(\beta\lceil N_{in}^2)) = P^2(\beta\lceil N_{out}^2).$$

These two statements follow directly by unwinding the definitions of P^1 and P^2, respectively. Specifically, for the first statement, we consider $P(\beta\lceil N_{out}^1)$, the probability that the composed network $\mathcal{N}$ generates an execution that, when projected on outputs of $\mathcal{N}^1$, starts with $\beta\lceil N_{out}^1$. We note that this probability is entirely determined by the sub-network $\mathcal{N}^1$, based on β_{in} projected on the inputs of $\mathcal{N}^1$. But this is just the definition of $P^1(\beta\lceil N_{out}^1)$.

Likewise, though a bit more subtly, for the second statement, we consider $P((\beta\lceil N_{out}^2)|(\beta\lceil N_{in}^2))$, which is the conditional probability that the composed network generates an execution that, when projected on outputs of $\mathcal{N}^2$, starts with $\beta\lceil N_{out}^2$, conditioned on the event that the inputs to $\mathcal{N}^2$ start with $\beta\lceil N_{in}^2$. This time, the probability is entirely determined by the sub-network $\mathcal{N}^2$, based on β projected on the inputs of $\mathcal{N}^2$.[9] But this is just the definition of $P^2(\beta\lceil N_{out}^2)$.

□

---

[8] To elaborate: According to our approach throughout this paper, we get a probability distribution of traces of $\mathcal{N}^2$ by fixing an infinite input execution of $\mathcal{N}^2$. The question here is, which input to choose? The infinite input β_{in} for the entire system $\mathcal{N}$ provides part of the answer, for inputs of $\mathcal{N}^2$ that are also inputs of $\mathcal{N}$. The other part is obtained from β projected on the inputs of $\mathcal{N}^2$ that are outputs of $\mathcal{N}^1$. Technically, we have to pad out β somehow, since we need an infinite input execution, but it doesn't matter how we do this, since the probability that $\mathcal{N}^2$ produces outputs consistent with β depends only on the portion of the input up to $length(\beta)$.

[9] Notice that this probability is entirely determined by the finite input $\beta\lceil N_{in}^2$—the firing states of the input neurons of $\mathcal{N}^2$ after time $length(\beta)$ do not matter.

The next lemma has a slightly simpler statement than Lemma 16.

Lemma 17. *Let β be a finite trace of $\mathcal{N}$ that is consistent with β_{in}. Then*

$$P(\beta) = P^1(\beta\lceil N^1) \times P^2(\beta\lceil N^2).$$

Proof. This follows from Lemma 16 because in each term on the right-hand-side of the equation in this lemma, the probability depends on the output traces only—the input traces are fixed. Formally, this uses Lemma 5.   □

Finally, Lemma 17 yields a kind of compositionality theorem for acyclic composition:

Theorem 3. *Beh($\mathcal{N}$) is determined by Beh($\mathcal{N}^1$) and Beh($\mathcal{N}^2$).*

We prove a more general compositionality result in Sect. 5.

4.2   Examples

We revisit our two examples of acyclic composition from Sects. 3.2 and 3.2, this time analyzing their behavior more precisely.

Boolean Circuits. Let $\mathcal{N}$ be the seven-neuron Boolean circuit from Sect. 3.2. Express $\mathcal{N}$ as the composition $\mathcal{N}^1 \times \mathcal{N}^2$, where

- $\mathcal{N}^1$ is the network resulting from the first two stages in the order of compositions described in Sect. 3.2. This computes Nand and Or of the two inputs.
- $\mathcal{N}^2$ is the final And network.

Fix β_{in} to be any infinite input execution of $\mathcal{N}$ with stable inputs, and let P be the probabilistic execution of $\mathcal{N}$ for β_{in}. In P, we should expect to have stable, correct outputs for a long while starting from time 4, because the depth of the entire network is 4. Here we consider just the situation at precisely time 4, that is, we consider the probabilities $P(\beta)$ for finite traces β of length exactly 4. Specifically, we would like to use Lemma 16 to help us show that the probability of a correct Xor output at time 4 is at least $(1 - \delta)^5$.

We work compositionally. In particular, we assume that, in the probabilistic execution of $\mathcal{N}^1$ for β_{in}, or any other stable input sequence, the probability of correct (Nand,Or) outputs at time 3 is at least $(1 - \delta)^4$. We also assume that, in the probabilistic execution of $\mathcal{N}^2$ on any input sequence, the probability that the output at time 4 is the And of its two inputs at time 3 is at least $1 - \delta$. We could prove these bounds for our two specific networks $\mathcal{N}^1$ and $\mathcal{N}^2$, but to emphasize the compositional reasoning, we ignore the internal workings of the two sub-networks and simply state the bounds here. We use these bounds to get our result about the composed network $\mathcal{N}$.

So define B to be the set of traces β of $\mathcal{N}$ of length 4 such that β gives a correct Xor output at time 4, as well as correct (Nand, Or) outputs at time 3. (These traces may differ in their firing states for the And neuron at any time, and also in their firing states for the Not and Or neurons at times other than those specified.) We will argue that $P(B) \geq (1 - \delta)^5$, which implies our desired result.

We have that $P(B) = \sum_{\beta \in B} P(\beta)$. By Lemma 16, this is equal to

$$\sum_{\beta \in B} P^1(\beta \lceil N_{out}^1) \times P^2(\beta \lceil N_{out}^2).$$

Here, P^1 and P^2 are defined as in Sect. 4.1, based on $\beta_{in}^1 = \beta_{in}$, and for each particular β, based on β_{in}^2 equal to $\beta \lceil N_{in}^2$, extended to an infinite sequence by adding 0's. Note that the choice of input sequence β_{in}^2 for $\mathcal{N}^2$ is uniquely determined by $\beta \lceil N_{out}^1$.

We break this expression up into the double summation:

$$\sum_{\beta^1} (\sum_{\beta^2} P^1(\beta^1 \lceil N_{out}^1) \times P^2(\beta^2 \lceil N_{out}^2))$$

Here, β^1 ranges over traces of $\mathcal{N}^1$ that are consistent with β_{in} and yield correct (Nand, Or) outputs at time 3. And for each particular β^1, β^2 ranges over traces of $\mathcal{N}^2$ that are consistent with the input sequence β_{in}^2 determined from $\beta^1 \lceil N_{out}^1 = \beta \lceil N_{out}^1$, and whose output at time 4 is the Xor of its inputs at time 3. This is equal to (collecting terms for each β^1):

$$\sum_{\beta^1} P^1(\beta^1 \lceil N_{out}^1) \sum_{\beta^2} P^2(\beta^2 \lceil N_{out}^2).$$

Now, for any particular β^1, we know that:

$$\sum_{\beta^2} P^2(\beta^2 \lceil N_{out}^2) \geq (1 - \delta),$$

by our assumptions about the behavior of $\mathcal{N}^2$. So the overall expression is at least

$$\sum_{\beta^1} P^1(\beta^1 \lceil N_{out}^1)(1 - \delta) = (1 - \delta) \sum_{\beta^1} P^1(\beta^1 \lceil N_{out}^1).$$

We also know that

$$\sum_{\beta^1} P^1(\beta^1 \lceil N_{out}^1) \geq (1 - \delta)^4,$$

by our assumption about the behavior of $\mathcal{N}^1$. So the overall expression is at least $(1 - \delta)(1 - \delta)^4 = (1 - \delta)^5$, as needed.

Attention Using WTA. We consider the composition of the WTA network and the $Filter$ network, as described in Sect. 3.2. Now let $\mathcal{N}^1$ denote the WTA network, $\mathcal{N}^2$ the $Filter$ network, and $\mathcal{N}$ their composition. We assume that the WTA network satisfies Theorem 1, with particular values of δ, t_c, t_s, γ, c_1 and

c_2. We assume that each And network within *Filter* is correct at each time with probability at least $1 - \delta'$.

Fix β_{in} to be any infinite input execution of $\mathcal{N}$ with stable x_i inputs such that at least one x_i is firing. The w_i inputs are unconstrained. Let P be the probabilistic execution of $\mathcal{N}$ generated from β_{in}. We want to prove that, according to P, with probability at least $(1 - \delta)(1 - \delta')^{nt_s}$, there is some $t \leq t_c$ such that: (a) the y outputs stabilize by time t to one steadily-firing output y_i, which persists through time $t + t_s - 1$, and (b) for this particular i, starting from time $t + 1$ and continuing for a total of t_s times, the z_i outputs correctly mirror the w_i inputs at the previous time, and all the other z neurons do not fire.

Again, we work compositionally. We assume that, in the probabilistic execution of the WTA network $\mathcal{N}^1$ on $\beta_{in} \lceil N_{in}$, the probability of correct, stable outputs as in Theorem 1 is at least $1 - \delta$. We also assume that, in the probabilistic execution of $\mathcal{N}^2$ on any input sequence, conditioned on any finite execution prefix, the probability of correct mirroring of inputs for the next t times is at least $(1 - \delta')^{nt_s}$. These assumptions could be proved for our two networks, but we simply assume them here.

Now define B to be the set of traces β of $\mathcal{N}$ of length $t_c + t_s - 1$ such that all the desired conditions hold in β, that is, there is some $t \leq t_c$ such that in β, (a) the y outputs stabilize by time t to one steadily-firing output y_i, which persists through time $t + t_s - 1$, and (b) for this particular i, starting from time $t + 1$ and continuing for a total of t_s times, the z_i outputs correctly mirror the w_i inputs at the previous time, and all the other z neurons do not fire. We will argue that $P(B) \geq (1 - \delta)(1 - \delta')^{nt_s}$. We follow the same pattern as in the Boolean circuit network example in Sect. 4.2.

We have that $P(B) = \sum_{\beta \in B} P(\beta)$. By Lemma 16, this is equal to

$$\sum_{\beta \in B} P^1(\beta \lceil N_{out}^1) \times P^2(\beta \lceil N_{out}^2).$$

Here, P^1 and P^2 are defined as in Sect. 4.1, based on $\beta_{in}^1 = \beta_{in} \lceil N_{in}^1$ and for each particular β, based on β_{in}^2 equal to $\beta \lceil N_{in}^2$, extended to an infinite sequence by adding 0's. Note that β_{in}^2 is uniquely determined by $\beta \lceil (N_{in} \cup N_{out}^1)$.

This expression is equal to:

$$\sum_{\beta^1} (\sum_{\beta^2} P^1(\beta^1 \lceil N_{out}^1) \times P^2(\beta^2 \lceil N_{out}^2)).$$

Here, β^1 ranges over traces of $\mathcal{N}^1$ that are consistent with β_{in} and for which there is some $t \leq t_c$ such that in β^1, the y outputs stabilize by time t to one steadily-firing output y_i, which persists through time $t + t_s - 1$. And for each particular β^1, β^2 ranges over traces of $\mathcal{N}^2$ that are consistent with the input sequence β_{in}^2 determined from β_{in} and $\beta^1 \lceil N_{out}^1 = \beta \lceil N_{out}^1$, and that satisfy the following correctness condition for $\mathcal{N}^2$: for the first t and associated i that witness the correctness condition for β^1, at times $t + 1, \ldots, t + t_s$, the z_i outputs correctly mirror the w_i inputs at the previous time, and all the other z neurons do not fire.

This is equal to (collecting terms for each β^1):

$$\sum_{\beta^1} P^1(\beta^1 \lceil N_{out}^1) \sum_{\beta^2} P^2(\beta^2 \lceil N_{out}^2).$$

Now, for any particular β^1, we know that:

$$\sum_{\beta^2} P^2(\beta^2 \lceil N_{out}^2) \geq (1 - \delta')^{nt_s},$$

by our assumptions about the behavior of $\mathcal{N}^2$. So the overall expression is at least

$$\sum_{\beta^1} P^1(\beta^1 \lceil N_{out}^1)(1 - \delta')^{nt_s} = (1 - \delta')^{nt_s} \sum_{\beta^1} P^1(\beta^1 \lceil N_{out}^1).$$

We also know that

$$\sum_{\beta^1} P^1(\beta^1 \lceil N_{out}^1) \geq (1 - \delta),$$

by our assumption about the behavior of $\mathcal{N}^1$. So the overall expression is at least $(1 - \delta)(1 - \delta')^{nt_s}$, as needed.

5   Theorems for General Composition

For general composition, the simple approach in Sect. 4 does not work. There, we were able to prove results such as Lemma 15, which decompose the behavior of the entire network $\mathcal{N}$ in terms of the behavior of the two sub-networks $\mathcal{N}^1$ and $\mathcal{N}^2$. This worked because the dependencies between the behaviors go only one way, from $\mathcal{N}^1$ to $\mathcal{N}^2$. In the general case, the dependencies go both ways, potentially leading to circularities.

Fortunately, since we are working in a synchronous model, we can break the circularities in another way, using discrete time. Namely, the behavior of each sub-network at time t depends only on the behavior of the other network at times up to $t - 1$. We exploit this limitation on dependencies to prove decomposition lemmas such as Lemma 19, leading to our main compositionality theorem, Theorem 5.

For this section, fix $\mathcal{N} = \mathcal{N}^1 \times \mathcal{N}^2$. We continue to avoid writing the cone notation $A()$.

5.1   Composition Results for Executions and Traces

For this subsection and the following, fix a particular input execution β_{in} for $\mathcal{N}$, which yields a particular probabilistic execution P. The main result of this subsection is Lemma 19. It says that the probability of a certain finite execution α of the entire network $\mathcal{N}$, conditioned on its trace β, is simply the product of the probabilities of the two projections of α on the two sub-networks, each conditioned on its projected trace. In other words, once we fix all the external behavior of the network, including the part of the behavior involved in interaction between the two sub-networks, the internal states of the neurons within the two sub-networks are determined independently. We begin with a straightforward lemma that treats the two sub-networks asymmetrically.

Lemma 18. *Let α be a finite execution of $\mathcal{N}$ that is consistent with β_{in}, and let $\beta = trace(\alpha)$. Then*

$$P(\alpha|\beta) = P((\alpha\lceil N_{int}^1)|\beta) \times P((\alpha\lceil N_{int}^2)|(\alpha\lceil N_{int}^1), \beta).$$

Proof. Standard conditional probability.   □

And now we remove the asymmetry, by identifying the portions of β on which the internal behavior of the two sub-networks actually depends.

Lemma 19. *Let α be a finite execution of $\mathcal{N}$ that is consistent with β_{in}, and let $\beta = trace(\alpha)$. Then*

$$P(\alpha|\beta) = P((\alpha\lceil N^1)|(\beta\lceil N^1)) \times P((\alpha\lceil N^2)|(\beta\lceil N^2)).$$

Proof. Lemma 18 says that

$$P(\alpha|\beta) = P((\alpha\lceil N_{int}^1)|\beta) \times P((\alpha\lceil N_{int}^2)|(\alpha\lceil N_{int}^1), \beta).$$

It suffices to show both of the following:

1. $P((\alpha\lceil N_{int}^1)|\beta) = P((\alpha\lceil N^1)|(\beta\lceil N^1))$.
   For this, note that

   $$P((\alpha\lceil N_{int}^1)|\beta) = P((\alpha\lceil N^1)|\beta),$$

   because β already includes the firing patterns for all the neurons in $N^1 - N_{int}^1 = N_{ext}^1$. And

   $$P((\alpha\lceil N^1)|\beta) = P((\alpha\lceil N^1)|(\beta\lceil N^1)),$$

   because the firing behavior of neurons in N^1 is independent of the behavior of the neurons in $N - N^1$, conditioned on β. Putting these two facts together yields the needed equality.
2. $P((\alpha\lceil N_{int}^2)|(\alpha\lceil N_{int}^1), \beta) = P((\alpha\lceil N^2)|(\beta\lceil N^2))$.
   For this, note that

   $$P((\alpha\lceil N_{int}^2)|(\alpha\lceil N_{int}^1), \beta) = P((\alpha\lceil N^2)|(\alpha\lceil N_{int}^1), \beta),$$

   because β already includes the firing patterns for all the neurons in $N^2 - N_{int}^2 = N_{ext}^2$. And

   $$P((\alpha\lceil N^2)|(\alpha\lceil N_{int}^1), \beta) = P((\alpha\lceil N^2)|\beta),$$

   because the firing behavior of neurons in N^2 is independent of the behavior of the neurons in N_{int}^1, conditioned on β. Finally,

   $$P((\alpha\lceil N^2)|\beta) = P((\alpha\lceil N^2)|(\beta\lceil N^2)),$$

   because of locality—the neurons in N^2 are the only ones that $\alpha\lceil N^2$ depends on. Putting these three facts together yields the needed equality.   □

5.2   Composition Results for One-Step Extensions

In this subsection, we describe how to break circularities in dependencies using discrete time, as a key step toward our general compositionality result. In particular, we prove two lemmas showing how one-step extensions of executions and traces of $\mathcal{N}$ can be expressed in terms of one-step extensions of executions and traces of $\mathcal{N}^1$ and $\mathcal{N}^2$.

Our first lemma is about extending a finite execution, either to a particular longer execution, or just to any execution with a particular longer trace.

Lemma 20. *1. Let α be a finite execution of $\mathcal{N}$ of length > 0 that is consistent with β_{in}. Let α' be the one-step prefix of α. Then:*

$$P(\alpha|\alpha') = P((\alpha\lceil N_{lc}^1)|(\alpha'\lceil N^1)) \times P((\alpha\lceil N_{lc}^2)|(\alpha'\lceil N^2)).$$

2. Let β be a finite trace of $\mathcal{N}$ of length > 0 that is consistent with β_{in}. Let α' be a finite execution of $\mathcal{N}$ such that $trace(\alpha')$ is the one-step prefix of β. Then:

$$P(\beta|\alpha') = P((\beta\lceil N_{out}^1)|(\alpha'\lceil N^1)) \times P((\beta\lceil N_{out}^2)|(\alpha'\lceil N^2)).$$

Proof. 1. The non-input neurons of $\mathcal{N}$ are those in $N_{lc} = N_{lc}^1 \cup N_{lc}^2$. The firing states of all of these neurons in the final configuration of α are determined independently. Thus, we have

$$P(\alpha|\alpha') = P((\alpha\lceil N_{lc}^1)|\alpha') \times P((\alpha\lceil N_{lc}^2)|\alpha').$$

Furthermore, the final firing states for the neurons in N_{lc}^1 depend only on the immediately previous states of the neurons in N^1, and similarly for N_{lc}^2 and N^2, so this last expression is equal to

$$P((\alpha\lceil N_{lc}^1)|(\alpha'\lceil N^1)) \times P((\alpha\lceil N_{lc}^2)|(\alpha'\lceil N^2)),$$

as needed.

2. The output neurons of $\mathcal{N}$ are those in $N_{out} = N_{out}^1 \cup N_{out}^2$. The firing states of all of these neurons in the final configuration of β are determined independently. Thus, we have

$$P(\beta|\alpha') = P((\beta\lceil N_{out}^1)|\alpha') \times P((\beta\lceil N_{out}^2)|\alpha').$$

Furthermore, the final firing states for the neurons in N_{out}^1 depend only on the immediately previous states of the neurons in N^1, and similarly for N_{out}^2 and N^2, so this last expression is equal to

$$P((\beta\lceil N_{out}^1)|(\alpha'\lceil N^1)) \times P((\beta\lceil N_{out}^2)|(\alpha'\lceil N^2)),$$

as needed.

$\square$

The second lemma is about extending a finite trace, either to an execution or to a longer trace. This is a bit more difficult because we are conditioning only on traces, which do not include the internal behavior of the two sub-networks.

Lemma 21. *1. Let α be a finite execution of $\mathcal{N}$ of length > 0 that is consistent with β_{in}. Let β' be the one-step prefix of $trace(\alpha)$. Then:*

$$P(\alpha|\beta') = P((\alpha\lceil N^1_{lc})|(\beta'\lceil N^1)) \times P((\alpha\lceil N^2_{lc})|(\beta'\lceil N^2)).$$

2. Let β be a finite trace of $\mathcal{N}$ of length > 0 that is consistent with β_{in}. Let β' be the one-step prefix of β. Then:

$$P(\beta|\beta') = P((\beta\lceil N^1_{out})|(\beta'\lceil N^1)) \times P((\beta\lceil N^2_{out})|(\beta'\lceil N^2)).$$

Proof. 1. Fix α and β' as described. Let α' be the one-step prefix of α. By Lemma 7, we have:

$$P(\alpha|\beta') = P(\alpha|\alpha') \times P(\alpha'|\beta').$$

Lemma 20 implies that

$$P(\alpha|\alpha') = P((\alpha\lceil N^1_{lc})|(\alpha'\lceil N^1)) \times P((\alpha\lceil N^2_{lc})|(\alpha'\lceil N^2)).$$

Lemma 19 implies that

$$P(\alpha'|\beta') = P((\alpha'\lceil N^1)|(\beta'\lceil N^1)) \times P((\alpha'\lceil N^2)|(\beta'\lceil N^2)).$$

Substituting, we get that:

$$P(\alpha|\beta') = P((\alpha\lceil N^1_{lc})|(\alpha'\lceil N^1)) \times P((\alpha\lceil N^2_{lc})|(\alpha'\lceil N^2)) \times P((\alpha'\lceil N^1)|(\beta'\lceil N^1))$$
$$\times P((\alpha'\lceil N^2)|(\beta'\lceil N^2)).$$

Rearranging terms and using Lemma 13, Part 3, we see that the right-hand side is equal to

$$P((\alpha\lceil N^1_{lc})|(\beta'\lceil N^1)) \times P((\alpha\lceil N^2_{lc})|(\beta'\lceil N^2)),$$

as needed.

2. Fix β and β' as described. Let B denote the set of executions α of $\mathcal{N}$ such that $trace(\alpha) = \beta$, i.e., such that $\alpha\lceil N_{ext} = \beta$. Note that what varies among the different executions in B is just the firing patterns of the neurons in $N_{int} = N^1_{int} \cup N^2_{int}$. Then $P(\beta|\beta')$ can be expanded as

$$\sum_{\alpha \in B} P(\alpha|\beta').$$

By Part 1, this is equal to

$$\sum_{\alpha \in B} (P((\alpha\lceil N^1_{lc})|(\beta'\lceil N^1)) \times P((\alpha\lceil N^2_{lc})|(\beta'\lceil N^2)).$$

Now define B^1 to be the set of executions α^1 of $\mathcal{N}^1$ such that $trace(\alpha^1) = \beta\lceil N^1$. Note that all that varies among these α^1 is the firing patterns of the neurons in N^1_{int}. Analogously, define B^2 to be the set of executions α^2 of $\mathcal{N}^2$

such that $trace(\alpha^2) = \beta \lceil N^2$. All that varies among these α^2 is the firing patterns of the neurons in N_{int}^2.

Now we project the B executions onto N^1 and N^2, and we get that the expression above is equal to:

$$\sum_{\alpha^1 \in B^1, \alpha^2 \in B^2} (P(\alpha^1|(\beta' \lceil N^1)) \times P(\alpha^2|(\beta' \lceil N^2))).$$

This sum can be split into the product of sums:

$$\sum_{\alpha^1 \in B^1} P(\alpha^1|(\beta' \lceil N^1)) \times \sum_{\alpha^2 \in B^2} P(\alpha^2|(\beta' \lceil N^2)).$$

This is, in turn, equal to

$$P((\beta \lceil N_{out}^1)|(\beta' \lceil N^1)) \times P((\beta \lceil N_{out}^2)|(\beta' \lceil N^2)),$$

as needed.   □

5.3   Compositionality

Finally we are ready to prove that our behavior notion Beh is compositional. In view of Theorem 2, it suffices to show that our auxiliary behavior notion Beh_2 is compositional. And in view of Lemma 14, it suffices to show that $Beh_2(\mathcal{N})$ is uniquely determined by $Beh_2(\mathcal{N}^1)$ and $Beh_2(\mathcal{N}^2)$, which we do in Lemma 24. To accomplish this, we show (in Lemma 23) how to express $Beh_2(\mathcal{N})$ in terms of $Beh_2(\mathcal{N}^1)$ and $Beh_2(\mathcal{N}^2)$.

Recall that the definition of $Beh_2(\mathcal{N})$ specifies, for each infinite input execution β_{in} of $\mathcal{N}$, a collection of conditional probabilities, one for each finite trace β of $\mathcal{N}$ of length > 0 that is consistent with β_{in}. Fix any such input execution, β_{in}, which generates a particular probabilistic execution P of $\mathcal{N}$. Then consider an arbitrary finite trace β of $\mathcal{N}$ of length $t > 0$ that is consistent with β_{in}. Let β' be the length $t-1$ prefix of β. We show how to express $P(\beta|\beta')$ in terms of the conditional probabilities that arise from probability distributions P^1 and P^2 on infinite executions of $\mathcal{N}^1$ and $\mathcal{N}^2$, respectively. These distributions P^1 and P^2 are defined from certain input executions of $\mathcal{N}^1$ and $\mathcal{N}^2$, respectively. We define these input executions and distributions as follows.

– Input execution β_{in}^1 and distribution P^1 for $\mathcal{N}^1$:
   Define the infinite input execution β_{in}^1 of $\mathcal{N}^1$ as follows. First, note that $N_{in}^1 \subseteq N_{in} \cup N_{out}^2$, that is, every input of $\mathcal{N}^1$ is either an input of $\mathcal{N}$ or an output of $\mathcal{N}^2$. Define the firing patterns of the neurons in $N_{in}^1 \cap N_{in}$ using β_{in}, that is, define $\beta_{in}^1 \lceil (N_{in}^1 \cap N_{in}) = \beta_{in} \lceil N_{in}^1$. And for the firing patterns of the input neurons in $N_{in}^1 \cap N_{out}^2$, use β', that is, define $\beta_{in}^1 \lceil (N_{in}^1 \cap N_{out}^2) = \beta' \lceil (N_{in}^1 \cap N_{out}^2)$ for times $0, \ldots, t-1$, and the default 0 for times $\geq t$. Define P^1 to be the probability distribution that is generated by $\mathcal{N}^1$ from input execution β_{in}^1.

– Input execution β_{in}^2 and distribution P^2 for $\mathcal{N}^1$:
Analogous, interchanging 1 and 2.

Lemma 22. *Define β, β', P^1, and P^2 as above. Then:*

$$P(\beta|\beta') = P^1((\beta\lceil N_{out}^1)|(\beta'\lceil N^1)) \times P^2((\beta\lceil N_{out}^2)|(\beta'\lceil N^2)).$$

Proof. Lemma 21, Part 2, tells us that:

$$P(\beta|\beta') = P((\beta\lceil N_{out}^1)|(\beta'\lceil N^1)) \times P((\beta\lceil N_{out}^2)|(\beta'\lceil N^2)).$$

So it suffices to show that

$$P((\beta\lceil N_{out}^1)|(\beta'\lceil N^1)) = P^1((\beta\lceil N_{out}^1)|(\beta'\lceil N^1)),$$

and similarly for $\mathcal{N}^2$.

The two expressions for $\mathcal{N}^1$ look very similar; their equivalence follows by unwinding definitions. First, the left-hand expression is based on P, which is generated by the execution of the entire network $\mathcal{N}$ for input β_{in}. Thus, β_{in} defines the inputs of $\mathcal{N}^1$ that are also inputs of $\mathcal{N}$, but not those that are outputs of $\mathcal{N}^2$—the latter emerge from P. Then we consider the conditional probability $P((\beta\lceil N_{out}^1)|(\beta'\lceil N^1))$, which means that we now assume that the external behavior of $\mathcal{N}^1$ through time $t-1$ is β', and consider the (conditional) probability that the firing pattern produced by P for the outputs of $\mathcal{N}^1$ at time t coincides with what is given in β.

On the other hand, the right-hand expression is based on P^1, which is generated by the execution of just the sub-network $\mathcal{N}^1$ for input β_{in}^1. Then we consider the conditional probability $P^1((\beta\lceil N_{out}^1)|(\beta'\lceil N^1))$, which means that we again assume that the external behavior of $\mathcal{N}^1$ through time $t-1$ is β', and now consider the (conditional) probability that the firing pattern produced by P^1 for the outputs of $\mathcal{N}^1$ at time t coincides with what is given in β.

Note that in P, we may have different input sequences to $\mathcal{N}^1$ starting from time t, depending on what is produced by network $\mathcal{N}$ for input β_{in}. In P^1, those inputs are always 0, as in the definition of β_{in}^1. This difference does not matter, because we are concerned only with the outputs of $\mathcal{N}^1$ through time t, and these outputs depend only on inputs to $\mathcal{N}^1$ through time $t-1$.

It follows that these two conditional probabilities are the same. $\square$

Lemma 22 is a nice statement of how the probabilities decompose, and we generalize this in Lemma 25. However, it is not quite in the right form to prove compositionality of Beh_2. This is because the expressions on the right-hand-side calculate conditional probabilities for $\beta\lceil N_{out}^1$ and $\beta\lceil N_{out}^2$, which describe behavior of only output neurons of the two networks, whereas Beh_2 is defined in terms of probabilities for traces that include inputs as well as outputs. So, we need a technical modification of the lemma.

Specifically, define γ^1 to be the length-t trace of $\mathcal{N}^1$ such that $\gamma^1\lceil N_{out}^1 = \beta\lceil N_{out}^1$ and $\gamma^1\lceil N_{in}^1$ is a prefix of β_{in}^1. That is, γ^1 pastes together the output from $\beta \lceil N_{out}^1$ with the input used in the definition of P^1. Note that $\beta' \lceil N^1$ is the one-step prefix of γ^1. Define γ^2 analogously.

Now we can state a lemma that expresses conditional probabilities for $\mathcal{N}$ with input β_{in} in terms of conditional probabilities for $\mathcal{N}^1$ with input β_{in}^1 and $\mathcal{N}^2$ with input β_{in}^2.

Lemma 23. *Define β, β', P^1, P^2, γ^1, and γ^2 as above. Then:*

$$P(\beta|\beta') = P^1(\gamma^1|(\beta' \lceil N^1)) \times P^2(\gamma^2|(\beta' \lceil N^2)).$$

Proof. By Lemma 22, we have that

$$P(\beta|\beta') = P^1((\beta \lceil N_{out}^1)|(\beta' \lceil N^1)) \times P^2((\beta \lceil N_{out}^2)|(\beta' \lceil N^2)).$$

So it suffices to show that the corresponding terms are the same, that is, that:

$$P^1((\beta \lceil N_{out}^1)|(\beta' \lceil N^1)) = P^1(\gamma^1|(\beta' \lceil N^1)),$$

and similarly for $\mathcal{N}^2$. The first case follows because the definition of P^1 fixes the firing patterns for the neurons in N_{in}^1 through time t, in a way that is consistent with γ^1, and the traces γ^1 and β agree on the neurons in N_{out}^1. Similarly for the second case. □

Now we can conclude compositionality:

Lemma 24. *For all compatible pairs of networks $\mathcal{N}^1$ and $\mathcal{N}^2$, $Beh_2(\mathcal{N})$ is determined by $Beh_2(\mathcal{N}^1)$ and $Beh_2(\mathcal{N}^2)$.*

Proof. Follows directly from Lemma 23. □

Theorem 4. *Beh_2 is compositional.*

Proof. By Lemmas 24 and 14. □

Theorem 5. *Beh is compositional.*

Proof. By Theorems 4 and 2. □

We end this section with a generalization of Lemma 22 that applies to all four combinations of executions and traces. The proof is similar to that for Lemma 22, based on earlier Lemmas 20 and 21. We will use this in Sect. 5.4.

Lemma 25. *Let α be a finite execution of $\mathcal{N}$ of length > 0 that is consistent with β_{in}. Let α' be its one-step prefix. Let $\beta = trace(\alpha)$ and $\beta' = trace(\alpha')$. Let P_1 and P_2 be as defined earlier in this section. Then*

1. $P(\alpha|\alpha') = P^1((\alpha \lceil N_{lc}^1)|(\alpha' \lceil N^1)) \times P^2((\alpha \lceil N_{lc}^2)|(\alpha' \lceil N^2)).$
2. $P(\beta|\alpha') = P^1((\beta \lceil N_{out}^1)|(\alpha' \lceil N^1)) \times P^2((\beta \lceil N_{out}^2)|(\alpha' \lceil N^2)).$
3. $P(\alpha|\beta') = P^1((\alpha \lceil N_{lc}^1)|(\beta' \lceil N^1)) \times P^2((\alpha \lceil N_{lc}^2)|(\beta' \lceil N^2)).$
4. $P(\beta|\beta') = P^1((\beta \lceil N_{out}^1)|(\beta' \lceil N^1)) \times P^2((\beta \lceil N_{out}^2)|(\beta' \lceil N^2)).$

5.4   Examples

Toy Example for Cyclic Composition. We consider the toy cyclic composition example from Sect. 3.2. We analyze just one case in detail, namely, where x_1 fires at time 0 and x_2 does not. We prove that, with probability at least $(1 - \delta)^7$, both x_1 and x_2 fire at time 4.

The input firing sequence β_{in} is trivial here, since the composed network $\mathcal{N}$ has no input neurons. For this example, we assume that, in the initial configuration, x_1 fires and the other three neurons do not fire. With these restrictions, we have a single probability distribution P for infinite executions of $\mathcal{N}$. We argue compositionally, in terms of executions.

So let E be the set of executions of length 4 in which both x_1 and x_2 fire at time 4. We will show that $P(E) \geq (1 - \delta)^7$. For this, we define several other sets of executions. Each set is included in the previous one.

- E_0, the set of executions of length 0 consisting of just the initial configuration, in which x_1 is firing and the other neurons are not firing.
- E_1, the set of executions of length 1 whose one-step prefix is in E_0 and in which, in the last configuration, a_1 is firing.
- E_2, the set of executions of length 2 whose one-step prefix is in E_1 and in which, in the last configuration, x_2 is firing.
- E_3, the set of executions of length 3 whose one-step prefix is in E_2 and in which, in the last configuration, x_2 and a_2 are both firing.
- E_4, the set of executions of length 4 whose one-step prefix is in E_3 and in which, in the last configuration, x_1, x_2 and a_2 are all firing.

Then we can see that

$$P(E) \geq P(E_4) = P(E_4|E_3)P(E_3|E_2)P(E_2|E_1)P(E_1|E_0)P(E_0)$$
$$= P(E_4|E_3)P(E_3|E_2)P(E_2|E_1)P(E_1|E_0).$$

We need lower bounds for the four conditional probabilities. For example, consider $P(E_4|E_3)$. Let α' be any execution in E_3; we will argue that $P(E_4|\alpha') \geq (1 - \delta)^3$, and use Total Probability to conclude that $P(E_4|E_3) \geq (1 - \delta)^3$. We have:

$$P(E_4|\alpha') = \sum_{\alpha} P(\alpha|\alpha'),$$

where α ranges over the length-4 executions in E_4 that extend α'. By Lemma 25, we may break this down in terms of the two sub-networks and write:

$$P(\alpha|\alpha') = P^1((\alpha\lceil N_{lc}^1)|(\alpha'\lceil N^1)) \times P^2((\alpha\lceil N_{lc}^2)|(\alpha'\lceil N^2)),$$

where P^1 and P^2 are defined from $\beta' = trace(\alpha')$ as in Sect. 5.3.

We can rewrite $\sum_{\alpha} P(\alpha|\alpha')$ as

$$\sum_{\alpha^1} \sum_{\alpha^2} P^1((\alpha^1\lceil N_{lc}^1)|(\alpha'\lceil N^1)) \times P^2((\alpha^2\lceil N_{lc}^2)|(\alpha'\lceil N^2)),$$

where α^1 ranges over all one-step extensions of $\alpha' \lceil N^1$ such that x_2 fires in the final configuration, and α^2 ranges over all one-step extensions of $\alpha' \lceil N^2$ in which x_1 and a_2 both fire in the final configuration. This summation is equal to

$$\sum_{\alpha^1} P^1((\alpha^1 \lceil N_{lc}^1)|(\alpha' \lceil N^1)) \times \sum_{\alpha^2} P^2((\alpha^2 \lceil N_{lc}^2)|(\alpha' \lceil N^2)).$$

The first term is $\geq (1 - \delta)$ because we care only that x_2 fires in the final configuration, and we have assumed that it fires in the previous configuration. The second term is $\geq (1 - \delta)^2$, because we care that both x_1 and a_2 fire in the final configuration, and we have assumed that a_2 and x_2 fire in the previous configuration. So we have:

$$P(E_4|\alpha') = \sum_{\alpha^1} P^1((\alpha^1 \lceil N_{lc}^1)|(\alpha' \lceil N^1)) \times \sum_{\alpha^2} P^2((\alpha^2 \lceil N_{lc}^2)|(\alpha' \lceil N^2)) \geq (1-\delta)(1-\delta)^2 = (1-\delta)^3.$$

Thus, we have shown that $P(E_4|E_3) \geq (1 - \delta)^3$, Similar arguments can be used to show that $P(E_3|E_2) \geq (1 - \delta)^2$, $P(E_2|E_1) \geq (1 - \delta)$, and $P(E_1|E_0) \geq (1 - \delta)$. Combining all the terms we get that $P(E_4) \geq (1 - \delta)^7$, as needed.

6 Hiding for Spiking Neural Networks

Now we define our second operator for SNNs, the *hiding operator*. This operator is designed to "hide" some previously externally-visible behavior so it becomes invisible outside the network. Formally, the hiding operator simply reclassifies some output neurons as internal. The hiding operator can be used in conjunction with a composition operator; for example, we often want to compose two networks and then hide the neurons that were used to communicate between them.

6.1 Hiding Definition

Given a network $\mathcal{N}$ and a subset V of the output neurons N_{out} of $\mathcal{N}$, we define a new network $\mathcal{N}' = hide(\mathcal{N}, V)$ to be exactly the same as $\mathcal{N}$ except that all the outputs in V are now reclassified as internal neurons. That is, all parts of the definition of $\mathcal{N}'$ and $\mathcal{N}$ are identical except that $N'_{out} = N_{out} - V$ and $N'_{int} = N_{int} \cup V$. The effect of the hiding operator is to make the hidden neurons ineligible for combining with other neurons in further composition operations.

We give a result in the style of Lemma 24, here saying that the external behavior of $hide(\mathcal{N}, V)$ is determined by the external behavior of $\mathcal{N}$ and V.

Theorem 6. *For every network $\mathcal{N}$ and subset $V \subseteq N_{out}$, $Beh(hide(\mathcal{N}, V))$ is determined by $Beh(N)$ and V.*

Proof. Let $\mathcal{N}' = hide(\mathcal{N}, V)$. Fix any infinite input execution β_{in} for $\mathcal{N}'$, and let P' denote the probabilistic execution of $\mathcal{N}'$ generated from β_{in}. Consider any finite trace β of $\mathcal{N}'$ that is consistent with β_{in}. We must express $P'(\beta)$ in terms of the probability distribution of traces generated by $\mathcal{N}$ on some input execution.

To do this, note that the executions of $\mathcal{N}$ are identical to those of $\mathcal{N}'$—only the classification of neurons in V is different. In particular, the input execution β_{in} is also an input execution of $\mathcal{N}$. Let P denote the probabilistic execution generated of $\mathcal{N}$ generated from β_{in}. Then P', the probabilistic execution of $\mathcal{N}'$, is identical to P, the probabilistic execution of $\mathcal{N}$. So we can write $P'(\beta) = P(\beta)$.

This is not quite what we need, because β is not actually a trace of $\mathcal{N}$—it excludes firing patterns for neurons in V. But we can define B to be the set of traces γ of $\mathcal{N}$ such that $\gamma \lceil (N'_{ext}) = \beta$, that is, B is the set of traces of $\mathcal{N}$ that project to yield β but allow any firing behavior for the neurons in V. Then we have

$$P'(\beta) = \sum_{\gamma \in B} P(\gamma).$$

This is enough to show the needed dependency.   □

6.2   Examples

Boolean Circuits. Let $\mathcal{N}$ be the 5-gate Nand circuit from Sect. 3.2. Let V be the singleton set consisting of just the And neuron within the circuit. We consider the network $\mathcal{N}' = hide(\mathcal{N}, V)$, which is the same as the Nand circuit except that the And neuron is now regarded as internal. Thus, $\mathcal{N}'$ has two internal neurons: the And neuron, and the internal neuron a of $\mathcal{N}$. Fix β_{in} to be any infinite input execution (for both $\mathcal{N}$ and $\mathcal{N}'$) with stable inputs, and let P and P' be the probabilistic executions of $\mathcal{N}$ and $\mathcal{N}'$, respectively, generated from β_{in}.

In P', we should expect to have stable correct Nand outputs for a long time starting from time 3. Here we consider just finite traces β of length exactly 3, and focus on the output at exactly time 3. Thus, we consider the probabilities $P'(\beta)$ for finite traces β of length exactly 3, and we would like to show that the probability of a correct Nand output at time 3 is at least $(1 - \delta)^3$. We use the connection between P and P' to help us show this.

Namely, we assume that, in P, the probability of both a correct And output at time 1 and a correct Nand output at time 3 is at least $(1 - \delta)^3$. This could be proved for the Nand circuit separately, but we simply assume it here.

Now define event B to be the set of traces β of $\mathcal{N}'$ of length 3 such that β gives a correct Nand output at time 3. Our assumption about P implies that $P(B) \geq (1 - \delta)^3$. We argue that $P'(B) \geq (1 - \delta)^3$, which implies our desired result.

We have that $P'(B) = \sum_{\beta \in B} P'(\beta)$. We know that $P'(\beta) = P(\beta)$ for each trace β of $\mathcal{N}'$. Therefore, we have that $P'(B) = \sum_{\beta \in B} P(\beta) = P(B)$. Since we have that $P(B) \geq (1 - \delta)^3$, it follows that $P'(B) \geq (1 - \delta)^3$, as needed.

7   Problems for Spiking Neural Networks

In this section, we define a formal notion of a *problem* to be solved by a stochastic Spiking Neural Network. Problems are stated in terms of the input/output behavior that should be exhibited by a network. Namely, for every input, a problem specifies a set of *possibilities*, each of which is a probability distribution on outputs. We define what it means for an SNN to *solve* a problem. We prove that this notion of "solves" respects our composition and hiding operators.

7.1 Problems and Solving Problems

We define a *problem* $\mathcal{R}$ for a pair (N_{in}, N_{out}) of disjoint sets of neurons to be a mapping that assigns, to each infinite sequence β_{in} of firing patterns for N_{in}, a nonempty set $\mathcal{R}(\beta_{in})$ of *possibilities*. Each possibility $R \in \mathcal{R}(\beta_{in})$ is a mapping that specifies, for every finite sequence β of firing patterns for $N_{in} \cup N_{out}$ that is consistent with β_{in}, a probability $R(\beta)$. Thus, the problem $\mathcal{R}$ assigns to each input a set of "possible" probability distributions on outputs.

The probabilities assigned by a particular possibility R must satisfy certain constraints, designed to guarantee that they generate an actual probability distribution on the set of infinite sequences of firing patterns for $N_{in} \cup N_{out}$. Namely, we require that R assign probability 1 to some particular β of length 0, and that the probabilities assigned to the one-step extensions of any β must add up to the probability of β.

Now suppose that $\mathcal{N}$ is a network with input and output neurons N_{in} and N_{out}, and $\mathcal{R}$ is a problem for (N_{in}, N_{out}). Then we say that that $\mathcal{N}$ *solves* $\mathcal{R}$ provided that, for any infinite input execution β_{in} for $\mathcal{N}$, there is some possibility $R \in \mathcal{R}(\beta_{in})$ for which the following holds: Let P denote the probabilistic execution of $\mathcal{N}$ for β_{in}. Then for every finite trace β of $\mathcal{N}$, $P(\beta) = R(\beta)$. In other words, R is exactly the trace distribution derived from the probabilistic execution of $\mathcal{N}$ for input β_{in}.

7.2 Composition of Problems

We would like a theorem of the following form: If $\mathcal{N}^1$ solves problem $\mathcal{R}^1$ and $\mathcal{N}^2$ solves problem $\mathcal{R}^2$, then the composition of networks $\mathcal{N} = \mathcal{N}^1 \times \mathcal{N}^2$ solves the composition of problems $\mathcal{R} = \mathcal{R}^1 \times \mathcal{R}^2$. For this, we must first define the composition of two problems, $\mathcal{R} = \mathcal{R}^1 \times \mathcal{R}^2$.

So let $\mathcal{R}^1$ be a problem for the pair (N_{in}^1, N_{out}^1) and $\mathcal{R}^2$ a problem for the pair (N_{in}^2, N_{out}^2). Assume that $\mathcal{R}^1$ and $\mathcal{R}^2$ are *compatible*, in the sense that $N_{out}^1 \cap N_{out}^2 = \emptyset$. Then the composition $\mathcal{R}$ is defined to be a problem for the pair (N_{in}, N_{out}), where $N_{out} = N_{out}^1 \cup N_{out}^2$ and $N_{in} = N_{in}^1 \cup N_{in}^2 - N_{out}$. The composed problem $\mathcal{R}$ should be defined as a mapping that assigns, to each infinite sequence β_{in} of firing patterns for N_{in}, a nonempty set $\mathcal{R}(\beta_{in})$ of *possibilities*. Each possibility $R \in \mathcal{R}(\beta_{in})$ should be a mapping that specifies, for every finite sequence β of firing patterns for $N_{in} \cup N_{out}$ that is consistent with β_{in}, a probability $R(\beta)$.

We define the $\mathcal{R}$ mapping by considering each β_{in} separately; so fix any β_{in}. We describe how to define the set $\mathcal{R}(\beta_{in})$ of possibilities for β_{in}.

To define $\mathcal{R}(\beta_{in})$, we start by selecting (in an arbitrary way) a single possibility $R^1(\beta_{in}^1) \in \mathcal{R}^1(\beta_{in}^1)$ for each firing pattern β_{in}^1 for N_{in}^1, and likewise a single possibility $R^2(\beta_{in}^2) \in \mathcal{R}^2(\beta_{in}^2)$ for each firing pattern β_{in}^2 for N_{in}^2.[10] We use this entire collection of choices for $R^1(\beta_{in}^1)$ and $R^2(\beta_{in}^2)$, for all values of β_{in}^1 and β_{in}^2, to construct a single, particular possibility R for β_{in}. Then we define $\mathcal{R}(\beta_{in})$ to be the set of all possibilities for β_{in} that can be constructed in this way, based on all choices for the possibilities $R^1(\beta_{in}^1)$ and $R^2(\beta_{in}^2)$.

So fix the possibilities $R^1(\beta_{in}^1) \in \mathcal{R}^1(\beta_{in}^1)$ and $R^2(\beta_{in}^2) \in \mathcal{R}^2(\beta_{in}^2)$ arbitrarily, as just described. Constructing the possibility R for β_{in} requires us to define $R(\beta)$ for every finite sequence β of firing patterns of $N_{in} \cup N_{out}$ that is consistent with β_{in}. We do this recursively. For the base, consider β of length 0, where β is consistent with β_{in}. Let β_{in}^1 be the infinite sequence of all-0 firing patterns for N_{in}^1, and β_{in}^2 be the infinite sequence of all-0 firing patterns for N_{in}^2. Then we define $R(\beta) = 1$ if

$$R^1(\beta_{in}^1)(\beta \lceil N_{out}^1) = 1 \text{ and } R^2(\beta_{in}^2)(\beta \lceil N_{out}^2) = 1,$$

and 0 otherwise. That is, we assign probability 1 to the length-0 sequence β that is consistent with β_{in}, and in which the output firing states are the same as those to which $R^1(\beta_{in}^1)$ and $R^2(\beta_{in}^2)$ assign probability 1.

For the recursive step, consider β of length ≥ 1, where β is consistent with β_{in}, and let β' be the one-step prefix of β. We define $R(\beta)$ in terms of $R(\beta')$. Namely, let β_{in}^1 be the infinite sequence of firing patterns for N_{in}^1 that are constructed from the following: (a) for neurons in $N_{in}^1 \cap N_{in}$, use $\beta_{in} \lceil N_{in}^1$, and (b) for neurons in $N_{in}^1 \cap N_{out}^2$, use $\beta' \lceil (N_{in}^1 \cap N_{out}^2)$ for times $0, \ldots, t-1$, and the default 0 for times $\geq t$, Define β_{in}^2 analogously. Then define $R(\beta) = R(\beta') \times T^1 \times T^2$, where T^1 is the conditional probability $R^1(\beta_{in}^1)((\beta \lceil N_{out}^1) | (\beta' \lceil N^1))$ and T^2 is the conditional probability $R^2(\beta_{in}^2)((\beta \lceil N_{out}^2) | (\beta' \lceil N^2))$.[11]

Theorem 7. *If $\mathcal{N}^1$ solves problem $\mathcal{R}^1$ and $\mathcal{N}^2$ solves problem $\mathcal{R}^2$, then the composition of networks $\mathcal{N} = \mathcal{N}^1 \times \mathcal{N}^2$ solves the composition of problems $\mathcal{R} = \mathcal{R}^1 \times \mathcal{R}^2$.*

Proof. Since $\mathcal{N}^1$ solves $\mathcal{R}^1$, we know that, for every infinite input execution β_{in}^1 for $\mathcal{N}^1$, there is a possibility in $\mathcal{R}^1(\beta_{in}^1)$ that is identical to the trace distribution derived from the probabilistic execution of $\mathcal{N}^1$ for β_{in}^1. Denote this possibility by $R^1(\beta_{in}^1)$. Likewise, since $\mathcal{N}^2$ solves $\mathcal{R}^2$, we know that, for every infinite input execution β_{in}^2 for $\mathcal{N}^2$, there is a possibility in $\mathcal{R}^2(\beta_{in}^2)$ that is identical to the trace distribution derived from the probabilistic execution of $\mathcal{N}^2$ for input β_{in}^2. Denote this possibility by $R^2(\beta_{in}^2)$. To show that $\mathcal{N}$ solves $\mathcal{R}$, we must show that, for every infinite input execution β_{in} for $\mathcal{N}$, there is some possibility $R \in \mathcal{R}(\beta_{in})$ such that R is identical to the trace distribution derived from the probabilistic execution of $\mathcal{N}$ for input β_{in}.

---

[10] Unwinding the definitions a bit, possibility $R^1(\beta_{in}^1)$ is a mapping from sequences of firing patterns that are consistent with β_{in}^1 to probabilities, and analogously for $R^2(\beta_{in}^2)$.

[11] Again unwinding the definitions, $R^1(\beta_{in}^1)$ is the possibility chosen for input β_{in}^1. The conditional probability $R^1(\beta_{in}^1)((\beta \lceil N_{out}^1) | (\beta' \lceil N^1))$ describes the probability that $\mathcal{N}^1$ extends $\beta' \lceil N^1$ to yield the outputs specified by β. Analogously for T^2.

So fix an input execution β_{in} for $\mathcal{N}$, and define P to be the trace distribution generated by $\mathcal{N}$ for input β_{in}. Also define distribution R for β_{in} using the recursive approach in the definition of composition of problems, but now based on the particular selections R^1 and R^2 just defined. We claim that $P = R$. To show this, we must show that, for any finite trace β of $\mathcal{N}$ that is consistent with β_{in}, $P(\beta) = R(\beta)$. We do this by induction on the length of β.

For the base, consider β of length 0. The definition of $P(\beta)$ yields 1 if β is the initial output configuration of $\mathcal{N}$ and 0 otherwise. The initial output configuration is the unique configuration C for which $C\lceil N_{out}^1 = F_0^1\lceil N_{out}^1$ and $C\lceil N_{out}^2 = F_0^2\lceil N_{out}^2$ (here using the general notation for initial firing patterns). On the other hand, the definition of $R(\beta)$ yields 1 if β is the unique output configuration of $\mathcal{N}$ for which $R^1(\beta_{in}^1)(\beta\lceil N_{out}^1) = 1$ and $R^2(\beta_{in}^2)(\beta\lceil N_{out}^2) = 1$, where β_{in}^1 and β_{in}^2 are infinite sequences of all-0 firing patterns, and 0 for other output configurations. By definition of R^1 and R^2, this is, again, just the initial output configuration of $\mathcal{N}$. This implies that $P(\beta) = R(\beta)$.

For the inductive step, consider β of length ≥ 1, and let β' be the one-step prefix of β. By the inductive hypothesis, we may assume that $P(\beta') = R(\beta')$. We must show that $P(\beta) = R(\beta)$.

Fix β_{in}^1 and β_{in}^2 as in the recursive definition of $R(\beta)$. Then by the definition of $R(\beta)$, we have

$$R(\beta) = R(\beta') \times R^1(\beta_{in}^1)((\beta\lceil N_{out}^1)|(\beta'\lceil N^1)) \times R^2(\beta_{in}^2)((\beta\lceil N_{out}^2)|(\beta'\lceil N^2)).$$

Also, for the same β_{in}^1 and β_{in}^2, fix P^1 and P^2 to be the probabilistic traces for $\mathcal{N}^1$ and $\mathcal{N}^2$, respectively. Then by Lemma 22 and Lemma 6, we have

$$P(\beta) = P(\beta') \times P^1((\beta\lceil N_{out}^1)|(\beta'\lceil N^1)) \times P^2((\beta\lceil N_{out}^2)|(\beta'\lceil N^2)).$$

The assumption that $\mathcal{N}^1$ solves $\mathcal{R}^1$ with the particular possibility $R^1(\beta_{in}^1)$ implies that the two conditional distributions P^1 and $R^1(\beta_{in}^1)$ are identical, so

$$P^1((\beta\lceil N_{out}^1)|(\beta'\lceil N^1)) = R^1(\beta_{in}^1)((\beta\lceil N_{out}^1)|(\beta'\lceil N^1)).$$

Similarly, P^2 and $R^2(\beta_{in}^2)$ are identical, so

$$P^2((\beta\lceil N_{out}^2)|(\beta'\lceil N^2)) = R^2(\beta_{in}^2)((\beta\lceil N_{out}^2)|(\beta'\lceil N^2)).$$

Since all three pairs of corresponding terms in the two equations are equal, we conclude that their products are equal, that is, $P(\beta) = R(\beta)$, as needed.   □

7.3   Hiding of Problems

Next, we define a hiding operator on problems, analogous to the hiding operator on networks. Namely, given a problem $\mathcal{R}$ for (N_{in}, N_{out}), and a subset V of the output neurons N_{out} of $\mathcal{R}$, we define a new "hidden" problem $\mathcal{R}' = hide(\mathcal{R}, V)$ for (N_{in}', N_{out}'), where $N_{out}' = N_{out} - V$ and $N_{in}' = N_{in}$. The hidden problem $\mathcal{R}'$ should be defined as a mapping that assigns, to each infinite sequence β_{in} of firing patterns for $\mathcal{N}'$, a nonempty set $\mathcal{R}'(\beta_{in})$ of *possibilities*. Each possibility $R' \in \mathcal{R}'(\beta_{in})$ should be a mapping that specifies, for every finite sequence β of firing patterns for $N'_{in} \cup N'_{out}$ that is consistent with β_{in}, a probability $R'(\beta)$.

We define this mapping by considering each β_{in} separately; so fix any β_{in}. To define the set $\mathcal{R}'(\beta_{in})$, we start by selecting (in an arbitrary way) a single possibility $R \in \mathcal{R}(\beta_{in})$ We use R to define the possibility R' for $\mathcal{N}'$ and input β_{in}. Since there may be many ways to define R, $\mathcal{R}'$ may wind up containing many different possibilities.

Constructing the possibility R' requires us to define $R'(\beta)$ for every finite sequence β of firing patterns of $N'_{in} \cup N'_{out}$ that is consistent with β_{in}. This construction is much simpler than that for composition: Let B denote the set of finite sequences γ of firing patterns for N_{ext} such that $\gamma\lceil(N'_{in} \cup N'_{out}) = \beta$. Then define

$$R'(\beta) = \sum_{\gamma \in B} R(\gamma).$$

Theorem 8. *If network $\mathcal{N}$ solves problem $\mathcal{R}$, and $V \in N_{out}$, then network $\mathcal{N}' = hide(\mathcal{N}, V)$ solves problem $\mathcal{R}' = hide(\mathcal{R}, V)$.*

Proof. Since $\mathcal{N}$ solves $\mathcal{R}$, we know that, for every infinite input execution β_{in} for $\mathcal{N}$, there is a possibility in $\mathcal{R}(\beta_{in})$ that is identical to the trace distribution derived from execution of $\mathcal{N}$ for input β_{in}. Denote this possibility by $R(\beta_{in})$. To show that $\mathcal{N}'$ solves $\mathcal{R}'$, we must show that, for every input execution β_{in} for $\mathcal{N}'$, there is some possibility in $\mathcal{R}'(\beta_{in})$ that is identical to the trace distribution derived from the probabilistic execution of $\mathcal{N}'$ for input β_{in}.

So fix an input execution β_{in} for $\mathcal{N}'$. Define P' to be the trace distribution generated by $\mathcal{N}'$ for input β_{in}. Also define distribution R' for β_{in} as in the definition of hiding of problems, now based on the particular selection $R(\beta_{in})$ just defined. We claim that $P' = R'$. This means that for any finite trace β of $\mathcal{N}'$ that is consistent with β_{in}, $P'(\beta) = R'(\beta)$.

To see this, let B denote the set of finite sequences γ of firing patterns for $N_{in} \cup N_{out}$ such that $\gamma\lceil(N'_{in} \cup N'_{out}) = \beta$. Then $P'(\beta) = \sum_{\gamma \in B} P(\gamma)$ and $R'(\beta) = \sum_{\gamma \in B} R(\beta_{in})(\gamma)$. Since $\mathcal{N}$ solves $\mathcal{R}$ with the particular possibility $R(\beta_{in})$, it follows that for each such γ, $P(\gamma) = R(\beta_{in})(\gamma)$. Consequently, the two summations are equal, as needed.   □

7.4   Examples

In this section, we define three problems satisfying our formal definition of problems. They are the Winner-Take-All (WTA) problem, the Filter problem, and an Attention problem that can be solved by combining solutions to the WTA and Filter problems.

The Winner-Take-All Problem. We define the Winner-Take-All problem formally using notation that corresponds to the statement of Theorem 1: we write it as $WTA(n, \delta, t_c, t_s)$, using four parameters from the theorem statement. The problem definition allows considerable freedom, in the choice of which output ends up firing, in the time when the stable interval begins, and in what happens outside the stable interval.

The set N_{in} is $\{x_1, \ldots, x_n\}$, and N_{out} is $\{y_1, \ldots, y_n\}$. For each infinite sequence β_{in} of firing patterns for N_{in}, the WTA problem specifies a set of probability distributions on sequences of firing patterns for $N_{in} \cup N_{out}$ that are consistent with β_{in}.

So consider any particular β_{in}. If the firing pattern for N_{in} in β_{in} is not stable or does not have at least one firing neuron, then we allow all distributions that are consistent with β_{in}. Now consider the case where β_{in} is stable with at least one firing neuron. Then the possibilities for β_{in} are exactly the distributions that satisfy the following condition: With probability $\geq 1 - \delta$, there is some $t \leq t_c$ such that the y outputs stabilize by time t to one steadily-firing output y_i, and this firing pattern persists through time $t + t_s - 1$. Notice that these distributions may differ in many ways, for example, they may give equal probabilities to each output choice, or may favor some over others. They may exhibit different times, or probability distributions of times, for when the stable interval begins. They may exhibit different types of behavior before and after the stable interval.

We argue that our WTA network from Sect. 2.4 solves the formal problem $WTA(n, \delta, t_c, t_s)$. Specifically, we consider our network with the weighting factor γ satisfying the inequality $\gamma \geq c_1 \log(\frac{nt_s}{\delta})$, and with $t_c \approx c_2 \log n \log(\frac{1}{\delta})$. And we allow initial firing patterns for the internal and output neurons to be arbitrary; so technically, we are talking about a class of networks, not a single network. Then Theorem 1 implies that each of these networks solves the $WTA(n, \delta, t_c, t_s)$ problem.

The Filter Problem. We define the Filter problem as $Filter(n, \delta)$. The set N_{in} is $\{w_i, y_i | 1 \leq i \leq n\}$ and the set N_{out} is $\{z_i | 1 \leq i \leq n\}$. The Filter problem is intended to say that, for every i, $1 \leq i \leq n$, the output neuron z_i should fire at any time $t \geq 1$ exactly if both the corresponding inputs w_i and y_i fired at time $t - 1$. Thus, it acts like n And networks.

Formally, for each infinite sequence β_{in} of firing patterns for N_{in}, the $Filter(n, \delta)$ problem specifies a set of probability distributions on sequences of firing patterns for $N_{in} \cup N_{out}$ that are consistent with β_{in}.

So consider any particular β_{in}. Then the possibilities for β_{in} are exactly the distributions that satisfy the following condition, here expressed in terms of conditional probabilities (which could be translated into absolute probabilities): Let β be any finite sequence over $N_{in} \cup N_{out}$ of length $t \geq 1$ that is consistent with β_{in}, and let C_t be the final configuration of β. Let β' be the one-step prefix of β, and C_{t-1} be the final configuration of β'. Suppose that, for every i, $1 \leq i \leq n$, $C_t(z_i) = C_{t-1}(w_i) \wedge C_{t-1}(y_i)$. That is, β extends β' with correct outputs at the final time t. Then $P(\beta|\beta') \geq 1 - \delta$. The differences among these distributions may involve different conditional probabilities (for example, different for different outputs), as long as they satisfy the given inequality.

Our simple *Filter* network of Sect. 3.2 solves the formal *Filter* problem, with $\delta = 1 - (1 - \delta')^n$, where δ' is the failure probability for a single And gate at a single time, according to notation used in Sect. 3.2.

The Attention Problem. We define the Attention problem formally as

$$Attention(n, \delta, t_c, t_s) = WTA(n, \delta', t_c, t_s) \times Filter(n, \delta'').$$

Here δ, δ', and δ'' are related so that $(1 - \delta) = (1 - \delta')(1 - \delta'')^{t_s}$. The set N_{in} is $\{x_i, w_i | 1 \leq i \leq n\}$, and N_{out} is $\{y_i, z_i | 1 \leq i \leq n\}$.

By the definition of composition of problems, the guarantees of $Attention(n, \delta, t_c, t_s)$ combine those of $WTA(n, \delta', t_c, t_s)$ and $Filter(n, \delta'')$. That is, for any input sequence β_{in} in which the x inputs are stable, $Attention(n, \delta, t_c, t_s)$ specifies that, with probability at least $(1 - \delta')$, the y outputs converge to a single firing output corresponding to some firing x input within time t_c, and this configuration persists for time t_s. $Attention(n, \delta, t_c, t_s)$ also specifies that, with probability at least $(1 - \delta'')^{t_s}$, the z outputs always exhibit correct And behavior with respect to the previous time's y and w firing behavior. Together, these two properties imply that, assuming stable x inputs, with probability at least $(1 - \delta) = (1 - \delta')(1 - \delta'')^{t_s}$, the *Attention* network produces stable behavior of the part of the y outputs, and moreover, during the stable interval, the network produces z outputs that correctly mirror the w inputs corresponding to the chosen y output.

Theorem 7 implies that any compatible solutions to $WTA(n, \delta', t_c, t_s)$ and $Filter(n, \delta'')$ can be composed to yield a solution to the composed problem $Attention(n, \delta, t_c, t_s)$. In particular, the solutions to these problems that we presented in Sects. 2.4 and 3.2 can be composed in this way.

We can also define a version of the Attention problem in which we hide the y outputs, formally, $hide(Attention(n, \delta, t_c, t_s), \{y_1, \ldots, y_n\})$. The guarantees specified by this problem are similar to those of the $Attention(n, \delta, t_c, t_s)$ problem, except that the behavior of the y neurons is not mentioned explicitly. Essentially, this problem says that, with probability at least $(1 - \delta) = (1 - \delta')(1 - \delta'')^{t_s}$, the network correctly mirrors the inputs corresponding to some y output, throughout the stable interval. The same composition of solutions as above, with hiding of the y outputs, solves this version of the problem.

8   Conclusions

In this paper, we have presented a formal, mathematical foundation for modeling and reasoning about the behavior of synchronous, stochastic Spiking Neural Networks. This foundation is based on a simple version of the SNN model in which a neuron's only state is a Boolean value indicating whether the neuron is currently firing. We have provided definitions for networks and their externally-visible behavior. We have defined composition and hiding operators for building new SNNs from others, and have proved fundamental theorems saying that these operators preserve externally-visible behavior. We have also defined a formal notion of a problem to be solved by an SNN, and have given basic results showing how the composition and hiding operators affect the problems that are solved by networks.

Future work will include using this formal foundation as a basis for describing and verifying properties of particular SNNs. We have already carried out rather formal proofs for some of our brain network algorithms (see, e.g., [17]). However, these have been done in terms of models that were specially-tailored to the problem at hand, and not in terms of a general modeling framework; we believe that working in terms of a general framework will contribute toward building a coherent general theory for SNN algorithms. A good starting point for such applications might be a study of brain-like mechanisms for focusing attention, based on simpler mechanisms such as our Winner-Take-All and Filter networks.

In the basic SNN model used in this paper, each neuron has a state that is just a Boolean indicating whether or not it is currently firing. We plan to extend the definitions and results to allow a neuron to have more elaborate state. For example, as in [34], a neuron's state might include history of its recent incoming potential or recent firing behavior. Also, as in [14], we may want to allow a neuron's state to include some Boolean flags that may turn the neuron on or off for performing certain activities, such as learning; in the neuroscience literature, such mechanisms are known as "eligibility traces" [4]. It remains to carefully extend the definitions and results in this paper to these more elaborate cases; this paper should provide a useful blueprint for these extensions. With such model extensions in hand, it will be interesting to revisit work by Valiant, Navlakha, Papadimitriou, and their collaborators, such as [3,31,38]), trying to recast it in terms of our general concurrency theory framework.

Acknowledgments. We thank our co-authors on our papers based on SNNs, especially Merav Parter, Lili Su, Brabeeba Wang, Yael Hitron, C. J. Chang, and Frederik Mallmann-Trenn, for providing many concrete examples that inspired our general model. We also thank Victor Luchangco and Jesus Lares for reading and contributing comments on earlier drafts of this paper.

References

1. Chou, C.N., Wang, M.B.: ODE-inspired analysis for the biological version of Oja's rule in solving streaming PCA. In: Thirty-third Annual Conference on Learning Theory (COLT), July 2020. arXiv:1911.02363. Accessed November 2019
2. Chou, C.N., Wang, M.B., Yu, T.: A general framework for analyzing stochastic dynamics in learning algorithms, June 2020. arXiv:2006.06171
3. Dasgupta, S., Stevens, C.F., Navlakha, S.: A neural algorithm for a fundamental computing problem. Science **358**(6364), 793–796 (2017). http://courses.csail.mit.edu/6.852/brains/papers/DasguptaStevensNavlakha.pdf
4. Gerstner, W., Lehmann, M., Liakoni, V., Corneil, D., Brea, J.: Eligibility traces and plasticity on behavioral time scales: experimental support of neohebbian three-factor learning rules. Front. Neural Circ. **12**(53) (2018)

5. Haddad, S., Varacca, D. (eds.): 32nd International Conference on Concurrency Theory, CONCUR 2021, 24–27 August 2021, Virtual Conference. LIPIcs, vol. 203. Schloss Dagstuhl - Leibniz-Zentrum für Informatik (2021). https://www.dagstuhl. de/dagpub/978-3-95977-203-7

6. Hitron, Y., Musco, C., Parter, M., Lynch, N.: Random sketching, clustering, and short-term memory in spiking neural networks. In: 11th Innovations in Theoretical Computer Science (ITCS 2020), Seattle, Washington, January 2020

7. Hitron, Y., Parter, M.: Counting to ten with two fingers: compressed counting with spiking neurons. In: European Symposium on Algorithms (ESA), Munich, Germany, September 2019

8. Kaynar, D.K., Lynch, N., Segala, R., Vaandrager, F.: The Theory of Timed I/O Automata. Synthesis Lectures on Computer Science, 2nd edn. Morgan and Claypool Publishers (2010)

9. Lazzaro, J., Ryckebusch, S., Mahowald, M.A., Mead, C.A.: Winner-take-all networks of $o(n)$ complexity. Technical report, DTIC Document (1988)

10. Lee, D.K., Itti, L., Koch, C., Braun, J.: Attention activates winner-take-all competition among visual filters. Nat. Neurosci. **2**(4), 375–381 (1999)

11. Legenstein, R., Naeger, C., Maass, W.: What can a neuron learn with spike-timing-dependent plasticity? Neural Comput. **17**(11), 2337–2382 (2005)

12. Lombo, A.E., Lares, J.E., Castellani, M., Chou, C.N., Lynch, N., Berggren, K.K.: A superconducting nanowire-based architecture for neuromorphic computing (2022, submitted)

13. Lynch, N.: Distributed Algorithms. Morgan Kaufmann Publishers, Inc., San Mateo (1996)

14. Lynch, N., Mallmann-Trenn, F.: Learning hierarchically structured concepts. Neural Netw. **143**, 798–817 (2021)

15. Lynch, N., Musco, C., Parter, M.: Computational tradeoffs in biological neural networks: self-stabilizing winner-take-all networks. In: Proceedings of the 8th Conference on Innovations in Theoretical Computer Science (ITCS) (2017). https://arxiv.org/abs/1610.02084

16. Lynch, N., Musco, C., Parter, M.: Neuro-RAM unit with applications to similarity testing and compression in spiking neural networks. In: Proceedings of the 2017 Internal Symposium on Distributed Computing (DISC) (2017). https://arxiv.org/abs/1706.01382

17. Lynch, N., Musco, C., Parter, M.: Winner-take-all computation in spiking neural networks, April 2019. arXiv:1904.12591

18. Lynch, N., Segala, R., Vaandrager, F.: Hybrid I/O automata. Inf. Comput. **185**(1), 105–157 (2003). Technical report MIT-LCS-TR-827d, MIT Laboratory for Computer Science, Cambridge, MA 02139, 13 January 2003

19. Lynch, N., Segala, R., Vaandrager, F.: Observing branching structure through probabilistic contexts. SIAM J. Comput. **37**(4), 977–1013 (2007)

20. Lynch, N., Vaandrager, F.: Forward and backward simulations – part I: untimed systems. Inf. Comput. **121**(2), 214–233 (1995)

21. Lynch, N., Vaandrager, F.: Forward and backward simulations – part II: timing-based systems. Inf. Comput. **128**(1), 1–25 (1996)

22. Lynch, N.A., Tuttle, M.R.: Hierarchical correctness proofs for distributed algorithms. In: Proceedings of the Sixth Annual ACM Symposium on Principles of Distributed Computing (PODC 1987), Vancouver, British Columbia, Canada, pp. 137–151 (1987)

23. Lynch, N.A., Tuttle, M.R.: An introduction to input/output automata. CWI-Q. **2**(3), 219–246 (1989). Centrum voor Wiskunde en Informatica, Amsterdam, The Netherlands. Technical Memo MIT/LCS/TM-373, Laboratory for Computer Science, Massachusetts Institute of Technology, Cambridge, MA 02139, November 1988

24. Maass, W.: Networks of spiking neurons: the third generation of neural network models. Neural Netw. **10**(9), 1659–1671 (1997)

25. Maass, W.: Neural computation with winner-take-all as the only nonlinear operation. In: Advances in Neural Information Processing Systems (NIPS), vol. 12, pp. 293–299 (1999)

26. Maass, W.: On the computational power of winner-take-all. Neural Comput. **12**, 2519–2535 (2000)

27. Maass, W.: Noise as a resource for computation and learning in networks of spiking neurons. Proc. IEEE **102**(5), 860–880 (2014)

28. Maass, W., Schmitt, M.: On the complexity of learning for spiking neurons with temporal coding. Inf. Comput. **153**(1), 26–46 (1999)

29. Mcculloch, W., Pitts, W.: A logical calculus of ideas immanent in nervous activity. Bull. Math. Biophys. **5**, 127–147 (1943)

30. Musco, C.: The power of randomized algorithms: from numerical linear algebra to biological systems. Ph.D. thesis, Electrical Engineering and Computer Science, Massachusetts Institute of Technology, Cambridge, MA 02139, June 2018. Neural algorithms work covered in Chapter 5

31. Papadimitriou, C.H., Vempala, S.S.: Random projection in the brain and computation with assemblies of neurons. In: 10th Innovation in Theoretical Computer Science (ITCS 2019), San Diego, CA, pp. 57:1–57:19, January 2019. https://www.cc.gatech.edu/vempala/papers/assemblies.pdf

32. Segala, R.: Modeling and verification of randomized distributed real-time systems. Ph.D. thesis, Laboratory for Computer Science, Massachusetts Institute of Technology, Cambridge, MA 02139, June 1995

33. Segala, R., Lynch, N.: Probabilistic simulations for probabilistic processes. Nordic J. Comput. **2**(2), 250–273 (1995)

34. Su, L., Chang, C.J., Lynch, N.: Spike-based winner-take-all computation: fundamental limits and order-optimal circuits. Neural Comput. **31**(12), 2523–2561 (2019)

35. Toomey, E.: Superconducting nanowire electronics for alternative computing. Ph.D. thesis, Department of Electrical Engineering and Computer Science, Massachusetts Institute of Technology, Cambridge, MA 02139, May 2020

36. Toomey, E., Segall, K., Castellani, M., Colangelo, M., Lynch, N., Berggren, K.K.: A superconducting nanowire spiking element for neural networks. Nano Lett. (2020). https://doi.org/10.1021/acs.nanolett.0c03057

37. Trappenberg, T.: Fundamentals of Computational Neuroscience. OUP, Oxford (2009)

38. Valiant, L.G.: Circuits of the Mind. Oxford University Press, Oxford (2000)

39. Wang, B.: Mathematical analysis of static and plastic biological neural circuits. Master's thesis, Department of Electrical Engineering and Computer Science, Massachusetts Institute of Technology, Cambridge, MA, May 2020

40. Wang, B., Lynch, N.: Integrating temporal information to spatial information in a neural circuit (2019). arXiv:1903.01217

State Identification and Verification with Satisfaction

Joshua Moerman[1]([✉])(iD) and Thorsten Wißmann[2](iD)

[1] Open Universiteit, Heerlen, The Netherlands
joshua.moerman@ou.nl
[2] Radboud University, Nijmegen, The Netherlands
thorsten.wissmann@ru.nl
https://joshuamoerman.nl, https://thorsten-wissmann.de

Abstract. We use SAT-solving to construct adaptive distinguishing sequences and unique input/output sequences for finite state machines in the flavour of Mealy machines. These sequences solve the state identification and state verification problems respectively. Preliminary experiments evaluate our implementation and show that this approach via SAT-solving works well and is able to find many short sequences.

Keywords: SAT solving · Finite State Machines · State Identification · Conformance Testing · Mealy machines

1 Introduction

In a paper by Lee and Yannakakis [LY94], the notion of *adaptive distinguishing sequence* (ADS) is developed. Such a sequence is a (single) experiment which can determine exactly in which state a given finite state machine (FSM) is. The experiment consists of input symbols for the FSM, which may depend on the outputs of the FSM observed so far (making it *adaptive*). The goal of the experiment is to determine exactly in which state the given FSM is at the start of the experiment (making it *distinguishing*). We use the formalism of Mealy machines to model FSMs; but the techniques can also be adapted to Moore machines and DFAs. Whether such an experiment exists for the whole machine can be decided efficiently. In the special case where we have prior knowledge that the machine is in one of two states, such a sequence always exists and can also be found efficiently. Despite these positive results, the general problem is hard:

Theorem [LY94, Theorem 3.4]. *Given an FSM and a set of possible initial states, it is* PSPACE-*complete to tell whether there is an experiment that identifies the initial state.*

Nonetheless, the problem is of practical interest. For instance, the L$^\sharp$ algorithm [VGRW22] learns an opaque FSM based on its input/output behaviour, that is without having access to the internal transition structure. It does so by

N. Jansen et al. (Eds.): Vaandrager Festschrift 2022, LNCS 13560, pp. 450–466, 2022.
https://doi.org/10.1007/978-3-031-15629-8_23

successively exhibiting distinct states in the FSM that differ in their behaviour, that is, states that are provably *apart*. Whenever a longer trace of the FSM is observed, the algorithm has to *identify* whether this leads to the same state as one of the exhibited states so far. Hence, it would be useful if there is a single experiment from which we could determine in which state the FSM is. In such a learning algorithm, the queries are often the bottleneck, since they interact with embedded devices with restricted communication speed. So even though the learning can be done in polynomial time, it may be worth some extra computation to reduce the query size or the number of resets.

In this paper, we will use SAT solvers to construct two types of experiments: adaptive distinguishing sequences and unique input/output sequences. The problem of deciding the existence of these sequences is PSPACE-complete. Our motivation typically asks for *short* experiments, and so we will fix a bound (polynomial in the size of the automaton). This bound ensures that the problem is in NP and so a reduction to SAT is possible. This preference towards short experiments is perfectly in line with the setting of learning where one can run multiple short experiments instead of a single long one.

Dedication

This paper is dedicated to Frits Vaandrager who was our supervisor and co-author.

Frits was the first author's PhD supervisor: In the very first week of my PhD, he gave me a very well-defined task: read the paper by Lee and Yannakakis [LY94] and implement their algorithm. This was a fun start of my research and brought us useful insights in the area of model learning. I am very thankful to Frits that he gave me such interesting problems at the start.

Frits is the supervisor of the second author's postdoc studies: since starting in Nijmegen, Frits introduced me to the realm of automata learning and testing. Those numerous research discussions finally led to the $L^\sharp$ algorithm [VGRW22], which makes great use of adaptive (and ordinary) distinguishing sequences.

Now, we once again return to those basic concepts of finite state machines, as there is still more to discover about adaptive distinguishing sequences and unique input/output sequences.

2   State Identification and Verification

As commonly done in (software) engineering, we model the systems of interest as (deterministic) finite state machines for a fixed finite input alphabet I and output alphabet O.

Definition 2.1. *A finite state machine M (FSM) consists of*

1. *a finite set Q, called the* state space,
2. *a function $\delta\colon Q \times I \to Q$, called the* transition function, *and*
3. *a function $\lambda\colon Q \times I \to O$, called the* output function.

For states $q, q' \in Q$, we write $q \xrightarrow{a/o} q'$ to denote $\delta(q, a) = q'$ and $\lambda(q, a) = o$, we call a the input and o the output of the transition. An example FSM is visualized in Fig. 1a on page page 4. We do not require a specified initial state in the definition of FSM since it is not relevant for the task of state identification and verification. In fact, in this task, we are given an FSM in some unknown state and need to derive from the I/O behaviour, in which state the FSM is.

Definition 2.2. *The transition and output functions for an FSM inductively extend to words:*

$$\delta: Q \times I^* \to Q; \qquad \delta^*(q, \epsilon) := q; \qquad \delta^*(q, aw) := \delta^*(\delta(q, a), w)$$
$$\lambda: Q \times I^* \to O^*; \qquad \lambda^*(q, \epsilon) := \epsilon; \qquad \lambda^*(q, aw) := \lambda(q, a) \cdot \lambda^*(\delta(q, a), w)$$

The semantics, i.e. observable behaviour, of a state $q \in Q$ are given as a function $[\![q]\!]: I^* \to O^*$ defined as

$$[\![q]\!](w) := \lambda^*(q, w).$$

Two states q_1 and q_2 are apart [GJ21], i.e., have different observable behaviour, written $w \vdash q_1 \# q_2$, if $w \in I^*$ is an input word on which their semantics differ:

$$[\![q_1]\!](w) \neq [\![q_2]\!](w).$$

Since we are only concerned with observable behaviour, we assume that machines are *minimal*, meaning that all distinct states in the given FSM are apart.

2.1 Testing Problems

We are in a setting where we are provided with a known machine M but do not know in which state it currently is:

State identification: The task is to determine the state the M currently is in. We are allowed to interact with the M by inputting symbols from I and observing the output O. It is fine if those tests alter the current state of M. It is our task to determine the state M was in when we were presented it.

State verification: Given a distinguished state $q \in Q$, the task is to verify whether the FSM is in q.

In either problem, there is no way of resetting the machine. The experiment may consist of multiple inputs and may depend on the previously produced outputs of the machine. In the present paper we focus on state identification and verification since they appear as important subtasks in *model learning* (also called machine identification) and in *conformance testing* and *fault detection*; a survey on these problems is given by Lee and Yannakakis [LY96][1].

---

[1] Lee and Yannakakis wrote two papers with similar titles [LY94, LY96]. The one from 1994 contains the polytime ADS algorithm in detail and the one from 1996 contains a survey with related problems, results (such as bounds), and applications.

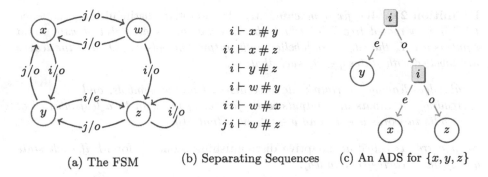

(a) The FSM   (b) Separating Sequences   (c) An ADS for $\{x, y, z\}$

Fig. 1. Example of an FSM with inputs $I = \{i, j\}$ and outputs $O = \{e, o\}$ in which all states are pairwise apart.

2.2   Separating and Distinguishing Sequences

The solutions of the state identification and verification problems boil down to finding clever input sequences such that the output allows us to reason about the states traversed:

Definition 2.3. *For a machine M, a word $w \in I^*$ is*

1. *a separating sequence for two states $p, q \in Q$ if $w \vdash p \# q$.*
2. *a unique input/output sequence (UIO) of a state $p \in Q$ if $w \vdash p \# q$ for all other states $q \in Q$.*
3. *a preset distinguishing sequence (PDS) if $w \vdash p \# q$ for all distinct states $p, q \in Q$.*

Note how each definition requires $w \vdash p \# q$, with the only difference being the quantification over p and q. This also means that a PDS is automatically a UIO and a UIO is automatically a separating sequence. See Fig. 1b for examples of separating sequences.

Separating sequences can be found very efficiently [SMJ16]. Unfortunately, both UIO sequences and PDSs are very hard to find:

Theorem [LY94]. *It is* PSPACE-*complete to decide if a given machine has a PDS and it is* PSPACE-*complete to decide whether a given state in a given machine has a UIO.*

Under the assumption that NP $\neq$ PSPACE, this PSPACE-completeness implies that these sequences are not bounded by any polynomial (otherwise we could find them in NP time).

To overcome this hardness, Lee and Yannakakis looked more closely at the *adaptive* distinguishing sequence. In this sequence of inputs, the choice of input may depend on the output of the machine for the earlier inputs. It is a decision tree rather than just a sequence. The adaptive nature makes it so that after each letter a (possibly) smaller set of states is relevant, and so it becomes easier to continue the experiment.

Definition 2.4. *We fix a machine* M. *An* adaptive distinguishing sequence *(ADS) is a rooted tree* T *of which the internal nodes are labelled with input symbols* $a \in I$, *the edges are labelled with output symbols* $o \in O$, *and the leaves are labelled with states* $q \in Q$, *such that:*

- *all edges leaving a certain node have distinct output symbols, and*
- *reading the inputs and outputs while following the path to a leaf labelled* q, *results in words* $w \in I^*$ *and* $v \in O^*$ *such that* $\lambda(q, w) = v$.

Such a tree is called an adaptive distinguishing sequence for M *if each state* $q \in Q$ *has a corresponding leaf.*

Theorem [LY94, Theorem 3.1]. *Deciding whether a machine has an ADS can be done in polynomial time.*

Example 2.5. We consider the example from Fig. 1a and show that there is no ADS for M. If the ADS would start with i (i.e. i in the root node), then it cannot distinguish w and z because $\delta(w, i) = \delta(z, i)$ and $\lambda(w, i) = \lambda(z, i)$. Similarly, starting with j fails to distinguish y and w. Thus, there is no ADS for the entire FSM of Fig. 1a. However, we can distinguish states for a smaller subset, for example the tree depicted in Fig. 1c distinguishes $\{x, y, z\}$ (and also $\{x, y, w\}$).

A preset distinguishing sequence is also an adaptive distinguishing sequence. And when one follows the root to a leaf in an ADS for the FSM, one obtains a UIO for the state labelled by the leaf. So the existence of these types of sequences are ordered:

$$\text{PDS} \implies \text{ADS (for } M\text{)} \implies \text{UIOs (for all states)}$$

None of the converse implications holds in general: For a minimal FSM M, all pairs of states have a separating sequence, but not every state may have a UIO. Even if every state has a UIO, there may be no ADS for M. And even if there is an ADS, there may be no PDS.

These sequences are related by the testing problems mentioned above. If an ADS exists for the entire FSM, then state identification can be solved with it. Similarly, state verification can be solved with UIO sequences if they exist.

2.3   Identification in a Subset of States

In the context of model learning, we may have additional insight about the FSM in state identification and verification. Given a (partly unknown) machine M in an unknown state, we may already exclude some states based on previous observations, leading to the simplified version of the state identification task:

Local state identification: Given a known machine M that is currently in a state in the subset $Q_0 \subseteq Q$, the task is to identify the current state exactly.

For $Q_0 = Q$, this is the original problem posed above, and if we have only two states (i.e., $Q_0 = \{p, q\}$), then identification problem can be solved with separating sequences. For the general problem where Q_0 is an arbitrary subset of Q, we adjust the previous sequence definitions:

Definition 2.6. *For a machine M and a subset $Q_0 \subseteq Q$, an Q_0-local adaptive distinguishing sequence is an ADS that mentions all states $p \in Q_0$ in its leaves. Likewise, an Q_0-local UIO of a state p is a sequence w such that $w \dashv p \# q$ for all $q \in Q_0$ other than p.*

Surprisingly, finding an ADS for Q_0 is PSPACE-complete, that is, harder than finding an ADS for $Q_0 = Q$, visualized in Fig. 2. This comes from the fact that even if there is no ADS for the full state set Q, there may be one for a subset. An example for such an FSM is depicted in Fig. 1a which does not have an ADS for $Q = \{w, x, y, z\}$ but for the subset $Q_0 = \{x, y, z\}$ (Fig. 1c).

Fig. 2. The general problem of finding ADSs is PSPACE-complete. But at the extreme cases, where Q_0 consists of either two states or all states, the problem is in P.

3 Reduction to SAT Solving

SAT solving is concerned with the problem of finding a satisfying assignment for a boolean propositional formula. This is a fundamental problem in computer science and enjoys a lot of applications [BHvMW09]. Although the problem is NP-complete, there exist implementations which work very well in practice.

Most solvers require the input to be in *conjunctive normal form (CNF)*, which is a conjunction of *clauses*. In turn, a clause is a disjunction of literals, where a literal is a proposition variable or a negation of a proposition variable. Every formula has an equivalent formula in CNF. For instance, we often deal with an implication such as

$$(x_1 \wedge \cdots \wedge x_k) \implies y$$

which is equivalent to the clause

$$\neg x_1 \vee \cdots \vee \neg x_k \vee y.$$

When the conversion to CNF is straightforward (which is the case for implications), we only present the original formula.

Some care is required when turning arbitrary formulas into CNF, as the formula can get substantially bigger. In order to avoid very big CNF formulas, it is sometimes beneficial to introduce auxiliary variables, as we will later do.

Cardinality Constraints. It is very common to require that at most one of a set of literals is satisfied, and such a constraint is called a *cardinality constraint*. Such constraints can be encoded directly in CNF in a variety of ways, we use the following definitions:

$$\text{at-least-1}(x_1, \ldots, x_n) := (x_1 \vee \cdots \vee x_n)$$
$$\text{at-most-1}(x_1, \ldots, x_n) := \bigwedge_{i \neq j} (\neg x_i \vee \neg x_j)$$
$$\text{exactly-1}(x_1, \ldots, x_n) := \text{at-least-1}(x_1, \ldots, x_n) \wedge \text{at-most-1}(x_1, \ldots, x_n)$$

Non-boolean Variables. Often, we want to express not just boolean values, but a variable x with a bounded domain such as $\{1, \ldots, k\}$. We do this with a *one-hot encoding* (also called direct encoding or sparse encoding), meaning that we introduce k variables $x_1, \ldots, x_k$, where x_i means that x has value i. This works in conjunction with the constraint $\text{exactly-1}(x_1, \ldots, x_k)$.

As a convention, we use subscripts for indices used in a one-hot encoding and superscripts otherwise. For example, when we guess a word of length l from an alphabet I, we introduce the variables x_a^i for $1 \leq i \leq l$ and $a \in I$.

We will now translate the problem of finding UIO sequences and ADSs into SAT. We will encode these problems directly in CNF.

3.1 State Verification via UIO Sequences

We fix a machine M with state space Q and a state $q_0 \in Q$. Our task is to find a UIO sequence for q_0, bounded by a length l.

The encoding of finding a UIO sequence of length l is quite straightforward: We guess the sequence, and determine the outputs of all the states when provided with this sequence, and check that those outputs differ in at least one place with the output of q_0.

Encoding. We introduce the variables listed in Table 1[2]. We could, theoretically, encode everything in propositional logic with only the variables $\mathfrak{a}_a^{q_0,i}$. However, by introducing the other variables, the resulting CNF formula is much smaller and easier to construct.

---

[2] We use $\mathfrak{Fraktur}$ letters to distinguish variables in our encoding, such as $\mathfrak{a}$, from variables ranging over sets used as indices, such as a symbol $a \in I$. The symbols are chosen so that $\mathfrak{a}$ stands for alphabet, $\mathfrak{s}$ stands for state, $\mathfrak{o}$ stands for output and $\mathfrak{d}$ stands for difference.

Table 1. Variables for the encoding of the UIO sequence for a fixed state q_0.

Variable	Range	Meaning
$\mathfrak{a}_a^{q_0,i}$	for $1 \leq i \leq l, a \in I$	The UIO sequence has symbol a on index i.
$\mathfrak{s}_{q'}^{q,i}$	for $q, q' \in Q, 1 \leq i \leq l$	State q transitions to q' after reading the first i symbols from the UIO sequence.
$\mathfrak{o}_o^{q,i}$	for $q \in Q, 1 \leq i \leq l, o \in O$	When state q reads the first i symbols from the UIO sequence, then the last transition has output o.
$\mathfrak{d}^{q,i}$	for $1 \leq i \leq l, q \in Q \setminus \{q_0\}$	Auxiliary variable denoting that the runs of q_0 and q for the first i symbols of the UIO sequence end with different outputs.

One-Hot Encoded Variables. For all the one-hot encoded variables, we require that exactly one variable is satisfied.

$$\bigwedge_{1 \leq i \leq l} \text{exactly-1}(\{\mathfrak{a}_a^{q_0,i} \mid a \in I\})$$

$$\wedge \bigwedge_{q \in Q} \bigwedge_{0 \leq i \leq l} \text{exactly-1}(\{\mathfrak{s}_{q'}^{q,i} \mid q' \in Q\})$$

$$\wedge \bigwedge_{q \in Q} \bigwedge_{0 \leq i \leq l} \text{exactly-1}(\{\mathfrak{o}_o^{q,i} \mid o \in O\})$$

Successor States and Output. If the state q is in state q' after i symbols, it should output $\lambda(q', a)$ on the current symbol a:

$$\bigwedge_{q \in Q} \bigwedge_{1 \leq i \leq l} \bigwedge_{a \in I} \left(\mathfrak{s}_{q'}^{q,i-1} \wedge \mathfrak{a}_a^{q_0,i} \implies \mathfrak{o}_{\lambda(q',a)}^{q,i}\right)$$

Similarly, we encode that the successor state is consistent with the guessed word:

$$\bigwedge_{q \in Q} \bigwedge_{1 \leq i \leq l} \bigwedge_{a \in I} \left(\mathfrak{s}_{q'}^{q,i-1} \wedge \mathfrak{a}_a^{q_0,i} \implies \mathfrak{s}_{\delta(q',a)}^{q,i}\right)$$

In the above formulas, when $i = 1$, we use a new variable $\mathfrak{s}_{q'}^{q,0}$ as short-hand notation for

$$\mathfrak{s}_{q'}^{q,0} := \begin{cases} \top & \text{if } q = q' \\ \bot & \text{if } q \neq q'. \end{cases}$$

Differences. So far, we have encoded a word and the according outputs starting from each state. In order to find UIOs, we need that the outputs of q_0 are different from the outputs of others states q (at some index i). First we encode what it means for a difference to occur, using the variables $\mathfrak{d}^{q',i}$:

$$\bigwedge_{q' \in Q \setminus \{q_0\}} \bigwedge_{1 \leq i \leq l} \bigwedge_{o \in O} \left(\mathfrak{d}^{q',i} \wedge \mathfrak{o}_o^{q_0,i} \implies \neg \mathfrak{o}_o^{q',i}\right)$$

In words this reads: if a difference is claimed (i.e., $\mathfrak{d}^{q,i}$ is guessed to be true), and if q_0 outputs o, then q' may not do so. We do not need to encode the converse direction explicitly.

Finally, we require at least one difference for each state:

$$\bigwedge_{q' \in Q \setminus \{q_0\}} \text{at-least-1}\left(\mathfrak{d}^{q',1}, \mathfrak{d}^{q',2}, \ldots, \mathfrak{d}^{q',l}\right)$$

Putting it Together. Denote the conjunction of all above clauses by

$$\text{UIO}(M, l, q_0).$$

Lemma 3.1. *Given a machine M, a length l, and a state q_0, the CNF formula* $\text{UIO}(M, l, q_0)$ *is satisfiable if and only if q_0 has a UIO sequence of length l.*

Improvements. In order to keep the above encoding simple, we have omitted the following improvements from the above presentation. The improvements are explained in more detail in the implementation.

Only Encode Reachable States. As presented, the variables $\mathfrak{s}_{q'}^{q,i}$ are created for all $q' \in Q$. This is unnecessary, and only the states reachable from q in exactly i steps have to be considered. Similarly for the outputs.

Searching Multiple UIOs. In many situations, we may want to find UIO sequences for multiple states. It is then beneficial to re-use most of the constructed formula. This can be achieved with *incremental SAT-solving* [ES03b].

Extending UIOs to Obtain New UIOs. If a UIO sequence w for state q has been found, then this could possibly lead to UIO sequences for predecessors of q. Namely, if q' is a state with a transition $q' \xrightarrow{a/o} q$ and the input/output pair (a, o) is unique among the predecessors of q, then aw is a UIO sequence for q'.

To use this idea, we define the *UIO implication graph* as follows. The nodes are the states in Q, and there is an edge from q to q' if a UIO sequence for q can be extended (by 1 symbol) to a UIO for q'. This graph can be precomputed and many UIOs can be found by traversing this graph. Note, however, that the found UIOs may not be of minimal length.

Incrementing the Length. The presented encoding works with a fixed bound. It is useful to start with a low bound and increment this bound one-by-one. This way, we can find short UIOs for many states, and only need to construct large formulas for the states which have no short UIOs.

3.2   State Identification via Adaptive Distinguishing Sequences

If we want to identify the current state of an FSM, we can construct an ADS for a fixed machine M with states Q in a similar way. We fix a subset $Q_0 \subseteq Q$ of potential initial states and a bound l on the length of the sequence. (The length of an ADS is the *depth* of the tree.)

The encoding of an ADS is less straightforward than for UIO sequences, because we are not searching for a single word, but for a tree structure. To tackle this problem, we recall a remark by Lee and Yannakakis [LY96, Section IV.A] which relates adaptive distinguishing sequences to sets of sequences:

"[..] we can satisfy the separation property with all sets Z_i being singletons if and only if A has an adaptive distinguishing sequence."

The sets Z_i contain sequences, and if there exists an ADS, these sets are singletons. So, instead of searching for a tree, we may as well search for one sequence per state (together with additional requirements). We rephrase this result in the following lemma.

Lemma 3.2. *The following are in one-to-one correspondence:*

1. *An adaptive distinguishing sequence for $Q_0 \subseteq Q$*
2. *A map $f\colon Q_0 \to I^*$ such that for all $q, q' \in Q_0$ with $q \neq q'$:*
   (a) $f(q) \vdash q \# q'$ (i.e. $f(q)$ is a Q_0-local UIO for q).
   (b) if wa is a prefix of $f(q)$ and $[\![q]\!](w) = [\![q']\!](w)$, then wa is also a prefix of $f(q')$.

Proof (Sketch). Given an ADS for Q_0, define $f\colon Q_0 \to I^*$ as the map that sends $q \in Q_0$ to word $v \in I^*$ on the internal nodes leading to q in the ADS. This map satisfies the two properties: (a) For $q' \in Q_0$ with $q \neq q'$, the definition of ADS implies $[\![q]\!](v) \neq [\![q']\!](v)$. (b) If wa is a prefix of v, and $[\![q]\!](w) = [\![q']\!](w)$, then q' must also be in the subtree of the ADS to which w leads and whose node is labelled a.

Conversely, we can recursively build an ADS from such a map $f\colon Q_0 \to I^*$: if $|Q_0| < 2$ the ADS is trivial. If Q_0 has at least two elements there must be some $a \in I$ that is the prefix of all $f(q)$, $q \in Q_0$ by (b). Thus, the root is labelled a and it has a subtree for each element of $\{[\![q]\!](i) \mid q \in Q_0\} \subseteq O$. The subtree reached via $o \in O$ is recursively constructed for $Q_0' := \{q \in Q_0 \mid [\![q]\!](a) = o\}$ and $f'\colon Q_0' \to I^*$, $f'(q) = w$ with $aw = f(q)$.   □

Encoding. We introduce the variables listed in Table 2. The encoding is similar to that of UIO sequences. There is one crucial difference: here every state q has an associated word $f(q)$ in the sense of Lemma 3.2. In order to achive that these words describe a tree, these input words $f(q)$, $f(q')$ for different states q, q' must be the same, as long as the two states also produce the same output symbols, as described by the condition in Lemma 3.2.

Table 2. Variables used for the ADS encoding

Variable	Range	Meaning
$\mathfrak{a}_a^{q,i}$	for $q \in Q_0, 1 \leq i \leq l, a \in I$	On the word for state q the ith symbol is a.
$\mathfrak{s}_{q'}^{q,i}$	for $q \in Q_0, q' \in Q, 0 \leq i \leq l$	State q transitions to q' after reading the first i symbols from its word.
$\mathfrak{o}_o^{q,i}$	for $q \in Q_0, 1 \leq i \leq l, o \in O$	State q outputs o after reading i symbols from its word.
$\mathfrak{d}^{q,q',i}$	for $q, q' \in Q_0, 1 \leq i \leq l$	Auxiliary variable denoting that there is a difference between the outputs of q and q' at position i.
$\overline{\mathfrak{d}}^{q,q',i}$	for $q, q' \in Q_0, 1 \leq i \leq l$	Auxiliary variable denoting that there is a difference between the outputs of q and q at position i or earlier. This is used to allow different input symbols.

One-Hot Encoded Variables. We again start by requiring that every one-hot encoded variable has exactly one value enabled:

$$\bigwedge_{q \in Q_0} \bigwedge_{1 \leq i \leq l} \text{exactly-1}(\{\mathfrak{a}_a^{q,i} \mid a \in I\})$$

$$\wedge \bigwedge_{q \in Q_0} \bigwedge_{0 \leq i \leq l} \text{exactly-1}(\{\mathfrak{s}_{q'}^{q,i} \mid q' \in Q\})$$

$$\wedge \bigwedge_{q \in Q_0} \bigwedge_{0 \leq i \leq l} \text{exactly-1}(\{\mathfrak{o}_o^{q,i} \mid o \in O\})$$

Successor States and Outputs. Similarly to the UIO sequences, we require that the guessed successor states and outputs are consistent with the transition and output function:

$$\bigwedge_{q \in Q_0} \bigwedge_{1 \leq i \leq l} \bigwedge_{q' \in Q} \bigwedge_{a \in I} \left(\mathfrak{s}_{q'}^{q,i-1} \wedge \mathfrak{a}_a^{q,i} \implies \mathfrak{s}_{\delta(q',a)}^{q,i}\right) \wedge \left(\mathfrak{s}_{q'}^{q,i-1} \wedge \mathfrak{a}_a^{q,i} \implies \mathfrak{o}_{\lambda(q',a)}^{q,i}\right)$$

Differences. If the solver claims one of the $\mathfrak{d}^{q,q',i}$ to be true, then there must be an actual difference in output:

$$\bigwedge_{q \neq q' \in Q_0} \bigwedge_{1 \leq i \leq l} \bigwedge_{o \in O} \left(\mathfrak{d}^{q,q',i} \wedge \mathfrak{o}_o^{q,i} \implies \neg \mathfrak{o}_o^{q',i}\right)$$

And we encode the fact that there is at least one difference for each pairs of states $q, q' \in Q_0$.

$$\bigwedge_{q \neq q' \in Q_0} \text{at-least-1} \left(\mathfrak{d}^{q,q',1}, \mathfrak{d}^{q,q',2}, \ldots, \mathfrak{d}^{q,q',l}\right)$$

Shared Prefixes. Finally, we have to assert that the words of two states are the same as long as there is no observed difference in output. First, we encode the "closure" of difference:

$$\bigwedge_{q \neq q' \in Q_0} (\overline{\eth}^{q,q',1} \implies \eth^{q,q',1}) \wedge \bigwedge_{2 \leq i \leq l} (\overline{\eth}^{q,q',i} \implies (\eth^{q,q',i} \vee \overline{\eth}^{q,q',i-1}))$$

In words this means that $\overline{\eth}^{q,q',j}$ may only hold true if some difference $\eth^{q,q',i}$ holds true earlier (i.e., for some $i \leq j$). (We only need to encode one direction of the implication.)

Second, states must use the same inputs as long as $\overline{\eth}^{q,q',i}$ is still false. Note that the first symbols are always equal.

$$\bigwedge_{q \neq q' \in Q_0} \bigwedge_{a \in I} (\mathfrak{a}_a^{q,1} \implies \mathfrak{a}_a^{q',1}) \wedge \bigwedge_{2 \leq i \leq l} (\neg \overline{\eth}^{q,q',i-1} \wedge \mathfrak{a}_a^{q,i} \implies \mathfrak{a}_a^{q',i})$$

Putting it Together. Denote the conjunction of the above clauses by

$$\mathsf{ADS}(M, l, Q_0).$$

Lemma 3.3. *Given a machine M, a length $l \in \mathbb{N}$ and a subset Q_0, the formula $\mathsf{ADS}(M, l, Q_0)$ is satisfiable if and only if there exists an ADS for Q_0 of depth l.*

Improvements. Some of the same improvements mentioned for the UIO sequence apply here as well. Nevertheless, there is one interesting optimization specifically for the ADS problem.

Encoding Distinct Successors. As long as two states $q, q' \in Q_0$ produce the same outputs for an input word $w \in I^*$, i.e. a path in the ADS, the states must *not* transition to the same state $\delta(q, w) = \delta(q', w)$, because this would make the states indistinguishable. In the Lee and Yannakakis algorithm, this is called *validity* of a split or transition. Every ADS has this validity property, so the ADS found by the solver will also have this property. We can encode this property explicitly to help the solver to prune the search. The following clauses state that as long as there is no difference and one state transitions to q'', then the other state is not allowed to transition to q''.

$$\bigwedge_{q \neq q' \in Q_0} \bigwedge_{2 \leq i \leq l} \bigwedge_{q'' \in Q} (\neg \overline{\eth}^{q,q',i-1} \wedge \mathfrak{s}_{q''}^{q,i} \implies \neg \mathfrak{s}_{q''}^{q',i})$$

In one instance, the solving time was reduced from 90 min to a mere 2 min. It is not unlikely that other such redundant clauses can be added to improve the runtime.

4 Preliminary Experimental Results

4.1 Implementation

The encoding is implemented in Python and the solving is done through the PySAT package [IMM18]. This package supports several SAT solvers, such as MINISAT [ES03a], GLUCOSE [AS09]. The implementation can be found at

https://github.com/Jaxan/satuio.

Throughout the experiments, the SAT solver we use is GLUCOSE3, as this worked well enough on some preliminary tests. PySAT also allows different encodings for the cardinality constraints as explained in Sect. 3. We stick to the default encoding provided by PySAT, which is based on sequential counters [Sin05].

The experiments are run on a 2020 MacBook Air (with an M1 chip) on a single core. We use Python version 3.10.2 and PySAT version 0.1.7.dev16.

4.2 Benchmarks

We use finite state machines from the open automata wiki [NSVK18]. This wiki contains many models from a variety of real-world domains, such as internet communication protocols, smart cards, and embedded systems. We pick the following two sets of models.

Small Models from Protocols. We have picked the models which are learned from the DTLS implementations [FJM+20] and MQTT implementations [TAB17] with fewer than 50 states. Both DTLS and MQTT are internet protocols with many (open source) implementations. These are state machines with fewer than 50 states and have between 6 and 11 inputs.

Big Model from an Embedded System. In order to test the scalability of the encoding, we use the biggest model from the automata wiki, which is the ESM controller [SMVJ15]. This is a state machine in control of printer hardware and has 3410 states and 78 inputs. This was used in a case study for automata learning, and the automata wiki also includes the intermediate hypotheses, which we use as a family of models of increasing size.

4.3 UIO Experiments

For the UIO sequences, we will compare our efficiency to an algorithm by Naik [Nai97]. We only have implemented their base algorithm, which is a nontrivial enumerative search. It searches UIO sequences for all states at the same time, returning sequences as it finds them.

For each small benchmark, we run both algorithms with a time limit of 3 s. For the bigger benchmarks, we set a time limit of 10 min. We report how many

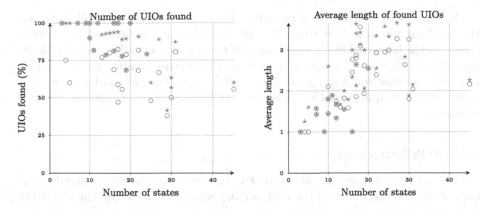

Fig. 3. Results for the small benchmark, comparing our tool (⋆) and Naik's algorithm (○) (timeout = 3 s). The number of UIOs found as fraction of the state space is plotted left and the average length of the found UIOs is plotted right. Note that there may be several models with the same number of states.

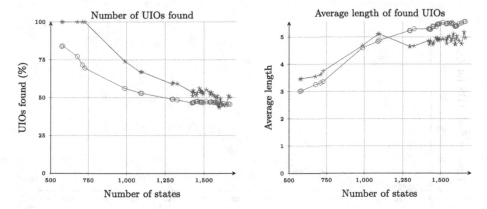

Fig. 4. Results for the big benchmark, comparing our tool (⋆) and Naik's algorithm (○) (timeout = 10 min). The number of UIOs found as fraction of the state space is plotted left and the average length of the found UIOs is plotted right.

UIOs each algorithm finds within that time. Note that some models have states without UIO sequences, meaning that a search may take a very long time (as the upper bound on the length is exponential). This is the reason it is necessary to set a time bound, even for the small models. Also note that both algorithms search in a non-deterministic way, and so one can be lucky or unlucky in specific instances.

The results are shown in Figs. 3 and 4. In almost all instances, our algorithm was able to find more UIO sequences than the baseline algorithm. However, the baseline algorithm results, on average, in shorter sequences. This may be because it finds fewer, or because it finds the shortest ones first.

We also note that our tool can often find UIO sequences for all states for the small models in a short time (3 s) and that the UIO sequences are generally short. In the big benchmark, the found UIO sequences are still relatively short, but after the first five models, we do not find UIO sequences for all states. This is partly because not every state has a UIO sequence, and partly because it is becoming computationally harder to find them when the number of states increase.

4.4 ADS Experiments

For the ADS we do not have an alternative implementation. So we include some experiments to see how well the SAT solving scales. We only run the algorithm for the big benchmark with 3410 states and 78 inputs. (This machine does not admit an ADS for all states.) For the set of potential initial states, Q_0, we pick a random subset of specified size and set the bound (i.e., depth of the tree) to be 7.

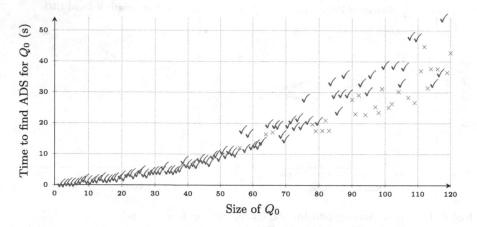

Fig. 5. Finding ADSs for a random subset Q_0, of increasing size. The state machine used here is the big benchmark with 3410 states and 78 inputs. The checkmarks ($\checkmark$) indicate satisfiability and the crosses ($\times$) indicate unsatisfiability.

Figure 5 shows the runtime for finding an ADS of given size in the big benchmark. We observe that for small sets Q_0 the solver is able to find adaptive distinguishing sequences in mere seconds. But already for 120 states (which is a small fraction of the total 3410 states), the algorithm needs almost a full minute to find an ADS or to prove unsatisfiability.

We also observe that bigger sets Q_0 more often lead to unsatisfiability. For these sets, a bigger bound could provide an ADS, at the cost of more computation time. Interestingly, we see that the solver can prove unsatisfiability a bit faster than satisfiability.

5 Conclusions and Future Work

We have presented and evaluated a reduction of UIO and ADS computation to satisfiability checking of CNF formulae, such that the ADS and UIO can be determined from the satisfying assignment of the formula. The experiments show that the reduction is able to find many UIO sequences and ADSs. For the UIO sequences it is competitive with a non-trivial search algorithm by Naik [Nai97]. Unfortunately, for the larger benchmark, the computation time is still rather large. The experiments also show that, if sequences are found, they are often short, even in larger models.

The reduction may add some overhead compared to direct implementations for searching these sequences, but it is a versatile solution. The high level encoding into logic allows us to change the requirements easily, without having to integrate these changes in a search algorithm. One such variation is an extension to partiality, meaning that the FSM might have an unknown behaviour for certain input letters $a \in I$. This is the setting in the $L^\sharp$ learning algorithm [VGRW22], where all observations are gathered in a tree, which happens to be a partial FSM. Here, the partiality expresses that the behaviour for certain inputs is still unknown, as those inputs have not yet been tested. We are optimistic that the our generic encoding techniques can also help finding adaptive distinguishing sequences for partial Mealy machines and other flavours of finite-state machines that arise in the future.

Acknowledgements. We would like to thank Alexander Fedotov for providing an implementation of Naik's algorithm in Java. We are grateful for the many suggestions by the referees that helped improving the present paper.

References

[AS09]   Audemard, G., Simon, L.: Predicting learnt clauses quality in modern SAT solvers. In: Proceedings of the 21st International Joint Conference on Artificial Intelligence IJCAI, pp. 399–404 (2009)

[BHvMW09] Biere, A., Heule, M., van Maaren, H. (eds.).: Handbook of Satisfiability, volume 185 of Frontiers in Artificial Intelligence and Applications. IOS Press (2009)

[ES03a]   Eén, N., Sörensson, N.: An extensible sat-solver. In: Theory and Applications of Satisfiability Testing, 6th International Conference, SAT 2003. Selected Revised Papers, volume 2919 of LNCS, pp. 502–518. Springer (2003). https://doi.org/10.1007/978-3-540-24605-337

[ES03b]   Eén, N., Sörensson, N.: Temporal induction by incremental SAT solving. Electron. Notes Theor. Comput. Sci. **89**(4), 543–560 (2003)

[FJM+20]   Fiterau-Brostean, P., Jonsson, B., Merget, R., de Ruiter, J., Sagonas, K., Somorovsky, J.: Analysis of DTLS implementations using protocol state fuzzing. In: USENIX Security Symposium, pp. 2523–2540. USENIX Association (2020)

[GJ21]   Geuvers, H., Jacobs, B.: Relating apartness and bisimulation. Logical Meth. Comput. Sci. **17**(3) (2021). https://doi.org/10.46298/lmcs-17(3:15)2021

[IMM18]   Ignatiev, A., Morgado, A., Marques-Silva, J.: PySAT: a python toolkit for prototyping with SAT oracles. In: SAT, volume 10929 of LNCS, pp. 428–437 (2018). https://doi.org/10.1007/978-3-319-94144-826

[LY94]   Lee, D., Yannakakis, M.: Testing finite-state machines: state identification and verification. IEEE Trans. Comput. **43**(3), 306–320 (1994). https://doi.org/10.1109/12.272431

[LY96]   Lee, D., Yannakakis, M.: Principles and methods of testing finite state machines - a survey. Proc. IEEE **84**, 1090–1123 (1996). https://doi.org/10.1109/5.533956

[Nai97]   Naik, K.: Efficient computation of unique input/output sequences in finite-state machines. IEEE/ACM Trans. Netw. **5**(4), 585–599 (1997)

[NSVK18] Neider, D., Smetsers, R., Vaandrager, F., Kuppens, H.: Benchmarks for automata learning and conformance testing. In: Margaria, T., Graf, S., Larsen, K.G. (eds.) Models, Mindsets, Meta: The What, the How, and the Why Not? LNCS, vol. 11200, pp. 390–416. Springer, Cham (2019). https://doi.org/10.1007/978-3-030-22348-9_23

[Sin05]   Sinz, C.: Towards an optimal CNF encoding of boolean cardinality constraints. In: van Beek, P. (ed.) CP 2005. LNCS, vol. 3709, pp. 827–831. Springer, Heidelberg (2005). https://doi.org/10.1007/11564751_73

[SMJ16]   Smetsers, R., Moerman, J., Jansen, D.N.: Minimal separating sequences for all pairs of states. In: Dediu, A.-H., Janoušek, J., Martín-Vide, C., Truthe, B. (eds.) LATA 2016. LNCS, vol. 9618, pp. 181–193. Springer, Cham (2016). https://doi.org/10.1007/978-3-319-30000-9_14

[SMVJ15] Smeenk, W., Moerman, J., Vaandrager, F., Jansen, D.N.: Applying automata learning to embedded control software. In: Butler, M., Conchon, S., Zaïdi, F. (eds.) ICFEM 2015. LNCS, vol. 9407, pp. 67–83. Springer, Cham (2015). https://doi.org/10.1007/978-3-319-25423-4_5

[TAB17]   Tappler, M., Aichernig, B.K., Bloem, R.: Model-based testing IoT communication via active automata learning. In: ICST, pp. 276–287. IEEE Computer Society (2017)

[VGRW22] Vaandrager, F., Garhewal, B., Rot, B., Wißmann, T.: A new approach for active automata learning based on apartness. In: Tools and Algorithms for the Construction and Analysis of Systems - 28th International Conference, TACAS: Lecture Notes in Computer Science. Springer **04**, 2022 (2022). https://doi.org/10.1007/978-3-030-99524-9_12

A Note on the Message Complexity of Cidon's Distributed Depth-First Search Algorithm

Saidgani Musaev and Wan Fokkink[✉]

Vrije Universiteit, Amsterdam, The Netherlands
w.j.fokkink@vu.nl

Abstract. The same distributed depth-first search algorithm was proposed independently by Lakshmanan, Meenakshi, and Thulasiraman, who gave $4E - N$ as upper bound on the worst-case message complexity of the algorithm, and by Cidon, who gave $3E$ as upper bound. We determine the exact worst-case message complexity and show that the upper bound of $3E$ by Cidon is too strict.

1 Introduction

In distributed computing, often information needs to be gathered from all nodes in the network, requiring the construction of a sink tree toward a designated root node. One approach is to build a depth-first search (DFS) tree. Awerbuch [1] defined a token-based distributed DFS (DDFS) algorithm, which is an improvement of an earlier DDFS algorithm by Cheung [2]. Lakshmanan, Meenakshi, and Thulasiraman [5] and Cidon [3] independently proposed the same improvement upon Awerbuch's algorithm; in line with [4,8], we will refer to this improved version as Cidon's algorithm. The traversal of the token through the network is started by the root of the DFS tree. Before a node p sends the token for the first time, it sends information messages to its neighbors, to try to avoid that these neighbors send the token to p in the future. Unlike Awerbuch's algorithm, Cidon's algorithm does not include acknowledgments in response to such information messages, and p may forward the token without delay. As a result, p can receive a spurious token from a neighbor q. The key observation in [3,5] is that this situation can be recognized at p and q, and can be resolved without loss of time.

Lakshmanan, Meenakshi, and Thulasiraman proved that $4E - N$ is an upper bound on the worst-case message complexity of their algorithm, where E is the number of edges and N the number of nodes in the network. Cidon proved a sharper upper bound of $3E$, where his line of reasoning is that no edge ever carries more than three messages (tokens or information messages) during executions of the algorithm. Tsin [9] showed that Cidon's analysis of the worst-case message complexity is flawed, by giving an execution in which four messages are sent through one of the edges. Tsin however did not present an execution that violates Cidon's worst-case message complexity of $3E$.

© The Author(s), under exclusive license to Springer Nature Switzerland AG 2022
N. Jansen et al. (Eds.): Vaandrager Festschrift 2022, LNCS 13560, pp. 467–471, 2022.
https://doi.org/10.1007/978-3-031-15629-8_24

We determine the exact worst-case message complexity of Cidon's algorithm. Furthermore, we provide an execution on complete network topologies that violates Cidon's bound of $3E$, for $N \geq 5$.

With pleasure we dedicate this paper to Frits Vaandrager, on the occasion of his 60th birthday. His research works play a pivotal role in the formal analysis of communication protocols and algorithms for distributed systems. Notably, in [10] he proved correct a distributed algorithm, somewhat related to depth-first search, in which all nodes in a distributed network report their weights to a designated root node via a spanning tree, so that this root can determine the sum of all these weights.

2   Cidon's DDFS Algorithm

Consider a connected distributed network consisting of $N > 1$ nodes and E bidirectional edges, with message passing communication. A token-based DDFS algorithm builds a DFS tree in the network by forwarding a token through the entire network in a depth-first fashion, starting from the designated root node. Each nonroot selects as parent in the DFS tree the neighbor from which it receives the token for the first time. The token is forwarded between nodes according to two rules: (1) the token is not forwarded to the same neighbor twice; and (2) a nonroot only forwards the token to its parent if there is no other option left. After having visited all nodes, the token eventually returns to the root who cannot forward the token anymore, and the algorithm terminates.

The message-optimal token-based DDFS algorithm of Sharma, Iyengar, and Mandyam [7] keeps the list of IDs of all visited nodes in the token. The token is not forwarded to neighbors whose IDs are in this list. This guarantees that the token only travels up and down the $N - 1$ tree edges of the DFS tree, so that the message complexity is $2N - 2$. However, since the token contains a list of IDs, the algorithm has a relatively high bit complexity. The variant of this algorithm by Makki and Havas [6] in some cases sends fewer token messages up the DFS tree, but still has the same the worst-case message and bit complexity as [7].

In Cidon's algorithm [3,5], each node p, when it holds the token for the first time, informs its neighbors that it has seen the token. Two neighbors of p are spared this information message: the node to which p will send the token next and, if p is a nonroot, p's parent. Next, p forwards the token (without delay, unlike Awerbuch's algorithm [1]) and records to which node $forward_p$ it forwarded the token last. A third rule is added to the forwarding procedure: (3) the token is not forwarded to neighbors from which an information message has been received. If p receives the token from a node $q \neq forward_p$, then it dismisses the token and marks the edge pq as a frond edge, meaning that it is not a tree edge. No further action from p is required, because q will eventually receive the information message from $forward_q = p$. Then in turn q marks the edge pq as a frond edge and continues to forward the token to another node (if possible).

If it is assumed that a message takes at most one time unit to reach its destination, then the worst-case time complexity of Cidon's algorithm is $2N - 2$

time units, because at least once per time unit the token is forwarded through a tree edge, and the $N-1$ tree edges all carry two tokens. Frond edges may carry two information messages and two tokens, so an upper bound on the worst-case message complexity is $4E$. Lakshmanan, Meenakshi, and Thulasiraman proved a sharper bound of $4E - N$. Cidon argued that actually in each execution, edges carry at most three messages, meaning that $3E$ would be an upper bound on the worst-case message complexity. However, Tsin [9] showed there exist executions in which four messages are sent through the same edge. But he did not present an execution that takes more than $3E$ messages.

3   On the Message Complexity of Cidon's Algorithm

We present an execution of Cidon's algorithm on a complete network topology (i.e., there is a bidirectional edge between each pair of distinct nodes) that takes $4E-2N+1$ messages. This execution violates Cidon's bound of $3E$ if $E > 2N-1$, which is the case for a complete graph, meaning that $E = \frac{N(N-1)}{2}$, if $N \geq 5$.

The idea behind the execution is simply to delay the arrival of an information message through an edge until a token has been sent into the same edge in the opposite direction. We assume fully asynchronous message communication: there is no upper bound on the time between the sending and reception of the same message. Let $p_0, \ldots, p_{N-1}$ be the $N \geq 3$ nodes in the complete network, where p_0 is the designated root of the DFS tree. In the end, p_{i-1} is the parent of p_i in the DFS tree for $i = 1, \ldots, N-1$. Initially, p_0 sends $N-2$ information messages to $p_2, \ldots, p_{N-1}$ and the token to p_1. When the token from p_{i-1} arrives at p_i for $i = 1, \ldots, N-1$, p_i sends $N-3$ information messages to all nodes except $p_{i-1}, p_i, p_{(i+1) \bmod N}$ and the token to $p_{(i+1) \bmod N}$. So ultimately, when $i = N-1$, p_{N-1} sends the token p_0. Note that at that moment, all information messages are still in transit. Note moreover that eventually p_0 will dismiss the token from p_{N-1}. The network configuration, with $N = 4$, can now be depicted as follows, where t represents a token and i an information message in transit.

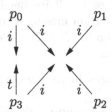

Next, for $j = 0, \ldots, N-4$, p_{N-1} receives the information message from p_j and then sends the token to p_{j+1}. Finally, p_{N-1} receives the information message from p_{N-3} and then sends the token back to its parent p_{N-2}. After this chain of events, the network configuration, with $N = 4$, can be depicted as follows.

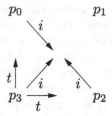

Now, for $i = N - 2, \ldots, 1$, p_i performs the following chain of events. First it receives the token from p_{i+1}. Next, for $j = i+2, \ldots, N+i-2$, p_i sends the token to $p_{j \bmod N}$ and then receives the information message from $p_{j \bmod N}$. Finally, p_i sends the token to its parent p_{i-1}. After this chain of events, the network configuration, with $N = 4$, can be depicted as follows.

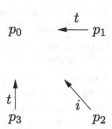

To conclude, p_0 performs the following chain of events. First it receives the token from p_1. Next, for $j = 2, \ldots, N - 2$, p_0 sends the token to p_j and then receives the information message from p_j. Finally, p_0 sends the token p_{N-1} and receives the token from p_{N-1}, after which the execution terminates.

We analyze the number of messages sent in the execution described above, for general N.

- Each node sends the token to all its neighbors, which adds up to $N(N-1) = N^2 - N$ token messages in total.
- p_0 sends information messages to all its neighbors except p_1, while p_i for $i = 1, \ldots, N - 1$ sends information messages to all its neighbors except p_{i-1} and $p_{(i+1) \bmod N}$. This adds up to $(N - 2) + (N - 1)(N - 3) = N^2 - 3N + 1$ information messages in total.

So the overall number of messages in the execution on a complete network is $2N^2 - 4N + 1$.

To determine a precise upper bound on the worst-case message complexity of Cidon's algorithm, consider a general distributed network. Let N^* denote the number of nonroots that have at least two edges. We can perform an execution like the one we exhibited on a complete graph, in which information messages are delayed as much as possible. In such an execution, each node sends tokens to all its neighbors, adding up to $2E$ token messages. Furthermore, the root sends information messages to all but one of its neighbors. And each nonroot with at least two edges sends information messages to all but two of its neighbors, while each nonroot with one edge sends no information messages. This adds up to $2E - (N + N^*)$ information messages. So $4E - (N + N^*)$ messages in total. (For complete networks this boils down to $2N^2 - 4N + 1$, because then $E = \frac{N(N-1)}{2}$ and $N^* = N - 1$.)

4   Conclusion

We argued that the precise upper bound on the worst-case message complexity of Cidon's algorithm is $4E - (N + N^*)$, where N^* denotes the number of nonroots that have at least two edges. In particular, we presented an execution on a complete network topology that violates Cidon's bound of $3E$, in case $N \geq 5$.

Tsin observed a second flaw in Cidon's algorithm: a node may consider a neighbor its child in the DFS tree while in reality it is not. For instance, at the end of the execution on a complete network that was described in detail in this paper, p_0 would falsely consider p_{N-1} its child. This problem is avoided by Lakshmanan, Meenakshi, and Thulasiraman, who distinguish token messages traveling down the DFS tree from token messages traveling up the DFS tree. We did not take this subtlety into account here because it has no effect on the message complexity.

References

1. Awerbuch, B.: A new distributed depth-first-search algorithm. Inf. Process. Lett. **20**(3), 147–150 (1985)
2. Cheung, T.-Y.: Graph traversal techniques and the maximum flow problem in distributed computation. IEEE Trans. Softw. Eng. **9**(4), 504–512 (1983)
3. Cidon, I.: Yet another distributed depth-first search algorithm. Inf. Process. Lett. **26**(6), 301–305 (1988)
4. Fokkink, W.J.: Distributed Algorithms: An Intuitive Approach, 2nd edn. MIT Press, Cambridge (2018)
5. Lakshmanan, K.B., Meenakshi, N., Thulasiraman, K.: A time-optimal message-efficient distributed algorithm for depth-first search. Inf. Process. Lett. **25**(2), 103–109 (1987)
6. Makki, S.A.M., Havas, G.: Distributed algorithms for depth-first-search. Inf. Process. Lett. **60**(1), 7–12 (1996)
7. Sharma, M.B., Iyengar, S.S.: An efficient distributed depth-first-search algorithm. Inf. Process. Lett. **32**(4), 183–186 (1989)
8. Tel, G.: Introduction to Distributed Algorithms, 2nd edn. Cambridge University Press, Cambridge (2000)
9. Tsin, Y.H.: Some remarks on distributed depth-first search. Inf. Process. Lett. **82**(4), 173–178 (2002)
10. Vaandrager, F.: Verification of a distributed summation algorithm. In: Lee, I., Smolka, S.A. (eds.) CONCUR 1995. LNCS, vol. 962, pp. 190–203. Springer, Heidelberg (1995). https://doi.org/10.1007/3-540-60218-6_14

Minesweeper is Difficult Indeed!
Technology Scaling for Minesweeper Circuits

Alex Thieme[1] and Twan Basten[1,2]($\boxtimes$) (iD)

[1] Eindhoven University of Technology, Eindhoven, The Netherlands
`a.a.basten@tue.nl`
[2] ESI (TNO), Eindhoven, The Netherlands

Abstract. Various aspects of playing minesweeper have been proven to be (co-)NP-complete through reductions from circuit-SAT and UNSAT. The proofs use quite involved minesweeper templates to simulate Boolean formulas and circuits. We provide a set of much simpler synthesis templates, leading to much smaller circuit simulations in minesweeper.

Keywords: Games · Complexity · Circuit simulation

1 Introduction

Minesweeper was and is a popular single-player computer game first released by Microsoft in Windows 3.1 [14]. As for many games, the question was raised whether or not the game is efficiently solvable, i.e., whether or not there is a polynomial-time algorithm to compute a winning strategy. For many games, this is actually not the case (assuming P $\neq$ NP). Minesweeper is among the games for which it turns out that there is no efficient solution strategy.

Minesweeper consistency is the decision problem asking the question whether or not a partial minesweeper configuration can be completed to a valid minesweeper instance. Kaye [6] introduced minesweeper consistency and showed its NP-completeness through reduction from circuit-SAT. circuit-SAT is the problem to decide whether or not a one-output Boolean circuit is satisfiable, i.e., whether or not a Boolean valuation of the circuit's inputs exists such that the output becomes 1. Kaye's reduction uses a set of minesweeper templates, corresponding to gates and wiring elements, to simulate Boolean circuits in minesweeper.

Scott et al. [8] argue that repeatedly checking minesweeper consistency is not the only possible way of playing minesweeper, implying that Kaye's reasoning does not show NP-completeness of playing minesweeper. They define the minesweeper inference problem, asking the question whether or not for a given partial minesweeper instance that is known to be consistent, there is a covered square that is derivably safe or unsafe. Scott et al. use templates similar to those of Kaye to show that minesweeper inference is co-NP-complete, by reduction from Boolean unsatisfiability, UNSAT. UNSAT is the problem to decide whether a Boolean formula built from and, or, and not operators and variables

© The Author(s), under exclusive license to Springer Nature Switzerland AG 2022
N. Jansen et al. (Eds.): Vaandrager Festschrift 2022, LNCS 13560, pp. 472–490, 2022.
https://doi.org/10.1007/978-3-031-15629-8_25

cannot be satisfied. UNSAT is the complement of Boolean satisfiability, SAT, the problem whether or not a Boolean formula is satisfiable.

All the circuit-simulation minesweeper templates proposed by Kaye and Scott et al. use safe squares as boundaries to create and isolate information flows. We provide circuit-synthesis templates that use mines to create information flows. Mines form a strict isolating boundary so that no information leaks to neighboring squares. This leads to more compact and easier to understand templates and circuits. For instance, a 2-input circuit with three literals and two or gates that fits within a 57×21 minesweeper instance with the templates and synthesis approach of this paper, takes 204×84 squares with the templates of Scott et al.[1]. The key ideas underlying the minesweeper circuit-simulation templates and circuit-synthesis approach developed in this paper are the following:

- Mines are used to create the information flow in Boolean circuits and to isolate these flows from their environment.
- Inversion (logical negation) is done with a 3×3 kernel that also serves as a building block for wires. Consequently, explicit not gates are not needed for circuit synthesis; inversion can be done in the circuit wiring as appropriate.
- A simple 3×3 kernel suffices to create four logic states; this kernel serves as a basis for compact gate templates and wire crossings.

We illustrate how the provided templates can be used to prove NP-completeness of minesweeper consistency, by reducing SAT to minesweeper consistency. This re-establishes the result of [6], but in contrast to Kaye, we consider the original version of minesweeper in which the number of hidden mines is given. This leads to some extra constraints on the templates and the synthesis to ensure that the number of mines in the minesweeper instance generated from a SAT instance is predetermined and independent of the valuation of the Boolean variables in the SAT instance. These constraints are similar to those introduced by Scott et al. for the templates used for proving co-NP-completeness of minesweeper inference. Also Scott et al. consider the original minesweeper version with a given number of mines. Our templates and synthesis approach can replace the templates and synthesis of Scott et al. in their co-NP-completeness proof.

The paper is organized as follows. The next section discusses relevant related work. Section 3 introduces some notations. Section 4 precisely defines the minesweeper consistency and inference problems. In Sect. 5, we provide templates for circuit simulation in minesweeper. Section 6 elaborates templates for synthesis. These templates satisfy design principles that facilitate automated synthesis and that ensure that the number of mines in the generated minesweeper instance is predetermined. Section 7 provides the synthesis approach and proves NP-completeness of minesweeper consistency. Finally, Sect. 8 concludes.

---

[1] The exact dimensions of such a circuit with the templates of [8] depends on the number of inversions needed. With our templates the dimensions only depend on the numbers of variables, literals, and (or-)gate layers.

2   Related Work

Information on the history of minesweeper and the rules of the game can be found on Wikipedia [14]. The book by Garey and Johnson [4] is the classical text on NP-completeness. Boolean satisfiability, SAT, is the original decision problem shown NP-complete by Cook [2]. Brief introductions to NP-completeness and proving NP-completeness through reduction can be found in, for instance, [8] and on Wikipedia [16], which also contains a list of NP-complete games and puzzles [15]. Ref. [8] also provides a nice tutorial-style introduction to co-NP-completeness and its relation to NP-completeness. The complexity of games is a popular and fun topic of study. The work of Demaine and colleagues [1,5], for example, provides systematic frameworks for analyzing the complexity of games, at the same time proving complexity results for a wide selection of well-known games, including many of the classic Nintendo games.

Kaye [6] introduced minesweeper consistency and showed its NP-completeness through reduction from circuit-SAT. Kaye's circuit templates are quite involved. An and gate, for instance, has 23×13 squares and a wire crossing is built from and and not gates (24 in total). He later published some further, simplified templates [7], but they remain quite large. Kaye's reduction from circuit-SAT to minesweeper does not guarantee a predefined number of hidden mines. We re-establish the NP-completeness of minesweeper consistency by reduction from SAT for the original version of minesweeper with a given number of hidden mines. This illustrates that this extra piece of information does not fundamentally simplify minesweeper.

The latter was also already observed by Scott et al. [8]. Scott et al. argue that Kaye's reasoning does not prove NP-completeness of playing minesweeper. Kaye assumed that minesweeper is played by iteratively solving minesweeper consistency. Scott et al. observe that there may be other strategies to play minesweeper. They therefore introduce the minesweeper inference problem, which precisely captures the essence of minesweeper game play. They show that minesweeper inference is co-NP-complete (and hence that playing minesweeper is most likely not NP-complete). They do so by reducing UNSAT to minesweeper inference, for the original version of minesweeper with a given number of hidden mines.

The templates of Scott et al. are similar to those of Kaye, but they are designed for synthesizing circuits for the original minesweeper game with a given number of hidden mines. The dimensions of all templates are multiples of three, the number of mines in each template is always the same, independent of the valuation of inputs of the circuit element being simulated, and all the predefined mines are derivable. An or gate, for instance, consists of 24×18 squares with exactly 58 mines of which 43 are predefined and derivable; a crossing consists of 15×9 squares with 21 mines, of which 14 predefined and derivable. Our gate templates are also designed for synthesis and ensure that the number of mines in a synthesized circuit is known. But our templates use mines to create and isolate information flows, where Scott et al. use safe squares to create flows. The use of mines to create flows leads to substantially smaller templates than the templates of Scott et al. Our or gate has 7×9 squares with 32 mines, of which

29 predetermined and derivable; our crossing has 6×6 squares with 19 mines, 16 derivable and 3 depending on the valuation.

The synthesis approach of Scott et al. is based on rectangular tiles. Our synthesis is based on layers, corresponding to the levels in a tree representation of the Boolean formula being synthesized. Moreover, we integrate negation in the wiring. With the already mentioned choice to use mines to create information flows, these aspects lead to substantially smaller minesweeper circuits than those of Scott et al.

3   Notations

This section introduces some notations needed in the remainder.

First, we define some notations for natural numbers and grids. Let $\mathbb{N}$ denote the natural numbers and $\mathbb{N}_0$ the natural numbers extended with 0. For any natural numbers $k, l \in \mathbb{N}$, let $[k] = \{n \in \mathbb{N}_0 \mid n < k\}$ and $[k, l] = [k] \times [l]$; the neighborhood $N : [k, l] \to 2^{[k,l]}$ is defined for any $(i, j) \in [k, l]$ as $N(i, j) = \{(i + p, j + q) \in [k, l] \setminus \{(i, j)\} \mid p, q \in \{-1, 0, 1\}\}$.

Second, we introduce some notations for Boolean formulas and circuits. Let $\mathbb{B} = \{0, 1\}$ be the set of Boolean values; let V be a set of variables. A Boolean formula f is an expression built from variables from V, the (infix) binary operators $\cdot$ (and, often left implicit in formulas) and $+$ (or), the (postfix) unary operator $'$ (not), and parentheses. A (Boolean) valuation is a function $b : V \to \mathbb{B}$ that assigns a Boolean value to all variables. Boolean formula f is satisfiable if and only if a valuation b of its variables $x_0, \ldots, x_{n-1} \in V$ (for some $n \in \mathbb{N}$) exists so that the formula evaluates to true, i.e., $f(b(x_0), \ldots, b(x_{n-1})) = 1$. Boolean circuits generalize Boolean formulas by allowing shared subformulas and multiple outputs. We omit a precise definition, because our reasoning is based on the subset of Boolean circuits that correspond to Boolean formulas. The Boolean operators are also referred to as (logic) gates in the context of Boolean circuits.

4   Minesweeper Consistency and Inference

The notations introduced provide a basis for defining both minesweeper consistency and minesweeper inference. We use a $\star$ to denote mines.

Definition 1 (The minesweeper consistency problem [6][2]). *Assume given a $k \times l$ grid, for $k, l \in \mathbb{N}$ and a number of hidden mines $M \in [kl + 1]$. A consistent minesweeper instance is a function $m : [k, l] \to [9] \cup \{\star\}$ such that $M = |\{(i, j) \in [k, l] \mid m(i, j) = \star\}|$ and, for all $(i, j) \in [k, l]$, $m(i, j) = \star$ or $m(i, j) = |\{(p, q) \in N(i, j) \mid m(p, q) = \star\}|$. The minesweeper consistency problem then is the question whether a partial minesweeper solution, given in the form*

---

[2] Kaye does not include the number of still hidden mines in his problem definition; in line with the original minesweeper game, we include this information, following Scott et al. [8].

of a partial function $mp : [k, l] \hookrightarrow [9] \cup \{\star\}$ and a number of mines $\#m \in \mathbb{N}_0$ hidden in the covered squares $[k, l] \setminus \mathrm{dom}(mp)$, can be extended to a total function $m : [k, l] \rightarrow [9] \cup \{\star\}$ with $|\{(i, j) \in [k, l] \setminus \mathrm{dom}(mp) \mid m(i, j) = \star\}| = \#m$ that is a consistent minesweeper instance. If so, that partial minesweeper solution is said to be consistent.

Definition 2 (The minesweeper inference problem[8]). *Assume given a partial minesweeper solution $mp : [k, l] \hookrightarrow [9] \cup \{\star\}$ derived from a consistent minesweeper instance $m : [k, l] \rightarrow [9] \cup \{\star\}$ such that $mp(i, j) = m(i, j)$ for all $(i, j) \in \mathrm{dom}(mp)$, with the number of still hidden mines $\#m = |\{(i, j) \in [k, l] \setminus \mathrm{dom}(mp) \mid m(i, j) = \star\}|$. The minesweeper inference problem is then the question whether there is a covered grid square $(i, j) \in [k, l] \setminus \mathrm{dom}(mp)$ for which it can be inferred from mp and $\#m$ whether $m(i, j) = \star$ (i.e., the square is unsafe and contains a mine) or $m(i, j) \in [9]$ (i.e., the square is safe).*

Kaye [6] showed that minesweeper consistency is NP-complete, although he did so for the minesweeper version in which the number of hidden mines is not given. In Sect. 7, we prove NP-completeness of the above version of minesweeper consistency. The fact that also this version of minesweeper consistency is NP-complete, despite the extra available information, was already observed by Scott et al. in [8] and can be proven using the minesweeper circuit-simulation templates provided in that paper. The main contribution of Scott et al. is that they show co-NP-completeness of minesweeper inference. The reason to re-establish NP-completeness of the above version of minesweeper consistency in this paper is to illustrate the use of the provided minesweeper templates in a well defined circuit-synthesis approach.

5   Simulating Circuits in Minesweeper

The essence of the complexity proofs for minesweeper consistency and inference is the observation that it is possible to simulate circuits in minesweeper. Figure 1[3] shows minesweeper templates for the three Boolean operators defined earlier. The designs are based on the following principles:

1. Mines are used to isolate gates from their environment. This is essential for the compactness of their design.
2. A mine is interpreted as a logic 1 and a value in [9], i.e., a safe square – no mine, as a logic 0. This is opposite to the interpretation of Kaye and Scott et al.. Because of duality, the interpretation of the Boolean constants in terms of mines and safe squares is not essential though, and it could be swapped.
3. The leftmost template in Fig. 1 shows a not gate. At its core is a triplet of two covered squares and one safe square. The triplet is bordered by mines. This pattern provides logical negation and it returns frequently (in adapted forms) in the other templates to be presented.

---

[3] All minesweeper figures have been made using the logigames minesweeper solver, https://www.logigames.com/minesweeper/solver.

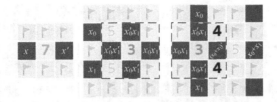

Fig. 1. Boolean operators/logic gates in minesweeper. Predefined mines are denoted by red flags, safe squares by grey squares numbered with the number of neighboring mines (omitting 0s, not seen in this figure), and covered squares by blue squares. (Color figure online)

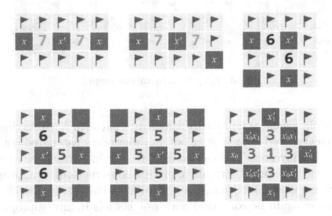

Fig. 2. Various wiring elements

4. The two rightmost templates in Fig. 1 show an and an or gate. At their core is a 3×3 kernel with an uncovered 3 at its center, two mines and two safe squares in the corners, and four covered squares. This design ensures that the four covered squares can contain only a single mine. By appropriately connecting inputs and outputs to this core, four different states can be represented, allowing to code any two-variable Boolean function. Inputs and outputs follow the not pattern. For instance, the $(x_0, 5, x_0'x_1)$ and $(x_0, 5, x_0'x_1')$ input patterns in the and gate and the $((x_0 + x_1)'(= x_0'x_1'), 5, x_0 + x_1)$ output pattern of the or gate are instances of the not pattern.

The templates in Fig. 1 are annotated with possible consistent valuations of the (relevant) covered squares. The correctness of the annotations is easily verified against the minesweeper rules (see [14]). The annotations confirm that the templates simulate not, and, and or gates, respectively. The 3×3 not gate and the 4×5 and gate are much smaller than the 13×4 and 23×13 not and gates given originally by Kaye in [6]. Kaye did not provide an or gate in [6].

To create circuits, we need wires to connect gates. Figure 2 shows a variety of wiring elements. The top three elements show wires, the two leftmost elements at the bottom show splits, and the bottom right element shows an inverting crossing.

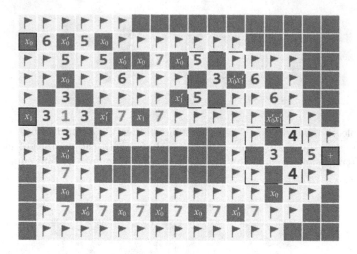

Fig. 3. $x_0'x_1' + x_0$ in minesweeper

The wire and split elements repeatedly use the not pattern. A wire is simply an even number of concatenated not gates; an odd number of concatenated not gates gives an inverting wire/inverter. This can be used to obtain either positive or negative instances of a variable or subformula in circuit construction, as appropriate. The inverting crossing uses a 3×3 kernel very similar to the kernels used for the gates. The crossing can again be combined with not kernels in any appropriate way to obtain positive or negative instances of subformulas.

Figure 3 shows an example of a circuit simulation in minesweeper, using the gate templates and (variants of the) wiring elements.

6   Templates for Circuit Synthesis

The templates given in the previous section allow the manual construction of circuits in minesweeper, and they suffice to prove the original NP-completeness result of [6]. They cannot be (easily) used for automated synthesis though, and they are not suitable to prove the earlier mentioned complexity results for the version of minesweeper in which the number of hidden mines is known.

To support synthesis of Boolean circuits and derive the needed templates, we observe that any Boolean formula can be represented as a binary tree. Figure 4 (left) shows the tree representation of the example circuit of Fig. 3. We use the ideas presented in the previous section and the tree representation of Boolean formulas to develop templates that support synthesis of circuits along the lines of the tree representation. We define four groups of templates, one for gate layers, one for wires, one to create a layer of literals, and one to create wiring layers. But first, we provide a straightforward transformation on Boolean formulas that simplifies the synthesis and set out some design principles for templates.

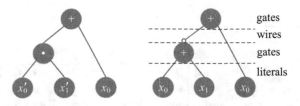

Fig. 4. Tree representations for Boolean formula $x_0'x_1' + x_0$ (left) and the equivalent formula $(x_0 + x_1)' + x_0$ (right)

6.1 Removing and Gates from Boolean Circuits

Two key laws in Boolean algebra are De Morgan's laws: $x_0x_1 = (x_0' + x_1')'$ and $x_0 + x_1 = (x_0'x_1')'$. The first one shows that and gates can be replaced by or gates if inputs and outputs are inverted. Figure 4 (right) shows the result of this transformation for the example circuit. Any resulting double negations can be removed. After this transformation, the tree representation of the Boolean circuit consists of layers of (or) gates and wires. Wires may be inverting. The tree is built on leaves of literals. The root may or may not be inverted; it is not for the example circuit because it already had an or gate at the root. The transformation simplifies the synthesis problem, because the resulting representation has only one type of gate. Moreover, negation is a basic building block in the minesweeper emulation of circuits that can be integrated in the wires where needed.

6.2 Design Principles for Templates

Our synthesis templates satisfy a number of design principles to facilitate synthesis, with a few small exceptions as explained later.

1. The templates are designed per layer in the tree representation of a Boolean formula and have a fixed width to support the layer structure. Trees are laid out from left (leaves, inputs) to right (top, output).
2. The inputs of the simulated circuit element are part of the template; the outputs are not. Templates can be connected by overlapping output and input squares as appropriate.
3. Information flows are isolated by single-file rows of mines, bordered on one side by safe squares. This ensures that all predefined mines in the templates are derivable when the predefined safe squares in the generated minesweeper instance are uncovered.
4. The templates ensure that the content of precisely the covered squares is not derivable.
5. The templates have a given fixed number of mines on the covered squares for all possible assignments of mines to these covered squares. This ensures that the number of mines in a generated minesweeper instance is known.

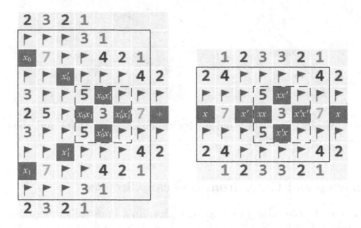

Fig. 5. Gate templates for synthesis

6.3 Templates for Gate Layers

We create two gate templates to build gate layers from the tree representation of a circuit, one or gate and one wire. The 'wire gate' is needed to cross a gate layer when the tree representing a circuit has no gate at a particular position in that layer. Figure 5 shows the two gate-layer templates. The templates consist of the squares inside the solid rectangles. They are shown with some additional context to ease understanding.

1. The gate templates have a fixed width of seven squares, meaning that a gate layer is seven squares wide. Both templates use the 3×3 and-gate kernel already presented in the previous section. The or template is built from this 3×3 kernel following De Morgan's law for the or operator. The inputs of the or template are five squares apart, to easily connect to the literal layer, elaborated in the next subsection. The wire template is essentially an and kernel with a single input. The input and output are inverted so that the template has the same width as the or template.

2. The or template has 29 predefined mines; the wire template has 18 predefined mines. As mentioned, these predefined mines form single-file lines bordered on one side by safe squares, which ensures that all these mines are derivable.

3. The or template has precisely 3 mines on the covered squares, one for each pair of covered squares forming the inverted inputs and one in the and kernel. The wire template has precisely 2 mines on the covered squares, one for the inverted input and one for the and kernel. Note that the covered squares marked xx' and $x'x$ are derivably safe, with value 5, deviating from the design principles outlined earlier. But uncovering these two squares does not reveal any extra information about the other covered squares. The template can be redesigned by uncovering these squares or with mines on these squares, resulting in a straight wire. We chose to present this template for gate layers based on the and-gate kernel.

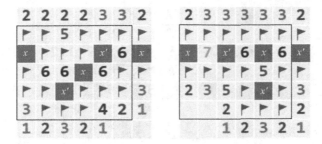

Fig. 6. Wire templates for synthesis: wire (left), inverting wire (right)

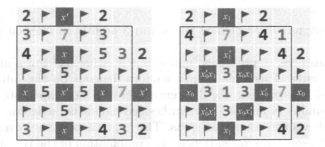

Fig. 7. Templates for the literal layer: split (left), crossing (right)

6.4 Wire Templates

Figure 6 shows two wire templates for synthesis, a wire and an inverting wire. The wire templates are used in connecting the literal layer to the first gate layer and in wiring layers between gate layers, as further explained below.

1. The wire templates have a width of six squares, to support fixed-width layers.
2. The inverting wire has an extra not kernel, the vertical $(x, 5, x')$ triple, to ensure that the number of mines in the template is predetermined, independent of the content of the covered squares.
3. The wire template has 18 predefined mines, the inverting wire 16. Both templates have 2 additional mines on the covered squares, as can be seen from the annotations.

6.5 Templates for the Literal Layer

Figure 7 shows two templates for constructing the literal layer for a circuit. These templates are inspired by the split and crossing already presented in Fig. 2.

1. Both templates have a width of six squares. This ensures that all lines of mines in a literal layer are single-file lines, so that the predefined mines in such a layer are derivable.

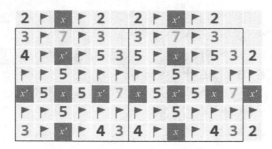

Fig. 8. Fixing the mine count in the literal layer

2. The crossing has 16 predefined mines and 3 additional ones on the covered squares.
3. The split also has 16 predefined mines, but it either has 1 or 4 mines on the covered squares. This mine count therefore depends on the valuation of x. When used for synthesis, the difference needs to be compensated to ensure that the number of mines in the synthesized circuit is predetermined.
4. Figure 8 shows two connected splits. The valuations of the covered squares in these two splits are duals. Hence, the combination of the two splits always has 5 covered mines. This is even so when the splits are connected through a (normal, non-inverting) wire. This can be used to create a literal layer with a predetermined number of mines, independent of the valuation of variables.

Figure 9 shows the layout of a literal layer in minesweeper. A literal layer has a vertical wire for each variable in the Boolean formula for the circuit being synthesized. For each literal in the formula, a horizontal wire is created. The vertical wires create the variables sublayer of the literal layer and are built from crossings stacked on top of each other, with one split at the appropriate place to derive the needed literal. The resulting horizontal wires have connections both to the left and to the right. Figure 10 shows the construction for the running example.

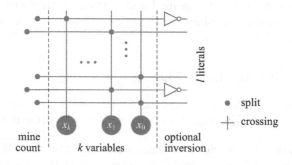

Fig. 9. The layout of the literal layer

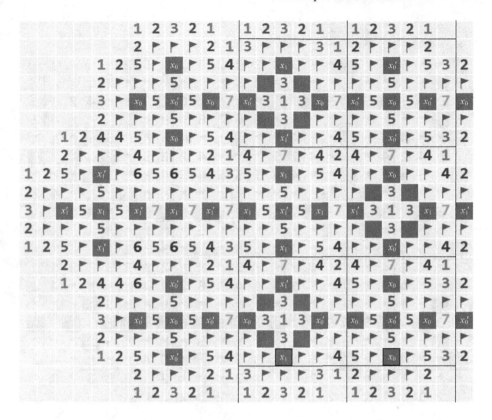

Fig. 10. The literal layer of the example circuit: variables and mine count

The variable sublayer is connected to splits in a mine-count sublayer on its left. Adding one split for every horizontal wire implies that each horizontal wire has precisely two splits. This ensures a predetermined mine count in this pair, as explained. The additional splits are laid out alternatingly in two vertical stacks to make sure that all predefined mines are in single-file lines (and hence derivable). This alternating layout is achieved by shifting every other split to the left through a simple wire as already shown in Fig. 2, top left. Note that this simple wire can be seen as a 4×3 template with 8 predefined mines and 1 additional covered mine (see also Fig. 12, top left). As a result of the construction up to this point, every horizontal wire in the mine-count and variable sublayers is built from crossings, simple wires, and precisely two splits; see Fig. 10 for the running example. This ensures a predetermined mine count in this part of the literal layer. (The borders seen in Fig. 10 are explained and accounted for in Sect. 7, that elaborates the reduction from SAT to minesweeper consistency.)

To complete the literal layer, we need to ensure that the literals produced as inputs for the circuit are properly inverted where needed. This can be done by creating a sublayer with the wire templates given already in Fig. 6. Figure 11 shows the inversion sublayer for the running example. The figure illustrates how

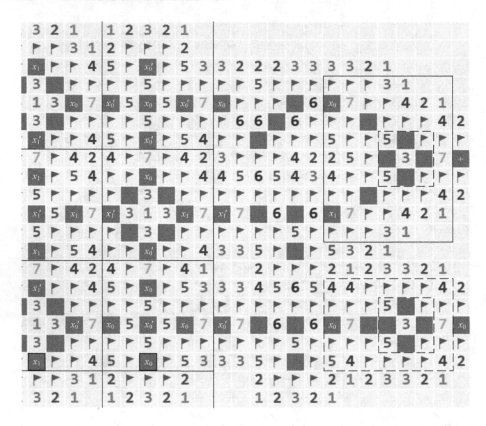

Fig. 11. The literal layer of the example circuit: connection to the first gate layer, optional inversion

it connects the literal layer to the first gate layer of the circuit. Since the wiring templates have a predetermined number of mines, the literal layer as a whole also has a predefined number of mines.

6.6   Templates for Connecting Layers

One more set of templates is needed for circuit synthesis, namely templates to create wiring layers between gate layers. The layers need to account for vertical displacements, preferably using as little horizontal space as needed (for compactness of the resulting circuits). Two important observations are, first, that the literals coming from the literal layer are vertically 6 squares apart, and, second, that the output of an or gate is 3 squares lower or higher than its inputs. As a result, the vertical displacements that need to be realized in generating a tree-shaped circuit in line with the tree representation of Fig. 4 are all $3 + 6n$ squares, for some $n \in \mathbb{N}_0$. Figure 12 shows the templates for vertical displacement, including a simple wire template to be used when no displacement is needed. Figure 13 shows their use in the example circuit.

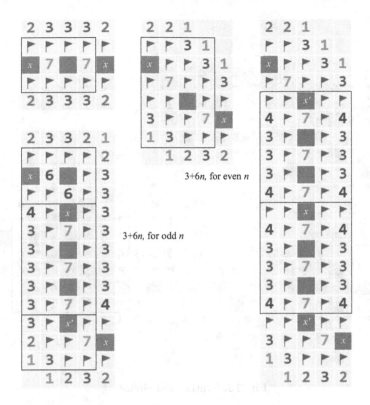

Fig. 12. Wiring elements for vertical displacements of 0 resp. $3 + 6n$ rows ($n \in \mathbb{N}_0$)

1. All templates act as normal wires. As explained, inversion may be needed in the wiring layers. This could be done in the displacement wires. For simplicity, this is not done though. Optional inversion can be achieved using the earlier wire templates also used in connecting the literal layer to the first gate layer of the circuit. Figure 13 shows that this optional inversion is applied directly to the outputs of the gate layer being connected to the next gate layer (in line with the tree representation in Fig. 4). The displacement templates can then be used to realize the needed displacement. Note that the bottom half of a wiring layer uses templates that are mirrored vertically. This is needed to avoid undesired connections between circuit parts that would prevent derivability of the predefined mines.
2. The wire template without displacement (Fig. 12, top left) is four squares wide, has 8 predefined mines and 1 covered mine; it is used when the input gate layer does not have an or gate but only a wire, as in the bottom part of Fig. 13.
3. The templates for non-zero displacements are split in two cases. This is needed to ensure the combination of derivability of predefined mines, a predetermined number of mines in total for each of the templates, and compactness of the templates.

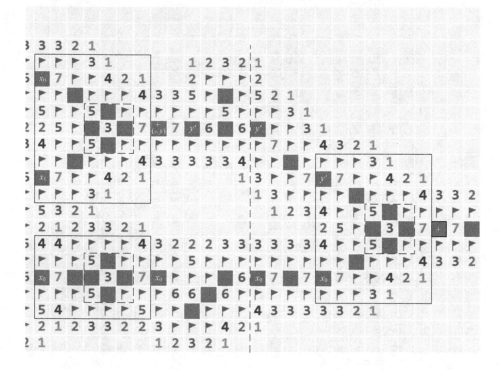

Fig. 13. Synthesized circuit

4. The template for a displacement of $3 + 6n$ squares, for even $n \in \mathbb{N}_0$, including $n = 0$, consists of a 4×6 kernel template that realizes a displacement of 3 (Fig. 12, top middle) and a 5×6 optional block that can be repeated n times, as needed (Fig. 12, right). It has $14 + 14n$ predefined mines and $1 + 3m$, with $m = n/2$, additional mines on its covered squares.

5. The template for $3 + 6n$, for odd $n \in \mathbb{N}$, also consists of a 4×6 kernel and a 4×6 repeatable block that is included n times. It has $14 + 12n$ predefined mines and $3 + 3m$, with $m = \lfloor n/2 \rfloor$, additional mines on its covered squares.

6. The displacement sublayer of a wiring layer is four squares wide. The repeatable block in the template for even n has a width of five squares, meaning that these blocks extend into the gate layer to the right of the displacement sublayer when used in a circuit. This does not cause any problems because, due to the tree-shaped construction, that is empty space where no other circuit elements appear.

Figure 13 shows the synthesized circuit for our example. It has two gate layers, in line with the tree representation of Fig. 4. These two layers are connected by a wiring layer, consisting of an inversion sublayer and a displacement sublayer.

Note that the circuit has an inverter connected to its output, despite the fact that this inversion is not needed. The reason for including this not kernel at the output, also if the circuit does not need it, is that in this way also at the output the number of mines is independent of the Boolean valuation of the output. As a result, the number of mines is predetermined for the entire circuit (shown in its entirety in Figs. 10, 11, and 13).

7   NP-completeness of Minesweeper Consistency

To illustrate the use of the templates given in the previous section, we prove the NP-completeness of minesweeper consistency by reduction from SAT. An approach to synthesize minesweeper circuits from a Boolean formula, as already sketched in the previous section, is the key ingredient of the reduction.

Definition 3 (SAT). *SAT is the decision problem whether or not a Boolean formula is satisfiable.*

The reduction from SAT to minesweeper consistency consists of two steps. Given a Boolean formula, first, the conversion illustrated in Fig. 4 is applied. Second, a consistent minesweeper instance is generated that simulates the Boolean circuit corresponding to the resulting formula, as follows.

Assume that the circuit to be synthesized has $k \in \mathbb{N}$ variables, $l \in \mathbb{N}$ literals, and $h \in \mathbb{N}$ gate layers. The literal layer determines the height and layout of the minesweeper instance, so we start with the construction of this literal layer.

1. The height of the generated minesweeper instance is determined by the number of literals l. Since the split and crossing templates for the literal layer are 6×6 squares, the height becomes $3 + 6l$ squares, including a bottom border of two squares and a top border of one square.
2. Each variable needs precisely one vertical wire in the variables sublayer. Each wire is constructed from crossings with one split at the appropriate point to split off the horizontal literal wire. The resulting variables sublayer has a width of $6k$ squares.
3. The mine-count sublayer is constructed following the alternating layout of splits shown in Fig. 10. With at least one gate layer, we have at least two literals, meaning that the width of the mine-count sublayer is 12 squares.
4. The inversion sublayer creating the correct literals and connecting the literal layer to the first gate layer is constructed appropriately from wires and inverting wires, leading to a width of 6 squares.
5. The dimensions of the resulting literal layer thus are $(18 + 6k) \times (3 + 6l)$.

Before proceeding with the circuitry of the circuit being synthesized, we compute the mine count in the literal layer.

1. We start with the borders. The bottom border has three mines for each variable. The top border has no mines itself, but the top splits and crossings have one extra mine compared to the standard templates on the position of the topmost safe square marked 7 in those templates. Hence, for each variable, we have 4 mines due to the borders of the generated minesweeper instance, $4k$ mines in total.

2. Next, observe that we have $kl - l$ crossings, with 19 mines each. So the crossings contribute $19l(k - 1)$ mines.
3. We also have precisely l split pairs that each have 5 mines on their covered squares. A split in the mine-count sublayer has 23 mines and a split in the variables sublayer has 16 mines. So the splits contribute $44l$ mines.
4. A wire used in the alternating layout of the splits in the mine-count sublayer has 9 mines. We have $\lfloor l/2 \rfloor$ such wires, contributing $9\lfloor l/2 \rfloor$ mines in total.
5. The inversion sub-layer contributes $20l_w + 18l_i$ mines, where l_w is the number of normal wires used and l_i is the number of inverting wires used.
6. The total mine count of the literal layer is $4k + 19l(k - 1) + 44l + 9\lfloor l/2 \rfloor + 20l_w + 18l_i = 4k + 19kl + 25l + 9\lfloor l/2 \rfloor + 20l_w + 18l_i$.

The core circuitry of the circuit being synthesized is built from gate and wiring layers as indicated in Fig. 4.

1. The gate and wiring layers can be attached one by one to the literal layer. At the end, an inverter is added and the output of the circuit is chosen appropriately to be either the input or the output of this inverter. All parts of the grid not covered by instances of templates contain only safe squares of which the correct valuation can be derived from the mine assignment for the predefined mines in the templates.
2. Each gate layer is 7 squares wide; each wiring layer is 10 squares wide. The final inverter results in an additional 3 squares width. With h gate layers, this leads to a width of $7h + 10(h - 1) + 3 = 17h - 7$ squares.
3. The mine count in the circuitry depends on the layout of the tree representation of the formula being converted. It can be computed by counting the number of used gate, wire, and displacement templates, multiplying these template counts with the appropriate mine counts derived earlier in Sect. 6, and adding 7 for the final inverter. The two-square bottom and one-square top boundaries that extend from the literal layer to the circuitry part do not contain any mines (besides the ones that are part of a template and hence already accounted for).

Summarizing the above, given a Boolean formula f with k variables, l literals, and h gate layers in its tree representation, the outlined synthesis approach results in a partial minesweeper instance pm_f with dimensions $(11 + 6k + 17h) \times (3 + 6l)$, a predetermined mine count M_f (that depends on the characteristics of the circuit being synthesized), and a designated output square $(i, j)_f$ for some $(i, j) \in [11 + 6k + 17h, 3 + 6l]$, with all squares in all the template instances, including the borders in the literal layer, uncovered/flagged as indicated in the templates, and all grid squares outside the scope of the used templates (which are all safe) uncovered as well. The mine count of still hidden mines $\#m_f$ of this partial minesweeper solution is obtained by subtracting the number of flagged squares in the partial solution from M_f. We now have the following result.

Proposition 1. *A given Boolean formula f is satisfiable if and only if the partial minesweeper solution $pm_f \cup \{(i,j)_f \mapsto \star\}$ with mine count $\#m_f - 1$, i.e., the generated partial minesweeper solution with a mine allocated to the designated circuit output, is consistent.*

The two-step conversion presented up to this point is polynomial in the size of the Boolean formula, because it consists of simple substitutions of nodes and edges in the tree representation of the Boolean formula (by other nodes and edges in the first step and minesweeper templates in the second step).

Finally, it is clear that minesweeper consistency is in NP. Given a minesweeper instance m with mine count M as defined in Definition 1, the consistency conditions given in Definition 1 can be checked in a single traversal of the grid.

Combining Proposition 1 with the observations in the last two paragraphs then gives the following result.

Theorem 1 (Complexity of minesweeper consistency). *Minesweeper consistency is NP-complete.*

8 Conclusions

In this paper, we have given minesweeper templates for simulating and synthesizing circuits. The templates and synthesized circuits are much smaller than the templates and circuit simulations proposed in earlier work. We used the templates to prove NP-completeness of minesweeper consistency, for the original version of minesweeper, in line with Kaye's original result for the version of minesweeper without a given number of hidden mines presented in [6]. Since our templates and synthesis approach predetermine the number of mines in the generated minesweeper instance and because all predefined mines are derivable, the templates can also be used in the proof of Scott et al. in [8], which shows that minesweeper inference is co-NP-complete. Given the small 3×3 kernels that form the basis for our templates, we do not expect that any further (substantial) reduction of the size of minesweeper circuits is possible.

Frits Vaandrager. This paper is part of a Festschrift to celebrate the 60th birthday of Frits Vaandrager. Twan Basten had the pleasure of collaborating with Frits on several occasions. He got to know Frits as a person that looks beyond the purely scientific aspects of his work. Frits is a socially involved person, to whom it is important to not only communicate the societal importance of computer science but also the beauty and the fun of it. Already in 1998, Frits published an opinion piece [10] in which he argued the need to bring logic and theoretical computer science closer to society, through independent academic programs and collaboration with industry. He invested time and effort in developing educational setups (e.g., [3]) and in developing and teaching a model-checking module for high schools [9]. And he actively advocates the importance of theoretical computer science for society at large, as illustrated through this

TV fragment on Dutch national TV [12]. Fun is never far away with Frits. When writing a Uppaal tutorial [11], he decided to take a puzzle of gossiping girls as an illustrative example. And in a column on recreational formal methods [13], he explored the use of SAT solvers to analyze vacuum cleaning scenarios. The current paper intends to be recreational as well. We hope it is a fun read for Frits and other readers alike, and that it as such may contribute to popularizing (theoretical) computer science.

References

1. Aloupis, G., Demaine, E., Guo, A., Viglietta, G.: Classic Nintendo games are (computationally) hard. Theor. Comput. Sci. **586**, 135–160 (2015). https://doi.org/10.1016/j.tcs.2015.02.037
2. Cook, S.: The complexity of theorem proving procedures. In: Proceedings 3rd ACM Symposium on Theory of Computing, STOC, pp. 151–158. ACM (1971). https://doi.org/10.1145/800157.805047
3. Fehnker, A., Vaandrager, F., Zhang, W.: Modeling and verifying a Lego car using hybrid I/O automata. In: Proceedings 3rd International Conference on Quality Software, QSIC 2003, pp. 280–289. IEEE Computer Society (2003)
4. Garey, M., Johnson, D.: Computers and Intractability: A Guide to the Theory of NP-Completeness. Freeman W.H., New York (1979)
5. Hearn, R., Demaine, E.: Games, Puzzles, and Computation. A K Peters/CRC Press, Boca Raton (2009). https://doi.org/10.1201/b10581
6. Kaye, R.: Minesweeper is NP-complete. Math. Intelligencer **22**(2), 9–15 (2000). https://doi.org/10.1007/BF03025367
7. Kaye, R.: Richard Kaye's minesweeper pages (2022). https://web.mat.bham.ac.uk/R.W.Kaye/minesw/minesw.htm
8. Scott, A., Stege, U., van Rooij, I.: Minesweeper may not be NP-complete but is hard nonetheless. Math. Intelligencer **33**(4), 5–17 (2011). https://doi.org/10.1007/s00283-011-9256-x
9. Vaandrager, F., Jansen, D., Koopmans, E.: Een module over model checking voor het VWO. In: Proceedings NIOC 2009, pp. 135–137. Hogeschool Utrecht (2009). in Dutch
10. Vaandrager, F.: Logica is prachtig hulpmiddel bij oplossen informaticaproblemen. Automatisering Gids **32**(13), 17 (1998). in Dutch
11. Vaandrager, F.: A first introduction to Uppaal. Quasimodo Handb. Deliverable D5.12 (2011). ICT-FP7-STREP-214755 project Quasimodo
12. Vaandrager, F.: Alan Turing: grondlegger van informatica. In: RTL Late Night. RTL (2015). https://www.rtlxl.nl/programma/rtl-late-night/65b22fda-4ef4-bb8d-0c90-80f670646220. TV program (fragment). in Dutch
13. Vaandrager, F., Verbeek, F.: Recreational formal methods: designing vacuum cleaning trajectories. Bull. EATCS **113**, 100–109 (2014)
14. Wikipedia: Microsoft Minesweeper (2022). https://en.wikipedia.org/wiki/Microsoft_Minesweeper
15. Wikipedia: NP-complete games and puzzles (2022). https://en.wikipedia.org/wiki/List_of_NP-complete_problems#Games_and_puzzles
16. Wikipedia: NP-completeness (2022). https://en.wikipedia.org/wiki/NP-completeness

Goodbye ioco

Jan Tretmans[1,2(✉)] and Ramon Janssen[1,3]

[1] Radboud University, Institute iCIS, Nijmegen, The Netherlands
`jan.tretmans@tno.nl, ramonjanssen@cs.ru.nl`
[2] ESI (TNO), Eindhoven, The Netherlands
[3] BetterBe, Enschede, The Netherlands

Abstract. Model-based testing involves testing a system under test for conformance to a model that specifies its behaviour. An important aspect for model-based testing is the *implementation relation* that defines precisely when a system under test conforms to its model. The implementation relation **ioco** has often been used and studied in model-based testing when models are expressed as labelled transition systems, and there are tools implementing **ioco**-based test generation. An alternative, slightly different implementation relation is **uioco**, which is more recent, has been less studied, and there are no tools for it. We will compare **ioco** and **uioco** on a couple of aspects, viz. intuition, the decision whether a test observation is correct, the definition of a consistent refinement relation, the construction of a canonical implementation for each specification, and the relation to other input-output implementation relations. For all these aspects, we conclude that **uioco** is the preferred implementation relation, so, goodbye **ioco**, hello **uioco**.

1 Introduction

Systematic testing plays an important role in the quest for improved quality and reliability of software systems. Software testing, however, is often an error-prone, expensive, and time-consuming process. Estimates are that testing consumes up to 50% of the total software development effort. The tendency is that this effort is still increasing due to the continuing quest for better software quality, and the ever growing size and complexity of systems. The situation is aggravated by the fact that the complexity of testing tends to grow faster than the complexity of the systems being tested, in the worst case even exponentially. Whereas development and construction methods for software allow the building of ever larger and more complex systems, there is a real danger that testing methods cannot keep pace with these construction and development methods. This may seriously hamper the development and testing of future generations of software systems.

Software testing involves checking of required and desired properties of a software product by systematically executing and experimenting with the software, while stimulating it with inputs, and observing and checking its outputs. Model-Based Testing (MBT) is one of the technologies to meet the challenges imposed on software testing. MBT is a form of black-box testing where a System

Under Test (SUT) is tested for conformance to a model. The model specifies, in a formal way, what the system is allowed to do and what it shall not do. As such, the model is the basis for the algorithmic generation of test cases and for the evaluation of test results. The main virtue of model-based testing is that it allows test automation that goes well beyond the mere automatic execution of manually crafted test cases. It allows for the algorithmic generation of large amounts of test cases, including test oracles for the expected results, completely automatically from the model of required behaviour.

An important prerequisite for MBT is the precise definition of what it means for an SUT to conform to its model. Conformance is expressed using an implementation relation or conformance relation. Although an SUT is a black box, we can assume it could be modelled by some model instance in a domain of implementation models. This assumption is commonly referred to as the testability assumption [10]. This assumption allows reasoning about SUTs as if they were formal models, and it makes it possible to define a conformance relation as a formal relation between the domain of specification models and the domain of implementation models.

One of the formal theories for model-based testing uses Labelled Transition Systems (LTS) as models and **ioco** (input-output-conformance) as implementation relation [17,18]. An LTS is a structure with states, representing the states of the actual system, and with transitions between states representing the actions that the system may perform. Actions can be inputs, outputs, or internal steps. The implementation relation **ioco** expresses that an SUT conforms to its specification if the SUT never produces an output that cannot be produced by the specification in the same situation. A particular, virtual output is quiescence, actually expressing the absence of real outputs. Such absence of outputs is considered an observable event. Moreover, **ioco** allows underspecification: after inputs for which the specification model does not specify anything, the implementation may show arbitrary behaviour. The **ioco**-testing theory for LTS provides a test generation algorithm that is sound and exhaustive, i.e., the (possibly infinitely many) test cases generated from an LTS model detect all and only **ioco**-incorrect implementations. The **ioco**-testing theory constitutes a well-defined theory of model-based testing, and it forms the basis for various practical MBT tools, like TorX [6], TGV [14], Uppaal-Tron [15], Axini Test Manager [4], JTorx [5], and TorXakis [19].

Another implementation relation on LTS, akin to **ioco**, is **uioco**, for universal **ioco**. The relation **uioco** was introduced in [7] and it differs from **ioco** in how it deals with *nondeterministic underspecification*, which will be explained later. For specification models without nondeterministic underspecification the two relations coincide. The relation **uioco** is the newer one, it has been less studied in the literature, and there are no tools directly implementing test generation for **uioco**.

In this paper we will compare the implementation relations **ioco** and **uioco**, first, by explaining some examples and showing how the relations deal with non-deterministic underspecification in Sect. 3, and, second, by comparing them on some more formal criteria. The latter include test observations and decidability of whether these are correct or not in Sect. 4, the definition of a refinement relation consistent with the implementation relation in Sect. 5, the construction of a standard, canonical implementation for each specification in Sect. 6, and the relation to other input-output implementation relations in Sect. 7. From this analysis we conclude that **uioco** is the better choice, so, goodbye **ioco**.

This paper does not contain any new technical results. It re-explains and re-interprets results from [11], partly from [12], and from the forthcoming thesis by the second author [13]. In those papers, however, the main topic is the conjunction of models to express the union of test suites, whereas the main conclusion of this paper is only presented as a scattered, collateral result. Yet, the comparison of **ioco** and **uioco** is in itself a valuable result, which deserves a separate paper.

2 Preliminaries

Model-based testing deals with systems under test (SUT), implementations, models, implementation relations, test cases, test generation algorithms, and soundness and exhaustiveness of the generated test cases with respect to the implementation relations. An important aspect is the chosen implementation relation. This section introduces two implementation relations on labelled transition systems, viz. **ioco** and **uioco**, which are part of the **ioco**-theory for model-based testing; see [17,18] for a more elaborate treatment of this theory.

Models. In the **ioco/uioco**-test theory, specification models, implementations, and test cases are all expressed as labelled transition systems.

Definition 1. *A labelled transition system with inputs and outputs is a 5-tuple* $\langle Q, L_I, L_U, T, q_0 \rangle$ *where Q is a countable, non-empty set of states; L_I is a countable set of input labels; L_U is a countable set of output labels, such that $L_I \cap L_U = \emptyset$; $T \subseteq Q \times (L_I \cup L_U \cup \{\tau\}) \times Q$, with $\tau \notin L_I \cup L_U$, is the transition relation; and $q_0 \in Q$ is the initial state.*

The labels in L_I and L_U represent the inputs and outputs, respectively, of a system, i.e., the system's possible interactions with its environment. Inputs are usually decorated with '?' and outputs with '!'. We use $L = L_I \cup L_U$ when we abstract from the distinction between inputs and outputs.

The execution of an action is modelled as a transition: $(q, \mu, q') \in T$ expresses that the system, when in state q, may perform action μ, and go to state q'. This is more elegantly denoted as $q \xrightarrow{\mu} q'$. Transitions can be composed: $q \xrightarrow{\mu} q' \xrightarrow{\mu'} q''$, which is written as $q \xrightarrow{\mu \cdot \mu'} q''$.

Internal transitions model some internal action or computation of a system that is not visible to the environment of the system. Internal actions are labelled with the special action τ ($\tau \notin L$). Consequently, the observable behaviour of a system is captured by the system's ability to perform sequences of observable actions. Such a sequence of observable actions, say σ, is obtained from a sequence

of actions under abstraction from the internal action τ, and it is denoted by $\overset{\sigma}{\Longrightarrow}$.
If, for example, $q \xrightarrow{a \cdot \tau \cdot \tau \cdot b \cdot c \cdot \tau} q'$ $(a, b, c \in L)$, then we write $q \overset{a \cdot b \cdot c}{\Longrightarrow} q'$ for the τ-abstracted sequence of observable actions. We say that q is able to perform the
trace $a \cdot b \cdot c \in L^*$, where the set of all finite sequences over L is denoted by L^*,
with ϵ denoting the empty sequence. If $\sigma_1, \sigma_2 \in L^*$ are finite sequences, $\sigma_1 \cdot \sigma_2$ is
the concatenation of σ_1 and σ_2. Some more, standard notations and definitions
are given in Definitions 2 and 3.

Definition 2. *Let* $p = \langle Q, L_I, L_U, T, q_0 \rangle$ *be a labelled transition system with*
$q, q' \in Q$, $\mu, \mu_i \in L \cup \{\tau\}$, $a, a_i \in L$, *and* $\sigma \in L^*$.

$$
\begin{array}{lll}
q \xrightarrow{\mu} q' & \Longleftrightarrow_{\text{def}} & (q, \mu, q') \in T \\[4pt]
q \xrightarrow{\mu_1 \cdot \ldots \cdot \mu_n} q' & \Longleftrightarrow_{\text{def}} & \exists q_0, \ldots, q_n : q = q_0 \xrightarrow{\mu_1} q_1 \xrightarrow{\mu_2} \ldots \xrightarrow{\mu_n} q_n = q' \\[4pt]
q \xrightarrow{\mu_1 \cdot \ldots \cdot \mu_n} & \Longleftrightarrow_{\text{def}} & \exists q' : q \xrightarrow{\mu_1 \cdot \ldots \cdot \mu_n} q' \\[4pt]
q \xrightarrow{\mu_1 \cdot \ldots \cdot \mu_n} \!\!\!\! \not\;\; & \Longleftrightarrow_{\text{def}} & not\ \exists q' : q \xrightarrow{\mu_1 \cdot \ldots \cdot \mu_n} q' \\[4pt]
q \overset{\epsilon}{\Longrightarrow} q' & \Longleftrightarrow_{\text{def}} & q = q' \text{ or } q \xrightarrow{\tau \cdot \ldots \cdot \tau} q' \\[4pt]
q \overset{a}{\Longrightarrow} q' & \Longleftrightarrow_{\text{def}} & \exists q_1, q_2 : q \overset{\epsilon}{\Longrightarrow} q_1 \xrightarrow{a} q_2 \overset{\epsilon}{\Longrightarrow} q' \\[4pt]
q \overset{a_1 \cdot \ldots \cdot a_n}{\Longrightarrow} q' & \Longleftrightarrow_{\text{def}} & \exists q_0 \ldots q_n : q = q_0 \overset{a_1}{\Longrightarrow} q_1 \overset{a_2}{\Longrightarrow} \ldots \overset{a_n}{\Longrightarrow} q_n = q' \\[4pt]
q \overset{\sigma}{\Longrightarrow} & \Longleftrightarrow_{\text{def}} & \exists q' : q \overset{\sigma}{\Longrightarrow} q' \\[4pt]
q \overset{\sigma}{\not\Longrightarrow} & \Longleftrightarrow_{\text{def}} & not\ \exists q' : q \overset{\sigma}{\Longrightarrow} q'
\end{array}
$$

In our reasoning about labelled transition systems we will not always distinguish between a transition system and its initial state. If $p = \langle Q, L_I, L_U, T, q_0 \rangle$,
we will identify the labelled transition system p with its initial state q_0, and,
e.g., we write $p \overset{\sigma}{\Longrightarrow}$ instead of $q_0 \overset{\sigma}{\Longrightarrow}$.

Definition 3. *Let p be a (state of a) labelled transition system, P a set of states,*
$A \subseteq L$ *a set of labels, and* $\sigma \in L^*$.

1. $traces(p)$ $=_{\text{def}}$ $\{\sigma \in L^* \mid p \overset{\sigma}{\Longrightarrow}\}$
2. p **after** σ $=_{\text{def}}$ $\{p' \mid p \overset{\sigma}{\Longrightarrow} p'\}$
3. P **after** σ $=_{\text{def}}$ $\bigcup \{p \text{ **after** } \sigma \mid p \in P\}$

The class of labelled transition systems with inputs in L_I and outputs in
L_U is denoted as $\mathcal{LTS}(L_I, L_U)$, or just $\mathcal{LTS}$ when L_I and L_U are assumed to be
globally known. For technical reasons we restrict this class to *strongly converging*
and *image finite* systems. Strong convergence means that infinite sequences of
τ-actions are not allowed to occur. Image finiteness means that the number of
non-deterministically reachable states shall be finite, i.e., for any σ, p **after** σ
shall be finite.

Input-Output Transition Systems. In the **ioco/uioco**-testing theory a specification model is a labelled transition system in $\mathcal{LTS}$. In order to formally reason
about a System Under test (SUT) the assumption is made that the SUT behaves as
if it were some kind of behavioural, formal model. This assumption is referred to
as the testability assumption and this model is called an implementation model.

In the **ioco/uioco**-testing theory the testability assumption is that a system under test behaves as if it were a labelled transition system that is always able to perform any input action, i.e., all inputs are enabled in all states. Such a system is defined as an *input-output transition system*. The class of such input-output transition systems is denoted by $\mathcal{IOTS}(L_I, L_U) \subseteq \mathcal{LTS}(L_I, L_U)$.

Definition 4. *An* input-output transition system *is a labelled transition system with inputs and outputs* $\langle Q, L_I, L_U, T, q_0 \rangle$ *where all input actions are enabled in any reachable state:* $\forall \sigma, q : q_0 \overset{\sigma}{\Longrightarrow} q$ *implies* $\forall a \in L_I : q \overset{a}{\Longrightarrow}$

Quiescence. A state of a system where no outputs or internal actions are enabled, and consequently the system is forced to wait until its environment provides an input, is called *suspended*, or *quiescent* [20]. An observer looking at a quiescent system does not see any outputs. This particular observation of seeing nothing can itself be considered as an event, which is denoted by δ $(\delta \notin L \cup \{\tau\})$; $p \overset{\delta}{\longrightarrow} p$ expresses that p allows the observation of quiescence. Also these transitions can be composed, e.g., $p \overset{\delta \cdot ?a \cdot \delta \cdot ?b \cdot !x}{=\!=\!=\!=\!=\!=\!\Longrightarrow}$ expresses that initially p is quiescent, i.e., does not produce outputs, but p does accept input action $?a$, after which there are again no outputs; when then input $?b$ is performed, the output $!x$ is produced. We use L_δ for $L \cup \{\delta\}$, and traces that may contain the quiescence action δ are called *suspension traces*. Suspension traces are the observations that we can make of an SUT during testing: we observe sequences of inputs, outputs, and quiescence, the latter in practice by setting a time-out and observing that no output arrived before the time-out expired.

Definition 5. *Let* $p = \langle Q, L_I, L_U, T, q_0 \rangle \in \mathcal{LTS}$.

1. *A state* q *of* p *is* quiescent, *denoted by* $\delta(q)$, *if* $\forall \mu \in L_U \cup \{\tau\} : q \overset{\mu}{\not\longrightarrow}$
2. $\Delta(p) =_{\text{def}} \langle Q, L_I, L_U \cup \{\delta\}, T \cup T_\delta, q_0 \rangle$,
   with $T_\delta =_{\text{def}} \{q \overset{\delta}{\longrightarrow} q \mid q \in Q, \delta(q)\}$
3. *The* suspension traces *of* p *are* $Straces(p) =_{\text{def}} \{\sigma \in L_\delta^* \mid \Delta(p) \overset{\sigma}{\Longrightarrow} \}$

From now on we will include δ-transitions in the transition relations, i.e., we consider $\Delta(p)$ instead of p, unless otherwise indicated. Definitions 2 and 3 also apply to transition systems with label set L_δ.

The Implementation Relation **ioco**. An implementation relation is intended to precisely define when an implementation model is correct with respect to a specification model. For implementation models we consider $\mathcal{IOTS}$ and for specification models we choose $\mathcal{LTS}$, so an implementation relation **imp** is generically written as **imp** $\subseteq \mathcal{IOTS} \times \mathcal{LTS}$.

The first specific implementation relation that we consider is **ioco**, which is abbreviated from input-output conformance. Informally, an implementation $i \in \mathcal{IOTS}$ is **ioco**-conforming to specification $s \in \mathcal{LTS}$ if after any suspension trace of s, the outputs (including quiescence) observed with i are included in those of s. After a trace that is not a suspension trace of s, nothing is specified: i is free to perform any ouput (implementation freedom, partial specification, or underspecification).

Definition 6. *Let q be a state in a transition system, Q be a set of states, $i \in \mathcal{IOTS}$, and $s \in \mathcal{LTS}$, then*

1. $out(q)$ $=_{def}$ $\{x \in L_U \mid q \xrightarrow{x} \} \cup \{ \delta \mid \delta(q)\}$
2. $out(Q)$ $=_{def}$ $\bigcup \{out(q') \mid q' \in Q\}$
3. $i \text{ **ioco** } s \Longleftrightarrow_{def} \forall \sigma \in Straces(s) : out(i \text{ **after** } \sigma) \subseteq out(s \text{ **after** } \sigma)$
   $\Longleftrightarrow \forall \sigma \in traces(\Delta(s)) : out(\Delta(i) \text{ **after** } \sigma) \subseteq out(\Delta(s) \text{ **after** } \sigma)$

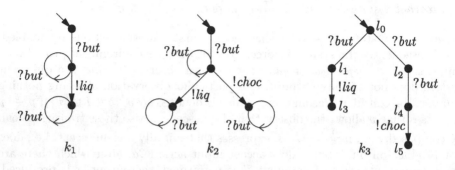

Fig. 1. Example labelled transition systems.

Example 1. Figure 1 presents three examples of labelled transition systems modelling candy machines. There is an input action for pushing a button $?but$, and there are outputs for obtaining chocolate $!choc$ and liquorice $!liq$: $L_I = \{?but\}$ and $L_U = \{!liq, !choc\}$.

Since $k_1, k_2 \in \mathcal{IOTS}(L_I, L_U)$ they can be both specifications and implementations; k_3 is not input-enabled, and can only be a specification. We have that $out(k_1 \text{ **after** } ?but) = \{!liq\} \subseteq \{!liq, !choc\} = out(k_2 \text{ **after** } ?but)$ and indeed $k_1 \text{ **ioco** } k_2$, but $k_2 \text{ **io$\not$co** } k_1$. For k_3 we have $out(k_3 \text{ **after** } ?but) = \{!liq, \delta\}$ since $\delta(l_2)$, and $out(k_3 \text{ **after** } ?but \cdot ?but) = \{!choc\}$, so both $k_1, k_2 \text{ **io$\not$co** } k_3$.

The importance of having suspension actions δ in the set of traces over which **ioco** quantifies is illustrated in Fig. 2. It holds that $out(r_1 \text{ **after** } ?but \cdot ?but) = out(r_2 \text{ **after** } ?but \cdot ?but) = \{!liq, !choc\}$, but we have $out(r_1 \text{ **after** } ?but \cdot \delta \cdot ?but) = \{!liq, !choc\} \supset \{!choc\} = out(r_2 \text{ **after** } ?but \cdot \delta \cdot ?but)$. So, without δ in these traces r_1 and r_2 would be considered implementations of each other in both directions, whereas with δ, $r_2 \text{ **ioco** } r_1$ but $r_1 \text{ **io$\not$co** } r_2$.

Proposition 1. *Let $i, i_1, i_2 \in \mathcal{IOTS}$, $s, s_1, s_2 \in \mathcal{LTS}$.*

1. $i_1 \text{ **ioco** } i_2$ iff $Straces(i_1) \subseteq Straces(i_2)$
2. $i_1 \text{ **ioco** } i_2$ and $i_2 \text{ **ioco** } s$ imply $i_1 \text{ **ioco** } s$
3. **ioco** *is a preorder on $\mathcal{IOTS}$, i.e., it is reflexive and transitive.*
4. *In general,* **ioco** $\subseteq \mathcal{IOTS} \times \mathcal{LTS}$ *is neither reflexive nor transitive.*

The Implementation Relation **uioco.** The implementation relation **ioco** allows partial specifications: the behaviour of the implementation after traces not in the specification, i.e., underspecified traces, is not specified. The implementation relation **uioco** (<u>u</u>niversal <u>i</u>nput-<u>o</u>utput <u>co</u>nformance) has a slightly different way of dealing with underspecified traces.

Definition 7. *Let $i \in \mathcal{IOTS}$ and $s \in \mathcal{LTS}$.*

1. *$Utraces(s)$ $=_{\text{def}}$ $\{\sigma \in Straces(s) \mid \forall \sigma_1, \sigma_2 \in L_\delta^*,\ a \in L_I :$*
   $$\sigma = \sigma_1 \cdot a \cdot \sigma_2 \text{ implies } \text{ not } s \text{ after } \sigma_1 \text{ refuses } a\ \}$$
   where s after σ_1 refuses a $\iff_{\text{def}}$ $\exists s' : s \xoverset{\sigma_1}{\Longrightarrow} s'$ and $s' \xoverset{a}{\not\Longrightarrow}$
2. *i uioco s $\iff_{\text{def}}$ $\forall \sigma \in Utraces(s) : out(\Delta(i) \text{ after } \sigma) \subseteq out(\Delta(s) \text{ after } \sigma)$*

Example 2. Consider k_3 of Fig. 1 as a specification. Since k_3 is not input-enabled, it is a partial specification. For example, $?but \cdot ?but \cdot ?but$ is an underspecified trace, and any implementation behaviour is allowed after it. On the other hand, $?but$ is clearly specified; the allowed outputs after it are $!liq$ and δ. For the trace $?but \cdot ?but$ the situation is less clear. According to **ioco**, $?but \cdot ?but \in Straces(k_3)$ and the expected output is $out(k_3 \text{ after } ?but \cdot ?but) = \{!choc\}$. According to **uioco**, however, $?but \cdot ?but \notin Utraces(k_3)$, so $?but \cdot ?but$ is an underspecified trace, and any implementation behaviour is allowed after it.

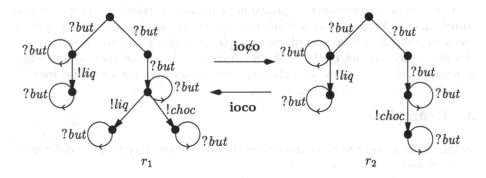

Fig. 2. More labelled transition systems.

Proposition 2.

1. **ioco** $\subset$ **uioco**
2. *For deterministic specifications, i.e., $\mid s$ after $\sigma \mid \leq 1$ for all $\sigma \in L_\delta^*$, and on $\mathcal{IOTS}$,* **ioco** = **uioco**

Example 3. Because $Utraces(s) \subseteq Straces(s)$ it is evident that **uioco** is not stronger than **ioco**. That it is strictly weaker follows from the following example. Take k_3 in Fig. 1 as a (partial) specification, and consider r_1 and r_2 from Fig. 2 as implementations. Then r_2 **io¢o** k_3 because $!liq \in out(r_2$ **after** $?but\cdot?but)$ and $!liq \notin out(k_3$ **after** $?but\cdot?but)$. But $?but\cdot?but \notin Utraces(k_3)$ and indeed it holds that r_2 **uioco** k_3. Also r_1 **io¢o** k_3, but in this case also r_1 **uio¢o** k_3. The reason for this is that we have $?but\cdot\delta\cdot?but \in Utraces(k_3)$, $!liq \in out(r_1$ **after** $?but\cdot\delta\cdot?but)$ and $!liq \notin out(k_3$ **after** $?but\cdot\delta\cdot?but)$.

Testing. For testing, based on an implementation relation **imp**, be it **ioco** or **uioco**, we have to define what test cases are, i.e., what is the domain of test cases *TEST*, and how they are executed on implementations. Then test-generation algorithms can be developed that generate test suites, i.e., sets of test cases, from a specification model: $\Pi_{\mathbf{imp}} : \mathcal{LTS} \rightarrow \mathcal{P}(TEST)$. Such a generated test suite shall detect only incorrect implementations, i.e., the test suite shall be *sound*:

$$i \textbf{ imp } s \quad \text{implies} \quad i \textbf{ passes } \Pi_{\mathbf{imp}}(s)$$

and in the limit it shall detect all incorrect implementations, i.e., it shall be *exhaustive* (though this is usually not achievable in practical testing):

$$i \textbf{ passes } \Pi_{\mathbf{imp}}(s) \quad \text{implies} \quad i \textbf{ imp } s$$

Test generation depends on the specific implementation relation, so for **ioco** and **uioco** different test generation algorithms have to be developed. In this paper we focus on comparing **ioco** and **uioco** as implementation relations, so testing and test generation are not further elaborated; see [18] for the further formalization of testing and for a sound and exhaustive test-generation algorithm for **ioco**.

3   Examples

In this section, some more examples are discussed that illustrate the differences between **ioco** and **uioco**.

Example 4. Revisiting Example 2 of Sect. 2 with k_3 of Fig. 1 as a partial specification, we clearly have that $?but\cdot?but\cdot?but \notin Straces(k_3)$, and consequently $?but\cdot?but\cdot?but \notin Utraces(k_3)$. Hence, it is an underspecified trace for **ioco** as well as for **uioco**, and it is underspecified in the left branch of k_3 as well as in the right branch, so any implementation behaviour is allowed after it.

On the other hand, $?but$ is clearly a specified trace for both **ioco** and **uioco**, $?but \in Straces(k_3)$ and $?but \in Utraces(k_3)$, and the allowed outputs after it are $!liq$ and δ.

For the trace $?but\cdot?but$, the relations differ. In the left branch of k_3, i.e., going to state l_1, $?but\cdot?but$ is underspecified, whereas in the right branch of k_3, i.e., going to state l_2, $?but\cdot?but$ is specified. So we have *nondeterministic underspecification* and this is where **ioco** and **uioco** differ. For **ioco**,

$?but\cdot?but$ is specified, $?but\cdot?but \in Straces(k_3)$, and the expected output is $out(k_3 \textbf{ after } ?but\cdot?but) = \{!choc\}$, but for **uioco**, $?but\cdot?but$ is underspecified, $?but\cdot?but \notin Utraces(k_3)$ because $k_3 \textbf{ after } ?but \textbf{ refuses } ?but$, and any implementation behaviour is allowed after it.

The relation **ioco** states that $?but\cdot?but$ is not an underspecified trace, because there exists a state where it is specified, whereas **uioco** states that $?but\cdot?but$ is underspecified, because there exists a state where it is underspecified. One could say that underspecification is existential for **uioco** and universal for **ioco** and, the other way around, that specified traces are existential for **ioco** and universal for **uioco**, hence $\underline{U}traces$ for *universal* traces and **u̲ioco**.

Note that, though $?but\cdot?but$ is underspecified for **uioco**, we cannot remove the right branch of k_3. The right branch specifies that the expected output is $!choc$ after $?but\cdot\delta\cdot?but \in Utraces(k_3)$.

Fig. 3. **ioco** and **uioco** examples.

Example 5. Consider specification s_2 in Fig. 3. We again have that for **ioco**, $?but\cdot?but$ is specified, whereas for **uioco** it is underspecified. Now we can remove branches: for **ioco**, the left branch can be removed, i.e., s_2 is for **ioco** equivalent to its right branch. For **uioco**, s_2 is equivalent to its left branch, i.e., all **uioco** conforming implementations are the same.

Example 6. Consider specification s_1 in Fig. 3, where explicit quiescence labels have been added. The trace $?but\cdot\delta\cdot?but$ is underspecified for **ioco** as well as for **uioco**: $?but\cdot\delta\cdot?but \notin Straces(s_1)$ and $?but\cdot\delta\cdot?but \notin Utraces(s_1)$. Yet, the only possible output for an **ioco**-conforming implementation i after $?but\cdot\delta\cdot?but$ is $!choc$. This is the case, since $out(s_1 \textbf{ after } ?but\cdot?but) = \{!choc\}$, and the trace $?but\cdot\delta\cdot?but$ will lead to the same states as $?but\cdot?but$, because any δ-action is the result of a δ-loop in the transition system. In other words, if there would be some output $!y \neq !choc$ after $?but\cdot\delta\cdot?but$ then $!y$ would also be in $out(i \textbf{ after } ?but\cdot?but)$ which would make the implementation **ioco** nonconforming. Consequently, $out(i \textbf{ after } ?but\cdot\delta\cdot?but)$ must be $\{!choc\}$, though trace $?but\cdot\delta\cdot?but$ might seem underspecified.

So, apparently, for **ioco** we have to do some "jumping around" in the transition system of the specification. Though after $?but \cdot \delta$ it might seem that we are in the right branch of s_1, we also still have to consider the left branch to judge about conforming behaviour. This "jumping around" has some peculiar unintuitive and formal consequences as will be shown later.

For **uioco**, the trace $?but \cdot ?but$ is also underspecified, so this problem does not occur.

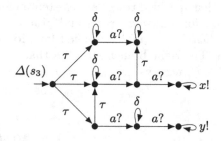

Fig. 4. Non-implementable **ioco** specification s_3.

Example 7. Consider s_3 in Fig. 4, introduced by Bourdonov and Kossatchev [8], with $L_I = \{a?\}$ and $L_U = \{x!, y!\}$. Specification s_3 is non-implementable for **ioco**, as can be shown as follows [11]. Assume an implementation $i \in \mathcal{IOTS}$ with i **ioco** s_3. We have that $\delta \cdot a? \cdot \delta \cdot a? \in Straces(i)$, because:

(1) $\epsilon \in Straces(i)$;

(2) then $out(\Delta(i) \text{ after } \epsilon) \neq \emptyset$; moreover, $out(\Delta(s_3) \text{ after } \epsilon) = \{\delta\}$, so it must be that $out(\Delta(i) \text{ after } \epsilon) = \{\delta\}$, and consequently $\delta \in Straces(i)$;

(3) then also $\delta \cdot a? \in Straces(i)$ since i is input-enabled;

(4) analogous to *(2)*: $out(\Delta(s_3) \text{ after } \delta \cdot a?) = \{\delta\}$, thus $out(\Delta(i) \text{ after } \delta \cdot a?) = \{\delta\}$, so also $\delta \cdot a? \cdot \delta \in Straces(i)$;

(5) analogous to *(3)*: $\delta \cdot a? \cdot \delta \cdot a? \in Straces(i)$, as i is input-enabled.

Let $out(i \text{ after } \delta \cdot a? \cdot \delta \cdot a?) = X$, then, because $\delta \cdot a? \cdot \delta \cdot a? \in Straces(i)$, it holds that $X \neq \emptyset$ (since there is either a 'real' output $x!$ or $y!$, and if not, there is output δ). Moreover, since δ-transitions are always added as loops in $\Delta(i)$, we can leave them out, and the resulting traces will at least have the same outputs as after $\delta \cdot a? \cdot \delta \cdot a?$:

$$out(\Delta(i) \text{ after } \delta \cdot a? \cdot a?) \supseteq X \quad \text{and} \quad out(\Delta(i) \text{ after } a? \cdot \delta \cdot a?) \supseteq X$$

Furthermore, if i **ioco** s_3 holds, then we must have that

$$out(\Delta(i) \text{ after } \delta \cdot a? \cdot a?) \subseteq out(\Delta(s_3) \text{ after } \delta \cdot a? \cdot a?) = \{x!\}$$
$$out(\Delta(i) \text{ after } a? \cdot \delta \cdot a?) \subseteq out(\Delta(s_3) \text{ after } a? \cdot \delta \cdot a?) = \{y!\}$$

Combining all these constraints for X, we conclude that there is no possible X satisfying all of them. This implies that the conforming implementation i cannot exist: s_3 is a specification that has no conforming implementations at all. Apparently, there exist *unimplementable* specifications. In [13] an even smaller unimplementable specification of only 6 states and one output is given.

For **uioco**, there are no unimplementable specifications. Specification s_3 could be implemented by an implementation with just an $a?$-loop in the initial state. Since the traces $a?\cdot a?$, $\delta\cdot a?\cdot a?$, and $a?\cdot\delta\cdot a?$ are underspecified for **uioco**, outputs $x!$ and $!y$ do not have to appear.

4 Test Observations

During testing, test cases are executed on an SUT and observations are made of what happens during test execution. Based on these observations a verdict is assigned whether the system passed or failed the test. As argued in Sect. 2, the observations for testing systems modelled as $\mathcal{IOTS}$ are *suspension traces*, i.e., sequences of inputs, outputs, and occurrences of quiescence. So, for each suspension trace we must decide whether it is allowed, i.e., whether it is correct or not according to the specification model together with the implementation relation. If we can derive from the specification with the implementation relation such a set of allowed suspension traces, then conformance can be expressed by trace inclusion: an SUT conforms iff each trace observed during testing is contained in this set of allowed suspension traces.

The relations **ioco** and **uioco**, however, are not defined as trace inclusion, but as inclusion of *out*-sets after some suspension traces; see Def. 6 and 7. So, these definitions have to be transformed into a trace-based characterization, so that we can express **ioco** and **uioco** as inclusion of suspension traces. This trace characterization is based upon the so-called *conformal traces* introduced in [8]. A conformal trace is a suspension trace which may occur in some correct implementation. These are not necessarily the same as the suspension traces of the specification, since underspecified traces of the specification may occur in an implementation and some traces of the specification can be disallowed as in Example 6. The set of all conformal traces of a specification constitutes its *trace characterization*. For both **ioco** and **uioco** this leads to a trace-based inclusion relation.

Definition 8. *Let* $\sigma \in L_\delta^*$, $s \in LTS$, *and* **imp** *an implementation relation.*

1. *Trace* σ *is a* conformal trace *of* s *with respect to* **imp** *if there exists an* **imp**-*correct implementation that has this trace:*

$$\sigma \; \mathbf{cfl_{imp}} \; s \quad \Longleftrightarrow_{\mathrm{def}} \quad \exists i \in \mathcal{IOTS} : \; i \; \mathbf{imp} \; s \; \text{ and } \; \sigma \in Straces(i)$$

2. *The* **imp**-*trace characterization of* s *is* $\langle s \rangle_{\mathbf{imp}} =_{\mathrm{def}} \{\sigma \in L_\delta^* \mid \sigma \; \mathbf{cfl_{imp}} \; s\}$

Theorem 1. *Let* $i \in \mathcal{IOTS}$, $s \in \mathcal{LTS}$.

1. $\langle i \rangle_{\mathbf{ioco}} = \langle i \rangle_{\mathbf{uioco}} = Straces(i)$
2. i **ioco** s iff $\langle i \rangle_{\mathbf{ioco}} \subseteq \langle s \rangle_{\mathbf{ioco}}$
3. i **uioco** s iff $\langle i \rangle_{\mathbf{uioco}} \subseteq \langle s \rangle_{\mathbf{uioco}}$

For **ioco** as well as for **uioco**, we can easily determine whether an observed suspension trace of the SUT is allowed, once we have the corresponding trace characterization of the specification s. The definition of trace characterization, however, though well-defined, is not at all constructive. So, we have to find a way to constructively obtain the trace characterization from s, preferably represented as some automaton or labelled transition system obtained by transformation from s. This is rather intricate as it involves both adding and removing traces of s. This is where **ioco** and **uioco** actually differ.

ioco-*Trace Characterization.* In [11], a construction for an **ioco**-trace characterization from s is given. It involves quite a number of intermediate transformations on labelled transition systems, and it is rather complicated, in particular, because the intermediate transformation steps may generate inconsistent systems, which cannot represent valid behaviour of suspension traces. Examples of inconsistency are that there are suspension traces in which quiescence cannot be followed by another quiescence (called *quiescence stability*), that quiescence cannot be removed (*quiescence reducibility*), or that there is a state that has no outputs and no quiescence (*non-blockingness*). Given that quiescence is modelled as a δ-loop for all states that have no outputs (Def. 5), such inconsistencies cannot lead to a valid set of suspension traces; for a formal elaboration of inconsistency in terms of *suspension languages*, see [11]. The transformation steps to obtain an **ioco**-trace characterization are the following:

1. Δ: *deltafication*, i.e., adding explicit quiescence actions;
2. *det*: *determinization*;
3. Ξ: *demonic completion*, i.e., adding explicit underspecification and making the system input-complete; the resulting system may violate *quiescence reducibility*;
4. ζ: recover quiescence reducibility and stability, but this may result in loosing *non-blockingness*;
5. η: recovers non-blockingness, and delivers the final, consistent labelled transition system.

Theorem 2. $\langle s \rangle_{\mathbf{ioco}} = traces(\eta(\zeta(\Xi(det(\Delta(s))))))$

So, this gives a construction for a concrete transition system representing the conformal traces of the **ioco**-trace characterization. This construction is not only complicated, but also complex: due the exponential complexity of *det* and ζ it has a double exponential upper bound.

This high complexity in itself is already problematic. Moreover, it only holds for finite models, whereas many realistic models have an infinite state space, e.g., models expressed in a process algebraic language with recursion [19], or as symbolic transition system using data parameters with infinite domains [9].

Computing an explicit transition system representation is then infeasible. The usual way of dealing with such an infinite state space is constructing the state space as far as necessary. For example, to check whether a given suspension trace σ is a conformal trace of specification s, instead of constructing the full, transformed transition system, we could attempt to construct only the initial part with depth up to the length of σ, to check whether $\sigma \in \langle s \rangle_{\text{ioco}}$. Unfortunately, this does not work for a labelled transition system representing the **ioco**-trace characterization: finding out whether a given trace is **ioco**-conformal is undecidable, even if q **after** ℓ for every state q and action ℓ is finite and computable. Any trace σ may be non-conformal because some extension of σ of unknown length leads to an inconsistent state further in the transition system. The entire state space of the specification must be checked for inconsistent states to detect non-conformal traces. Investigating an initial part is not sufficient, by construction of η. Consider the specification s_3 in Fig. 4, which has no conforming implementations, so $\langle s \rangle_{\text{ioco}} = \emptyset$, and in particular $\epsilon \notin \langle s \rangle_{\text{ioco}}$. But to find this out we have to explore the whole transition system of s_3, and we cannot restrict to the states reachable after ϵ.

Theorem 3. *Determining whether σ $\mathbf{cfl}_{\text{ioco}}$ s holds is undecidable.*

uioco-*Trace Characterization.* For **uioco**, the construction of a labelled transition system representing the **uioco**-trace characterization $\langle s \rangle_{\text{uioco}}$ turns out to be much simpler. The difference with **ioco** is that the order of applying demonic completion Ξ and determinization det is reversed for **uioco**: determinization is performed on the demonically completed specification. This exactly reflects the difference between **ioco** and **uioco** in dealing with underspecified inputs. The resulting labelled transition system is already consistent, so that the transformations ζ and η are not necessary anymore. The result is a consistent labelled transition system exactly representing the **uioco**-trace characterization. Moreover, since determinization det preserves traces, we can even leave it out.

Theorem 4. $\langle s \rangle_{\text{uioco}} = traces(\Xi(\Delta(s)))$

Hence, we can check **uioco**-conformal traces directly by checking suspension trace inclusion, after performing demonic completion on the specification. This is PSPACE-complete [16]. Moreover, in contrast to the **ioco**-trace characterization, the **uioco**-trace characterization is decidable. To check whether a suspension trace is conformal to specification s, we construct $\Xi(\Delta(s))$ and see whether σ is a trace. For infinite s, we can construct only the needed part: we only need to explore the δ-transitions and demonically-completed input actions that are traversed when following trace σ through s.

Theorem 5. *Determining whether σ $\mathbf{cfl}_{\text{uioco}}$ s holds is decidable, under the condition that q **after** ℓ is computable for all q and ℓ.*

Note that there are specifications with the same suspension traces, but with different **uioco**-trace characterizations, because the branching structure of the specification does matter. Consider specification s_2 of Fig. 3. Consider also only the right branch of this specification and call it s_2'. Then $Straces(s_2) = Straces(s_2')$, but $\langle s_2 \rangle_{\text{uioco}} \neq \langle s_2' \rangle_{\text{uioco}}$, e.g., the trace $?but \cdot ?but \cdot !liq \in \langle s_2 \rangle_{\text{uioco}}$, but $?but \cdot ?but \cdot !liq \notin \langle s_2' \rangle_{\text{uioco}}$. This means that there is no transformation possible from $Straces(s_2)$ to its **uioco**-trace characterization. The transformation to obtain the **uioco**-trace characterization must really occur on the labelled transition system of s_2.

Also the other way around holds: systems with different sets of suspension traces may have the same **uioco**-trace characterization. In the example above, Fig. 3, consider the left branch and call it s_2''. Then $Straces(s_2) \neq Straces(s_2'')$, but $\langle s_2 \rangle_{\text{uioco}} = \langle s_2'' \rangle_{\text{uioco}}$.

Conclusion. The implementation relations **ioco** and **uioco** can both be expressed as trace-based relations, but the construction for **uioco** is much simpler, it has lower complexity, and checking whether an observed suspension trace is allowed according to the specification, is decidable, whereas it is not decidable for **ioco**.

More on Testing. Ideally, after executing a test case, we wish to give the verdict *pass* if and only if the observed suspension trace is allowed, i.e., is conformal. For **ioco**, this is only possible by looking at the whole transition system of the specification, which, of course, is not possible for infinite specifications. The **ioco**-test generation of [18], however, is a so-called *on-the-fly* (or *on-line*) algorithm: it only looks, lazily, at the transition system of s as far as necessary for the actions of the test case. Consequently, this algorithm will not always give the desired verdict for each individual suspension trace, i.e., *pass* if and only if the observed trace is conformal. Yet, this algorithm is *sound* and *exhaustive*. Soundness holds for individual suspension traces: if a trace leads to a *fail* then the trace is non-conformal. Exhaustiveness of the algorithm in [18], however, does not apply to individual traces but to the whole test suite, i.e., the set of all generated test cases: a trace in a generated test case may lead to *pass* though it is non-conformal, but then some other test case will detect the non-conformance of the implementation.

Consider again the specification in Fig. 4. The algorithm of [18] will generate a test case to test what happens after trace ϵ, and this test case will have the verdict *pass* for an implementation that reacts with δ after ϵ, though δ is not a conformal trace. But there will be more test cases: a test case to test that

after $\delta \cdot a?$ the output is δ,

after $\delta \cdot a? \cdot a?$ the output is $x!$,

after $a?$ the output is δ,

after $a? \cdot a?$ the output is $x!$ or $y!$, and

after $a? \cdot \delta \cdot a?$ the output is $y!$.

Now, following an analogous reasoning as in Example 7, no implementation can pass all these test cases, so any implementation will eventually fail with the whole test suite generated with the algorithm of [18], which is consistent with the specification in Fig. 4 having no **ioco**-conforming implementations.

For passive testing, or monitoring, however, this argumentation does not hold. During monitoring we observe only one trace, and the verdict shall be *pass* if and only if the observed trace is allowed, i.e., is conformal. Because deciding whether a trace is **ioco**-conformal is undecidable, **ioco** is unsuitable as an implementation relation for monitoring.

5   Refinement

An implementation relation defines which implementations in $\mathcal{IOTS}$ are correct with respect to a specification in $\mathcal{LTS}$. It compares two different entities, implementations in $\mathcal{IOTS}$ and specifications in $\mathcal{LTS}$, and, consequently, it does not make sense to consider properties like reflexivity or transitivity. Yet, it does make sense to compare specifications between themselves, e.g., to express which specifications are equivalent, to do stepwise refinement, or to perform test selection by specification weakening. Stepwise refinement is a manner of system development where the starting point is an abstract specification model, which is refined in a step-by-step manner, adding more implementation details in each step, leading to more concrete specification models, until a very concrete model is obtained where all implementation freedom has been fixed, and which can be transformed into an executing realization. Each refinement step reduces the set of possible implementations, and refinement steps shall be reflexive and transitive: each refinement is a correct refinement of itself, and if s_1 is a refinement of s_2 and s_2 is a refinement of s_3 then s_1 shall be a refinement of s_3. Refinement is formalized by a *refinement relation* on specification models and it is defined in a straightforward way by relating each specification to its set of conforming implementations. Reflexivity and transitive follow then immediately from the reflexivity and transitivity of $\subseteq$, so refinement is a preorder on $\mathcal{LTS}$. This can be done for any implementation relation.

Definition 9. *Let* $s, s_1, s_2 \in \mathcal{LTS}$ *and* $\mathbf{imp} \subseteq \mathcal{IOTS} \times \mathcal{LTS}$.

1. $Imp_{\mathbf{imp}}(s)$ $=_{\mathrm{def}}$ $\{i \in \mathcal{IOTS} \mid i \ \mathbf{imp} \ s\}$
2. $s_1 \preceq_{\mathbf{imp}} s_2$ $\Longleftrightarrow_{\mathrm{def}}$ $Imp_{\mathbf{imp}}(s_1) \subseteq Imp_{\mathbf{imp}}(s_2)$
3. $s_1 \simeq_{\mathbf{imp}} s_2$ $\Longleftrightarrow_{\mathrm{def}}$ $Imp_{\mathbf{imp}}(s_1) = Imp_{\mathbf{imp}}(s_2)$

Furthermore, $\mathcal{P}(\mathcal{IOTS})$ with partial order $\subseteq$ is a *lattice*, with least upper bound (join) $\cup$, greatest lower bound (meet) $\cap$, top element $\mathcal{IOTS}$, and bottom element $\emptyset$. This lattice can be lifted to the domain of $\simeq$-equivalence classes of specifications. In this way, conjunction and disjunction of specifications can be introduced as the meet and join in this lattice, respectively.

Definition 10. *Let* $s_1, s_2 \in \mathcal{LTS}$ *and* $\mathbf{imp} \subseteq \mathcal{IOTS} \times \mathcal{LTS}$.

1. *The conjunction of* s_1 *and* s_2 *for* $\mathbf{imp}$ *is*

$$s_1 \wedge_{\mathbf{imp}} s_2 \quad =_{\mathrm{def}} \quad Imp_{\mathbf{imp}}(s_1) \cap Imp_{\mathbf{imp}}(s_2)$$

2. *The disjunction of s_1 and s_2 for* **imp** *is*

$$s_1 \vee_{\mathbf{imp}} s_2 \quad =_{\text{def}} \quad Imp_{\mathbf{imp}}(s_1) \cup Imp_{\mathbf{imp}}(s_2)$$

3. *The universal, or top specification is*

$$s_{\top_{\mathbf{imp}}} \text{ such that } Imp_{\mathbf{imp}}(s_{\top_{\mathbf{imp}}}) = \mathcal{IOTS}$$

4. *The unimplementable, or bottom specification is*

$$s_{\perp_{\mathbf{imp}}} \text{ such that } Imp_{\mathbf{imp}}(s_{\perp_{\mathbf{imp}}}) = \emptyset$$

The top specification for **ioco** and **uioco** is the so-called *chaos* model, denoted by $\chi \in \mathcal{IOTS} \subseteq \mathcal{LTS}$. The model *chaos* allows any behaviour: For any $i \in \mathcal{IOTS}$, i **ioco** χ and i **uioco** χ hold. The bottom specification for **ioco** is the $\simeq$-equivalence class of all labelled transition systems that do not allow any implementation: $[\![s_3]\!]_{\simeq_{\mathbf{ioco}}}$, with s_3 of Fig. 4. Note that an unimplementable specification is a correct refinement of any other specification, which might seem counter-intuitive.

The bottom specification for **uioco** does not exist in $\mathcal{LTS}$: any specification model $s \in \mathcal{LTS}$ has an implementation $i \in \mathcal{IOTS}$ with i **uioco** s, as follows from Theorems 1.3 and 4. So, for **uioco**, either Def. 10 must be restricted to a *semi-lattice*, i.e., a lattice without bottom element, or an artifical bottom element must be added.

Refinement, conjunction, and disjunction for **ioco** and **uioco** are easily defined as above, but these definitions, just as for conformal traces in the previous section, do not help at all in checking a refinement or constructing a conjunction. That is why we link refinement to conformal traces. If an implementation relation **imp** can be expressed as inclusion of **imp**-trace characterizations, then this also holds for refinement. This means that for checking refinement and calculating conjunction and disjunction we can use **ioco**- and **uioco**-trace characterizations.

Proposition 3. *If* **imp** $\subseteq \mathcal{IOTS} \times \mathcal{LTS}$ *can be expressed as* **imp**-*trace characterization inclusion, i.e., i* **imp** *s iff $\langle i \rangle_{\mathbf{imp}} \subseteq \langle s \rangle_{\mathbf{imp}}$*
then $s_1 \preceq_{\mathbf{imp}} s_2$ iff $\langle s_1 \rangle_{\mathbf{imp}} \subseteq \langle s_2 \rangle_{\mathbf{imp}}$

Conclusion. For **ioco** as well as for **uioco**, a refinement preorder for specification models can be defined, such that a refined model allows less conforming implementations. Also conjunction and disjunction of models can be defined. To check refinement or to compute conjunction we can use **ioco**- and **uioco**-trace characterizations. In Sect. 4, we showed that this is much easier and more feasible for **uioco** than for **ioco**.

More on Disjunction. Disjunction of two specifications expresses that an implementation can implement one or the other (or both). Nondeterministic behaviour in a model means that one of the behaviours can be nondeterministically chosen. One of the core problems of **ioco** is that nondeterministic choice does not act as disjunction.

Example 8. Consider the specification s_2 of Fig. 3, take the left branch of s_2 as specification s_2', and the right branch as specification s_2''. According to Def. 10, disjunction $s_2' \vee s_2''$ combines the conforming implementations of s_2' and s_2''. The nondeterministic choice of behaviours s_2' and s_2'' is s_2. An implementation i that can do the trace $?but \cdot ?but \cdot !liq$ does not **ioco**-conform to the nondeterministic choice of s_2' and s_2'', but it does conform to $s_2' \vee s_2''$ because it is in $Imp_{\mathbf{ioco}}(s_2')$.

More on **uioco**. The implementation relation **uioco** is defined on $\mathcal{IOTS} \times \mathcal{LTS}$. It can be extended to a relation *on* $\mathcal{LTS}$ by adding the converse of the requirement on *out*-sets for *in*-sets, by adding the requirement that all inputs specified must be implemented [21]:

$$s_1 \ \mathbf{uioco}' \ s_2 \quad \Longleftrightarrow_{\mathrm{def}} \quad \forall \sigma \in Utraces(s_2): \quad out(\, s_1 \ \mathbf{after} \ \sigma\,) \subseteq out(\, s_2 \ \mathbf{after} \ \sigma\,)$$
$$\wedge \ in(\, s_1 \ \mathbf{after} \ \sigma\,) \supseteq in(\, s_2 \ \mathbf{after} \ \sigma\,)$$

where $in(\, s \ \mathbf{after} \ \sigma\,) =_{\mathrm{def}} \{a \in L_I \mid \text{ not } p \ \mathbf{after} \ \sigma \ \mathbf{refuses} \ a\,\}$

Though this looks intuitive, **uioco'** is not **uioco**-refinement: $\mathbf{uioco}' \subset \preceq_{\mathbf{uioco}}$, since implicit underspecification and the explicit use of the chaos specification χ lead to the same set of conforming implementations, but implicit underspecification does not **uioco'**-relate to χ.

6   Canonical Implementations

Refinement relations are reflexive, so any specification is a correct refinement of itself. For implementation relations **ioco** and **uioco** we would also like to have a kind of quasi-reflexivity, so that for each specification we can construct in a standard way a canonical implementation that behaves as much as possible like the specification. For **ioco** and **uioco**, however, such a construction is not immediately obvious, since implementations and specifications come from different domains.

Also for canonical implementations we can revert to trace characterizations. From Theorem 1 it follows that, given specification $s \in \mathcal{LTS}$, for an implementation $i \in \mathcal{IOTS}$ with $Straces(i) = \langle s \rangle_{\mathbf{ioco}}$ it holds that i **ioco** s, and analogously, for an implementation $i \in \mathcal{IOTS}$ with $Straces(i) = \langle s \rangle_{\mathbf{uioco}}$ it holds that i **uioco** s.

So we have to construct an implementation $i \in \mathcal{IOTS}$ with the given set of $Straces(i)$. The first step is constructing a labelled transition system with explicit δ-transitions, following Theorems 2 for **ioco** and 4 for **uioco**, respectively. The second step involves transforming δ-actions, which are not allowed in $\mathcal{IOTS}$, to internal τ-transitions such that quiescence occurs in the right states. Such a construction is given in [11] and not repeated here.

Consequently, also for canonical-implementation construction there is the huge difference in complexity and feasibility of constructions for **ioco** and **uioco**. For **ioco** the construction is practically, and for infinite specifications also theoretically, infeasible for almost any realistic specification, whereas for **uioco** the construction can be performed lazily and on-the-fly, constructing the canonical implementation from $\varXi(\varDelta(s))$ as far as needed.

Note that for input-enabled specifications the situation is simplified according to Proposition 1: on $\mathcal{IOTS}$, **ioco** is a preorder. Also note that canonical-implementation construction is complete for **uioco**, but partial for **ioco**: there are specifications s that do not have any conforming implementation, which means that $\langle s \rangle_{\mathbf{ioco}} = \emptyset$, and, consequently, $Straces(i) = \emptyset$. There is no implementation in $\mathcal{IOTS}$ with $Straces(i) = \emptyset$ since for any i always $\epsilon \in Straces(i)$.

7   Relating Relations

Next to **ioco**, **uioco**, and its refinements, there are other relations on labelled transition systems with inputs and outputs, in particular, alternating simulation and different versions of alternating trace containment originating from game theory and formal verification of component-based systems [2,3]. Figure 5 relates the relations **ioco**, **uioco'**, alternating simulation $\leq_{as}$, alternating trace containment $\leq_{atc}$, and the interpretation of alternating trace containment $\leq_{\forall\forall\exists\exists}^{tb}$ from [12].

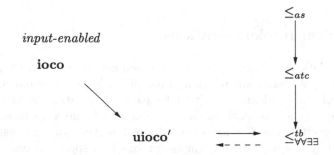

Fig. 5. (from [12]) Relating **ioco**, **uioco**, alternating simulation $\leq_{as}$, alternating trace containment $\leq_{atc}$, and the interpretation of alternating trace containment $\leq_{\forall\forall\exists\exists}^{tb}$. An arrow from relation A to relation B denotes that A is stronger than B. The dashed arrow only holds if quiescence is explicitly added to the models related by $\leq_{\forall\forall\exists\exists}^{tb}$. Relation **ioco** is only defined if the first argument is input-enabled; **uioco'** is the extended **uioco** relation *on* $\mathcal{LTS}$. Moreover, all relations without arrows between them are different, as is shown by counter-examples in [12].

Alternating simulation $\leq_{as}$ is the only branching-time relation, the others are linear-time relations. Linear-time relations are more natural to serve as implementation relation for testing since test observations are usually linear, i.e., traces. Branching-time relations like alternating simulation, are not black-box observational. Testing such a relation involves unrealistic testing actions, like freezing and copying states and undo-ing actions [1]. Yet, a branching-time relation could be used for refining and verifying a system, in which case it is desirable that this activity is sound with respect to the implementation relation used for testing. In principle, the relations $\leq_{as}$ and **uioco**$'$ are not related, but if quiescence δ is explicitly added and treated as a normal output action, then $\leq_{as} \subseteq$ **uioco**$'$. This means that any design activity done on the basis of $\leq_{as}$, e.g., the construction of an implementation, is sound with respect to testing with **uioco**. For **ioco** this is not the case: $\leq_{as}$ and **ioco** are unrelated, whether quiescence is added or not.

We conclude that **uioco** is the better fit in the spectrum of input-output relations, and that **ioco** is too strong to act as an implementation relation for testing: a system designed or verified with any of the other relations might be rejected when tested based on **ioco**.

8   Concluding Remarks

We have compared the implementation relations **ioco** and **uioco**:

- Both **ioco** and **uioco** can be expressed as trace-based relations, but the construction for **uioco** is much simpler, it has lower complexity, and checking whether an observed suspension trace is allowed according to the specification, is decidable, whereas it is not decidable for **ioco**.
- For **ioco** as well as for **uioco** a refinement preorder can be defined, such that a refined model allows less conforming implementations. Also conjunction and disjunction of models can be defined. As for trace-based relations, checking of refinement and computation of conjunction are much simpler and more feasible for **uioco** than for **ioco**.
- The relations **ioco** and **uioco** both allow the construction of a canonical implementation, but, as before, there is the huge difference in complexity and feasibility of constructions for **ioco** and **uioco**. For **ioco** the construction is practically, and for infinite specifications also theoretically, infeasible for almost any realistic specification, whereas for **uioco** the construction can be performed lazily and on-the-fly, constructing the canonical implementation from $\varXi(\Delta(s))$ as far as needed.
- The relation **uioco** is the better fit in the spectrum of input-output relations, whereas **ioco** is too strong to act as an implementation relation for testing. A system designed or verified for correctness using, for example, alternating simulation might be rejected when tested based on **ioco**, but not if tested with **uioco**.
- In the examples of Sect. 3 we have seen that some specifications are unimplementable, and that sometimes we have to "jump around" in the whole model to decide about conforming behaviour.

Altogether, we conclude that **uioco** is the better choice as implementation relation for model-based testing, so, goodbye **ioco**, hello **uioco**.

Acknowledgements. We thank Piërre van de Laar, Tim Willemse, and the anonymous reviewers for their valuable feedback and suggestions.

And, of course, we wish to thank Frits Vaandrager. Not only is this work dedicated to him, on the occasion of his 60th birthday, but Frits also played a major role in our analysis of the secrets of ioco and uioco, if not through his feedback and discussions on our research, then surely through the daily dose of optimism and the amusing conversations during the coffee breaks. We thank Frits for his inspiration, support, and pleasant collaboration, and for giving us quiescence. Without these this contribution would not have been written. Frits, thank you, and happy birthday!

References

1. Abramsky, S.: Observational equivalence as a testing equivalence. Theor. Comput. Sci. **53**(3), 225–241 (1987)
2. de Alfaro, L., Henzinger, T.: Interface automata. In: Gruhn, V. (ed.) Joint 8th European Software Engineering Conference and 9th ACM SIGSOFT Symposium on the Foundation of Software Engineering – ESEC/FSE-01. SIGSOFT Software Engineering Notes, vol. 26, pp. 109–120. ACM Press, New York, NY, USA (2001). http://doi.acm.org/10.1145/503271.503226
3. Alur, R., Henzinger, T.A., Kupferman, O., Vardi, M.Y.: Alternating refinement relations. In: Sangiorgi, D., de Simone, R. (eds.) CONCUR 1998. LNCS, vol. 1466, pp. 163–178. Springer, Heidelberg (1998). https://doi.org/10.1007/BFb0055622
4. Axini: Testautomatisering. http://www.axini.com
5. Belinfante, A.: JTorX: a tool for on-line model-driven test derivation and execution. In: Esparza, J., Majumdar, R. (eds.) TACAS 2010. LNCS, vol. 6015, pp. 266–270. Springer, Heidelberg (2010). https://doi.org/10.1007/978-3-642-12002-2_21
6. Belinfante, A., et al.: Formal test automation: a simple experiment. In: Csopaki, G., Dibuz, S., Tarnay, K. (eds.) Testing of Communicating Systems. ITIFIP, vol. 21, pp. 179–196. Springer, Boston, MA (1999). https://doi.org/10.1007/978-0-387-35567-2_12
7. van der Bijl, M., Rensink, A., Tretmans, J.: Compositional testing with IOCO. In: Petrenko, A., Ulrich, A. (eds.) FATES 2003. LNCS, vol. 2931, pp. 86–100. Springer, Heidelberg (2004). https://doi.org/10.1007/978-3-540-24617-6_7
8. Bourdonov, I., Kossatchev, A.: Specification completion for IOCO. Program. Comput. Softw. **37**(1), 1–14 (2011). Original Russian Text Published in Programmirovanie 2011
9. Frantzen, L., Tretmans, J., Willemse, T.A.C.: A symbolic framework for model-based testing. In: Havelund, K., Núñez, M., Roşu, G., Wolff, B. (eds.) FATES/RV -2006. LNCS, vol. 4262, pp. 40–54. Springer, Heidelberg (2006). https://doi.org/10.1007/11940197_3
10. Gaudel, M.-C.: Testing can be formal, too. In: Mosses, P.D., Nielsen, M., Schwartzbach, M.I. (eds.) CAAP 1995. LNCS, vol. 915, pp. 82–96. Springer, Heidelberg (1995). https://doi.org/10.1007/3-540-59293-8_188
11. Janssen, R., Tretmans, J.: Matching implementations to specifications: the corner cases of *ioco*. In: ACM/SIGAPP Symposium on Applied Computing – Software Verification and Testing Track, pp. 2196–2205. SAC 2019, ACM, New York, NY, USA (2019)

12. Janssen, R., Vaandrager, F., Tretmans, J.: Relating alternating relations for conformance and refinement. In: Ahrendt, W., Tapia Tarifa, S.L. (eds.) IFM 2019. LNCS, vol. 11918, pp. 246–264. Springer, Cham (2019). https://doi.org/10.1007/978-3-030-34968-4_14

13. Janssen, R.: Refinement and partiality for model-based testing. Ph.D. thesis, Radboud University, Nijmegen, The Netherlands (2022)

14. Jard, C., Jéron, T.: TGV: theory, principles and algorithms: a tool for the automatic synthesis of conformance test cases for non-deterministic reactive systems. Softw. Tools Technol. Transfer **7**(4), 297–315 (2005)

15. Larsen, K., Mikucionis, M., Nielsen, B., Skou, A.: Testing real-time embedded software using UPPAAL-TRON: an industrial case study. In: Wolf, W. (ed.) EMSOFT 2005 – ACM International Conference On Embedded Software, pp. 299–306. ACM (2005)

16. Stockmeyer, L.J., Meyer, A.R.: Word problems requiring exponential time. In: Proceedings of the 5th Annual ACM Symposium on Theory of computing (STOC), pp. 1–9. ACM (1973)

17. Tretmans, J.: Test generation with inputs, outputs and repetitive quiescence. Softw.-Concepts Tools **17**(3), 103–120 (1996)

18. Tretmans, J.: Model based testing with labelled transition systems. In: Hierons, R.M., Bowen, J.P., Harman, M. (eds.) Formal Methods and Testing. LNCS, vol. 4949, pp. 1–38. Springer, Heidelberg (2008). https://doi.org/10.1007/978-3-540-78917-8_1

19. Tretmans, J., van de Laar, P.: Model-based testing with TorXakis – the mysteries of dropbox revisited. In: Strahonja, V., Hertweck, D., Kirinić, V. (eds.) Central Eur. Conf. on Information and Intelligent Systems – CECIIS, pp. 247–258. Faculty of Organization and Informatics, University of Zagreb, Varaždin, Croatia (2019)

20. Vaandrager, F.: On the relationship between process algebra and input/output automata. In: Logic in Computer Science, pp. 387–398. Sixth Annual IEEE Symposium, IEEE Computer Society Press (1991)

21. Volpato, M., Tretmans, J.: Towards quality of model-based testing in the ioco framework. In: International Workshop on Joining AcadeMiA and Industry Contributions to Testing Automation – JAMAICA 2013, pp. 41–46. ACM, New York, NY, USA (2013)

Process Algebras and Flocks of Birds

Rocco De Nicola[1], Luca Di Stefano[2], Omar Inverso[3], and Serenella Valiani[1(✉)]

[1] IMT School of Advanced Studies, Lucca, Italy
`serenella.valiani@imtlucca.it`
[2] Univ. Grenoble Alpes, Inria, CNRS, Grenoble INP, LIG, Grenoble, France
[3] Gran Sasso Science Institute (GSSI), L'Aquila, Italy

Abstract. Many natural and artificial systems studied across a variety of disciplines, from biology to social sciences, consist of relatively simple agents with a partial knowledge of the system as a whole, where complex collective dynamics that are difficult to anticipate emerge from local interaction. We argue how formal methods broadly understood can be of assistance in such studies with a systematic approach to specification and analysis. To convey our argument, we elaborate a proof of concept inspired from an instance of emergent behaviour commonly observed in flocks of birds.

1 Introduction

Sophisticated *collective* dynamics can be observed in a variety of biological systems [18], such as herds of animals [25], colonies of insects [28], flocks of birds and schools of fish [23], but also in artificial systems such as political parties [27], smart cities [29], cyber-physical systems, and many others [8,15,21]. The study of such systems poses several challenges, such as intuitive specification and fast validation of different hypotheses on so-called *emergent behaviour* and other complex properties.

In this paper, we argue that concepts, methods, and tools from the wider area of formal methods, to which Frits Vaandrager has dedicated most of his research efforts, can be of assistance in such activities. In particular, with the right ingredients, an integrated approach to formal specification and verification can open up to seemingly distant disciplines, where there could be plenty to be gained. The right ingredients here consist of a domain-specific formal language and effective verification procedures.

We consider a well-known example of collective behaviour known as *flocking*, that spontaneously emerges from the movement of birds in a flock. It is a fascinating natural phenomenon studied in a variety of disciplines, including ethology [22], optimization [1], economics [11], biology [18], and many others.

Flocking was considered as the combined effect of conflicting forces in the 1950s s by Emlen, who proposed a model where an attractive force, which causes the birds to move closer to each other, is combined with a repulsive force that limits the size of the flock [17]. In the late 1980s, Reynolds refined this concept by introducing three separate rules, namely *cohesion*, *alignment*, and *separation*,

N. Jansen et al. (Eds.): Vaandrager Festschrift 2022, LNCS 13560, pp. 512–523, 2022.
https://doi.org/10.1007/978-3-031-15629-8_27

where flockmates move closer to each other when far apart, adapt their movements according to those of their neighbours, and avoid collisions by keeping a minimum distance from each other, respectively [23]. In practice, the combined effect of Reynold's rules can generate collective patterns of movement that resemble those of flocks of birds in the nature. Reynold's flocking model is an interesting example of bottom-up modelling of sophisticated collective behaviour via simple local rules. Indeed, the idea that collective behaviour can be expressed in terms of local interactions in a natural way is also backed up by more recent studies, from biology [12,18] to physics [3,4].

Elaborating an accurate model of flocking is outside the scope of this paper. Rather, we are interested in the study of minimalistic models that can mimic the dynamics described above at least in part. We focus on cohesion, which is commonly acknowledged as a core property of flocking [13,26,28]. Cohesion is usually defined based on the capability of each bird to determine a flock centroid (e.g., in Reynold's model, the barycentre of birds in the cohesion zone [23]). We would like to see whether it would be possible to achieve something similar to cohesion with minimal specifications, for instance by simply having birds approach pairwise non-deterministically.

We thus develop an initial model of flocking behaviour using a process algebra for collective systems [14] (Sect. 2). We carry out the analysis of cohesion using sequential emulation [16], spotting a corner case in the specifications which prevents cohesion (Sect. 3). We use the counterexample produced by our analysis to refine the specifications, and re-analyse cohesion (Sect. 4). We report some final considerations in Sect. 5.

2   A Simplified Model of a Flocking Behaviour

Let us now consider a minimalistic model of flocking behaviour, where each bird b looks at another bird a in the flock, estimates the future position of a based on a's current movement, and aims at moving towards that position (Fig. 1). To account for inertia, the new direction of b is averaged with its previous direction. To avoid collisions, in case the position where b wants to move is already occupied by another flockmate, b slows down. Assuming that all birds in the flock behave like this, we would like to know whether such rules would be sufficient to achieve cohesion.

Cohesion is usually defined based on the capability of each bird to determine a flock centroid (e.g., in Reynold's model, the barycentre of birds in the cohesion zone [23]). In our model, instead, a bird tries to approach a point where another bird in the system is likely going to be in the future.

We formalise the description given above by relying on the process description language LAbS [14]. A simplified version of the formal specifications is shown in Algorithm 1. Lines 2–6 describe the *interface*, i.e. the set of features, or *attributes*, that a bird exposes to the rest of the system. Here, the interface contains two attributes x and y describing the position of a bird on a two-dimensional grid, and two attributes dir_x and dir_y representing the movement vectors of the bird

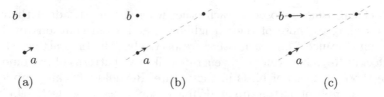

Fig. 1. Bird b targets bird a (a), looks at a's direction (b), and gets closer (c).

along the two axes. Each attribute has a range of feasible values. The position attributes may range over the interval $[0, G]$ and the direction attributes over $[-D, D+1]$. G and D are two parameters that respectively denote the size of the grid where the birds move, and the maximum length of the movement vectors (see Fig. 4 for the possible directions with $D = 1$). The symbol $\leftarrow$ denotes assignments to attributes. To model non-deterministic initialisation, attributes are assigned ranges of values rather than specific ones. Each agent also has an implicit attribute id, which is a unique identifier between 0 and the number of agents in the system.

The behaviour of each bird is defined in lines 8–27. The recursive definition at line 8 indicates that each bird repeatedly performs the same actions, given in process **Move**. This process is in turn defined as a sequence of assignments. Please note the symbol $:=$ that denotes assignments to local variables, and the enclosing curly braces that enforce atomicity.

The **Move** process consists of two parts. The first part (lines 11–19) implements the mechanism presented at the beginning of the section (Fig. 1). First, we non-deterministically select one agent by means of the *pick 1* command and assign it to a variable p (line 11). Then, we check whether this agent is *isolated* or not. We define p to be isolated when its distance from every other agent is larger than a parameter δ (line 12). Note that, in general, an attribute name decorated with an id (e.g., x_p) evaluates to the value of the attribute for the agent with the given id. If the selected bird p is not isolated, the bird will approach it; otherwise, the bird will keep moving in its current direction. Also note that we define the distance operator $d(\cdot)$ at line 12 as the *Manhattan distance*, or ℓ_1-norm [7]: the distance between two points is the sum of the absolute differences between their components. Specifically, given two points $\mathbf{b}, \mathbf{p}$ in a two-dimensional space, we have $d((x_{\mathbf{b}}, y_{\mathbf{b}}), (x_{\mathbf{p}}, y_{\mathbf{p}})) = |x_{\mathbf{b}} - x_{\mathbf{p}}| + |y_{\mathbf{b}} - y_{\mathbf{p}}|$, which corresponds to the combined length of the segments shown in Fig. 2. Starting from line 14 the bird estimates the future position (ax, ay) of the agent *appId* to approach by multiplying its direction vector by a parameter ω. It then approximates a movement vector *adir* towards that position by comparing $(\mathbf{x}, \mathbf{y})$ and (ax, ay) component-wise with a tolerance parameter ε. We only report the instructions for the x component of the vector; the y component is computed similarly.

In the second part of the **Move** process (lines 22–26), the bird updates its own attributes. Specifically, the bird's new direction is the average between the previous one and the vector *adir* computed beforehand. Please note that the

Listing 1: Initial specifications for a flock of birds.

```
1  agent Bird {
2      Interface =
3          x ← 0..G;
4          y ← 0..G;
5          dir_x ← −D..D + 1;
6          dir_y ← −D..D + 1
7
8      Behaviour = Move; Behaviour
9
10     Move = {
11         p := pick 1;
12         pIsIsolated := forall Bird b, b ≠ p ⇒ d((x_p, y_p), (x_b, y_b)) > δ;
13         appId := if pIsIsolated then id else p;
14         ax := x_appId + ω · dir_x_appId;
15         sgn_x := if x > ax then 1 else −1;
16         adir_x :=  if a = id then
17                 |  dir_x
18               else
19                 |  if |x − ax| < ε then 0 else sgn_x · D;
20         # assign ay, sgn_y, adir_y as above
21
22         dir_x ← (dir_x + adir_x)/2;
23         dir_y ← (dir_y + adir_y)/2;
24         posIsFree := forall Bird b, (x_b ≠ x + dir_x) ∨ (y_b ≠ y + dir_y);
25         x ← if posIsFree then x + dir_x else x
26         y ← if posIsFree then y + dir_y else y
27     }
28 }
```

division used here is an integer division with rounding. Finally, the bird checks whether the cell it would reach by moving along its new direction is free: if so, the bird moves there by updating its attributes x and y; otherwise, it stays in its current cell (lines 24–26).

3   Analysis of Cohesion

We now carry out the analysis of cohesion for the model of flocking behaviour given in the previous section. The key element of our verification flow is a symbolic encoding of the specifications into a sequential imperative program, which we call an *emulation program* [16]. The encoding reduces the problem of checking whether the system satisfies the given property to checking reachability in the emulation program. This has the twofold advantage of detaching the specification language from the verification technique, and allowing to automatically re-use program analysis tools for general-purpose languages.

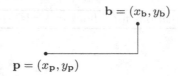

Fig. 2. Manhattan distance between two points in two dimensions.

The emulation program uses a minimal set of features (i.e., loops and statically-sized arrays), and can be concretised with limited effort into different target languages, depending on the verification technology of preference; it also embeds an explicit scheduler, which allows to apply specific scheduling policies. We target the C language and rely on bounded model checking [9] for the actual analysis; we choose round-robin scheduling, i.e., agents perform their actions in a round-robin fashion. We call *epoch* an execution fragment in which every agent in the system performs precisely one action. This allows us to consider verification bounds in terms of epochs. The verification flow described above is implemented in our prototype tool SLiVER[1], that takes care of generating the emulation program from the specifications of the system under analysis, instrumenting the emulation program for verification to be carried out by the back end model checker, and translating any counterexample from the model checker into a human-readable output with respect to the initial system specifications.

In order to assess cohesion, we set up a scenario with two separate groups of birds positioned at a certain distance from each other (Fig. 3), and check whether, given enough epochs for the system to evolve, the two groups end up forming a single flock. We thus instantiate the system of Listing 1 with four agents, a grid of size $G = 1024$ (lines 3–4), movement vectors of max modulo $D = 1$ for the possible directions of agents (lines 5–6), a sensitivity $\omega = 10$ to estimate the future position of the bird to approach (line 14), a distance $\delta = 32$ to determine whether an agent is isolated (line 12), and a tolerance parameter $\varepsilon = 5$ to approximate the approach vector (line 19). We non-deterministically position the two groups of birds into two smaller sub-grids of size 9×9, the birds in the left-hand group oriented bottom to top, and those in the right-hand group oriented right to left. The two regions are 40 cells apart, therefore the Manhattan distance between any two birds from different groups is initially at most 76 cells. Figure 5a shows a feasible initial state under these constraints. We enforce these constraints by specifying them as quantified predicates in a dedicated section of the specifications (Listing 2).

With the above set up, we use our prototype to check whether, after B steps, every execution of the system reaches a state where all birds are at most k cells apart (lower values of k indicating a more compact flock and thus a stronger cohesion). To express this property, we decorate the specifications of Listing 1 as shown in Listing 3. Since birds are initially not farther than 76 cells, we start checking the property for a cohesion distance k of 75, to check whether

---

[1] The tool is available at https://github.com/labs-lang/sliver.

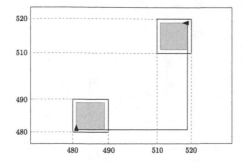

Fig. 3. Initial areas, in grey, where agents can position themselves. (Color figure online)

Fig. 4. Possible directions of a bird with movement vectors of max. size $D=1$.

the birds can get barely closer together than in the initial state. Indeed, our tool immediately produces a counterexample showing that the specifications of Listing 1 fail to guarantee even such minimal degree of cohesion.

The counterexample is shown in Fig. 5. Intuitively, since each bird keeps approaching a bird within the same group, the groups will stay separate indefinitely if they don't meet by accident, and thus the flock will never achieve cohesion. Figure 5a shows the initial state of the system. During the first epoch, first the 1-orange and 2-blue agents choose to approach the 3-red and 4-green ones, respectively, altering their direction accordingly (Figs. 5b). Then, the 3-red and 4-green agents make the symmetrical choice (Fig. 5c). At this point, the two subgroups have parallel direction vectors and the cohesion property is still unsatisfied, as the red agent is more than 75 cells apart from the green one. From now on, agents in each subgroup keep selecting each other as the agent to approach, meaning that the subgroups keep moving parallel to each other and never achieve the desired degree of cohesion (Fig. 5d).

4   Revising the Model

The counterexample obtained in Sect. 3 shows that when adopting the behaviour of Listing 1 the birds may never achieve cohesion, as they will completely ignore the other birds outside their group. In this section we modify the specification of Listing 1 to address this problem so that each bird can also approach agents outside its own group. We then repeat the analysis to check whether the revised specifications improve cohesion.

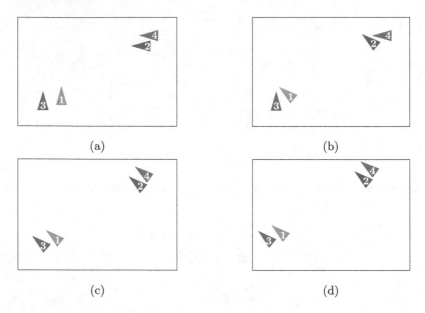

Fig. 5. Two groups of birds failing to achieve cohesion. (Color figure online)

Intuitively, as a possible way to improve cohesion, a bird should be able to alternately approach other birds from his own group and from the other group. To accommodate this, we change the specifications as shown in Listing 4. An attribute groupId initialized to either 0 or 1 keeps track which group a bird initially belongs to. Another attribute, check, is initialized to 0 and is used to guide the selection of the bird to be approached (lines 4–5). Finally, line 11 of Listing 1 is replaced by lines 9–10 of Listing 4. After this change, the non-deterministic selection of the bird p to be approached is constrained by a predicate, introduced by the keyword where. This predicate states that, if the attribute check is currently set to 0, the agent may pick any bird indiscriminately. However, if check is set to 1, then the agent must pick a bird whose groupId is different from its own (line 9). Then, the agent flips the value of check (line 10). This means that a bird will necessarily pick somebody outside its own initial group at least every other epoch.

We repeat the same experiment described in Sect. 3 on the specifications revised as above to verify flocks of 4, 6, and 8 agents with the same parameters listed in Sect. 3, increasing the verification bound until obtaining a positive verdict. Figure 6 reports the minimum number of epochs needed to reach a positive verdict for varying systems and values of k. The number of epochs grows linearly as the cohesion distance k decreases and does not blow up as the number of birds increases, suggesting that achieving cohesion does not become particularly harder for larger flocks, at least not for such simple specifications.

Figure 7 reports additional measurements on the amount of time and memory needed to obtain the positive verdicts reported in Fig. 6, where we can observe

---

Listing 2: Initial scenario with two separate groups of birds.

```
1 assume {
2     DifferentPositions =
          forall Bird a, forall Bird b, a = b ∨ xₐ ≠ x_b ∨ yₐ ≠ y_b
3     GridLeft =
          forall Bird b, (id_b mod 2 = 0) ∨ ((480 < x_b < 490) ∧ (480 < y_b < 490))
4     GridRight =
          forall Bird b, (id_b mod 2 ≠ 0) ∨ ((510 < x_b < 520) ∧ (510 < y_b < 520))
5     AlignmentLeft = forall Bird b, (id_b mod 2 = 0) ∨ (dirx_b = 0 ∧ diry = 1)
6     AlignmentRight =
          forall Bird b, (id_b mod 2 ≠ 0) ∨ (dirx_b = −1 ∧ diry = 0)
7 }
```

Listing 3: Cohesion property.

```
1 check {
2     Cohesion = finally forall Bird b, forall Bird c, d((x_b, y_b), (x_c, y_c)) < k
3 }
```

---

that the performance quickly degenerates when increasing the number of birds and of epochs; the model checker must in fact exhaustively explore the state space up to a bound which is given by the number of epochs multiplied by the number of agents. Changing the back end technology can affect the efficiency of analysis significantly [16], but comparing different techniques is outside the scope of this paper.

We performed all the experiments in a virtualized environment on a dedicated machine running 64-bit GNU/Linux with kernel 5.4.0 and equipped with four 2-GHz Xeon E7-4830v4 10-core processors and 512 GB of physical memory.

Listing 4: Revised version of the specifications in Listing 1.

```
1 agent Bird {
2     Interface =
3         ...
4         groupId ← 0..2;
5         check ← 0
6
7     Behaviour = Move; Behaviour
8     Move = {
9         p := pick 1 where (check = 0) ∨ (groupId ≠ groupId_p);
10        check ← (check + 1) mod 2;
11        ...
12    }
13 }
```

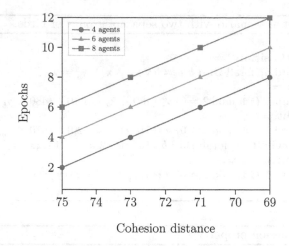

Fig. 6. Number of epochs to achieve cohesion at different distances.

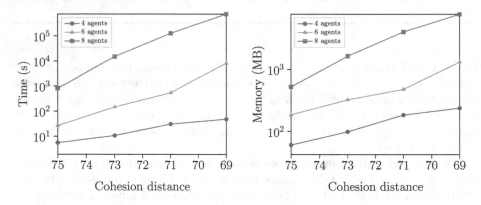

Fig. 7. Resources needed to verify cohesion varying cohesion distance.

5   Conclusion

The main point we intend to make with this paper is that existing methodologies, techniques, and tools from the wider area of formal methods, when appropriately combined, can be of assistance in the study of different classes of so-called collective systems of interest in a variety of disciplines. To support our argument, we have shown how formal languages and modern verification procedures can be combined to study the behaviour of flocks of birds. The technical contribution of this paper is clearly only a proof of concept to support our argument, but in our opinion points out relevant research directions which it may be worthwhile pursuing.

With respect to the specific scenario considered in this paper, we plan to devise further refined models of flocking behaviour and formally verify different properties, possibly working on the back end verification technique to improve efficiency, considering distributed analysis or large-scale simulation with computing clusters. We certainly plan to apply our methodology to other classes of systems, either artificial or natural, and would like to try to interact with researchers from different areas in the long run.

From a technical standpoint, our approach can be improved in several ways. With respect to scalability, techniques for *parameterized* model checking may help, as they would enable us to demonstrate that a property holds for all systems larger than a threshold. So far, these techniques have been demonstrated on models and languages with limited agent capabilities [5,19,20]; the question whether they may be adapted to more high-level languages such as LAbS is open. Orthogonal approaches such as symmetry reduction and partial order reduction [2,10] could facilitate the verification of larger systems, but their integration in our verification flow might require considerable efforts. Lastly, in this paper we have only experimented with bounded analysis. Indeed, our verification workflow can accommodate other kinds of back end technologies. It would be interesting to experiment with unbounded verification of properties using state-of-the-art inductive techniques such as k-induction [24] or PDR [6].

References

1. Alaliyat, S., Yndestad, H., Sanfilippo, F.: Optimisation of Boids swarm model based on genetic algorithm and particle swarm optimisation algorithm (comparative study). In: Squazzoni, F., Baronio, F., Archetti, C., Castellani, M. (eds.) 28th European Conference on Modelling and Simulation, ECMS 2014, Brescia, Italy, 27–30 May 2014, pp. 643–650. European Council for Modeling and Simulation (2014). https://doi.org/10.7148/2014-0643
2. Alur, R., Brayton, R.K., Henzinger, T.A., Qadeer, S., Rajamani, S.K.: Partial-order reduction in symbolic state space exploration. In: Grumberg, O. (ed.) CAV 1997. LNCS, vol. 1254, pp. 340–351. Springer, Heidelberg (1997). https://doi.org/10.1007/3-540-63166-6_34
3. Ballerini, M., et al.: Interaction ruling animal collective behavior depends on topological rather than metric distance: evidence from a field study. Proc. Nat. Acad. Sci. **105**(4), 1232–1237 (2008). https://doi.org/10.1073/pnas.0711437105, www.pnas.org/doi/abs/10.1073/pnas.0711437105
4. Bialek, W., et al.: Statistical mechanics for natural flocks of birds. Proc. Natl. Acad. Sci. **109**(13), 4786–4791 (2012)
5. Blondin, M., Esparza, J., Jaax, S.: PEREGRINE: a tool for the analysis of population protocols. In: Chockler, H., Weissenbacher, G. (eds.) CAV 2018. LNCS, vol. 10981, pp. 604–611. Springer, Cham (2018). https://doi.org/10.1007/978-3-319-96145-3_34
6. Bradley, A.R.: SAT-based model checking without unrolling. In: Jhala, R., Schmidt, D. (eds.) VMCAI 2011. LNCS, vol. 6538, pp. 70–87. Springer, Heidelberg (2011). https://doi.org/10.1007/978-3-642-18275-4_7
7. Brezis, H.: Functional Analysis, Sobolev Spaces and Partial Differential Equations. Universitext, Springer, New York (2011). https://doi.org/10.1007/978-0-387-70914-7

8. Casadei, R., Viroli, M.: Programming actor-based collective adaptive systems. In: Ricci, A., Haller, P. (eds.) Programming with Actors. LNCS, vol. 10789, pp. 94–122. Springer, Cham (2018). https://doi.org/10.1007/978-3-030-00302-9_4

9. Clarke, E., Kroening, D., Lerda, F.: A tool for checking ANSI-C programs. In: Jensen, K., Podelski, A. (eds.) TACAS 2004. LNCS, vol. 2988, pp. 168–176. Springer, Heidelberg (2004). https://doi.org/10.1007/978-3-540-24730-2_15

10. Clarke, E.M., Emerson, E.A., Jha, S., Sistla, A.P.: Symmetry reductions in model checking. In: Hu, A.J., Vardi, M.Y. (eds.) CAV 1998. LNCS, vol. 1427, pp. 147–158. Springer, Heidelberg (1998). https://doi.org/10.1007/BFb0028741

11. Cont, R., Bouchaud, J.P.: Herd behavior and aggregate fluctuations in financial markets. Macroecon. Dyn. 4(2), 170–196 (2000)

12. Couzin, I.D., Krause, J., James, R., Ruxton, G.D., Franks, N.R.: Collective memory and spatial sorting in animal groups. J. Theor. Biol. 218(1), 1–11 (2002)

13. Craig, W.: Appetites and aversions as constituents of instincts. Biol. Bull. 34(2), 91–107 (1918)

14. De Nicola, R., Di Stefano, L., Inverso, O.: Multi-agent systems with virtual stigmergy. Sci. Compu. Program. 187, 102345 (2020). https://doi.org/10.1016/j.scico.2019.102345

15. Deneubourg, J.L., Goss, S., Franks, N., Sendova-Franks, A., Detrain, C., Chrétien, L.: The dynamics of collective sorting robot-like ants and ant-like robots. In: From Animals to Animats: Proceedings of the First International Conference on Simulation of Adaptive Behavior, pp. 356–365 (1991)

16. Di Stefano, L., De Nicola, R., Inverso, O.: Verification of distributed systems via sequential emulation. ACM Trans. Softw. Eng. Methodol. 31(3), 1–41 (2022). https://doi.org/10.1145/3490387

17. Emlen, J.T.: Flocking behavior in birds. The Auk 69(2), 160–170 (1952)

18. Grégoire, G., Chaté, H., Tu, Y.: Moving and staying together without a leader. Phys. D: Nonlinear Phenom. 181(3–4), 157–170 (2003)

19. Konnov, I., Veith, H., Widder, J.: SMT and POR beat counter abstraction: parameterized model checking of threshold-based distributed algorithms. In: Kroening, D., Păsăreanu, C.S. (eds.) CAV 2015. LNCS, vol. 9206, pp. 85–102. Springer, Cham (2015). https://doi.org/10.1007/978-3-319-21690-4_6

20. Kouvaros, P., Lomuscio, A.: A counter abstraction technique for the verification of robot swarms. In: Bonet, B., Koenig, S. (eds.) 29th Conference on Artificial Intelligence (AAAI), pp. 2081–2088. AAAI (2015)

21. Kube, C.R., Bonabeau, E.: Cooperative transport by ants and robots. Robot. Auton. Syst. 30(1–2), 85–101 (2000)

22. Norris, K.S., Schilt, C.R.: Cooperative societies in three-dimensional space: on the origins of aggregations, flocks, and schools, with special reference to dolphins and fish. Ethol. Sociobiol. 9(2–4), 149–179 (1988)

23. Reynolds, C.W.: Flocks, herds and schools: a distributed behavioral model. In: Stone, M.C. (ed.) Proceedings of the 14th Annual Conference on Computer Graphics and Interactive Techniques, SIGGRAPH 1987, Anaheim, 27–31 July 1987, pp. 25–34. ACM (1987). https://doi.org/10.1145/37401.37406

24. Sheeran, M., Singh, S., Stålmarck, G.: Checking safety properties using induction and a SAT-solver. In: Hunt, W.A., Johnson, S.D. (eds.) FMCAD 2000. LNCS, vol. 1954, pp. 127–144. Springer, Heidelberg (2000). https://doi.org/10.1007/3-540-40922-X_8

25. Sumpter, D.J.: The principles of collective animal behaviour. Philos. Trans. Royal Soc. B: Biol. Sci. 361(1465), 5–22 (2006)

26. Trotter, W.: Instincts of the Herd in Peace and War. TF Unwin Limited (1920)
27. Valentini, G., Hamann, H., Dorigo, M., et al.: Self-organized collective decision making: the weighted voter model. In: AAMAS, pp. 45–52 (2014)
28. Wheeler, W.M.: The Social Insects: Their Origin and Evolution. Routledge, Abingdon (2015)
29. Zedadra, O., Guerrieri, A., Jouandeau, N., Spezzano, G., Seridi, H., Fortino, G.: Swarm intelligence and IoT-based smart cities: a review. In: Cicirelli, F., Guerrieri, A., Mastroianni, C., Spezzano, G., Vinci, A. (eds.) The Internet of Things for Smart Urban Ecosystems. IT, pp. 177–200. Springer, Cham (2019). https://doi.org/10.1007/978-3-319-96550-5_8

The Integration of Testing and Program Verification

A Position Paper

Petra van den Bos and Marieke Huisman[✉][iD]

Formal Methods and Tools, University of Twente, Enschede, The Netherlands
m.huisman@utwente.nl

Abstract. Formal analysis techniques for software systems are becoming more and more powerful, and have been used on non-trivial examples. We argue that the next step forward is to combine these different techniques in a single framework, which makes it possible to (i) analyse different parts of the system with different techniques, (ii) apply different techniques on a single component, and (iii) seamlessly combine the results of the various analysis. We describe our vision of how this integration can be achieved for the analysis techniques of testing and deductive verification. We end with an overview of research challenges that need to be addressed to achieve this vision.

1 Introduction

As our society depends more and more on software in every aspect of our daily lives, we have become crucially dependent on software functioning correctly and reliably, and without doing us any harm. Over the last decades, many different techniques have been developed that can help us to obtain such guarantees. These techniques range from running a few test cases to full formal verification of the software's properties. With this wide range of approaches that we have available, we see that the amount of effort that is required to use such a technique is typically counterbalanced by the guarantees that are provided by it. In particular for powerful techniques, the required formal description might be even larger than the software system or program itself. Therefore, to make effective use of this wide range of techniques, we need to find a way to balance and combine the effort and effectiveness of the different approaches in an optimal way.

To achieve this balance, we argue that an integration of those different techniques is necessary. This integration should enable the following ways of verifying a system:

- different system parts can be analyzed with different techniques;
- a formal technique used to analyze a system part can be replaced by another; and
- the analysis results can be combined seamlessly.

N. Jansen et al. (Eds.): Vaandrager Festschrift 2022, LNCS 13560, pp. 524–538, 2022.
https://doi.org/10.1007/978-3-031-15629-8_28

There are many different reasons why the integration of formal techniques for software analysis is necessary:

- Usually some parts of a system are more critical than others. Critical parts should be verified thoroughly, using techniques with strong guarantees, while other parts can be analyzed with easy-to-apply techniques that provide weaker guarantees.
- By allowing the flexible use of techniques with proportionally required efforts and provided guarantees, the threshold for applying formal techniques is lowered. Consequently, a general boost in software quality can be expected, because some sort of formal techniques can easily be applied to large parts of the system.
- Software is almost never a static artifact, but changes continuously, while it also runs in changing environment. These changes result in different needs for correctness guarantees. Ease in swapping of applied techniques will support this change.
- Without clear results from the analysis effort, it is hard to know where to improve the software. Hence, when combining techniques, combining the analysis results is essential to transfer the knowledge obtained in the analysis effort to the development of the system. By combining analysis results, again, a boost in quality of the software is to be expected, as this will provide more pointers for improvement, than separate results for parts alone. Also we think that combining results is a smaller challenge than applying one analysis technique on the whole system.

To exemplify what such an integration would encompass, this paper sketches what the integration would look like for the authors' research areas: testing and deductive verification. This way, we provide a concrete view on how the integration could work. Deductive verification [17], or program verification, is a static analysis method applied on the code level of a system. Testing consists of executing the system and observing whether the systems behaviour is as expected. We distinguish between two different testing techniques: automated testing, where test cases are written by humans (e.g. developers), and model-based testing, where test cases are derived algorithmically from a formal model [28,38].

To understand how testing and verification can be integrated, we first discuss the testing and deductive verification in more detail, with their strengths and weaknesses (Sect. 2). Then we sketch what our ideal approach to integrating testing and verification would look like (Sect. 3), and after that we discuss what we see as the open research challenges that need to be addressed to reach this goal (Sect. 4). We have grouped these challenges in three categories: challenges that are related to how these techniques can be combined, challenges that need to be addressed in the area of testing, and challenges that need to be addressed in the area of deductive verification.

2   Strengths and Weaknesses of Testing and Verification

This section gives a brief overview of automated testing, model-based testing, and deductive verification, and for each of these formal analysis techniques we discuss strengths and weaknesses.

General Strengths and Weaknesses of Testing. Testing is the most applied app-roach for validating software, and has already shown its practical value on many relevant case studies [1,10,20,24,39,41] An important advantage is that testing can be applied independently from the programming language(s) and internal details of the system implementation, by focusing on the (black-box) input-output behaviour of the system. As long as there is an interface that can be used by the test cases, testing works. Furthermore, by only modeling or select-ing tests for the most relevant or important aspects of a system, the time needed for testing can be reduced. A general drawback of testing is that testing is always limited to a finite number of runs of the program with a finite length, and thus exhaustively testing all possible behaviours of the system is usually impossible. Moreover, because testing looks at actual, concrete runs of a system, some situa-tions require the tests to be run multiple times, to uncover previously undetected problems in the code, e.g. when the software runs on different types of hardware, or in threads that can be interleaved in many orders.

Automated Testing. Automated testing [5] is more lightweight than model-based testing and deductive verification, in terms of effort and expertise required. It comprises executing hand-written test cases automatically. The test cases are small programs that execute some system code, e.g. by calling a method/func-tion/procedure, and then checking that the result of this execution, e.g. a part of the system state, is as expected.

Because these test cases can be executed automatically, e.g. by using a testing framework as JUnit, the tests can be run any time, and many times. This allows for testing after any change made to the system, although execution time poten-tially increases with the number of tests, making this infeasible and impractical. Test cases are relatively easy to write. First of all they can check a very specific property of the system which requires only limited knowledge of the system. Second, test cases are usually written in a language developers are familiar with. Furthermore, one can start applying automated testing by just writing the first test case, and expand the set over time.

However, as the set of test cases grows, the maintenance of this set becomes an issue. A lack of overview may lead to (almost) duplicate test cases, or parts of the system without test cases. Code coverage measurements can help to detect this, but improving the set of test cases is still a manual task. Moreover, a change in the system may require a change in many test cases to get all test cases succeeding again. The 'guarantee' automated testing provides is often expressed in the lines of code executed by at least one test case. The lines of code reached by any test case can be measured easily, but no semantic or formal guarantee, e.g. expressed as a specification of behaviour or functionality, is obtained by just executing a set of test cases.

We note that, as a set of test cases selected based on an educated guess and domain knowledge about the system, can find some initial bugs quickly, automated testing is, especially in the initial stages of building a system, a very easy to use, and effective technique.

Model-Based Testing. Model-based testing [11] is a testing technique rooted in formal methods [38], where the specification of the system's behaviour to be tested is given as a formal model. Tests are derived automatically, using a test generation algorithm. The choice of algorithm determines the guarantees that can be provided after executing the set of generated tests. The formal model provides the overview that automated testing often lacks. Model-based testing can be scaled to larger systems by increasing the abstraction level of the model, i.e. by generating tests at the level of the user or component interface, instead of generating unit tests.

In this paper we consider white-box testing on the unit level, for automated testing, and black-box model-based testing on the higher levels. In white-box testing, test generation algorithms may use information from the code, e.g. to generate a test for both branches of an if-statement. For black-box testing we just assume that the system can be tested via some interface. A model then specifies the system by only using this interface.

Guarantees provided by test generation algorithm can consist of structural model coverage guarantees [9,10], or semantic guarantees, e.g. in the form of test purposes [40]. Although these guarantees are based on executions of the system, and hence do not provide a complete guarantee of correctness, they are much stronger than automated testing, by expressing the guarantee on the level of the model instead of the collection of test executions. The main disadvantage of model-based testing is the requirement of the existence of a model: constructing it is usually a larger effort than writing a few test cases, and requires more expertise, because modelling languages are usually formal languages, e.g. finite state machines or labeled transition systems. Lastly, test generation algorithms are usually designed for a specific formal modelling language, as the guarantee they provide is linked to the language. Moreover, the powerful guarantees usually imply more required restrictions, e.g. only control flow but no (unbounded) data. More research is needed to integrate and lift test generation algorithms and their guarantees.

Deductive Verification. In contrast to running tests, program verification (a.k.a. deductive verification) [17] makes a static analysis of the program, based on the code only, and in this analysis it considers all possible behaviours of the program. Thus, any property that is established by program verification holds for all executions of the program, and will remain to hold if the program is deployed on different hardware (provided that any assumptions that are made for the verification are guaranteed by the hardware). Typically, the user writes the desired properties as special annotations of the program code. Typical examples of annotations are pre- and postconditions of single methods, or global invariant properties that hold throughout the execution of a program. Also loop invariants are often written as program annotations. The verifier then uses (variants and extension of) Hoare logic proof rules [18] to verify that a program respects its specification. This makes program verification a powerful analysis technique, which can be used for a large range of different properties.

However, to establish these general properties, often the prover needs to be guided by a large number of auxiliary annotations, i.e., properties that are supposed to hold at a particular point in the program, such as loop invariants, which have to be provided by the user manually. Adding all these auxiliary properties to guide the prover requires substantial expertise in program verification, and can take a large amount of time, which makes it hard to apply this technique on large-scale, industrial applications. As the verification is closely connected to the semantics of the program language that is used to develop the software, any extension of the program language requires also an extension of the verification support. Moreover, to make the provers underlying the verification technique work automatically, we often need to make abstractions over the state space of the program. For example, most deductive verification tools will abstract the computer type `int` into the mathematical type of integers, while the type `float` is abstracted to reals (if supported at all).

Despite these challenges, in recent years, enormous progress has been made to improve program verification tools, making them work for large parts of realistic languages (such as Java [3, 11–13] and C [25]), and even considering complex language features such as concurrency [7]. These state-of-the-art program verifiers have been used on relevant case studies, such as the widely used TIMsort algorithm [34], a parallel nested depth-first search algorithm [31], as used in parallel model checking, and implementations of prefix sum algorithms [35], a basic library function used for many GPU algorithms.

Strengths and Weaknesses of Testing and Verification. Finally, we would like to stress that there are two inherent properties of testing and verification that are hard to adapt and need to be considered when applying the techniques:

- The quality of testing and verification depends on the quality of the requirements that are formalised. Only requirements that are explicitly formulated and specified can be tested and/or verified. We note that if the user of the formal technique does not write the specification, he may still choose a tool or algorithm that provides a generic specification, e.g. no "crash" or no null pointer exceptions, but for stronger guarantees a formal property specification is necessary.
- Testing and verification are *post hoc* techniques, that require a (partial) implementation to do the analysis, as no results can be obtained for a non-existent implementation. Nevertheless, having a specification can help to guide the implementation effort significantly.

3   Our Vision

As discussed above, in order to effectively scale the use of formal analysis techniques, and to make them better applicable and easier to apply, we need to integrate formal techniques. This way techniques can be combined and switched between, depending on the required strengths of the correctness guarantees.

First of all, for this approach to work, it is essential to identify the different parts that make up the system, and to have support to analyse these parts in isolation, as well as to analyse the interaction between the different parts. Ideally, at each of these levels, we have different techniques that we can apply (i.e. support for both testing and verification), such that a user/developer can decide which technique to use.

To decide what technique would be appropriate, different considerations are relevant. During the development phase, it is important that one is able to get quick push-button feedback whether the implementation is "on track", i.e., according to the specification, and testing is often the right approach for this. Once the implementation is finalised, it depends on the nature of the program part whether testing, i.e., analysis of some executions, is sufficient, or whether it should be fully verified. As verification takes more effort, this would typically be the case for crucial data structures, or parts that are highly safety-critical. However, it can also be useful elsewhere, for example if in a later stage, a bug is detected, which did not manifest during testing. Verification will then provide the means to analyse the executions that were not covered by testing.

Below we propose a scheme to apply and integrate testing and deductive verification for analyzing a software system. The scheme is visualized in Fig. 1.

1. A model M describes system level behaviour on the level of user interactions. Model-based test generation algorithms can be used to generate system level test cases.
2. The model M is decomposed into model parts $M_0, M_1, \ldots, M_n$ describing only a part of the system. These model parts can be of any format that helps describing a part of the system in more detail. A model part M_i corresponds to an implementation part I_i.
3. From a model part M_i contracts C_i are generated. These contracts are used to either check the validity of implementation parts with deductive verification, or to generate implementations using a correct-by-construction approach. Both the models M_i and contract C_i can be used to generate tests for sub-parts that are not analyzed with deductive verification or derived by correct-by-construction techniques.

We motivate and explain this scheme as follows:

1. We use testing for the analysis of system level behaviour, since testing allows for abstraction, i.e. the model can describe the system at the level of user interactions instead of at code level. Appropriate test generation algorithms need to be selected from the abstract model, for generating test cases, to run concrete executions in the system.

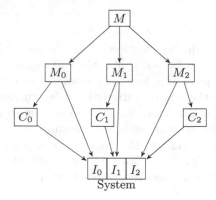

Fig. 1. Scheme for integration of testing and deductive verification

2. To perform more detailed analysis, model M is decomposed into model parts M_i, describing an implementation part at code level. Part-specific details may be added at this stage, but is important to maintain the link with the global model M, such that it remains possible to merge the part-specific analysis results into an overall analysis result. A system is divided into implementation parts, where a part can be of different forms, e.g. a system component, a process, or a function/behaviour of the system. The model parts M_i should match the implementation parts I_i.

3. To allow for flexible use of testing and deductive verification in analyzing implementation parts, both should be used at code level, in a way that they strengthen each other. By generating contracts from the model parts, the effort of using deductive verification is reduced. If generation cannot generate a full contract, the contract may be augmented manually. Moreover, development effort can also be reduced, by using these contracts, and possibly also the model parts, for code generation in a correct-by-construction approach.

In the next section we will describe the challenges that we believe need to be solved in testing, verification, and their combination, in order to implement this scheme.

4 Challenges

To realise the vision outlined above, there are still a number of important research challenges that need to be addressed. This section lists some of these challenges, and divides them into three categories: challenges for integration, challenges for testing, and challenges for deductive verification.

4.1 Challenges for Integration

Challenge 1 (Common Specification Language). As mentioned above, a system developer should be able to seamlessly switch between different formal analysis mechanisms. This requires that all the desired properties are specified in a single specification formalism, which should combine both data and control-flow related properties. It should provide enough abstraction to describe the system-level behaviour to be used for model-based testing, but also should allow to capture precise code-level details. Existing specification languages typically support a single analysis technique; examples of specification languages are automata and process algebras [38] for model-based testing and JML [26,27] and ACSL [6] for contract-based specifications (for deductive verification). An interesting approach in this direction is the ppDATE specification language, which enhances the control-oriented property language of DATE, with data-oriented pre- and postconditions [4].

Challenge 2 (Connected Specifications at Different Abstraction Levels). As our specifications can express both system-wide level properties, as well as properties about the code, we also need to develop techniques that allow to make the transition between these two levels: given a model that describes the abstract system-level behaviour, and a method or function that implements one step in this overall process, we need to define suitable refinement and abstraction techniques that allow to switch between the different levels, while making sure that the various levels are properly connected. In particular, this means that we need to investigate techniques that (i) can generate contracts from model-level specifications, and (ii) can generate system-level model descriptions from individual method contracts, combined with a high-level program that shows the pattern in which the methods are called.

The particular challenge that we need to handle here is that the different levels focus also on different aspects of the behaviour: the system-wide level is more focusing on the control-flow, while the concrete implementation-level focuses also on data-oriented properties.

In this context, we would also like to mention our recent work on Alpinist [36]. Alpinist takes as input an annotated and verified program, and it then applies an optimisation to both to the annotations and the code, such that the resulting optimised program can still be verified and has a better performance. We believe that similar ideas can be used in the context of program refinements: a high-level description is annotated and verified, and then via several refinement steps transformed into efficiently executable code, which can still be verified.

Challenge 3 (Code-level Generation). In addition to having specifications at different levels, we also would like to understand how system-level models can be refined into executable code (with suitable annotations). Program synthesis is an active research area, with a large number of open challenges. We have already explored this idea in a limited setting, where high-level system descriptions are given as choreographies, i.e. sequential programs that describe communications between processes. These sequential programs can then be decomposed into parallel programs [8,23]. The functional correctness that was deductively verified for the sequential program is preserved in the decomposition into parallel programs. The approach has been implemented in the tool VeyMont [8]. The current approach still works in a fairly restricted setting, in particular the processes need to be named explicitly, and their number is hence bounded. In future work we plan to support an unbounded number of processes.

Challenge 4 (Educated Choice of Analysis Technique). As mentioned a-bove, given an implementation part, we can apply both testing and verification. Testing will often be much less work, but only provides guarantees for the executions that have been tested, while verification in principle considers all possible executions, but also requires much extra effort. Therefore, we believe that it is important to develop heuristics that provide an estimate about the expected investment versus the payoff of applying the different techniques. These heuristics could depend for example on how a part of the code is used within the application, on the complexity of the computations that are being done, or on the sensitivity to changes elsewhere in the program.

Challenge 5 (Error Propagation at Different Specification Levels). If we have specifications at different levels that describe different aspects of the code, we also need to have ways to provide error messages at these different specification levels. For example, if there is an error in the implementation, then we should also be able to indicate that this error exists in the system-level model. To support this, this error has to be propagated up and described at the appropriate level, such that the system-level model developer can understand that it is the responsibility of the code developer to fix the issue.

Challenge 6 (Using Testing Results for Verification). We believe that the information that is obtained during the testing phase can be used to extract information about the code, and to *generate auxiliary annotations* with possible intermediate properties, which can help to speed up the analysis process. Of course, this requires also some way to interact with the developer to discard annotations that are wrongly inferred. Notice that such a technique also can help during the testing phase itself: if the system infers unexpected or wrong properties, they could also point to an error in the implementation.

4.2   Challenges for Testing

Challenge 7 (Maintenance of Test Cases and Models). Almost always systems are subject to change. Consequently, the test cases used for automated testing, or the models used for test generation, need to be updated as well. With automated testing, the test set will grow with the system, but the tests need to remain a good indicator for the quality of the system, while time spent on test execution is manageable. A challenge here is to detect and reduce similar test cases to reduce execution time, while adding test cases for new parts of the system to guarantee the quality of these new parts. For model-based testing, the same holds: the model needs to be updated to reflect the changed software, and the challenge is to understand what parts need to be updated, or added; (de)composition of models (see next challenge) may help to keep an overview of the system, as small model parts are easier to understand than one monolithic model. We note that verification annotations also need to be updated when code changes, but as this all happens at the code level, the correspondence is much more obvious and direct.

Challenge 8 (Composition and Decomposition of Models). A monolithic model describing the system as a whole is difficult to construct and hard to maintain. Like in deductive verification, a more modularized approach is helpful, as specifying small parts that can be combined is much easier than reasoning about the system and all its interactions as a whole. Besides such composition methods, decomposition also helps in specifying a model, as a composed model. For example, after composing behavioral features into one model, this model can be decomposed in a different way, e.g. components and processes. Moreover, a model can describe the system behavior on a global, abstract level, and then be decomposed into parts, possibly with gaps that need to be filled in with implementation level details.

Challenge 9 (Test Selection). Selecting the right tests is important to reduce test execution time, while maximizing the discovery of bugs in the system. Tests should be selected based on the risk and impact a bug can have on some part of the system. However, establishing these risks, impacts, and the parts of the system that are at risk, is usually a rather informal educated guess. Moreover, this risk then needs to be translated into a formal selection criterion. In case of automated testing, a categorization of test cases could be used to distinguish the system parts that they analyse. In case of model-based testing, test selection boils down to choosing the right test generation algorithm. Moreover, the available choices in algorithms usually depend on the modelling formalism. In this direction, a more technical challenge is to find better test generation algorithms. They should allow for flexible scaling in the number of test cases, and provide a scaling in the guarantees offered as well. Additionally, better algorithms should be developed for expressive modelling and specification languages that include both control flow and (unbounded) data, as such languages will help with the integration of testing and verification.

4.3   Challenges for Deductive Verification

Challenge 10 (Language Features). In order to make deductive verification usable in an industrial setting, the verifiers need to extend their support for different language features, such as exception support (see [33] for initial ideas in this direction), floating point numbers (currently partially supported by some tools, such as KeY [2], Frama-C [29] and Why3 [15]), strings, input/output, reflection, streams, and logging mechanisms. Part of this is an engineering effort, but to support verification of for example reflection and streams, also new verification techniques need to be developed.

Challenge 11 (Annotation Generation). A major bottleneck for deductive verification is the amount of annotations that needs to be written. We conjecture that for a large part of code, suitable annotations to prove memory safety can be generated automatically, using e.g. techniques for loop invariant generation, but also by developing suitable heuristics that recognise boilerplate code patterns. The literature already contains ample work on loop invariant generation, see e.g. [16, 19, 22, 37], however these papers often focus on automatically inferring loop invariants for loops doing complex numerical calculations, while they ignore many standard code patterns, for example a loop manipulating all single elements in an array (with [16] as a noteworthy exception). Therefore, we believe that the combination with recognising frequently occurring code patterns will be important to actually make progress on this challenge.

Moreover, when reasoning about concurrent software, such as is done by for example VerCors [7], Viper [30] and VeriFast [21], we typically require permission annotations, which allow us to prove data race freedom: permission annotations indicate whether a thread has (shared) read access to a heap location, or (exclusive) write access. Some initial techniques have been developed to infer these permission annotations [14]. However, also here for many programs, permissions are following standard patterns, and can be generated automatically, and we believe that good heuristics can lead to good progress here.

Challenge 12 (Multi-language Software). Moreover, modern software is often composed of modules written in different programming languages, that communicate via a well-defined communication interface. Deductive verification tools typically support single languages, and it is a major effort to add support for a new programming language. We believe that an important step forward will be to develop deductive verifiers with multi-language support, that easily can be extended for new programming languages. One possible approach that we see to achieve this is by developing verification techniques for a core language, and for any newly added language, we only need to define an embedding into this core language. Of course, this raises additional challenges: how to reason about language features that are not easily embedded into the core language, at what level to write the specifications, and how to ensure that verification errors are reported at the right level (ideally, at the level of the source language, rather than at the core)?

Challenge 13 (Generating Unit Tests). There is a close correspondence between code contracts and unit tests: a precondition indicates under which circumstances the test should be executed (the required test set-up), while the postcondition corresponds to the test goal. This idea has been explored for sequential programs in tool such as JMLUnitNG [42], and the test case generator of Whiley [32]. However, it is still an open challenge how to extend this technique to a concurrent setting, where the testing has to consider possible interleaving with other threads. Moreover, if one uses permission-based annotations to capture the access permissions of threads, it would also be interesting to include these permission annotations in the generated test cases, but this requires setting up a runtime framework to keep track of access permissions.

Challenge 14 (Explicit Platform-dependent Assumptions). When we verify a program, we often make implicit assumptions about the underlying computation model, in order to keep the verification tractable. It is an important challenge to be able to make these assumptions explicit, such that we know which parts of the system are verified in a platform-independent manner, and which parts are platform-dependent. If we have this information, then it means that we only have to re-test those parts of the system that are platform-dependent when the system is deployed on a different platform.

5 Conclusion

This position paper motivated the need for integration of formal techniques: their combination will increase their effectiveness, and enable the right level of analysis guarantees required for a sufficient level of trust in the correct functioning of the analyzed system. We proposed a scheme for integrated use of automated testing, model-based testing, and deductive verification to show how this integration can be used concretely. Finally, we identified a number of research challenges that need to be dealt with, in order for this integration to become reality.

References

1. Aarts, F., Kuppens, H., Tretmans, J., Vaandrager, F., Verwer, S.: Learning and testing the bounded retransmission protocol. In: Heinz, J., Higuera, C., Oates, T. (eds.) Proceedings of the Eleventh International Conference on Grammatical Inference, vol. 21. Proceedings of Machine Learning Research. University of Maryland, College Park, pp. 4–18. PMLR (2012). https://proceedings.mlr.press/v21/aarts12a.html
2. Abbasi, R., Schiffl, J., Darulova, E., Ulbrich, M., Ahrendt, W.: Deductive verification of floating-point Java programs in KeY. In: TACAS 2021. LNCS, vol. 12652, pp. 242–261. Springer, Cham (2021). https://doi.org/10.1007/978-3-030-72013-1_13
3. Ahrendt, W., Beckert, B., Bubel, R., Hähnle, R., Schmitt, P.H., Ulbrich, M.: Deductive Software Verification the KeY Book, vol. 10001. Springer, Cham (2016). https://doi.org/10.1007/978-3-319-49812-6
4. Ahrendt, W., Chimento, J.M., Pace, G.J., Schneider, G.: Verifying data- and control-oriented properties combining static and runtime verification: theory and tools. Formal Methods Syst. Des. 51(1), 200–265 (2017). https://doi.org/10.1007/s10703-017-0274-y
5. Ammann, P., Outt, J.: Introduction to Software Testing. Cambridge University Press, Cambridge (2016)
6. Baudin, P., et al.: ACSL: ANSI/ISO C Specification Language, Version 1.14 (2018)
7. Blom, S., Darabi, S., Huisman, M., Oortwijn, W.: The VerCors tool set: verification of parallel and concurrent software. In: Polikarpova, N., Schneider, S. (eds.) IFM 2017. LNCS, vol. 10510, pp. 102–110. Springer, Cham (2017). https://doi.org/10.1007/978-3-319-66845-1_7
8. van den Bos, P., Jongmans, S.: VeyMont: parallelising verified programs instead of verifying parallel programs. Manuscript
9. van den Bos, P., Tretmans, J.: Coverage-based testing with symbolic transition systems. In: Beyer, D., Keller, C. (eds.) TAP 2019. LNCS, vol. 11823, pp. 64–82. Springer, Cham (2019). https://doi.org/10.1007/978-3-030-31157-5_5

10. van den Bos, P., Vaandrager, F.W.: State identification for labeled transition systems with inputs and outputs. Sci. Comput. Program. **209**, 102678 (2021). https://doi.org/10.1016/j.scico.2021.102678. https://www.sciencedirect.com/science/article/pii/S016764232100071X. ISSN 0167-6423

11. Broy, M., Jonsson, B., Katoen, J.-P., Leucker, M., Pretschner, A. (eds.): Model-Based Testing of Reactive Systems. LNCS, vol. 3472. Springer, Heidelberg (2005). https://doi.org/10.1007/b137241

12. Cok, D.R.: OpenJML: software verification for Java 7 using JML, Open-JDK, and Eclipse. In: Dubois, C., Giannakopoulou, D., Méry, D. (eds.) 1st Workshop on Formal Integrated Development Environment (F-IDE). EPTCS, vol. 149, pp. 79–92 (2014). https://doi.org/10.4204/EPTCS.149.8. https://dx.doi.org/10.4204/EPTCS.149.8

13. Cok, D.R.: OpenJML: JML for Java 7 by extending OpenJDK. In: Bobaru, M., Havelund, K., Holzmann, G.J., Joshi, R. (eds.) NFM 2011. LNCS, vol. 6617, pp. 472–479. Springer, Heidelberg (2011). https://doi.org/10.1007/978-3-642-20398-5_35

14. Dohrau, J., Summers, A.J., Urban, C., Münger, S., Müller, P.: Permission inference for array programs. In: Chockler, H., Weissenbacher, G. (eds.) CAV 2018. LNCS, vol. 10982, pp. 55–74. Springer, Cham (2018). https://doi.org/10.1007/978-3-319-96142-2_7

15. Fumex, C., Marché, C., Moy, Y.: Automating the verification of floating-point programs. In: Paskevich, A., Wies, T. (eds.) VSTTE 2017. LNCS, vol. 10712, pp. 102–119. Springer, Cham (2017). https://doi.org/10.1007/978-3-319-72308-2_7

16. Galeotti, J., Furia, C., May, E., Fraser, G., Zeller, A.: Inferring loop invariants by mutation, dynamic analysis, and static checking. IEEE Trans. Softw. Eng. **41**, 1019–1037 (2015)

17. Hähnle, R., Huisman, M.: Deductive software verification: from pen-and-paper proofs to industrial tools. In: Steffen, B., Woeginger, G. (eds.) Computing and Software Science. LNCS, vol. 10000, pp. 345–373. Springer, Cham (2019). https://doi.org/10.1007/978-3-319-91908-9_18

18. Hoare, C.: An axiomatic basis for computer programming. Commun. ACM **12**(10), 576–580 (1969). ISSN 0001-0782

19. Hoder, K., Kovács, L., Voronkov, A.: Invariant generation in vampire. In: Abdulla, P.A., Leino, K.R.M. (eds.) TACAS 2011. LNCS, vol. 6605, pp. 60–64. Springer, Heidelberg (2011). https://doi.org/10.1007/978-3-642-19835-9_7

20. Huertas, T., Quesada-López, C., Martínez, A.: Using model-based testing to reduce test automation technical debt: an industrial experience report. In: Rocha, Á., Ferrás, C., Paredes, M. (eds.) ICITS 2019. AISC, vol. 918, pp. 220–229. Springer, Cham (2019). https://doi.org/10.1007/978-3-030-11890-7_22

21. Jacobs, B., Smans, J., Piessens, F.: Solving the VerifyThis 2012 challenges with VeriFast. Int. J. Softw. Tools Technol. Transfer **17**(6), 659–676 (2014). https://doi.org/10.1007/s10009-014-0310-9

22. Janota, M.: Assertion-based loop invariant generation. In: 1st International Workshop on Invariant Generation (WING) (2007)

23. Jongmans, S.S., van den Bos, P.: A predicate transformer for choreographies. In: Sergey, I. (ed.) ESOP 2022. LNCS, vol. 13240. Springer, Cham (2022). https://doi.org/10.1007/978-3-030-99336-8_19

24. Karlsson, S., Čaušević, A., Sundmark, D., Larsson, M.: Model-based automated testing of mobile applications: an industrial case study. In: 2021 IEEE International Conference on Software Testing, Verification and Validation Workshops (ICSTW), pp. 130–137 (2021). https://doi.org/10.1109/ICSTW52544.2021.00033

25. Kosmatov, N., Marché, C., Moy, Y., Signoles, J.: Static versus dynamic verification in Why3, Frama-C and SPARK 2014. In: Margaria, T., Steffen, B. (eds.) ISoLA 2016. LNCS, vol. 9952, pp. 461–478. Springer, Cham (2016). https://doi.org/10.1007/978-3-319-47166-2_32

26. Leavens, G.T., Baker, A.L., Ruby, C.: Preliminary design of JML: a behavioral interface specification language for Java. ACM SIGSOFT Softw. Eng. Notes 31(3), 1–38 (2006)

27. Leavens, G., et al.: JML reference manual. Department of Computer Science, Iowa State University, February 2007. https://www.jmlspecs.org

28. Lee, D., Yannakakis, M.: Principles and methods of testing finite state machines-a survey. Proc. IEEE 84(8), 1090–1123 (1996). https://doi.org/10.1109/5.533956

29. Mattsen, S., Cuoq, P., Schupp, S.: Driving a sound static software analyzer with branch-and-bound. In: 13th IEEE International Working Conference on Source Code Analysis and Manipulation, SCAM 2013, Eindhoven, Netherlands, 22–23 September 2013, pp. 63–68. IEEE Computer Society (2013). https://doi.org/10.1109/SCAM.2013.6648185

30. Müller, P., Schwerhoff, M., Summers, A.J.: Viper: a verification infrastructure for permission-based reasoning. In: Jobstmann, B., Leino, K.R.M. (eds.) VMCAI 2016. LNCS, vol. 9583, pp. 41–62. Springer, Heidelberg (2016). https://doi.org/10.1007/978-3-662-49122-5_2

31. Oortwijn, W., Huisman, M., Joosten, S.J.C., van de Pol, J.: Automated verification of parallel nested DFS. In: TACAS 2020. LNCS, vol. 12078, pp. 247–265. Springer, Cham (2020). https://doi.org/10.1007/978-3-030-45190-5_14

32. Pearce, D.J., Utting, M., Groves, L.: An introduction to software verification with Whiley. In: Bowen, J.P., Liu, Z., Zhang, Z. (eds.) SETSS 2018. LNCS, vol. 11430, pp. 1–37. Springer, Cham (2019). https://doi.org/10.1007/978-3-030-17601-3_1

33. Rubbens, R., Lathouwers, S., Huisman, M.: Modular transformation of Java exceptions modulo errors. In: Lluch Lafuente, A., Mavridou, A. (eds.) FMICS 2021. LNCS, vol. 12863, pp. 67–84. Springer, Cham (2021). https://doi.org/10.1007/978-3-030-85248-1_5

34. de Gouw, S., Rot, J., de Boer, F.S., Bubel, R., Hähnle, R.: OpenJDK's Java.utils.Collection.sort() is broken: the good, the bad and the worst case. In: Kroening, D., Păsăreanu, C.S. (eds.) CAV 2015. LNCS, vol. 9206, pp. 273–289. Springer, Cham (2015). https://doi.org/10.1007/978-3-319-21690-4_16

35. Safari, M., Oortwijn, W., Joosten, S., Huisman, M.: Formal verification of parallel prefix sum. In: Lee, R., Jha, S., Mavridou, A., Giannakopoulou, D. (eds.) NFM 2020. LNCS, vol. 12229, pp. 170–186. Springer, Cham (2020). https://doi.org/10.1007/978-3-030-55754-6_10

36. şakar, Ö., Safari, M., Huisman, M., Wijs, A.: Alpinist: an annotation-aware GPU program optimizer. In: Fisman, D., Rosu, G. (eds.) TACAS 2022. LNCS, vol. 13244, pp. 332–352. Springer, Cham (2022). https://doi.org/10.1007/978-3-030-99527-0_18

37. Sharma, R., Dillig, I., Dillig, T., Aiken, A.: Simplifying loop invariant generation using splitter predicates. In: Gopalakrishnan, G., Qadeer, S. (eds.) CAV 2011. LNCS, vol. 6806, pp. 703–719. Springer, Heidelberg (2011). https://doi.org/10.1007/978-3-642-22110-1_57

38. Tretmans, J.: Model based testing with labelled transition systems. In: Hierons, R.M., Bowen, J.P., Harman, M. (eds.) Formal Methods and Testing. LNCS, vol. 4949, pp. 1–38. Springer, Heidelberg (2008). https://doi.org/10.1007/978-3-540-78917-8_1

39. Tretmans, J.: On the existence of practical testers. In: Katoen, J.-P., Langerak, R., Rensink, A. (eds.) ModelEd, TestEd, TrustEd. LNCS, vol. 10500, pp. 87–106. Springer, Cham (2017). https://doi.org/10.1007/978-3-319-68270-9_5
40. de Vries, R.G., Tretmans, J.: Towards formal test purposes. Formal Approaches Test. Softw. FATES 1, 61–76 (2001)
41. Zafar, M.N., Afzal, W., Enoiu, E., Stratis, A., Arrieta, A., Sagardui, G.: Model-based testing in practice: an industrial case study using graphwalker. In: 14th Innovations in Software Engineering Conference (Formerly Known as India Software Engineering Conference), ISEC 2021, Bhubaneswar, Odisha, India. Association for Computing Machinery (2021). https://doi.org/10.1145/3452383.3452388. ISBN 9781450390460
42. Zimmerman, D.M., Nagmoti, R.: JMLUnit: the next generation. In: Beckert, B., Marché, C. (eds.) FoVeOOS 2010. LNCS, vol. 6528, pp. 183–197. Springer, Heidelberg (2011). https://doi.org/10.1007/978-3-642-18070-5_13

Discovering Directly-Follows Complete Petri Nets from Event Data

Wil M. P. van der Aalst[✉]

Process and Data Science (PADS), RWTH Aachen University, Aachen, Germany
wvdaalst@pads.rwth-aachen.de
https://www.vdaalst.com

Abstract. Process mining relies on the ability to discover high-quality process models from event data describing only example behavior. Process discovery is challenging because event data only provide positive examples and process models may serve different purposes (performance analysis, compliance checking, predictive analytics, etc.). This paper focuses on the *discovery* of *accepting Petri nets* under the assumption that both the event log and process model are *directly-follows complete*. Based on novel insights, two new variants ($\alpha^{1.1}$ and $\alpha^{2.0}$) of the well-known *Alpha* algorithm ($\alpha^{1.0}$) are proposed. These variants overcome some of the limitations of the classical algorithm (e.g., dealing with short-loops and non-unique start and ending activities) and shed light on the boundaries of the "directly-follows completeness" assumption. These insights can be leveraged to create new process discovery algorithms or improve existing ones.

Keywords: Process Discovery · Process Models · Petri Nets

1 Introduction

Process mining is increasingly adopted by larger organizations to find and remove inefficiencies, bottlenecks, and compliance issues [1]. There are over 40 process mining vendors (cf. www.processmining.org) and more than half of the Fortune-500 corporations are already using process mining [16]. Thousands of organizations are extracting event data from systems such SAP, Salesforce, Oracle, ServiceNow, and Workday to apply process mining. Despite the widespread use of process mining, many challenges remain, ranging from data extraction and scalability to discovering better process models and providing better diagnostics.

Although most process mining tools support the discovery of higher-level models visualized in terms of BPMN (Business Process Model and Notation) (next to conformance checking and predictive analytics), in practice process analysts and managers mostly use the so-called *Directly-Follows Graphs* (DFGs) to get initial insights. In a DFG all activities and their frequencies are shown. The activities are connected through directed edges that show how often one activity is followed by another activity within the same case (i.e., process instance). These edges can also be annotated with durations (minimum, maximum, mean, etc.), because events have timestamps. The creation of DFGs is simple and

N. Jansen et al. (Eds.): Vaandrager Festschrift 2022, LNCS 13560, pp. 539–558, 2022.
https://doi.org/10.1007/978-3-031-15629-8_29

highly scalable. However, there are also many limitations (e.g., producing complex underfitting process models), as discussed in [2].

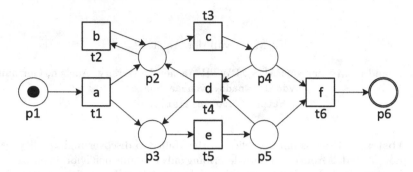

Fig. 1. Accepting Petri net AN_1 discovered for $L_1 = [\langle a,c,e,f\rangle^5, \langle a,e,c,f\rangle^4, \langle a,b,c, e,f\rangle^4, \langle a,b,e,c,f\rangle^3, \langle a,e,b,c,f\rangle^3, \langle a,b,b,c,e,f\rangle^3, \langle a,b,b,e,c,f\rangle^2, \langle a,e,b,b,c,f\rangle^2, \langle a,c, e,d,c,e,f\rangle^2, \langle a,e,c,d,c,e,f\rangle^2, \langle a,c,e,d,b,c,e,f\rangle^2, \langle a,e,c,d,b,b,c,e,f\rangle^2, \langle a,b,c,e,d,c, e,f\rangle, \langle a,b,e,c,d,e,c,f\rangle, \langle a,e,b,c,d,c,e,f\rangle, \langle a,b,c,e,d,e,c,f\rangle, \langle a,b,c,e,d,c,e,d, b,e,b,c,f\rangle, \langle a,c,e,d,c,e,d,e,c,f\rangle]$ using the new Alpha algorithm.

To overcome the limitations of DFGs, dozens (if not hundreds) of process discovery techniques have been developed. The core idea is very simple. The input (i.e., an event log) can be viewed as a *multiset of traces*. Each trace corresponds to a case, i.e., one execution of the process for a patient, order, student, package, etc. A trace is represented as a sequence of activities. Since multiple cases may exhibit the same sequence, we need to consider multisets. $L_1 = [\langle a,c,e,f\rangle^5, \langle a, e,c,f\rangle^4, \ldots]$ in the caption of Fig. 1 describes such an event log, e.g., there are five cases following the sequence $\langle a,c,e,f\rangle$. Note that in this compact representation, we abstract from timestamps, resources, costs, etc. Based on such input, we would like to produce models such as the accepting Petri net AN_1 shown in Fig. 1. AN_1 is able to produce all the traces in L_1. Note that activity e is concurrent to b and c such that c and e occur the same number of times (at least once) and b can occur any number of times.

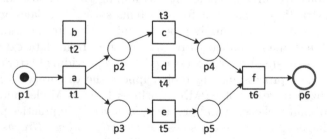

Fig. 2. Accepting Petri net AN_1' discovered for L_1 using the classical Alpha algorithm.

The original *Alpha* algorithm [1,5] was the first algorithm able to discover concurrent process models from event logs. The algorithm assumes that the underlying process can be represented as a free-choice structured workflow net without short loops. For this class of process models, the algorithm guarantees to return the correct process model assuming a directly-follows complete event log [5]. For process models outside this class, the results are unpredictable. The discovered model may be underfitting or not sound. The limitations were already investigated in the original paper. One of the problems is the inability to discover short loops. This is illustrated in Fig. 2, which shows the process model when applying the original, over twenty year old, Alpha algorithm. The self-loop involving b and the length-two loops involving d cause problems. Activities b and d are disconnected and it is impossible to replay parts of the event log L_1. The Alpha algorithm has more problems, some of which can be resolved by using more information [24, 25]. However, these extensions are complex and impose more assumptions.

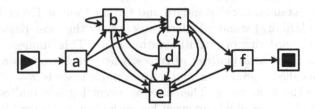

Fig. 3. Directly-Follows Graph (DFG) based on L_1.

In this paper, we take a different route. We simply assume that the Directly-Follows Graph (DFG) is all the information we have. For event log L_1, we assume that the DFG in Fig. 3 is all we have. Moreover, we look beyond the traditional subclasses of Petri nets. We do not assume workflow nets or the free-choice property. Instead, we focus on *structural directly-follows complete* accepting Petri nets. The accepting Petri net AN_1 shown in Fig. 1 is an example of this class of models. Therefore, we consider both directly-follows complete event logs and structural directly-follows complete process models. This provides novel insights and also leads to *two new versions of the Alpha algorithm* that are as compact and simple as the original algorithm, but more powerful.

The remainder of this paper is organized as follows. Section 2 introduces event logs and accepting Petri nets. Section 3 discusses different notions of directly-follows completeness and Sect. 4 lists the typical subclasses of Petri nets considered. Section 5 presents an improved version of the original algorithm that drops the workflow net assumption. Section 6 changes the core part of the algorithm allowing for the discovery of short loops. The paper ends with a discussion (Sect. 7) and conclusion (Sect. 8).

2   Preliminaries

In this section, we introduce basic concepts, but assume that the reader is (somewhat) familiar with the basics of Petri nets and process mining. For completeness, we refer to [1] for process mining and [13, 14] for an extensive introduction to Petri nets.

In process mining, multisets and sequences play an important role. $\mathcal{B}(X) = X \to \mathbb{N}$ is a multiset over X. For example, if $X = \{a, b, c\}$, then $[a^3, b^2, c] \in \mathcal{B}(X)$, $[a^4, b^2] \in \mathcal{B}(X)$, $[a^6] \in \mathcal{B}(X)$ are three multisets each consisting of six elements. X^* is the set of sequences over X, e.g., $\sigma = \langle a, b, a, b, c \rangle \in X^*$. We use the standard operations on multisets and sequences, e.g., $\{x \in \sigma\} = \{a, b, c\}$ and $[x \in \sigma] = [a^2, b^2, c]$.

We start by introducing *event logs*. An event log is a collection of events typically grouped in *cases*, ordered by *time*, and labeled by *activity names*. In its simplest form each event has a case identifier, an activity name, and a timestamp. Events can have many more attributes, e.g., costs, resource, location, etc. There are also more sophisticated event log notions, e.g., partially ordered events, events with explicit uncertainty, and events that may refer to any number of objects of different types, see, for example, the eXtensible Event Stream (XES, www.xes-standard.org) standard and Object Centric Event Log (OCEL, www.ocel-standard.org) standard. Here, we consider the most basic setting and only consider the ordering of activities within cases. This implies that an event log can be described as a *multiset of traces*, where each trace is a *sequence of activities* (also called a *process variant*). An example trace is $\sigma = \langle a, b, a \rangle$. Many cases can have the same trace. Therefore, an event log is a multiset of traces. E.g. $L = [\langle a, b, a \rangle^{12}, \langle b, a, a \rangle^8]$ is an event log with 60 events describing the traces of 20 cases distributed over two process variants.

Definition 1 (Event Log). $\mathcal{U}_{act}$ *is the universe of activity names. A trace* $\sigma = \langle a_1, a_2, \ldots, a_n \rangle \in \mathcal{U}_{act}^*$ *is a sequence of activities. An event log* $L \in \mathcal{B}(\mathcal{U}_{act}^*)$ *is a multiset of traces.*

In the caption of Fig. 1, there is another (larger) example of an event log $L_1 = [\langle a, c, e, f \rangle^5, \langle a, e, c, f \rangle^4, \langle a, b, c, e, f \rangle^4, \langle a, b, e, c, f \rangle^3, \ldots]$, e.g., there are five cases corresponding to trace $\langle a, c, e, f \rangle$, four cases corresponding to $\langle a, e, c, f \rangle$, etc.

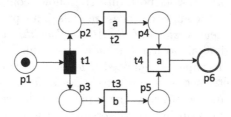

Fig. 4. An accepting Petri net $AN_2 = (N, M_{init}, M_{final})$ with $M_{init} = [p1]$, $M_{final} = [p6]$, and $lang(AN_2) = \{\langle a, b, a \rangle, \langle b, a, a \rangle\}$.

We use *accepting Petri nets* to model processes. Figure 4 shows an example accepting Petri net AN_2 allowing for two traces: $\langle a, b, a \rangle$ and $\langle b, a, a \rangle$. The Petri net has six places $P = \{p1, p2, p3, p4, p5, p6\}$ (represented by circles), four transitions $T = \{t1, t2, t3, t4\}$ (represented by squares), and 10 arcs $F = \{(p1, t1), (t1, p2), \ldots, (t4, p6)\}$. Transitions can be labeled, e.g., $l(t2) = a$ and $l(t3) = b$.

Definition 2 (Labeled Petri Net). *A labeled Petri net is a tuple* $N = (P, T, F, l)$ *with* P *the set of places,* T *the set of transitions,* $P \cap T = \emptyset$, $F \subseteq (P \times T) \cup (T \times P)$ *the flow relation, and* $l \in T \nrightarrow \mathcal{U}_{act}$ *a labeling function.* $\bullet t = \{p \in P \mid (p, t) \in F\}$ *is the set of input places and* $t\bullet = \{p \in P \mid (t, p) \in F\}$ *is the set of output places of a transition* $t \in T$. *The same notation can be used for input and output transitions of a place* $p \in P$: $\bullet p = \{t \in T \mid (t, p) \in F\}$ *and* $p\bullet = \{t \in T \mid (p, t) \in F\}$.

Note that the labeling function may be partial and that multiple transitions may have the same label. For AN_2 in Fig. 4, $t1 \notin dom(l)$ and $l(t2) = l(t4)$. It a transition t has no label, i.e., $t \notin dom(l)$, we also write $l(t) = \tau$ and say the transition is *silent* or *invisible*. In Fig. 4, $\bullet p1 = \emptyset$, $p1\bullet = \{t1\}$, $\bullet t1 = \{p1\}$, $t1\bullet = \{p2, p3\}$, etc. States in Petri nets are called *markings* that mark certain places with *tokens* (represented by black dots). Technically, a marking is a multiset of places $M \in \mathcal{B}(P)$. An *accepting* Petri net has an *initial marking* M_{init} and a *final marking* M_{final}.

Definition 3 (Accepting Petri Net). *An accepting Petri net is a triplet* $AN = (N, M_{init}, M_{final})$ *where* $N = (P, T, F, l)$ *is a labeled Petri net,* $M_{init} \in \mathcal{B}(P)$ *is the initial marking, and* $M_{final} \in \mathcal{B}(P)$ *is the final marking.* $\mathcal{U}_{AN}$ *is the set of accepting Petri nets.*

In AN_2 depicted in Fig. 4, $M_{init} = [p1]$ is the initial marking, and $M_{final} = [p6]$. A transition is called *enabled* if each of the input places has a token. An enabled transition may *fire* (i.e., occur), thereby consuming a token from each input place and producing a token for each output place. For example, firing $t1$ in the initial making leads to marking $[p2, p3]$. There are 6 reachable markings starting from $M_{init} = [p1]$: $[p1]$, $[p2, p3]$, $[p2, p5]$, $[p3, p4]$, $[p4, p5]$, and $[p6]$.

Definition 4 (Reachable Markings and Enabled Firing Sequences). *Let* $AN = (N, M_{init}, M_{final}) \in \mathcal{U}_{AN}$ *be an accepting Petri net with* $N = (P, T, F, l)$. $M_1 \xrightarrow{t} M_2$ *denotes that in* $M_1 \in \mathcal{B}(P)$ *transition* $t \in T$ *is enabled and firing* t *results in marking* $M_2 \in \mathcal{B}(P)$. $M_1 \xrightarrow{\sigma} M_n$ *with* $\sigma = \langle t_1, t_2, \ldots t_{n-1} \rangle \in T^*$ *denotes that there are markings* $M_2, \ldots M_{n-1} \in \mathcal{B}(P)$ *such that* $M_i \xrightarrow{t_i} M_{i+1}$ *for* $1 \leq i < n$, *i.e., there is an enabled firing sequence* σ *leading from* M_1 *to* M_n. $efs(AN) = \{\sigma \in T^* \mid \exists_{M \in \mathcal{B}(P)} M_{init} \xrightarrow{\sigma} M\}$ *is the set of enabled firing sequences.* $rmk(AN) = \{M \in \mathcal{B}(P) \mid \exists_{\sigma \in T^*} M_{init} \xrightarrow{\sigma} M\}$ *is the set of reachable markings.*

Definition 5 (Liveness and Boundedness). *Let* $AN = (N, M_{init}, M_{final}) \in \mathcal{U}_{AN}$ *be an accepting Petri net with* $N = (P, T, F, l)$. AN *is live if for any reachable marking* $M \in rmk(AN)$ *and every transition* $t \in T$, *there exists a marking reachable from* M *enabling* t. AN *is bounded if* $rmk(AN)$ *is finite (i.e., there is a* k *such that no place can have more than* k *tokens).* AN *is safe if for any* $M \in rmk(AN)$ *and* $p \in P$: $M(p) \leq 1$ *(i.e., each place holds at most 1 token in any reachable marking).*

Accepting Petri net AN_1 in Fig. 1 has six reachable markings and is safe, but not live. AN_2 depicted in Fig. 4 also has six reachable markings and is safe, but not live. Adding a short-circuiting transition t_{sc} connecting $p6$ to $p1$ (i.e., $\bullet t_{sc} = \{p6\}$ and $t_{sc}\bullet = \{p1\}$) in Figs. 1 and 4 makes both nets live.

Definition 6 (Complete Firing Sequences). *Let $AN = (N, M_{init}, M_{final}) \in \mathcal{U}_{AN}$ be an accepting Petri net with $N = (P, T, F, l)$. $cfs(AN) = \{\sigma \in T^* \mid M_{init} \xrightarrow{\sigma} M_{final}\}$ is the set of complete firing sequences of AN, i.e., all firing sequences starting in the initial marking M_{init} and ending in the final marking M_{final}.*

For the accepting Petri net AN_2 in Fig. 4, $cfs(AN_2) = \{\langle t1, t2, t3, t4\rangle, \langle t1, t3, t2, t4\rangle\}$. The accepting Petri net AN_1 in Fig. 1, allows for arbitrary long complete firing sequences. Hence, $cfs(AN_1) = \{\langle t1, t3, t5, t6\rangle, \langle t1, t2, t3, t5, t6\rangle, \langle t1, t2, t5, t2, t2, t3, t6\rangle, \ldots\}$ has infinitely many elements.

Firing a transition t corresponds to executing activity $l(t)$ if $t \in dom(l)$. To map complete firing sequences to traces, we apply labeling function l such that visible transitions are mapped onto activities and visible transitions are skipped. For AN_2, i.e., the accepting Petri net in Fig. 4, and the two corresponding complete firing sequences $\sigma_1 = \langle t1, t2, t3, t4\rangle$ and $\sigma_2 = \langle t1, t3, t2, t4\rangle$: $l(\sigma_1) = \langle a, b, a\rangle$ and $l(\sigma_2) = \langle b, a, a\rangle$. Note that firing $t1$ cannot be observed and $t2$ and $t4$ are mapped onto the same activity a.

Definition 7 (Traces of an Accepting Petri Net). *Let $AN = (N, M_{init}, M_{final}) \in \mathcal{U}_{AN}$ be an accepting Petri net. $lang(AN) = \{l(\sigma) \mid \sigma \in cfs(AN)\}$ are the traces possible according to AN.*

For the accepting Petri net AN_2 in Fig. 4, $lang(AN_2) = \{\langle a, b, a\rangle, \langle b, a, a\rangle\}$. The accepting Petri net AN_1 in Fig. 1, allows for infinitely many traces: $lang(AN_1) = \{\langle a, c, e, f\rangle, \langle a, b, c, e, f\rangle, \langle a, b, e, b, b, c, f\rangle, \ldots\}$.

An accepting Petri net is *sound*, if there are no dead transitions and, from any reachable state, it is possible to reach the final state.

Definition 8 (Soundness). *Let $AN = (N, M_{init}, M_{final}) \in \mathcal{U}_{AN}$ be an accepting Petri net with $N = (P, T, F, l)$. AN is sound if and only if (1) for any $t \in T$ there exists a $\sigma \in efs(AN)$ such that $t \in \sigma$ (i.e., t is not dead), and (2) for any $\sigma_1 \in efs(AN)$ there exists a $\sigma_2 \in T^*$ such that $\sigma_1 \cdot \sigma_2 \in cfs(AN)$ (i.e., from any reachable marking, it is possible to reach the final state).*

Discovering a process model from a collection of example traces is one of the main process mining tasks. Ideally, the discovered process model is sound.

Definition 9 (Process Discovery). *A discovery algorithm $disc \in \mathcal{B}(\mathcal{U}_{act}^*) \to \mathcal{U}_{AN}$ produces an accepting Petri net for each event log.*

Many algorithms described in literature implement a discovery function $disc \in \mathcal{B}(\mathcal{U}_{act}^*) \to \mathcal{U}_{AN}$, e.g., [4,5,9–11,17–21,24–27]. Not all are explicitly discovering accepting Petri nets. However, also process trees can be converted into accepting Petri nets and if an explicit final marking is missing it can often be added.

Definition 10 (Conformance Checking). *Let $\mathcal{U}_{diag}$ be the universe of conformance diagnostics. A conformance checking algorithm conf $\in \mathcal{B}(\mathcal{U}_{act}{}^*) \times \mathcal{U}_{AN} \to \mathcal{U}_{diag}$ produces conformance diagnostics given an event log and accepting Petri net as input.*

Conformance checking is a topic in itself [1,3,12,22]. Therefore, we do not detail the type of diagnostics $\mathcal{U}_{diag}$. Most conformance measures are normalized to $[0,1]$ where values close to 0 are bad and values close to 1 are good.

Conformance diagnostics may focus on (1) *recall*, also called (replay) fitness, which aims to quantify the fraction of observed behavior that is allowed by the model, (2) *precision*, which aims to quantify the fraction of behavior allowed by the model that was actually observed (i.e., avoids "underfitting" the event data), (3) *generalization*, which aims to quantify the probability that new unseen cases will fit the model (i.e., avoids "overfitting" the event data), and (4) *simplicity*, which refers to Occam's Razor and can be made operational by quantifying the complexity of the model (number of nodes, number of arcs, understandability, etc.).

Let's try to operationalize recall and precision. Recall is concerned with traces in the event log not possible in the model, i.e., $L_{nofit} = [\sigma \in L \mid \sigma \notin lang(AN)]$. Precision is concerned with traces possible in the model, but not appearing in the event log, i.e., $L_{miss} = \{\sigma \in lang(AN) \mid \sigma \notin L\}$. However, this is not so simple. The event log contains only example behavior (a sample) and any model with loops has infinitely many traces. In such cases L_{miss} has infinitely many elements by definition. If the model aims to describe the mainstream behavior, then L_{nofit} may contain exceptional behavior that was left out deliberately. Moreover, traces may be partly fitting and one often wants to strike a balance between precision (avoiding "underfitting" the sample event data) and generalization (avoiding "overfitting" the sample event data).

These considerations make *process mining different from many other model-learning techniques* such as synthesis, system identification, grammatical inference, regular inference, automata learning [6–8,15,23]. The field of model learning can be structured using three dimensions: (a) only positive examples versus positive and negative examples, (b) input data is complete (in some form) or not, (c) passive learning (just observations) versus active learning (interactions). Process mining focuses on passive learning using only positive examples with only weak completeness guarantees. This makes it very difficult. For example, it is impossible to actively test hypotheses.

A detailed discussion of process discovery and conformance checking techniques (including possible quality criteria) is outside the scope of this paper (see [1,3,12,22] for details).

3 Directly-Follows Completeness

Most process discovery algorithms heavily rely on the *directly-follows relation*, i.e., activities following each other directly, either in the event log or process model. The goal is to find models that have the same directly-follows relation as seen in the event log. The motivation to do this is simple. *One cannot expect to see all possible traces in an event log.* The event log only contains a sample. However, it is reasonable to assume that one can witness the complete directly-follows relation in the event log, i.e., if a can be followed by b we should see it at least once in the input data.

In the section, we define different *directly-follows completeness* notions, also considering the structure of the accepting Petri net.

Consider event log $L_1 = [\langle a, c, e, f \rangle^5, \langle a, e, c, f \rangle^4, \langle a, b, c, e, f \rangle^4, \langle a, b, e, c, f \rangle^3,$ $\langle a, e, b, c, f \rangle^3, \langle a, b, b, c, e, f \rangle^3, \langle a, b, b, e, c, f \rangle^2, \langle a, e, b, b, c, f \rangle^2, \langle a, c, e, d, c, e, f \rangle^2,$ $\langle a, e, c, d, c, e, f \rangle^2, \langle a, c, e, d, b, c, e, f \rangle^2, \langle a, e, c, d, b, b, c, e, f \rangle^2, \langle a, b, c, e, d, c, e, f \rangle,$ $\langle a, b, e, c, d, e, c, f \rangle, \langle a, e, b, c, d, c, e, f \rangle, \langle a, b, c, e, d, e, c, f \rangle, \langle a, b, c, e, d, c, e, d, c, e,$ $d, b, e, b, c, f \rangle, \langle a, c, e, d, c, e, d, e, c, f \rangle]$ and accepting Petri net AN_1 shown in Fig. 1. Assume that L_1 was obtained by repeatedly *simulating* the accepting Petri net AN_1. In this case, we have a *known ground truth*, because we want the discovery algorithm *disc* to discover AN_1 based on L_1, i.e., $disc(L_1) = AN_1$. However, due to the two loops and concurrency, there are many possible traces. The *self-loop* involving b and the *length-two loops* involving d allow for an arbitrary number of b's, c's, d's, and e's in a single trace. Hence, one *cannot* expect to observe all possible traces. In fact, this is impossible. One can try to increase the sample (i.e., the number traces in the event log), but the foundational problem remains: we only have example traces. However, event log L_1 is *directly-follows complete* with respect to model AN_1. This is reflected by the *Directly-Follows Graph* (DFG) in Fig. 3. To explain directly-follows completeness, we first define some core concepts.

Definition 11 (Adding Artificial Start and End Activities). $\blacktriangleright \notin \mathcal{U}_{act}$ is an artificial start activity, $\blacksquare \notin \mathcal{U}_{act}$ is an artificial end activity, $\mathcal{U}_{act}^{\hat{}} = \mathcal{U}_{act} \cup \{\blacktriangleright , \blacksquare\}$. For any $\sigma \in \mathcal{U}_{act}^*$, $\hat{\sigma} = \langle \blacktriangleright \rangle \cdot \sigma \cdot \langle \blacksquare \rangle$. For any $L \in \mathcal{B}(\mathcal{U}_{act}^*)$, $\hat{L} = [\hat{\sigma} \mid \sigma \in L]$. For any $S \subseteq \mathcal{U}_{act}^*$, $\hat{S} = \{\hat{\sigma} \mid \sigma \in S\}$.

The "hat notation" adds artificial starts and ends to traces, languages, and event logs. For $L_2 = [\langle a, b, a \rangle^5, \langle b, a, a \rangle^4]$: $\hat{L}_2 = [\langle \blacktriangleright, a, b, a, \blacksquare \rangle^5, \langle \blacktriangleright, b, a, a, \blacksquare \rangle^4]$.

Definition 12 (Log-Based Directly-Follows Relation). Let $L \in \mathcal{B}(\mathcal{U}_{act}^*)$ be an event log.

- $act(L) = [\sigma(i) \mid \sigma \in L \wedge 1 \le i \le |\sigma|]$ is the multiset of activities in the event log (note that $\sigma(i)$ is the i-th element in the sequence σ).
- $df(L) = [(\sigma(i), \sigma(i+1)) \mid \sigma \in \hat{L} \wedge 1 \le i < |\sigma|]$ is the multiset of directly-follows relations in the event log (note that the artificial start activity $\blacktriangleright$ and end activity $\blacksquare$ have been added to the traces in $\hat{L}$).
- $a_1 \Rightarrow_L a_2$ if and only if $(a_1, a_2) \in df(L)$, $a_1 \not\Rightarrow_L a_2$ if and only if $(a_1, a_2) \notin df(L)$, and $a_1 \Leftrightarrow_L a_2$ if and only if $a_1 \Rightarrow_L a_2$ and $a_2 \Rightarrow_L a_1$.

Take again $L_2 = [\langle a, b, a \rangle^5, \langle b, a, a \rangle^4]$: $act(L_2) = [a^{18}, b^9]$, $df(L_2) = [(\blacktriangleright, a)^5,$ $(\blacktriangleright, b)^4, (a, a)^4, (a, b)^5, (b, a)^9, (a, \blacksquare)^9]$. Hence, we can write $\blacktriangleright \Rightarrow_{L_2} a$, $b \Rightarrow_{L_2} a$, $b \not\Rightarrow_{L_2} b$, $a \Rightarrow_{L_2} \blacksquare$, etc. Similar relations can be obtained for process models as is defined next.

Definition 13 (Behavioral Model-Based Directly-Follows Relation).
Let $AN = (N, M_{init}, M_{final}) \in \mathcal{U}_{AN}$ be an accepting Petri net with $S = lang(AN)$ as possible traces.

- $act^b(AN) = \{\sigma(i) \mid \sigma \in S \land 1 \leq i \leq |\sigma|\}$ is the set of activities possible according to the model's behavior.
- $df^b(AN) = \{(\sigma(i), \sigma(i+1)) \mid \sigma \in \hat{S} \land 1 \leq i < |\sigma|\}$ is the set of directly-follows relations possible according to the model's behavior.
- $a_1 \Rightarrow^b_{AN} a_2$ if and only if $(a_1, a_2) \in df^b(AN)$, $a_1 \not\Rightarrow^b_{AN} a_2$ if and only if $(a_1, a_2) \notin df^b(AN)$, and $a_1 \Leftrightarrow^b_{AN} a_2$ if and only if $a_1 \Rightarrow^b_{AN} a_2$ and $a_2 \Rightarrow^b_{AN} a_1$.

For the accepting Petri net AN_2 in Fig. 4, we find $act^b(AN_2) = \{a, b\}$, $df^b(AN_2) = \{(\blacktriangleright, a), (\blacktriangleright, b), (a, a), (a, b), (b, a), (a, \blacksquare)\}$. Hence, we can write $\blacktriangleright \Rightarrow^b_{AN_2} a$, $b \Rightarrow^b_{AN_2} a$, $b \not\Rightarrow^b_{AN_2} b$, $a \Rightarrow^b_{AN_2} \blacksquare$, etc.

Next, we consider a novel concept that takes the *structure* of the accepting Petri net into account. For this, we only consider sound models where all transitions have a label (no silent transitions). Each place has a set of input and output transitions. These are in a *structural* directly-follows relation. If $t_1 \in \bullet p$ and $t_2 \in p\bullet$, then we expect – based on the structure – that activity $l(t_1)$ can be directly followed by activity $l(t_2)$. If multiple places in the Petri net can be enabled concurrently, the same is expected to hold for the input transitions of one place and the output transitions of another concurrently marked place.

Definition 14 (Structural Model-Based Directly-Follows Relation).
Let $AN = (N, M_{init}, M_{final}) \in \mathcal{U}_{AN}$ be a sound accepting Petri net with $N = (P, T, F, l)$ and $dom(l) = T$.

- $act^s(AN) = \{l(t) \mid t \in T\}$ is the set of activities in the model (consider only structure and not behavior).
- $df^s(AN) = \{(l(t_1), l(t_2)) \mid \exists_{M \in rmk(AN)} \exists_{p_1, p_2 \in M} t_1 \in \bullet p_1 \land t_2 \in p_2\bullet\} \cup \{(\blacktriangleright, l(t)) \mid \exists_{p \in M_{init}} t \in p\bullet\} \cup \{(l(t), \blacksquare) \mid \exists_{p \in M_{final}} t \in \bullet p\}$ is the set of directly-follows relations possible according to the model's structure.
- $a_1 \Rightarrow^s_{AN} a_2$ if and only if $(a_1, a_2) \in df^s(AN)$, $a_1 \not\Rightarrow^s_{AN} a_2$ if and only if $(a_1, a_2) \notin df^s(AN)$, and $a_1 \Leftrightarrow^s_{AN} a_2$ if and only if $a_1 \Rightarrow^s_{AN} a_2$ and $a_2 \Rightarrow^s_{AN} a_1$.

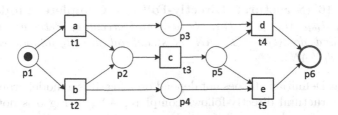

Fig. 5. Accepting Petri net AN_3 that is *not* structural directly-follows complete.

$act^s(AN) = act^b(AN)$ by definition for sound accepting fully labeled Petri nets. However, $df^s(AN)$ and $df^b(AN)$ do not need to be the same. Consider for example accepting Petri net AN_3 in Fig. 5. $df^s(AN_3) = \{(\blacktriangleright, a), (\blacktriangleright, b), (a, c),$ $(a, d), (a, e), (b, c), (b, d), (b, e), (c, d), (c, e), (d, \blacksquare), (e, \blacksquare)\}$, but $df^b(AN_3) = \{(\blacktriangleright$ $, a), (\blacktriangleright, b), (a, c), (b, c), (c, d), (c, e), (d, \blacksquare), (e, \blacksquare)\}$, i.e., the relations corresponding to places $p3$ and $p4$ are missing.

Based on accepting Petri net AN_3 in Fig. 5, we consider two related event logs: $L_3 = [\langle a, c, d\rangle^{10}, \langle b, c, e\rangle^{10}]$ and $L_3' = [\langle a, c, d\rangle^5, \langle a, c, e\rangle^5, \langle b, c, d\rangle^5, \langle b, c, e\rangle^5]$. Event log L_3 could have been generated by simulating AN_3, but L_3' could not (e.g., $\langle a, c, e\rangle$ is not possible). However, both have the same directly-follows relations (shown in Fig. 6). Both event logs are directly-follows complete for AN_3.

Definition 15 (Directly-Follows Complete Log). *Let $L \in \mathcal{B}(\mathcal{U}_{act}{}^*)$ be an event log and $AN = (N, M_{init}, M_{final}) \in \mathcal{U}_{AN}$ be an accepting Petri net. L is directly-follows complete for AN if $df(L) = df^b(AN)$.*

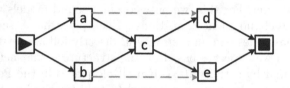

Fig. 6. Directly-follows graph based on the behavior of the accepting Petri net in Fig. 5. Note that the long-term dependencies between a and d, and b and e are missing because these activities never directly follow one another.

Note that $df(L_3) = df(L_3') = df^b(AN_3) = \{(\blacktriangleright, a), (\blacktriangleright, b), (a, c), (b, c), (c, d),$ $(c, e), (d, \blacksquare), (e, \blacksquare)\}$. Hence, both event logs are directly-follows complete with respect to AN_3.

Obviously, models like AN_3 are difficult to discover. Region-based techniques are able to find the places $p3$ and $p4$, but are unusable for real-life data sets because they produce complex overfitting process models and are not scalable. Therefore, we are interested in the class of *structural directly-follows complete* accepting Petri nets.

Definition 16 (Structural Directly-Follows Complete Model). *Let $AN = (N, M_{init}, M_{final}) \in \mathcal{U}_{AN}$ be a sound accepting Petri net with $N = (P, T, F, l)$ and $dom(l) = T$. AN is structural directly-follows complete if $df^s(AN) = df^b(AN)$.*

Note that Definition 16 does not depend on a log. It is a model property. AN_1 in Fig. 1 is structural directly-follows complete, AN_3 in Fig. 5 is not. Figure 7 shows that the free-choice property and structural directly-follows completeness are independent.

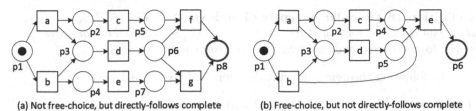

(a) Not free-choice, but directly-follows complete   (b) Free-choice, but not directly-follows complete

Fig. 7. Two accepting Petri net: (a) AN_4 is *not* free-choice, but structural directly-follows complete (e.g., d can be directly followed by both f and g) and (b) AN_5 is free-choice, but *not* structural directly-follows complete (despite $p4$, activity b is never directly followed by e).

4 Subclasses of Accepting Petri Nets Relevant for Process Mining

Properties such as soundness, liveness, and boundedness are behavioral properties. Structural directly-follows completeness is both structural and behavioral. In this section, we list properties relevant for process mining that are structural.

Definition 17 (Structural Properties). *Let* $N = (P, T, F, l)$ *be Petri net.*

- *N is a state machine if for all $t \in T$: $|\bullet t| \leq 1$ and $|t\bullet| \leq 1$.*
- *N is a marked graph if for all $p \in P$: $|\bullet p| \leq 1$ and $|p\bullet| \leq 1$.*
- *N is free-choice if for all $t_1, t_2 \in T$ with $\bullet t_1 \cap \bullet t_2 \neq \emptyset$: $\bullet t_1 = \bullet t_2$.*
- *N is uniwired if for all $t_1, t_2 \in T$: $|t_1 \bullet \cap \bullet t_2| \leq 1$.*
- *N is join-free if for all $p \in P$ and $t \in p\bullet$: $|\bullet p| \leq 1$ or $|\bullet t| \leq 1$.*
- *N is free of self-loops if for all $t \in T$: $\bullet t \cap t\bullet \neq \emptyset$.*
- *N is free of length-two loops if for all $t_1, t_2 \in T$: $t_1\bullet \cap \bullet t_2 = \emptyset$ or $t_2\bullet \cap \bullet t_1 = \emptyset$.*
- *N is free of PT handles if for all $p \in P$ and $t \in T$ there are no two elementary paths from p to t sharing only p and t.*
- *N is free of TP handles if for all $p \in P$ and $t \in T$ there are no two elementary paths from t to p sharing only p and t.*
- *N is a workflow net if there is one source place $p_{\blacktriangleright} \in P$ and one sink place $p_{\blacksquare} \in P$ such that $\bullet p_{\blacktriangleright} = p_{\blacksquare}\bullet = \emptyset$ and all nodes are on a path from $p_{\blacktriangleright}$ to $p_{\blacksquare}$.*

Note that these properties consider only the net structure (i.e., the initial marking and behavior are not considered). Free-choice nets separate choice and synchronization and most process discovery algorithms aim to produce free-choice nets (note that process trees and basic BPMN models with XOR and AND gateways correspond to free-choice nets). Block-structured process models (e.g., process trees) are also free of PT and TP handles. The basic Alpha algorithm has difficulties dealing with self-loops, length-two loops, and non-free-choice constructs. Workflow nets have places explicitly indicating the start and the end of the process.

In the remainder, we focus on *regular accepting Petri nets* as our target model. Such nets have desirable properties such as safeness, soundness, and have no silent or duplicate activities.

Definition 18 (Regular Accepting Petri Nets). $AN = (N, M_{init}, M_{final}) \in \mathcal{U}_{AN}$ *is a regular accepting Petri net if AN is safe, sound, and l is bijective (i.e., a one-to-one correspondence between transitions and activities).*

The following theorem is a generalization of Theorem 4.1 in [5].

Theorem 1. *Let $AN = (N, M_{init}, M_{final}) \in \mathcal{U}_{AN}$ be a regular accepting Petri net. For any two transitions $t_1, t_2 \in T$ such that $t_1 \bullet \cap \bullet t_2 = \emptyset$: if $l(t_1) \Rightarrow_{AN}^b l(t_2)$, then $l(t_2) \Rightarrow_{AN}^b l(t_1)$.*

Proof. For simplicity, we assume that l is the identity function (this can be achieved by renaming transitions using bijection l). Let $a, b \in T$, $a \bullet \cap \bullet b = \emptyset$, and $a \Rightarrow_{AN}^b b$. We need to prove that $b \Rightarrow_{AN}^b a$. If $a = b$, this holds trivially. Hence, we assume $a \neq b$. Because $a \Rightarrow_{AN}^b b$, there is a trace $\sigma_1 \cdot \langle a, b \rangle \cdot \sigma_2 \in lang(AN)$. Because $a \bullet \cap \bullet b = \emptyset$, $\sigma_1 \cdot \langle b \rangle$ is enabled. If $\sigma_1 \cdot \langle b, a \rangle$ is not enabled, then b removes a token from an input place of a without returning it (remember that AN is safe). However, if a consumes the token first, then b can no longer fire (leading to a contradiction), i.e., $\sigma_1 \cdot \langle b, a \rangle$ is enabled. Therefore, $\sigma_1 \cdot \langle b, a \rangle \cdot \sigma_2 \in lang(AN)$ and $b \Rightarrow_{AN}^b a$.   □

5   The $\alpha^{1.0}$ and $\alpha^{1.1}$ Algorithms

The original Alpha algorithm was developed over two decades ago [5]. We refer to the original algorithm as $\alpha^{1.0}$. It was described in publications such as [1,5] and during the development of $\alpha^{1.0}$ it was already proven that any Structured Workflow Net (SWN) without self-loops can be "rediscovered", i.e., a directly-follows complete event log obtained by simulating SWN contains enough information for the algorithm to discover the SWN again (modulo renaming of places). An SWN is free-choice, join-free, has a source and sink place, and no implicit places (cf. Definition 17). As pointed out in [1,5], $\alpha^{1.0}$ has many known limitations. The algorithm assumes that the event log is directly-follows complete and that all behavior observed should be captured in the model (i.e., no noise and infrequent behavior). Moreover, it has problems dealing with short loops and processes that cannot be expressed as a workflow net.

Over the last two decades, there have been many proposals to "repair" $\alpha^{1.0}$ e.g., [24, 25]. However, these alternative approaches assume information that goes beyond the directly-follows relation and most of them are much more complicated (with many case distinctions). In this paper, we propose two variants of $\alpha^{1.0}$: $\alpha^{1.1}$ and $\alpha^{2.0}$. These are as simple as the original algorithm, but allow for the discovery of a larger class of process models. In this section, we introduce $\alpha^{1.1}$ which is close to $\alpha^{1.0}$ and only changes the initial and final parts of the process model to allow for non-workflow nets.

Definition 19 ($\alpha^{1.1}$ Algorithm). *The $\alpha^{1.1}$ algorithm implements a function $disc_{\alpha^{1.1}} \in \mathcal{B}(\mathcal{U}_{act}{}^*) \to \mathcal{U}_{AN}$ that returns an accepting Petri net $disc_{\alpha^{1.1}}(L)$ for any event log $L \in \mathcal{B}(\mathcal{U}_{act}{}^*)$. Let $A = act(L)$ and $\hat{A} = A \cup \{\blacktriangleright, \blacksquare\}$.*

1. $Cnd(L) = \{(A_1, A_2) \mid A_1 \subseteq \hat{A} \wedge A_1 \neq \emptyset \wedge A_2 \subseteq \hat{A} \wedge A_2 \neq \emptyset \wedge$
   $(\forall_{a_1 \in A_1} \forall_{a_2 \in A_2}\ a_1 \Rightarrow_L a_2 \wedge a_2 \not\Rightarrow_L a_1) \wedge (\forall_{a_1, a_2 \in A_1}\ a_1 \not\Rightarrow_L a_2) \wedge (\forall_{a_1, a_2 \in A_2}$
   $a_1 \not\Rightarrow_L a_2)\}$ are the candidate places,
2. $Sel(L) = \{(A_1, A_2) \in Cnd(L) \mid \forall_{(A_1', A_2') \in Cnd(L)}\ A_1 \subseteq A_1' \wedge A_2 \subseteq A_2' \implies$
   $(A_1, A_2) = (A_1', A_2')\}$ are the selected maximal places,
3. $P = \{p_{(A_1, A_2)} \mid (A_1, A_2) \in Sel(L)\}$ is the set of all places,
4. $T = \{t_a \mid a \in A\}$ is the set of transitions,
5. $F = \{(t_a, p_{(A_1, A_2)}) \mid (A_1, A_2) \in Sel(L) \wedge\ a \in A_1 \cap A\} \cup \{(p_{(A_1, A_2)}, t_a) \mid$
   $(A_1, A_2) \in Sel(L) \wedge\ a \in A_2 \cap A\}$ is the set of arcs,
6. $l = \{(t_a, a) \mid a \in A\}$ is the labeling function,
7. $M_{init} = [p_{(A_1, A_2)} \in P \mid \blacktriangleright \in A_1]$ is the initial marking, $M_{final} = [p_{(A_1, A_2)} \in P \mid$
   $\blacksquare \in A_2]$ is the final marking, and
8. $disc_{\alpha^{1.1}}(L) = ((P, T, F, l), M_{init}, M_{final})$ is the discovered accepting Petri net.

The first two steps are most important. Set $Sel(L)$ defines the set of places in terms of preceding and succeeding activities. Steps 3–8 are mostly bookkeeping, i.e., all the elements in $Sel(L)$ are mapped onto places with the corresponding connections. $\blacktriangleright$ and $\blacksquare$ are placeholders for the start and end of the process and are not mapped onto transitions, but define the initial and final marking.

Figure 8 shows a simple example highlighting the difference between $\alpha^{1.0}$ and $\alpha^{1.1}$. For the event log $L = [\langle a, b \rangle^{10}, \langle b, a \rangle^{10}]$, the $\alpha^{1.1}$ algorithm specified in Definition 19 generates the correct regular accepting Petri net shown in Fig. 8(a). $\alpha^{1.0}$ tries to create a workflow net with only one initially marked place (cf. Fig. 8(b)). The model in Fig. 8(b) is unable to replay any of the traces in the event log, whereas the model in Fig. 8(a) is able to replay all and does not allow for unseen behavior. The original algorithm does not allow for concurrent initial and final activities and also does not allow for initial and final activities occurring at different positions. For $L = [\langle a, b \rangle^{10}, \langle b, a \rangle^{10}]$: $\blacktriangleright \Rightarrow_L a$, $\blacktriangleright \Rightarrow_L b$, $a \Rightarrow_L b$, $b \Rightarrow_L a$, $a \Rightarrow_L \blacksquare$, and $b \Rightarrow_L \blacksquare$. Hence, $Cnd(L) = Sel(L) = \{(\{\blacktriangleright\}, \{a\}), (\{\blacktriangleright\}, \{b\}), (\{a\}, \{\blacksquare\}), (\{b\}, \{\blacksquare\})\}$. Note that $p1$ corresponds to $(\{\blacktriangleright\}, \{a\})$, etc.

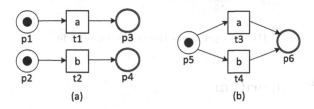

(a)   (b)

Fig. 8. Improvement over the original algorithm: (a) shows the correct model AN_6 obtained by $\alpha^{1.1}$ and (b) shows the incorrect model AN_6' obtained by $\alpha^{1.0}$ for the event log $L = [\langle a, b \rangle^{10}, \langle b, a \rangle^{10}]$.

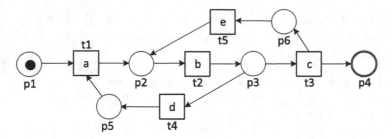

Fig. 9. $\alpha^{1.0}$ produces an incorrect model for $L_4 = [\langle a,b,c\rangle^{10}, \langle a,b,d,a,b,c\rangle^5,$ $\langle a,b,c,e,b,c\rangle^5, \langle a,b,d,a,b,c,e,b,c\rangle^2, \langle a,b,c,e,b,d,a,b,c\rangle^2]$. Note that none of the traces can be replayed.

Another event log where $\alpha^{1.0}$ fails and $\alpha^{1.1}$ produces the desired model is $L_4 = [\langle a,b,c\rangle^{10}, \langle a,b,d,a,b,c\rangle^5, \langle a,b,c,e,b,c\rangle^5, \langle a,b,d,a,b,c,e,b,c\rangle^2,$ $\langle a,b,c,e,b,d,a,b,c\rangle^2]$ for which $\blacktriangleright \Rightarrow_L a$, $a \Rightarrow_L b$, $b \Rightarrow_L c$, $b \Rightarrow_L d$, $c \Rightarrow_L e$, $c \Rightarrow_L \blacksquare$, $d \Rightarrow_L a$, and $e \Rightarrow_L b$. $Sel(L) = \{(\{\blacktriangleright,d\},\{a\}),(\{a,e\},\{b\}),(\{b\},\{c,d\}),(\{c\},\{e,\blacksquare\})\}$ describes the four places, e.g., $p_{(\{\blacktriangleright,d\},\{a\})}$ is initially marked, $\bullet p_{(\{\blacktriangleright,d\},\{a\})} = \{d\}$, and $p_{(\{\blacktriangleright,d\},\{a\})}\bullet = \{a\}$. Figure 9 shows the incorrect model produced by the $\alpha^{1.0}$ algorithm. Figure 10 shows the correct model produced by the $\alpha^{1.1}$ (and later $\alpha^{2.0}$) algorithm. Note that the latter model is able to replay all traces.

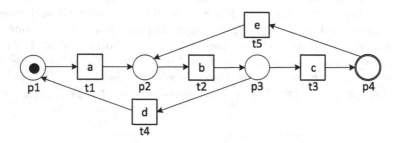

Fig. 10. $\alpha^{1.1}$ produces the desired model for L_4.

6   The $\alpha^{2.0}$ Algorithm

The $\alpha^{1.1}$ algorithm overcomes some of the limitations of the original $\alpha^{1.0}$ algorithm, but for "internal places" the characteristics are essentially the same and short-loops are still a problem. For $L_1 = [\langle a,c,e,f\rangle^5, \ldots]$ in Fig. 1, still the incorrect accepting Petri net AN'_1 (Fig. 2) is discovered due to the self-loop involving b and the length-two loop involving c and d. The requirements used in $Cnd(L)$ (Definition 19) are always violated for short loops. For any $(A_1, A_2) \in Cnd(L)$: if $a \Rightarrow_L a$, then a cannot be part of A_1 and a cannot be part of A_2. For any loop of length 2 involving a and b, we have $a \Rightarrow_L b$ and $b \Rightarrow_L a$ and the condition $\forall_{a_1 \in A_1} \forall_{a_2 \in A_2}\ a_1 \Rightarrow_L a_2\ \wedge\ a_2 \not\Rightarrow_L a_1$ used in the computation of $Cnd(L)$ is violated for places connecting a and b.

For L_1, we have $b \Rightarrow_{L_1} b$ due to the self-loop involving b, and $c \Rightarrow_{L_1} d$ and $d \Rightarrow_{L_1} c$ due to the length-two loop involving c and d. Therefore, there cannot be a place connecting b to itself or a place connecting c to d or d to c. This can be solved by changing only the first step of the $\alpha^{1.1}$ algorithm specified in Definition 19.

Definition 20 ($\alpha^{2.0}$ Algorithm). *The $\alpha^{2.0}$ algorithm implements a function $disc_{\alpha^{2.0}} \in \mathcal{B}(\mathcal{U}_{act}{}^*) \to \mathcal{U}_{AN}$ that only differs from $disc_{\alpha^{1.1}}$ in the first step (computation of $Cnd(L)$). The rest is the same as in Definition 19.*

$$Cnd^{2.0}(L) = \{(A_1, A_2) \mid A_1 \subseteq \hat{A}\ \wedge\ A_2 \subseteq \hat{A}\ \wedge \tag{1}$$

$$(\forall_{a_1 \in A_1} \forall_{a_2 \in A_2}\ a_1 \Rightarrow_L a_2)\ \wedge \tag{2}$$

$$(\exists_{a_1 \in A_1 \setminus A_2} \exists_{a_2 \in A_2 \setminus A_1}\ a_2 \not\Rightarrow_L a_1)\ \wedge \tag{3}$$

$$(\forall_{a_1 \in A_1}\ \forall_{a_2 \in A_1 \setminus A_2}\ a_1 \not\Rightarrow_L a_2)\ \wedge \tag{4}$$

$$(\forall_{a_1 \in A_2 \setminus A_1}\ \forall_{a_2 \in A_2}\ a_1 \not\Rightarrow_L a_2)\} \tag{5}$$

Candidate places are again represented by pairs of sets of activities. $(A_1, A_2) \in Cnd^{2.0}(L)$ should still be such that elements of A_1 are in a directly-follows relation with elements of A_2. However, it is no longer required that the reverse never holds, i.e., we no longer demand that $\forall_{a_1 \in A_1} \forall_{a_2 \in A_2}\ a_2 \not\Rightarrow_L a_1$. Instead, we assume the weaker requirement that $\exists_{a_1 \in A_1 \setminus A_2} \exists_{a_2 \in A_2 \setminus A_1}\ a_2 \not\Rightarrow_L a_1$. This implies that $A_1 \neq \emptyset$ and $A_2 \neq \emptyset$. Note that $a_1 \in A_1 \setminus A_2$ and $a_2 \in A_2 \setminus A_1$ such that $a_2 \not\Rightarrow_L a_1$ ensures that there is an activity a_1 producing a token for the place without removing it and an activity a_2 consuming a token from the place without putting it back.

Consider the event log $L = [\langle a, b, d \rangle^{10}, \langle a, b, c, b, d \rangle^3, \langle a, b, c, b, c, b, d \rangle^2, \langle a, b, c, b, c, b, c, b, d \rangle]$. The $\alpha^{2.0}$ algorithm discovers the loop of length two and returns the correct Petri net. The model returned by $\alpha^{1.0}$ and $\alpha^{1.1}$ only allows for trace $\langle a, b, d \rangle$ and leaves c disconnected from the rest.

The $\alpha^{2.0}$ algorithm is also able to discover the regular accepting Petri net AN_1 shown in Fig. 1. Note that $\alpha^{2.0}$ inherits all the improvements of the $\alpha^{1.1}$ algorithm. Actually, the algorithm is able to discover all structural directly-follows complete models in this paper. Describing the exact conditions under which the $\alpha^{2.0}$ algorithm is able to rediscover the correct model based on a directly-follows complete event log is outside the scope of the paper. However, the examples clearly show that the class of correctly discovered process models is extended significantly.

The $\alpha^{1.1}$ and $\alpha^{2.0}$ algorithms have been implemented in ProM by Aaron Küsters. (The reader can download the ProM Nightly Build from www.promtools.org.) Experiments show that for most event logs more places can be discovered compared to the original algorithm, i.e., there are fewer transitions without any connecting places. Since there is no guarantee that all places are fitting for arbitrary processes, a check has been added to remove places that cannot replay a predefined percentage of cases.

7   Discussion

The $\alpha^{2.0}$ algorithm is able to rediscover accepting Petri nets such as AN_1 in Fig. 1, AN_4 in Fig. 7(a), AN_6 in Fig. 8(a) based on a directly-follows complete event log. The $\alpha^{2.0}$ algorithm is of course *unable to discover models from event logs that are not directly-follows complete*. It fully depends on $\Rightarrow_L$, but this is a reasonable assumption. What has not been observed cannot be discovered! The $\alpha^{2.0}$ algorithm is also *unable to discover models that are not structural directly-follows complete*. The notion of structural directly-follows complete was introduced in this paper. Accepting Petri net AN_3 in Fig. 5 is not structural directly-follows complete because $a \not\Rightarrow_L d$ and $b \not\Rightarrow_L e$ although there are places ($p3$ and $p4$) connecting these activities. Accepting Petri net AN_5 in Fig. 7(b) is not structural directly-follows complete, because $b \not\Rightarrow_L e$ while there is a place ($p4$) connecting b to e.

Such problems are unavoidable when assuming directly-follows completeness. Therefore, directly-follows-based algorithms like the $\alpha^{2.0}$ algorithm need to be supported by pre- and post-processing techniques. Here, we discuss some examples.

An obvious *preprocessing* step is the filtering of activities and variants as described in [2]. The approach is to first remove infrequent or chaotic activities and then order the remaining variants by frequency (selecting the most frequent ones). Note that most event logs follow a Pareto distribution, i.e., most of the behavior is explained by a limited number of activities and variants.

An obvious *postprocessing* step is to remove places that do not fit. One can use the $\alpha^{2.0}$ algorithm and then check every place individually. This can be done very efficiently. For a place p, one can first look at the sum of the absolute frequencies of the activities represented by $\bullet p$ and compare this with the sum of the absolute frequencies of the activities represented by $p\bullet$. If there is a substantial mismatch, the place can be discarded or repaired. It is also possible to project the event log onto activities $\bullet p \cup p\bullet$ and perform token-based replay or alignments. This can be done very efficiently for a single place. It is possible to set a threshold to retain only the places that fit a minimum percentage of traces. In general, process mining tools should avoid producing models that have known problems.

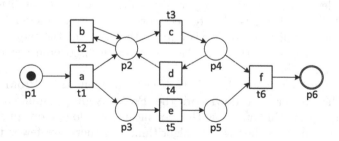

Fig. 11. Accepting Petri net AN_1' having the same directly-follows relations as AN_1, i.e., $df^b(AN_1) = df^b(AN_1')$.

It is also possible to improve discovery by exploiting the fact that we are interested in *safe* accepting Petri nets, i.e., there should not be two tokens in the same place for a particular case. This can be exploited to rule out certain constructs and speed-up the implementation of the algorithm and postprocessing.

It is important to note that there are processes that are behaviorally different, but have the same directly-follows relation. Figure 11 shows an accepting Petri net AN_1' such that $df^b(AN_1) = df^b(AN_1')$, i.e., the corresponding DFGs are identical (the DFG shown in Fig. 3) although the behaviors are different. This shows the weakness of any algorithm relying on directly-follows relations only.

Figure 12(a) maps the arcs of the DFG shown in Fig. 3 (based on event log L_1) onto the places of accepting Petri net AN_1 in Fig. 1. Figure 12(b) maps the same arcs onto the places of accepting Petri net AN_1' in Fig. 11. Note the difference in the connections between d and e. Figure 12 nicely illustrates that bidirectional arcs either correspond to concurrency or loops of length two. Often it is clear whether bidirectional arcs correspond to concurrency or loops of length two. However, this cannot always be decided based on just the DFG as the example shows.

Another possible refinement is to consider more elements of $Cnd^{2.0}(L)$. We now consider only the maximal elements when applying $Sel(L)$ to the candidates generated in the first step. However, if we can quickly check places on projected event logs, it is possible to select the "largest one" of good quality. Instead of replaying, we can first check the total number of produced and consumed tokens for a place. Given $(A_1, A_2) \in Cnd^{2.0}(L)$, we can compare $\sum_{\sigma \in L} \sum_{a \in A_1} |[a \in \sigma]|$ (tokens produced for the candidate place) and $\sum_{\sigma \in L} \sum_{a \in A_2} |[a \in \sigma]|$ (tokens consumed from the candidate place). If these values are very different, we can discard candidate (A_1, A_2). Instead, we pick the maximal candidate not having obvious quality problems.

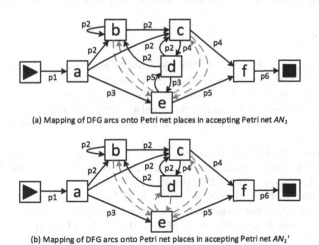

(a) Mapping of DFG arcs onto Petri net places in accepting Petri net AN_1

(b) Mapping of DFG arcs onto Petri net places in accepting Petri net AN_1'

Fig. 12. Mapping the Directly-Follows Graph (DFG) based on L_1 onto the places of AN_1 and AN_1'.

Finally, there is the observation that regular accepting Petri nets (cf. Definition 18) *cannot* produce arbitrary directly-follows relations $\Rightarrow^b_{AN}$. There is no regular accepting Petri net AN with $df^b(AN) = \{(\blacktriangleright, a), (a, b), (a, c), (b, c), (c, \blacksquare)\}$. This knowledge can be used to replace problematic edges in the directly-follows relation by silent activities before applying the $\alpha^{2.0}$ algorithm. In this example, one should replace (a, c) by (a, τ) and (τ, c) and then the $\alpha^{2.0}$ algorithm produces the desired result.

8   Conclusion

Discovering accepting Petri nets from example data in such a way that the resulting model is not overfitting or underfitting is extremely challenging. One cannot assume that all possible behaviors are in the sample log. Therefore, one needs to resort to assumptions like directly-follows completeness. The original Alpha algorithm ($\alpha^{1.0}$) was based on this assumption. In this paper, we tried to push the boundaries of what can be discovered using this assumption and also introduced the new concept of *structural* directly-follows completeness. The insights obtained led to two new variants of the original $\alpha^{1.0}$ algorithm: $\alpha^{1.1}$ and $\alpha^{2.0}$. The $\alpha^{2.0}$ can correctly discover short-loops and non-workflow-net structures. Combining these with the usual pre- and post-processing steps (i.e., filtering and local checks) results in a discovery algorithm that is practically usable. Future work aims at extensive experimentation of the presented approach and detecting/repairing structures in directly-follows relations that cannot stem from a process corresponding to regular accepting Petri net.

Acknowledgment. Funded by the Alexander von Humboldt (AvH) Stiftung and the Deutsche Forschungsgemeinschaft (DFG, German Research Foundation) under Germany's Excellence Strategy – EXC 2023 Internet of Production – 390621612.

References

1. van der Aalst, W.M.P.: Process Mining: Data Science in Action. Springer-Verlag, Berlin (2016). https://doi.org/10.1007/978-3-662-49851-4_1
2. van der Aalst, W.M.P.: A practitioner's guide to process mining: limitations of the directly-follows graph. In: International Conference on Enterprise Information Systems (Centeris 2019), volume 164 of Procedia Computer Science, pp. 321–328. Elsevier (2019)
3. van der Aalst, W.M.P., Adriansyah, A., van Dongen, B.: Replaying history on process models for conformance checking and performance analysis. WIREs Data Min. Knowl. Discovery **2**(2), 182–192 (2012)
4. van der Aalst, W.M.P., Rubin, V., Verbeek, H.M.W., van Dongen, B.F., Kindler, E., Günther, C.W.: Process mining: a two-step approach to balance between underfitting and overfitting. Softw. Syst. Model. **9**(1), 87–111 (2010). https://doi.org/10.1007/s10270-008-0106-z
5. van der Aalst, W.M.P., Weijters, A.J.M.M., Maruster, L.: Workflow mining: discovering process models from event logs. IEEE Trans. Knowl. Data Eng. **16**(9), 1128–1142 (2004)

6. Aarts, F., Heidarian, F., Kuppens, H., Olsen, P., Vaandrager, F.: Automata learning through counterexample guided abstraction refinement. In: Giannakopoulou, D., Méry, D. (eds.) FM 2012. LNCS, vol. 7436, pp. 10–27. Springer, Heidelberg (2012). https://doi.org/10.1007/978-3-642-32759-9_4

7. Aarts, F., Heidarian, F., Vaandrager, F.: A theory of history dependent abstractions for learning interface automata. In: Koutny, M., Ulidowski, I. (eds.) CONCUR 2012. LNCS, vol. 7454, pp. 240–255. Springer, Heidelberg (2012). https://doi.org/10.1007/978-3-642-32940-1_18

8. Angluin, D., Smith, C.H.: Inductive inference: theory and methods. Comput. Surv. **15**(3), 237–269 (1983)

9. Augusto, A., Conforti, R., Marlon, M., La Rosa, M., Polyvyanyy, A.: Split miner: automated discovery of accurate and simple business process models from event logs. Knowl. Inf. Syst. **59**(2), 251–284 (2019). https://doi.org/10.1007/s10115-018-1214-x

10. Bergenthum, R., Desel, J., Lorenz, R., Mauser, S.: Process mining based on regions of languages. In: Alonso, G., Dadam, P., Rosemann, M. (eds.) BPM 2007. LNCS, vol. 4714, pp. 375–383. Springer, Heidelberg (2007). https://doi.org/10.1007/978-3-540-75183-0_27

11. Carmona, J., Cortadella, J., Kishinevsky, M.: A region-based algorithm for discovering Petri nets from event logs. In: Dumas, M., Reichert, M., Shan, M.-C. (eds.) BPM 2008. LNCS, vol. 5240, pp. 358–373. Springer, Heidelberg (2008). https://doi.org/10.1007/978-3-540-85758-7_26

12. Carmona, J., van Dongen, B., Solti, A., Weidlich, M.: Conformance Checking: Relating Processes and Models. Springer-Verlag, Berlin (2018). https://doi.org/10.1007/978-3-319-99414-7

13. Desel, J., Esparza, J.: Free Choice Petri Nets, volume 40 of Cambridge Tracts in Theoretical Computer Science. Cambridge University Press, Cambridge, UK (1995)

14. Desel, J., Reisig, W.: Place/transition nets. In: Reisig, W., Rozenberg, G. (eds.) Lectures on Petri Nets I: Basic Models. Lecture Notes in Computer Science, vol. 1491, pp. 122–173. Springer-Verlag, Berlin (1998). https://doi.org/10.1007/3-540-65306-6_15

15. Ehrenfeucht, A., Rozenberg, G.: Partial (set) 2-structures - part 1 and part 2. Acta Informatica **27**(4), 315–368 (1989). https://doi.org/10.1007/BF00264612

16. Kerremans, M., Srivastava, T., Choudhary, F.: Gartner market guide for process mining, Research Note G00737056 (2021). https://www.gartner.com

17. Leemans, S.J.J., Fahland, D., van der Aalst, W.M.P.: Discovering block-structured process models from event logs: a constructive approach. In: Colom, J.M., Desel, J. (eds.) Applications and Theory of Petri Nets 2013. Lecture Notes in Computer Science, vol. 7927, pp. 311–329. Springer-Verlag, Berlin (2013)

18. Leemans, S.J.J., Fahland, D., van der Aalst, W.M.P.: Discovering block-structured process models from event logs containing infrequent behaviour. In: Lohmann, N., Song, M., Wohed, P. (eds.) BPM 2013. LNBIP, vol. 171, pp. 66–78. Springer, Cham (2014). https://doi.org/10.1007/978-3-319-06257-0_6

19. Leemans, S.J.J., Fahland, D., van der Aalst, W.M.P.: Scalable process discovery and conformance checking. Softw. Syst. Model. **17**(2), 599–631 (2018). https://doi.org/10.1007/s10270-016-0545-x

20. Mannel, L.L., van der Aalst, W.M.P.: Finding complex process-structures by exploiting the token-game. In: Donatelli, S., Haar, S. (eds.) PETRI NETS 2019. LNCS, vol. 11522, pp. 258–278. Springer, Cham (2019). https://doi.org/10.1007/978-3-030-21571-2_15

21. Solé, M., Carmona, J.: Process mining from a basis of state regions. In: Lilius, J., Penczek, W. (eds.) PETRI NETS 2010. LNCS, vol. 6128, pp. 226–245. Springer, Heidelberg (2010). https://doi.org/10.1007/978-3-642-13675-7_14

22. Syring, Anja F., Tax, Niek, van der Aalst, W.M.P.: Evaluating conformance measures in process mining using conformance propositions. In: Koutny, Maciej, Pomello, Lucia, Kristensen, Lars Michael (eds.) Transactions on Petri Nets and Other Models of Concurrency XIV. LNCS, vol. 11790, pp. 192–221. Springer, Heidelberg (2019). https://doi.org/10.1007/978-3-662-60651-3_8

23. Vaandrager, F.: Model learning. Commun. ACM 60(2), 86–95 (2002)

24. Wen, L., van der Aalst, W.M.P., Wang, J., Sun, J.: Mining process models with non-free-choice constructs. Data Min. Knowl. Disc. 15(2), 145–180 (2007)

25. Wen, L., Wang, J., van der Aalst, W.M.P., Huang, B., Sun, J.: Mining process models with prime invisible tasks. Data Knowl. Eng. 69(10), 999–1021 (2010)

26. van der Werf, J.M.E.M., van Dongen, B.F., Hurkens, C.A.J., Serebrenik, A.: Process discovery using integer linear programming. Fund. Inform. 94, 387–412 (2010)

27. van Zelst, S.J., van Dongen, B.F., van der Aalst, W.M.P., Verbeek, H.M.W.: Discovering workflow nets using integer linear programming. Computing 100(5), 529–556 (2017). https://doi.org/10.1007/s00607-017-0582-5

Fair Must Testing for I/O Automata

Rob van Glabbeek[⊠][iD]

School of Computer Science and Engineering, University of New South Wales,
Sydney, Australia
rvg@cs.stanford.edu

Abstract. The concept of must testing is naturally parametrised with a
chosen completeness criterion or fairness assumption. When taking weak
fairness as used in I/O automata, I show that it characterises exactly the
fair preorder on I/O automata as defined by Lynch & Tuttle.

Keywords: I/O automata · Must testing · Fairness

*This paper is dedicated to Frits Vaandrager at the occasion of his 60th birthday.
I fondly remember my days at CWI as a starting computer scientist, sharing an
office with Frits. Here I had the rare privilege of sharing all my ideas with Frits
at the time they were formed, and receiving instantaneous meaningful feedback.
This feedback has had a great impact on my work.*

*I take the opportunity to also pass best wishes and warmest thoughts to Frits
from Ursula Goltz, whom I am visiting while finishing this paper. My joint work
with Ursula was inspired by my work with Frits on connecting Petri nets and
process algebra.*

1 Introduction

May- and must-testing was proposed by De Nicola & Hennessy in [2]. It yields
semantic equivalences where two processes or automata are distinguished if and
only if they react differently on certain tests. The tests are processes that additionally feature success states. Such a test T is applied to a process A by tak-
ing the CCS parallel composition $T|A$, and implicitly applying a CCS restric-
tion operator to it that removes the remnants of uncompleted communication
attempts. The outcome of applying T to A is deemed successful if and only if
this composition yields a process that may, respectively must, reach a success
state. It is trivial to recast this definition of may- and must-testing equivalence
using the CSP parallel composition ‖ [8] instead of the one from CCS.

I/O automata [9] are a model of concurrency that distinguishes output
actions, which are under the control of a given automaton, from input actions,
which are stimuli from the environment on which an automaton might react. The
parallel composition ‖ of I/O automata, exactly like the one of CSP, imposes
synchronisation on actions the composed automata have in common. However, it

N. Jansen et al. (Eds.): Vaandrager Festschrift 2022, LNCS 13560, pp. 559–574, 2022.
https://doi.org/10.1007/978-3-031-15629-8_30

allows forming the composition $A \| B$ only when A and B have no output actions in common. This makes it impossible to synchronise on actions c where both A and B have the option not to allow c in certain states.

Must testing equivalence for CCS and CSP partially discerns *branching time*, in the sense that is distinguishes the processes $\tau.(a + b)$ and $\tau.a + \tau.b$ displayed in Fig. 1. This is not the case for I/O automata, as the synchronisations between test and tested automaton that are necessary to make such distinctions are ruled out by the restriction described above.

It is not a priori clear how a given process or automaton *must* reach a success state. For all we know it might stay in its initial state and never take any transition leading to this success state. To this end one must employ an assumption saying that under appropriate circumstances certain enabled transitions will indeed be taken. Such an assumption is called a *completeness criterion* [5]. The theory of testing from [2] implicitly employs a default completeness criterion that in [7] is called *progress*. However, one can parameterise the notion of must testing by the choice of any completeness criterion, such as the many notions of *fairness* classified in [7].

Lynch & Tuttle [9] defined a trace and a fair preorder on I/O automata, which were meant to reason about safety and liveness properties, respectively, just like the may- and must testing preorders of [2]. Unsurprisingly, as formally shown in Sect. 5 of this paper, the trace preorder on I/O automata is characterised exactly by may testing. Segala [12] has studied must-testing on I/O automata, employing the default completeness criterion, and found that on a large class of I/O automata it characterises the *quiescent trace preorder* of Vaandrager [13]. It does not exactly characterise the fair preorder, however.

In my analysis this is due to the choice of progress as the completeness criterion employed for must testing, whereas the fair preorder of I/O automata is based on a form of weak fairness. In this work I study must testing on I/O automata based on the same form of weak fairness, and find that it characterises the fair preorder exactly.

Although I refer to must-testing with fairness as the chosen completeness criterion as *fair must testing*, it should not be confused with the notion of *fair testing* employed in [1,10]. The latter is also known as *should testing*. It incorporates a concept of fairness that is much stronger than the notion of fairness from I/O automata, called *full fairness* in [7].

In [6] another mode of testing was proposed, called *reward testing*. Reward-testing equivalence combines the distinguishing power of may as well as must testing, and additionally makes some useful distinctions between processes that are missed by both may and must testing [6]. As for must testing, its definition is naturally parametrised by a completeness criterion. When applied to I/O automata, using as completeness criterion the form of fairness that is native to I/O automata, it turns out that reward testing is not stronger than must testing, and also characterises the fair preorder.

2 I/O Automata

An I/O automaton is a labelled transition system equipped with a nonempty set of start states, with each action that may appear as transition label classified as an input, an output or an internal action. Input actions are under the control of the environment of the automaton, whereas output and internal actions, together called *locally-controlled* actions, are under the control of the automaton itself. I/O automata are *input enabled*, meaning that in each state each input action of the automaton can be performed. This indicates that the environment may perform such actions regardless of the state of the automaton; an input transition merely indicates how the automaton reacts on such an event. To model that certain input actions have no effect in certain states, one uses self-loops.

I/O automata employ a partition of the locally-controlled actions into *tasks* to indicate which sequences of transitions denote *fair* runs. A run is fair unless it has a suffix on which some task is enabled in every state, yet never taken.

Definition 1. An *input/output automaton* (or *I/O automaton*) A is a tuple $(acts(A), states(A), start(A), steps(A), part(A))$ with

- $acts(A)$ a set of *actions*, partitioned into three sets $in(A)$, $out(A)$ and $int(A)$ of *input actions*, *output actions* and *internal actions*, respectively,
- $states(A)$ a set of *states*,
- $start(A) \subseteq states(A)$ a nonempty set of start states,
- $steps(A) \subseteq states(A) \times acts(A) \times states(A)$ a *transition relation* with the property that $\forall s \in states(A). \forall a \in in(A). \exists (s, a, s') \in steps(A)$, and
- $part(A) \subseteq \mathscr{P}(local(A))$ a partition of the set $local(A) := out(A) \cup int(A)$ of *locally-controlled actions* of A into *tasks*.

Let $ext(A) := in(A) \cup out(A)$ be the set of *external actions* of A.

An action $a \in acts(A)$ is *enabled* in a state $s \in states(A)$ if $\exists (s, a, s') \in steps(A)$. A task $T \in part(A)$ is *enabled* in s if some action $a \in T$ is enabled is s.

Definition 2. An *execution* of an I/O automaton A is an alternating sequence $\alpha = s_0, a_1, s_1, a_2, \ldots$ of states and actions, either being infinite or ending with a state, such that $s_0 \in start(A)$ and $(s_i, a_{i+1}, s_{i+1}) \in steps(A)$ for all $i < length(\alpha)$. Here $length(\alpha) \in \mathbb{N} \cup \{\infty\}$ denotes the number of action occurrences in α. The sequence $a_1, a_2, \ldots$ obtained by dropping all states from α is called $sched(\alpha)$. An execution α of A is *fair* if, for each suffix $\alpha' = s_k, a_{k+1}, s_{k+1}, a_{k+2}, \ldots$ of α (with $k \in \mathbb{N} \wedge k \leqslant length(\alpha)$) and each task $T \in part(A)$, if T is enabled in each state of α', then α' contains an action from T.

In [9] two semantic preorders are defined on I/O automata, here called $\sqsubseteq_T$ and $\sqsubseteq_F$, the *trace* and the *fair preorder*. In [9] $S \sqsubseteq_T I$ and $S \sqsubseteq_F I$ are denoted "*I implements S*" and "*I solves S*", respectively. Here S is an I/O automaton that is (a step closer to) the specification of a problem, and I one that is (a step closer to) its implementation. The preorder $\sqsubseteq_T$ is meant to reason about safety properties: if $S \sqsubseteq_T I$ then I has any safety property that S has. In the same way, $\sqsubseteq_F$ is for reasoning about liveness properties. In [12] and much subsequent work $S \sqsubseteq_F I$ is written as $I \sqsupseteq_F S$. Here I put I on the right, so as to orient the refinement symbol $\sqsubseteq$ in the way used in CSP [8], and in the theory of testing [2].

I/O automata are a typed model of concurrency, in the sense that two automata will be compared only when they have the same input and output actions.

Definition 3. Let $trace(\alpha)$ be the finite or infinite sequence of external actions resulting from dropping all internal actions in $sched(\alpha)$, and let $fintraces(A)$ be the set $\{trace(\alpha) \mid \alpha \text{ is a finite execution of } A\}$. Likewise $fairtraces(A) := \{trace(\alpha) \mid \alpha \text{ is a fair execution of } A\}$. Now

$$S \sqsubseteq_T I \quad :\Leftrightarrow \quad in(S) = in(I) \wedge out(S) = out(I) \wedge \quad fintraces(I) \subseteq fintraces(S)$$
$$S \sqsubseteq_F I \quad :\Leftrightarrow \quad in(S) = in(I) \wedge out(S) = out(I) \wedge fairtraces(I) \subseteq fairtraces(S).$$

One writes $A \equiv_T B$ if $A \sqsubseteq_T B \wedge B \sqsubseteq_T A$, and similarly for $\equiv_F$.

By [7, Thm. 6.1] each finite execution can be extended into a fair execution. As a consequence, $A \sqsubseteq_F B \Rightarrow A \sqsubseteq_T B$.

The parallel composition of I/O automata [9] is similar to the one of CSP [8]: participating automata A_i and A_j synchronise on actions in $acts(A_i) \cap acts(A_j)$, while for the rest allowing arbitrary interleaving. However, it is defined only when the participating automata have no output actions in common.

Definition 4. A collection $\{A_i\}_{i \in I}$ of I/O automata is *strongly compatible* if

- $int(A_i) \cap acts(A_j) = \varnothing$ for all $i, j \in I$ with $i \neq j$, and
- $out(A_i) \cap out(A_j) = \varnothing$ for all $i, j \in I$ with $i \neq j$,
- no action is contained in infinitely many sets $acts(A_i)$.

The *composition* $A = \prod_{i \in I} A_i$ of a countable collection $\{A_i\}_{i \in I}$ of strongly compatible I/O automata is defined by

- $int(A) := \bigcup_{i \in I} int(A_i)$,
- $out(A) := \bigcup_{i \in I} out(A_i)$,
- $in(A) := \bigcup_{i \in I} in(A_i) - out(A)$,
- $states(A) := \prod_{i \in I} states(A_i)$,
- $start(A) := \prod_{i \in I} start(A_i)$,
- $steps(A)$ is the set of triples $(\vec{s_1}, a, \vec{s_2})$ such that, for all $i \in I$, if $a \in acts(A_i)$ then $(\vec{s_1}[i], a, \vec{s_2}[i]) \in steps(A_i)$, and if $a \notin acts(A_i)$ then $\vec{s_1}[i] = \vec{s_2}[i]$, and
- $part(A) := \bigcup_{i \in I} part(A_i)$.

Clearly, composition of I/O automata is associative: when writing $A_1 \| A_2$ for $\prod_{i \in \{1,2\}} A_i$ then $(A\|B)\|C \cong A\|(B\|C)$, for some notion of isomorphism $\cong$, included in $\equiv_T$ and $\equiv_F$. Moreover, as shown in [9], composition is monotone for $\sqsubseteq_T$ and $\sqsubseteq_F$, or in other words, $\sqsubseteq_T$ and $\sqsubseteq_F$ are precongruences for composition:

$$\text{if } A_i \sqsubseteq_T B_i \text{ for all } i \in I, \text{ then } \prod_{i \in I} A_i \sqsubseteq_T \prod_{i \in I} B_i, \text{ and}$$
$$\text{if } A_i \sqsubseteq_F B_i \text{ for all } i \in I, \text{ then } \prod_{i \in I} A_i \sqsubseteq_F \prod_{i \in I} B_i.$$

The first condition of strong compatibility is not a limitation of generality. Each I/O automaton is $\equiv_T$ and $\equiv_F$-equivalent to the result of bijectively renaming its internal actions. Hence, prior to composing a collection of automata, one could rename their internal actions to ensure that this condition is met. Up to $\equiv_T$ and $\equiv_F$ the composition would be independent on the choice of these renamings.

3   Testing Preorders

Testing preorders [2] are defined between *automata* A, defined as in Definition 1, but without the partition $part(A)$ and without the distinction between input and output actions, and therefore also without the input enabling requirement from Item 4. The parallel composition of automata is as in Definition 4, but without the requirement that the participating automata have no output actions in common.

Definition 5. An *automaton* A is a tuple $(acts(A), states(A), start(A), steps(A))$ with

- $acts(A)$ a set of *actions*, partitioned into two sets $ext(A)$ and $int(A)$ of *external actions* and *internal actions*, respectively,
- $states(A)$ a set of *states*,
- $start(A) \subseteq states(A)$ a nonempty set of start states, and
- $steps(A) \subseteq states(A) \times acts(A) \times states(A)$ a *transition relation*.

A collection $\{A_i\}_{i \in I}$ of I/O automata is *compatible* if

- $int(A_i) \cap acts(A_j) = \varnothing$ for all $i, j \in I$ with $i \neq j$, and
- no action is contained in infinitely many sets $acts(A_i)$.

The *composition* $A = \prod_{i \in I} A_i$ of a countable collection $\{A_i\}_{i \in I}$ of compatible I/O automata is defined by

- $int(A) := \bigcup_{i \in I} int(A_i)$,
- $ext(A) := \bigcup_{i \in I} ext(A_i)$,
- $states(A) := \prod_{i \in I} states(A_i)$,
- $start(A) := \prod_{i \in I} start(A_i)$, and
- $steps(A)$ is the set of triples $(\vec{s_1}, a, \vec{s_2})$ such that, for all $i \in I$, if $a \in acts(A_i)$ then $(\vec{s_1}[i], a, \vec{s_2}[i]) \in steps(A_i)$, and if $a \notin acts(A_i)$ then $\vec{s_1}[i] = \vec{s_2}[i]$.

A *test* is such an automaton, but featuring a special external action w, not used elsewhere. This action is used to mark *success states*: those in which w is enabled. The parallel composition $T\|A$ of a test T and an automaton A, if it exists, is itself a test, and $[T\|A]$ denotes the result of reclassifying all its non-w actions as internal. An execution of $[T\|A]$ is *successful* iff it contains a success state.

Definition 6. An automaton A *may pass* a test T, notation A **may** T, if $[T\|A]$ has a successful execution. It *must pass* T, notation A **must** T, if each complete execution[1] of $[T\|A]$ is successful. It *should pass* T, notation A **should** T, if each finite execution of $[T\|A]$ can be extended into a successful execution.

Write $A \sqsubseteq_{\mathrm{may}} B$ if $ext(A) = ext(B)$ and A **may** T implies B **may** T for each test T that is compatible with A and B. The preorders $\sqsubseteq_{\mathrm{must}}$ and $\sqsubseteq_{\mathrm{should}}$ are defined similarly.

The may- and must-testing preorders stem from [2], whereas should-testing was added independently in [1] and [10]. I have added the condition $ext(A) = ext(B)$ to obtain preorders that respect the types of automata. A fourth mode of testing, called *reward testing*, was contributed in [6]. It has no notion of success state, and no action w; instead, each transition of a test T is tagged with a real number, the reward of taking that transition. A negative reward can be seen as a penalty. Each transition (s, a, s') of $[T\|A]$ with $a \in acts(T)$ inherits its reward from the unique transition of T it projects to; in case $a \notin acts(T)$ it has reward 0. The reward $reward(\alpha)$ of an execution α is the sum of the rewards of the actions in α.[2] Now $A \sqsubseteq_{\mathrm{reward}} B$ if $ext(A) = ext(B)$ and for each test T that is compatible with A and B and for each complete execution β of $[T\|B]$ there exists a complete execution α of $[T\|A]$ such that $reward(\alpha) \leqslant reward(\beta)$.

In the original work on testing [2,6] the CCS parallel composition $T|A$ was used instead of the CSP parallel composition $T\|A$; moreover, only those executions consisting solely of internal actions mattered for the definitions of passing a test. The present approach is equivalent, in the sense that it trivially gives rise to the same testing preorders.

The may-testing preorder can be regarded as pointing in the opposite direction as the others. Using CCS notation, one has $\tau.P \sqsubsetneq_{\mathrm{may}} \tau.P + \tau.Q$, yet $\tau.P + \tau.Q \sqsubsetneq_{\mathrm{must}} \tau.P$, $\tau.P + \tau.Q \sqsubsetneq_{\mathrm{should}} \tau.P$ and $\tau.P + \tau.Q \sqsubsetneq_{\mathrm{reward}} \tau.P$. The inverse of the may-testing preorder can be characterised as *survival testing*. Here a state in which w is enabled is seen as a *failure state* rather than a success state, and automaton A *survives* test T, notation A **surv** T, if no execution of $[T\|A]$ passes through a failure state. Write $A \sqsubseteq_{\mathrm{surv}} B$ if $ext(A) = ext(B)$ and A **surv** T implies B **surv** T for each test T that is compatible with A and B. By definition, $A \sqsubseteq_{\mathrm{surv}} B$ iff $B \sqsubseteq_{\mathrm{may}} A$.

The only implications between reward, must and may/survival testing are

$$A \sqsubseteq_{\mathrm{reward}} B \;\Rightarrow\; A \sqsubseteq_{\mathrm{must}} B \qquad \text{and} \qquad A \sqsubseteq_{\mathrm{reward}} B \;\Rightarrow\; A \sqsubseteq_{\mathrm{surv}} B \,.$$

Namely, any must test T witnessing $A \not\sqsubseteq_{\mathrm{must}} B$ can be coded as a reward test by assigning a reward $+1$ to all transitions of T leading to a success state (and 0 to all other transitions). Likewise any survival test T witnessing $A \not\sqsubseteq_{\mathrm{surv}} B$ can be coded as a reward test by assigning a reward -1 to all transitions of T leading to a failure state.

---

[1] The original work on must testing [2] defined an execution to be complete if it either is infinite, of ends in a state without outgoing transitions. Here I will consider the concept of a complete execution as a parameter in the definition of must testing.

[2] If α is infinite, its reward can be $+\infty$ or $-\infty$; see [6] for a precise definition.

The notions of may- and should-testing are unambiguously defined above, whereas the notions of must- and reward testing depend on the definition of a complete execution. In [5] I posed that transition systems or automata constitute a good model of distributed systems only in combination with a *completeness criterion*: a selection of a subset of all executions as complete executions, modelling complete runs of the represented system.

The default completeness criterion, employed in [2,6] for the definition of must- and reward testing, deems an execution complete if it either is infinite, of ends in deadlock, a state without outgoing transitions. Other completeness criteria either classify certain finite executions that do not end in deadlock as complete, or certain infinite executions as incomplete.

The first possibility was explored in [5,7] by considering a set B of actions that might be blocked by the environment in which an automaton is running. Now a finite execution can be deemed complete if all transitions enabled in its last state have labels from B. The system might stop at such a state if indeed the environment blocks all those actions. Since in the application to must- and reward testing, all non-w transitions in $[T\|A]$ are labelled with internal actions, which cannot be blocked by the environment, the above possibility of increasing the set of finite complete executions does not apply.

The second possibility was extensively explored in [7], where a multitude of completeness criteria was defined. Most of those can be used as a parameter in the definition of must- and reward testing. So far, the resulting testing preorders have not been explored.[3]

4   Testing Preorders for I/O Automata

Since I/O automata can be seen as special cases of the automata from Sect. 3, the definitions of Sect. 3 also apply to I/O automata. The condition $ext(A) = ext(B)$ should then be read as $in(A) = in(B) \land out(A) = out(B)$. The only place where it makes an essential difference whether one works with I/O automata or general automata is in judging compatibility between automata and tests. Given two I/O automata A and B, let $A \sqsubseteq^{\mathrm{LTS}}_{\mathrm{must}} B$ be defined by first seeing A and B as general automata (by dropping the partitions $part(A)$ and $part(B)$), and then applying the definitions of Sect. 3, using the default completeness criterion. In contrast, let $A \sqsubseteq^{Pr}_{\mathrm{must}} B$ be defined as Sect. 3, but only allowing tests that are themselves I/O automata (seeing the special action w as an output action), and that are strongly compatible with A and B. The superscript Pr stands for "progress", the name given in [7] to the default completeness criterion. The difference between $\sqsubseteq^{\mathrm{LTS}}_{\mathrm{must}}$ and $\sqsubseteq^{Pr}_{\mathrm{must}}$ is illustrated in Fig. 1.

Here A and B are automata with $acts(A) = acts(B) = \{\tau, a, b\}$, and T is a test with $acts(T) = \{a, b, w\}$. The short arrows point to start states. Test T witnesses that $A \not\sqsubseteq^{\mathrm{LTS}}_{\mathrm{must}} B$, for A **must** T, yet $\neg(B$ **must** $T)$. Here it is crucial that $a \in acts(T)$, even though this action labels no transition of T, for otherwise

---

[3] The paper [4] explores these testing preorders; it was written after the present paper.

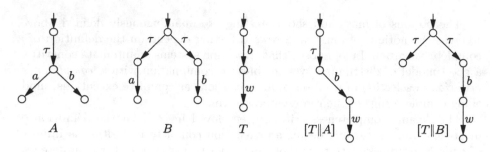

Fig. 1. Classic example of how branching time is discerned by must testing

the a-transition of A would return in $[T\|A]$ and one would not obtain A **must** T. To see A, B and T as I/O automata, one needs to take $in(A) = in(B) = in(T) = \emptyset$, and thus $a, b \in out(A) \cap out(B) \cap out(T)$. However, this violates the strong compatibility of T with A and B, so that T is disqualified as an appropriate test. There is no variant of T that is strongly compatible with A and B and yields the same result; in fact $A \equiv_{\text{must}}^{Pr} B$.

5   May Testing

For may-testing on I/O automata there is no difference between $\sqsubseteq_{\text{may}}^{\text{LTS}}$—allowing any test that is compatible with A and B—and $\sqsubseteq_{\text{may}}$—allowing only tests that are strongly compatible with A and B. These preorders both coincide with the trace preorder $\sqsupseteq_T$.

Theorem 1. $A \sqsubseteq_{\text{may}}^{\text{LTS}} B$ iff $A \sqsubseteq_{\text{may}} B$ iff $B \sqsubseteq_T A$.

Proof. Suppose $B \sqsubseteq_T A$, i.e., $in(A) = in(B) \wedge out(A) = out(B)$ and $fintraces(A) \subseteq fintraces(B)$, and let T be any test compatible with A and B. The automaton T need not be an I/O automaton, and even if it is, it need not be strongly compatible with A and B. It is well-known that $\sqsubseteq_T$ is a precongruence for composition [8], so $fintraces(T\|A) \subseteq fintraces(T\|B)$. Since C **may** T (for any C) iff w occurs in a trace $\sigma \in fintraces(T\|C)$, it follows that A **may** T implies B **may** T. Thus $A \sqsubseteq_{\text{may}}^{\text{LTS}} B$.

That $A \sqsubseteq_{\text{may}}^{\text{LTS}} B$ implies $A \sqsubseteq_{\text{may}} B$ is trivial.

Now suppose $A \sqsubseteq_{\text{may}} B$. Then $in(A) = in(B) \wedge out(A) = out(B)$. Let $\sigma = a_1 a_2 \ldots a_n \in fintraces(A)$. Let T be the test automaton

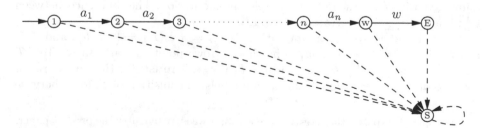

with $out(T) := in(A) \uplus \{w\}$, $in(T) := out(A)$ and $int(T) := \varnothing$. To make sure that T is an I/O automaton, the dashed arrows are labelled with all input actions of T, except for a_i (if $a_i \in in(T)$) for the dashed arrow departing from state i. By construction, T is strongly compatible with A and B. Now C **may** T (for any C) iff $\sigma \in \mathit{fintraces}(C)$. Hence A **may** T, and thus B **may** T, and therefore $\sigma \in \mathit{fintraces}(B)$. $\qquad\qquad\square$

6 Must Testing Based on Progress

Definition 7. An I/O automaton T is *complementary* to I/O automaton A if $out(T) = in(A) \uplus \{w\}$, $in(T) = out(A)$ and $int(T) \cap int(A) = \varnothing$.

In this case T and A are also strongly compatible, so that $T \| A$ is defined, and $in(T \| A) = \varnothing$. I now show that for the definition of $\sqsubseteq^{Pr}_{\text{must}}$ it makes no difference whether one restricts the tests T that may be used to compare two I/O automata A and B to ones that are complementary to A and B.

For use in the following proof, define the relation $\equiv$ between I/O automata by $C \equiv D$ iff $states(C) = states(D) \wedge start(C) = start(D) \wedge steps(C) = steps(D)$. Note that $T \| A \equiv T' \| A$ implies that A **must** T iff A **must** T'.

Proposition 1. $A \sqsubseteq^{Pr}_{\text{must}} B$ iff $in(A) = in(B) \wedge out(A) = out(B)$ and A **must** T implies B **must** T for each test T that is complementary to A and B.

Proof. Suppose $A \sqsubseteq^{Pr}_{\text{must}} B$. Then $in(A) = in(B) \wedge out(A) = out(B)$ and A **must** T implies B **must** T for each test T that is strongly compatible with A and B, and thus certainly for each test T that is complementary to A and B.

Now suppose $in(A) = in(B) \wedge out(A) = out(B)$ but $A \not\sqsubseteq^{Pr}_{\text{must}} B$. Then there is a test T, strongly compatible with A and B, such that A **must** T, yet $\neg(B$ **must** $T)$. It suffices to find a test T'' with the same properties that is moreover complementary to A and B.

First modify T into T' by adding $ext(A) \backslash ext(T)$ to $in(T')$, while adding a loop (s, a, s) to $steps(T')$ for each state $s \in states(T')$ and each $a \in ext(A) \setminus ext(T)$. Now $T \| A = T' \| A$ and $T \| B = T' \| B$, and thus A **must** T', yet $\neg(B$ **must** $T')$. Moreover, $ext(A) = ext(B) \subseteq ext(T')$.

Modify T' further into T'' by reclassifying any action $a \in in(T') \cap in(A)$ as an output action of T'' and any $a \in ext(T') \backslash (ext(A) \uplus \{w\})$ as an internal action of T''. How $part(T'')$ is defined is immaterial. Then $T' \| A \equiv T'' \| A$ and $T' \| B \equiv T'' \| B$, and thus A **must** T'', yet $\neg(B$ **must** $T'')$. Now $out(T'') = in(A) \uplus \{w\}$, $in(T'') = out(A)$, $int(T'') \cap int(A) = \varnothing$ and $int(T'') \cap int(B) = \varnothing$. $\qquad\square$

Using the characterisation of Proposition 1 as definition, the preorder $\sqsubseteq^{Pr}_{\text{must}}$ on I/O automata has been studied by Segala [12, Sect. 7]. There it was related to the *quiescent trace* preorder $\sqsubseteq_Q$ defined by Vaandrager [13]. Similar as for the preorders of Sect. 2, I write $S \sqsubseteq_Q I$ for what was denoted $I \sqsubseteq_Q S$ in [12], and $I \sqsubseteq_{qT} S$ in [13].

Definition 8. An execution α is *quiescent* if it is finite and its last state enables only input actions. Let $qtraces(A) := \{trace(\alpha) \mid \alpha$ is a quiescent execution of $A\}$. Now

$$S \sqsubseteq_Q I :\Leftrightarrow S \sqsubseteq_T I \wedge qtraces(I) \subseteq qtraces(S).$$

An I/O automaton is *finitely branching* iff each of its states enables finitely many transitions; it is *strongly convergent* if it has no infinite execution α with $trace(\alpha)$ finite, i.e., no execution with an infinite suffix of only internal actions.

Theorem 2 ([12, Thm. 7.3]). Let A and B be finitely branching and strongly convergent I/O automata. Then $A \sqsubseteq_{must}^{Pr} B$ iff $A \sqsubseteq_Q B$.

Note that an execution is quiescent iff it is fair and finite. By [12, Thm. 5.7], if A is strongly convergent then $A \sqsubseteq_F B$ implies $A \sqsubseteq_Q B$. (For let $A \sqsubseteq_F B$. If $\sigma \in qtraces(B)$, then $\sigma \in fairtraces(B) \subseteq fairtraces(A)$ so A has a fair execution α with $trace(\alpha) = \sigma$. As A is strongly convergent, α is finite. Hence $\sigma \in qtraces(A)$.) This does not hold when dropping the side condition of strong convergence. Take $A = \rightarrow\!\bigcirc$ and $B = \rightarrow\!\bigcirc\!\!\supset\tau$ with $acts(A) = \varnothing$ and $acts(B) = int(B) = \{\tau\}$. Then $A \equiv_F B$, yet $A \not\sqsubseteq_Q B$ (and $A \not\sqsubseteq_{must}^{Pr} B$).

Even restricted to finitely branching and strongly convergent I/O automata, $A \sqsubseteq_Q B$ does not imply $A \sqsubseteq_F B$. This is illustrated by [12, Examples 5.1 and 5.2].

7 Must Testing Based on Fairness

As explained in Sect. 3, the notion of must testing is naturally parametrised by the choice of a completeness criterion. As I/O automata are already equipped with a completeness criteria, namely the notion of fairness from Definition 2, the most appropriate form of must testing for I/O automata takes this concept of fairness as its parameter, rather than the default completeness criterion used in Sect. 6.

A problem in properly defining a must-testing preorder $\sqsubseteq_{must}^F$ involves the definition of the operator [ ] employed in Definition 6. In the context of standard automata, this operator reclassifies all its external actions, except for the success action w, as internal. When applied to I/O automaton A, it is not a priori clear how to define $part([A])$, for this is a partition of the set of locally-controlled actions into tasks, and when changing an input action into a locally-controlled action, one lacks guidance on which task to allocate it to. This was a not a problem in Sect. 6, as there the must-testing preorder $\sqsubseteq_{must}^{Pr}$ depends in no way on *part*.

Below I inventorise various solutions to this problem, which gives rise to three possible definitions of $\sqsubseteq_{must}^F$. Then I show in Sect. 9 that all three resulting preorders coincide, so that it doesn't matter on which of the definitions one settles. Moreover, these preorders all turn out to coincide with the fair preorder $\sqsubseteq_F$ that comes with I/O automata.

My first (and default) solution is to simply drop the operator [ ] from Definition 6:

Definition 9. An I/O automaton A *must pass* a test T *fairly*—A **must**$^F T$—if each fair execution of $T\|A$ is successful. Write $A \sqsubseteq^F_{\text{must}} B$ if $in(A) = in(B) \wedge out(A) = out(B)$ and A **must**$^F T$ implies B **must**$^F T$ for each test T that is strongly compatible with A and B.

This is a plausible approach, as none of the testing preorders discussed in Sects. 3, 4, 5 and 6 would change at all were the operator [ ] dropped from Definition 6. This is the case because the set of executions, successful executions and complete executions of an automaton A is independent of the status (input, output or internal) of the actions of A.

The above begs the question why I bothered to employ the operator [ ] in Definition 6 in the first place. The main reason is that the theory of testing [2] was developed in the context of CCS, where each synchronisation of an action from a test with one from a tested process yields an internal action τ. Definition 6 recreates this theory using the operator $\|$ from CSP [8] and I/O automata [9], but as here synchronised actions are not internal, they have to be made internal to obtain the same effect. A second reason concerns the argument used towards the end of Sect. 3 for not parametrising notions of testing with a set B of actions that can be blocked; this argument hinges on all relevant actions being internal.

My second solution is to restrict the set of allowed tests T for comparing I/O automata A and B to those for which $in(T\|A) = in(T\|B) = \varnothing$. This is the case iff $in(T) \subseteq out(A)$ and $in(A) \subseteq out(T)$. In that case $[T\|A]$ and $[T\|B]$ are trivial to define, as the set of locally-controlled actions stays the same. Moreover, it makes no difference whether this operator is included in the definition of **must** or not, as the set of fair executions of a process is not affected by a reclassification of output actions as internal actions.

Definition 10. Write $A \,{}^\varnothing{\sqsubseteq}^F_{\text{must}} B$ if $in(A)=in(B) \wedge out(A)=out(B)$ and moreover A **must**$^F T$ implies B **must**$^F T$ for each test T that is strongly compatible with A and B, and for which $in(T\|A) = in(T\|B) = \varnothing$.

A small variation of this idea restricts the set of allowed tests even further, namely to the ones that are complementary to A and B, as defined in Definition 7. This yield a fair version of the must-testing preorder employed in [12].

Definition 11. Write $A \,{}^{\text{cm}}{\sqsubseteq}^F_{\text{must}} B$ if $in(A) = in(B) \wedge out(A) = out(B)$ and A **must**$^F T$ implies B **must**$^F T$ for each T that is complementary to A and B.

As a last solution I consider tests T that are not restricted as in Definitions 10 or 11, while looking for elegant ways to define $[T\|A]$ and $[T\|B]$. First of all, note that no generality is lost when restricting to tests T such that $ext(A)(= ext(B)) \subseteq ext(T)$, regardless how the operator [ ] is defined. Namely, employing the first conversion from the proof of Proposition 1, any test T that is strongly compatible with I/O automata A and B can converted into a test T' satisfying this requirement, and such that $T\|A = T'\|A$ and $T\|B = T'\|B$.

An application of [ ] to $T\|A$ consists of reclassifying external actions of $T\|A$ as internal actions. However, since for the definition of the testing preorders it makes no difference whether an action in $T\|A$ is an internal or an output action, one can just as well use an operator $[\ ]'$ that merely reclassifies input actions of $T\|A$ as output actions. Note that $in(T\|A) \subseteq in(T)$, using that $ext(A) \subseteq ext(T)$. Let T^* be a result of adapting the test T by reclassifying the actions in $in(T\|A)$ from input actions of T into output actions of T; the test T^* is not uniquely defined, as there are various ways to fill in $part(T^*)$.

Observation 1. Apart from the problematic definition of $part([T\|A]')$, the I/O automaton $[T\|A]'$ is the very same as $T^*\|A$.

In other words, the reclassification of input into output actions can just as well be done on the test, instead of on the composition of test and tested automaton. The advantage of this approach is that the problematic definition of $part([T\|A]')$ is moved to the test as well. Now one can use $T^*\|A$ instead of $[T\|A]'$ in the definition of must testing for any desired definition of $part(T^*)$. This amounts to choosing any test T^* with $in(T^*\|A) = \varnothing$. It makes this solution equivalent to the one of Definition 10.

8   Action-Based Must Testing

The theory of testing from [2] employs the success action w merely to mark success states; an execution is successful iff it contains a state in which w is enabled. In [3] this is dubbed *state-based testing*. Segala [11] (in a setting with probabilistic automata) uses another mode of testing, called *action-based* in [3], in which an execution is defined to be successful iff it contains the action w.

Although the state-based and action-based may-testing preorders obviously coincide, the state-based and action-based must-testing preorders do not, at least when employing the default completeness criterion. An example showing the difference is given in [3]. It involves two automata A and B, which can in fact be seen as I/O automata, such that $A \not\sqsubseteq^{Pr}_{must} B$, yet $A \stackrel{ab}{\equiv}^{Pr}_{must} B$. Here $\stackrel{ab}{\equiv}^{Pr}_{must}$ is the action-based version of $\equiv^{Pr}_{must}$.

So far I have considered only state-based testing preorders on I/O automata. Let $\stackrel{ab}{\sqsubseteq}^{F}_{must}$ be the action-based version of $\sqsubseteq^{F}_{must}$. It is defined as in Definition 9, but using **must**$^{F}_{ab}$ instead of **must**^{F}. Here A **must**$^{F}_{ab}$ T holds iff each fair trace of $T\|A$ contains the action w. Below I will show that when taking the notion of fairness from [9] as completeness criterion, state-based and action-based must testing yields the same result, i.e., $\stackrel{ab}{\sqsubseteq}^{F}_{must}$ equals $\sqsubseteq^{F}_{must}$. In fact, I need this result in my proof that $\sqsubseteq^{F}_{must}$ coincides with $\sqsubseteq_F$.

9   Fair Must Testing Agrees with the Fair Traces Preorder

The following theorem states that the must-testing preorder on I/O automata based on the completeness criterion of fairness that is native to I/O automata, in each of the four forms discussed in Sects. 7 and 8, coincides with the standard preorder of I/O automata based on reverse inclusion of fair traces.

Theorem 3. $A \overset{ab}{\sqsubseteq}^F_{must} B$ iff $A \sqsubseteq^F_{must} B$ iff $A \overset{\varnothing}{\sqsubseteq}^F_{must} B$ iff $A \overset{cm}{\sqsubseteq}^F_{must} B$ iff $A \sqsubseteq_F B$.

Proof. Suppose $A \sqsubseteq_F B$, i.e., $in(A) = in(B) \land out(A) = out(B)$ and $fairtraces(B) \subseteq fairtraces(A)$, and let T be any test that is strongly compatible with A and B. Since $\sqsubseteq_F$ is a precongruence for composition (cf. Sect. 2), $fairtraces(T\|B) \subseteq fintraces(T\|A)$. Since for action-based must testing C **must**$^F_{ab} T$ (for any C) iff w occurs in each fair trace $\sigma \in fairtraces(T\|C)$, it follows that A **must**$^F_{ab} T$ implies B **must**$^F_{ab} T$. Thus $A \overset{ab}{\sqsubseteq}^F_{must} B$.

Now suppose $A \overset{ab}{\sqsubseteq}^F_{must} B$. In order to show that $A \sqsubseteq^F_{must} B$, suppose that A **must**$^F T$, where T is a test that is strongly compatible with A and B. Let the test T^* be obtained from T by (i) dropping all transitions $(s, a, s') \in steps(T)$ for s a success state and $a \neq w$, and (ii) adding a loop (s, a, s) for each success state s and $a \in in(T)$. Since for state-based must testing it is irrelevant what happens after encountering a success state, one has

$$C \text{ must}^F T \text{ iff } C \text{ must}^F T^* \tag{1}$$

for each I/O automaton C. Moreover, I claim that for each C one has

$$C \text{ must}^F T^* \text{ iff } C \text{ must}^F_{ab} T^*. \tag{2}$$

Here "if" is trivial. For "only if", let α be a fair execution of $T^*\|C$, and suppose, towards a contradiction, that α contains a success state (s, r), with s a success state of T^* and r a state of C, but does not contain the success action w. Let α' be the suffix of α starting with the first occurrence of (s, r). Then all states of α' have the form (s, r'), and the action w is enabled in each of these states. Let $\mathcal{T} \in part(T^*\|C)$ be the task containing w. Since w is a locally controlled action of T^*, by Definition 4 all members of $\mathcal{T}$ must be locally controlled actions of T^*. No such action can occur in α'. This contradicts the assumption that α is fair (cf. Definition 2), and thereby concludes the proof of (2).

From the assumption A **must**$^F T$ one obtains A **must**$^F_{ab} T^*$ by (1) and (2), and B **must**$^F_{ab} T^*$ by the assumption that $A \overset{ab}{\sqsubseteq}^F_{must} B$. Hence B **must**$^F T$ by (2) and (1). Thus $A \sqsubseteq^F_{must} B$.

That $A \sqsubseteq^F_{must} B$ implies $A \overset{\varnothing}{\sqsubseteq}^F_{must} B$ is trivial.

That $A \overset{\varnothing}{\sqsubseteq}^F_{must} B$ implies $A \overset{cm}{\sqsubseteq}^F_{must} B$ is also trivial.

Finally, suppose $A \overset{cm}{\sqsubseteq}^F_{must} B$. Then $in(A) = in(B) \land out(A) = out(B)$. Let $\sigma = a_1 a_2 \ldots a_n \in fairtraces(B)$. Let T be the test automaton

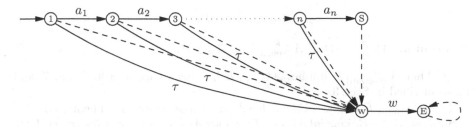

with $out(T) := in(A) \uplus \{w\}$, $in(T) := out(A)$ and $int(T) := \{\tau\}$. The dashed arrows are labelled with all input actions of T, except for a_i (if $a_i \in in(T)$) for the dashed arrow departing from state i. By construction, T is complementary to A and B. Now C **must** T (for any C) iff $\sigma \notin \textit{fairtraces}(C)$. Hence B **may not** T, and thus A **may not** T, and therefore $\sigma \in \textit{fairtraces}(A)$.

The case that $\sigma = a_1 a_2 \cdots \in \textit{fairtraces}(B)$ is infinite goes likewise, but without the state s in T. Hence $A \sqsubseteq_F B$. $\square$

10   Reward Testing

The reward testing preorder taking the notion of fairness from Definition 2 as underlying completeness criterion can be defined on I/O automata by analogy of Definitions 9, 10 or 11. Here I take the one that follows Definition 9, as it is clearly the strongest, i.e., with its kernel making the most distinctions.

Definition 12. Write $A \sqsubseteq_{\text{reward}}^F B$ if $in(A) = in(B) \wedge out(A) = out(B)$ and for each reward test T that is strongly compatible with A and B and for each fair execution β of $T\|B$ there is a fair execution α of $T\|A$ with $\textit{reward}(\alpha) \leqslant \textit{reward}(\beta)$.

When taking progress as underlying completeness criterion, reward testing is stronger than must testing; the opening page of [6] shows an example where reward testing makes useful distinctions that are missed by may as well as must testing. When moving to fairness as the underlying completeness criterion, must testing no longer misses that example, and in fact must testing becomes equally strong as reward testing. In order to show this, I will use the following notation.

Definition 13. Let A_1 and A_2 be two strongly compatible I/O automata. A state $\vec{s}$ of $A_1\|A_2$ is a pair $(\vec{s}[1], \vec{s}[2])$ with $\vec{s}[k] \in states(A_k)$ for $k = 1, 2$. Let $\alpha = \vec{s}_0, a_1, \vec{s}_1, a_2, \ldots$ be an execution of $A_1\|A_2$. The projection $\alpha[k]$ of α to the kth component A_k, for $k = 1, 2$, is obtained from α by deleting "$, a_i, \vec{s}_i$" whenever $a_i \notin acts(A_k)$, and replacing the remaining pairs $\vec{s}_i$ by $\vec{s}_i[k]$.

Moreover, if σ is a sequence of external actions of $A_1\|A_2$, then $\sigma \upharpoonright A_k$ is what is left of σ after removing all actions outside $acts(A_k)$.

Note that if $\sigma = trace(\alpha)$, for α an execution of $A_1\|A_2$, then $\sigma \upharpoonright A_k = trace(\alpha[k])$. Moreover, if α is an execution of $T\|A$, were T is a test and A a tested automaton, then all rewards of the actions in α are inherited from the ones in $\alpha[1]$, so that

$$\textit{reward}(\alpha) = \textit{reward}(\alpha[1]). \tag{3}$$

Theorem 4. $A \sqsubseteq_{\text{reward}}^F B$ iff $A \sqsubseteq_{\text{must}}^F B$ iff $A \sqsubseteq_F B$.

Proof. That $A \sqsubseteq_{\text{reward}}^F B$ implies $A \sqsubseteq_{\text{must}}^F B$ has been shown in [6, Thm. 7] and is also justified in Sect. 3.

That $A \sqsubseteq_{\text{must}}^F B$ implies $A \sqsubseteq_F B$ has been demonstrated by Theorem 3.

Suppose $A \sqsubseteq_F B$, i.e., $in(A) = in(B) \wedge out(A) = out(B)$ and $\textit{fairtraces}(B) \subseteq \textit{fairtraces}(A)$, and let T be any test that is strongly compatible with A and B. Let β be a fair execution of $T\|B$. By [9, Prop. 4], $\beta[1]$ is a fair execution of

T, and $\beta[2]$ is a fair execution of B. Since $A \sqsubseteq_F B$, automaton A has a fair execution γ with $trace(\gamma) = trace(\beta[2])$. Let $\sigma := trace(\beta)$. Then σ is a sequence of external actions of $T\|A$ such that $\sigma\!\restriction\!T = trace(\beta[1])$ and $\sigma\!\restriction\!A = \sigma\!\restriction\!B = trace(\beta[2]) = trace(\gamma)$. By [9, Prop. 5], there exists a fair execution α of $T\|A$ such that $trace(\alpha) = \sigma$, $\alpha[1] = \beta[1]$ and $\alpha[2] = \gamma$. By (3) one has $reward(\alpha) = reward(\alpha[1]) = reward(\beta[1]) = reward(\beta)$. Thus $A \sqsubseteq_{\mathrm{reward}}^{F} B$. $\qquad\square$

11   Conclusion

When adapting the concept of a complete execution, which plays a central rôle in the definition of must testing, to the weakly fair executions of I/O automata, must testing turns out to characterise exactly the fair preorder on I/O automata. Moreover, reward testing, which under the default notion of a complete execution is much more discriminating than must testing, in this setting has the same distinguishing power. Interesting venues for future investigation include extending these connections to timed and probabilistic settings.

References

1. Brinksma, E., Rensink, A., Vogler, W.: Fair testing. In: Lee, I., Smolka, S.A. (eds.) CONCUR 1995. LNCS, vol. 962, pp. 313–327. Springer, Heidelberg (1995). https://doi.org/10.1007/3-540-60218-6_23
2. De Nicola, R., Hennessy, M.: Testing equivalences for processes. Theoret. Comput. Sci. **34**, 83–133 (1984). https://doi.org/10.1016/0304-3975(84)90113-0
3. Deng, Y., van Glabbeek, R.J., Hennessy, M., Morgan, C.C.: Characterising testing preorders for finite probabilistic processes. Log. Methods Comput. Sci. **4**(4), 4 (2008). https://doi.org/10.2168/LMCS-4(4:4)2008
4. van Glabbeek, R.J.: Just testing. https://theory.stanford.edu/~rvg/abstracts.html#160
5. van Glabbeek, R.J.: Justness: a completeness criterion for capturing liveness properties (extended abstract). In: Bojańczyk, M., Simpson, A. (eds.) FoSSaCS 2019. LNCS, vol. 11425, pp. 505–522. Springer, Cham (2019). https://doi.org/10.1007/978-3-030-17127-8_29
6. van Glabbeek, R.J.: Reward testing equivalences for processes. In: Boreale, M., Corradini, F., Loreti, M., Pugliese, R. (eds.) Models, Languages, and Tools for Concurrent and Distributed Programming. LNCS, vol. 11665, pp. 45–70. Springer, Cham (2019). https://doi.org/10.1007/978-3-030-21485-2_5
7. van Glabbeek, R.J., Höfner, P.: Progress, justness and fairness. ACM Comput. Surv. **52**(4), 69 (2019). https://doi.org/10.1145/3329125
8. Hoare, C.A.R.: Communicating Sequential Processes. Prentice Hall, Hoboken (1985)
9. Lynch, N.A., Tuttle, M.R.: An introduction to input/output automata. CWI Q. **2**(3), 219–246 (1989). https://groups.csail.mit.edu/tds/papers/Lynch/CWI89.pdf
10. Natarajan, V., Cleaveland, R.: Divergence and fair testing. In: Fülöp, Z., Gécseg, F. (eds.) ICALP 1995. LNCS, vol. 944, pp. 648–659. Springer, Heidelberg (1995). https://doi.org/10.1007/3-540-60084-1_112

11. Segala, R.: Testing probabilistic automata. In: Montanari, U., Sassone, V. (eds.) CONCUR 1996. LNCS, vol. 1119, pp. 299–314. Springer, Heidelberg (1996). https://doi.org/10.1007/3-540-61604-7_62
12. Segala, R.: Quiescence, fairness, testing, and the notion of implementation. Inf. Comput. **138**(2), 194–210 (1997). https://doi.org/10.1006/inco.1997.2652
13. Vaandrager, F.W.: On the relationship between process algebra and input/output automata. In: Proceedings of the Sixth Annual Symposium on Logic in Computer Science (LICS 1991), Amsterdam, The Netherlands, 15–18 July 1991. IEEE Computer Society, pp. 387–398 (1991). https://doi.org/10.1109/LICS.1991.151662

Passive Automata Learning: DFAs and NFAs

Hans Zantema[1,2]([✉])

[1] Department of Computer Science, TU Eindhoven,
P.O. Box 513, 5600 MB Eindhoven, The Netherlands
h.zantema@tue.nl
[2] Radboud University Nijmegen,
P.O. Box 9010, 6500 GL Nijmegen, The Netherlands

Abstract. It is a natural question to find a DFA or NFA for which a given set of words should be accepted and another given set should not be accepted. In this short note we investigate how to find a smallest automaton for both types by means of SMT solving, and compare the results.

1 Introduction

The question how to learn an automaton has extensively been studied. A landmark in this research is the algorithm L^* from Angluin [2]. Here a DFA is learned by asking two types of questions: *membership queries* by which it is asked whether a word is in the language, and *equivalence queries* by which it is asked whether a given DFA accepts the language. This was the starting point of a large amount research in this direction. A recent variant includes $L^\#$ [8] in which the focus is on *apartness*: proving inequality of observations rather than equivalence. Instead of for DFAs, a similar approach for NFAs has been investigated in [3].

But all these variants exploit *active* learning: the learner starts from scratch and has a strategy to ask questions to be answered by an oracle. This is in contrast to *passive* learning, where a set of positive examples is given that has to be accepted and a set of negative examples that has to be not accepted. A most natural question in this area is finding a smallest DFA satisfying these requirements. This question has proven to be NP-complete in [4]. As it is NP-complete, indeed it is not expected that it can be solved for larger instances. But wit the current developments in SAT/SMT solving it makes sense to get a feeling until which size passive learning is feasible. The goal of this note is to investigate this, based on randomly generated examples sets, both for DFAs and NFAs.

Encoding DFA passive learning by pure SAT solving has been elaborated in [5]. Similar work for NFAs has been done in [6]. For both holds that the encoding is in pure SAT, and the emphasis is on developing specific tricks to improve results.

© The Author(s), under exclusive license to Springer Nature Switzerland AG 2022
N. Jansen et al. (Eds.): Vaandrager Festschrift 2022, LNCS 13560, pp. 575–580, 2022.
https://doi.org/10.1007/978-3-031-15629-8_31

In this note we will achieve comparable results by a direct encoding in SMT and using the standard SMT solver Z3. Surprisingly, an approach very similar to ours for DFAs was described independently in [7]. We have special interest for comparing DFAs and NFAs: for a given positive set and negative set of examples we search for both a smallest compatible DFA and a smallest compatible NFA. As expected, often the NFA will have less states. On the other hand, for a fixed n searching for an NFA of n states is in general more expensive than searching for a DFA of n states, so in advance it is unclear what will be most expensive in computation time: finding a smallest DFA or finding a smallest NFA. If the main goal is to find a simple compatible regular language that can be used to predict whether a fresh string will be in the language or not, finding this language quickly is more important than the type of description of the language. In this view it is a natural question to compare the computation times for the two formats. Our experiments show that often finding a smallest NFA is found quicker, but not always.

2   Finding a Smallest DFA

Assume that two disjoint sets A^+ and A^- of words over an alphabet Σ are given, and a number n. We will construct a boolean formula that is satisfiable if and only if a DFA of n states exists such that all words in A^+ are accepted and all words in A^- are not accepted. We specify the set Q of states to be $\{1, 2, \ldots, n\}$, of which 1 is defined to be the initial state, and the DFA will be given by two functions $\delta : Q \times \Sigma \to Q$ and $F : Q \to \mathbb{B}$, where $\mathbb{B}$ stand for the Booleans.

In the usual DFA definition δ is extended to $\delta^* : Q \times \Sigma^* \to Q$, and a word w is defined to be accepted if $F(\delta^*(1, w))$ is true.

Instead of defining δ^* in our encoding we compute the set P of all prefixes of words from $A^+ \cup A^-$, including these word themselves. The key idea is to specify a function $D : P \to Q$ for which we have $D(w) = \delta^*(1, w)$ for all $w \in P$. We do this by collecting the requirements $D(\epsilon) = 1$ and $D(w) = \delta(D(w'), a)$ for every $w \in P$ that can be written as $w'a$ for $w' \in \Sigma^*$ and $a \in \Sigma$, note that $w' \in P$ since P is closed under prefixes.

It is interesting to realize that this set P has a tree structure and yields a partial compatible automaton that is typically not minimal, but gives an upper bound for the minimal size of a compatible DFA. SAT based minimization of such a partial automaton for the setting of Mealy machines is described in [1].

Finally we have the acceptance requirements $F(D(w))$ for all $w \in A^+$ and $\neg F(D(w))$ for all $w \in A^-$. Consider the formula consisting of the conjunction of all these requirements. By construction it is satisfiable if and only if a DFA of n states exists such that all words in A^+ are accepted and all words in A^- are not accepted.

This is encoded directly in Z3 by not only numbering the elements of Q but also the elements of P and Σ and declaring three functions

$$\delta : \mathsf{Int} \times \mathsf{Int} \to \mathsf{Int}, \ F : \mathsf{Int} \to \mathbb{B}, \ D : \mathsf{Int} \to \mathsf{Int}.$$

Apart from the already mentioned parts of the formula also the requirements $0 < \delta(i,j) \leq n$ are added for all $i = 1, 2, \ldots, n$ and all $j = 1, 2, \ldots, \#\Sigma$. Summarizing, the full formula reads as follows:

$$D(\epsilon) = 1 \wedge \bigwedge_{w=w'a \in P} D(w) = \delta(D(w'), a) \wedge$$

$$\bigwedge_{w \in A^+} F(D(w)) \wedge \bigwedge_{w \in A^-} \neg F(D(w)) \wedge$$

$$\bigwedge_{i=1}^{n} \bigwedge_{j=1}^{k} 0 < \delta(i,j) \leq n.$$

Here n is the number of states of the DFA to be searched, $k = \#\Sigma$, and the elements of P are numbered, and identified with their numbers. Essentially the same encoding was described in [7], where also register automata and IORAs were considered and the focus was on comparison with active learning, while we focus on comparison with NFAs on randomly generated data.

Now our program repeats building this formula for increasing n, starting by $n = 2$, applies Z3, until Z3 results in establishing SAT. Then Z3 also gives the satisfying assignment, by which the full DFA is specified.

3   Finding a Smallest NFA

Again assume that two disjoint sets A^+ and A^- of words over an alphabet Σ are given, and a number n. Now we will construct a boolean formula that is satisfiable if and only if an NFA of n states exists such that all words in A^+ are accepted and all words in A^- are not accepted. Here we take the standard definition of an NFA with a single initial state and no ϵ steps. Again we specify the set Q of states to be $\{1, 2, \ldots, n\}$, of which 1 is defined to be the initial state, and the NFA will be given by two functions δ and $F : Q \to \mathbb{B}$, specifying the transition function and the final states. But now we have $\delta : Q \times Q \times \Sigma \to \mathbb{B}$, where $\delta(q, q', a)$ states that there is an a-step from q to q'. Again we define and number the set P of all prefixes of words from $A^+ \cup A^-$, and in our SMT formula we declare a function $D : P \times Q \to \mathbb{B}$, in which $D(w, q)$ states that there is path from 1 to q consecutively labeled by the symbols of w. So a string $w \in P$ is defined to be accepted if and only if a state q exists satisfying both $F(q)$ and $D(w, q)$. This results in the following formula that is satisfiable if and only if a compatible NFA of n states exist:

$$D(\epsilon, 1) \wedge \bigwedge_{i=2}^{n} \neg D(\epsilon, i) \wedge$$

$$\bigwedge_{i=1}^{n} \bigwedge_{w=w'a \in P} \left(D(w, i) \leftrightarrow \bigvee_{j=1}^{n} (D(w', j) \wedge \delta(j, i, a)) \right) \wedge$$

$$\bigwedge_{w \in A^+} (\bigvee_{i=1}^{n} (F(i) \wedge D(w, i))) \wedge \bigwedge_{w \in A^-} (\neg \bigvee_{i=1}^{n} (F(i) \wedge D(w, i))),$$

in which again the elements of P are numbered, and identified with their numbers.

Again our program repeats building this formula for increasing n, starting by $n = 2$, applies Z3, until Z3 results in establishing SAT. The full NFA is obtained from the resulting satisfying assignment.

4   Results

Our main goal is to get a feeling for which sizes of DFAs and NFAs this approach is feasible, and how they compare. To do so, we randomly generated several sets A^+ and A^- and applied the above approach. This generation has two parameters: the sizes of A^+ and A^-, and the lengths of the words. As expected, for A^+ and A^- consisting of a few short words the resulting DFAs and NFAs are small and are found very quickly, while for A^+ and A^- consisting of a great number of long words small corresponding DFAs and NFAs are established not to exist and for larger automaton sizes the procedures run out of time. Our goal is to get an impression of the border between these two extremes by executing the above approach for a great number of randomly generated sets A^+ and A^-. Instead of generating big tables describing all detailed results for many cases and computation times in milliseconds, we prefer to focus on general conclusions on the one hand, and on the details of one single particular representative example on the other hand.

Generally speaking, the DFA approach turns out to be feasible if the resulting DFA has up to 9 or 10 states if the words are not too long, say up to 7, for longer words (length 10 or 12) it hardly goes beyond 7 states. The NFA approach turns out to be feasible if the resulting NFA has up to 8 states if the words are not too long, say up to 7, for longer words it hardly goes beyond 6 states. There is a lot of variation in computation time. For a fixed pair of sets A^+ and A^- sometimes the smallest DFA is found much faster than the smallest NFA, and sometimes the other way around.

We agree that these sizes are quite limited. For more structured sets A^+ and A^- than our randomly generated samples one may expect higher sizes. Also one may think of further optimizations on our most basic encodings by which the sizes may slightly increase. On the other hand, the DFA and NFA we will give now for one particular example clearly show that the results of our approach are far beyond what may be expected from guessing or from approaches without computer support.

To get a feeling of what can be achieved we now elaborate one particular example in which both randomly generated A^+ and A^- consist of 20 words of length at most 7:

$$A^+ =$$

$\{ba, bba, baba, bbaba, baaaa, bbbaba, bababa, abaaba, baaaba, baabbba, bbababa,$

$baababa, aaababa, bbbbbaa, ababbaa, bababaa, aababaa, aabbaaa, baabaaa, bbaaaaa\},$

$$A^- =$$

$\{aab, aba, aaa, abba, aaba, abaaa, babbba, aabbba, aaabba, abbaba, aabaaa,$

$baaaaa, aaaaaa, bbbabba, abbabba, babbaba, aabbaba, bbbaaba, bbaaaba, aaaaaba\}.$

It turns out that a smallest compatible DFA consist of 10 states, which is found by the above approach in 419 s, of which nearly all time is used by Z3 for proving that the formula for 9 states is unsatisfiable. The final formula for 10 states has size 4 kB, and satisfiability is found by Z3 in a fraction of a second. The corresponding DFA is the following, in which as usual the initial state is indicated by an incoming arrow and the final states are indicated by double circles.

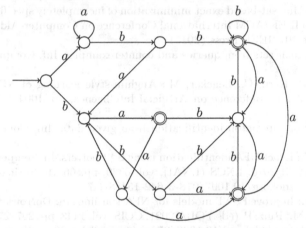

Now we switch to NFAs for the same sets A^+ and A^-. It turns out that a smallest compatible NFA consists of 7 states, which is found by the above approach in 47 s, of which nearly all time is used by Z3 for proving that the formula for 6 states is unsatisfiable. The final formula for 7 states has size 140 kB, and satisfiability is found by Z3 in 2 s. The corresponding NFA is the following:

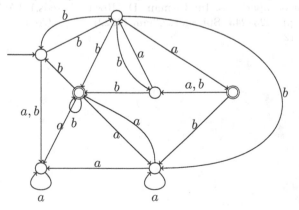

Both the minimal DFA and minimal NFA may be not unique, and distinct compatible minimal automata may be describe distinct languages. Indeed in the above example the resulting DFA and NFA describe distinct languages, for instance, the word *bbb* is accepted by the NFA, but not by the DFA.

In our approach for both the DFAs and NFAs by far the most computation time is consumed by proving that the formula for an automaton of size $n - 1$ is unsatisfiable, for n being the smallest value for which there is a solution. Hence if the goal is to find a compatible automaton that does not need to be a guaranteed smallest one, a good policy is still to consider the procedure for increasing n, but simply stop it if it takes long, and then continue by the next n.

References

1. Abel, A., Reineke, J.: MeMin: sat-based exact minimization of incompletely specified mealy machines. In: 2015 IEEE/ACM International Conference on Computer-Aided Design (ICCAD), pp. 94–101. IEEE Press (2015)
2. Angluin, D.: Learning regular sets from queries and counterexamples. Inf. Comput. **75**, 87–106 (1987)
3. Bollig, B., Habermehl, P., Kern, C., Leucker, M.: Angluin-style learning of NFA. In: IJCAI International Joint Conference on Artificial Intelligence, pp. 1004–1009 (2009)
4. Gold, E.M.: Complexity of automaton identification from given data. Inf. Control **37**(3), 302–320 (1978)
5. Heule, M.J.H., Verwer, S.: Exact DFA identification using SAT solvers. In: Sempere, J.M., García, P. (eds.) ICGI 2010. LNCS (LNAI), vol. 6339, pp. 66–79. Springer, Heidelberg (2010). https://doi.org/10.1007/978-3-642-15488-1_7
6. Lardeux, F., Monfroy, E.: Improved SAT models for NFA learning. In: Dorronsoro, B., Amodeo, L., Pavone, M., Ruiz, P. (eds.) OLA 2021. CCIS, vol. 1443, pp. 267–279. Springer, Cham (2021). https://doi.org/10.1007/978-3-030-85672-4_20
7. Smetsers, R., Fiterău-Broştean, P., Vaandrager, F.: Model learning as a satisfiability modulo theories problem. In: Klein, S.T., Martín-Vide, C., Shapira, D. (eds.) LATA 2018. LNCS, vol. 10792, pp. 182–194. Springer, Cham (2018). https://doi.org/10.1007/978-3-319-77313-1_14
8. Vaandrager, F., Garhewal, B., Rot, J., Wissmann, T.: A new approach for active automata learning based on apartness. In: Fisman, D., Rosu, G. (eds.) TACAS 2022. LNCS, vol. 13243, pp. 223–243. Springer, Cham (2022). https://doi.org/10.1007/978-3-030-99524-9_12

Author Index

Printed in the United States
by Baker & Taylor Publisher Services

Printed in the United States
by Baker & Taylor Publisher Services